T0331095

Earnings Management, Fintech-Driven Incentives and Sustainable Growth

Traditional research about Financial Stability and Sustainable Growth typically omits Earnings Management (as a broad class of misconduct), Complex Systems Theory, Mechanism Design Theory, Public Health, psychology issues, and the externalities and psychological effects of Fintech. Inequality, Environmental Pollution, Earnings Management opportunities, the varieties of complex Financial Instruments, Fintech, Regulatory Fragmentation, Regulatory Capture and real-financial sector-linkages are growing around the world, and these factors can have symbiotic relationships. Within the Complex Systems Theory framework, this book analyzes these foregoing issues, and introduces new behavior theories, Enforcement Dichotomies, and critiques of models, regulations and theories in several dimensions. The issues analyzed can affect markets, and evolutions of systems, decision-making, internal markets and risk-perception within government regulators, operating companies and investment entities, and thus they have public policy implications. The legal analysis uses applicable US case-law and statutes (which have been copied by many countries and are similar to those of many common-law countries).

Using *Qualitative Reasoning, Capital Dynamics Theory* (a new approach introduced in this book), *Critical Theory* and elements of *Mechanism Design Theory*, the book aims to enhance cross-disciplinary analysis of the above-mentioned issues; and to help researchers build better systems/artificial intelligence/mathematical models of Consumer Behavior, Retailing Trends, International Contagion, Financial Stability, Portfolio Management, Policy-Analysis, Asset Pricing, Contract Theory, Enforcement Theory and Fraud Detection.

The primary audience for this book consists of university professors, PhD students and PhD degree-holders (in industries, government agencies, financial services companies and research institutes). The book can be used as a primary or supplementary textbook for graduate courses in Regulation; Fintech/Artificial-Intelligence, Capital Markets; Law & Economics, International Political Economy and or Mechanism Design (Applied Math, Operations Research, Computer Science or Finance).

Michael I. C. Nwogugu is an author, entrepreneur and consultant and has held senior corporate management and Board-of-Director positions in both the US and Nigeria. Mr. Nwogugu wrote the following books: *Risk in the Global Real Estate Market; Illegal File-sharing Networks, Digital Goods Pricing and Decision Analysis; Anomalies in Net Present Value, Returns and Polynomials and Regret Theory in Decision Making; Indices, Index Funds and ETFs: Exploring HCI, Nonlinear Risk and Homomorphisms;* and *Complex Systems, Multi-sided Incentives and Risk Perception in Companies.* Mr. Nwogugu's research articles are cited in: *International Journal of Approximate Reasoning; Applied Mathematics & Computation; Journal of Business Research; European Journal of Operational Research; PNAS (USA); Physica-A; Annual Review of Psychology; Neural Computing & Applications; Europhysics Letters; Information Fusion; Economic Modeling; Mathematical Methods of Operations Research; Computers & Industrial Engineering; British Journal of Applied Science & Technology; American Journal of Applied Sciences; International Journal of Environment & Public Health; Journal of Experimental Psychology – Learning, Memory & Cognition;* and *Expert Systems With Applications,* among others. Mr. Nwogugu earned degrees from the University of Nigeria (Nigeria), City University of New York (USA), and Columbia University (New York City, USA).

Earnings Management, Fintech-Driven Incentives and Sustainable Growth

On Complex Systems, Legal and Mechanism Design Factors

Michael I. C. Nwogugu

Routledge
Taylor & Francis Group

LONDON AND NEW YORK

First published 2020
by Routledge
2 Park Square, Milton Park, Abingdon, Oxon OX14 4RN

and by Routledge
605 Third Avenue, New York, NY 10017

First issued in paperback 2021

Routledge is an imprint of the Taylor & Francis Group, an informa business

Publisher's Note
The publisher has gone to great lengths to ensure the quality of this
reprint but points out that some imperfections in the original copies
may be apparent.

British Library Cataloguing-in-Publication Data
A catalogue record for this book is available from the British Library

Library of Congress Cataloging-in-Publication Data
A catalog record for this book has been requested

ISBN 13: 978-1-03-208577-7 (pbk)
ISBN 13: 978-1-4094-5696-4 (hbk)

Typeset in Times New Roman
by Apex CoVantage, LLC

Contents

Introduction[1]

Earnings management and the efficiency of *Incentive Mechanisms* and Fintech (and their significant impact on economic planning/modelling, public policy and quality of life) remain significant problems in both developed and developing economies around the world; and have substantial implications for sustainability (economic, social, urban and environmental sustainability), economic growth, risk regulation, risk management, systemic risk and financial stability; all of which affect pension plans, household wealth and government policies. Unfortunately, legislatures and the executive branches of government and the judiciaries in most countries have not been able to properly address this problem. Most regulations that were intended to reduce earnings management and or improve the efficiency of *Incentive Mechanisms* and Fintech have been ineffective or costly to implement. The nature, evolution and psychological effects of associated *Incentive Mechanisms* and Fintech (for both individuals and corporate entities) have become dominant institutions that affect sustainability, risk-taking and risk management.

This book differs from all other books on Earnings Management, *Inequality* and Sustainable Growth in the following ways:

i) The approaches used include "*Qualitative Reasoning*" (see: Forbus (2019), Halpern (2003), and Bredeweg and Struss (Winter 2003)), *Critical Theory*, "*Capital Dynamics Theory*" (introduced in this book), *Mechanism Design* and *Complex Systems Theory*.

ii) This book introduces "*Asset-Quality Management*" and *Incentive-effects Management* as distinct classes of actionable *Disclosure-Misconduct* (civil and or criminal liability) or ethics violations (some of which were formerly bundled together as "*Earnings Management*").

iii) This book does not focus on specific types and instances of earnings management, but rather, focuses on behavioral biases, and the *Incentive Mechanisms* and institutions that can facilitate Earnings Management and Incentive-effects Management (as broadly defined), *Inequality* and *Fintech Gaps* (explained herein and below); and or affect Sustainable Growth, *Enforcement* and "*Capital Dynamics Theory*". This book addresses the behavioral effects of accounting rules and the auditee-firms' and auditors' Group Decisions (causes and effects) that pertain to *Disclosure-Misconduct* within the context of the firm, regulatory regimes and sustainability – all of which often have *Multiplier Effects*. Collectively, such analysis can help improve Computer Science, Physics, Decision Sciences and Artificial Intelligence models that are used to identify or predict financial statement fraud, Corporate Bankruptcy and or *Non-Compliance*, and to model Portfolio Management, Financial Stability, Asset Pricing, Household Dynamics/Allocations, Consumer Behavior, Retailing Trends, "Personal Growth", Organizational Psychology trends, *International Contagion* (of Cultures, Beliefs, Usage-of-Trade, technologies, market-volatility, Corporate Governance; enforcement patterns; etc.), and Public Policy.

iv) Various parties have estimated that more than 80 percent of all equity and futures trading in the USA and perhaps other countries is now automated/algorithmic[2]; and one implication is that most "traditional" research on *Market Microstructure, Risk-Perception,* Household dynamics/allocations, *Preferences* and *Reasoning* is misleading or incomplete. This book helps in bridging that gap.

v) This book addresses the efficiency of regulations that affect the incentives (of firms, employees; and auditors) to perpetrate Earnings Management, Incentive-effects Management and or Asset-Quality Management.

vi) The book addresses the macroeconomic, Public Health and International Political Economy dimensions of Earnings Management, Asset-Quality Management and Incentive-Effects Management – including *Inequality* and Environmental Auditing.

vii) The book introduces *Economic Psychology* and "*Behavioral Operations Research*" theories that pertain to two classes of assets that generate or can generate more than 60 percent of all earnings management and asset quality management and substantial Sustainability problems, and ironically also generate a substantial portion of economic growth in many developed countries – which are Intangible Assets and Real Estate. The book analyzes issues in the *Global Real Estate Markets* and the *Global Intangibles Economy* that related to Antitrust, Group Decisions, Behavioral Biases, Consumer Behavior, and the efficiency of Incentive Mechanisms.

viii) The book addresses Earnings Management, Asset-Quality Management and Incentive-Effects Management and their "*Multiplier Effects*" in developing countries and Less-Developed Countries.

ix) The book addresses critical issues that pertain to Trust, Perception and Cooperation in markets, and to Preferences, Beliefs and Reasoning (all of which are widely debated in HCI, Fintech and AI).

x) From Mechanism Design, Contract Theory, Dynamical Systems, Sustainability and Complex Systems Theory perspectives, this book addresses the following classes of issues:

1) *Multi-sided Incentives* that can reduce or increase earnings management, asset-quality management, sustainability and incentive-effects management – such as Incentives, Fintech and ARS auctions. Such incentives actively involve two or more persons or classes of persons.

2) *"Many-person Re-generative Institutions"* such as Intangibles/Goodwill accounting rules; Fintech, AI, legal processes; etc.

3) *"Many-person Mechanisms"* that affect behaviors of Human/Automated Agents and can reduce or increase harmful group collusion, and the incentives for transparency and truthfulness.

4) The elicitation of: i) "best" preferences for organizations; ii) preferences of groups in organizations.

5) Complex adaptive systems.

Earnings Management, Incentive-Effects Management, violations of Securities Laws and associated *Multiplier Effects* (economic, psychological, political, social, contagion and capital markets) have been analysed from various perspectives including the following:

i) Psychology (Economic Psychology and Organizational Psychology) and Consumer Behavior.

ii) Retailing – e.g. Retail financial services; franchising; Household Dynamics/Allocations; etc.

iii) Telecommunications and Networks – e.g. contagion in online social networks; investor networks; etc.

iv) *Corporate Finance* – see: Agrawal and Cooper (2017).

v) *Financial Engineering* – see: Kamran, Zhao, Ali and Sabir (2018).

vi) *Management-Science* – see: Chapman and Steenburgh (2010) and Chen, Wu, et al. (2017).

vii) *Operations-Research* (Fintech and Artifical Intelligence) – see: Königsgruber and Palan (2015); Koskivaara (2000) and Calvo, Ivorra and Liern (2017).

viii) *Applied Math, Decision Sciences* and *Artifical Intelligence* – see: Zhou and Kapoor (2011); Dbouk and Zaarour (2017); Dikmen and Kukkocaoglu (2010) and Ngai, Hu, et al. (2011).

ix) *Computer Science* (Fintech and Artifical Intelligence) – see: Long, Song and Cui (2017) and Trigo, Belfo and Estébanez (2016).

x) *Political Geography* – see: Gross et al. (2016).

xi) *Political Economy* – see: Ding, Li and Wu (2018); Abeysekera (2003); Boczko (2000) and Gross, Königsgruber, et al. (2016).

xii) *Physics* – see: Ma, Zhuang and Li (2011); Battiston and Glattfelder (2009); Kuzubas, Ömercikoglu and Saltoglu (2014) and Li, An, Gao, et al. (2014).

xiii) *Game Theory* (Math) – see: Shuotong and Yanxi (2012).

xiv) *Public Policy* – see: Gross, et al. (2016).

xv) *Economics* – see: Marinovic (2013) and Cumming and Johan (2013).

xvi) *Finance* (Bankruptcy Prediction, Portfolio Management and Asset Pricing) – see Veganzones and Severin (June 2017); Drabkova (2016); Kwag and Stephens (2009) and Sun (2009).

xvii) *Corporate Governance* – see Badia, Dicuonzo, et al. (2019) and Zambon, Marasca and Chiucchi (2019).

xviii) *Law* – see: Ma (2013).
 xix) *Accounting Information Systems* – see: Chen, Wu, et al. (2017).

The common elements among these approaches are as follows: i) Networks; ii) public policy; and iii) relationships between corporate financial policies and capital markets dynamics; and iv) identification of patterns of misconduct. However, most of these studies: i) don't distinguish among *Earnings Management*, *"Asset-Quality Management"* and *"Incentive-Effects Management"*; and or don't analyze asset-quality management and Incentive-Effects Management; ii) don't analyze the Public Health, *Inequality* and other macroeconomic implications of such misconduct; iii) don't analyze affected institutions and Incentive Mechanisms; and iv) don't analyze Contract Theory issues.

Earnings management, Asset-quality Management and Incentive-Effects Management typically occur and or are amplified within the context of, and often distort organizations, *Incentive-Mechanisms*, *Contracting-Frameworks*, *Networks-of-Contracts*, markets and benefits of Fintech. *Contract Theory* and *Mechanism Design Theory* have been jointly studied from various perspectives including Economics/Finance, Operations Research, Mathematical Psychology, Computer Science, Game Theory and Applied Math – see: Hoppe and Schmitz (2018); Niederhoff and Kouvelis (2019); Hong, Wernz and Stillinger (2016); Wu, Zhao and Tang (2014); Li, Liu and Chen (2018); Lin and Chou (1990); Park and Kim (2014); Goetz et al. (2019); Fang and Yuan (2018); Madureira et al. (2014); Meneguzzi et al. (2011, 2012); Zohar and Rosenschein (2008); Terán, Aguilar and Cerrada (2017); and Wei et al. (2018). However, the models in most of these foregoing articles and literature are static, don't incorporate relevant variables; don't consider varying "states" and often complex "joint" effects of variables; and they don't consider Industrial Organization effects of contracts/mechanisms – see Nwogugu (2007a;b), Nwogugu (2019a;b) and Nwogugu (2006).

Various types of *Inequality* have been analyzed from Physics, Applied Mathematics, Taxation, Econometrics and Economics perspectives (with the common themes being Networks, transactions and wealth-concentration), and the associated literatures are cited in Chapter 3 in this book.

With regards to Public Policy and affected populations, the theories introduced and issues analyzed in this book collectively (and directly or indirectly) affect more than two billion people in several continents; and more than €310 trillion of corporate, government and household assets; and more than €10 trillion of daily transactions around the world (e.g. loans/bonds/notes; money-markets; stock markets; swaps/derivatives; Structured Products; commodities; credit transactions; Equity-Based Incentives (EBIs) and employee incentives; employee costs/taxes; performance benchmarking; etc.).

The primary audience for this book is as follows:

 i) University professors.
 ii) PhD-degree-holders who work in industry, think-tanks, consulting firms, financial services companies and government agencies.
 iii) PhD students.

The book can also be used as a primary or supplemental textbook for graduate courses in Behavioral Operations Research; Risk Management; Applied Mathematics; Complex Adaptive Systems; Behavioral Political Economy; Accounting; Law & Economics; Mathematical Psychology and Organizational Psychology.

In some chapters in this book, "*Incentive Mechanisms*" and Game-Theory Models are introduced or discussed (by explaining how they function). These are in the nature of one or more of the following:

i) *Game-Theory strategies* – similar to how Supermodularity and Complementarity can be represented by $\partial^2 f/\partial z_i \partial z_j \geq 0$; for all $i \neq j$; where and z_i and z_j are strategies of participants in the action space and each action is chosen from an interval $z_i, z_j \, \varepsilon \, [a,b]$; and the payoff function ($f(.)$) depends on actions/strategies of two or more types of participants z_i and z_j in the action space ($i = 1 \ldots \ldots \ldots n$; $j=1 \ldots \ldots \ldots \ldots n$).

ii) *Invariants* – which are used to characterize key elements of *Groups*.

iii) *Decision elements* – wherein groups of these "mechanisms" can also be weighted and converted into decision-scores for decision making.

iv) *Dynamical Systems* elements.

1.1 "Capital dynamics theory"

"*Capital Dynamics Theory*" is a new approach introduced herein, and it relates corporate financial policies, Behavioral Operations Research, Game-Theory type analysis of Managerial Risk Preferences, *Contract Theory*, "*Accounting Biases*" and Earnings Management on one hand, to Sustainable Growth, *Fintech-Gaps*, AI, Financial Stability, *Complex Systems Theory* and capital markets. *Fintech-Gaps* consists of the psychological effects of Fintech and associated Artificial Intelligence, inefficiencies inherent in the use of Fintech/AI, "*Fintech/AI Externalities*", and *Externalities* that can affect Fintech.

Capital Dynamics Theory introduces "*Asset-Quality Management*" and *Incentive-Effects Management* as distinct classes of actionable *Disclosure-Misconduct* (civil and or criminal liability) or ethics violations, some of which were formerly bundled together as "*Earnings Management*"; and as distinct types of *Incentive-Mechanisms* and Disclosure-Misconduct that can affect macroeconomic/macrofinancial and political trends and human psychology – that is the "*Three-Factor Evolution Model*", an Emergent phenomena.

Capital Dynamics Theory analyzes the Public Health, Environmental Pollution, *Inefficient Resource Allocation* and *Inequality* (the "*Four-Factor Symbiosis Model*", an Emergent phenomena) implications of Earnings Management, Asset-Quality Management, Incentive-Effects Management around the world; explains how these four factors are intertwined and can affect Sustainable Growth, and links them to corporate scandals and economic/financial crisis.

Capital Dynamics Theory can help improve Computer Science, Physics, Decision Sciences and Artificial Intelligence models that are used to identify or predict financial statement fraud, securities fraud and or *Non-Compliance* (as a physical and evolutionary phenomenon); and to model Portfolio Management, Financial Distress, Household Dynamics, Consumer Behavior, Retailing Trends, Organizational Psychology Trends, *International Contagion* (of culture, market-volatility, Corporate Governance; Usage-of-Trade, enforcement patterns; etc.), "Personal Growth", Public Policy, Financial Instability, Stock-market Fluctuations and or Asset Pricing.

1.2 The types of *multi-sided incentive mechanisms* that are analyzed in this book

On *Incentive Mechanisms*, see: Liu et al. (2016), Zhao, Yang and Li (2012), Wang (2018) and Jarungrattanapong (2018). *Multi-sided Incentive Mechanisms* are mechanisms: i) that affect two or more distinct parties that may or may not be related; ii) that are defined partly or wholly by contracts, statutes, regulations, codes/standards or usage-of-trade (all of which can be deemed to be types contracts and quasi-contracts); iii) for which performance and use patterns can evolve over time; iv) that can have incentive, social, economic and or psychological effects; v) that may be public goods or non-public goods; vi) that in most cases, are enacted or implemented or executed in order to achieve defined objectives (sometimes there can be un-intended *Incentive Mechanisms*); vii) that can elicit desired preferences and behaviors from agents and or groups, or otherwise influence behaviors and decisions. Thus, the following instruments and processes are types of "*Multi-sided Incentive Mechanisms*":

i)   *Earning Management* – the methods, processes, motivations and outcomes (affects shareholders; employees; third-party investors; regulators; competitors). See: Hosseini et al. (2016) and Nwaeze (2011). Kamran et al. (2018) noted that earnings management is a mechanism.

ii) *Asset-Quality Management* and *Incentive-Effects Management* – the methods, processes, motivations and outcomes can affect shareholders, employees, third-party investors, regulators and competitors. See: Hosseini et al. (2016); Nwaeze (2011) and Girth and Lopez (2018).

iii) *Accounting Earnings* and *IASB/IFRS Accounting Regulations* (affects shareholders; third-party investors; employees; external auditors; regulators; financial institutions; Boards of Directors; and competitors). See the comments in Greenwood, Baylis and Tao (2017); Kang and Lin (2011); Christensen et al. (2015) and Peng (2011).

iv) *Intangible Assets* – such as Patents, Trademarks, Copyrights; Brands; Contract Rights; Human Capital; Trade-Area Rights; etc. (affects shareholders; employees; third-party investors; regulators; competitors). See: Chari, Golosov and Tsyvinski (2012); Grabowski, DiMasi and Long (2015); Nyadzayo, Matanda and Ewing (2011) and Barnes (2006).

v)   *The Structure of, and Relationships Among Institutions in a Country* – Bushman and Piotroski (2006) noted that a country's country-level institutions (e.g. securities laws, political economy and legal/judicial system) create incentives (and incentive mechanisms) that determine the properties of reported accounting numbers and also influence the behavior of regulators, corporate executives, investors and other market participants. Further, such incentives ultimately shape the properties of reported accounting numbers.

vi)   *Real Estate Contracts* – such as lease agreements; mortgage agreements; property management agreements; Purchase/sale agreements; maintenance agreements; etc. (affects shareholders; employees; third-party investors; financial institutions; regulators; competitors). See: Chinloy and Winkler (2010); Benjamin, de la Torre and Musumeci (1995), Girth and Lopez (2018); Nwogugu (2007a;b) and Darrington and Howell (2011).

vii) *Real Estate Processes* (affects shareholders; employees; third-party investors; regulators; competitors). See: Chinloy and Winkler (2010); Benjamin, de la Torre and Musumeci (1995), Nwogugu (2007a;b;c) and Darrington and Howell (2011).

viii) *Structured Products Agreements* – for example, bond/note agreements; trust agreements; swaps/derivatives agreements; custodian agreements; etc. (affects sponsor; servicers; trustees; shareholders; employees; third-party investors; financial institutions; regulators; and competitors). The *Structured Products* referred to in this book are primarily: 1) those that are created through "express" asset securitization using Special Purpose Vehicles ("SPVs" – such as trusts, Limited Partnerships; LLCs; etc.) that own securities/interests, baskets-of-securities, commodities, foreign currencies and or swaps/futures/options contracts; and 2) those that are created through "synthetic" asset securitization (without SPVs/SIVs)[3] wherein the values of the structured products are linked to an index, currency, commodity, securities or other benchmark. A third type of Structured Product is that which is issued by an operating company in industry or in the financial services sector – usually to hedge or finance its operations at lower cost. See: Iacobucci and Winter (2005); Pinto and Alves (2016), and Nwogugu (2007b;c). Asset-backed securities are a type of *Structured Products* (see Table 0.1). *Structured Products* are used extensively around the world to finance governments and companies, and to create "targeted" investments for investors.

ix)   *Asset Securitization* – the combined agreements for asset-backed securities and mortgage-backed securities (affects sponsor; trustees; servicers; shareholders; employees; third-party investors; financial institutions; regulators; competitors). See: Iacobucci and Winter (2005); Pinto and Alves (2016), and Nwogugu (2007b;c).

x)   *Auction Rate Securities (ARS)* – the combination of the agreements and processes for ARS auctions (affects shareholders; employees; third-party investors; securities regulators and other government agencies; financial institutions; Boards of Directors; third-party investors; and competitors). See: Miyake (1998); Girth and Lopez (2018) and Sun and Yang (2014). ARS are used extensively around the world to finance governments and companies.

xi) *TARP/CPP Financial Instruments* – those were "investments" made by the US government to stabilize the US economy during the Global Financial Crisis (2008–2014). As explained in Chapter 5 in this book, the economic, political, social and psychological *Multiplier Effects* of the TARP/CPP program continue to this day in various ways.

xii) *Chinese VIEs (Variable Interest Entities).*

xiii) *Chinese Reverse-Merger companies.*

xiv) *Structured Synthetic Exchange Traded Funds (SSETFs).*

xv) *Mutual Funds* in various countries that invest in domestic and or international securities and financial instruments.

xvi) *Enforcement and prosecution efforts and processes.*

xvii) *Auditing Agreements* – the agreements between auditee-entities (companies and government agencies) on one hand, and auditing firms and management consulting firms (affects auditing/consulting firms; shareholders; employees; third-party investors; regulators; financial institutions; Boards of Directors; competitors). See: Asare, van Buuren and Majoor (2018), Singh and Larkin (2015), Girth and Lopez (2018), The Institute of Internal Auditors Research Foundation (2014) and Shapiro (2005).

xviii) Matheisen (2018) (Encyclopedia of Corporate Governance; http://e.viaminvest.com/A0BigPicture/1CorpGovProblem/A3IncentiveMechanisms.asp) noted that the following are also *Incentive Mechanisms*: Decision Systems; Performance Monitoring; Incentive Based Compensation; Bankruptcy System; Ownership Structure; Creditor Structure; Capital Structure; the market for corporate control; the market for management services; and product market competition.

xix) In addition, *Auditor Liability-Allocation Systems*, the *Auditor-Work Allocation System* and *Auditor-Fee Allocation System* can be Incentive Mechanisms (affects auditing/consulting firms; shareholders; employees; third-party investors; regulators; financial institutions; Boards of Directors; competitors). See: Asare, van Buuren and Majoor (2018); Singh and Larkin (2015); The Institute of Internal Auditors Research Foundation (2014); Girth and Lopez (2018) and Shapiro (2005).

Most of these foregoing Incentive Mechanisms are based on, or are experienced through, or are effected through, or can be significantly affected/disrupted by Fintech and Artificial Intelligence.

Generally, the *multi-sided incentives* analyzed in this book can be divided into two groups, each of which affect sustainability, economic growth and Financial Stability (in both the financial and real sectors of the economy) and which are as follows:

• *Multi-sided Compensatory Separable Incentives*: Two-sided and multi-sided compensatory incentives include equity-based incentives (e.g. employee stock options; DERs); franchising contracts; multiple-listing real estate brokerage contracts; debt contracts; some types of strategic alliances and joint ventures; etc. Some of these incentives are "stable" or "unstable" or oscillate between both states in time-varying patterns.

•   *Multi-Sided Non-Separable Incentive Mechanisms*: such as some types of Dutch Auctions (e.g. auctions for Auction-Rate-Securities and telecom Spectrum-licenses), strategic alliances; joint ventures; asset securitizations; some types of structured products; etc. These incentives are many-person mechanisms that involve two or more geographically dispersed "persons" (and often many persons) wherein the outcome is determined by the behaviors of the grantor/auctionor and the grantees/auctionees. The payoff-functions of the grantor/auctionor and the grantees/auctionees are mathematically "non-separable". This class of incentives are critical because: i) they often serve as formal or informal economic indicators; ii) they affect the corporate strategies and budgeting of for-profit and non-profit organizations; iii) they affect or can affect government monetary and fiscal policies; iv) they affect financial stability; v) they often directly or indirectly affect the budgets, changes of wealth-allocations, and intra-group relationships of households. Some of these incentive mechanisms are "stable" or "unstable" or oscillate between both states in time-varying patterns.

1.3 Problems inherent in mechanism design theory

Some academic articles that study *Mechanism Design Theory* (MDT) and its relation to *Contract Theory* (both of which are widely used in Fintech, Automated Systems and Artificial Intelligence) are cited in Hong, Wernz and Stillinger (2016). The Bergemann and Morris (2005) critique of MDT noted the following prior criticisms of MDT:

a)   Hurwicz (1972) discussed the need for "nonparametric" mechanisms (independent of parameters of the model).
b)   Wilson (1985) stated that a desirable property of a trading rule is that it "does not rely on features of the agents' common knowledge, such as their probability assessments".
c)   Dasgupta & Maskin (2000) "seek auction rules that are independent of the details such as functional forms or distribution of signals – of any particular application and that work well in a broad range of circumstances".
d)   An important paper of Neeman (2004) shows how rich type spaces can be used to relax implicit common knowledge assumptions in a Mechanism Design context.

Glachant (1998) stated that its criticism of MDT is in fact, similar to the criticism by Coase in *"The Problem of Social Cost"* of the Pigovian tradition.

Crew and Kleindorfer (2000) noted the following weaknesses in MDT: i) there is no assurance of regulatory commitment (commitment means that the regulator will allow the mechanism to continue to function as designed with regard to outcomes and profits); ii) planners/designers have not been able to accurately model the environment in which mechanisms function; iii) economic design theory does not address the constraints inherent in regulatory processes.

Nwogugu (2008a) noted that the literature on *Mechanism Design Theory* has some major gaps and inaccuracies, some of which are as follows:

1) Erroneously assumes that all agents truthfully disclose their preferences; and that all agents disclose their preferences at the same rate and at the same time.

2) Does not account for the value accruing to the agent or principal or participant, by withholding information about their preferences.

3) Erroneously assumes that the mechanism is fair and un-biased. In reality, even completely automated mechanisms have biases. Most mechanisms involve some human intervention and/or human processes, and existing mechanism design theory does not account for human biases, and processes such as altruism, regret, aspirations, etc., both in the participants and in the humans involved as part of the mechanism.

4) Does not account for varying levels of "privateness" of agents' information – rather, erroneously assumes binary situations in which information is either public or private.

5) Mechanism design theory does not incorporate the effects of regulation on agents and on the mechanism; and does not account for constitutionality of mechanisms.

6) Erroneously assumes that all agents are "*rational*" and self-interested. There can be many reasons for agents' irrationality and propensity to act for the benefit of the society – e.g. Altruism; Public Service; contractual relations/ obligations; job responsibilities; etc.

7) Erroneously assumes some minimum level of uniformity of agents' preferences; but on the contrary, Agents' preferences vary widely.

8) Does not account for differences in agents' information processing capabilities.

9) Erroneously assumes that the mechanism is monolithic in time, space and expense – in reality some mechanisms are dispersed in space (various locations) and time (requires participation, interaction and various disclosures at various times) and expenses (cost of participation varies across participants, time and locations).

10) Erroneously assumes that monitoring costs, compliance costs, switching costs, access costs, decision costs (costs of contemplating a decision) and sanctions (for non-compliance with the mechanism) are minimal or non-existent. In reality, these types of costs are both monetary/physical and non-monetary/ psychological and have significant effects on the efficiency of mechanisms.

11) Erroneously assumes that agents have quasi linear utility functions and are risk-neutral. In reality, agents' attitudes towards risk vary dramatically and depend on many factors. Furthermore, agents' utility functions are more likely to be non-linear because the agent will react to the mechanism

(economically, psychologically and socially), and react to the prospect of other participants, and also react to perceived opportunity costs, in addition to his/her normal utility function.

12) Erroneously assumes that the *social choice functions* inherent in mechanism designs have linear *"benefit effects"*; where a benefit effect is the economic gain or loss of social welfare across all agents and across the society/economy, as the mechanism functions during a specified time interval. Hence, benefit effect is defined with respect to time and to the entire economy. *Benefit effects* are likely to be non-linear because: a) agents vary in terms of wealth, utility functions, risk aversion, time horizon, preferences, etc.; b) the economy is not static, and changes in various elements of the economy are not discrete; c) not all eligible agents or permitted agents or financially capable agents will participate in the mechanism.

13) Erroneously assumes that the *social choice functions* inherent in mechanism designs have uniform and same "impact effects" across all agents; where an impact effect is the magnitude of the monetary and non-monetary impact of the mechanism on all agents. Erroneously assumes that all *social choice functions* inherent in mechanisms have linear effects on agents' utilities and participation strategies

14) Erroneously assumes that all eligible, financially capable and permitted agents will participate in the mechanism, and will participate at the same time.

15) Erroneously defines the success of mechanisms primarily in terms of utility. This approach does not sufficiently incorporate other elements and result of mechanisms – psychological gains/losses, emotions, social capital, reputation effects, aspirations, perceptions-of-achievement; Risk Perception; Political Capital; Regulatory Capture; etc. Furthermore, utility as used in mechanism design theory is relatively static. McCauley (2002) states that there are several problems in the use of utility. Most mechanism design theories are based on *equilibrium* as a relevant "state" and as an objective; and the concept of *equilibrium* is "static". In reality true *equilibrium* does not exist, and cannot be achieved in mechanisms due to: a) continuous changes in agents' preferences, wealth, access to information, etc.; b) transaction costs and opportunity costs; c) mental states of agents; d) time constraints; e) government regulations and/or industry standards/practices; f) agents' varying reactions to incentives over time.

16) Mechanisms are defined and designed only in terms of agents' preferences, public actions, and private actions. This approach does not incorporate the effects of agents' reactions to incentives, and values of hidden information to agents, and agents' information processing capabilities, the mechanism's information processing capabilities, regulation and government enforcement.

17) Contrary to mechanism design theory, the set of all possible preferences of agents is not finite. Within this context of mechanisms and group action, the definition of *"finite"* should be based on achievability (*True and Reasonable Possibilities*), and not on mathematical ranges.

18)   Erroneously assumes that each agent's and all agents' preferences are static over time; and mechanisms are *preference formation-independent* (ie the mechanism does not affect the agents' processes of forming their preferences). In reality, most mechanisms are interactive, and the agent's preferences change over time as he/she interacts with both the mechanism and other agent-participants and non-participants.

19)   Erroneously assumes that the mechanism is removed from, and is distinct from the agents – in reality, the agents typically form a major part of the mechanism (as in auctions, online file sharing networks, multiple listing systems, etc.).

20)   Erroneously assumes that the mechanism's main role is either *allocation* and or *co-ordination*. In reality many mechanisms serve other economic and non-economic purposes (some of which are unintended) such as: a) psychological reassurance (voting, auctions, etc.); b) information dissemination; c) comparison – which increases social welfare by reducing overall agents' search costs; d) entertainment.

21)   Erroneously assumes that mechanisms can be *deliberation-proof* (in equilibrium, all agents don't have any incentive to strategically deliberate). In most existing mechanisms, agents deliberate while using the mechanism; and real *equilibrium* is rare in many contexts.

1.4 The differences among Earnings Management, "Asset-Quality Management" and "Incentive-Effects Management"

There are or can be significant differences among the following three types of misconduct:

i)   *Earnings Management* – that is, traditional real earnings management and accrual-based earnings management by the firm's employees/managers and or board members. There are two generally accepted types of Earnings Management in the literature which are as follows: 1) Accrual Manipulation ("AM") wherein the perpetrators use subjective and manipulated estimates of balance sheet accruals to manage earnings; and 2) manipulation of real activities ("Real Earnings management" or "REM"), wherein the perpetrators manipulate real activities – such as shifting sales between periods, changing/moving inventory, etc. REM is deemed to be more difficult to detect than AM. Most books and articles on earnings management focus on describing the various types of AM and REM earnings management but don't propose any solutions for curbing or eliminating such misconduct.

Intangibles-Disclosure Management differs from Accruals-Manipulation because: i) Intangibles-Disclosure Management is intertwined with the organizational structure of the firm; ii) Intangibles-Disclosure Management can simultaneously affect the Balance Sheet, Income Statement and Cash

Flow Statement; iii) Intangibles-Disclosure Management can have substantial effect on investors' perception of the quality of the firm's assets.

ii) *"Asset-Quality Management"* – wherein the firm's employees/managers and or board-members deliberately execute transactions and or accounting journal entries that falsely distort (and in most cases inflate and exaggerate) the quality of the firm's assets and or liabilities. Asset-Quality Management (AQM) also refers to: 1) mis-classification of the firm's non-performing obligations/loans; 2) misclassification of the firm's investments (quality; use; holding period; value; etc.). Such transactions and or journal entries may or may not involve earnings management; but are always or often illegal (because of existing laws; or the *mens rea*; or specific intent elements; etc.) or unethical (because of their detrimental effects and adverse effects on social welfare). Most if not all earnings management books/articles completely omit the analysis of Intangibles as a "third method" for earnings management and as a method for profiting from earnings management in the short term and long term ("Intangibles Disclosure management") which is a type of "Asset-Quality Management". Intangibles-Disclosure Management differs from Accruals-Manipulation because: 1) Intangibles-Disclosure Management is intertwined with the organizational structure of the firm; 2) Intangibles-Disclosure Management can simultaneously affect the Balance Sheet, Income Statement and Cash Flow Statement; 3) Intangibles-Disclosure Management can have substantial effect on investors' perception of the quality of the firm's assets. Intangibles-Disclosure Management is a type of "Asset Quality Management".

iii) *"Incentive-Effects Management"* – wherein the firm's employees/managers and or board members deliberately enact/implement policies and or execute transactions and or accounting journal entries that falsely distort (and in most cases inflate and exaggerate) the effects, timing and or values of various types of *Incentive Mechanisms* and or Equity-based incentives (EBIs) and or cash incentives; and or affect the efficiency of the *Incentive Mechanisms* mentioned herein and above. Such transactions and or journal entries may or may not involve earnings management; but are always or often illegal (because of existing laws; or the *mens rea*; or knowledge or specific-intent elements; etc.) or unethical (because of their detrimental effects and adverse effects on social welfare).

Equity-based incentives (EBIs) and to a lesser extent, cash incentives, are the primary means that managers/employees use to realize the benefits of earnings management, asset-quality management and incentive-effects management, all of which have adverse effects on social welfare – such as unjustified wealth transfers (to EBI-holders and un-affiliated investors); disruption costs at both the company and industry levels; increased transaction costs; increased volatility of stocks; inflation; increased perceived risk; distorted values of assets; etc.

History and the post-Sarbanes Oxley Act (SOX; USA) regime (and similar regimes in many countries where similar statutes were enacted) have shown that regulating earnings management is very difficult and can be costly with attendant adverse multiplier effects in the economy. Thus, a more effective approach is to identify and eliminate the methods and instruments that perpetrators use to benefit from earnings management, and to provide substantial incentives for elimination of earnings management.

While earnings management can be achieved with many types of assets, this book focuses on Intangibles and real estate because: i) historically and in most countries, a significant percentage of all earnings management, (and asset-quality management and incentive-effects management) are related to, or based on real estate and or Intangible assets; and ii) among all corporate assets, real estate and intangibles are some of the most susceptible to external influences.

1.5 Sustainability, economic growth and the standardization of contracts

Standardization of contracts can affect economic growth, Sustainability, Inequality and Economic Growth as noted by various academic researchers – see Sussman (1999), Van Assche and Schwartz (2013), Patterson (2010), Engert and Hornuf (2018), Aguirre (2017), Ayotte and Bolton (2011), Baffi (2007, 2012), He, Xue and Zhou (2019), Vo et al. (2019), Sheng (2019), Eenmaa-Dimitrieva and Schmidt-Kessen (2019), Dekker, Kawai and Sakaguchi (2018), Iossa and Martimort (2018) and Sprinkle, Williamson and Upton (2008). Sussman (1999) noted that ". . . The main implications of contract standardization are that (i) financial history matters in the growth process, (ii) early formation of the system may create a drag on economic growth and (iii) the effect may be non-monotonic because the system may be modernized at some point . . .". In the realm of Fintech, local bar associations and trade associations have developed standardized or quasi-standardized agreements for transactions and strategic alliances. In the realm of ARS, CDS and Investment Vehicles, various trade associations in many countries (such as FINRA, ISDA and ICMA in the US and the UK) have developed standardized contracts for swaps/derivatives, other Financial Instruments, securities brokers and securities brokerage customers. In the realm of outsourcing contracts, maintenance contracts and procurement contracts, lawyers' associations and various trade associations in many countries have developed standardized contracts.

1.6 *Accounting Biases, Structural Effects,* enforcement patterns and industry structure

Accounting Biases is a relatively new line of research and has been studied from Behavioral Accounting, Management Science (see: Khan and Lo [2018]; Chen and Jorgensen [2018]; Kwon [2005] and Marquardt and Zur [2015]), Behavioral Operations Management and Operations Research (see: Nan and Wen [2014]) perspectives. Specific *Accounting Biases* were introduced in several chapters in this book. Chen and Jorgensen (2018) noted that *Accounting Biases* can affect competition and Industry Structure in various industries. Using a study of mergers/acquisitions, Marquardt and Zur (2015) found evidence that financial accounting quality is positively related to the efficient allocation of the economy's capital resources.

Structural Effects (used in various chapters in this book) are behavior patterns, psychological effects and human responses that arise solely because of the nature/structure of Incentive-Mechanisms, regulations/statutes and or organizations. *Structural Effects* can affect competition and Industry Structure in various industries because: i) they affect the relationships of, and collaboration among firms in industries, and firms' responses to competitive pressures and their regulatory environment; ii) they affect firms' executive compensation, decision-making, opportunity-set, Internal Capital Markets and allocations of resources and capital; iii) they affect product development, marketing and human resources deliberations and managerial decisions; v) they affect the functioning, responsibilities and liability of boards of directors; v) they affect firms' perceived risk and liability-allocation in expected or existing disputes.

Enforcement Theory has been analyzed from Operations Research, Political Philosophy and Law perspectives, and the associated literatures are cited in Chapter 2 in this book. *Enforcement Patterns* (e.g. enforcement of accounting regulations, commodities-trading regulations and securities laws; corporate laws; etc.) can also affect competition and Industry Structure in various industries because: i) they affect the nature of competition and collaboration among firms in industries; ii) they affect firms' allocations of resource and capital; iii) they affect product development, marketing and human resources decisions; iv) they affect the functioning, responsibilities and liability of boards of directors; v) they affect firms' perceived risk and liability-allocation in expected or existing disputes.

Thus, by extension, *Accounting Biases, Structural Effects* and *Enforcement Patterns* can have both direct and indirect effects on economic growth and Sustainability.

1.7 The unreliability of empirical research in psychology (including mathematical psychology), complex systems, behavioral political economy and behavioral operations research

The significant un-reliability and distortion of empirical research and the "*Reproducibility/Replicability Crisis*" in Science, Behavioral Operations Research, Behavioral Accounting, Behavioral Political Economy and Psychology (including Mathematical Psychology) was addressed in Open Science Collaboration (August 28, 2015); István (2016); Zeng, Shen and Zhou (2017); Cairney and Geyer (2017); Bohannon (August 28, 2015); Banks, Kepes and McDaniel (2015); Banks et al. (2016, in press); Bosco et al. (2016, in press); John, Loewenstein and Prelec (2012); Masicampo and Lalande (2012); O'Boyle, Banks and Gonzalez-Mule (2016); Schmidt and Hunter (2015); Świątkowski and Dompnier (2017); Loken and Gelman (2017); Ioannidis (2005); Johnson (2013); Aguinis, Cascio and Ramani (2017); Drummond

(2009); Replicability Research Group (2015); Baker (2016); Chang and Li (2015); Collins (2016); Cristea and Ioannidis (2018); Feest (2016); Sterling (1959); Wasserstein and Lazar (2016); McShane et al. (2018); Stanford Encyclopedia of Philosophy (December 3, 2018); and BEC Crew (August 28, 2015).[4]

1.8 Problems inherent in prior empirical studies of earnings management and securities fraud

Many empirical studies of earnings management analyze quarterly financial statements of publicly traded companies in order to attempt to show existing or new methods of earnings management. These approaches are wrong for the following reasons:

i)   Those studies suffer from the *"Reproducibility/Replicability Crisis"* mentioned herein and above.

ii) These studies focused on creation and duration of "discretionary accruals" as major indices/proxies of earnings management.

iii) Most of the studies omitted most types of Asset-Quality Management and Incentive-Effects Management.

iv) The studies typically covered a specific period of time, or focused on one industry – and thus their results are limited to such time-periods and or industries and cannot be generalized (as illustrated by the Global Financial Crisis of 2007–2012 and the Asian Financial Crisis of 1997–1999, past statistical relationships are not guaranteed to re-occur in the future).

v)   The studies often used "matched samples".

vi) Most of the studies didn't adequately discuss the relationships among earnings management, economic growth, Sustainability, and Financial Stability.

1.9 The chapters: EBIS, elements of global real estate, and the above-mentioned *incentive-mechanisms* are intangible assets or liabilities; and intangible assets and real estate may account for as much as sixty percent of all earnings management and asset-quality management globally, and a substantial percentage of global economic growth

By their nature, most of the foregoing *Incentive-Mechanisms* (instruments, policies/regulations and processes mentioned in Section 1.2 herein and above) are intangible assets or liabilities; and can substantially affect various dimensions of Sustainability and Sustainable Growth as summarized as follows:

i)   *Economic/financial Sustainability* – the crash-risks of financial markets and commodity markets; market volatility; financial stability; prices; sustainable economic growth; etc.

ii) *Social Sustainability* – social networks; social un-rest; labor relations; the formation of families/households; household mobility (both geographical and social mobility); etc.

iii) *Urban Sustainability* – quality of life in urban areas; financing and maintenance of urban systems; sanitation; healthcare; transportation networks; household savings; housing-finance and housing-affordability; etc.

iv) *Environmental Sustainability* – environmental pollution; climate change; climate finance; environmental disclosures; etc.

As explained in Chapters 2, 5, 6, 7 and 8 in this book, *Sustainability*, Economic Growth and Public Policy are or can be significantly affected by:

i) Financial Development and Financial Contracting (i.e. "Auction Rate Securities", Mutual Funds, ETFs, Structured Products Vehicles, government bail-out programs; Equity-Based Incentives; the regulation of Financial Instruments; Reverse-Merger companies; VIEs; etc.).

ii) Real estate and associated infrastructure, *Structural Effects* and human biases.

iii) Intangible assets, intangibles accounting regulations (i.e. IFSR/IASB accounting regulations) and associated *Structural Effects* and human biases.

iv) Accounting Biases and *Enforcement Patterns*.

v) Mechanism Design, Contract Theory and the standardization of Contracts.

As explained in Chapter 3 in this book, it's estimated that more than 60 percent of all earnings management, asset-quality management and incentive-effects management in corporate entities pertain to real estate and or intangible assets. As explained in Chapter 3 in this book, in recent history, the largest corporate perpetrators of earnings management, asset-quality management and corporate scandals, and the largest financially/operationally distressed companies, and the largest successful startup companies, and the largest failed startup companies all owned significant intangible assets and or real estate related assets; and used substantial volumes of EBIs.

Equity-Based Incentives are the primary means and channel through which employees and managers benefit from Earnings Management, Asset-Quality Management, Incentive-Effects Management. Using observations from the 240 largest non-financial firms in the UK, Kuang (2008) found that managers are more likely to engage in earnings management when they hold a larger proportion of their compensation in performance-vested stock options (PVSOs); and that vesting-targets (and vesting requirement) influence the relationship between earnings management and PVSO compensation – and Efendi, Srivastava and Swanson (2007) made similar conclusions and Nwogugu (2006) noted that Employee Stock Options fundamentally change Production Functions and Service Functions. The term EBIs refers to all Common-Stock based and equity-based incentives, and include Contingent Rights; Stock Warrants (to purchase equity); *Phantom stock plans* ("PSPs"; also known as "Shadow Stock Plans"); *Stock Appreciation Rights*

("SARs"); equity-linked incentives; *Restricted Stock Units* ("RSUs"); *Dividend Equivalent Rights* (DERs); *Employee-Stock-Options* ("ESOs"); some types of convertible securities (which provide incentives to investors and or the issuer-firm's managers); etc. Even some types of share-repurchases by companies and climate-finance instruments are EBIs – simply because they are partly or wholly based on the company's equity and can provide significant incentives for employees/managers that own the subject company's ESOs and stocks. The underlying commonalities are that: i) in the context of their use in companies, all EBIs have either actual or "implicit" strike-prices in the form of actual monetary amounts, or the occurrence of an event, or the achievement of a performance target, or the passage of time; ii) ESOs are economically and structurally similar to other types of "non-ESO-EBIs" such as PSPs, SARs, DERs, RSUs, and some types of stock-repurchases (which generally tends to increase per-share metrics/measures) and the non-ESO-EBIs are based on the company's equity and they have or can have direct or indirect incentive effects on employees (or other holders); iii) it's possible to effect fraudulent and illegal transactions (such as earnings management, *back-dating, re-loading* and *re-pricing*) when using DERs, RSUs, Phantom Stock, SARs, contingent performance rights and when executing some types of share-repurchases. Although the costs associated with the grant of EBIs are expensed in most countries, EBIs create substantial Intangibles in the form of greater employee motivation and productivity, incentives to innovate, greater product/service quality, employee job-satisfaction, greater goal congruence, etc. These intangibles are typically recognized only when the subject company is acquired (under the present IFRS/IASB accounting rules, such Intangibles cannot be recorded when or after the EBIs are granted). See: DeLong (2002).[5] Hand (2003: 305–306) and Damodaran (September 2009) also concur that EBIs create Intangibles that are often un-recognized in financial statements due to accounting rules. Damodaran (September 2009) noted that firms that have significant Intangible assets (e.g. pharmaceutical companies, internet companies, technology firms, etc.) use much more EBIs than the typical firm; and also noted the flaws in the accounting treatment of earnings and book value in these high-EBI firms. Damodaran (September 2009) argued that R&D expenses should be capitalized and then expensed/amortized; and that in some circumstances, advertising expenses and SG&A costs (selling, general and administrative expenses) should also be capitalized and amortized over a fixed period. Nakamura (1999) also indicated that EBIs are intangibles. This relationship between EBIs and Intangibles is well established – in its ruling 2009, the US Court of Appeals for the Ninth Circuit (USA) held that the costs of EBIs were the costs of creating Intangibles[6] within the context of international operations and transfer pricing. In 2010, the same Court reversed itself but the 2010 decision applies only to a limited context – transfer pricing and international operations and R&D collaboration between two related companies, and the ruling applies to a US Treasury Department rule that was enacted in 2003. Hence, the 2010 US Court of Appeals decision does not apply to un-related companies that share R&D costs, or to domestic R&D cost allocation, or to traditional domestic allocation of other costs incurred for the creation of intangibles. Also the question before the court in *Xilinx* was the treatment of these EBI expenses under the rules that were in effect from 1997 to 1999, for the 2003 amendment by the US Treasury. In 2003, the US Treasury Department amended its regulations to state that stock-based compensation must be taken into account as a cost of developing intangibles subject to transfer pricing adjustment under these rules. Bell, Landsman, Miller and Yeh (2002) found that the stock market values EBI expenses as Intangibles. Bell, Landsman, et al. (2002); Dottling, Ladika & Perotti (2016); Fehr and Schmidt (2000); and Fehr and Falk (2002) observed that investors perceive EBIs as intangibles.

Some elements of real estate such as leasehold-interests; lease agreements; property management agreements; purchase/sale agreements; brokerage agreement; easements, franchise rights, etc., are or can be formally classified as Intangible Assets. See the comments in IAAO (2016).[7]

Chapter 2 in this book analyzes and surveys *Enforcement Theory*, and explains why *Real Options Theory* is not applicable to the selection of disputes for litigation (litigation pertaining to IASB/IFRS and US FASB accounting regulations and securities law violations mostly in common law countries). *Enforcement Theory* has evolved from an arcane sub-field of Political Philosophy to an established approach in Law and Political Economy. Chapter 2 also introduces psychology and behavioral Operations Research theories of human biases and enforcement patterns; and explains why *Selective Enforcement* invalidates *Trial Selection Theory* (a sub-set of *Enforcement Theory*). Many academic studies of Asset Pricing, Structural Changes and Financial Stability completely omitted the issue of *Non-Compliance* and *Enforcement* (as physical and economic phenomena) inspite of the fact that Intangible Assets account for more than 50 percent of stock-market value in most developed countries (and an increasing percentage in many developing countries). There have been very few theoretical studies of the use of *Real Options Theory* in the rules-enforcement context, and *Chapter 2* critiques Grundfest and Huang (2006) which is one of such rare studies.

Chapter 3 in this book discusses Public Health, Environmental Pollution, *Inefficient Resource Allocation* and *Inequality* (the "*Four-Factor Symbiosis Model*", an Emergent phenomenon) implications of Earnings Management, Asset-Quality Management, Incentive-Effects Management around the world; explains how these four factors are intertwined and can affect Sustainable Growth, and links them to corporate scandals and economic/financial crisis.

Chapter 4 explains why earnings management, asset-quality management, incentive-effects management and illegal insider trading are types of "*Leakages*" (macroeconomic; International Political Economy; social) and can cause or increase economic recessions, Systemic risk and Financial Instability. The chapter explains and introduces testable hypothesis about some of the evolving and symbiotic relationships between macroeconomic factors on one hand, and earnings management and Incentive-Effects Management on the other (including Standardized Contracts, asset securitization and some Structured Products Vehicles transactions).

Chapter 5 discusses the asset-misclassification, Earnings Management, Asset-Quality Management, Incentive-Effects Management and *Inequality Effects* inherent in the following Financial Instruments and within the context of *Standardized Contracts*: i) Mutual Funds; ii) Auction Rate Securities; iii) the TARP/CPP related securities that were issued to US government agencies during the Global Financial Crisis of 2007–2014, as part of the US government's failed *"Economic/financial stabilization" programs* and bailouts/bail-ins of financial institutions; iv) Structured Products; and v) SSETFs (Structured Synthetic ETFs). These Financial Instruments and vehicles are not "securities" (and Mutual Funds and SSETFs units are hybrid Contract-Intangibles and neither debt nor equity) and their legal classification has wide ranging implications for Public Policy, firms' "Internal Markets", *Optimal Financial Contracting*, many research fields and practitioners. These Financial Instruments and vehicles have been directly and indirectly used to finance economic development and corporate growth in many countries; and they have or can have economic and psychological *Multiplier Effects* and *Inequality Effects* that can spillover into other countries/continents. *Chapter 5* also summarizes and critiques the literature on *Optimal Financial Contracting*.

Chapter 6 analyzes earnings management, asset quality management and incentive-effects management pertaining to REITs and in RECs (non-REIT companies that own substantial real estate). The Chapter introduces testable Psychology and behavioral Operations Research hypothesis/theories of human biases, *Operations Gaps*, *Contract Theory*, enforcement patterns and *"Structural Effects"* (including Game Theory and antitrust related hypothesis). Since REITs and some regulated-RECs are subject to stringent regulations and accounting biases, such entities have substantial incentives to manipulate their reported earnings, cash flow and assets; all of which can cause information asymmetry and have Financial Stability and Industrial Organization implications. See: Chen and Tzang (1988). As mentioned in Nwogugu (2007c) there are substantial securities law problems inherent in the REIT format. In many countries, the use of the REIT format increases the propensity for employees to commit fraud and falsify records in order to comply with the numerous REIT tax codes. See: Devaney and Weber (2005) and McDonald, Nixon and Slawson (2000). The REIT ownership-concentration rule (9 percent in the US) effectively limits the amount and type of equity compensation that can be paid to managers, and hence provides substantial incentives for REITs' managers to seek other forms of illegal gain. Some REITs attempt to solve this problem by issuing "Phantom Stock". The nature and circumstances of RECs' and REITs' Property Management Agreements provide opportunities for fraud. These Management Agreements are typically executed without any open bidding or any transparent process. Lapses in compliance with Management Agreements that otherwise would have been sufficient grounds for lawsuits and or other enforcement actions, are sometimes ignored, to the detriment of the holders of RECs'/REIT's Beneficial Interests. The low costs of non-compliance with REIT statutes (loss of REIT status, loss of shareholders, shareholder turnover and the resultant declines in share prices) serves as a powerful motivator to commit fraud. Furthermore, because the

REIT must payout a minimum percentage of its earnings, and hence, has to rely on external financing for growth and acquisitions, its management has substantial incentives to increase non-cash expenses (such as depreciation and amortization), create reserves (to manage earnings), expense otherwise capitalizable costs, and also to reduce reported income. The transaction costs involved in implementing such penalties (for De-REITing) are relatively low. In the event of non-compliance with REIT qualification rules, there are no lawsuits, and the REIT simply de-REITs. The theories introduced in this chapter also apply to publicly traded companies that own substantial commercial real estate such as retailing chains, restaurant chains, hotel companies and large healthcare companies – the perceptions, prospects and profitability of these entities are sensitive to the quality and use-value of their real estate holdings.

Intangibles/Goodwill account for more than 50 percent of the stock market capitalization and more than 30 percent of the disclosed assets of companies in most developed countries (and increasingly substantial percentages in emerging markets countries such as South Korea, China and Brazil). As a result, the enforcement of Goodwill/Intangibles disclosure regulations affects investors' and regulators' perceptions of companies, and thus, the propensity for systemic risk, Financial Contagion and market crashes. Under the past and present US GAAP and IFRS/IASB accounting rules, it is possible to manipulate the accounting treatment of mergers, acquisitions, joint ventures, strategic alliances and "investments" in order to manipulate reported earnings, assets, goodwill, intangibles and equity. The rapid and continuing growth in cross-border transactions, continuing expansion of the Internet; and the increasing inter-connectedness of companies/subsidiaries across national borders and the growing popularity of IFRS/IASB accounting standards has increased the probability of Systemic Risk. In many countries, Intangibles/Goodwill accounting standards (e.g. "ASC-805: Business Combinations" and "ASC-350: Goodwill and Intangible Assets" in the US FASB rules; and "IFRS-3R: Business Combinations" and "IAS-38: Intangible Assets" in IASB/IFRS standards) are *Incentive Mechanisms* and have been expressly and/or impliedly incorporated into various type of statutes/regulations, and thus have the effect of enforceable law.

Chapter 7 explains some of the behavioral and Fintech-amplified problems that may arise in the use and enforcement of Intangibles/Goodwill accounting rules and within the context of Financial Stability, Sustainability, Earnings Management, Systemic Risk, Complex Adaptive Systems and Industry Structure. *Chapter 7* introduces economic psychology theories that can explain these foregoing phenomena in addition to Corporate Growth, fraud/misconduct and *Non-Compliance*. *Chapter 7* also explains how the Intangibles/Goodwill accounting regulations can be manipulated to perpetrate Incentive Effects Management and Earnings Management. Thus, Intangibles/Goodwill accounting standards should be reformed to reduce managerial discretion, un-necessary market-volatility and distortion-effects of news; to promote Accounting-Principles (such as consistency, comparability and transparency), and to reflect the economic realities of transactions.

Chapter 8 discusses the asset-misclassification, earnings management, asset-quality management and incentive-effects management perpetrated by *Chinese VIEs* (variable interest entities) and *Chinese Reverse-Merger Companies* (CRMs) since 2000 and in stock markets in Canada, USA, Singapore, China and Thailand. These vehicles have been used to finance economic development and growth in Chinese industries; and they have or can have economic and psychological *Multiplier Effects* and *Inequality* that can continue to spillover into other countries/continents (such as Mexico and ASEAN countries). *Chapter 8* also introduces economic psychology theories that pertain to fraud, News-Contagion, *Fintech-Enabled Phenomena* and *Mass-Cognition*. The Chapter explains why *Third-generation Prospect Theory* (and related approaches) is invalid. *Structural Change* and *Asset Pricing* implications are also discussed.

1.10 Behavioral bias indicators

When aggregated at the national economy level, human behavioral biases such as those introduced in Chapters 2, 6, 7 and 8 (including *Capital Dynamics Theories*) in this book combine to create a class of complex-systems, behavioral operations research, macroeconomic and macrofinance indicators which are hereby referred to as the "*Behavioral Bias Indicators*". These indicators have not been properly recognized in the economics/finance, political economy, behavioral operations research or psychology literatures and are not tracked. Niamir, Filatova, et al. (2018); Nakagawa, Oiwa and Takeda (2012); Korniotis and Kumar (1993); Acquier, Daudigeos and Pinkse (2017); Schnellenbach and Schubert (2015); Pennings and Wansink (2004); and Rosenbaum, Billinger, et al. (2012) concluded or implied that human biases can affect national economies, although the links they established or theorized were indirect and they didn't discuss the issue of *Behavioral Bias Indicators*.

Notes

1 This chapter contains excerpts from Michael C. Nwogugu's article that is cited as follows: Nwogugu, M. (2008). Securitization is illegal: Racketeer influenced and corrupt organizations, usury, antitrust and tax issues. *Journal of International Banking Law & Regulation*, 23(6), 316–332.
2 *See*: "The Vast Majority of All Futures Trading Is Now Automated". By Brian Merchant. April 26, 2019. https://www.gizmodo.com.au/2019/04/the-vast-majority-of-all-futures-trading-is-now-automated/.
   See: "80% of the Stock Market Is Now on Autopilot". By Yun Li. June 29, 2019. https://www.cnbc.com/2019/06/28/80percent-of-the-stock-market-is-now-on-autopilot.html.
   See: "Robots Are killing Off Wall Street's traders". By Laura French. October 29, 2014. https://www.worldfinance.com/markets/technology/robots-are-killing-off-wall-streets-traders.
   See: "Cracking the Street's New Math, Algorithmic trades are sweeping the stock market". http://www.businessweek.com/magazine/content/05_16/b3929113_mz020.htm.
   See: The Future of Algorithmic Trading. https://www.experfy.com/blog/the-future-of-algorithmic-trading.

See: "The Growth and Future of Algorithmic Trading". July 19, 2018. https://blog.quantinsti.com/growth-future-algorithmic-trading/.

See: "Algorithmic Trading a 'Prerequisite' for Surviving Tomorrow's Markets – With Technology, Data Sciences and Automated Trading Beginning to Play a Big Role, This Skill Is Fast Becoming a Prerequisite". By Nitesh Khandelwal. Updated on February 17, 2019. https://www.business-standard.com/article/pf/algorithmic-trading-a-prerequisite-for-surviving-tomorrow-s-markets-119021601197_1.html.

See: "The Quickening Evolution of Trading – In Charts: Automated Algorithms Are on the Rise, With High-Frequency Trading Volumes Picking Up". By Robin Wigglesworth, April 11, 2017. https://www.ft.com/content/77827a4c-1dfc-11e7-a454-ab04428977f9.

See: "How Important Is Algorithmic Trading in the Retail Market?: The Computerization of the Financial Markets Industry Began as Far Back as the Early 1970s and Program Trading Became Widely . . ." https://financefeeds.com/important-algorithmic-trading-retail-market/.

See: "Agent-Human Interactions in the Continuous Double Auction". IBM T.J.Watson Research Center, August 2001. http://spider.sci.brooklyn.cuny.edu/~parsons/courses/840-spring-2005/notes/das.pdf.

Gjerstad, S. & Dickhaut, J. (January 1998). Price formation in double auctions. *Games and Economic Behavior*, 22(1), 1–29. http://www.sciencedirect.com/science/article/pii/S0899825697905765.

See: Technical Committee of the International Organization of Securities Commissions (July 2011). "Regulatory Issues Raised by the Impact of Technological Changes on Market Integrity and Efficiency". IOSCO Technical Committee. http://www.iosco.org/library/pubdocs/pdf/IOSCOPD354.pdf.

See: Shen, J. & Yu, J. (2014). "Styled Algorithmic Trading and the MV-MVP Style". http://papers.ssrn.com/sol3/papers.cfm?abstract_id=2507002.

See: Shen, J. (2017). "Hybrid IS-VWAP Dynamic Algorithmic Trading via LQR". http://papers.ssrn.com/sol3/papers.cfm?abstract_id=2984297.

See: "How to Build Robust Algorithmic Trading Strategies". AlgorithmicTrading.net. https://algorithmictrading.net/project/robust-algorithmic-trading-strategies/.

3 *See*: Lexis Nexis. (2018). *Structured Products – Overview*. www.lexisnexis.com/uk/lexispsl/bankingandfinance/document/391289/5FBC-77G1-F185-X0TV-00000-00/Structured_products_overview#.

4 This article stated in part "A landmark study involving one hundred scientists from around the world has tried to replicate the findings of 270 recent findings from highly ranked psychology journals and by one measure, only 36 percent turned up the same results. That means that for over half the studies, when scientists used the same methodology, they could not come up with the same results. . . . And earlier this year, a separate study found that the prevalence of irreproducible preclinical research exceeds fifty percent, resulting in approximately US$28,000,000,000/year spent on pre-clinical research that is not reproducible – in the United States alone".

5 DeLong (2002) stated in part ". . . As was recently noted, 'Without institutions to bring together people with resources and people with ideas, new ventures can be launched only by the narrow circle of people who have both'. Options are just such an institution, and an important one, and the proposals to treat them as expenses would meddle destructively with a complex financial and entrepreneurial ecosystem. . . ."

6 *See*: Ernst & Young (July 2010). "IRS Concedes Stock Option Issue in Veritas Following Ninth Circuit's Opinion in Xilinx". Available at: http://www.ey.com/Publication/vwLUAssets/ITA_26July2010/$FILE/ITA_IRS_concedes_stock_option.pdf.

See: Sullivan & Cromwell (May 29, 2009). "Court Addresses Employee Stock Option Expenses for Transfer Pricing Purposes – Ninth Circuit Overturns Tax Court and Holds That Expenses Attributable to Employee Stock Options Are 'Cost'

of Developing Intangibles for Transfer Pricing Purposes". Available at: http://
www.sullcrom.com/files/Publication/1123f4bf-af4b-4d0b-a948-2e0cbf147a73/
Presentation/PublicationAttachment/83790441-f801-4766-bfcc-2eabc306273e/SC_
Publication_Court_Addresses_Employee_Stock_Option_Expenses_for_Transfer_
Pricing_Purposes.pdf.
  See: *Xilinx, Inc.* vs. *Commissioner;* 2009 WL1459501 (USA; 9th Cir. 2009).
  See: Sullivan & Cromwell (March 24, 2010). "Court Addresses (Again) Employee Stock
Option Expenses for Transfer Pricing Purposes – Ninth Circuit Overturns Tax Court and
Holds That Expenses Attributable to Employee Stock Options Are 'Costs' of Developing
Intangibles for Transfer Pricing Purposes – Ninth Circuit Reverses Itself and Holds That
the Arm's-Length Standard Controls in Determining If Employee Stock Option Expenses
Must Be Shared Among Related Parties Under Pre-2003 US Transfer Pricing Rules. Avail-
able at: http://www.sullcrom.com/files/Publication/68c25802-e2d4-483c-8662-102f0af7
bdbf/Presentation/PublicationAttachment/b88f2c64-3d86-44d5-998c-1484ea00283a/SC_
Publication_Court_Addresses_Employee_Stock_Option_Expenses.pdf.
  See: Xilinx, Inc. vs. *Commissioner* (2010 U.S. App. LEXIS 5795 (March 22, 2010)).
  See: O'Driscoll, D. (November 1, 2005). Allocation of Employee Stock Options to
Cost-Sharing Agreement. *The Tax Adviser. See*: US Internal Revenues Service (2008).
"Cost Sharing Stock Based Compensation (UIL 482.11–13)". http://www.irs.gov/busi
nesses/article/0,,id=180309,00.html.
7 *See*: IAAO (2016). "Understanding Intangible Assets and Real Estate: A Guide for Real
Property Valuation Professionals". https://www.iaao.org/library/2017_Intangibles_web.pdf.

Bibliography

Abeysekera, I. (2003). Political economy of accounting in intellectual capital reporting.
  The European Journal of Management and Public Policy, 2(1), 2003, 65–79.
Acquier, A., Daudigeos, T. & Pinkse, J. (2017). Promises and paradoxes of the sharing econ-
  omy: An organizing framework. *Technological Forecasting & Social Change*, 125, 1–10.
Agrawal, A. & Cooper, T. (2017). Corporate governance consequences of accounting scan-
  dals: Evidence from top management, CFO and auditor turnover. *Quarterly Journal of
  Finance*, 07(01), 1650014.
Aguinis, H., Cascio, W. & Ramani, R. (2017). Science's reproducibility and replicability
  crisis: International business is not immune. *Journal of International Business Studies*,
  48, 653–663.
Aguirre, A. (2017). Contracting institutions and economic growth. *Review of Economic
  Dynamics*, 24, 192–217.
Asare, S., van Buuren, J. & Majoor, B. (2018). The joint role of auditors' and auditees'
  incentives and disincentives in the resolution of detected misstatements. *Auditing:
  A Journal of Practice & Theory*, in press.
Ayotte, K. & Bolton, P. (2011). Covenant lite lending, liquidity, and standardization of
  financial contracts. Chapter in: Bolon, P. ed., *Research Handbook on the Economics of
  Property Law* (Edward Elgar Publishing Ltd.), pp. 174–189.
Badia, F., Dicuonzo, G., et al. (2019). Integrated reporting in action: Mobilizing intellec-
  tual capital to improve management and governance practices. *Journal of Management
  and Governance*, 23(2), 299–320.
Baffi, E. (2007). *The Economics of Standard Form Contracts* (Università degli Studi "Gug-
  lielmo Marconi", Italy).
Baffi, E. (2010). *Some Characteristic Features of Mass Contracting* (Università degli Studi
  "Roma Tre" – Faculty of Law", Italy).

Baffi, E. (2012). Contracting in modern world. *Aperta Contrada*. www.apertacontrada. it/2012/11/13/contracting-in-modern-world/.

Baker, M. (2016). 1,500 scientists lift the lid on reproducibility. *Nature*, 533(7604), 452–454.

Banks, G., Kepes, S. & McDaniel, M. (2015). Publication bias: Understand the myths concerning threats to the advancement of science. Chapter in: Lance, C.E. & Vandenberg, R.J., eds., *More Statistical and Methodological Myths and Urban Legends* (Routledge, New York), pp. 36–64.

Banks, G., O'Boyle Jr., E., Pollack, J.M., White, C.D., Batchelor, J.H., Whelpley, C.E., Abston, K.A. et al. (2016). Questions about questionable research practices in the field of management: A guest commentary. *Journal of Management*, 12: 331–338.

Barnes, D. (2006). A new economics of trademarks. *Northwestern Journal of Technology and Intellectual Property*, 5, 22–33.

Battiston, S. & Glattfelder, J.B. (2009). Backbone of complex networks of corporations: The flow of control. *Physics Review-E*, 80, 036104.

Bell, T., Landsman, W., Miller, B. & Yeh, S. (2002). The valuation implications of employee stock option accounting for profitable computer software firms. *The Accounting Review*, 77(4), 971–996.

Benjamin, J., de la Torre, C. & Musumeci, J. (1995). Controlling the incentive problems in real estate leasing. *The Journal of Real Estate Finance and Economics*, 10(2), 177–191.

Bergemann, D. & Morris, S. (2005). Robust mechanism design. *Econometrica*, 73(6), 1771–1813.

Bizjak, J., Lemmon, M. & Naveen, L. (2008). Does the use of peer groups contribute to higher pay and less efficient compensation? *Journal of Financial Economics*, 90(2), 152–168.

Boczko, T. (2000). A critique on the classification of contemporary accounting: Towards a political economy of classification – the search for ownership. *Critical Perspectives on Accounting*, 11, 131–153.

Bosco, F., Aguinis, H., Field, J., Pierce, C.A. & Dalton, D.R. (2016). Harking's threat to organizational research: Evidence from primary and meta-analytic sources. *Personnel Psychology*, 69(3), 709–750.

Bredeweg, B. & Struss, P. (Winter 2003). Current Topics in Qualitative Reasoning. *AI Magazine*, pp. 13–17.

Brounen, D. & Eichholtz, P. (2005). Corporate real estate ownership implications: International performance evidence. *Journal of Real Estate Finance & Economics*, 30, 429–445.

Bushman, R. & Piotroski, J. (2006). Financial reporting incentives for conservative accounting: The influence of legal and political institutions. *Journal of Accounting and Economics*, 42(1–2), 107–148.

Cairney, P. & Geyer, R. (2017). A critical discussion of complexity theory: How does 'complexity thinking' improve our understanding of politics and policymaking? *Complexity, Governance and Networks*, 3(2), 1–11.

Calvo, C., Ivorra, C. & Liern, V. (2017). Controlling risk through diversification in portfolio selection with non-historical information. *Journal of the Operational Research Society*, 69(10), 1543–1548.

Chang, A. & Li, P. (2015). Is economics research replicable? Sixty published papers from thirteen journals say 'usually not'. *Finance and Economics Discussion Series*, 2015(83), 1–26.

Chapman, C. & Steenburgh, T. (2010). An investigation of earnings management through marketing actions. *Management Science*, 57(1), 214.

Chari, V., Golosov, M. & Tsyvinski, A. (2012). Prizes and patents: Using market signals to provide incentives for innovations. *Journal of Economic Theory*, 147(2), 781–801.

Chen, F. & Gao, G. (2006). Ownership structure, corporate governance, and fraud: Evidence from China. *Journal of Corporate Finance*, 12, 424–448.

Chen, H. & Jorgensen, B. (2018). Market exit through divestment – The effect of accounting bias on competition. *Management Science*, 64(1), 1–493.

Chen, K. & Tzang, D. (1988). Interest rate sensitivity of real estate investment trusts. *Journal of Real Estate Research*, 3(3), 13–22.

Chen, Y., Wu, C., Chen, Y., Li, H. & Chen, H. (2017). Enhancement of fraud detection for narratives in annual reports. *International Journal of Accounting Information Systems*, 26, 32–45.

Chinloy, P. & Winkler, D. (2010). Contract incentives and effort. *Journal of Real Estate Research*, 32(4), 397–412.

Christensen, H., Lee, E., Walker, M. & Zeng, C. (2015). Incentives or standards: What determines accounting quality changes around IFRS adoption? *European Accounting Review*, 24(1), 31–61.

Collins, H. (2016). Reproducibility of experiments: Experiments' regress, statistical uncertainty principle, and the replication imperative. Chapter 4 in: Atmanspacher, H. & Maasen, S. eds., *Reproducibility: Principles, Problems, Practices, and Prospects* (John Wiley & Sons), pp. 65–82.

Crew, M. & Kleindorfer, P. (2000). *A Critique of the Theory of Incentive Regulation: Implications for the Design of Performance Based Regulation for Postal Service*. Working Paper.

Cristea, I. & Ioannidis, J. (2018). P-values in display items are ubiquitous and almost invariably significant: A survey of top science journals. *PLoS One*, 13(5), e0197440. doi: 10.1371/journal.pone.0197440.

Cumming, D. & Johan, S. (2013). Listing Standards and Fraud. *Managerial & Decision Economics*, 34(7–8), 451–470.

Damodaran, A. (September 2009). *Valuing Companies with Intangible Assets*. Working Paper, NYU Stern School of Business, New York. http://pages.stern.nyu.edu/~adamodar/pdfiles/papers/intangibles.pdf.

Darrington, J. & Howell, G. (2011). Motivation and incentives in relational contracts. *Journal of Financial Management of Property and Construction*, 16(1), 42–51.

Dasgupta, P., & Maskin, E. (2000). Efficient Auctions, *Quarterly Journal of Economics*, 115, 341–388.

Davidson, W., Xie, B., Xu, W. & Ning, Y. (2007). The influence of executive age, career horizon and incentives on pre-turnover earnings management. *Journal of Management & Governance*, 11(1), 45–60.

Dbouk, B. & Zaarour, I. (2017). Towards a Machine Learning Approach for Earnings Manipulation Detection. *Asian Journal of Business and Accounting*, 10(2), 215–220.

Dekker, H., Kawai, T. & Sakaguchi, J. (2018). Contracting abroad: A comparative analysis of contract design in host and home country outsourcing relations. *Management Accounting Research*, 40, 47–61.

DeLong, J. (2002). *The Stock Options Controversy and the New Economy* (Competitive Enterprise Institute, Washington, DC).

Deng, Y. & Gyourko, J. (1999). *Real Estate Ownership by Non-Real Estate Firms: The Impact on Firm Returns*. www.usc.edu/schools/sppd/lusk/research/pdf/wp_1999_103.pdf.

Denis, D., Hanouna, P. & Sarin, A. (2006). Is there a dark side to incentive compensation? *Journal of Corporate Finance*, 12(3), 467–488.

Devaney, M. & Weber, W. (2005). Efficiency, scale economies, and the risk/return performance of real estate investment trusts. *Journal of Real Estate Finance & Economics*, 31(3), 301–317.

Dikmen, B. & Kukkocaoglu, G. (2010). The detection of earnings manipulation: The three-phase cutting plane algorithm using mathematical programming. *Journal of Forecasting*, 29(5), 442–466.

Ding, R., Li, J. & Wu, Z. (2018). Government affiliation, real earnings management, and firm performance: The case of privately held firms. *Journal of Business Research*, 83(C), 138–150.

Drabkova, Z. (2016). Models of detection of manipulated financial statements as part of the internal control system of the entity. *ACRN Oxford Journal of Finance and Risk Perspectives*, 5(1), 227–235.

Drozd, L. & Serrano-Padia, R. (2018). Financial contracting with enforcement externalities. *Journal of Economic Theory*, 178, 153–189.

Drummond, C. (2009). *Replicability Is Not Reproducibility: Nor Is It Good Science*. Proceedings of the Evaluation Methods for Machine Learning Workshop at the 26th ICML, Montreal, Canada.

Eenmaa-Dimitrieva, H. & Schmidt-Kessen, M. (2019). Creating markets in no-trust environments: The law and economics of smart contracts. *Computer Law & Security Review*, 35(1), 69–88.

Efendi, J., Srivastava, A. & Swanson, E. (2007). Why do corporate managers misstate financial statements? The role of option compensation and other factors. *Journal of Financial Economics*, 85(3), 667–708.

Engert, A. & Hornuf, L. (2018). Market standards in financial contracting: The Euro's effect on debt securities. *Journal of International Money and Finance*, 85, 145–162.

Fang, X. & Yuan, F. (2018). The coordination and preference of supply chain contracts based on time-sensitivity promotional mechanism. *Journal of Management Science and Engineering*, 3(3), 158–178.

Feest, U. (2016). The experimenters' regress reconsidered: Replication, tacit knowledge, and the dynamics of knowledge generation. *Studies in History and Philosophy of Science Part-A*, 58, 34–45.

Fehr, E. & Falk, A. (2002). Psychological foundations of incentives. *European Economic Review*, 46(4–5), 687–724.

Fehr, E. & Schmidt, K. (2000). Fairness, incentives, and contractual choices. *European Economic Review*, 44(4–6), 1057–1068.

Firth, M., Rui, O. & Wu, W. (2011). Cooking the books: Recipes and costs of falsified financial statements in China. *Journal of Corporate Finance*, 17(2), 371–390.

Fizaine, F. (2018). Toward generalization of futures contracts for raw materials: A probabilistic answer applied to metal markets. *Resources Policy*, 59, 379–388.

Forbus, K. (2019). Qualitative Representations: How People Reason and Learn About the Continuous World (MIT Press, USA).

Friewald, N., Jankowitsch, R. & Subrahmanyam, M. (2017). Transparency and liquidity in the structured product market. *Review of Asset Pricing Studies*, 7(2), 316–326.

Girth, A. & Lopez, L. (2018). Contract design, complexity, and incentives: Evidence from U.S. federal agencies. *American Review of Public Administration*, in press.

Glachant, M. (1998). The use of regulatory mechanism design in environmental policy: A theoretical critique in: F. Duchin, S. Faucheux, J. Gowdy, I. Nicolai (Eds.), *Firms and Sustainability* (Edward Elgar Publishers). http://www.cerna.ensmp.fr/Documents/MG-inFaucheux.pdf.

Goetz, R., Yatsenko, Y., Hritonenko, N., Xabadia, A. & Abdulai, A. (2019). The dynamics of productive assets, contract duration and holdup. *Mathematical Social Sciences*, 97, 24–37.

Grabowski, H., DiMasi, J. & Long, G. (2015). The roles of patents and research and development incentives in biopharmaceutical innovation. *Health Affairs*, 34(2). https://www.healthaffairs.org/doi/full/10.1377/hlthaff.2014.1047.

Greenwood, M., Baylis, R. & Tao, L. (2017). Regulatory incentives and financial reporting quality in public healthcare organisations. *Accounting & Business Research*, 47, 831–855.

Gross, C., Königsgruber, R., Pantzalis, C. & Pero, P. (2016). The financial reporting consequences of proximity to political power. *Journal of Accounting and Public Policy*. doi: 10.1016/j.jaccpubpol.2016.06.007.

Grundfest, J. & Huang, P. (2006). The Unexpected Value of Litigation: A Real Options Perspective. *Stanford Law Review*, 58(5), 1267–1336.

Hand, J. (2003). Increasing returns-to-scale of intangibles. Chapter in: Hand, J.R.M. & Lev, B., eds., *Intangible Assets: Values, Measures and Risks* (Oxford Management Readers).

Halpern, J. (2003). *Reasoning about Uncertainty* (MIT Press, USA).

He, Q., Xue, C. & Zhou, S. (2019). Does contracting institution affect the patterns of industrial specialization in China? *China Economic Review*, 54, 191–203.

Hong, S., Wernz, C. & Stillinger, J. (2016). Optimizing maintenance service contracts through mechanism design theory. *Applied Mathematical Modelling*, 40(21–22), 8849–8861.

Hoppe, E. & Schmitz, P. (2018). Hidden action and outcome contractibility: An experimental test of moral hazard theory. *Games & Economic Behavior*, 109, 544–564.

Hosseini, M., Chalestori, K., Rezahi Hi, S. & Ebrahimi, E. (2016). A study on the relationship between earnings management incentives and earnings response coefficient. *Procedia Economics and Finance*, 36, 232–243.

Hurwicz, L. (1972): "On Informationally Decentralized Systems," in R. Radner and C. McGuire (eds.), *Decision and Organization*. Amsterdam: North-Holland, 297–336.

IAAO. (2016). *Understanding Intangible Assets and Real Estate: A Guide for Real Property Valuation Professionals*. www.iaao.org/library/2017_Intangibles_web.pdf.

Iacobucci, E. & Winter, R. (2005). Asset securitization and asymmetric information. *The Journal of Legal Studies*, 34(1), 161–206.

The Institute of Internal Auditors Research Foundation. (2014). *Job Satisfaction for Internal Auditors: How to Retain Top Talent* (The Institute of Internal Auditors, Florida, USA).

Ioannidis, J. (2005). Why most published research findings are false. *PLOS Medicine*, 2(8), e124. doi: 10.1371/journal.pmed.0020124.

Iossa, E. & Martimort, D. (2018). Corruption in PPPs, incentives and contract incompleteness. *International Journal of Industrial Organization*, 44, 85–100.

István, B. (2016). Empirical research and practice-oriented physics for the humanities and sciences. *Comparative Literature & Culture*, 18(2).

Jarungrattanapong, R. (2018). Joint-liability and dynamic incentive mechanisms in microlending: Evidence from lab-in-the-field experiments in Thailand. *Kasetsart Journal of Social Sciences*, in press.

Jin, L. & Kothari, S. (2012). Effect of personal taxes on managers' decisions to sell their stock. *Journal of Accounting and Economics*, 46(1), 23–46.

John, L.K., Loewenstein, G. & Prelec, D. (2012). Measuring the prevalence of questionable research practices with incentives for truth telling. *Psychological Science*, 23, 524–532.

Johnson, V. (2013). Revised standards for statistical evidence. *Proceedings of the National Academy of Sciences*, 110, 19313–19317.

Kamran, M., Zhao, Z. & Ali, H. & Sabir, F. (2018). Does earnings management mediate the impact of financial policies on market value of firms? A comparative study of China and Pakistan. *International Journal of Financial Engineering*, 05(01), 1850006.

Kang, G. & Lin, J. (2011). Effects of the type of accounting standards and motivation on financial reporting decision. *Journal of Accounting Business and Management*, 18(2).

Khan, U. & Lo, A. (2018). Bank lending standards and borrower accounting conservatism. *Management Science*, in press.

Königsgruber, R. (2010). A political economy of accounting standard setting. *Journal of Management & Governance*, 14(4), 277–295.

Königsgruber, R. & Palan, S. (2015). Earnings management and participation in accounting standard-setting. *Central European Journal of Operations Research*, 23(1), 31–52.

Korniotis, V. & Kumar, A. (1993). Do behavioral biases adversely affect the economy? *Review of Financial Studies*, 24(5), 1513–1559.

Koskivaara, E. (2000). Artificial neural network models for predicting patterns in auditing monthly balances. *Journal of the Operational Research Society*, 51(9), 1060–1069.

Kuang, Y. (2008). Performance-vested stock options and earnings management. *Journal of Business Finance & Accounting*, 35(9–10), 1049–1078.

Kuzubas, T., Ömercikoglu, I. & Saltoglu, B. (2014). Network centrality measures and systemic risk: An application to the Turkish financial crisis. *Physica-A: Statistical Mechanics and Its Applications*, 405, 203–215.

Kwag, S. & Stephens, A. (2009). Investor reaction to earnings management. *Managerial Finance*, 36(1), 44–56.

Kwon, Y. (2005). Accounting conservatism and managerial incentives. *Management Science*, 51(11), 1593–1732.

Lhaopadchan, S. (2010). Fair value accounting and intangible assets: Goodwill impairment and managerial choice. *Journal of Financial Regulation & Compliance*, 18(2), 120–130.

Li, H., An, H., Gao, X., Huang, J. & Xu, Q. (2014). On the topological properties of the cross shareholding networks of listed companies in China: Taking shareholders' cross-shareholding relationships into account. *Physica-A*, 406, 80–88.

Li, W., Liu, Y. & Chen, Y. (2018). Modeling a two-stage supply contract problem in a hybrid uncertain environment. *Computers & Industrial Engineering*, 123, 289–302.

Lin, E. & Chou, M. (1990). Optimal contracts. *Applied Mathematics Letters*, 3(2), 65–68.

Ling, D., Naranjo, A. & Ryngert, M. (2012). Real estate ownership, leasing intensity, and value: Do stock returns reflect a firm's real estate holdings? *The Journal of Real Estate Finance and Economics*, 44(1–2), 184–202.

Liow, K. (1995). Property in corporate financial statements: The U.K. evidence. *Journal of Property Research*, 12, 13–28.

Liow, K. & Nappi-Choulet, I. (2008). A combined perspective of corporate real estate. *Journal of Corporate Real Estate*, 10(1), 54–67.

Liu, J., Gao, R., Cheah, C.Y.J. & Luo, J. (2016). Incentive mechanism for inhibiting investors' opportunistic behavior in PPP projects. *International Journal of Project Management*, 34(7), 1102–1111.

Loken, E. & Gelman, A. (2017). Measurement error and the replication crisis. *Science*, 355(6325), 584–585.

Long, W., Song, L. & Cui, L. (2017). Relationship between capital operation and market value management of listed companies based on random forest algorithm. *Procedia Computer Science*, 108, 1271–1280.

Ma, M. (2013). The perils and prospects of China's variable interest entities: Unraveling the murky rules and the institutional challenges posed. *Hong Kong Law Journal*, 43, 1061–1064.

Ma, Y., Zhuang, X.T. & Li, L. (2011). Research on the relationships of the domestic mutual investment of China based on the cross-shareholding networks of the listed companies. *Physica-A*, 390, 749–759.

Madureira, A., Pereira, I., Pereira, P. & Abraham, A. (2014). Negotiation mechanism for self-organized scheduling system with collective intelligence. *Neurocomputing*, 132, 97–110.

Marinovic, I. (2013). Internal control system, earnings quality and the dynamics of financial reporting. *The RAND Journal of Economics*, 44, 145–167.

Marquardt, C. & Zur, E. (2015). The role of accounting quality in the M&A market. *Management Science*, 61(3), 487–705.

Masicampo, E. & Lalande, D. (2012). A peculiar prevalence of *p* values just below .05. *The Quarterly Journal of Experimental Psychology & Aging*, 65, 2271–2279.

McCauley, J. (2002). Adam Smith's invisible hand is unstable: Physics and dynamics reasoning applied to economic theorizing. *Physica A: Statistical Mechanics and its Applications*, 314(1–4), 722–727.

McDonald, C., Nixon, T. & Slawson, C. (2000). The changing asymmetric information component of REIT spreads: A study of anticipated announcements. *Journal of Real Estate Finance & Economics*, 20(2), 195–210.

McShane, B., Gal, D., Gelman, A., Robert, C. & Tackett, J.L. (2018). *Abandon Statistical Significance*. arXiv.org.

Meneguzzi, F., Modgil, S., Oren, N., Miles, S., Luck, M. & Faci, N. (2012). Applying electronic contracting to the aerospace aftercare domain. *Engineering Applications of Artificial Intelligence*, 25, 1471–1487.

Miyake, M. (1998). On the incentive properties of multi-item auctions. *International Journal of Game Theory*, 27(1), 1–19.

Nakagawa, R., Oiwa, H. & Takeda, F. (2012). The economic impact of herd behavior in the Japanese loan market. *Pacific-Basin Finance Journal*, 20(4), 600–613.

Nakamura, L. (July/August 1999). Intangibles: What put the new in the new economy? *Federal Reserve Bank of Philadelphia Business Review*, 3–16.

Nan, L. & Wen, X. (2014). Financing and investment efficiency, information quality, and accounting biases. *Operations Research*, 60(9), 2111–2380.

Neeman, Z. (2004). The Relevance of Private Information in Mechanism Design, *Journal of Economic Theory*, 117, 55–77.

Ngai, E., Hu, Y., Wong, Y.H., Chen, Y. & Sun, X. (2011). The application of data mining techniques in financial fraud detection: A classification framework and an academic review of literature. *Decision Support Systems*, 50(3), 559–569.

Niamir, L., Filatova, T., Voinov, A. & Bressers, H. (2018). Transition to low-carbon economy: Assessing cumulative impacts of individual behavioral changes. *Energy Policy*, 118, 325–345.

Niederhoff, J. & Kouvelis, P. (2019). Effective and necessary: Individual supplier behavior in revenue sharing and wholesale contracts. *European Journal of Operational Research*, 277(3), 1060–1071.

Nwaeze, E. (2011). Are incentives for earnings management reflected in the ERC: Large sample evidence. *Advances in Accounting*, 27(1), 26–38.

Nwogugu, M. (2006). Employee stock options, production functions and game theory. *Applied Mathematics & Computation*, 181(1), 552–562.

Nwogugu, M. (2007a). Issues in disintermediation in the real estate brokerage industry. *Applied Mathematics & Computation*, 186(2), 1054–1064.

Nwogugu, M. (2007b). Some issues in securitization and disintermediation. *Applied Mathematics & Computation*, 186(2): 1031–1039.

Nwogugu, M. (2007c). Some securities law problems inherent in REITs. *Journal of International Banking Law & Regulation*, 22(11), 594–602.

Nwogugu, M. (2008a). Securitization is illegal: Racketeer influenced and corrupt organizations, usury, antitrust and tax issues. *Journal of International Banking Law & Regulation*, 23(6), 316–332.

Nwogugu, M. (2008b). Some corporate governance problems pertaining to REITs – Part two. *Journal of International Banking Law & Regulation*, 23(3), 142–155.

Nwogugu, M. (2019a). Human computer interaction, incentive conflicts and methods for eliminating index arbitrage, index-related mutual fund arbitrage and ETF arbitrage. Chapter 9 in: Nwogugu, M., *Indices, Index Funds and ETFs HCI: Exploring HCI, Nonlinear Risk and Homomorphisms* (Palgrave Macmillan, London, UK).

Nwogugu, M. (2019b). Economic policy, complex adaptive systems, human-computer interaction and managerial psychology: Popular-index ecosystems. Chapter 12 in: Nwogugu, M., *Indices, Index Funds and ETFs HCI: Exploring HCI, Nonlinear Risk and Homomorphisms* (Palgrave Macmillan, London, UK).

Nyadzayo, M., Matanda, M. & Ewing, M. (2011). Brand relationships and brand equity in franchising. *Industrial Marketing Management*, 40, 1103–1115.

O'Boyle, E., Banks, G. & Gonzalez-Mule, E. (2016). The chrysalis effect: How ugly initial results metamorphoze into beautiful articles. *Journal of Management*, 43(2), 376–399.

Open Science Collaboration. (2015). Estimating the reproducibility of psychological science. *Science*, 349(6251), aac4716.

Park, S. & Kim, J. (2014). A mathematical model for a capacity reservation contract. *Applied Mathematical Modelling*, 38(5–6), 1866–1880.

Patterson, M. (2010). Standardization of standard-form contracts: Competition and contract implications. *William and Mary Law Review*, 52(2), 327–340.

Peng, W., Wei, J. & Yang, Z. (2011). Tunneling or propping: Evidence from connected transactions in China. *Journal of Corporate Finance*, 17(2), 306–325.

Pennings, J. & Wansink, B. (2004). Channel contract behavior: The role of risk attitudes, risk perceptions, and channel members' market structures. *The Journal of Business*, 77(4), 697–724.

Pinto, J. & Alves, P. (2016). The economics of securitization: Evidence from the European markets. *Investment Management and Financial Innovations*, 13(1), 112–126.

Replicability Research Group. (2015). *Replicability vs. Reproducibility*. Tel Aviv University, Department of Statistics and Operations Research. www.replicability.tau.ac.il/index.php/replicability-in-science/replicability-vs-reproducibility.html.

Rosenbaum, S., Billinger, S., Stieglitz, N., Djumanov, A. & Atykhanov, Y. (2012). Market economies and pro-social behavior: Experimental evidence from Central Asia. *The Journal of Socio-Economics*, 41(1), 64–71.

Roulac, S. (2003). Corporate-owned real estate represents a substantial investment universe. *Journal of Real Estate Portfolio Management*, 9(2), 167–178.

Schmidt, F.L. & Hunter, J.E. (2015). *Methods of Meta-Analysis: Correcting Error and Bias in Research Findings*, 3rd ed. (Sage, Newbury Park, CA).

Schnellenbach, J. & Schubert, C. (2015). Behavioral political economy: A survey. *European Journal of Political Economy*, 40B, 395–417.

Sham, H., Sing, T. & Tsai, I. (2009). Are there efficiency gains for larger Asian REITs? *Journal of Financial Management of Property and Construction*, 14(3), 231–247.

Shapiro, A. (2005). Who pays the auditor calls the tune? Auditing regulation and clients' incentives. *Seton Hall Law Review*, 35, 1029–1049.

Sheng, J. (2019). Neoliberal environmentality and incentive-coordinated REDD+ contracts. *Land Use Policy*, 81, 400–407.

Shuotong, X. & Yanxi, L. (2012). Game analysis of earnings management considered managerial risk preferences. Chapter in: Zhang, Y., ed., *Future Communication, Computing, Control and Management*. Lecture Notes in Electrical Engineering, Volume 142 (Springer, Berlin and Heidelberg).

Singh, R. & Larkin, I. (2015). Auditor conservatism, incentive compensation, and the quality of financial reporting. *Journal of Law Economics and Organization*, 31(4), 721–751.

Sprinkle, G., Williamson, M. & Upton, D. (2008). The effort and risk-taking effects of budget-based contracts. *Accounting, Organizations and Society*, 33, 436–452.

Stanford Encyclopedia of Philosophy. (December 3, 2018). *Reproducibility of Scientific Results*. https://plato.stanford.edu/entries/scientific-reproducibility/.

Stein, S., Gerding, E.H., Rogers, A.C., Larson, K. & Jennings, N.R. (2011). Algorithms and mechanisms for procuring services with uncertain durations using redundancy. *Artificial Intelligence*, 175(14–15), 2021–2060.

Sterling, T. (1959). Publication decisions and their possible effects on inferences drawn from tests of significance – or vice versa. *Journal of the American Statistical Association*, 54(285), 30–34.

Sun, B. (2009). *Asset Returns with Earnings Management*. Board of Governors of the Federal Reserve System, USA. International Finance Discussion Papers, Number 988. https://pdfs.semanticscholar.org/aa00/39e86ed742989269bb10d460f95d36c767b9.pdf.

Sun, N. & Yang, Z. (2014). An efficient and incentive compatible dynamic auction for multiple complements. *Journal of Political Economy*, 122(2), 422–466.

Sussman, O. (1999). Economic growth with standardized contracts. *European Economic Review*, 43, 1797–1818.

Świątkowski, W. & Dompnier, B. (2017). Replicability crisis in social psychology: Looking at the past to find new pathways for the future. *International Review of Social Psychology*, 30(1), 111–124.

Terán, J., Aguilar, J. & Cerrada, M. (2017). Integration in industrial automation based on multi-agent systems using cultural algorithms for optimizing the coordination mechanisms. *Computers in Industry*, 91, 11–23.

Thevenot, M. (2012). The factors affecting illegal insider trading in firms with violations of GAAP. *Journal of Accounting and Economics*, 53(1–2), 375–390.

Trigo, A., Belfo, F. & Estébanez, R. (2016). Accounting information systems: Evolving towards a business process oriented accounting. *Procedia Computer Science*, 100, 987–994.

Tuzel, S. (2010). Corporate real estate holdings and the cross-section of stock returns. *Review of Financial Studies*, 23(6), 2268–2302.

Van Assche, A. & Schwartz, G. (2013). Contracting institutions and ownership structure in international joint ventures. *Journal of Development Economics*, 103, 124–132.

Veganzones, D. & Severin, E. (June 2017). *The Impact of Earnings Management on Bankruptcy Prediction Models: An Empirical Research*. Available at SSRN: https://ssrn.com/abstract=2980144 or http://dx.doi.org/10.2139/ssrn.2980144.

Vo, D., Nguyen, P., Nguyen, H., Vo, A. & Nguyen, T. (2019). Derivatives market and economic growth nexus: Policy implications for emerging markets. *The North American Journal of Economics and Finance*, in press.

Wang, F. (2018). Forest algorithm based staff incentive mechanism design of non-public enterprise from the perspective of positive organizational behavior. *Cognitive Systems Research*, 52, 132–137.

Wasserstein, R. & Lazar, N. (2016). The ASA's statement on p-values: Context, process and purpose. *The American Statistician*, 70(2), 129–133.

Wei, W., Wang, J., Chen, X., Yang, J. & Min, X. (2018). Psychological contract model for knowledge collaboration in virtual community of practice: An analysis based on the game theory. *Applied Mathematics & Computation*, 329, 175–187.

Wilson, R. (1985). Incentive Efficiency in Double Auctions, *Econometrica*, 53, 1101–1115.

Wu, Z., Zhao, R. & Tang, W. (2014). Optimal contracts for the agency problem with multiple uncertain information. *Knowledge-Based Systems*, 59, 161–172.

Zambon, S., Marasca, S. & Chiucchi, M. (2019). Special issue on "the role of intellectual capital and integrated reporting in management and governance: A performative perspective". *Journal of Management and Governance*, 23(2), 291–297.

Zeng, A., Shen, Z. & Zhou, J. (2017). The science of science: From the perspective of complex systems. *Physics Reports*, 714–715, 1–73.

Zhao, H., Yang, X. & Li, X. (2012). An incentive mechanism to reinforce truthful reports in reputation systems. *Journal of Network and Computer Applications*, 35(3), 951–961.

Zhou, W. & Kapoor, G. (2011). Detecting evolutionary financial statement fraud. *Decision Support Systems*, 50(3), 570–575.

Zohar, A. & Rosenschein, J. (2008). Mechanisms for information elicitation. *Artificial Intelligence*, 172(16–17), 1917–1939.

2

Complex adaptive systems, enforcement theory, and applicability of *real options theory* to the selection of disputes (accounting regulations and securities laws) for litigation[1]

This chapter surveys the literature on *Real Options Theory* (ROT) and aspects of *Enforcement Theory*; and discusses the non-applicability of ROT to the selection of disputes for litigation about compliance with Accounting Regulations (IASB/IFRS and US FASB regulations) and securities law violations (mostly in common-law countries). While *Enforcement Theory* is widely known as a subject-area of Political Philosophy, it is now being directly and indirectly studied in Law & Economics, Political Economy, Law, Complex Systems and Operations Research. In the context of elimination of earnings management, asset quality management and incentive effects management, *Enforcement Theory* is a core issue that covers the following:

i) Theories of enforcement of applicable regulations (e.g. securities laws; accounting regulations; stock exchange regulations; banking regulations; corporate governance standards; professional accounting codes of conduct; etc.).
ii) The economic theory of both public and private law enforcement. *Public enforcement* is by government agent and *private enforcement* is by private persons such as auditing firms, investors, securities analysts, CFOs and internal finance/accounting staff.
iii) *Behavioral biases* and effects that arise from, and or are amplified by the use of, or enforcement of accounting regulations and securities laws.
iv) The political circumstances of enforcement.
v) The relationships among these factors and their evolution.

While ROT has been touted as a viable alternative for valuing projects, decision-making and allocation of resources, the enforcement and efficiency of the US (FASB) and IASB accounting regulations (the "Accounting Regulations") and specifically, *Goodwill and Intangibles accounting regulations*[2] (GIAR) and securities laws in various countries raise several problems and psychological issues. GIAR are likely to increase the incidence of fraud and misconduct. The standard ROT analysis framework is not entirely applicable to enforcement of, and litigation about GIAR, Accounting Regulations or securities laws.

This chapter also introduces new economic psychology theories that can explain fraud, misconduct and non-compliance that may arise from the implementation of Accounting Regulations in general and more specifically, ASC 805 & 350, IFRS3R and IAS-38.

When aggregated at the national economy level, behavioral biases such as those introduced in this chapter create a class of critical macroeconomic and macrofinance indicators which are hereby referred to as the "*Behavioral Bias Indicators*". These indicators have not been properly recognized in the Complex Adaptive Systems, economics/finance, International Political Economy, Behavioral Operations Research or psychology literatures and are not tracked. Niamir et al. (2018); Nakagawa, Oiwa and Takeda (2012); Korniotis and Kumar (1993); Acquier, Daudigeos and Pinkse (2017); Schnellenbach and Schubert (2015); Pennings and Wansink (2004); and Rosenbaum et al. (2012) concluded or implied that human biases can affect national economies, although the links they established or theorized were indirect and they didn't discuss the issue of *Behavioral Bias Indicators*.

2.1 Complexity, complex adaptive systems and the rule-of-law: a survey of enforcement theories

The relationships among *Enforcement*, earnings management, securities law violations, Sustainability and Economic Growth are well documented in the literature – see: Laux and Stocken (2018); Wheeler (2019); Ji, Lu and Qu (2015); Bertomeu and Magee (2011); Graham, Harvey and Rajgopal (2005); Leung, Richardson and Taylor (2019); Guenther and Young (2000); Shevlin, Shivakumar and Urcan (2019); Do and Nabar (2018); Sinha (2019); Lemma, Feedman, et al. (2018); Roychowdhury, Shroff and Verdi (2019); Nagar, Schoenfeld and Wellman (2019); Trombetta and Imperatore (2014); Maso, Kanagaretnam, et al. (2018); Zhao and Chen (2009), and Lee (1987).

The literature on Complexity, Complex Adaptive Systems and the Rule-of-Law is developed; but has not sufficiently addressed Enforcement Theory.[3] The Complexity pertaining to these issues (Accounting regulations and securities laws) is or can be manifested in the following ways:

i)   Nonlinearity in relation to rule-of-law development.
ii)   Self-organization of institutions and organizations; and enforcement of laws by both private entities and public entities.
iii)   Change and theories of change.
iv)   Nonlinearity in relation to Deadweight Losses in the demand for, and enforcement of laws.
v)   Nonlinearity in relation to compliance with statutes and enforcement of laws.
vi)   Complex Networks and their dynamics.
vii)   *Network Effects* and the associated growth-and-evolution effects (on the mechanism/system and the users and their usage patterns).

The legal and economic environment in which Accounting Regulations, GIAR and securities laws function is a Complex Adaptive System because it has some or all of the following attributes:

i)   The relations between the system and its environment are non-trivial and or nonlinear.
ii) The system can be influenced by, or can adapt itself to its environment.
iii) The system has feedback or memory, and can adapt itself according to its history or feedback.
iv) The system is highly sensitive to initial conditions.
v)   The number of parts (and types of parts) in the system and the number of relations between the parts is non-trivial.

The results/conclusions of the empirical studies cited herein are subject to the usual limitations of statistical analysis and empirical research (some of which were mentioned in Chapter 1 in this book – that is, issues of lack of reproducibility of empirical studies).

Montero (2001) analyzed whether incomplete enforcement of a regulation has any impact on the choice between price (e.g. taxes) and quantity (e.g. tradeable quotas) instruments; and found that a second-best design that accounts for incomplete enforcement can be implemented with either a quantity or price instrument as long as the benefit and cost curves are known with certainty.

In 2014, FASB (USA)[4] issued a new release about Goodwill/Intangible accounting alternatives for private companies. During July 2012, the US Securities and Exchange Commission (SEC)[5] issued a 127-page final report on its work plan for IFRS but the report didn't make any recommendation about incorporating IFRS into the financial reporting system for US issuers.

2.1.1 Enforcement theory and real options theory in operations research

Although the existing literature on the enforcement of Accounting Regulations (including GIAR) and securities laws is substantial, there hasn't been much research on the applicability of Real Options Theory (ROT) to enforcement and litigation decisions. Marzo (2012) analyzed the usefulness of ROT in valuing intangible assets (IAs), and presented some criticisms of ROT. Deffains and Obidzinski (2009) analyzed Real Options for lawmakers. On *Enforcement Theory* in Operations Research, see: Trigeorgis and Tsekrekos (2018); Thies et al. (2018); Caulkins (1993); Drenovak et al. (2017); Oliviera (2017); and Wu and Hsu (2018). On *Real Options Theory* in Operations Research, see: Antunes and Gomez (2008); Ji and Gunasekaran (2014); Wu and Hsu (2018); Liu and Wang (2019); Acciaro (2014); and Banerjee, Güçbilmez and Pawlina (2014).

2.1.2 Enforcement theory: the incentives versus standards debate

Königsgruber and Palan (2015) noted that: i) enforcement and incentives are better predictors of accounting quality than financial reporting standards; ii) the way public policy is set, and in particular the participation of those affected by it, impacts upon the outcome of the policy – and thus it is inferable that Accounting standard setting processes (and participation by users) affects disclosure quality; iii) the possibility to participate in accounting standard setting doesn't lead to reduced earnings management. On the incentives versus standards debate, see: Ball, Robin and Wu (2003); Christensen (2012); and Christensen, Hail and Leuz (2013). On corporate lobbying and politics of accounting standards-setting and enforcement, see: Johnston and Jones (2006); Georgiou (2004); Königsgruber (2010); and Muehlbacher and Kirchler (2010).

2.1.3 The detection of earnings management and or fraud in corporate disclosures

The detection of earnings management, asset quality management and incentive effects management remains a hotly debated issue in several fields such as accounting (see: Chen et al. [2017]; Trigo, Belfo and Estébanez [2016]); finance (see: Banarescu [2015]); decision sciences (see: Zhou and Kapoor [2011]; Ngai et al. [2011]; Huang et al. [2008]; Chesney, Gold and Trautrims [2017]; Zhou and Kapoor [2011]; Holton [2009]; and Ravisankar et al. [2011]); Computer Science (see: Long, Song and Cui [2017]; Trigo, Belfo and Estébanez [2016]; Chouiekh and El Haj [2018]; West and Bhattacharya [2016]; and Zhang et al. [2018]); and operations research (see: Chen et al. [2017]); each of which seems to have adopted different approaches.

2.1.4 Enforcement of climate/emissions standards and environmental protection laws

On the enforcement of Climate/Emissions Standards and Environmental Protection Laws, see the discussion in Chapter 3 in this book; and see: Cárdenas (2012), Tjio (2009), and Coffee (2007).

2.1.5 The crash-risk of financial markets, and the enforcement of accounting regulations and securities laws

Many academic studies of the crash-risk of stock markets completely omitted the issue of enforcement of GIAR and *Accounting Regulations* despite the fact that according to Salinas (2009) and other authors,[6] during the last 15 years, Intangible assets accounted for 60–75 percent of the stock market capitalization values in most developed countries; and an increasing percentage of the stock market value in many developing countries (such as South Korea Brazil; China/Hong Kong; Mexico; Thailand; Singapore; etc.). Furthermore, Hand (2003: 305–306),[7] Damodaran (September 2009),[8] Bell, Landsman, Miller and Yeh (2002)[9] and Nakamura (1999)[10] noted that Equity-based Incentives create Intangibles that are often un-recognized in financial statements due to accounting rules. This relationship between EBIs and Intangibles is well established in the literature – as mentioned in Chapter 1 in this book, in its ruling during 2009, the US Court of Appeals for the Ninth Circuit (USA) held that the costs of EBIs were the costs of creating Intangibles[11] within the context of international operations and transfer pricing. In 2010, the same Court reversed itself but the 2010 decision applies only to a limited context – transfer pricing and international operations and R&D collaboration between two related companies, and the ruling applies to a US Treasury Department rule that was enacted in 2003.

Howson (2012) noted that China's securities regulator enforces insider trading prohibitions pursuant to non-legal and non-regulatory internal "guidance" and argues that the agency guidance is itself unlawful and unenforceable. Separately, many researchers have reported that the Chinese government adopts a *Selective Enforcement* approach, and protects perpetrators of earnings management. Schmidt et al. (2011) compared the enforcement of financial reporting standards in South Africa (Namibia) and Germany. Files (2012) analyzed the conditions under which the US Securities and Exchange Commission (SEC) exercises enforcement leniency after a restatement. Kedia and Rajgopal (2011) found that companies located closer to the US SEC and in geographical areas with greater past SEC enforcement activity (both factors were treated as proxies for firms' information about the US SEC's enforcement activities), were less likely to re-state their financial statements. Schmidt (2005) adopted a neo-institutional economics perspective on the phenomenon of whistle blowing and contrasted the regulatory models of the US, the UK and Germany, and suggested an appropriate statutory approach that can use whistle blowing to improve the enforcement of accounting standards in Germany and Europe.

The Intangibles/Goodwill accounting regulations (IASB/IFRS and US GAAP – ASC 805 and ASC 350 (Formerly SFAS 141R & 142); and IASB-38 And IFRS-3R) are discussed in Chapter 7 in this book. Goodwill/Intangibles and the associated impairment and or amortization have substantial and critical information content, which is not being disclosed properly. There remains significant controversy about Goodwill/Intangibles impairment and required testing. Nwogugu (2015) explained the many problems inherent in the Intangibles/Goodwill Accounting Rules. Sevin and Schroeder (2005) found significant evidence that there is substantial information content in identification and reporting of goodwill impairments and in the selection of goodwill amortization periods. Several academic studies have found that Intangibles/Goodwill accounting regulations are not consistent with market valuations. Comiskey and Mulford (2008) and Ketz (2004) found that the accounting rules/standards for Negative Goodwill are sub-optimal.

Martins (2011) acknowledged that the Goodwill/Intangibles accounting rules can create substantial litigation.

Hegarty, Gielen and Barros (September 2004) discussed various issues that arose from enforcement of accounting standards in the World Bank's Accounting and Auditing ROSC Program. United Nations (2008) discussed problems and issues inherent in the practical implementation of accounting and auditing standards.

The academic studies about the risks of market-crashes include Ascioglu et al. (2012); Bar-Yosef and Prencipe (2013); Eng and Lin (2012); An and Zhang (2013); Hutton, Marcus and Tehranian (2009); Francis, Hasan and Li (2014); Guo, Wang and Wu (2011); Kim and Zhang (2013); Kim, Li and Zhang (2011a, 2011b); Kim and Zhang (2014); Pinegar and Ravichandran (2010); Zeitun and Tian (2007); Hope (2003); Langevoort (1997) and Lopes and Alencar (2010).

2.1.6 Enforcement games, empirical studies, and psychological and political theories of enforcement

On Enforcement Games, see: Leshem and Tabbach (2012), Helbing (2010), Yeung et al. (2010), Ohtsubo et al. (2010), Lang and Wambach (2013), Fehr, Fischbacher and Gächter (2002), Scholz (1991), Mogy and Pruitt (1974), and Miller and Watson (2013).

On empirical studies of enforcement and compliance in different contexts, see: Fellner, Sausgruber and Traxler (2013), Segovia, Arnold and Sutton (2009), Gibbins, McCracken and Salterio (2008), *Pomerot* (March 2010), Agoglia, Doupnik and Tsakumis (2011), Van Gennip et al. (2013), Short et al. (2010), Zhang, Wang and Qyu (2011), Chen et al. (2011), Hope (2003), Rincke and Traxler (2011), Jayaraman (2012), Jackson and Roe (2009), Antunes, Cavalcanti and Villamil (2008), and Al-Shammari, Brown and Tarca (2008).

On psychological theories of enforcement of statutes and or implementation of accounting regulations, see: Piercey (2009); Trotman (2005); Tetlock (2002); De Dreu et al. (2006), and Bodenhuasen, Macrae and Hugenberg (2003), and Henrich and Boyd (2001).

On political theories of enforcement (analysis of crime, punishment, governance and compliance within the context of institutions and political factors), see: Bednar (2006); Tsebelis (1993), Weissing and Ostrom (1991); Urpelainen (2011) and De Mesquita and Stephenson (2006).

2.1.7 Compliance and non-compliance

On *Compliance* and *Non-Compliance* as physical phenomena, and associated modelling, see: Burgemeestre, Hulstijn and Tan (2011), Byrne and Callaghan (2014), Beer, Fisk and Rogers (2014), Brandau, Endenich, Trapp and Hoffjan (2013), Ezrachi and Stucke (2015), Harrington (2018), Hasmath and MacDonald (2018), Leung, Paolacci and Puntoni (2018), Lin, Lin and Tseng (2016), Saygin,

Chaminade, et al. (2012), Schwalbe (2018), Sikka and Hampton (2005), Srinidhi, Lim and Hossain (2009), and Vlachou and Pantelias (2017).

2.2 *Selective enforcement* invalidates many models/ theories in *trial selection theory*: behavioral issues

Trial Selection Theory is a branch of *Enforcement Theory*. The *Trial Selection Theory* literature is well developed and is summarized as follows. Chen et al. (2011); Heyes, Rickman and Tzavara (2004); Hylton (2002, 2008), Nwogugu (2008), Waldfogel (1998), Samuelson (1998), Chopard, Cortade and Langlais (2010), Cornell (1990), Wang, Kim and Yi (1994) and Marco (2005) analyzed the selection of disputes for litigation. Hylton and Lin (2009) surveyed the literature and evidence; and presented a model that includes *Priest-Klein Theory* and *Asymmetric Information Theory* as special cases. Hylton (1993), Heyes, Rickman and Tzavara (2004), Hylton (2006), and Hylton (2002) analyzed issues pertaining to litigation decisions. See the comments in Leung and Cooper (2003). Demolombe (2011), Balke, De Vos and Padget (2013); Burgemeestre, Hulstijn and Tan (2011); Chapman (2013); Zhang and Walton (2010); Bex and Walton (2012); Miller (2012); analyzed issues pertaining to *Trial Selection Theory*.

Unfortunately, the *Selective Enforcement* phenomenon invalidates or moots most theories and models in modern *Trial Selection Theory*, most of which don't consider *Selective Enforcement* (but rather, focus on probability distributions and static relationships in what are dynamic environments). *Selective Enforcement* (of accounting regulations and or securities laws) as a trend or government policy is relatively new as an academic research topic. *Selective Enforcement* refers to the deliberate choices by government prosecutors or private-parties to selectively investigate and or prosecute suspected perpetrators or to avoid doing so, often without regard to statutory requirements – all of which can lead to sub-optimal enforcement, *Harmful Multiplier Effects*, and false-positives and false-negatives in convictions. See the comments in: Lewellyn and Bao (2017); Brandau et al. (2013); Lavezzolo, Rodríguez-Lluesma and Elvira (2018); Attia, Lassoued and Attia (2016); Galligan (1997); Braam et al. (2015); Habib, Muhammadi and Jiang (2017); Chen, Li et al. (2011); Li, Selover and Stein (2011); Chen, Jiang et al. (2011); Jacoby, Li and Liu (2016); He (2016); Salmi and Heikkilä (2015); Srinidhi, Lim and Hossain (2009); Windsor (2017); Houqe, Monem and van Zijl (2012); Geiger et al. (2006); D'Amato et al. (2018); Earnhart and Glicksman (2015); Akpalu, Eggert and Vondolia (2009); Wang, Zhang and Chen (2011); and Cheng and Leung (2016). *Selective Enforcement* can arise from any of the following sources or causes:

i)   Political lobbying by companies.
ii) The *Social Capital* of *Multinational Corporations* (MNCs) and technology companies.

iii) Deliberate government policy especially in Transition Economies (e.g. China) and in established capitalist democracies that are exposed to campaign funding distortions (e.g. US).
iv) Estimated information, psychological, social and economic effects of investigation and or prosecution – for example, the effects of social media.
v) Concerns about International Relations (especially for MNCs and cross-listed companies).
vi) Prosecution costs.
vii) International trade policy and government protectionism (e.g. in China).
viii) National culture.
ix) Bribery and corruption.
x) Tribalism and or racism.
xi) Political elections.
xii) Social-Class "wars" (e.g. in India).
xiii) The government's budgetary and appropriations processes.

Chen, Jiang, Liang and Wang (2011), Cheng and Leung (2016), Zhang and Mauck (2018), and Chen, Li, Liang and Wang (2011) noted political costs of enforcement and *Selective Enforcement* by the Chinese government. Gastwirth (2011) observed that Goldman Sachs submitted inaccurate statistical evidence in its response to the US SEC's charges that it misled investors about a hedge fund manager's role in selecting a securities portfolio involving subprime mortgages. Kim (2014) analyzed the properties and relative efficiency of the inquisitorial system and the adversarial system of dispute resolution.

Choi and Pritchard (2012) analyzed how *Tellabs, Inc. v. Makor Issues & Rights, Ltd.* (a USA Supreme Court securities-law class-action precedent) affected lower court decisions when there is asymmetric probability of appellate review; and whether the US Supreme Court's directive caused the dismissal rates in the lower courts to converge. Choi (2007) noted that other authors provided evidence that the Private Securities Litigation Reform Act (PSLRA) of 1995 increased the significance of merit-related factors in determining the incidence and outcomes of securities fraud class actions.

Chen and Wang (2007) theoretically compared the British and American fee-shifting rules in their influences on the behavior of the litigants and the outcomes of litigation. Using docket-level US federal district court data, Boyd and Hoffman (2013) found that the filing of a motion significantly speeds case settlement; that granted motions are more immediately critical to settlement timing than motions denied; and that plaintiff victories have a stronger effect than defendant victories.

2.2.1 The regret effect

The *Regret Effect* is introduced here – and it proposes that both *Regret* and *Selective Enforcement* nullify the Von-Neumann-Morgenstern linearity axiom in the context of litigation. Barnett (2010) studied the risks and rewards involved in the litigation process, and noted that the '*Minimax Theorem*', the '*Maximax Principle*' and 'minimize the maximum regret principle' all follow the Von Neumann and Morgenstern linearity axiom.

2.2.2 Litigation/pre-litigation processes as incentive-mechanisms

The following studies used *Game Theory* for analyzing *Trial Selection*, and that implies that litigation processes (in arbitration, administrative law agencies and courts) are or can be *Incentive-Mechanisms*. Daughety and Reinganum (2000) modeled the adversarial provision of evidence as a game in which two parties engage in strategic sequential search, and characterized a court's decision based on the evidence provided. Klement and Neeman (2005) introduced a strategic model of liability and litigation under court errors wherein the model allows for endogenous choice of level of care and endogenous likelihood of filing and disputes. Baker and Mezzetti (2001) analyzed the strategic interaction between a defendant and a prosecutor during the plea bargaining process, and developed a four-stage game where the defendant's guilt or innocence is private information but the amount of resources available to the prosecutor is common knowledge. Friedman and Wittman (2007) developed game-theoretic foundations for bargaining in the context of a trial, wherein Plaintiff and defendant make simultaneous offers to settle, they settle where feasible; and otherwise, both litigants incur additional litigation cost and the judgment is imposed at trial. Prakken (2008) developed a formal reconstruction of a Dutch civil legal case in Prakken's formal model of adjudication dialogs in order to test whether *Artificial Intelligence & Law* models of legal dialogs in general, and Prakken's model in particular, are suitable for modelling particular legal procedures and legal dispute.

2.2.3 Regret invalidates trial selection theory: the settlement-regret effect

The *Settlement-Regret Effect* is introduced here – it is conjectured that when *Regret* is considered, the possibility of Settlement (more than the timing or structure of settlement) of a dispute: i) affects the pre- and post-judgment and settlement utilities and payoffs of the litigants; ii) affects the magnitude if any, of "deviations" from "accurate legal/litigation outcomes"; iii) is a major eroder of deterrence effects; iv) affects the government's or private-party's willingness-to-prosecute. Thus, *Regret* is a key element that affects Social Welfare. However, the omission or inadequate incorporation of Regret in *Trial Selection Theory* models, nullifies such models. Thus, the Friedman and Wickelgren (2010) Hypothesis is not entirely correct. Friedman and Wickelgren (2010) noted that allowing or promoting Settlement of lawsuits does not necessarily enhance social welfare; and that Settlement can lower social welfare because it reduces the accuracy of legal outcomes, which in turn reduces the ability of the law to deter harmful activity without chilling legitimate activity that might be mistaken for harmful activity (i.e. the welfare loss from the chilling of legitimate activity can outweigh the gains from litigation cost savings, even if there are no restrictions on the damage rule).

2.2.4 The incentives-population effect

The *Incentives-Population Effect* is introduced here – it is conjectured that the number of actual/potential litigants in a dispute affects: i) the litigants' willingness-to-proceed with the lawsuit, ii) the litigants' expected "Net Payoff", iii) the litigants' concepts of victory in the dispute; iv) the litigants' *Abandonment Option* (option to abandon the litigation). Avraham and Liu (2012) analyzed the non-breaching party's option to not sue for damages upon breach, when her/his expected payoff from suing is negative, given the contractual terms and her/his private information about her post-breach loss. Daughety and Reinganum (2010) studied how plaintiffs' pre-litigation incentives differ between lawsuits associated with stand-alone torts ("individual-based liability determination" or "IBLD") cases and lawsuits involving mass torts ("population-based liability determination" or "PBLD").

2.2.5 The self-serving bias and the optimism bias

The *Self-Serving Bias* has been noted in the Literature. Farmera and Pecorino (2002) incorporated *self-serving bias* into the Bebchuk (*RAND Journal of Economics* 15 (1984) 404) model in which trials result from asymmetric information; and they characterized the equilibrium.

The *Optimism Bias* is noted in the existing literature. Using Evolutionary Game Theory, Bar-Gill (2006) attempted to provide a theoretical explanation for the persistence of the *Optimism Bias* among litigants and their attorneys; and noted that optimistic lawyers succeed in extracting more favorable settlements by credibly threatening to resort to costly litigation, and thus equilibrium should include a positive level of Optimism.

2.2.6 The enforcement path effect

The *"Enforcement Path Effect"* is introduced here. Enforcement of accounting regulations can be done in one of several ways: i) by external auditors – who are charged with preparing audit reports that will be submitted to boards of directors and or government agencies; ii) by government prosecutors that file claims against non-compliant companies in administrative courts and criminal courts; iii) by private attorneys that are retained by shareholders or employees or boards of directors to file civil lawsuits or claims in administrative courts; iv) by investigative and enforcement agencies of government agencies such as the US SEC which performs for adjudicative and enforcement functions; v) by international agencies such as the World Bank and the UN that have developed programs for implementation of accounting standards (which constitute quasi-enforcement because recipients of their loans, guarantees and or grants typically have to participate in such programs). This chapter focuses exclusively on enforcement of the accounting regulations (IASB/IFRS) and securities laws in courts and government administrative agencies.

It is conjectured here that: i) there are sometimes conflicts when more than one path is used for one dispute/offense; ii) the Enforcement Path chosen affects transaction costs, deterrence effects and the probability of recurrence.

2.2.7 The transaction cost effect

The *Transaction Cost Effect* is introduced here. Many IFRS accounting regulations (the "Accounting Regulations") and ASC 805/350, IASB-38 and IFRS-3R (the "GIAR" or "*Goodwill/Intangible Regulations*") substantially increase the costs of investigation, enforcement and prosecution, because they place undue burden on prosecutors/investigators to prove management/employees' intent to defraud, willful mis-valuation of Intangibles, and willful and fraudulent allocation and re-allocation of assets among various classes of intangibles and among divisions/departments. In most circumstances, *Goodwill/Intangible Regulations* typically don't require third-party validation/certification of assets; and leave many facts and details and impairment decisions entirely up to management's discretion. ASC 805/350, IASB-38 and IFRS-3R don't specify detailed standards for the classification of expenses and assets and don't expressly require external auditor certification. Goodwill/Intangible Regulations don't require mandatory statements of basis/reasons for any changes of classifications of assets – this omission grants management substantial discretion to manipulate asset values.

2.2.8 The low-deterrence effect

The *Low-Deterrence Effect* is introduced here. In most jurisdictions, i) the Accounting Regulations and the GIAR do not provide any specific penalties (civil or criminal) for non-compliance; ii) rather, it's the securities laws, or bankruptcy laws or debtor/creditor laws that provide mechanisms for investigation and enforcement; but iii) the securities laws require "*Minimum Threshold Misconduct*" to trigger investigations and enforcement; iv) such "*Minimum Threshold Misconduct*" typically involves use of, or reliance on financial statements by third-parties, and or the context of sales/offerings of financial instruments. Without explicit evidence in the form of express statements by employees, the necessary elements of violation of and non-compliance with the Accounting Regulations and the GIAR are very difficult to detect and prove (or even assume or imply), under the US federal rules of evidence. See: Hylton (2006).

It is conjectured here that in many contexts and around the world, the *Minimum Threshold Misconduct* is actually very high, and the severity of the misconduct requires regulations/statutes that are much more proactive towards investigation and enforcement.

Hence, there is insufficient deterrence effect because any convictions or find-ings of liability will result in the use of relatively general sentencing guidelines which may not reflect the gravity of fraud/offenses pertaining to the Accounting Regulations and the GIAR in the new economy.

2.2.9 The dormancy effect

The *Dormancy Effect* is introduced here. The wording of many sections of the Accounting Regulations and the GIAR also raises the issue of venue for adjudica-tion of disputes. See: Macey and Ohara (2006). In the US, non-compliance with *the Accounting Regulations* and the *GIAR* can be prosecuted under federal securi-ties laws (civil and criminal penalties) only if the US Securities and Exchange Commission expressly incorporates such Regulations into its rule-making frame-work. Disputes that arise from the Accounting Regulations and the GIAR can also adjudicated under state common law, if plaintiffs are able to show that such Regulations have some force of law/norm. Hence, like other FASB/IASB pro-nouncements and rules, the Accounting Regulations and the GIAR are by their nature, relatively harmless, although they have substantial implications for social welfare, securities markets and many industries; and are arguably as important as, or more important than the Sarbanes Oxley Act (which applies to only companies that are listed on stock exchanges – this population consists of less than 5 percent of registered US companies). This *Dormancy Effect* that is implicit in FASB (and some IASB) rules creates substantial incentives for non-compliance by preparers of financial statements.

2.2.10 The deferred tax bias and the deferred tax controversy

The *Deferred Tax Bias* is introduced here. Goodwill/Intangibles Rules create sig-nificant Deferred Tax Assets/Liabilities because the application of these account-ing rules can result in substantial differences between the tax treatment and book treatment of amortization/expensing of Goodwill/Intangibles. There is no required retroactive re-statement of financial statement when companies change the prin-ciples of their tax statements and or book accounting. Hence, Management can then use such Deferred Tax Asset/Liability accounts to manipulate earnings over time. Chau et al. (2003); Chen, Kohlbeck and Warfield (2008); Dunse, Hutchin-son and Goodacre (2004); Finch (Sept. 2006). These Deferred Tax Asset/Liabil-ity accounts carry substantial information content (which has not been analyzed fully in the existing literature), which is likely to increase stock market volatility, because of its complexity and opaque nature.

The impact of ASC 805/350 and IFRS-3R on compliance with the statutory capital-reserve requirements for banking organizations (established under the Basel capital rules, and Title 12 of the US Code) can be significant. Under present banking regulations, bank organizations are not permitted to include Goodwill in their Tier-1 Capital; and banks must perform periodic tests of their manda-tory minimum capital. Banking organizations' compliance with ASC 805/350 has been primarily for financial reporting purposes. For example, since Goodwill is treated as a special item in the Title-12 (of the US Code) calculations, a change in accounting (such as ASC 805/350 and IFRS-3R) that keeps Goodwill on the banks' Balance Sheets indefinitely can provide significant incentives for banking organizations to manipulate the allocation of Goodwill to Reporting Units, and to reduce acquired-Goodwill. This is very likely to result in sub-optimal manage-ment decisions by banks regarding capital maintenance, and in disclosure that does not reflect the true risk of banks. See: Marston (2004).

During December 2008, US government bank regulators approved a new accounting rule that requires the deduction/netting of certain Deferred Tax Lia-bilities (that are associated with Goodwill) from acquired-Goodwill that in turn, is deducted from banks' Tier-1 capital.[12] This new rule is critical (given consoli-dations in the global financial services industry), and will have the net effect of increasing the amount of Goodwill that is included in banks' Tier-1 capital. The December 2008 banking rule (US) is likely to result in inadequate/inaccurate disclosure because Goodwill will remain opaque, and banks' management will continue to have significant discretion about the impairment of Goodwill; and are very likely to have substantial incentives for manipulation of the Goodwill-related Deferred Tax Liability account. The Deferred Tax Liability that is associated with Goodwill is partly based on the estimated impairment and or amortization of Goodwill (and the applicable tax rate), which in turn, is affected by ASC 805/350.[13] The US government's contention that the Deferred Tax Liability associated with Goodwill does not represent a claim on the assets of the banking organization is wrong, because technically, Goodwill-related Deferred Tax Liabilities are future tax liabilities that are created by the differences between the banking organiza-tion's income under GAAP and its income for tax purposes, which in turn arise from differences between GAAP accounting for Goodwill (FASB and IASB) and tax rules for Goodwill.

Proposition-1: if goodwill becomes impaired or is de-recognized under GAAP, then a banking organization's maximum exposure to loss is not equal to the carrying value of the goodwill less any associated deferred tax liability

Proof: the contention that if Goodwill becomes impaired or is de-recognized under GAAP, then a banking organization's maximum exposure to loss is equal to the carrying value of the Goodwill less any associated Deferred Tax Liability, is wrong, because the Deferred Tax Liability represents a future tax claim on the company's assets, and the associated Deferred Tax Liability is derived from, and is less than the expensed/amortized Goodwill.

Let:

G_a = total Goodwill at beginning of period t.

G_t = Goodwill expensed/amortized under tax rules in period t.

G_g = Goodwill expensed/amortized under GAAP in period t.

T_t = the corporate income tax rate in period t.

D_{tl} = the Deferred Tax Liability associated with expensed/amortized Goodwill in period t.

D_{ta} = the Deferred Tax Asset associated with expensed/amortized Goodwill in period t.

I_g = the bank's taxable income after Goodwill is amortized/expensed under GAAP.

I_t = the bank's taxable income after Goodwill is amortized/expensed under tax rules.

L = the banking organization's Maximum Loss from the impairment/amortization of Goodwill in period t.

I_i = the bank's Pretax Income before amortization or expensing of Goodwill under either GAAP or tax rules.

Then:

$G_t, G_g \; \varepsilon \; G_a$

If all Goodwill is expensed in period t, then $G_t, G_g = G_a$

$I_t, I_g \leq I_i$

$I_i - G_t = I_t$

$I_i - G_g = I_g$

$D_{ta} = (I_t - I_g)*T_t$; and substituting, $D_{ta} = [(I_i - G_t) - (I_i - G_g)]*T_t = [-G_t + G_g]*T_t$

$D_{tl} = (I_g - I_t)*T_t$; and substituting, $D_{tl} = [(I_i - G_g) - (I_i - G_t)]*T_t = [-G_g + G_t]*T_t$

Therefore, $D_{tl} \leq G_g, G_t$

Also, once G_t or G_g is expensed, D_{tl} has no continuing relation to G_a, and D_{tl} will change only if future estimated income tax rates change. Similarly, once G_t or G_g is expensed, D_{ta} has no continuing relation to G_a, and D_{ta} will change only if future estimated income tax rates change. D_{tl} and D_{ta} are not a "reduction" of Goodwill, but rather, are tax items that are derived from taxable income and hence, D_{tl} and D_{ta} will vary as tax rates change due to changes in the banking organization's taxable income – ie. if $T_t \neq T_{(t+1)}$ $\neq \dots \dots \dots T_{(t+n)}$. The Goodwill-related Deferred Tax Liability for prior periods was derived from Goodwill that was already expensed/amortized in prior periods (i.e. t-1, t-2, t-3, etc.), and is not relevant for the calculation of the maximum loss in period t.

Therefore, $L = G_a$

Furthermore, the criteria for the calculation of Goodwill-related Deferred Tax Liabilities may not be based on the nature/permanence of underlying assets, finance ability or quality of assets or the type/structure/risk of the banking organization that generated the acquired-Goodwill.

2.3 The applicability of *real options theory* to dispute-selection that pertains to accounting regulations and or securities law: a critique of Grundfest and Huang (2006) and other academic research about real options

Grundfest and Huang (2006) attempted to analyze the dispute-selection process and the litigation process from a real options perspective. There have been very few related studies – on *Real Options Theory* in Operations Research, see: Antunes and Gomez (2008); Ji and Gunasekaran (2014); Wu and Hsu (2018); Liu and Wang (2019); Acciaro (2014); and Banerjee, Güçbilmez and Pawlina (2014). The Grundfest and Huang (2006) study is notable and is applicable to the debate about Accounting Regulations and the GIAR disclosure and securities law violations for several reasons. Securities laws obviously generate substantial civil and criminal litigation around the world. Accounting Regulations (including GIAR) can generate substantial civil and criminal litigation because of their ambiguities, behavioral effects, and because they facilitate and create opportunities for earnings management and asset-quality management – some of which are explained in Jordan, Clark and Vann (2007); Nwogugu (2006/2013); Nwogugu (2015); Comiskey and Mulford (2008); Finch (Sept. 2006); Garcia-Meca and Martinez (2007); Ketz (2004); Lewis, Lippitt and Mastracchio (2001); Seetharaman et al. (2006); Hake (2004), and Sevin and Schroeder (2005).

However, the process of selection of disputes pertaining to Accounting Regulations or securities laws cannot benefit from *Real Options Theory* for the reasons stated herein. Unlike the Sarbanes–Oxley Act (and similar statutes in other countries), most Accounting Regulations (and some securities law statutes) don't contain any penalties, or specification of venue, or procedural rules. There has to be some minimum level of initiative and cooperation from employees or external auditors in order for Accounting Regulations and securities laws to be implemented successfully and for any non-compliance to be reported; and there has to be a minimum amount of cooperation by employees and the external auditor in order for any investigation or enforcement efforts to be meaningful or successful (collectively, the "*Minimum Cooperation*"). There has to be a minimum amount of common-truthfulness (coordinated or un-coordinated) among statements and evidence provided by employees, the external auditor, the internal accounting system and managers, in order for any enforcement to be efficient and effective (the "*Minimum Truthfulness*"). See: Deffains and Obidzinski (2006). Thus, only a relatively very small part of the investigation and enforcement of Accounting Regulations or securities laws can be analyzed with ROT.

Employees have an option to alert the government or management about non-compliance with accounting rules and securities laws. The external auditor has the option to issue negative reports and to alert management and or the government about non-compliance with Accounting Regulations and or securities laws. Managers have the option to start an internal investigation about non-compliance with

Accounting Regulations and or securities laws or to report any non-compliance to state or federal government prosecutors. The Company's Board of Directors have the option to request for an internal investigation or to alert government agencies/ prosecutors about non-compliance. In medium and large companies, the Company's Board of Directors will typically request for reports from the company's Internal Audit group. The company and its managers have the option to impose a gag order on employees about reporting non-compliance. Employees have the option to serve as witnesses in the initial investigation by the government prosecutors. The government prosecutor has the option to investigate any allegations of non-compliance. The government prosecutor has the option to prosecute the allegations in court or at an administrative agency (such as the US SEC). The government prosecutor has the option to select a litigation forum (e.g. State court, the US SEC, or a federal court) that will maximize the probability of successful enforcement and reduce litigation costs. The adjudicator at the forum has the option to dismiss the case and or to amend the pleadings and the number of parties in the dispute. The adjudicator has the option to grant or reject summary judgment motions. The adjudicator has the option to grant or reject pre-trial motions, and to issue evidentiary rulings. The adjudicator has the option to order a trial. Each litigant has the option to settle the dispute. The adjudicator has the option to establish minimum burdens of proof. The adjudicator has the option to enter interlocutory orders. The adjudicator has the option to issue guidelines and rules to the jury, if any. The jury has the option to demand for more evidence. The jury has the option to enter various types of decisions. The adjudicator has the option to modify the jury's decision(s). The litigating parties have the option to appeal any judgments.

The clear elements of the foregoing litigation decision process are as follows. Some of the steps/decision points are simultaneous and are not entirely sequential. Some of the simultaneous steps/options are either mutually exclusive or are mutually preclusive after a few steps (a choice in one of the real options, precludes any choices made in the other simultaneous real option, after a few steps in the decision-tree). Judges and arbitrators have substantial discretion and their orders can drastically reduce or increase the value of any real option (or decision stage) or evidence. The quality of the control environment and internal controls is critical to the gathering of evidence and establishment of culpability. Decisions by insiders (employees, and the board of directors) to report non-compliance will be modified by consideration of compensation, protection of benefits, labor union issues, and possible negative effects on the Company's Stock price. Evidence in the form of human testimony is a key element of culpability. Proving the intent element (of fraud, misrepresentation, or tax evasion or conversion) will be difficult and will require direct human testimony and direct evidence – and not inferences, probabilities and or circumstantial evidence. Altruism, reputation, social capital and non-monetary utility can be major factors in choices made by litigants, witnesses and the government prosecutor.

As explained in Nwogugu (2003b, 2019), the *Put-Call Parity Theorem* is inaccurate. See: Knoll (2002).

Contrary to Grundfest and Huang (2006), most Accounting Regulations and securities laws create situations where disputes almost cannot be resolved by settlement and real options analysis cannot be applied. Under many Accounting Regulations (including GIAR) and some securities laws, there are many opportunities for mis-statements which increases the variability of discovery costs. In disputes about the implementation of Accounting Regulations and securities laws, the amount of required fact finding can be relatively substantial. See: Sevin and Schroeder (2005) and Nwogugu (2011). While evidence is a key element of determination of culpability for non-compliance with Accounting Regulations, evidentiary standards (state or federal rules of evidence) are not built into Accounting Regulations and some securities laws – hence there is likely to be substantial divergences among judges and appellate panels in applying evidentiary standards. In disputes about Accounting Regulations and securities laws, the uncertainty in proceeding with any stage of litigation does not increase the value of any "real option" because there are discovery costs, and issues of permissible management's discretion. In disputes that pertain to securities laws and Accounting Regulations, the societal value of prosecution almost always outweighs the value of settlement or non-prosecution because at the present time and in most countries, Accolunting Regulations and many securities laws donot contain any specific penalties, discovery is likely to be multi-faceted, and may uncover additional patterns of misconduct.

Grundfest and Huang (2006) erroneously assume that there are only two parties in every litigation – on the contrary, many lawsuits, administrative law cases and arbitration claims involve three or more parties, and the number of parties typically change as the case progresses.

The principles introduced in Grundfest and Huang (2006) are grossly inaccurate for the following reasons. The Grundfest and Huang (2006) models erroneously assume that each plaintiff must spend some money in order to commence litigation – in many cases, lawyers accept contingency fees and the plaintiff's time that is spent on the dispute is often done after work hours, or the plaintiff typically compensates by working longer hours.

Contrary to most assumptions in the Grundfest and Huang (2006) models, lawsuits always have some *information asymmetry* and there is almost never *perfect knowledge* about facts – hence the assumption that plaintiff and defendant have the same amount of information at any time is completely false. It's this information asymmetry that often precludes settlement and may result in the lawsuit. The second type of information asymmetry problem in litigation arises from three issues – the lawyers' information processing capabilities, the plaintiff's and the defendant's perceptions of fairness of proceedings and their lawyer's abilities, and the plaintiff's/defendant's constant re-evaluations of their respective options to terminate the lawyer's services. The Grundfest and Huang (2006) models don't address these types of information problems.

The Grundfest and Huang (2006: 1275) models erroneously assume that litigants in any dispute are identical, risk neutral, and share common knowledge about all characteristics of a lawsuit (such as expected value; each party's cash/ psychological/social litigation costs; available information and the changes in such information; etc.). In reality, different litigants have different reasons for litigating or for seeking settlement; and there is often substantial information asymmetry among litigants. Contrary to Grundfest and Huang (2006: 1275), litigants almost never have equal bargaining power and almost never face the same litigation expenses. Each litigant's litigation strategy typically varies in terms of how he/she gathers information, the facts to be established and the objectives of litigation (e.g. monetary award; delay; publicity; cost savings; clarification; divestments, etc.).

In the real options scheme described by Grundfest and Huang (2006), the Variance of information is a key element. However, Variance as applied in this context is not useful. In the investigation and discovery processes, most relevant information does not change as would be typically imagined in order for variance to be meaningful. Most relevant information in litigation are in the form of "true" or "false" states. As shown in Nwogugu (2003b) and Nwogugu (2013), Variance and standard deviation are inaccurate measures of risk or variation. The *Minimum Cooperation* and *Minimum Truthfulness* renders Variance useless. Within the enforcement, investigation and litigation contexts, there is a *"Truth-telling Problem"* that renders Variance meaningless – because where witnesses can hide or twist or refuse to disclose information, the Variance is useless as a measure. There is also an *"Evidentiary ruling Problem"* that reduces the usefulness/applicability of Variance because the judge's/arbitrator's orders can render evidence meaningless. A high "Variance" of information will not necessarily and always increase the settlement value or litigation value of a lawsuit, because the judge has the discretion to issue orders, and judges are not always bound by precedent, and the specific information may be deemed (by the judge or jury or the opposing litigant) to have low probative value.

Grundfest and Huang's (2006: 1276) definition of *"Negative Expected Value"* ("NEV") lawsuits is inaccurate, because it does not account for the utility value of lawsuits, and the non-monetary value of lawsuits (e.g. Revenge, altruism, deterrence-effect, publicity-value, Social-Capital effects, intentional delay, strategic avoidance, fairness, deferral of costs, nuisance-value, etc.). Grundfest and Huang's (2006) contention that a NEV lawsuit is merely an out of the money call option that the plaintiff will pursue if the cost of obtaining the option is less than the option's value, is inaccurate. This is because in most instances, the duration/term, Strike price, applicable Interest Rate, and payout of such alleged Call Option are all highly uncertain and somewhat very vague.

Grundfest and Huang's (2006) contention that every NEV lawsuit can become credible if the Variance of information to be disclosed (during litigation) is high, is also inaccurate. As explained above, Variance is not an accurate or appropriate measure in this context. A high "Variance" of information will not necessarily and always increase the settlement value or litigation value of a lawsuit, because the judge has discretion to issue orders, judges are not always bound by precedent, and the information may be deemed (by the judge or jury or the opposing litigant) to have low probative value. The definition of Variance also includes the possibility of substantial low-value information, and thus, the magnitude of Variance cannot be used to justify the credibility of value of any lawsuit. The *Minimum Cooperation* and *Minimum Truthfulness* can reduce the relevance of the concept of NEV lawsuits. Within the context of investigating or litigating non-compliance with Accounting Regulations and or securities laws, relevant information will have to be obtained from the company's staff, its auditors and from the company's accounting information systems.

Because most Accounting Regulations (e.g. GAAP, IFRS, FASB) and some securities laws don't have any punitive schemes (unlike Sarbanes–Oxley Act), they must be enforced with the application of statutes and common-law for torts, criminal laws and Evidence. This mandatory simultaneous application of rules can increase litigation costs, result in sub-optimal deterrence effects; result in sub-optimal application of rules of evidence and distort litigation objectives.

Contrary to Grundfest and Huang (2006), the sequence in which litigants incur litigation expenses does not have any material effect on the settlement value of the lawsuit, even if each party's litigation costs are constant and the sequence of expenditures is similar for both litigants. This is because there are segments of litigation that don't have any settlement value or litigation value. Second, the litigants are subject to the judge's discretion (which can render certain stages and expenses meaningless). Third, there is often substantial information asymmetry between and among litigants. If most of the utility that one or more litigants derive from continuing litigation consists of primarily non-monetary utility, then the sequence of the litigants' expenditures is much less irrelevant (or is irrelevant) and will have a reduced effect on, or will not affect the Settlement Value or Litigation Value of the lawsuit.

Contrary to the Grundfest and Huang (2006) models' assumptions, the plaintiff's option to abandon the lawsuit after Stage-One has to be adjusted for the probability of, and amount of judge-ordered court-costs upon abandonment, and the associated opportunity costs. The Grundfest and Huang (2006) models do not consider the defendant's option to abandon the lawsuit – in some cases, a defendant's abandonment of a lawsuit does not equate to a finding of liability. Second, default judgments are typically issued on the basis of forum procedures, and not on facts or merits of the dispute, and the appeals courts can re-open cases where default judgments were entered for many reasons. Furthermore, the defendant may have strategic reasons for abandoning a lawsuit, and such abandonment may result in greater total utility (monetary and non-monetary utility) than continuing litigation.

Grundfest and Huang (2006) models erroneously assume that compliance with rules of civil procedure is guaranteed in judicial proceedings (and other adjudicative proceedings). In some instances, civil procedure rules serve merely as a guide/reference and are not strictly applied.

Contrary to Grundfest and Huang (2006), the risk of litigation varies over time in a manner that is not a one-directional, uniform manner. In the Grundfest and

Huang (2006) models, litigation risk is expressed in terms of litigation costs and variance. Chapter 4 in this book explains why Variance is not a good measure of risk. In the litigation arena, where there is information asymmetry, information processing differentials, subjection to judicial interpretation, possibility of transfer of costs (e.g. Discovery costs, and by awarding court costs and damages) and subjection to terminal rulings by judges, risk is multi-faceted and multi-criteria in nature. Information value is a key element of risk – value of any specific information toward achieving conviction/guilt or acquittal/dismissal or settlement.

The Grundfest and Huang (2006) models erroneously assume that conviction or a finding of liability automatically equates to payout by the losing party in the lawsuit. In Grundfest and Huang (2006), the assumption that litigants are identical and risk-neutral agents that share common knowledge about all of a lawsuit's characteristics (e.g. the lawsuit's expected value, the type and value of information that might be disclosed during the litigation, the variance of the value of that information, and each party's litigation costs) is very inaccurate. It is well documented in the literature that each lawsuit has some measure of information asymmetry; and there are differences in knowledge among litigants in any one lawsuit.

In Grundfest and Huang (2006), the assumption that opposing litigants have equal bargaining power and also have equal litigation expenditures is major but an inaccurate assumption that renders many of the models useless. In most instances (and even with the existence of companies that finance litigation), opposing litigants have very different financial resources, levels of knowledge and available time to devote to the litigation.

2.4 The foregoing critiques of Grundfest and Huang (2006) also apply to other academic research about real options

Unfortunately, the problems and weaknesses inherent in the Grundfest and Huang (2006) analysis which are discussed herein are also evident in Heyes, Rickman and Tzavara (2004); Stephenson (2008); Bar-Gill (2005); Deffains and Obidzinski (2006); Parisi et al. (2004); Hansen, Krarup and Russell (2006); Fon and Parisi (2007) (real options implicit in both rule-making and the resulting regulations); Mahoney and Sanchirico (2005) (real options implicit in both rule-making and the resulting regulations); and Engelen (2004; Jan. 2005; 1997); 2003) – and thus, most, or all the theories and theorems developed in these articles are wrong, misspecified or incomplete.

2.5 Conclusion

The changes in national economies and the global economy raise very critical economic, accounting and public policy issues that have certainly not been sufficiently analyzed in existing literature, and have not been addressed by existing Accounting Regulations and securities laws in various countries; and harmonization (e.g. IASB) hasn't resolved these issues. Accounting Regulations and securities laws have significant implications for courts, administrative law agencies, international capital flows, international contracts, arbitral fora, investors, international development organizations (e.g. UNDP; IFC; WTO; etc.), international donors and financial institutions, particularly in an era where Intangible Assets constitute more than 30 percent of the total asset values of many private and exchange-traded companies. Harmonization of Accounting Regulations and securities laws can be developed and enforced through both new and existing international organizations (World Bank, BIS, UNDP, WTO; etc.). *Real Options Theory* has very limited application and relevance to the "selection of disputes" that pertain to Intangibles and the enforcement of securities laws and Accounting Regulations.

Notes

1 This chapter contains excerpts from the author Michael I. C. Nwogugu's article that is cited as follows: Nwogugu, M. (2015). Real options, enforcement of goodwill/intangibles rules and associated behavioral issues. *Journal of Money Laundering Control*, 18(3), 330–351.
2 ASC-805, *Business Combinations*, and ASC-350, *Goodwill and Intangible Assets;* IFRS-3R (*Business Combinations*) and IAS 38 *Intangible Assets* (accounting for Intangible Assets) (collectively, the "Goodwill/Intangibles Accounting Regulations" or "GIAR").
3 *See*: Andrews, Pritchett and Woolcock (2017); Byrne and Callaghan (2014); Bamberger, Vaessen and Raimondo (2016); Room (2011); Kirman (2016); Salzano and Colander (2007); OECD (2016); Finch (2013); Durlauf (2012); Bayoumi, Pickford and Subacchi (2016); Kuhlman and Mortveit (2014); LoPucki (1997); Melnik et al. (2013); Miklashevich (2003); Perc, Donnay and Helbing (2013); Post and Eisen (2000); Ruhl and Ruhl (1997); Williams and Arrigo (2002); Young (1997); Arthur (1999); Sherblom (2017); Tse, Friesen and Kalaycı (2016); Gates (2016); De Martino and Marsili (2006); Bouchaud (2009); and Bardoscia, Livan and Marsili (2017).
4 *See*: FASB. (2014). *Intangibles – Goodwill and Other (Topic 350): Accounting for Goodwill – a Consensus of the Private Company Council.* www.fasb.org/jsp/FASB/ Document_C/DocumentPage?cid=1176163744355&acceptedDisclaimer=true.
5 *See*: US SEC. (July 2012). *Work Plan for the Consideration of Incorporating International Financial Reporting Standards into the Financial Reporting System for U.S. Issuers – Final Staff Report.* www.sec.gov/spotlight/globalaccountingstandards/ifrs-work-plan-final-report.pdf.
6 *See*: Ballow, J., Thomas, R. & Roos, G. (Accenture) (2004). *Future Value: The $7 Trillion Challenge.* www.accenture.com/SiteCollectionDocuments/PDF/manage.pdf. Noting that "Nearly sixty percent of the aggregate value of the US stock market is based on investor expectations of future growth. And because this future value tends to be concentrated in industries and companies that are built on intangible assets, it is critical to find better ways to recognize, report and manage these assets."
  See: Hulten, C. (2008). *Intangible Capital and the "Market to Book Value" Puzzle.* www.conference-board.org/pdf_free/workingpapers/E-0029-08-WP.pdf. The conference Board – Economics Program Working Paper Series. Also see: http://raw.rutgers. edu/docs/intangibles/Papers/Intangible%20Capital%20and%20the%20Market%20 to%20Book%20ValuePuzzle.pdf.
  See: Hassett, K. & Shapiro, R. (2012). *What Ideas Are Worth: The Value of Intellectual Capital and Intangible Assets in the American Economy.* www.sonecon.com/

docs/studies/Value_of_Intellectual_Capital_in_American_Economy.pdf. (noting that "The value of the intangible assets – which includes intellectual capital plus economic competencies – in the U.S. economy totals an estimated $14.5 trillion in 2011. The ten industries whose intellectual capital represents at least fifty percent of their market value – the ten most intellectual-capital intensive industries – are media; telecommunications services; automobiles and components; household and personal products; food, beverages and tobacco; commercial and professional services; software and services; healthcare equipment and services; pharmaceuticals, biotech and life sciences; and consumer services.").

See: Bond, S. & Cummins, J.G. *The Stock Market and Investment in the New Economy: Some Tangible Facts and Intangible Fictions*. www.brookings.edu/~/media/Projects/BPEA/Spring%202000/2000a_bpea_bond.PDF.

See: OCEAN TOMO (2015). *2015 Annual Study of Intangible Asset Market Value*. https://www.oceantomo.com/blog/2015/03-05-ocean-tomo-2015-intangible-asset-market-value/ (noting that as of 2015, Intangible Assets accounted for about 87 percent of the stock market values of S&P 500 companies).

7   *See*: Hand, J. (2003). Increasing returns-to-scale of intangibles. Chapter in: Hand, J.R.M. & Lev, B., eds., *Intangible Assets: Values, Measures, and Risks* (Oxford Management Readers).

See: Nakamura, L. (July/August 1999). Intangibles: What put the new in the new economy? *Federal Reserve Bank of Philadelphia Business Review*, 3–16.

See: DeLong, J. (2002). *The Stock Options Controversy and the New Economy* (Competitive Enterprise Institute, Washington DC).

8   *See*: Damodaran, A. (September 2009). *Valuing Companies with Intangible Assets*. Working Paper, NYU Stern School of Business, New York. http://pages.stern.nyu.edu/~adamodar/pdfiles/papers/intangibles.pdf.

9   *See*: Bell, T., Landsman, W., Miller, B. & Yeh, S. (2002). The valuation implications of employee stock option accounting for profitable computer software firms. *The Accounting Review*, 77(4), 971–996.

10   *See*: Nakamura (July/August 1999) (supra).

11   *See*: Ernst & Young. (July 2010). *IRS Concedes Stock Option Issue in Veritas Following Ninth Circuit's Opinion in Xilinx*. www.ey.com/Publication/vwLUAssets/ITA_26July2010/$FILE/ITA_IRS_concedes_stock_option.pdf.

See: Sullivan & Cromwell. (March 24, 2010). *Court Addresses (Again) Employee Stock Option Expenses for Transfer Pricing Purposes – Ninth Circuit Overturns Tax Court and Holds That Expenses Attributable to Employee Stock Options Are "Costs" of Developing Intangibles for Transfer Pricing Purposes – Ninth Circuit Reverses Itself and Holds that the Arm's-Length Standard Controls in Determining if Employee Stock Option Expenses Must Be Shared Among Related Parties Under Pre-2003 US Transfer Pricing Rules*. www.sullcrom.com/files/Publication/68c25802-e2d4-483c-8662-102f0af7bdbf/Presentation/PublicationAttachment/b88f2c64-3d86-44d5-998c-1484ea00283a/SC_Publication_Court_Addresses_Employee_Stock_Option_Expenses.pdf.

See: *Xilinx, Inc.* vs. *Commissioner* (2010 U.S. App. LEXIS 5795 (March 22, 2010)).

See: O'Driscoll, D. (November 1, 2005). *Allocation of employee stock options to cost-sharing agreement*. The Tax Adviser.

12   *See*: www.forexhound.com/article.cfm?articleID=120795 which states in part: "the federal banking and thrift regulatory agencies today approved a final rule that would permit a banking organization to reduce the amount of Goodwill it must deduct from Tier-1 Capital by any associated deferred tax liability. Under the final rule, the regulatory capital deduction for Goodwill would be equal to the maximum capital reduction that could occur as a result of a complete write-off of the Goodwill under generally accepted accounting principles (GAAP). The final rule is in substance the same as the

proposal issued in September. The final rule will be effective 30 days after publication in the Federal Register. However, banking organizations may adopt its provisions for purposes of regulatory capital reporting for the period ending December 31, 2008."

See: US Treasury Department and the Federal Deposit Insurance Corporation. (2008). *Minimum Capital Ratios; Capital Adequacy Guidelines; Capital Maintenance; Capital: Deduction of Goodwill Net of Associated Deferred Tax Liability.* www.forexhound. com/Uploads/FEDREPORT.pdf. US Department of The Treasury (Office of the Comptroller of the Currency) 12 CFR Part 3, Docket ID OCC-2008–0025, RIN 1557-AD13.

See: Federal Reserve System, 12 CFR Parts 208 and 225; Regulations H and Y; Docket No. R-1329.

Federal Deposit Insurance Corporation – 12 CFR Part 325; RIN 3064-AD32.

See: *U.S. v. Winstar*, 518 U.S. 839 (1996).

13 See: The US Treasury Department's information statement (www.forexhound.com/ Uploads/FEDREPORT.pdf).

Bibliography

Aakre, S., Helland, L. & Hovi, J. (2014). When does informal enforcement work? *Journal of Conflict Resolution*, 60(7), 1312–1340.

Acciaro, M. (2014). Real option analysis for environmental compliance: LNG and emission control areas. *Transportation Research Part D: Transport and Environment*, 28, 41–50.

Agoglia, C., Doupnik, T. & Tsakumis, G. (2011). Principles-based versus rules-based accounting standards: The influence of standard precision and audit committee strength on financial reporting decisions. *The Accounting Review*, 86(3), 747–767.

Akpalu, W., Eggert, H. & Vondolia, G. (2009). Enforcement of exogenous environmental regulation, social disapproval and bribery. *The Journal of Socio-Economics*, 38(6), 940–945.

Al-Shammari, B., Brown, P. & Tarca, A. (2008). An investigation of compliance with international accounting standards by listed companies in the Gulf Cooperation Council member States. *The International Journal of Accounting*, 43(4), 425–447.

An, H. & Zhang, T. (2013). Stock price synchronicity, crash risk, and institutional investors. *Journal of Corporate Finance*, 21, 1–15.

Andrews, M., Pritchett, L. & Woolcock, M. (2017). *Building State Capability: Evidence, Analysis, Action* (Oxford University Press, UK).

Andrighetto, G. & Conte, R. (2012). Cognitive dynamics of norm compliance. From norm adoption to flexible automated conformity. *Artificial Intelligence and Law*, 20(4), 359–381.

Antunes, A., Cavalcanti, T. & Villamil, A. (2008). The effect of financial repression and enforcement on entrepreneurship and economic development. *Journal of Monetary Economics*, 55(2), 278–297.

Antunes, C. & Gomez, A. (2008). Operational research models and methods in the energy sector. *European Journal of Operational Research*, 97(3), 997–998.

Arthur, W.B. (1999). Complexity and the economy. *Science*, 284, 107–109.

Ascioglu, A., Hegde, S., Krishnan, G. & McDermott, J. (2012). Earnings management and market liquidity. *Review of Quant. Finance & Accounting*, 38, 257–274.

Attia, M., Lassoued, N. & Attia, A. (2016). Political costs and earnings management: Evidence from Tunisia. *Journal of Accounting in Emerging Economies*, 6(4), 388–407.

Avraham, R. & Liu, Z. (2012). Private information and the option to not sue: A reevaluation of contract remedies. *Journal of Economics & Organization*, 28(1), 77–102.

Baker, S. & Mezzetti, C. (2001). Prosecutorial resources, plea bargaining, and the decision to go to trial. *Journal of Economics & Organization*, 17(1), 149–167.

Balke, T., De Vos, M. & Padget, J. (2013). I-ABM: Combining institutional frameworks and agent-based modelling for the design of enforcement policies. *Artificial Intelligence & Law*, 21(4), 371–398.

Ball, R., Robin, A. & Wu, J. (2003). Incentives versus standards: Properties of accounting income in four East Asian countries. *Journal of Accounting & Economics*, 36(1–3), 235–270.

Bamberger, M., Vaessen, J. & Raimondo, E. (2016). *Dealing with Complexity in Development Evaluation: A Practical Approach.*

Banarescu, A. (2015). Detecting and preventing fraud with data analytics. *Procedia Economics & Finance*, 32, 1827–1836.

Banerjee, S., Güçbilmez, U. & Pawlina, G. (2014). Optimal exercise of jointly held real options: A Nash bargaining approach with value diversion. *European Journal of Operational Research*, 239(2), 565–578.

Bardoscia, M., Livan, G. & Marsili, M. (2017). Statistical mechanics of complex economies. *Journal of Statistical Mechanics*, 2017, 043401. doi: 10.1088/1742-5468/aa6688.

Bar-Gill, O. (2005). Pricing legal options: A behavioral perspective. *Review of Law & Economics*, 1, 203–223. www.bepress.com/rle/vol1/iss2/art2.

Bar-Gill, O. (2006). The evolution and persistence of optimism in litigation. *Journal of Economics & Organization*, 22(2), 490–507.

Barnett, T. (2010). Applying the Kelly criterion to lawsuits. *Law, Probability and Risk*, 9(2), 139–147.

Barnett, T. (2011). Obtaining a fair arbitration outcome. *Law, Probability and Risk*, 10(2), 123–131.

Bar-Yosef, S. & Prencipe, A. (2013). The impact of corporate governance and earnings management on stock market liquidity in a highly concentrated ownership capital market. *Journal of Accounting, Auditing and Finance*, 26, 199–227.

Bayoumi, T., Pickford, S. & Subacchi, P. (2016). *Managing Complexity: Economic Policy Cooperation After the Crisis* (Brookings Institution Press, Washington, DC, USA).

Bednar, J. (2006). Is full compliance possible? Conditions for shirking with imperfect monitoring and continuous action spaces. *Journal of Theoretical Politics*, 18, 347–375.

Beer, J., Fisk, A. & Rogers, W. (2014). Toward a Framework for Levels of Robot Autonomy in Human-Robot Interaction. *Journal of Human-Robot Interaction*, 3(2), 74–102.

Bertomeu, J. & Magee, R. (2011). From low-quality reporting to financial crises: Politics of disclosure regulation along the economic cycle. *Journal of Accounting and Economics*, 52(2–3), 209–227.

Bex, F. & Walton, D. (2012). Burdens and standards of proof for inference to the best explanation: Three case studies. *Law, Probability and Risk*, 11(2–3), 113–133.

Bodenhuasen, G., Macrae, C. & Hugenberg, K. (2003). Social cognition. Chapter in: Weiner, I., Million, T. & Lerner, M.J., eds., *Handbook of Psychology: Personality and Social Psychology*, Volume 5 (John Wiley & Sons, Hoboken, NJ, USA).

Bouchaud, J. (2009). The (unfortunate) complexity of the economy. *Physics World*, 22(4), 2058–7058, 22, 28. doi: 10.1088/2058-7058/22/04/39.

Boyd, C. & Hoffman, D. (2013). Litigating toward settlement. *Journal of Law, Economic & Organization*, 29(4), 898–929.

Braam, G., Nandy, M., Weitzel, U. & Lodh, S. (2015). Accrual-based and real earnings management and political connections. *The International Journal of Accounting*, 50(2), 111–141.

Brandau, M., Endenich, C., Trapp, R. & Hoffjan, A. (2013). Institutional drivers of conformity – Evidence for management accounting from Brazil and Germany. *International Business Review*, 22(2), 466–479.

Burgemeestre, B., Hulstijn, J. & Tan, Y. (2011). Value-based argumentation for justifying compliance. *Artificial Intelligence and Law*, 19(2–3), 149–186.

Byrne, D. & Callaghan, G. (2014). *Complexity Theory and the Social Sciences: The State of the Art.*

Cárdenas, E. (2012). Globalization of securities enforcement: A shift toward enhanced regulatory intensity in Brazil's capital market? *Brooklyn Journal of International Law*, 37(3), 803–813.

Caulkins, J. (1993). Local drug markets' response to focused police enforcement. *Operations Research*, 41(5), 816–1008.

Chapman, B. (2013). Incommensurability, proportionality, and defeasibility. *Law, Probability & Risk*, 12(3–4), 259–274.

Chen, D., Jiang, D., Liang, S. & Wang, F. (2011). Selective enforcement of regulation. *China Journal of Accounting Research*, 4(1–2), 9–27.

Chen, D., Li, J., Liang, S. & Wang, G. (2011). Macroeconomic control, political costs and earnings management: Evidence from Chinese listed real estate companies. *China Journal of Accounting Research*, 4(3), 91–106.

Chen, K. & Wang, J. (2007). Fee-shifting rules in litigation with contingency fees. *Journal of Law, Economic & Organization*, 23(3), 519–546.

Chen, Y., Wu, C., Chen, Y., Li, H. & Chen, H. (2017). Enhancement of fraud detection for narratives in annual reports. *International Journal of Accounting Information Systems*, 26, 32–45.

Cheng, L. & Leung, T. (2016). Government protection, political connection and management turnover in China. *International Review of Economics & Finance*, 45, 160–176.

Chesney, T., Gold, S. & Trautrims, A. (2017). Agent based modelling as a decision support system for shadow accounting. *Decision Support Systems*, 95, 110–116.

Choi, S. (2007). Do the merits matter less after the private securities litigation reform act? *Journal of Economics & Organization*, 23(3), 598–626.

Choi, S. & Pritchard, A. (2012). The Supreme Court's impact on securities class actions: An empirical assessment of Tellabs. *Journal of Economics & Organization*, 4, 850–881.

Chopard, B., Cortade, T. & Langlais, E. (2010). Trial and settlement negotiations between asymmetrically skilled parties. *International Review of Law & Economics*, 30(1), 18–27.

Chouiekh, A. & EL Haj, E. (2018). ConvNets for fraud detection analysis. *Procedia Computer Science*, 127, 133–138.

Christensen, H. (2012). Why do firms rarely adopt IFRS voluntarily? Academics find significant benefits and the costs appear to be low. *Review of Accounting Studies*, 17(3), 518–525.

Christensen, H., Hail, L. & Leuz, C. (2013). Mandatory IFRS reporting and changes in enforcement. *Journal of Accounting & Economics*, 56(2–3), 147–177.

Coffee, J. (2007). Law and the market: The impact of enforcement. *University of Pennsylvania Law Review*, 156(2), 229–256. www.law.upenn.edu/journals/lawreview/articles/volume156/issue2/Coffee156U.Pa.L.Rev.229%282007%29.pdf.

Comiskey, E. & Mulford, C. (2008). Negative goodwill: Issues of financial reporting and analysis under current and proposed guidelines. *Journal of Applied Research in Accounting and Finance (JARAF)*, 3(1), 33–42. http://smartech.gatech.edu/bitstream/1853/19231/1/fal_ga_tech_neg_goodwill_2007.pdf.

Cornell, B. (1990). The incentive to sue: An option-pricing approach. *The Journal of Legal Studies*, 19(1), 173–187.

Corrado, C., Hulten, C. & Sichel, D. (April 2006). Intangible capital and economic growth. *US Federal Reserve Board: Finance and Economics Discussion Series: 2006–24.* www.federalreserve.gov/Pubs/feds/2006/200624/index.html.

Corrado, C., Hulten, C. & Sichel, D. (2009). Intangible Capital and U.S. Economic Growth. Review of Income and Wealth, 55(3), 661–685.

D'Amato, A., Mazzanti, M., Nicolli, F. & Zoli, M. (2018). Illegal waste disposal: Enforcement actions and decentralized environmental policy. *Socio-Economic Planning Sciences,* 64, 56–65.

D'Arcy, A. (2006). *De Facto Accounting Harmonization Versus National Context – Goodwill Accounting in Germany and Japan.* Working Paper. www.unifr.ch/controlling/kolloquium/.

Daughety, A. & Reinganum, J. (2000). On the economics of trials: Adversarial process, evidence, and equilibrium bias. *Journal of Economics & Organization,* 16(2), 365–394.

Daughety, A. & Reinganum, J. (2010). Population-based liability determination, mass torts, and the incentives for suit, settlement, and trial. *Journal of Economics & Organization,* 26(3), 460–492.

De Martino, A. & Marsili, M. (2006). Statistical mechanics of socio-economic systems with heterogeneous agents. *Journal of Physics-A: Mathematical and General,* 39, R465. doi: 10.1088/0305-4470/39/43/R01.

De MEsquita, E. & Stephenson, M. (2006). Legal institutions and informal networks. *Journal of Theoretical Politics,* 18, 40–67.

DeDreu, C., Beersma, B., Stroebe, K. & Euwema, M. (2006). Motivated information processing, strategic choice and the quality of negotiated agreement. *Journal of personality and Social Psychology,* 90, 927–943.

Deffains, B. & Obidzinski, M. (2009). Real options theory for law makers. *Louvain Economic Review,* 75(1), 93–100.

Demolombe, R. (2011). Relationships between obligations and actions in the context of institutional agents, human agents or software agents. *Artificial Intelligence & Law,* 19(2–3), 99–115.

Do, C. & Nabar, S. (2018). Macroeconomic effects of aggregate accounting conservatism: A cross-country analysis. *Journal of International Financial Management & Accounting,* 30(1), 83–107.

Drenovak, M., Ranković, V., Ivanović, M., Urošević, B. & Jelic, R. (2017). Market risk management in a post-Basel II regulatory environment. *European Journal of Operational Research,* 257(3), 1030–1044.

Durlauf, S. (2012). Complexity, economics, and public policy. *Politics, Philosophy & Economics,* 11(1), 45–75.

Earnhart, D. & Glicksman, R. (2015). Coercive vs. cooperative enforcement: Effect of enforcement approach on environmental management. *International Review of Law and Economics,* 42, 135–146.

Eng, L. & Lin, Y. (2012). Accounting quality, earnings management and cross-listings: Evidence from China. *Review of Pacific Basin Financial Markets,* 15(2), 1–25.

Engelen, J. (1997). Is the enforcement of insider trading regulation enforceable? *European Journal of Crime, Criminal law and Criminal Justice,* 5(2), 105–111.

Engelen, J. (2004). Criminal behavior: A real option approach with an application to restricting illegal insider trading. *European Journal of Law & Economics,* 17(3), 329–352.

Engelen, J. (January 2005). *Modelling Criminal Behavior by Using a Real Options Approach.* Working Paper, Utrecht University, Netherlands.

Ezrachi, A. & Stucke, M. (2015). *Artificial Intelligence and Collusion: When Computers Inhibit Competition.* Oxford Legal Studies Research Paper No. 18/2015, University of Tennessee Legal Studies Research Paper No. 267.

Farmera, A. & Pecorino, P. (2002). Pretrial bargaining with self-serving bias and asymmetric information. *Journal of Economic Behavior & Organization*, 48(2), 163–176.

Fehr, E., Fischbacher, U. & Gächter, S. (2002). Strong reciprocity, human cooperation, and the enforcement of social norms. *Human Nature*, 13(1), 1–25.

Fellner, G., Sausgruber, R. & Traxler, C. (2013). Testing enforcement strategies in the field: Threat, moral appeal and social information. *Journal of the European Economic Association*, 3, 634–660.

Files, R. (2012). SEC enforcement: Does forthright disclosure and cooperation really matter? *Journal of Accounting & Economics*, 53(1), 353–374.

Financial Accounting Standards Board (FASB). (2001). *Statement of Financial Accounting Standards No. 142: Goodwill and Other Intangible Assets (2001). Statement of Financial Accounting Standards No. 141R – Business Combinations (2001)*. FASB, Stamford, CT.

Finch, J., ed. (2013). *Complexity and the Economy – Implications for Economic Policy* (Edward Elgar, Massachusetts, USA).

Finch, N. (2006). Intangible assets and creative impairment – An analysis of current disclosure practices by top Australian firms. *Journal of Law and Financial Management*, 5(2), 16–23.

Fon, V. & Parisi, F. (2007). On the optimal specificity of legal rules. *Journal of Institutional Economics*, 3(2), 147–164.

Francis, W., Hasan, I. & Li, L. (2014). *Abnormal Real Operations, Real Earnings Management, and Subsequent Crashes in Stock Prices*. Bank of Finland Research Discussion Papers #19.

Frankel, R., Seethamraju, T. & Zach, T. (2008). GAAP goodwill and debt contracting efficiency: Evidence from net worth covenants. *Review of Accounting Studies*, 13(1), 87–118.

Friedman, D. & Wittman, D. (2007). Litigation with symmetric bargaining and two-sided incomplete information. *Journal of Law, Economic & Organization*, 23(1), 98–126.

Friedman, E. & Wickelgren, A. (2010). Chilling, settlement, and the accuracy of the legal process. *Journal of Economics & Organization*, 26(1), 144–157.

Galligan, K. (1997). Political cost incentives for earnings management in the cable television industry. *Journal of Accounting & Economics*, 23(3), 309–337.

Garcia-Meca, E. & Martinez, I. (2007). The use of intellectual capital information in investment decisions: An empirical study using analyst reports. *The International Journal of Accounting*, 42(1), 57–81.

Gastwirth, J. (2011). Case comment: The need for careful analysis of the statistical summary in the response to the complaint in the *SEC v. Goldman Sachs* case. *Law, Probability & Risk*, 10(1), 77–87.

Gates, E. (2016). Making sense of the emerging conversation in evaluation about systems thinking and complexity science. *Evaluation and Program Planning*, 59, 62–73.

Ge, W. & Kim, J. (2013). Real earnings management and the cost of new corporate bonds. *Journal of Business Research*, 67(4), 641–647.

Geiger, M., O'Connell, B., Clikeman, P.M., Ochoa, E., Witkowski, K. & Basioudis, I. (2006). Perceptions of earnings management: The effects of national culture. *Advances in International Accounting*, 19, 175–199.

Georgiou, G. (2004). Corporate lobbying on accounting standards: Methods, timing and perceived effectiveness. *Abacus*, 40(2), 219–237.

Gibbins, M., McCracken, S. & Salterio, S. (2008). Auditor-client relationships and roles in negotiating financial reporting. *Accounting, Organizations & Society*, 33(4/5), 362–383.

Graham, J., Harvey, C. & Rajgopal, S. (2005). The economic implications of corporate financial reporting. *Journal of Accounting and Economics*, 40(1–3), 3–73.

Griffin, W. & Lev, A. (2007). *Tax Aspects of Corporate Mergers and Acquisitions* (Davis, Malm & D'Agostine P.C., Boston, MA, USA).

Grundfest, J. & Huang, P. (2006). The unexpected value of litigation: A real options perspective. *Stanford Law Review*, 58, 1267–1336.

Guenther, D. & Young, D. (2000). The association between financial accounting measures and real economic activity: A multinational study. *Journal of Accounting and Economics*, 29(1), 53–72.

Guo, W., Wang, F. & Wu, H. (2011). Financial leverage and market volatility with diverse beliefs. *Economic Theory*, 47(2–3), 337–364.

Habib, A., Muhammadi, A. & Jiang, H. (2017). Political connections and related party transactions: Evidence from Indonesia. *The International Journal of Accounting*, 52(1), 45–63.

Hake, E. (2004). The appearance of impairment: Verbelen and goodwill-financed mergers. *Journal of Economic Issues*, 38(2), 389–396.

Hansen, L., Krarup, S. & Russell, C. (2006). Enforcement and information strategies. *Journal of Regulatory Economics*, 30, 45–61.

Harrington, J. (2018). *Developing Competition Law for Collusion by Autonomous Price-Setting Agents*. Working Paper.

Hasmath, R. & MacDonald, A. (2018). Beyond special privileges: The discretionary treatment of ethnic minorities in China's welfare system. *Journal of Social Policy*, 47(2), 295–316.

He, G. (2016). Fiscal support and earnings management. *The International Journal of Accounting*, 51(1), 57–84.

Hegarty, J., Gielen, F. & Barros, A. (September 2004). *Implementation of International Accounting and Auditing Standards – Lessons Learned from the World Bank's Accounting and Auditing ROSC Program*.

Henrich, J. & Boyd, R. (2001). Why people punish defectors: Weak conformist transmission can stabilize costly enforcement of norms in cooperative dilemmas. *Journal of Theoretical Biology*, 208, 79–89.

Heyes, A., Rickman, N. & Tzavara, D. (2004). Legal expenses insurance, risk aversion and litigation. *International Review of Law & Economics*, 24, 107–119.

Holthausen, R. (2009). Accounting standards, financial reporting outcomes and enforcement. *Journal of Accounting Research*, 47, 447–458.

Holton, C. (2009). Identifying disgruntled employee systems fraud risk through text mining: A simple solution for a multi-billion dollar problem. *Decision Support Systems*, 46(4), 853–864.

Hope, C. (2003). Disclosure practices, enforcement of accounting standards and analyst's forecast accuracy: An international study. *Journal of Accounting Research*, 41(2), 235–284.

Houqe, M., Monem, R. & van Zijl, T. (2012). Government quality, auditor choice and adoption of IFRS: A cross country analysis. *Advances in Accounting*, 28(2), 307–316.

Howson, N.C. (2012). Enforcement without foundation? Insider trading and China's administrative law crisis. *American Journal of Comparative Law*, 60(4), 955–1002.

Huang, S., Yen, D., Yang, L. & Hua, J. (2008). An investigation of Zipf's law for fraud detection. *Decision Support Systems*, 46(1), 70–83.

Huefner, R.J. & Largay, J. (2004). *The Effect of the New Goodwill Accounting Rule on Financial Statements*. (New York State Society of CPAs, New York City, USA).

Hutton, A., Marcus, A. & Tehranian, H. (2009). Opaque financial reports, R square, and crash risk. *Journal of Financial Economics*, 94, 67–86.

Hylton, K. (2002). An asymmetric-information model of litigation. *International Review of Law & Economics*, 22, 153–175.

Hylton, K. (2008). When should a case be dismissed? The economics of pleading and summary judgment standards. *Supreme Court Economic Review*, 16, 39–49.

Hylton, K.N. & Lin, H. (2009). *Trial Selection Theory and Evidence: A Review*. Encyclopedia of Law and Economics: Procedural Law and Economics, Chris Sanchirico, ed., Vol. X, Edward Elgar Publishing; Boston Univ. School of Law Working Paper No. 09–27. SSRN: http://ssrn.com/abstract=1407557.

Institute of Chartered Accountants in England and Wales (ICAEW). (October 2007). *EU Implementation of IFRS and the Fair Value Directive: A Report for the European Commission*. http://ec.europa.eu/internal_market/accounting/docs/studies/2007-eu_implemen tation_of_ifrs.pdf.

International Accounting Standards Board (IASB). (2004). *Intangible Assets*. International Accounting Standards #38. (IASB, London, UK).

Jackson, H. & Roe, M. (2009). Public and private enforcement of securities laws: Resource based evidence. *Journal of Financial Economics*, 93, 207–238.

Jacoby, J., Li, J. & Liu, M. (2016). Financial distress, political affiliation and earnings management: The case of politically affiliated private firms. *The European Journal of Finance*.

Jarboe, K. (2007). *Athena Alliance Report: Measuring Intangibles: A Summary of Recent Activity*. www.athenaalliance.org/apapers/MeasuringIntangibles.htm.

Jayaraman, S. (2012). The effect of enforcement on timely loss recognition: Evidence from insider trading laws. *Journal of Accounting & Economics*, 53, 77–97.

Ji, G. & Gunasekaran, A. (2014). Evolution of innovation and its strategies: From ecological niche models of supply chain clusters. *Journal of the Operational Research Society*, 65(6), 888–903.

Ji, X., Lu, W. & Qu, W. (2015). Determinants and economic consequences of voluntary disclosure of internal control weaknesses in China. *Journal of Contemporary Accounting & Economics*, 11(1), 1–17.

Johnston, D. & Jones, D. (2006). How does accounting fit into a firm's political strategy? *Journal of Accounting & Public Policy*, 25(2), 195–228.

Jordan, C., Clark, S. & Vann, C. (2007). Using goodwill impairment to effect earnings management during SFAS 142's year of adoption and later. *Journal of Business & Economic Research*, 5(1). doi: 10.19030/jber.v5i1.2510.

Kacsuk, Z. (2011). The mathematics of patent claim analysis. *Artificial Intelligence and Law*, 19(4), 263–289.

Kedia, S. & Rajgopal, S. (2011). Do the SEC's enforcement preferences affect corporate misconduct? *Journal of Accounting & Economics*, 51(3), 259–278.

Ketz, E. (2004). Negative goodwill: An M&A "fix" that doesn't work. *Journal of Corporate Accounting & Finance*, 16(2), 47–50.

Kim, C. (2014). Adversarial and inquisitorial procedures with information acquisition. *Journal of Economics & Organization*, 30(4), 767–803.

Kim, J. & Zhang, L. (2013). Accounting conservatism and stock price crash risk: Firm-level evidence. *Contemporary Accounting Research*, 33(1), 412–441.

Kim, J. & Zhang, L. (2014). Financial reporting opacity and expected crash risk: Evidence from implied volatility smirks. *Contemporary Accounting Research*, 31(3), 851–875.

Kim, J.B., Li, Y. & Zhang, L. (2011a). Corporate tax avoidance and stock price crash risk: Firm-level analysis. *Journal of Financial Economics*, 100, 639–662.

Kim, J.B., Li, Y. & Zhang, L. (2011b). CFOs versus CEOs: Equity incentives and crashes. *Journal of Financial Economics*, 101, 713–730.

Kirman, A. (2016). Complexity and economic policy: A paradigm shift or a change in perspective? A review essay on David Colander and Roland Kupers's *Complexity and the Art of Public Policy*. *Journal of Economic Literature*, 54(2), 534–572.

Klement, A. & Neeman, Z. (2005). Against compromise: A mechanism design approach. *Journal of Economics & Organization*, 21(2), 285–314.

Knoll, M. (2002). Put-call parity and the law. *Cardozo Law Review*, 24, 61–72.

Königsgruber, R. (2010). A political economy of accounting standard setting. *Journal of Management & Governance*, 14(4), 277–295.

Königsgruber, R. & Palan, S. (2015). Earnings management and participation in accounting standard-setting. *Central European Journal of Operations Research*, 23(1), 31–52.

Kuhlman, C. & Mortveit, H. (2014). Attractor stability in non-uniform Boolean networks. *Theoretical Computer Science*, 559, 20–33.

Lang, M. & Wambach, A. (2013). The fog of fraud – Mitigating fraud by strategic ambiguity. *Games & Economic Behavior*, 8(1), 255–275.

Langevoort, D. (1997). Organized illusions: A behavioral theory of why corporations mislead stock market investors (and cause other social harms). *University of Pennsylvania Law Review*, 146, 101–156.

Lapointe-Antunes, P., Cormier, D. & Magnan, M. (2009). Value-relevance and timeliness of transitional goodwill impairment losses: Evidence from Canada. *The International Journal of Accounting*, 44(1), 56–78.

Laux, V. & Stocken, P. (2018). Accounting standards, regulatory enforcement, and innovation. *Journal of Accounting and Economics*, 65(2–3), 221–236.

Lavezzolo, S., Rodríguez-Lluesma, C. & Elvira, M. (2018). National culture and financial systems: The conditioning role of political context. *Journal of Business Research*, 85, 60–72.

Lee, C. (1987). Accounting infrastructure and economic development. *Journal of Accounting and Public Policy*, 6(2), 75–85.

Lemma, T., Feedman, M. et al. (2018). Corporate carbon risk, voluntary disclosure, and cost of capital: South African evidence. *Business Strategy and the Environment*, 28(1), 111–126.

Leung, E., Paolacci, G. & Puntoni, S. (2018). Man versus machine: Resisting automation in identity-based consumer behavior. *Journal of Marketing Research*, 55(6), 818–831.

Leung, P. & Cooper, B.J. (2003). The Mad Hatter's corporate tea party. *Managerial Auditing Journal*, 18(6/7), 505–516.

Leung, S., Richardson, G. & Taylor, G. (2019). The effect of the general anti-avoidance rule on corporate tax avoidance in China. *Journal of Contemporary Accounting & Economics*, 15(1), 105–117.

Lewellyn, K. & Bao, S. (2017). The role of national culture and corruption on managing earnings around the world. *Journal of World Business*, 52(6), 798–808.

Lewis, E., Lippitt, J. & Mastracchio, N. (2001). User's comments about SFAS 141 and 142 on business combinations and goodwill. *The CPA Journal*. www.nysscpa.org/cpajournal/2001/1000/features/f102601.htm.

Li, E. & Liu, L. (2012). *Intangible Assets and Cross-Sectional Stock Returns: Evidence from Structural Estimation*. https://pdfs.semanticscholar.org/d069/ae2fcf9d6947fb5b2d-869bd8f05c9a4cefa0.pdf.

Li, S., Selover, D. & Stein, M. (2011). "Keep silent and make money": Institutional patterns of earnings management in China. *Journal of Asian Economics*, 22(5), 369–382.

Lin, T., Lin, Y. & Tseng, W. (2016). Manufacturing suicide: The politics of a world factory. *Chinese Sociological Review*, 48(1), 1–32.

Liu, Z. & Wang, J. (2019). Supply chain network equilibrium with strategic supplier investment: A real options perspective. *International Journal of Production Economics*, 208, 184–198.

Long, W., Song, L. & Cui, L. (2017). Relationship between capital operation and market value management of listed companies based on random forest algorithm. *Procedia Computer Science*, 108, 1271–1280.

Lopes, A. & Alencar, R. (2010). Disclosure and cost of equity capital in emerging markets: The Brazilian case. *The International Journal of Accounting*, 45(4), 443–464.

LoPucki, L.M. (1997). The systems approach to law. *Cornell Law Review*, 82, 479–483.

Mahoney, P. & Sanchirico, C. (2005). General and specific legal rules. *Journal of Institutional & Theoretical Economics*, 161, 329–361.

Marco, T. (2005). The option value of patent litigation: Theory and evidence. *Review of Financial Economics*, 14, 323–351.

Martins, A. (2011). Impairment of goodwill and its fiscal treatment: More trouble for the Portuguese firms and tax courts? *European Journal of Management*, 11(2).

Marzo, G. (2011/2012). Intangibles and real options theory: A real measurement alternative? Chapter in: Zambon, S. & Marzo, G., eds., *Visualising Intangibles: Measuring and Reporting in the Knowledge Economy* (Ashgate Publishing Ltd, Aldershot, UK). www.edeos-cfr.it/Documenti/primaAshgate.pdf.

Maso, L., Kanagaretnam, K., et al. (2018). The influence of accounting enforcement on earnings quality of banks: Implications of bank regulation and the global financial crisis. *Journal of Accounting and Public Policy*, 37(5), 402–419.

Melnik, S., Ward, J., Gleeson, J. & Porter, M. (2013). Multi-stage complex contagions. *Chaos*, 23, 013124. doi: 10.1063/1.4790836.

Miklashevich, I. (2003). Mathematical representation of social systems: Uncertainty and optimization of social system evolution. *Non Linear Phenomena In Complex Systems*, 6(2), 678–686.

Miller, C. (2012). A comment on Saks and Neufeld: 'Convergent evolution in law and science: The structure of decision making under uncertainty'. *Law, Probability & Risk*, 11(1), 101–104.

Miller, D. & Watson, J. (2013). A theory of disagreement in repeated games with bargaining. *Econometrica*, 81(6), 2303–2350.

Mogy, R. & Pruitt, D. (1974). Effects of a threatener's enforcement costs on threat credibility and compliance. *Journal of Personality and Social Psychology*, 29(2), 173–180.

Montero, J. (2001). Prices versus quantities with incomplete enforcement. *Journal of Public Economics*, 85(3), 435–454.

Muehlbacher, S. & Kirchler, E. (2010). Tax compliance by trust and power of authorities. *International Economics Journal*, 24(4), 607–610.

Nagar, V., Schoenfeld, J. & Wellman, L. (2019). The effect of economic policy uncertainty on investor information asymmetry and management disclosures. *Journal of Accounting and Economics*, 67(1), 36–57.

Ngai, E., Hu, Y., Wong, Y.H., Chen, Y. & Sun, X. (2011). The application of data mining techniques in financial fraud detection: A classification framework and an academic review of literature. *Decision Support Systems*, 50(3), 559–569.

Nwogugu, M. (2003a). Corporate governance, legal reasoning and credit risk: The case of Encompass Services Inc. *Managerial Auditing Journal*, 18(4), 270–291.

Nwogugu, M. (2003b). Decision-making under uncertainty: A critique of options pricing models. *Journal of Derivatives & Hedge Funds* (now part of *Journal of Asset Management*), 9(2), 164–178.

Nwogugu, M. (2008). Some litigation decisions in commercial real estate leasing. *Corporate Ownership & Control*, 5(4), 240–242.

Nwogugu, M. (2006/2013). *Goodwill/Intangibles Rules, Earnings Management and Competition*. Working Paper. https://papers.ssrn.com/sol3/papers.cfm?abstract_id=1068123.

Nwogugu, M. (2013). Decision-making, sub-additive recursive "matching" noise and biases in risk-weighted index calculation methods in incomplete markets with partially observable multi-attribute preferences. *Discrete Mathematics, Algorithms & Applications*, 05, 1350020.

Nwogugu, M. (2015). Goodwill/intangibles accounting rules, earnings management, and competition. *European Journal of Law Reform*, 17(1), 117–137.

Nwogugu, M. (2019). *Human Computer Interaction, Misrepresentation and Evolutionary Homomorphisms in the XIV and Options-Based Indices in Incomplete Markets With Unaggregated Preferences and NT-Utilities Under a Regret-Minimization Regime*. Chapter 8 in: Nwogugu, M. (2019). *"Indices, Index Funds And ETFs: Exploring HCI, Nonlinear Risk and Homomorphisms"* (Palgrave Macmillan, UK).

OECD., ed. (September 29–30, 2016). *New Approaches to Economic Challenges – Insights into Complexity and Policy* (OECD Headquarters, Paris). Https://Www.Oecd.Org/Naec/Insights%20into%20Complexity%20and%20Policy.Pdf.

Ohtsubo, Y., Masuda, F., Watanabe, E. & Masuchi, A. (2010). Dishonesty invites costly third-party punishment. *Evolution & Human Behavior*, 31(4), 259–262.

Oliviera, F. (2017). Strategic procurement in spot and forward markets considering regulation and capacity constraints. *European Journal of Operational Research*, 261(2), 540–548.

Parisi, F., Fon, V. & Ghei, N. (2004). The value of waiting in lawmaking. *European Journal of Law & Economics*, 18, 131–148.

Perc, M., Donnay, K. & Helbing, D. (2013). Understanding recurrent crime as system-immanent collective behavior. *PLoS One*, 8(10), e76063.

Piercey, M.D. (2009). Motivated reasoning versus. numerical probability assessment: Evidence from an accounting context. *Organizational Behavior and Human Decision Processes*, 108(2), 330–341.

Pinegar, J. & Ravichandran, R. (2010). Raising capital in emerging markets with restricted Global Depositary Receipts. *Journal of Corporate Finance*, 16(5), 622–636.

Pomerot, B. (March 2010). *The Impact of Regulatory Scrutiny on the Resolution of Material Accounting Issues*. Paper presented at the CAAA Annual Conference 2010. SSRN: http://ssrn.com/abstract=1534349 or doi: 10.2139/ssrn.1534349.

Post, D.G. & Eisen, M. (2000). How long is the coastline of the law? Thoughts on the fractal nature of legal systems. *Journal of Legal Studies*, 29, 545–555.

Prakken, H. (2008). Formalizing ordinary legal disputes: A case study. *Artificial Intelligence & Law*, 16(4), 333–359.

Pricewaterhouse Coopers. (November 2007). *Similarities and Differences: A Comparison of IFRS, US GAAP and Indian GAAP*. http://petrofed.winwinhosting.net/upload/S&D.pdf.

Ravisankar, P., Ravi, V., Raghava Rao, G. & Bose, I. (2011). Detection of financial statement fraud and feature selection using data mining techniques. *Decision Support Systems*, 50(2), 491–500.

Rincke, J. & Traxler, C. (2011). Enforcement spillovers. *Review of Economics and Statistics*, 93(4), 1224–1234.

Room, G. (2011). *Complexity, Institutions and Public Policy* (Edward Elgar, Northampton, MA, USA).

Roychowdhury, S., Shroff, N. & Verdi, R. (2019). *The Effects of Financial Reporting and Disclosure on Corporate Investment: A Review*. SSRN Electronic Journal, 10.2139/ssrn.3364582.

Ruhl, J.B. & Ruhl, H. (1997). The arrow of the law in modern administrative states: Using complexity theory to reveal the diminishing returns and increasing risks the burgeoning of law poses to society. *University of California Davis Law Review*, 30, 405–426.

Salinas, G. (2009). *The International Brand Valuation Manual*, 1st ed. (John Wiley & Sons Ltd, Jersey City, NJ, USA).

Salmi, A. & Heikkilä, K. (2015). Managing relationships with public officials – A case of foreign MNCs in Russia. *Industrial Marketing Management*, 49, 22–31.

Salzano, M. & Colander, D. (2007). *Complexity Hints for Economic Policy* (Springer, Germany).

Samuelson, W. (1998). Settlements out of court: Efficiency and equity. *Group Decision & Negotiation*, 7(2), 157–177.

Saygin, A., Chaminade, T., Ishiguro, H., Driver, J. & Frith, C. (2012). The thing that should not be: Predictive coding and the uncanny valley in perceiving human and humanoid robot actions. *Social Cognitive and Affective Neuroscience*, 7(4), 413–422.

Schmidt, M. (2005). Whistle blowing regulation and accounting standards enforcement in Germany and Europe – An economic perspective. *International Review of Law and Economics*, 25(2), 143–168.

Schmidt, R., Sutherland, P., Van Schalkwyk, C., Lowe, T. & Bockmann, R. (2011). Monitoring and enforcement of financial reporting standards in South Africa and Germany: A comparative assessment. *Namibia Law Journal*, 3(1), 55–60. www.kas.de/upload/auslandshomepages/namibia/Namibia_Law_Journal/11-1/NLJ_section_5.pdf.

Scholz, J. (1991). Cooperative regulatory enforcement and the politics of administrative effectiveness. *American Political Science Review*, 85(1), 115–136.

Schwalbe, U. (2018). *Algorithms, Machine Learning, and Collusion*. Working Paper.

Seetharaman, A., Balachandran, M. & Saravanan, A. (2004). Accounting treatment of goodwill: Yesterday, today and tomorrow: Problems and prospects in the international perspective. *Journal of Intellectual Capital*, 5(1), 131–143.

Seetharaman, A., Sreenivasan, J., Sudha, R., Yee, T. (2006). Managing impairment of goodwill. *Journal of Intellectual Capital*, 7(3), 338–353.

Segovia, J., Arnold, V. & Sutton, S. (2009). Do principles- vs. rules-based standards have a differential impact on US auditors' decisions? *Advances in Accounting Behavioral Research*, 12, 61–84.

Sevin, S. & Schroeder, R. (2005). Earnings management: Evidence from SFAS #142 accounting. *Managerial Auditing Journal*, 20(1), 47–55.

Sherblom, S. (2017). Complexity-thinking and social science: Self-organization involving human consciousness. *New Ideas in Psychology*, 47, 10–15.

Shevlin, T., Shivakumar, L. & Urcan, O. (2019). Macroeconomic effects of corporate tax policy. *Journal of Accounting and Economics*, in press.

Short, M., Brantingham, J., Bertozzi, A. & Tita, G. (2010). Dissipation and displacement of hotspots in reaction-diffusion models of crime. *Proceedings of the National Academy of Sciences*, 107(9), 3961–3965.

Sikka, P. & Hampton, M.P. (2005). The role of accountancy firms in tax avoidance: Some evidence and issues. *Accounting Forum*, 29(3), 325–343.

Sinha, K. (2019). *Spillover Effects of State Regulated Corporate Disclosures on the Mortgage Market*. SSRN Electronic Journal, 10.2139/ssrn.3357771.

Srinidhi, B., Lim, C. & Hossain, M. (2009). Effects of country-level legal, extra-legal and political institutions on auditing: A cross-country analysis of the auditor specialization premium. *Journal of Contemporary Accounting & Economics*, 5(1), 34–46.

Stephenson, M. (2008). Evidentiary standards and information acquisition in public law. *American Law & Economics Review*, 10, 351–387.

Strutin, K. (December 8, 2013). *Calculating Justice: Mathematics and Criminal Law*. www.llrx.com/features/calculatingjustice.htm.

Swartz, L. (2008). *Multiple-Step Acquisitions: Dancing the Tax-Free Tango* (Cadwalader, Wickersham & Taft, New York City, USA).

Tetlock, P. (2002). Social functionalist frameworks for judgment and choice: Intuitive politicians, theologians and prosecutors. *Psychological review*, 109(3), 451–471.

Thies, C., Kieckhäfer, K., Spengler, T.S. & Sodhi, M.S. (2019). Operations research for sustainability assessment of products: A review. *European Journal of Operational Research*, 274(1), 1–21.

Tjio, H. (2009). Enforcing corporate disclosure. *Singapore Journal of Legal Studies*, 332–364.

Trigeorgis, L. & Tsekrekos, A. (2018). Real options in operations research: A review. *European Journal of Operational Research*, 270(1), 1–24.

Trigo, A., Belfo, F. & Estébanez, R. (2016). Accounting information systems: Evolving towards a business process oriented accounting. *Procedia Computer Science*, 100, 987–994.

Trombetta, M. & Imperatore, C. (2014). The dynamic of financial crises and its non-monotonic effects on earnings quality. *Journal of Accounting and Public Policy*, 33(3), 205–232.

Trotman, K. (2005). Discussion of judgment and decision making research in auditing: A task, person and interpersonal interaction perspective. *Auditing: A Journal of Practice and Theory*, 24, 73–87.

Tse, A., Friesen, L. & Kalaycı, K. (2016). Complexity and asset legitimacy in retirement investment. *Journal of Behavioral and Experimental Economics*, 60, 3–48.

Tsebelis, G. (1993). Penalty and crime: Further theoretical considerations and empirical evidence. *Journal of Theoretical Politics*, 5, 349–374.

United Nations (New York & Geneva). (2008). *Practical Implementation of International Financial Reporting Standards: Lessons Learned*. United Nations Conference on Trade and Development. www.unctad.org/en/docs/diaeed20081_en.pdf.

Urpelainen, J. (2011). The enforcement – exploitation trade-off in international cooperation between weak and powerful states. *European Journal of International Relations*, 17(4), 631–653.

Van Gennip, Y., Hunter, B., Ahn, R., Elliott, P., Luh, K., Halvorson, M., Reid, S. et al. (2013). Community detection using spectral clustering on sparse geosocial data. *SIAM Journal of Applied Mathematics*, 73(1), 67–83.

Vlachou, A. & Pantelias, G. (2017). The EU's emissions trading system, part-2: A political economy critique. *Capitalism Nature Socialism*, 28(3), 108–127.

Waldfogel, J. (1998). Reconciling asymmetric information and divergent expectations theories of litigation. *Journal of Law & Economics*, 41(2), 451–476.

Walker, D. (2007). Financial accounting and corporate behavior. *Washington & Lee Law Review*, 64(3), 927–937. http://scholarlycommons.law.wlu.edu/cgi/viewcontent.cgi?article=1199&context=wlulr.

Wang, G., Kim, J. & Yi, J. (1994). Litigation and pretrial negotiation under incomplete information. *Journal of Economics & Organization*, 10(1), 187–200.

Wang, J., Zhang, B. & Chen, T. (2011). The case study of China's environmental audit: Taking the Taihu Lake as an example. *Energy Procedia*, 5, 2108–2113.

Weissing, F. & Ostrom, E. (1991). Crime and punishment: Further reflections on the counterintuitive results of mixed equilibria games. *Journal of Theoretical Politics*, 3, 343–350.

West, J. & Bhattacharya, M. (2016). Intelligent financial fraud detection: A comprehensive review. *Computers & Security*, 57, 47–66.

Wheeler, B. (2019). Loan loss accounting and procyclical bank lending: The role of direct regulatory actions. *Journal of Accounting and Economics*, in press.

Williams, C. & Arrigo, B.A. (2002). *Law, Psychology and Justice: Chaos Theory and New (Dis)Order* (State University of New York Press, Albany).

Windsor, D. (2017). Interpreting China's model for business: Roles of corruption, favoritism, reliability, and responsibility. Chapter 3 in: Paulet, E. & Rawley, C. eds., *The China Business Model: Originality and Limits* (Chandos Publishing, The Netherlands), pp. 41–69.

Wu, J. & Hsu, Y. (2018). Decision analysis on entering the China pharmaceutical market: Perspectives from Taiwanese companies. *Computers & Industrial Engineering*, 125, 751–763.

Yeung, D., Zhang, Y., Yeung, P. & Mak, D. (2010). Dynamic game of offending and law enforcement: A stochastic extension. *International Game Theory Review*, 12(04), 471–481.

Young, T. (1997). The ABCs of crime: Attractors, bifurcations and chaotic dynamics. Chapter in: Milanovic, D., ed., *Chaos, Criminology and Social Justice: The New Orderly (Dis)Order* (Praeger Publishers, Westport, CT, USA).

Zeitun, R. & Tian, G. (2007). Does ownership affect a firm's performance and default risk in Jordan? *Corporate Governance*, 7(1), 66–82.

Zhang, B., Zhang, Q., Huang, Z., Li, M. & Li, L. (2018). A multi-criteria detection scheme of collusive fraud organization for reputation aggregation in social networks. *Future Generation Computer Systems*, 79(3), 797–814.

Zhang, J., Wang, P. & Qyu, B. (2012). Bank risk taking, efficiency and law enforcement: Evidence from Chinese city commercial banks. *China Economic Review*, 23, 284–295.

Zhang, N. & Walton, D. (2010). Recent trends in evidence law in China and the new evidence scholarship. *Law, Probability & Risk*, 9(2), 103–129.

Zhou, W. & Kapoor, G. (2011). Detecting evolutionary financial statement fraud. *Decision Support Systems*, 50(3), 570–575.

3

Industry 5.0/6.0: some public health, *inequality*, environmental pollution and *inefficient resource-allocation* implications

This chapter discusses the Public Health, *Inequality*, Environmental Pollution and *Inefficient Resource-Allocation* implications of Earnings Management, Incentive-Effects Management and Asset-Quality Management within the context of Industry 5.0/6.0, Artificial Intelligence (AI) and Fintech; all of which are intertwined and can have symbiotic relationships with each other. These relationships can be exacerbated by the following factors:

1) Earnings Management, Incentive Effects Management and the current systems/models of managerial compensation in many developed and developing countries exacerbates *Inequality* (*Income Inequality* increased around the world during 2000–2019). In most cases, managers' EBIs (equity-based incentives), cash incentives and total compensation packages don't have any downside risk.

2) Artificial Intelligence,[1] Fintech and associated human responses often amplify the adverse effects of Earnings Management, Incentive Effects Management and *Inequality* (i.e. rapid dissemination of news; automated trading rules that are based on accounting data; Index Arbitrage; harm inflicted on small unsophisticated investors; rich and sophisticated investors benefit from technology; etc.) all of which reduce sustainable growth and Sustainability. Managers have significant incentives to increase automation and AI in order to boost corporate profits and the values of their Incentive Compensation. AI, Automation and Fintech are creating a global *Labor-Social-Psychological Crisis* and are having often significant negative effects on allocation of capital (e.g. Automated Trading; Index Arbitrage; corporate budgeting; "Internal Capital Markets" of MNCs; etc.) and the nature of work, under-employment and unemployment – which in turn affects household dynamics, increases Inequality and reduces quality-of-life.

3) *Inequality* has disproportionately larger and negative *Multiplier Effects* on low-income households.

4) *Inequality* can amplify the negative effects of Environmental Pollution, Public Health problems/quasi-epidemics and inadequate healthcare access on low-income and middle-income households.

5) Earnings Management, Incentive-Effects Management, *Inequality* and Asset-Quality Management cause *Inefficient Resource Allocation. Inefficient Resource Allocation* can amplify the negative effects of Environmental Pollution, *Inequality*, Public Health problems/quasi-epidemics and inadequate healthcare access on low-income and middle-income households.

3.1 Existing literature

Elgar and Aitken (2011); Van Oort, van Lenthe and Mackenbach (2005); Schutte, et al. (2014) and Aldabe et al. (2011) discussed *Inequality*. Various types of *Inequality* have been analyzed from Physics,[2] Applied Mathematics,[3] Taxation,[4] Econometrics[5] and Economics[6] perspectives (with the common themes being networks, transactions and wealth-concentration). However, the theories and models in most of those articles/books are wrong because they don't sufficiently consider or account for Artificial Intelligence, Fintech, quality-of-life and the *Labor-Inequality Anomalies* and *International Trade Anomalies* discussed in this book; and because they impose rigid pre-conceived models on dynamic and complex relationships/events (e.g. unfortunately, most of the *Asset Exchange Models* and *Kinetic Theory Models* of *Inequality* that are studied in Physics and Mathematics don't fully capture the true causal-factors and relationships among them and dynamics of *Inequality* and wealth transfers, and they simply impose rigid pre-conceived frameworks on very dynamic and complex situations).

On the symbiotic and evolving relationships among Artificial Intelligence, Fintech, Sustainable Growth, Labor Dynamics and *Inequality*, see the comments in: Berg, Buffie and Zanna (2016); Acemoglu and Restrepo (2018); Adam and Galinsky (2012); André, Carmon, et al. (2018); Beer, Fisk and Rogers (2014); Bostrom (2014); Cummings (2017); Furman and Seamans (2018); Kosinski, Stillwell and Graepel (2013); Manyika and Bughin (2018); Manyika, Chui, et al. (2017); Manyika, Lund, et al. (2017); Müller and Bostrom (2016); Stone, Brooks, et al. (2016); Yeomans (2015); and Wu, Kosinski and Stillwell (2015).

Ma et al. (2011) and Lin, et al. (2013) discussed the effects of economic changes and financial market fluctuations on public health. Kopp et al. (2008) addressed the relationship between work stress and mental health problems. Some academic studies have found that many disease conditions often originate from mental health problems such as depression, anxiety and schizophrenia.

Davidson, Xie, Xu and Ning (2007) analyzed whether CEOs will be motivated to manage earnings prior to a turnover decision due to the "*horizon problem*" for CEOs nearing retirement age and for CEOs whose profit-based bonus is a large portion of their total compensation. They concluded that firms in which CEOs are nearing retirement age have large discretionary accruals in the year prior to turnover; but that firms with a larger proportion of profit-based bonus pay have larger discretionary accruals and such a result was not robust with the inclusion of control variables in the regressions. Efendi, Srivastava and Swanson (2007) analyzed the incentives that led to the rash of restated financial statements at the end of the

1990s market bubble; and they found that: i) the likelihood of a misstated financial statement increases greatly when the CEO has very sizable holdings of in-the-money stock options; ii) Misstatements are also more likely for firms that are constrained by an interest-coverage debt covenant, that raise new debt or equity capital, or that have a CEO who serves as board chair; iii) agency costs increased (Jensen, M.C., 2005a, Agency costs of overvalued equity. *Financial Management*, 34, 5–19) as substantially overvalued equity caused managers to take actions to support the stock price. Denis, Hanouna and Sarin (2006) found: i) a significant positive association between the likelihood of securities fraud allegations and a measure of executive stock option incentives; but the relationship was robust to the inclusion of other components of the compensation structure and to other possible determinants of fraud allegations; ii) that the positive relation between the likelihood of fraud allegations and option intensity is stronger in firms with higher outside blockholder and higher institutional ownership. These findings support the view that stock options increase the incentive to engage in fraudulent activity and that this incentive is exacerbated by institutional and block ownership. Using bivariate probit regression analysis, Firth, Rui and Wu (2011) studied the causes and consequences of falsified financial statements in China; and they found that: i) firms with high debt and that plan to make equity issues are more likely to manipulate their earnings and thus have to restate their financial reports in subsequent years; ii) corporate governance structures affect the occurrence and detection of financial fraud; iii) there are significant negative consequences to fraudulent financial statements – and restating firms suffered negative abnormal stock returns, increases in their cost of capital, wider bid – ask spreads, a greater frequency of modified audit opinions, and greater CEO turnover; and firms located in highly developed regions suffer more severe consequences when they manipulate their accounts. Burns and Kedia (2008) analyzed a sample of firms that announced restatements of their financial statements, and found no significant evidence of higher option exercises by executives in the mis-reported years – and Options exercises by executives were also increasing in the magnitude of the restatement; but for firms that are more likely to have made deliberate aggressive accounting choices, there was significant evidence of higher option exercises (higher by 20–60 percent compared to industry and size-matched non-restating firms).

Using data about exogenous state-level changes in unemployment insurance benefits, Dou, Khan and Zou (2016) found that firms manage long-run earnings upward in order to manage employees' perceptions of employment security; and they noted a significant reduction in abnormal accruals, increased recognition of special items and write downs, and greater likelihood of net income-reducing restatements, after an increase in state-level unemployment benefits. Dimitras, Kyriakou and Iatridis (2015) found that financially distressed companies that are audited by a big-4 audit-firm have lower discretionary accruals; Greek and Spanish companies reduce earnings management manipulation during recessions, while Portuguese, Irish and Italian companies reduce earnings management practices, but managers can be influenced to increase earnings management. Using a sample of 12,672 firms from nineteen countries during 1994–2010, Li and Zaiats (2017) found that dual class status is related to poorer information environment and increased accrual-based earnings management, and that managers of dual class firms have incentives to hide private control benefits from outside share-holders; and that dual class ownership reduces the mitigating impact of investor protection on earnings management.

3.1.1 Algorithm-Adoption, Algorithm-Aversion and Algorithm Collusion

One issue that hasn't been sufficiently addressed in the literature (AI; Mechanism Design; Dynamic Pricing) is intentional and unintentional collusion by autono-mous/intelligent pricing algorithms which sometimes results in increases in final prices (*"Intentional Algorithm Collusion"* and *"Unintentional Algorithm Collusion,"* respectively). *Algorithm Collusion* also occurs in other contexts. As of 2019, most countries had not developed antitrust or consumer protection laws for such collusion. Such statutes are increasingly necessary and critical for regular commerce – see the comments in Harrington (2018). *Algorithm Collusion* is rela-tively difficult to detect and prosecute. Also see the comments in: Calvano, Calzo-lari, Denicolò and Pastorello (2018); Ezrachi & Stucke (2015); Schwalbe (2018). In an empirical study with AI-based pricing algorithms in a controlled environment Calvano, Calzolari, et al. (February 2019) noted that even relatively simple pric-ing algorithms learned and engaged in price collusion by trial and error, without any prior knowledge of their operating environment and without communicating with each another, and without being specifically designed or instructed to collude. *Algorithm Collusion* can be partly attributed to: i) the design, "learning-process" and updating of each pricing algorithm (how data is gathered and processed by each algorithm in each time period); ii) the relevance or "weights" assigned to each specific data source by each pricing algorithm; iii) the use of common sources of data by the pricing algorithms; iv) the knowledge/training of the designers of each pricing algorithms (designers who have the same knowledge and use the same approaches/models are more likely to cause *Algorithm Collusion*).

On *Algorithm-Adoption* and *Algorithm-Aversion* (both of which are increas-ingly critical in economic, political and social interactions of both human and automated agents) see: Dietvorst, Simmons and Massey (2014, 2016); Komiak and Benbasat (2006); Leung, Paolacci and Puntoni (2018); Logg, Minson and Moore (2019); Mathur and Reichling (2016); Nguyen (2016); Stone, Brooks, et al. (2016); Saygin, Chaminade, et al. (2012); and Zhang and Dafoe (2019).

3.1.2 Universal Basic Income (UBI)

Universal Basic Income is an increasingly possible result of the growth and domi-nance of Artificial Intelligence, Automation and Fintech around the world and associated *"Contagions"* and *Multiplier Effects*; and the many problems caused by significant and increasing *Inequality*. See: Hoynes and Rothstein (2019) and Hughes (2014). By itself, UBI raises many Public Health (e.g. depression, phobias), energy crisis, household allocations/dynamics, human aspirations, competition and sustainable growth issues.

3.2 Cooperation+Trust

In Artificial Intelligence and Fintech, the term *Cooperation+Trust* is introduced here, and it refers to the joint time-varying evolution of online/offline Cooperation and Trust among Human Agents, Automated Agents and institutions, and within the constraints of Regulations, norms, culture, *Noise, Selective Memory* and Perception/Cognition. However, Berg, Buffie and Zanna (2016); Acemoglu and Restrepo (2018); Adam and Galinsky (2012); André, Carmon, et al. (2018); Beer, Fisk and Rogers (2014); Bostrom (2014); Cummings (2017); Furman and Seamans (2018); Kosinski, Stillwell and Graepel (2013); Manyika and Bughin (2018); Manyika, Chui, et al. (2017); Manyika, Lund, et al. (2017); Müller and Bostrom (2016); Stone, Brooks, et al. (2016); Yeomans (2015); Shi and Ma (2016); Tambayong (2011); Araújo and Mendes (2009); Janssen, Manning and Udiani (2014); Leimbach, Baumstark and Luderer (2015); and Wu, Kosinski and Stillwell (2015); and most of the literature omitted or didn't substantially analyze the issue of *Cooperation+Trust*.

3.3 The manipulation of balance sheet and income statement accounts for intangible assets and real estate constitute more than 60 percent of all earnings management, asset-quality management and incentive-effects management, and manipulation of sustainability-related accounts (economic, social, urban and environmental sustainability)

The existing literature and evidence indicate such trends. Intangibles have become a major component of the economies of most developed countries and many developing countries due to growth of the technology and service industries, innovation, increasing propensity to register intellectual property, and recognition of the value of intangibles worldwide. As mentioned in Chapter 1 in this book, and according to Salinas (2009) and other authors,[7] during the last fifteen years, Intangible assets accounted for 60–75 percent of the stock market capitalization values in most developed countries; and an increasing percentage of the stock market value in many developing countries (such as South Korea Brazil; China; Mexico; Thailand; Singapore; etc.) – these trends currently exist if Intangibles are measured as the difference between the stock market value and the book value of a company. Intangibles and Real Estate now account for more than 45 percent and 30 percent, respectively, of the total wealth/Assets in most developed countries, and increasingly in many developing countries – and the trend is likely to continue as more developing countries build up their economies. Acquisition/Merger transactions have increasingly recognized Intangibles, and hence Goodwill. Goodwill and Intangibles have been the subject of much debate in the accounting, economics, operations research and finance fields/professions during the last twenty years. Goodwill and Intangibles also present substantial opportunities for earnings management and asset-quality management, and can have substantial behavioral effects on management and employees. See the comments in Lhaopadchan (2010) and IAAO (2016).[8]

In many industries in both developed and developing countries, real estate related expenses (rent, property taxes, property insurance, property maintenance; utilities; mortgage interest) account for 15–40 percent of the operating expenses of companies; and real estate related assets accounts for 15–60 percent of the total assets of companies. Deng and Gyourko (1999) stated in part ". . . In the United States alone it is estimated that corporate users own nearly $2 trillion, or roughly half of all commercial property. Companies own not only their production facilities, but frequently their offices, warehouses, and retail outlets. Although many of these properties are suitable for a broad range of users, these operating companies choose to commit their scarce capital to the ownership and operation of real estate, rather than re-deploying this capital to their core operating businesses. . . ." Corporate-owned real estate has become a major element of corporate strategies for companies in industries such as healthcare, leisure, retailing, lodging, restaurants, transportation, etc. See: Roulac (2003); Liow and Nappi-Choulet (2008); Ling, Naranjo and Ryngert (2010); Deng and Gyourko (1999); Tuzel (2010); Brounen and Eichholtz (2005); Chen and Gao (2006); Liow (1995) and Sham, Sing and Tsai (2009). These companies have increasingly come to realize that commercial real estate decisions can have substantial effects on their financial performance and employee motivation. The growth of Real Estate Investment trusts (REITs) outside the US indicates continuing interest in developing real estate capital markets – many such REITs are very similar to, and have the same regulations as US REITs. However, the growth of real estate capital markets and increasing strategic use of corporate real estate present growing problems pertaining to earnings management and organizational psychology, much of which has not been addressed directly in the literature. Housing-related expenses (e.g. rent; mortgage payments; insurance payments; utilities; service charges; property taxes, and maintenance/ repairs; furniture/fixtures) typically account for 30–50 percent of the monthly expenses of most households; and housing wealth accounts for 50–95 percent of the total wealth of most households in both developing and developed countries – thus real estate can be a source of significant controversies among, and social, economic and psychological pressures on employees, corporate managers, portfolio managers and government regulators. Real Estate and Intangibles are the two major sources of bubbles and boom-and-bust cycles in economies; but they can also serve as growth engines for both regional and national economies in developed and developing countries. In most developed countries and some developing countries, residential and commercial real estate activities (rent; utilities; property

taxes; property insurance; mortgage interest/principal payments; property maintenance costs; brokerage fees; home improvement; renovations/remodeling)
account for more than 40 percent of the annual GDP.

*In recent history, the largest corporate perpetrators of earnings management,
asset-quality management and corporate scandals, and the largest financially/
operationally distressed companies all owned significant intangibles assets or
real estate; and used substantial volumes of equity-based incentives; and were
exchange-traded companies; and many owed substantial debts.*

The ten worst "discovered" corporate earnings management scandals[9] of all
time in the world and the years they were discovered were: Waste Management
(1998; USA); Enron (2001; USA); WorldCom (2002); Tyco (2002; USA); Health
South (2003; USA); Freddie Mac (2003; USA); American International Group
(AIG) (2005; USA); Lehman Brothers (2008; USA); Bernie Madoff (2008; USA);
Satyam Computer Services (2009; India). Other notable earnings management
scandals include Toshiba (2011; Japan); and Tesco (UK). During the three years
before their earnings management was discovered or announced, most of these
companies owned or purported to own significant real estate, real estate related
assets (e.g. mortgages; mortgage insurance premium contracts; assignments-of-
rents-and-leases/subleases; loan/mortgage guarantee contracts; etc.) or intangible
assets (including off-balance-sheet contracts; derivatives; contract rights; etc.);
and they also used substantial amounts of EBIs; and many were exchange-traded
companies and owed substantial debt.

A review of other data about the largest corporate bankruptcies in the world[10]
also indicates that during the three years before their bankruptcy filings: i) many
of those bankrupt companies owned or purported to own substantial intangible
assets and or real estate and or real estate related assets (e.g. mortgages; mortgage insurance contracts; assignments-of-rents-and-leases/subleases; loan/mort-
gage guarantee contracts; contract rights; etc.); ii) many of those companies used
substantial equity-based incentives; and iii) the bankruptcy filings of many of the
companies may have been delayed by earnings management and or asset-quality
management.

Appendix 3.3 (in the endnotes in Chapter 3) is a list of some of the Top-100
startups in the world and a review of data about rankings of successful startups[11]
around the world reveals that: i) many of those companies owned substantial
intangible assets and or real estate and or real estate related assets (e.g. leases;
rights-to-lease; contract rights; assignments-of-rents-and-leases/subleases; etc.);
ii) many of those companies used substantial amounts of EBIs for both their
employees and senior executives.

Appendix 3.1 is a list of the largest companies that were the subject of corporate
scandals that didn't result in insolvency. Appendix 3.2 lists some of the largest
companies in the world that became financially/operationally distressed (i.e. job
losses; insolvency or bankruptcy, or being nationalized or requiring a government
bailout through non-market loans). Appendix 3.4 lists some of the worst startup
failures around the world.

During the three years immediately before the scandals or financial distress were discovered or announced, many of those companies in Appendices 3.1, 3.2 and 3.4: i) perpetrated earnings management and or asset-quality management; ii) used significant amounts of EBIs for both their employees and senior executives; and iii) owned or purported to own substantial intangible assets (measured as the difference between the company's stock-market value and the Book Value of its equity; and including contract-rights; etc.) and or real estate and or real estate related assets (e.g. mortgages; mortgage insurance contracts; assignments-of-rents-and-lease/subleases; loan/mortgage guarantee contracts; etc.). Note that in the banking sector, the historical average total annual compensation expense has been about 40–65 percent of total annual revenues – and most of that consists of human capital.

Appendices 3.5 and 3.6 list some of the major financial and economic crises that occurred during the last few centuries (selected based on both monetary impact and the size of the affected human populations). Many of these crises were precipitated and or amplified by earnings management, asset-quality management and incentive-effects management.

Here, the values of Intangibles are measured as: i) the difference between the company's stock market value (or private equity value or Venture Capital value) on one hand, and its total "Net Assets" or the Book Value of its equity; and including contract-rights; etc.; or ii) the estimated market values of the company's intangible assets in a non-distress non-liquidation sale.

Note that Airbnb's and Uber's operations (and similar companies) are deemed to be illegal in the US and many countries, and both Uber and Airbnb and similar companies are being sued/prosecuted in many courts in many countries for various offenses.

3.4 Earnings management, incentive-effects management and asset-quality management cause public health problems and vice versa, all of which can have a symbiotic relationship with *inequality*

Earnings management, incentive-effects management and asset-quality management in organizations and investment companies (within the context of decisions, news, business dynamics and regulations) increase or can increase worker stress particularly for married workers, drug-dependent workers and employees who are going through non-work stress. The resulting adverse effects can be amplified in the worker's interactions with his/her family/children, friends and non-work destinations such as shops, restaurants, and public assembly spaces. Conversely, increased overall levels of stress/anxiety in communities/societies is likely to increase incidences of earnings management, incentive effects management and asset-quality management in organizations and investment companies partly because: i) healthcare costs will increase for which individuals/families will need cash;

ii) people will be more likely to be concerned about their social status, wealth and retirement income, and will be more likely to engage in misconduct. The resulting Income/Wealth Inequality can amplify environmental deterioration – due to depression, poor sanitation, poor waste management, etc.

Inequality and the associated uncertainty about future income/housing/healthcare can cause severe mental health problems (e.g. substance-abuse, anxiety/stress, phobias, depression, and schizophrenia), which can evolve into other illnesses such as heart disease, strokes, kidney diseases, obesity, hypertension, etc. On the public health effects of *Inequality*, see: Wu and Li (2017); Shapiro et al. (2017); and Schneider and Yaşar (2016). On mechanisms that can explain the effects of *Inequality* on environmental deterioration, see: Berthe and Elie (2015). The foundations of *Inequality* (and inability to improve one's living/economic conditions) sometimes begins with childhood conditions and psychological issues among university/tertiary-education students – see: Gong, Stinebrickner and Stinebrickner (2019) and Braveman and Gottlieb (2014).

At the individual level, earnings management, *incentive-effects management* and *asset-quality management* and associated changes and fear-of-apprehension can cause or increase individual health problems such as hypertension, substance-abuse, stroke, kidney damage, depression, schizophrenia, diabetes, obesity and cardiovascular problems. The treatment costs and durations of such illnesses and their effects on family members and friends amplify the economic, social and psychological costs.

When some of the *Behavioral Biases* that are introduced in chapters in this book are aggregated at the national or regional levels, they are or can become public health problems because they can cause depression, substance-abuse, anxiety, schizophrenia and other mental disorders. Clearly the political economy factors and the group-decisions of audit-firms and auditee-companies which are surveyed in Chapter 3 in this book, indicate that such patterns (and associated changes) can cause health problems.

Earnings management, incentive-effects management and asset-quality management can cause and increase disagreements among investors and corporate managers about the risks and values of various assets, which can result in increased volatility, increased market crash-risk, and increased risk of financial contagion, economic recessions and overall financial instability.

As mentioned earlier, Earnings management, asset-quality management and incentive-effects management were a major cause of some of the largest corporate failures/bankruptcies, financial crises and corporate scandals in the world which are listed in Appendices 3.1, 3.2, 3.3, 3.4 and 3.5. All of those events are major public health issues because they inflict trauma on large groups of people across countries and cause mental health problems (e.g. depression; phobias, disorientation; schizophrenia; decreased judgment; anxiety; etc.) which in turn can cause other illnesses such as heart disease, diabetes, obesity, vascular problems, strokes; hypertension, cancer, kidney diseases, etc. These illnesses constitute major drains on household wealth and government funds. Equally important is that these corporate failures/bankruptcies, financial crises and corporate scandals create *Inequality* in access to healthcare, access to jobs/income, access to health insurance, and in the quality-of-life of households (each of which can have adverse *Multiplier Effects* on human health and the propagation/spread of diseases), due to job layoffs, loss of health insurance coverage, loss of income, etc.

Earnings management, asset-quality management and incentive-effects management links public health and environmental pollution and climate change. A significant percentage of the enforcement and efficiency of environmental regulations, climate change standards and climate finance instruments (e.g. green bonds; emissions-permit trading; Carbon Credits; etc.) depends on external "independent" auditing of firms and government agencies by auditing firms. In weak/lax audit environments, firms are unlikely to fully or partially comply with these standards and regulations (which constitutes Earnings management, asset quality management and incentive effects management), which in turn will increase environmental pollution and harmful climate change which causes a wide variety of illnesses in humans and mammals (and affects the human food chain). The polluted-air problems in Bangkok (Thailand), Beijing (China), and large Indian cities are evidence.

Within the firm, earnings management, incentive-effects management and asset-quality management can cause increased disagreements within the board of directors and among corporate managers about almost every aspect of the company's operations. Managers of both private and exchange traded companies can also be affected by stock market changes because their company's reputation, ability to raise capital, perceived risk and incentives are often tied to, or are affected by stock market dynamics. The results can include ineffective strategies, inefficient capital allocation, operating losses, low employee motivation and financial distress. Collectively, these set of issues are critical public health problems that can substantially increase healthcare costs and reduce worker-productivity, innovation, economic growth, household savings and intrapreneurship/entrepreneurship.

According to Salinas (2009), Intangible assets constitute 60–75 percent of the market capitalization value of the major stock indices in the world; and as mentioned, real estate constitutes a major portion of the operating expenses and wealth of companies and households around the world. Thus intangibles and real estate are relevant to risk perceptions of investors and corporate managers; and changes in the disclosed values or perceived values and or perceived riskiness of Intangible assets and or real estate can affect individual and group psychology, which in turn can translate into mental illnesses and major public health crises (mental health illnesses such as depression and stress/anxiety can cause other illnesses such as diabetes, obesity, stroke, vascular problems, heart diseases, kidney diseases, etc.).

Nandi et al. (2012) and Guojonsdottir, Kristjansson and Olafsson (2011) showed that sudden noticeable change in overall regional or national economic conditions can cause severe illness and public health problems. Lin, Chen and Liu (2014); Lin et al. (2015); Liu (Nov. 2015); Cotti and Simon (2018); Ratcliffe and Taylor (2015); and Cottie, Dunn and Tefft (2015) found that sudden increases/

decreases in stock market volatility can cause severe illness, mental health problems and public health problems. Kopp et al. (2008) addressed the relationship between work stress and mental health problems. Nwogugu (2012); Kreiger and Higgins (2002); Moloughney (2004); Nettleton (1998), Bennett, Scharoun-Lee and Tucker-Seeley (2009) and other authors analyzed the public health and mental health problems caused by housing, mortgages and consumer debt. Some academic studies have found that many diseases conditions often originate from mental health problems such as depression, anxiety and schizophrenia. See the comments in: Whiteford, Ferrari et al. (2015); Murray et al. (2013); Zunzunegui et al. (2017); Bilala and Kaufman (2017). Vian and Crable (2017) discussed the effects of corruption on public health.

The *Goodwill/Intangibles accounting rules* (the Goodwill/Intangibles Rules) and IFRS/IASB accounting standards in general and the associated human biases and psychological effects (the *"Biases/Effects"*) including those introduced in chapters in this book, constitute substantial public health risks because they can cause mental health problems (e.g. depression, phobias, substance-abuse, and other mental illnesses) which can cause other illnesses (e.g. strokes or cardiac arrest; kidney diseases; obesity, etc.) due to the following reasons:

i)   Application of the Goodwill/Intangibles Rules and or the IFRS/IASB accounting regulations and many national accounting regulations and or the occurrence of the *Biases/Effects* can result in greater-than-normal creation of balance sheet accruals (in terms of both the number and size of accruals), and also greater-than-normal periodic changes in the values of accruals. All of these can substantially increase the volatility of stock prices of a company and its competitors in the industry. The criteria for creation of many of these accruals don't differentiate between temporary and permanent changes in values of the Intangibles. Many accruals can be changed at any time during the fiscal year, and the net result can be substantially increased volatility of stock prices, *Corporate Social Capital*, *Corporate Reputation* and *Corporate Brand Equity* (a firm's reputation or brand equity can significantly deteriorate in a matter of hours or days), all of which can spill over into related industries and even other countries. The channels for such transmissions can include investment policies in asset management companies, news media, research analysts' reports, international capital flows, corporate financial policies and *"Internal Capital Markets"* of Multinational corporations (MNCs); etc. The Goodwill/Intangibles Rules, IFRS/IASB regulations and the Biases/Effects can result in manipulation of asset impairments which affects the income statement, and thus, can increase the above-mentioned types of uncertainty and volatility.

ii) The Goodwill/Intangibles Rules and IFRS/IASB regulations or the occurrence of the *Biases/Effects* can cause significant mis-allocation of investments by the government and or private sector investors and or foreign investors.

iii) The *Goodwill/Intangibles accounting rules* and many IFRS/IASB accounting regulations cause "relatively opaque" financial statements and thus create significant uncertainty and disagreement (among investors, regulators and users of financial statements) in the interpretation and perceptions of financial statements and corporate risk, which in turn increases volatility and uncertainty in capital markets, which in turn can cause the above-mentioned mental health problems and other diseases.

iv) In the present era, the *Goodwill/Intangibles accounting rules* and or the IFRS/ IASB accounting regulations and or the occurrence of the *Biases/Effects* can reduce the attractiveness of Intangible assets and real estate from various perspectives – such as credit (difficult to value and monitor), collateral (low recovery value), etc.

Another rapidly emerging dimension of public health problems is that the current global and national institutional arrangements and agreements for environmental management and environmental auditing are insufficient and encourage environmental pollution. That in turn increases public health problems, costs and *Inequality*. Part of the problem is that environmental management processes and audits have been grossly politicized – governments have substantial incentives to, and want to understate pollution, avoid remediation costs, and avoid annoying large companies who are often donors to their political campaigns. Un-regulated and un-limited corporate lobbying against environmental regulations is also a major negative factor.

3.5 *Inequality*, inefficient capital/resource allocation and international political economy issues

The relationship between *Inequality* and *Inefficient Resource Allocation* is critical, symbiotic and evolving – and earnings management amplifies the many negative effects of both of them. The effects of *Inefficient Resource Allocation* continue to reverberate in both developed and developing countries – for example:

i) During 2005-2018, many local/municipal governments and state governments in the USA were either financially distressed or technically bankrupt.[12]

ii) The Global Financial Crisis of 2007–2014, and the Euro Crisis of 2010–2018, and the Arab Spring of 2011–2019 illustrated the many negative dimensions of *Inefficient Resource Allocation* (political, social, economic, financial, environmental and urban).

iii) Appendices 3.1, 3.2, 3.3, 3.4 and 3.5 list various economic/financial crisis around the world, bankrupt companies and financially distressed companies – all of which were partly or wholly attributable to *Inefficient Resource/Capital Allocation*.

iv) The budgetary processes of many national governments remain very inefficient and mired by "political costs", "Regulatory Capture", tribalism (in developing countries), and political lobbying. Many governments routinely incur deficits.

During 2000–2019 and around the world and by various measures and as confirmed by researchers, various types of *Inequality* (*Income Inequality*; *Wealth Inequality*; *Housing Inequality*; *Social Inequality*; etc.) increased significantly especially in developed countries, Japan, ASEAN countries and BRICS countries. Two relatively new dimensions of *Inequality* that have become critical (and amplify/propagate other types of *Inequality*) are *Environmental Pollution* and the *Global Pension Crisis* (i.e. inadequate pension/retirement benefits; pension deficits/liabilities at corporations and government agencies; ravaging effects of currency depreciation and inflation on pension benefits; etc.). See: MacDonald and Cairns (2011); Ongena and Zalewska (2018); Beetsma and Romp (2016); Cigno (2016); Echeverri, Abadía-Barrero and Palacios (2017); Freudenberg, Laub and Sutor (2018); Dolls et al. (2018); Gerrard et al. (2019); Feng, He and Sato (2011); Kurtbegu (2018); Staveley-O'Carroll and Staveley-O'Carroll (2017); Nakajima and Sasaki (2010); Chen et al. (2014); Broeders and Chen (2010) and Glaeser and Ponzetto (2014). Both *Environmental Pollution* and the *Global Pension Crisis* are partly driven by Earnings Management, Incentive-Effects Management and Asset-Quality Management (and associated Non-Compliance and Inefficient Capital/Resource Allocation) such as the following:

i)   Improper and fraudulent accounting disclosures about environmental pollution liabilities and non-compliance with environmental standards;

ii)   Corporate earnings management and asset-quality management that results in harmful volatility, mini stock-price and bond-price crashes in industry sectors which affect pension fund returns.

iii) Staveley-O'Carroll and Staveley-O'Carroll (2017) discussed the impact of pension system structure on international financial capital allocation. Florişteanu (2013) analyzed the effects of economic and social factors (e.g. including elements of Inequality) on Pension Systems. Willmore (2007) discussed Universal Pensions for developing countries.

iv)   While Acemoglu, Johnson and Robinson (2005) noted that institutions are a fundamental cause of long-run growth, it appears that in many countries, these same institutions have failed and are a primary cause of *Global Inequality* and inefficient capital allocation.

v)   There is significant evidence that around the world, there is substantial environmental pollution and climate change remains a threat. See the charts in Ritchie and Roser (2019) at https://ourworldindata.org/air-pollution; and United Nations pollution and climate change data at: https://unstats.un.org/unsd/ENVIRONMENT/interlinks.htm (Department of Economic & Social Affairs at UN); and World Health Organization data at www.who.int/air pollution/en/; and World Resources Institute's data at www.wri.org/resources/charts_graphs.

Earnings Management, Incentive-effects Management and Asset-Quality Management are major causes of *policy-distortion* (inaccurate data; psychological and political effects; debt-distortion), *Inefficient Capital/Resource Allocation* (inaccurate data; psychological and political effects; debt-distortion) and the resultant *Inequality Contagion* around the world (that is, *Inequality* can have economic, psychological and political *Multiplier Effects* that can easily spill over across national borders).

There has been increasing *Political Interference* in auditing in some countries such as China, wherein the central government and or local governments actively or implicitly support earnings management, asset-quality management and incentive-effects management at companies and government entities (mostly for political and economic gains). Some researchers have reported that the Chinese government has repeatedly refused to hand over the audit workpapers for Chinese companies that were cross-listed in US stock exchanges and were being investigated by the US SEC for securities fraud.[13] Also see: Jacoby, Li and Liu (2016); Chen et al. (2011); Fung, Raman and Zhu (2017); Bushman and Piotroski (2006); He (2016); Zhang and Mauck (2018); Anderson, Chi and Wang (2017); Cheng and Leung (2016); Belz, von Hagen and Steffens (2019); Lewellyn and Bao (2017); Brandau et al. (2013); Boubakri, El Ghoul and Saffar (2015); Ashraf (2017); Gungoraydinoglu, Çolak and Öztekin (2017) and Salmi and Heikkilä (2015).

As explained in Chapter 2 in this book, *Selective Enforcement* remains a big problem in both developing and developed countries and it can amplify earnings management, asset-quality management, Inequality and incentive-effects management – see: Chen et al. (2011).

As stated in Chapter 1 in this book, Chen and Jorgensen (2018) noted that *Accounting Biases* can affect competition and Industry Structure in various industries – several chapters in this book introduce *Accounting Biases* and *Structural Effects* that can have the same effects. Using a study of mergers/acquisitions, Marquardt and Zur (2015) found evidence that financial accounting quality is positively related to the efficient allocation of the economy's capital resources. See: Khan and Lo (2018); Chen and Jorgensen (2018); Kwon (2005); and Marquardt and Zur (2015), and Nan and Wen (2014). As stated in Chapter 1 in this book, *Enforcement Patterns* (e.g. enforcement of accounting regulations, commodities-trading regulations and securities laws; corporate laws; etc.) can also affect competition and Industry Structure in various industries because: i) they affect the nature of competition and collaboration among firms in industries; ii) they affect firms' allocations of resource and capital; iii) they affect product development, marketing and human resources decisions; iv) they affect the functioning, responsibilities and liability of boards of directors; v) they affect firms' perceived risk and liability-allocation in expected or existing disputes. Thus by extension, *Accounting Biases*, *Structural Effects* and *Enforcement Patterns* can have both direct and indirect effects on economic growth and Sustainability. When some of the *Structural Effects*, *Behavioral Biases* and *Accounting Biases* that are introduced in chapters in this book are aggregated at the national or regional levels, they are or can become *Inequality* causal factors because they can cause wage differentials and mental health problems (e.g. depression, substance-abuse, anxiety, schizophrenia and other mental disorders).

The IFRS/IASB accounting regulations and Goodwill/Intangibles Rules and or the occurrence of the *Biases/Effects* can substantially change and distort *National Income Accounting* data (e.g. Corporate Income; corporate taxes; real estate taxes; values of intangibles; etc.). That in turn, can change the government's and private sector estimates of economic conditions of regions and countries and the allocation of capital and resources, all of which can cause emotional distress, mental health problems and cardio-vascular health problems. For example, when there is substantial expensing of impairments of Intangible Assets, reported Corporate Profits will decline, and companies will tend to shrink their activities (e.g. lay off employees and reduce the hiring of new employees and corporate investment). That will tend to increase emotional distress, anxiety/ stress and depression among the population. Nakamura (2010) noted that the economic theory and practice underlying measurement of Intangible Assets remains controversial and incomplete.

Nwogugu (2015a) noted that *National Income Accounting* has distorted economic data, GDP/GNP and perceptions of economic activity in the USA – and the same problem may have occurred in other so-called "rich" countries. Some countries deliberately produce false/misleading economic data – which: i) affects estimates used in traditional auditing and environmental auditing; and ii) has or can have negative psychological effects on managers and auditors; and iii) encourages collusion between corporate/government managers and auditors; iv) negatively affects the allocation of capital by governments, companies and institutional investors (including international investors); v) negatively affects international trade and international capital flows; vi) increases various types of *Inequality*; vii) increases the probability that there will be *Inequality Contagion* (the movement/ spread of *Inequality* across regional and national borders).

Many Chinese and non-Chinese researchers have noted fraud and errors in the calculation of China's statistical data (national accounting data). See: Orlik (2014); Lyu et al. (2018); Ma et al. (2014); Liu, Zhang and Zhu (2016); Holz (2014); and Gao (2016). In 2019, Chen et al. (2019), a Brookings Institute research paper (paper's analysis covered 2008 to 2016), stated that the Chinese GDP was overstated by as much as 12 percent and that the real growth rate of the Chinese economy has been overstated by about two percentage points annually in recent years, and Chinese statisticians don't have the power to correct inflated GDP number/figures. Chen et al. (2019) contains relevant economic data about China such as *Aggregate TFP Growth*; *Debt-to-GDP*; *Aggregate Returns to Capital*; *Official and Adjusted Investment Rates*; *Fixed Asset Investment (FAI) vs. Fixed Capital Formation (FCF)*; *Sectoral GDP and Corporate Income Tax Revenue Growth*; *Corporate Income Tax Revenue/GDP*; *Wholesale and Retail GDP: Micro-Data/National Accounts*; *Growth in Value-Added Tax Revenues and GDP*; *Gap between Local and Aggregate GDP by Expenditure*;

and the *Gap between Local and Aggregate GDP by Sector*; many of which are negative (declining economy). Chen et al. (2019) noted that:

1) In China, local governments are rewarded for meeting growth and investment targets, and thus they have substantial incentives to falsify local economic data.
2) For many years, the sum of China's provincial GDP exceeded the national GDP number which is clear evidence of statistical inflation of economic data at the local level.
3) In China, the National Bureau of Statistics (NBS) has acknowledged that some local economic data were falsified and in 2017, the central Chinese government accused three provinces in China's north-east rust-belt of fabricating economic data.
4) Chinese government data overstated growth of nominal GDP by an average of 1.7 percent per year during 2008–2016, and thus the Chinese economy was 12 percent smaller in 2016 than official figures indicated.

On the public health effects of *Inequality*, see: Wu and Li (2017); Shapiro et al. (2017); and Schneider and Yaşar (2016). On mechanisms that can explain the effects of *Inequality* on environmental deterioration, see: Berthe and Elie (2015).

On the Political Economy and Group-Decisions of auditor-firms and auditee-companies, see: Srinidhi, Lim and Hossain (2009); Wu, Hsu and Haslam (2016); Booker (2018); Trotman, Bauer and Humphreys (2015); Wu, Hsu and Haslam (2016); Read and Yezegel (2018); Hwang and Chang (2010); Chen, Kelly and Salterio (2012); Kleinman and Palmon (2009); Robertson (2010); Houqe, Monem and Van Zijl (2012); Anderlini, Gerardi and Lagunoff (2016); Wang and Xin (2011); El Ghoul, Guedhami and Pittman (2016); Schneider (2018); and Schneider (2015). Clearly these foregoing factors/trends can cause various types of *Inequality* and *Inefficient Allocation of Capital/Resources* due to the following factors and other issues:

i) Such decisions affect the volumes of earnings management, asset quality management and incentive effects management.
ii) That in turn, leads to inefficient allocation of capital/resources, unjustified and inflated executive compensation, wrong human resources decisions; inefficient government policies; inefficient distribution/re-distribution of wealth; etc.
iii) The *Multiplier Effects* and associated *Symbiotic Relationships* created by such decisions include but are not limited to *Income Inequality*, social stratification, *Social Inequality*, *Gender Inequality*, *Housing Inequality*, environmental pollution, low *quality-of-life*; etc.; all of which can *spill over* into other countries.

Earnings Management, Incentive-Effects Management and *Asset-quality Management* can cause inefficient allocation of capital and resources (by government agencies, financial services companies, households and private companies), primarily because such misconduct:

   i) Distorts economic data and National Income Accounting.
  ii) Distorts fiscal policy and monetary policy which are often based on economic data and *National Income Accounting.*
 iii) Distorts firms' performance.
 iv) Distorts the incentive effects of incentives.
  v) Distorts managers' and government regulators' motives, cognition and decision-making abilities.
 vi) Can distort the time-value and or utility of money.
vii) Produces "windfall gains" that affect managers' risk perception and decision-making abilities.
viii) Can affect capital budgeting and the criteria for project selection.
 ix) Can distort the "internal capital markets" of firms and government agencies.
  x) Can increase volatility and uncertainty in all financial markets which makes it hard to create and implement effective monetary policies.

Earnings management and asset-quality management can cause significant investment losses for individual investors (most of whom are not "sophisticated"), pension deficits (which exist in many companies in developed countries), and corporate financial distress all of which can cause mental illnesses (e.g. depression, substance-abuse, and stress/anxiety can cause other illnesses such as diabetes, obesity, stroke, migraine, vascular problems, heart diseases, kidney diseases, etc.).
    See the charts and tables in the following:

 i) "*CEO Pay-Ratios* Have Little Relationship With The Operating Performance Of Companies". Source: www.ft.com/content/1ee790f0-5da8-11e9-b285-3acd5d43599e.
 ii) "US CEO Pay Ratios are Much Larger Than Those Of Other Countries". Source: www.ft.com/content/1ee790f0-5da8-11e9-b285-3acd5d43599e.
 iii) Household-debt-to-GDP Ratios Of Various Countries (2018). Source: https://tradingeconomics.com/country-list/households-debt-to-gdp.
 iv) Comparison of Household Savings Rates Across Countries (As of 2018) – https://tradingeconomics.com/china/personal-savingsi).
 v) Chen et al. (2019), Pi (Jan. 18, 2017), Bernanke and Olson (2016), Almås and Kjelsrud (2017); Saxena and Bhattacharya (2018); Chatterjee et al. (2016); Shah and Narain (2019); Bhattacharjee et al. (2017); and Keane and Thakur (2018) and Fernald, Malkin and Spiegel (March 2013).

3.6 The global pension and retirement savings crisis amplifies various types of inequality and public health problems

Given the growing percentage of indigenes aged more than sixty years around the world, differentials in retirement income are a relatively new type of *Inequality* in both developed and developing countries. In the US and many developed and developing countries, many pension funds are grossly underfunded[14] and some have drastically reduced their payouts to beneficiaries/participants. In the USA, Social Security funds are forecasted to be depleted by 2035.[15] See the comments in Citi GPS (Citibank) (2016). All that can increase *Income inequality*, *Housing Inequality*, *Social Inequality* and environmental problems.

The relationships among pension deficits, auditing, earnings management (and asset-quality management and incentive-effects management), tax avoidance/evasion and by extension, *Inequality*, are established in the literature – see: Chaudhry, Yong and Veld (2017); Chen, Ge and Zolotoy (2017); Josiah et al. (2014); Gordon and Gallery (2012); Thomas and Williams (2009); Vermeer, Styles and Patton (2012); Graham (2008); Laswad and Baskerville (2007); and Foltin (2017). On the political economy and reform of pension systems, see: Glaeser and Ponzetto (2014); Williamson, Howling and Maroto (2006); Ribeiro and Beetsma (2008); Ebrahim, Mathur and Gwilym (2014); Apostolakis, Kraanen and van Dijk (2016); Alonso-García and Devolder (2016); and Foltin (2017).

3.7 Extreme compensation disparity: CEO pay ratios are significant and have been increasing in many countries

The *CEO Pay Ratios* are at extreme levels and are increasing in many countries, and especially in the USA (see Tables 3.2, 3.3 and 3.4).[16] The Mishel and Schieder (August 2018)[17] report examined trends in CEO compensation in the USA, and noted that there has been growing *Income Inequality*. CEO Today Magazine (www. ceotodaymagazine.com/2019/04/ceos-earn-an-employees-entire-salary-in-just-days/) compared CEO pay ratios across several countries, and noted that CEO Compensation And CEO pay ratios in the USA exceed those of many countries.

Edgecliffe-Johnson (April 16, 2019)[18] noted that:

i) According to an April 2019 study of compensation patterns of US companies by Equilar (a compensation advisory firm), *Pay Inequality* is significant and *CEO Pay Ratios* (the ratio of CEO total compensation to the median employee's compensation at a company) are increasing.

ii) Public support in the US for reducing CEOs' compensation in the US has declined since 2009. The *CEO Pay Ratio* has attracted scrutiny by labor unions, activists and politicians.

iii) Equilar (a compensation advisory firm) analyzed compensation at some of the largest US companies (by revenue), and the US median *CEO Pay Ratio* was 254:1 in 2018, up from 235:1 in 2017. Berkshire Hathaway's *CEO Pay Ratio* was less than seven while Tesla's CEO Elon Musk was paid 40,668 times more than the median Tesla worker. Of the 100 CEOs analyzed by Equilar, the *CEO Pay Ratios* of eleven companies exceeded 1,000.

iv) According to the Equilar study, large performance-based incentives substantially increased the *CEO Pay Ratio* at many companies. Safra Catz and Mark Hurd, Oracle's co-CEOs each had $108 million incentive packages (mostly five years of stock option grants which when adjusted for their annualized value, would reduce the company's *CEO Pay Ratio* from 1,205:1 to 282:1). Discovery Communications CEO David Zaslav had a near-$100 million 10-year option package; while Disney's CEO Bob Iger got a $26 million grant of restricted stock units for its acquisition of Fox. At Tesla, all but $56,000 of Elon Musk's $2.284 billion compensation for 2018 was from a performance-based award that will pay out in full only if Tesla achieves several milestones including a $650 billion market capitalization.

v) The US SEC's *CEO Pay Ratio* disclosure requirement costs companies $1 billion in 2018. Other countries have enacted other disclosure rules, with the UK requiring companies (beginning from 2019) to compare their chief executive's compensation to those of their employees in the 25th, median and 75th percentiles of their UK staff.

Lifshey (2018)[19] found that:

  i) *CEO Pay Ratios* varied greatly between industries, and had little correlation to performance.
 ii) *CEO Pay Ratios* are not driving decisions about executive pay and compensation committees would continue to focus on financial performance.
iii) There is substantial variability in permitted methodologies for calculating the *CEO Pay Ratio*.
 iv) Many US companies doubt the efficiency of the *CEO Pay Ratio* and its ability to reduce compensation Inequality.
  v) The nature of industry has an important effect the *CEO Pay Ratio*. Companies in the consumer discretionary and consumer staples sectors had the higher average *CEO Pay Ratios* of 384 and 295 respectively; while *CEO Pay Ratios* in the energy, financials, and utilities industries were 59–80.
 vi) The *CEO Pay Ratio* is correlated to company revenues. The average *CEO Pay Ratio* was 32 for companies whose annual revenues were less than $300 million and was about 290 for companies whose annual revenues were $3 billion and higher.
vii) The number of company employees is positively correlated to the *CEO Pay Ratio*. Companies that have fewer than 500 employees had an average *CEO Pay Ratio* of 36 compared to companies that had more than 10,000 employee whose average *CEO Pay Ratio* was 337.
viii) The percentage of employees located outside the US was also correlated to *CEO Pay Ratios*. The lowest *CEO Pay Ratio* band had roughly 9 percent of its employees located outside of the US, while those companies that had more than a third of their workforce overseas had a CEO Pay ratio of over 150.

3.8 Inequality in the USA

Significant and growing *Inequality* (in its various dimensions) has been reported in many supposedly "rich" countries such as the USA.[20] Most of the research on *Inequality* omits earnings management and *Incentive-Effects Management* – see: Stergiopoulos, Hwan et al. (2015); Beeghley (2015); Braveman and Gottlieb (2014); Albouy and Zabek (Jan. 2016) and Osberg (2015). See Tables 3.1–3.9.

As of 2014–2017, only about 24 percent of the 19 million eligible households in the USA received rental/housing assistance[21] (and by 2018, there were more than 25 million eligible households); and only 3.2 million housing units were available at affordable rents for more than 11 million extremely low-income households and about 8 million low-income households spent a large portion of their income on rent, lived in substandard housing, or both (households that earned 30 percent or less of the area's median income, which ranges from $7,450 to $33,300). As of 2013–2017 the US was spending more than four times the amounts it spent on homeowner subsidies on affordable housing annually;[22] and the US spent about $46 billion annually on affordable housing – $40 billion on means-tested programs and another $6 billion in tax expenditures through the Low Income Housing Tax Credit (LIHTC) program. As of September 2018, at least 39 million US indigenes were receiving food stamps (SNAP benefits; etc.) – see: www.trivis onno.com/wp-content/uploads/Food-Stamps-Percent.jpg; www.trivisonno.com/wp-content/uploads/Food-Stamps-Monthly.jpg. As of 2018, more than 52 percent of the US population received government financial assistance that was specifically designated for low-income people (e.g. SNAP; healthcare benefits; housing benefits; transportation assistance; legal assistance; tax credits; etc.) and as much as 90 percent of US adults received government subsidies (e.g. tax credits; etc.).

Substantial environmental Pollution has been documented in the US, and its negative effects are amplified by Inequality (lack of access to healthcare, poor sanitation; poor housing and living conditions; etc.). See the charts in Ritchie and Roser (2019) at https://ourworldindata.org/air-pollution; and United Nations pollution and climate change data at https://unstats.un.org/unsd/ENVIRONMENT/interlinks.htm.

The above-mentioned *Pension Crisis* is prevalent in the USA. During 2000–2019, many US state governments and municipal/local governments were at various times at risk of becoming bankrupt and some had significant pension deficits/liabilities – all of which resulted in reduction of public services and government assistance to poor households, and thus increases in *Inequality* and Public Health problems.

During 1980–2018, outsourcing, globalization and the movement of jobs from the USA to Mexico and "low-cost" Asian countries (such as China) caused significant volumes of factory closures and *rural-to-urban* migration in the USA. The *Inequality* and negative public health effects of such migration have been well documented – see Johnson and Taylor (2019).

Thus, like most so-called "rich" capitalist democracies, the US remains a *Welfare State* (funded by government borrowings, corporate and personal taxes and by printing money) where people live far beyond their means by borrowing.

Gabler (2016)[23] noted that:

- The US Federal Reserve Board's 2016 survey of US indigenes found that 49 percent of part-time workers would prefer to work more hours at their current wage; 29 percent of Americans expected to earn a higher income in the coming year; and 43 percent of homeowners who have owned their home for at least a year believed its value has increased. The US Fed Reserve asked respondents how they would pay for a $400 emergency and 47 percent of respondents said that they would either borrow or sell something, or that they would not be able to come up with the $400 at all.
- A 2014 Bankrate survey in the USA, found that only 38 percent of Americans could cover a $1,000 emergency-room visit or $500 car repair with money they'd saved. Two reports published in 2015 by the Pew Charitable Trusts found, respectively, that 55 percent of US households didn't have enough liquid savings to replace a month's worth of lost income, and that of the 56 percent of people who worried about their finances in the previous year, 71 percent were concerned about having enough money to cover everyday expenses. A similar study conducted by Annamaria Lusardi (then of George Washington University), Peter Tufano (then of Oxford University), and Daniel Schneider (then of Princeton University), asked individuals whether they could "come up with" $2,000 within 30 days for an unanticipated expense, and about 25 percent could not, and another 19 percent could do so only if they sold possessions or obtained payday loans. The Bankrate survey reported that nearly half of college graduates could not cover that car repair or emergency-room visit through savings, and the study by Lusardi, Tufano, and Schneider found that nearly one-quarter of households making $100,000 to $150,000 a year claim not to be able to raise $2,000 in a month. Another study by Jacob Hacker (then of Yale University) measured the number of households that had lost a quarter or more of their "available income" in a given year (i.e. income minus medical expenses and interest on debt) and found that in each year from 2001 to 2012, at least one in five had suffered such a loss and couldn't compensate by digging into savings. Thus, nearly half of USA indigenes were "financially fragile".
- According to research funded by the Russell Sage Foundation, the inflation-adjusted net worth of the typical US household, one at the median point of wealth distribution, was $87,992 in 2003 and had declined to $54,500 by 2013, a 38 percent decline (although the housing crash of 2008 contributed, the decline for the lower quintiles began long before the recession).
- According to an analysis of Federal Reserve and TransUnion data by the personal-finance site ValuePenguin, credit-card debt in the US was about $5,700 per household in 2015. About 38 percent of households carried some debt, and among those, the average was more than $15,000.
- The personal savings rate in the USA peaked at 13.3 percent in 1971 before falling to 2.6 percent in 2005; and was 5.1 percent in 2015. About 30 percent of American adults don't save any of their income for retirement.
- In a 2015 survey of American finances published by Pew, 60 percent of respondents said they had suffered some sort of "economic shock" in the past

12 months – a drop in income, a hospital visit, the loss of a spouse, a major repair. About 34 percent of the respondents who made more than $100,000 a year said they felt strain as a result of an economic shock.

- The American Psychological Association's 2014 annual survey on stress in the United States found i) that 54 percent of Americans said they had just enough or not enough money each month to meet their expenses; and ii) that money was the top stressor in the US; iii) that 72 percent of adults reported feeling stressed about money at least some of the time, and about 25 percent rated their stress "extreme"; iv) 32 percent of the survey respondents said they couldn't afford to live a healthy lifestyle, and 21 percent said they were so financially strapped that they had forgone a doctor's visit, or considered doing so, in the previous year.
- A 2014 Pew survey stated that 55 percent of Americans spent as much as they earned each month, or more, and about 55 percent of the survey respondents said they had favorable financial circumstances.

Household consumer debt is significant and increasing in the US and many countries, and that exacerbates *Inequality* and puts additional psychological strain on households. The negative social, economic and psychological effects of debt are well documented in the literature. In the USA, increased *Uncertainty* about many aspects of life reduces human aspirations and employee motivation/productivity, and reduces the efficiency of most types of "Networks" in business.

Ironically as of 2018, there were more than US$18 trillion of Mutual Fund assets under management in the USA.

3.9 Inequality in China

Lovely, Liang and Zhang (2019) studied Economic Geography and *Inequality* in China and found that worker-location is a cause of *Wage Inequality* but that its impact has declined over time. On *Inequality* and economic growth in China, see Wu and Li (2017). While the consensus has been that during 1980–2018, China reduced its poverty levels by more than 66 percent (more than five hundred million people were supposedly "lifted" out of poverty),[24] such information is not entirely correct and the reality in China was and remains different as indicated by the following:

i) As confirmed by various studies by both Chinese and non-Chinese researchers, *Inequality*[25] actually increased in China during 1980–2018. See: Ravallion and Chen (2007); Ward (2016); Sicular et al. (2007); Elmer (23 May 2017); Knight, Li and Song (March 2004); IMF (2015); Wu and Li (2017) and Khan and Riskin (2001).

ii) Many Chinese and non-Chinese researchers have noted fraud and errors in the calculation of China's national economic/statistical data. There is documented evidence that China overstated its annual economic growth rates during 1990–2019 by as much as 12 percent per year in some years; and that there were often discrepancies between economic data from local governments and data from the central Chinese government.[26] See: Orlik (2014); Lyu, Wang, et al. (2018); Ma, Song, et al. (2014); Liu, Zhang and Zhu (2016); Holz (2004); Rawski (2001); Holz (2014); Gao (2016); Bernanke and Olson (2016); Fernald, Malkin and Spiegel (March 2013); Wu (Jan. 2014) and Chen, Chen, Hseih and Song (2019).

iii)   In China, consumer debt (and associated loan defaults) and government debt are significant and growing, which is a dangerous trend (China has become a debtor-nation, rather than a creditor-nation).

iv)   The unfair and sometimes brutal treatment of Chinese minorities by the Chinese government remains a critical issue.[27] During 2018–2019, there were news reports that the Chinese government forcibly incarcerated more than one million Uighurs in "re-education camps"; and had forcibly placed majority-Chinese persons in Uighur homes to live with them. These actions may not be the best ways to handle suspicions of Islamic terrorism.

v)   The Chinese *Houkou System* creates significant problems and *Inequality* which haven't been resolved by recent significant government reforms See: Afridi, Li and Ren (2015); Lin and Chen (2011); Tan (2014) and Sheehan (Feb. 22, 2017).

vi)   Sheehan (Feb. 22, 2017) noted that ". . . Local governments across China had a total of RMB 17 trillion ($2.5 trillion) worth of debt at the end of 2016 and this means that they are often unable to finance the necessary services to meet demand stemming from a large inflow of new residents. . . ."

vii)   China has essentially evolved into a welfare state. During 1980–2019, the Chinese government used a system of both hidden and explicit government welfare transfers and subsidies to Chinese households to "lift" people from poverty – and thus the change in Chinese households' income levels was not entirely organic. That involved significant *Labor-Inequality* and international trade issues wherein the taxes and profits generated from Chinese government-owned companies that exploited cheap migrant Chinese labor, were re-distributed by the Chinese government in perhaps sub-optimal ways that favored the urban Chinese.

viii)   The *quality-of-life* of the so-called Chinese urban middle class is relatively low and is declining – due to overcrowding, poor sanitation and significant environmental pollution in Chinese cities (e.g. in Beijing; Shanghai; etc.); illegal waste-dumps; illegal "waste processing plants"; expensive housing and over-crowded housing units; illegal structures/buildings and slums in large cities; the growing *Informal Economy* in Chinese cities; etc. During the last twenty years, there have been many documented reports of unsanitary and illegal working conditions and suicides at Chinese factories.[28] See: Lin, Lin and Tseng (2016).

ix)   On a comparative basis, the real income levels (adjusted for inflation, currency depreciation, bribery/corruption, government transfers/subsidies and perhaps taxes) of the so-called "new" Chinese middle class are not substantial. The economic prospects and wealth of the so-called Chinese urban/rural middle-class remain very unstable. That is confirmed by many factors including their low-quality jobs (more than 95 million jobs that are mostly assembly, process and clerical jobs) that don't involve transferable skills or technical knowledge in engineering, physical sciences or biological sciences; their high and increasing consumer/household debt; the *Import-Substitution Measures* and trade tariffs imposed on Chinese goods by the US government in 2018–2019 and by other countries; and the EU–Japan trade agreement that took effect in January 2019 (which is likely to reduce China-to-EU export/trade volumes); anti-globalization and nationalist movements in many "rich" and middle-class countries (which increases the probability of imposition of trade tariffs on Chinese goods/services and *Import Substitution*); increasing automation in many countries; the movement of manufacturing activities to southeast Asian (ASEAN) countries; etc.

x) Since 2008, China has had an ongoing *Debt Crisis* characterized by substantial and increasing corporate debt and consumer debt; corporate bankruptcies and state bailouts. According to the Bank for International Settlements, China's *total-debt/national-output ratio* increased from 140 percent in 2008 to 253 percent in 2018. According to the 2018 financial stability report published by the People's Bank of China, China's *household-debt-to-GDP ratio* increased from 17.9 percent in 2008 to 49 percent in December 2017 (according to the IMF, a national economy benefits the most from rising debt when its *household-debt-to-GDP ratio* is less than 10 percent). Although official Chinese government estimates of non-performing loans (NPL) were less than 2 percent during 2015–2018, industry and china analysts estimated that the true Chinese NPL-rate was at least 23 percent in 2018. More importantly, as of 2018–2019, a substantial amount of Chinese debt (more than 60 percent) was owned by Chinese government agencies and companies – and thus there can be negative *Domino Effects* and *Multiplier Effects* and associated *spillovers* to other countries. The Chinese government exercises strict and substantial control over all aspects of the Chinese economy including capital flows; encourages earnings management and *Selective Prosecution*; exercises control over the media and information flows and official economic data; and provides and controls state subsidies and formal/informal government bailouts. Through such control and questionable interventions, the Chinese government has been able to block what in democratic and capitalist economies would have been a series of disastrous economic and or financial crises.

xi) Urbanization in China (and the migration of Chinese peasant and low-skilled labor to large Chinese cities) increased substantially during 2000–2019. Such cheap labor has been the source of China's declining *Labor-Cost Advantage*. Unfortunately, that has resulted in "*Destructive Urbanization*" which is marked by un-sanitary conditions, serious environmental pollution, over-crowding, *Housing Inequality* and expensive homes, health problems, declining quality-of-life, *Income and Wealth Inequality*; etc. Despite all those urbanization problems, in 2018 the

Chinese government announced a plan to use a system of *"Urban Clusters"* (clusters of cities/towns) to boost its domestic economic growth.

xii) There were intermittent housing bubbles in China during 2009–2019. That had or could have had negative *Multiplier Effects* and *Symbiotic Relationships* in the Chinese economy.

xiii) Many researchers have noted risks in China's financial system – see: Song and Xiong (2018) and Bai, Hsieh and Qian (2006, 2016, 2019).

xiv) Environmental pollution (and illegal waste dumps and "waste processing plants") has been a major problem in China, especially in and around its large cities. In 2018, China implemented policies that drastically reduced the volumes of plastic and paper waste that it accepts from foreign countries for processing – much of the rejected waste was accepted by some south-east Asian countries where many illegal waste dumps and illegal waste processing facilities operate.

xv) In China, increased uncertainty reduces human aspirations and employee motivation/productivity, and reduces the efficiency of most types of "Networks" in business.

xvi) As confirmed in various studies by both Chinese and non-Chinese researchers, China's *Current Account* balances declined during 2014–2019.

3.10 Inequality in India

There continues to be significant and growing *Inequality* in India (which is often compounded by social networks, religion and the caste system) – see: Almås and Kjelsrud (2017); Saxena and Bhattacharya (2018); Chatterjee et al. (2016); Goel (2017); Agrawal (2014); Mehta and Hasan (2012); Zacharias and Vakulabharanam (2011); Falebita and Koul (2018); Roy and Pramanick (2019); Rath, Yu and Srinivas (2018); Schuetz and Venkatesh (2019); Ojha, Pradhan and Ghosh (2013); Shah and Narain (2019); Bhattacharjee et al. (2017); and Keane and Thakur (2018). As of 2019, less than 1 percent of India's population controlled at least 73 percent of its wealth and resources; and as of 2018, less than 10 percent of India's population controlled at least 79 percent of its wealth and resources.[29] Consider the following:

i) The Indian government's de-monetization program of 2017–2018 had a disproportionately negative effect on low-income households and un-banked populations, and increased *Inequality*.

ii) Similarly, the implementation of the *Goods and Services Tax* (GST) had a disproportionately negative effect on low-income households and un-banked populations – and due to back-lash, protests and economic slowdown in parts of India, the Indian government reduced the GST rates on various goods/services. See: Bala (2018) and Jalaja (2017).

iii) The Pradhan Mantri Jan Dhan Yojana (PMJDY) program for banking the "un-banked" was launched in 2014, has far-reaching implications for low-income households, but hasn't significantly improved the quality-of-life of many households. See: Bijoy (2018) and Agarwal, Alok et al. (2018).

iv) There is an understated debt crisis in India wherein state-owned banks have high NPL rates (which many suspect are understated).

v) Pesek (2019) noted that:

1) Unemployment in India was at historically very high levels as of July 2019.

2) Arvind Subramanian (a former International Monetary Fund [IMF] staffer and until 2018, the Modi government's chief economic adviser) stated that during 2012–2017, Indian GDP growth averaged about 4.5 percent and not the 7 percent range stated by the Indian government; and that India's rapid national growth does not match actual trends in investment rates, exports, corporate profits, credit financing and consumption. The Indian government has refuted most of these allegations.

3) The Modi government's promises to revise labor, land and corporate tax laws and to open India's retail sector to global operators have not been fulfilled.

4) FDI into India was just 1.5 percent of GDP in 2017 versus 6.3 percent in Vietnam and 3 percent in Malaysia.

5) Chronic shortfalls in domestic savings and investment makes India over-reliant on global/foreign capital.

6) A 2017 study by the Association of Chartered Certified Accountants estimated that India's Informal Economy is about 17 percent of its GDP.

Table 3.1 Number of US Households That Received US HUD Rental Assistance

HUD Rental Assistance Going to Families with Children, 2004–2015

Year	Households Receiving Assistance	Households with Kids	Share with Kids
2004	4,533,332	2,010,960	44.36%
2005	4,522,538	1,954,488	43.22%
2006	4,482,517	1,891,608	42.2%
2007	4,544,810	1,889,184	41.57%
2008	4,516,991	1,831,913	40.56%
2009	4,384,533	1,826,652	41.66%
2010	4,534,133	1,863,045	41.09%
2011	4,643,933	1,895,146	40.81%
2012	4,713,576	1,890,633	40.11%
2013	4,731,771	1,867,849	39.47%
2014	4,532,158	1,750,193	38.62%
2015	4,578,583	1,739,569	37.99%

Source: CBPP analysis of Department of Housing and Urban Development Picture of Subsidized Households. www.cbpp.org/research/housing/national-and-state-housing-fact-sheets-data. Missing values were interpolated using data from other years.

Notes: Families with children have at least one member under age 18 living in the home. All programs include all HUD programs with subsidies whose value varies based on the tenant's income except Housing Opportunities for People with AIDS/HIV and McKinney-Vento permanent housing.

Table 3.2 CEO compensation, CEO-to-worker compensation ratio, and stock prices (2017 dollars), 1965–2017

	CEO annual compensation (in thousands)*		Private-sector production/nonsupervisory workers annual compensation (in thousands)		Stock market (indexed to $2017)		CEO-to-worker compensation ratio***	
	Based on options realized	Based on options granted	All private-sector workers	Firms' industry**	S&P 500	Dow Jones	Based on options realized	Based on options granted
1965	902	688	40.9	n/a	588	6,078	20.0	14.5
1973	1,177	898	48.0	n/a	520	4,473	22.2	16.1
1978	1,612	1,230	49.1	n/a	325	2,780	29.7	21.6
1989	3,004	2,291	46.7	n/a	605	4,704	58.2	42.3
1995	5,830	6,468	46.8	56.3	850	7,058	112.3	123.2
2000	21,048	21,136	49.4	58.9	1,994	14,985	343.5	360.5
2007	19,503	13,583	51.4	61.2	1,714	15,290	327.4	226.9
2009	10,983	10,550	53.4	62.5	1,063	9,963	187.8	175.7
2013	15,903	12,193	52.9	62.2	1,696	15,487	278.6	204.7
2014	16,843	12,688	53.1	62.9	1,960	17,023	284.0	213.4
2015	16,564	12,716	53.9	64.2	2,088	17,814	271.6	208.5
2016	16,030	13,039	54.5	62.2	2,095	17,927	270.1	219.9
Projected 2017	18,855	13,264	54.6	62.4	2,398	21,292	311.7	220.7
2016 FH	15,200	12,768	54.5	62.2	2,095	17,927	257.3	215.7
2017 FH	17,880	12,988	54.6	62.4	2,398	21,292	298.9	216.5
Percent change							Change in ratio	
1965–1978	78.7%	78.7%	19.9%	n/a	-44.7%	-54.3%	9.8	7.1
1978–2000	1,205.5%	1,618.8%	0.7%	n/a	513.0%	439.1%	313.8	338.8
2000–2017	-10.4%	-37.2%	10.5%	6.0%	20.2%	42.1%	-31.8	-139.7
2009–2017	71.7%	25.7%	2.1%	-0.1%	125.6%	113.7%	123.9	45.0
1978–2017	1,069.5%	978.6%	11.2%	n/a	636.9%	666.0%	282.0	199.1
2016–2017	17.6%	1.7%	0.2%	0.3%	14.5%	18.8%	41.6	0.9

Source: Mishel, L. & Schieder, J. (August 2018) analysis of data from Compustat's ExecuComp database, the Federal Reserve Economic Data (FRED) database from the Federal Reserve Bank of St. Louis, the Bureau of Labor Statistics' Current Employment Statistics data series, and the Bureau of Economic Analysis NIPA tables

Notes: Projected value for 2017 is based on the change in CEO pay as measured from June 2016 to June 2017 applied to the full-year 2016 value. Projections for compensation based on options granted and options realized are calculated separately. "FH" denotes preliminary values from the "first half" of the year.

* CEO annual compensation is computed using the "options realized" and "options granted" compensation series for CEOs at the top 350 U.S. firms ranked by sales. The "options realized" series includes salary, bonus, restricted stock grants, options realized, and long-term incentive payouts for CEOs at the top 350 U.S. firms ranked by sales. The "options granted" series includes salary, bonus, restricted stock grants, value of options granted, and long-term incentive payouts.

** Annual compensation of the workers in the key industry of the firms in the sample.

*** Based on averaging specific firm ratios and not the ratio of averages of CEO and worker compensation.

3.11 Inequality contagion

Earnings management, incentive-effects management and asset-quality management are the primary means through which employees/managers benefit from Equity-based Incentives, and such misconduct:

i)   Increases Inequality because past and existing EBIs often produce significant "windfall gains" that are often un-related to the fundamental operating performance of companies, and EBI values contain substantial Market Noise

ii) Can amplify Inequality Contagion because they are used in standardized formats in multinational corporations (MNCs) many of whom have global operations in many countries.

iii) has significant effects on the efficiency and incentive-effects of EBIs, which in turn can be a major cause of public health problems (i.e. Mass Anxiety, depression; other mental health problems; hypertension; heart diseases; kidney diseases; volatility in stock markets and currency markets; etc.), *policy-distortion*, inefficient capital allocation and the resultant *Inequality Contagion* around the world. EBIs include employee stock options; Dividend Equivalent Rights (DERs); phantom stock; Stock Appreciation Rights (SARs); Stock Warrants; etc.

iv) Increases *Uncertainty* which reduces human aspirations and employee motivation/productivity, and reduces the efficiency of most types of "*Networks*" in business.

Another dimension of *Inequality* and *Inequality Contagion* is that the financial crises, corporate bankruptcies and corporate scandals (e.g. those listed in Appendices 3.1, 3.2, 3.3, 3.4 and 3.5) that are caused and or amplified by earnings management, incentive-effects management and asset-quality management, can also have the effect of causing and or expanding *Income/Wealth Inequality*, *Gender Inequality* and *Housing Inequality*. Such *Inequality* arises and or is propagated in various ways including but not limited to the following:

i)   Loss of, or reduced wages – particularly for mid and lower level employees.

ii) Loss of, or reduced benefits (particularly for mid and lower level employees) – which leads to reduced access to healthcare; loss of pension/retirement income; etc.

iii) Lost career progression opportunities, which often translates into lower income, and slower social mobility.

iv) Dismissed employees suffer evictions, liens and mortgage foreclosures, which is often reported to credit bureaus which in turn reduces career progress and opportunities.

v)   Difficulty in finding new jobs as industries shrink.

vi) Gender-based *Inequality* and discrimination.

vii) Unaffordability of housing, and sometimes inability to get housing benefits from the government.

 viii) Smaller social networks.
   ix) Employees' loss of Social Capital which affects their social mobility and opportunity sets.
    x) Employee's reduced borrowing capacity.
   xi) Increased consumer debt (borrowing by current and former employees) which often leads to mental health problems and inefficient decision making.
  xii) Current and former employees suffer from mental health problems such as depression, anxiety/stress, etc.
 xiii) Increased uncertainty reduces human aspirations and employee motivation/productivity, and reduces the efficiency of most types of "Networks" in business.

It is conjectured here that the channels for all the above-mentioned *Inequality Contagion* and cross-border spillovers of *Inequality* include but are not limited to international capital flows, international trade; corporate transactions; perceptions of other countries; copying institutions (laws; processes; etc.) in other countries; capital/currency controls; monetary and fiscal policies; cognition in decision making; etc. The academic literature has documented the many negative effects of *Income Inequality*, Social Inequality, *Housing Inequality* and *Wealth Inequality* and their often severe *Multiplier Effects* on households and economies. See the comments in Elgar and Aitken (2011); Van Oort, van Lenthe and Mackenbach (2005); Schutte et al. (2014) and Aldabe et al. (2011).

Inequality can be caused by many factors including but not limited to the following, some of which can have symbiotic relationships with each other:

    i) Wage differentials.
   ii) Excessive incentive compensation paid to managers – partly as a result of earnings management, asset-quality management and incentive effects management.
  iii) Localized inflation and general increases in prices particularly in large cities – which makes goods/services unaffordable for some households.
   iv) Localized inflation and general rises in prices and rents of housing units particularly in large cities (and partly due to excessive compensation caused by earnings management and asset quality management).
    v) The resultant corporate failures, financial crises and scandals (caused in part by earnings management and asset quality management) increase Income Inequality, Social Inequality and Housing Inequality (see below).
   vi) Lost employee benefits and employee pensions (caused in part by earnings management and asset quality management).
  vii) Distorted policy-making and inefficient capital/resource allocation which is based on corporate financial disclosures.
 viii) Uncertainty reduces human aspirations and employee motivation/productivity, and reduces the efficiency of most types of "Networks" in business.

3.12 Solving the inequality problem

This chapter discusses the relationships among *Inequality*, Earnings Management, Incentive-Effects Management, Inefficient Capital Allocation and Public Health. The following are ways to reduce or eliminate *Inequality*:

i) Reduce or eliminate Earnings Management, Asset-Quality Management and Incentives-Effect Management which are major sources/channels of "*Windfall Gains*" that are, or that amplify various types of *Inequality*.

ii) Increase *Matching* in the economy (in the labor, housing, marriage, leisure, borrowing/debt, savings/investment and education markets). The government and the private sector can create web-based *Matching* platforms that also sends alerts to consumers and companies.

iii) Governments should reform pension regulations/laws. Government agencies and companies should be compelled (via statutes and penalties) to: 1) eliminate all unfunded pension liabilities; and 2) mandatorily contribute substantial amounts towards workers' pensions/retirement which should be hedged against inflation, political risk and currency devaluation.

iv) *Equitable Redistribution* of wealth and tax reform. Governments should implement and increase "global taxes" on the super-rich – e.g. income tax rates of 65–75 percent and capital gains tax rates of 30–50 percent on the top-2 percent wealthy persons, where such taxes are coordinated among all or many countries by agreement. Governments should grant tax credits for voluntary wealth transfers by rich persons to "designated/classified unrelated poor persons" in the form of gifts and charitable donations. Governments should: 1) limit executive compensation – e.g. through taxation and by statutes (e.g. an executive's total compensation should not be more than a specified multiple of the average employee compensation at the company); 2) create statutory claw-backs of executive compensation where companies become financially distressed or don't meet their pension obligations or are fined large amounts for misconduct; 3) statutorily defer or block payment or realization (e.g. option exercise or stock sales) of any bonuses and executive incentive compensation at companies/organizations that have unfunded pension liabilities, and or excessive debts.

v) Eliminate the channels of *Inequality Contagion*.

vi) Nwogugu (2019) proposed a series of targeted government interventions in the form of "*Dedicated Tax-and-Spend Funds*" that can reduce *Inequality* and environmental pollution.

vii) Provide free secondary and tertiary education – re-training; acquisition of new skills; etc. The cost of education is significant and is increasing in many countries. For example in the US, the significant cost of a four-year university degree and the post-graduation education loan burdens are troubling, and provides strong incentives for university graduates to engage in conduct that amplifies *Inequality* and crime – e.g. Earnings Management, Incentive-Effects Management, etc.

viii) Change the structure of secondary and tertiary education to provide more free skills-based, vocational, entrepreneurship and technical training. For example, secondary-school students should be required to complete 3–4 comprehensive business plans for new technology ventures, and learn accounting/bookkeeping, 2–3 computer programming languages and 2–3 vocational skills (e.g. Welding; HVAC maintenance; auto repairs) before they graduate.

ix) Statutes should be created to compel large/medium sized companies (whose asset and or annual revenues exceed specific benchmarks) and government agencies (which are major causes/amplifiers of *Inequality*) to allocate capital to building low-cost housing and providing free medical care to their workers and their families. Governments should also consider providing free healthcare services to low-income persons. Compare the healthcare costs in the USA and Canada, and it seems that the privatization of healthcare in the US has increased costs significantly without matching increases in service quality.

x) Consider implementing *Universal Basic Income* (UBI) that is linked to jobs and skills-training (e.g. UBI is wholly or partially offset/reduced by existing income, and UBI recipients must work before receiving such UBI, and those that don't have any jobs must be available to be assigned to jobs by the government and must be undergoing free skills training).

xi) Provide more effective government and private-sector incentives for the construction of low-income housing and provision of free/low-cost healthcare. For example, the low-income housing system and the healthcare system in the US have failed with regard to providing affordable and effective services.

xii) Provide incentives for families to reduce the sizes of households – e.g. through cash incentives, birth-control training, penalties; etc.

xiii) Consider price controls for basic necessities such as food, housing, healthcare and transportation.

xiv) Provide relocation incentives to low-income families, and increase Labor Mobility (which improves matching in labor, education, real estate and marriage markets). Thus, programs such as the Houkou system in China should be radically reformed.

xv) Impose taxes on capital flows that cause or increase *Inequality* – such as illegal outflows from developing countries; MNCs' hoarding of cash in tax havens; etc.

xvi) Improve sanitation and waste management and reduce pollution in order to reduce healthcare costs and mental health problems, both of which increase *Inequality*.

xvii) Nwogugu (2015a) critiqued *National Income Accounting* which should be radically reformed to better measure economic activity and to develop better public policy.

xviii) Impose taxes/levies/tariffs on outsourcing and imported goods that displace and take jobs from domestic workers.

xix) Encourage Labor Unions and implement reasonable minimum-wage laws.

xx)   Statutorily eliminate or reduce dependence on, and use of *"Consumer Credit Scores"* and "Consumer Social Scores" (which often causes "red-lining" of neighborhoods and discrimination in employment and lending).

xxi)   Increase the efficiency of allocation-of-capital by government agencies, banks, pension funds and insurance companies. Without such efficiency, all types of capital will be improperly allocated to efforts, ventures and interventions that increase Inequality.

xxii)   Governments should impose jail sentences and criminal penalties (a sub-stantial percentage of the perpetrator's wealth) for misconduct that causes or amplifies *Inequality* – such as money-laundering, securities fraud and Incentive-Effects Management.

xxiii)   Governments should create new government-owned or government con-trolled companies, public-private partnerships and jobs in core industries such as agriculture, food processing, transportation, manufacturing, hous-ing, distribution/logistics and financial services (China's state-owned privatized companies that offer employee stock ownership have been major drivers of economic growth and implementers of government poli-cies). One major problem worldwide is that private companies haven't been able to efficiently allocate capital, jobs and compensation in some industries in ways that reduce *Inequality* (and they don't always transmit or implement government policies).

xxiv)   Reduce household/consumer debt, which often inflicts mental-health problems and associated negative *Multiplier Effects*. That can be done through efficient financial products and web-based "Spending Control" programs/systems for households.

xxv)   Government and the private sector should provide financial and market-ing support to expand and stabilize SMEs which remain the backbone of economic growth in many countries. That can be done through P2P loans, specialized web-based "SME Platforms" (e.g. ERP systems; online lend-ing; online marketing assistance; bookkeeping and online banking; etc.).

xxvi)   Replace microfinance with *"Group-based P2P Lending"* wherein a loan is granted to a group of persons who allocate the loan proceeds among their sole proprietorships or small businesses and share profits and losses. Around the world, Microfinance has been over-hyped and is causing problems especially in environments where the banks don't have the social/regulatory/technical infrastructure to assess and monitor risk, and or to recover loan-losses.

3.13 Environmental pollution, climate change and environmental auditing[30]

Environmental pollution and Climate Change have become critical issues around the world. Hook and Reed (Oct. 24, 2018) noted that the G7 countries pro-duce most of the plastic/paper waste in the world, a large percentage of which was shipped to China until 2018, after which a significant percentage is being shipped to southeast Asian counties, where many illegal waste dumps and waste-processing factories operate (see the tables/charts listed in Section 3.4 above). As of 2018, many *Multinational Corporations* (MNCs) (such as Apple; Alibaba; Facebook; Microsoft; Twitter; Instagram; Google/Alphabet; Deutsche Telecomm; Samsung; Lenovo; Airbnb, Uber, BT; Oracle; TMobile; Amazon; AT&T; etc., and other MNCs listed in Appendices 3.1–3.5) were not members of the United Nations Global Compact Initiative; and the *Sustainability* (economic; environmental, urban and social sustainability) disclosures and initiatives of many MNCs during 2010–2018 were woefully deficient.

Many MNCs (such as Facebook; Oracle; Alphabet/Google; Instagram; Deutsche Telecomm; Apple; Samsung; Lenovo; Airbnb, Uber, Alibaba, Ebay, WeChat; Snap; Baidu; Amazon; Mitsubishi; Microsoft; IBM; telecom companies; large international banks; automobile and aeroplane manufacturers; electronics manufacturers; etc., and other MNCs listed in Appendices 3.1–3.5) market, sell and *cause* the annual purchases of millions of cellphones, computers, hand-held devices, electronic parts, automobiles and auto-parts, plastic products and accessories around the world, many of which are made of non-biodegradable and or toxic (or potentially toxic) plastics/synthetics/materials and are manufactured under very questionable circumstances[31] in developing countries. Some MNC-affiliated foreign factories in emerging markets countries have reported suicides, fines for improper waste-management and labor law violations; and MNCs have been fined in several countries for the same and other violations/misconduct. Many MNCs outsource production of goods and or service delivery to services-contractors and manufacturers that are located in developing and under-developed countries/regions where labor and environmental laws and enforcement are much weaker than in developed countries – and those companies violate such laws. As of 2018, many of such MNCs didn't have any comprehensive and effective waste disposal, labor or environmental remediation policies/practices for those products (e.g. waste management for the computers, hand-held devices, batteries, car-parts; inks; metals; printer-cartridges and plastic products and other non-biodegradable products that are implicated in the use of their services/products).

Many MNCs (such as Facebook; Oracle; Lenovo; Samsung; Alphabet/Google; Airbnb, Uber, Alibaba, Ebay, WeChat; Snap; Apple; Baidu; Amazon; IBM; large international banks; Microsoft; automobile manufacturers; etc.) cause or facilitate the sales and use of products and equipment that consume significant amounts of energy that was generated from fossil fuels (the MNCs significantly increased the *carbon footprints* of households, companies and governments). Also the carbon footprints of many MNCs and their suppliers are significant and growing. As of 2018, most of those MNCs didn't have any programs to generate clean energy either for mass consumption, or to significantly reduce energy consumed by their operations and the products/service that they sell, or caused the purchases of (including ancillary and complementary products that are manufactured and sold by other companies).

MNCs' earnings management and asset-quality management and their other corporate governance problems (see Nwogugu [2019] and Appendices 3.1, 3.2, 3.3, 3.4 and 3.5 in this chapter) have or had or could have had "*governance contagion effects*" both in their industries and in other industries which in turn, can cause or increase systemic risk and financial instability (and also increase firms' cost-of-capital and perceived risk), all of which reduces economic/financial sustainability. The corporate governance, strategy, operations research and corporate finance literatures indicate that in many countries, many large and medium-sized companies hire senior executives and board members from, and copy the corporate governance policies and operational strategies of their competitors.

Thus legally, those MNCs may be partly liable for environmental pollution problems under tort law (e.g. Contribution; Product Liability; Negligence) and or Criminal Law – because the relevant elements exist (i.e. knowledge or *mens rea*; intent or omission; result; actual or proximate causation; and injury). Given that the statutes-of-limitations for legal claims against such offending companies have not expired, in some instances the monetary amount of such legal liabilities may exceed the total assets (and sometimes the equity market values) of such companies, which renders them technically insolvent. Companies that don't generate enough clean energy that exceeds the sum of their own direct energy consumption plus the energy consumption of their customers plus the allocated energy consumption of their regulators and suppliers, are henceforth referred to as "*Energy-Negative Companies*"; and companies that do the opposite are "*Energy Positive Companies*". Similarly, companies that don't have processes to adequately manage and dispose of waste that arise or are derived from their products/services are henceforth referred to as "*Waste-Negative Companies*"; and companies that do the opposite are "*Waste-Positive Companies*". Incorporating the foregoing portfolio selection criteria and equity/debt valuation factors into credit analysis and financial analysis can compel companies (and government agencies) to better manage their product development, energy consumption and "*energy-impact*".

The main catalysts for the use, perception and quality of sustainability reports issued by companies are as follows: i) sustainability rankings (of companies) that are published by various companies – including the investment/selection criteria of various "social impact funds", "green funds" and "green-indices" which have been growing in popularity; ii) the Non-Financial Reporting and CSR Resource Centre (https://docs.com/jernej-zavrl); iii) the guidelines of the Global Reporting Initiative's (GRI) *GRI Sustainability Reporting Guidelines*; iv) the *International Integrated Reporting Council* (IIRC); v) award schemes and international conferences; vi) international agreements and "commitments" such as the United Nations Global Compact Initiative (www.unglobalcompact.org/what-is-gc/participants); and vii) publicly available and widely circulated reports and surveys such as KPMG's "*Currents of change: The KPMG Survey of Corporate Responsibility Reporting – 2015*" (2015; https://assets.kpmg.com/content/dam/kpmg/pdf/2015/11/kpmg-international-survey-of-corporate-responsibility-reporting-2015.pdf) have highlighted issues of CSR and sustainability disclosures.

As of 2018, many MNCs (including exchange-traded MNCs) were not members of the United Nations Global Compact initiative (www.unglobalcompact.org/what-is-gc/participants). Many MNCs' (including exchange-traded MNCs) ESR/CSR disclosures and initiatives during 2010–2018 were woefully deficient and much below standards expected of multinational companies.

Like emissions permits and emissions taxes, the tax credits and *similar subsidies* granted to companies and households (for implementing "energy efficiency measures") are highly inefficient, and don't address the primary causes and sources of pollution. They encourage targeted and unaffordable consumption and import-substitution (many such products are imported and their consumption is often financed with debt); and are limited by the company's or household's own cash-expenditure/wealth. Many governments cannot afford to provide such tax-credits in sufficient amounts to create sustainable change. Under current regulatory systems (emissions-permits-trading; carbon taxes; subsidies; etc.), it's reasonably inferable that the implied prices of pollution, emissions permits and carbon-credits are relatively cheap and can be collusively manipulated downwards by polluting industries.

Unfortunately, in many developed and developing countries, many (if not most) environmental audits are done by government-agency employees or relatively small non-accounting firms (some are engineering firms) that are not subjected to the professional standards, penalties and discipline of the auditing/accounting profession. That causes or can cause *political interference* (wherein governments under-report environmental pollution for political gains), lapses in judgment and lax reporting, *Collusion*, *Price-fixing* (in the global markets for emissions permits, carbon credits, Green Bonds; climate derivatives; environmental auditing; etc.) and bribery. In some countries, these non-accounting environmental auditors are not subject to *Mandatory Auditor-Rotation, Auditor Fee-Allocation Mechanisms, Auditor Work-Allocation Mechanisms* or *Auditor Liability-Allocation Mechanisms*. Also, in some countries, the professional liability standards and penalties for auditing/accounting firms are more comprehensive and severe, have more public policy impact and have been more litigated than those of engineering professions (i.e. civil, chemical and environmental engineering).

In Environmental Auditing, "*Self-Auditing*" has or can have significant negative financial statement and accounting-audit implications; and can also affect the prices and trading of *Environmental Management Instruments* (EMIs) and *Climate Finance Instruments* (CFIs) (such as carbon credits; emissions permits; Green Bonds; etc.). On Self-Auditing, see: Demirel, Iatridis and Kesidou (2018), Sabonis-Helf (2003) and Quick and Schmidt (2018). The prices and trading of CFIs and EMIs partly depend on both aggregate pollution and each specific firm's pollution levels. Permitting *Self-Auditing* is like allowing the CFO of a company to prepare its official/statutory quarterly/annual audited financial statements and hoping that the CFO will always be truthful in harsh capital markets that severely punish companies for declining earnings or for missing earnings targets. The actual un-reported monetary liabilities for companies' non-compliance with environmental regulations and climate change regulations that is attributable to Self-Auditing may be in the trillions of Euros. It's now clear that the inefficient systems of "*Self-Auditing*" of environmental pollution (by polluting companies and government agencies) have woefully failed in many countries given increasing pollution and climate change around the world. There should be mandatory and independent environmental audits done by "independent" firms that are subject to penalties and regulations. Companies that pollute should bear the costs of such environmental audits. In Environmental Auditing, *Self-auditing* causes or can cause substantial Antitrust problems such as the following:

1) *Price-Fixing* in the global markets for *emissions-permits* and *carbon-credits*.
2) *Collusion* in the global markets for *emissions-permits* and *carbon-credits*.
3) *Collusion* – among employees of polluting companies; and between such employees and government agencies.
4) *Price-Fixing* for environmental audit fees.
5) *Conflicts-of-Interest* in polluting firms.
6) "*Regulatory Capture*" by polluting firms (who avoid or weaken regulations/ statutes, sometimes in connivance with government employees).
7) Regulatory Fragmentation (too many un-coordinated regulations and regulatory agencies) and Regulatory Failures (inefficient regulation).
8) *Extortion* by government agency employees.

In Environmental Auditing, other problems that may arise from *Self-Auditing* are as follows:

1) *Deadweight Losses* – in environmental auditing; and in the prices and the global markets for CFIs and EMIs.
2) *Truth-Telling Problems* – polluting-company managers and in some cases, government auditors have no or minimal incentives to tell the truth.
3) *Political Costs* – e.g. un-reported environmental pollution increases government's remediation expenditures, and or reduces amounts allocated by the government to social welfare programs. In many democracies and socialist countries, governments and politicians have significant incentives to politicize environmental pollution and Climate Change. Political Lobbying (and its impact on government budgets, legislation and enforcement) remains a big problem in many democracies.

Under the current regulatory regimes in some countries, each of these foregoing problems are very difficult to resolve because polluting-entities' managers' compensation, incentives and career advancement (and the fact that under *Self-Auditing* regulations in some countries, managers don't face any personal losses) compel them to lie, distort information and or collude. Also some governments gain political capital by suppressing environmental pollution and avoiding remediation costs. As of 2019, the U.S. Environmental Protection Agency (EPA) was operating a *Self-Auditing*[32] program which has been heavily criticized by various stakeholders. The US EPA, environmental groups, and other industry players have critiqued Self-Auditing and noted that: i) Self-auditing laws and associated secrecy protections result in polluters violating environmental statutes without suffering any penalties; and ii) Self-Auditing secrecy protections can cause decreased visibility of environmental practices and decisions which will result in increased complacency in compliance.

The fundamental issues are that:

i) Environmental Auditing can have significant financial statement effects and economic *Multiplier Effects*, because it can create significant financial liabilities, reduce the firm's perceived compliance with ESR/CSR principles and reduce the firm's Social Capital.

ii) Stock markets, debt markets and even private-placement markets severely punish companies that report declining, stagnant or below-expectations earnings or cashflow. Thus, Environmental Auditing and the associated Self-Auditing are or can be major channels for *Earnings Management, Asset-quality Management* and *Incentive-Effects Management*.

iii) Many environmental auditing firms are small and are relatively un-regulated and in many countries there no or minimal standards for professionals.

iv) Where government employees perform environmental audits, the *Political Costs* can be substantial because governments and politicians have significant incentives to manipulate environmental audits to improve their Political Capital and Social Capital and reduce amounts allocated to environmental remediation

v) Carbon Taxes, emissions taxes and emissions trading systems (tradable pollution permits/credits and subsidies) around the world have failed[33] woefully as indicated by rising CO_2, global warming and increasing pollution. As currently designed and implemented in many countries, Carbon Taxes, emissions taxes and emissions trading systems around the world are greatly inefficient and harmful but can be improved by efficient Environmental Auditing Mechanisms (e.g. environmental auditors should be subjected to *Auditor-Rotation, Auditor Work Allocation Mechanisms* or *Auditor Liability-Allocation Mechanisms*). Unfortunately in many countries, governments and households typically bear disproportionately larger costs of environmental pollution and climate change problems.

vi) Greater disclosure of environmental pollution may not improve compliance with environmental laws, but it provides: 1) necessary data for policy making; 2) better foundation for mechanisms such as Carbon Taxes, emissions taxes and emissions trading systems (tradable pollution permits/credits and subsidies); 3) some incentives for companies and government agencies to comply; 4) a foundation for imposing deterrent taxes which can be more effective compared to the destructive *"pollute-as-long-as-you-can-pay" mentality* (in companies, households and government agencies) that is implicit in Carbon Taxes, emissions taxes and emissions trading systems (tradable pollution permits/credits and subsidies); and which doesn't provide effective incentives to eliminate (not just reduce) pollution.

vii) Its clear that taxation/levies alone won't solve environmental pollution and waste problems, and they should be supplemented by the following measures:

1) Annual or semi-annual "*Pollution Audits*", "*Carbon-Credit Audits*" and "*Climate Change Audits*" of all polluting companies and government agencies.

2) Increased penalties, monetary fines and jail sentences for fraud or mis-representation by persons/companies and government employees.

3) A "*Constitutionally-Credible Shut-Down Operations*" program wherein any company or government agency that exceeds its pre-set environmental pollution or waste management limit will be shut down by the government. This is somewhat similar to the US FSOC's (USA) powers to take over any company that constitutes significant financial stability risks in the USA – but Nwogugu (2015b) noted that the US FSOC's orderly liquidation powers are un-constitutional.

See the comments in Sikka and Hampton (2005); Konrad Adeneaur Stiftung (2017); Condon and Sinha (2013); Asia Investor Group On Climate Change (2017); and Tang and Demmeritt (2018).[34] Thorwaldsson (Jan. 29, 2019) explained how *Income Inequality* can increase Climate-change and Environmental Pollution problems. On mechanisms that can explain the effects of *Inequality* on environmental deterioration, see Berthe and Elie (2015). On environmental pollution, effects of inadequate/inefficient Environmental Auditing and the relationship between Environmental Pollution and *Inequality*, see the comments in: Helm (2009); Tanuro (2008); Vlachou and Pantelias (2017); Zeng, Weishaar and Vedder (2018); Antimiani et al. (2013); Sijm, Neuhoff and Chen (2006); Frondel, Schmidt and Vance (2012); Grubb et al. (2015); Goulder and Stavins (2011); Monjon and Quirion (2011); Weishaar (2014); Pang and Duan (2016); Schneider, Kollmuss and Lazarus (2015); Tynkkynen (2014); Wang, Teng, Zhou and Cai (2017); Berthe and Elie (2015); Romer (1983); Furceri, Loungani and Zdzienicka (2018); and Kerr and Duscha (2014).

See the charts and tables in the following documents:

i) Trends in Disposals of Plastic Waste Around the World; China and Other Asian Countries Have Collectively Become the Main Importers of Paper Waste; and G7 Countries Generate Most of the Plastic and Paper Waste in the World (2018) – www.ft.com/content/360e2524-d71a-11e8-a854-33d6f82e62f8.

ii) Some companies that cause greenhouse gas emissions and the locations of their headquarters (this table doesn't include other polluting companies that are mentioned in this chapter) – https://decolonialatlas.wordpress.com/2019/04/27/names-and-locations-of-the-top-100-people-killing-the-planet/?fbclid=IwAR18_6rl4gVsLENbMmZS0P9BVLAdWk8rgjEKMbrVZvkCVAhOWFL45yUuUwY.

iii) Hook and Reed (Oct. 24, 2018).

Notes

1 *See*: Press, G. (2019). Four Observations from Recent Surveys About the State-of-Artificial Intelligence (AI). *Forbes*, https://www.forbes.com/sites/gilpress/2019/02/28/4-observations-from-recent-surveys-about-the-state-of-artificial-intelligence-ai/#401434114e7a.
   See: Nguyen, C. (2016). Chinese Restaurants Are Replacing Waiters with Robots. *Business Insider*, http://www.businessinsider.com/chinese-restaurant-robot-waiters-2016-7/.
   See: Mozur, P. (2019). One Month, 500,000 Face Scans: How China Is Using A.I. to Profile a Minority. *The New York Times*.
   See: Dafoe, Allan (2018). *AI Governance: A Research Agenda*.
2 *See*: Chatterjee et al. (2015); Yakovenko and Rosser (2009); Boghosian, Devitt-Lee and Wang (2016); Bagatella-Flores et al. (2015); Li and Boghosian (2017, 2014); Bejan and Errera (2017); Smerlak (2016); Weisbuch and Louzoun (2013); Chatterjee, Ghosh and Chakrabarti (2017) and Eliazar (2016).
3 *See*: Scheffer et al. (2017); Devitt-Lee et al. (2018); Vitali, Glattfelder and Battiston (2011); Berman, Shapira and Ben-Jacob (2015); Tavoni et al. (2011) and Berman, Ben-Jacob and Shapira (2016).
4 *See*: Stiglitz (2015).
5 *See*: Benhabib, Bisin and Zhu (2011) and Cagetti and De Nardi (2008).
6 *See*: Kopczuk (2015); Stiglitz (2012); Atkinson (2015); Ghatak (2015); Milanovic (2016); Cingano (2014) and Piketty and Saez (2014).
7 *See*: Ballow, J., Thomas, R. & Roos, G. (Accenture) (2004). *Future Value: The $7 Trillion Challenge*. www.accenture.com/SiteCollectionDocuments/PDF/manage.pdf. Noting that "Nearly sixty percent of the aggregate value of the US stock market is based on investor expectations of future growth. And because this future value tends to be concentrated in industries and companies that are built on intangible assets, it is critical to find better ways to recognize, report and manage these assets.
   See: Hulten, C. (2008). *Intangible Capital and the "Market to Book Value" Puzzle*. www.conference-board.org/pdf_free/workingpapers/E-0029-08-WP.pdf. The conference Board – Economics Program Working Paper Series. Also see: http://raw.rutgers.edu/docs/intangibles/Papers/Intangible%20Capital%20and%20the%20Market%20to%20Book%20ValuePuzzle.pdf.
   See: Hassett, K. & Shapiro, R. (2012). *What Ideas Are Worth: The Value of Intellectual Capital and Intangible Assets in the American Economy*. www.sonecon.com/docs/studies/Value_of_Intellectual_Capital_in_American_Economy.pdf. Noting that "The value of the intangible assets – which includes intellectual capital plus economic competencies – in the U.S. economy totals an estimated $14.5 trillion in 2011. . . . The ten industries whose intellectual capital represents at least fifty percent of their market value – the ten most intellectual-capital intensive industries – are media; telecommunications services; automobiles and components; household and personal products; food, beverages and tobacco; commercial and professional services; software and services; healthcare equipment and services; pharmaceuticals, biotech and life sciences; and consumer services."
   See: Bond, S. & Cummins, J. *The Stock Market and Investment in the New Economy: Some Tangible Facts and Intangible Fictions*. www.brookings.edu/~/media/Projects/BPEA/Spring%202000/2000a_bpea_bond.PDF.
   See: OCEAN TOMO (2015). *2015 Annual Study of Intangible Asset Market Value*. https://www.oceantomo.com/blog/2015/03-05-ocean-tomo-2015-intangible-asset-market-value/ (noting that as of 2015, Intangible Assets accounted for about 87 percent of the stock market values of S&P 500 companies).
8 *See*: IAAO. (2016). *Understanding Intangible Assets and Real Estate: A Guide for Real Property Valuation Professionals*. www.iaao.org/library/2017_Intangibles_web.pdf.

9 *See*: www.cpacanada.ca/en/members-area/profession-news/2015/june/the-10-worst-corporate-accounting-scandals.
   See: www.accounting-degree.org/scandals/.

10 *See*: *2017 Bankruptcies: The Biggest Names and Trends*, January 25, 2018. www.creditriskmonitor.com/blog/2017-bankruptcies-biggest-names-and-trends.
   See: *Twenty-Two Largest Bankruptcies in World History*, February 3, 2010. www.instantshift.com/2010/02/03/22-largest-bankruptcies-in-world-history/. This list of largest corporate bankruptcies in descending order as of 2010 included the following: Lehman Brothers (USA; Bankruptcy Date was 2008; Assets were $691 billion); Washington Mutual (USA; Bankruptcy Date was 2008; Assets were $327.9 billion); Worldcom (USA; Bankruptcy Date was July 21, 2002; Assets were $103.9 billion); General Motors (USA; Bankruptcy Date was 2009; Assets were $91 billion); CIT Group (USA; Bankruptcy Date was 2009; Assets were $71 billion); Enron (USA; Bankruptcy Date was 2001; Assets were $65.5 billion); Conseco (USA; Bankruptcy Date was 2002; Assets were $61 billion); Chrysler LLC (USA; Bankruptcy Date was April 30, 2009; Assets were $39 billion); Thornburg Mortgage (USA; Bankruptcy Date was 2009; Assets were $36.5 billion); Pacific Gas & Electric (USA; Bankruptcy Date was 2001; Assets were $36.1 billion); Texaco (USA; Bankruptcy Date was 1987; Assets were $34.9 billion); Financial Corporation Of America (USA; Bankruptcy Date was September 9, 1988; Assets were $33.8 billion); Refco (USA; Bankruptcy Date was October 10, 2005; Assets were $33.3 billion); IndyMac Bancorp (USA; Bankruptcy Date was July 31, 2008; Assets were $32.7 billion); Global Crossing (USA; Bankruptcy Date – January 28, 2002; Assets – $30.1 billion); Bank Of New England Corp. (USA; Bankruptcy Date was 1991; Assets were $29.7 billion); General Growth Properties (USA; Bankruptcy Date was April 16, 2009; Assets were $29.5 billion); Lyondell Chemical Company (USA subsidiary of LyondellBasell Industries) (Netherlands; Bankruptcy Date – 2009; Assets – $29.3 billion); Calpine Corporation (USA; Bankruptcy Date was December 20, 2005; Assets were $27.2 billion); New Century Financial Corporation (USA; Bankruptcy Date was 2007; Assets were $26.1 billion); UAL Corporation (USA; Bankruptcy Date was 2002; Assets were $25.1 billion); Delta Airlines (USA; Bankruptcy Date wa September 2005; Assets were $21.8 billion).
   See: *The Running List of 2018 Retail Bankruptcies – Retailers Filed for Bankruptcy at a Record Rate Last Year and That Trend Continues in 2018. Here's a look at which retailers have filed plans to restructure, find a buyer or liquidate through Chapter-11*, April 9, 2018. www.retaildive.com/news/the-running-list-of-2018-retail-bankruptcies/516864/.
   See: *Here Are the Eighteen Biggest Bankruptcies of the 'Retail Apocalypse' of 2017*, December 20, 2017. Kate Taylor. www.pulse.ng/bi/strategy/strategy-here-are-the-18-biggest-bankruptcies-of-the-retail-apocalypse-of-2017-id7755124.html.
   See: Dun & Bradstreet. (2017). *Global Bankruptcy Report 2017*. https://dnb.ru/media/entry/56/217433_Global_Bankruptcy_Report_2017_9-20-17.pdf.
   See: The great recession's twenty five biggest bankruptcies. *Forbes*. www.forbes.com/forbes/welcome/?toURL=https%3A//www.forbes.com/pictures/eegi45llhh/the-great-recessions-25-biggest-bankruptcies-2/&refURL=https%3A//www.google.com.ng/&referrer=https%3A//www.google.com.ng/.

11 *See*: The next billion-dollar startups – 2017. *Forbes*, September 26, 2017. www.forbes.com/sites/susanadams/2017/09/26/the-next-billion-dollar-startups-2017/#784a36e04447. This list of startups (most of whom raised $10-$200 million of capital in various startup phases) includes: BetterCloud; Blend; Brighthealth; Cohesity; Farmers Business Network; Flexport; Ginkgo Bioworks; Fundbox; Jive Communications; Interactions; LessaSleep; Livongo; Looker; Optoro; orbital Insight; Outreach; PillPack; Plaid; Postmates; SeatGeek; Segment; ServiceTrain; Spire; Vlocity; and Zola.

See: These are the most valuable start-ups in the world. *The Telegraph* (UK). www.telegraph.co.uk/finance/picture-galleries/11904378/These-are-the-most-valuable-start-ups-in-the-world.html.

See: The fifteen most valuable startups in the world. *Inc.com*, October 2014. www.inc.com/oscar-raymundo/most-valuable-startups-in-the-world.html.

See: These Are the Most Successful Startups in the World, May 3, 2018. www.dailyinfographic.com/these-are-the-most-successful-startups-in-the-world. This article states in part "There are currently 214 (two hundred and fourteen) "unicorns," or privately-held startups worth more than $1 billion (one billion US dollars). While every company that qualifies as a unicorn is wildly successful, some are doing better than others. Tech giant *Uber* is at the top of the list, with a staggering net worth of $68 billion dollars. Most of the companies are tech-related, too. Healthcare and real estate both have unicorn companies, but it's nowhere near the number of successful tech companies. Taking a look at the map, it's clear that unicorns are spread disproportionately among countries. The United States and China, the world's biggest economic superpowers, are home to the highest number of unicorns. In fact, the top ten most valuable startups all come from either the U.S. or China, and those ten are have forty percent of the total worth of all 214 unicorns combined.".

12 See: *Thirty-Two (32) States Now Officially Bankrupt: $37.8 Billion Borrowed from Treasury to Fund Unemployment; CA, MI, NY Worst*. www.zerohedge.com/article/32-states-now-officially-bankrupt-378-billion-borrowed-treasury-fund-unemployment-ca-mi-ny-w.

See: Bankrupt Cities, Municipalities List and Map, July 2013. www.governing.com/gov-data/municipal-cities-counties-bankruptcies-and-defaults.html.

13 *See*: Gillis, P. *Longtop Financial Technologies Case Study – Accounting fraud in China*. Peking University's Guanghua School of Management. www.paulgillis.org/longtop_financial_technolog.pdf.

See: Gillis, P. *Auditing Cash in China*. Peking University's Guanghua School of Management. www.chinaaccountingblog.com/weblog/auditing-cash-in-china.html.

See: Norris, F. (May 26, 2011). *The Audacity of Chinese Frauds*. www.nytimes.com/2011/05/27/business/27norris.html?pagewanted=all&_r=0.

See: https://en.wikipedia.org/wiki/Apple_Pay; and www.apple.com/apple-pay/.

See: Citron Reports on Longtop Financial (NYSE:LFT). www.paulgillis.org/citronresearchcom__citron.pdf.

See: Hempton, J. (Bronte Capital) (May 20, 2011). *Longtop Financial: Lessons in the Morphology of Sin, Loss of Virginity, and Your 17 Year Old Daughter*. www.businessinsider.com/john-hempton-longtop-financial-2011-5. Also see www.brontecapital.com/files/sma/Client_Letter_201105.pdf.

See: SEC Charges China-Based Longtop Financial Technologies for Deficient Filings – For Immediate Release – 2011–241, November 10, 2011. Washington, DC.

14 *See: Huge Pension Fund Deficits Are a Global Crisis in Waiting*, February 16, 2018. http://theconversation.com/huge-pension-fund-deficits-are-a-global-crisis-in-waiting-88420. The article stated in part: "The pension industry is already in a deep financial crisis and could well be the trigger for another global financial and economic meltdown. This has largely been overlooked. . . . According to a Citibank report from 2016, the twenty largest OECD countries alone have a US$78 trillion shortfall in funding pay-as-you-go and defined benefit public pensions' obligations. This shortfall is far from trivial. It is equivalent to about 1.8 times the value of these countries' collective national debt."

See: Public Policy: The Time Bomb Inside Public Pension Plans, August 2018. https://knowledge.wharton.upenn.edu/article/the-time-bomb-inside-public-pension-plans/.

See: Mooney, A. & Smith, P. (December 2, 2018). Global retirement crisis is main threat to investment industry, warn chiefs. *Financial Times*. www.ft.com/content/380e322e-c83b-36cc-8d7a-222ad9219a3b.

See: Chan, S. (June 4, 2016). World faces pensions crisis, warns OECD. *The Telegraph* (UK). www.telegraph.co.uk/business/2016/06/04/world-faces-pensions-crisis-warns-oecd/.

See: Brown, A. (January 13, 2019). The pension fund problem just got much worse: A simple extrapolation of the recent trend lines suggest a crisis around 2023, as assets are wiped out even if returns rebound. *Bloomberg*. www.bloomberg.com/opinion/articles/2019-01-13/pension-fund-crisis-has-a-start-date.

15 Davidson, K. (April 22, 2019). Social security costs to exceed income in 2020, trustees say – The trust fund to be depleted by 2035, they add. *Wall Street Journal*. www.wsj.com/articles/social-security-trust-fund-to-be-depleted-in-2035-trustees-say-11555946113?mod=e2fb&fbclid=IwAR3vZb24KIyRAt2-H_27reRldilY_aljsXI3ulHxZKw7NUUV_t_eKp9CEM.

16 *See*: CEOs earn an employees entire salary in just days: New research by Small BusinessPrices.co.uk has revealed how much CEOs earn compared to their employees around the world. *CEO Today Magazine*, April 1, 2019. www.ceotodaymagazine.com/2019/04/ceos-earn-an-employees-entire-salary-in-just-days/.

17 *See*: Mishel, L. & Schieder, J. (August 2018). *CEO Compensation Surged in 2017*. www.epi.org/publication/ceo-compensation-surged-in-2017/.

18 *See*: Edgecliffe-Johnson, A. (April 16, 2019). US companies reveal pay gap between bosses and workers: Among 100 chiefs analysed, 11 made more than 1,000 times that of the median employee. *Financial Times*. www.ft.com/content/1ee790f0-5da8-11e9-b285-3acd5d43599e?fbclid=IwAR1UFzli6LFUCW8p6kc0RAjGjtEQOZId3e3fV-1XmTZH2cKbrqoFi93otfw.

19 *See*: Lifshey, D. (October 14, 2018). *The CEO Pay Ratio: Data and Perspectives from the 2018 Proxy Season*. Pearl Meyer & Partners, LLC. https://corpgov.law.harvard.edu/2018/10/14/the-ceo-pay-ratio-data-and-perspectives-from-the-2018-proxy-season/.

20 *See*: Verkhivker, A. (June 4, 2018). *Housing Is the Real Culprit for America's Inequality*. www.forbes.com/sites/alexverkhivker/2018/06/04/housing-is-the-real-culprit-for-americas-inequality/#84b046639b96.

See: Kuhn, M., Schularick, M. & Steins, U. (April 29, 2019). *Wealth Inequality in America: A Race Between the Stock and the Housing Market*. https://promarket.org/wealth-inequality-in-america-race-between-the-stock-and-the-housing-market/.

See: Florida, R. (April 13, 2018). *Is Housing Inequality the Main Driver of Economic Inequality? A Growing Body of Research Suggests That Inequality in the Value of Americans' Homes Is a Major Factor – Perhaps the Key Factor – in the Country's Economic Divides*. www.citylab.com/equity/2018/04/is-housing-inequality-the-main-driver-of-economic-inequality/557984/.

21 *See*: Poethig, E. (2014). *One in Four: America's Housing Assistance Lottery*. www.urban.org/urban-wire/one-four-americas-housing-assistance-lottery.

22 *See*: Florida, R. (April 17, 2015). *The U.S. Spends Far More on Homeowner Subsidies Than It Does on Affordable Housing*. www.citylab.com/equity/2015/04/the-us-spends-far-more-on-homeowner-subsidies-than-it-does-on-affordable-housing/390666/.

See: Collinson, R., Ellen, I. & Ludwig, J. (April 2015). *Low-Income Housing Policy*. NBER Working Paper No. 21071.

23 Gabler, N. (May 2016). *The Secret Shame of Middle-Class Americans: Nearly Half of Americans Would Have Trouble Finding $400 to Pay for an Emergency. I'm One of Them*. www.theatlantic.com/magazine/archive/2016/05/my-secret-shame/476415/?fbclid=IwAR1wpJzqRHWDdZaEbc_S4mA82WGap2uBw8hms_CiOQjdZyPsHwmhYyNzSYQ&utm_campaign=the-atlantic&utm_content=5c402b7d4b738500015134cc_ta&utm_medium=social&utm_source=facebook.

24 *See*: Stuart, E. (August 19, 2015). China has almost wiped out urban poverty. Now it must tackle inequality. *The Guardian*. www.theguardian.com/business/economics-blog/2015/aug/19/china-poverty-inequality-development-goals.

   See: China, the millennium development goals, and the post-2015 development agenda. *Cn.undp.org*. www.cn.undp.org/content/dam/china/docs/Publications/UNDP-CH_discussionpaper-MDGPost2015.pdf.

   See: Poverty Profile of People's Republic of China. Asian Development Bank (ADB). www.adb.org/publications/poverty-profile-peoples-republic-china.

25 *See: Poverty Around the World – Global Issues*. www.globalissues.org/article/4/poverty-around-the-world#WorldBanksPovertyEste.

   See: Fu, J. (March 2, 2010). Urban-rural income gap widest since reform. *China Daily*. www.chinadaily.com.cn/china/2010-03/02/content_9521611.htm.

   See: Canaves, S. (April 13, 2009). Facts about poverty in China challenge conventional wisdom. *The Wall Street Journal*. https://blogs.wsj.com/chinarealtime/2009/04/13/facts-about-poverty-in-china-challenge-conventional-wisdom/.

   See: The Rural Poor Shunned by China's Top Schools. *Newsweek.com*, August 21, 2010. www.newsweek.com/2010/08/21/the-rural-poor-are-shut-out-of-china-s-top-schools.html.

26 *See*: LaoHu Economics Blog (Sept. 13, 2015). "Should We Believe China's GDP Data?". See laohueconomics.com/new-china-economics-blog/2015/9/11/should-we-believe-chinas-economic-data.

   See: Pi, X. (Jan. 18, 2017). "China's Economic Data: The Taste of Mystery Meat." Bloomberg News QuickTake. See www.bloomberg.com/quicktake/chinas-economic-data.

   See: International Monetary Fund. World Economic Outlook Database 2016. See www.imf.org/external/pubs/ft/weo/2016/01/weodata/index.aspx.

   See: Kawa, Luke (Nov. 2, 2015). "Six Ways to Gauge How Fast China's Economy Is Actually Growing." Bloomberg. See www.bloomberg.com/news/articles/2015-11-02/six-ways-to-gauge-how-fast-china-s-economy-is-actually-growing.

27 *See*: MacDonald and Hasmath (2019); and Hasmath and MacDonald (2018).

   See: Samuel, S. (August 28, 2018). *China Is Treating Islam Like a Mental Illness: The Country Is Putting Muslims in Internment Camps – and Causing Real Psychological Damage in the Process*. www.theatlantic.com/international/archive/2018/08/china-pathologizing-uighur-muslims-mental-illness/568525/?fbclid=IwAR18d845Jdv NQEXq5ccLaUGZusDJB2do51UP8NwgL5gcOFxCNbbM8XncNC8.

28 *See*: Malone, A. & Jones, R. (December 6, 2010). Revealed: Inside the Chinese suicide sweatshop where workers toil in 34-hour shifts to make your iPod. *Daily Mail* (London). www.dailymail.co.uk/news/article-1285980/Revealed-Inside-Chinese-suicide-sweatshop-workers-toil-34-hour-shifts-make-iPod.html.

   See: Carlson, N. (April 7, 2010). What it's like to work in China's gadget sweatshops where your iPhones and iPads are made. *Business Insider*. www.businessinsider.com/what-its-like-to-work-if-chinas-gadget-sweatshops-where-your-iphones-and-ipads-are-made-2010–4?utm_source=Daily+Buzz&utm_campaign=81432d578c-nl_emv_db_04082010_a&utm_medium=email.

   See: The Foxconn Suicides. *wsj.com*, May 28, 2010. WSJ opinion. http://online.wsj.com/article/SB10001424052748704269204575270031332376238.html?mod=googlenews_wsj.

   See: Jamie Fullerton (Jan. 7, 2018). "Suicide at Chinese iPhone factory reignites concern over working conditions". https://www.telegraph.co.uk/news/2018/01/07/suicide-chinese-iphone-factory-reignites-concern-working-conditions/.

   See: Apple suppliers maintain tight security to avoid leaks: Foxconn said to have "special status" in China. *MacNN*, February 17, 2010. www.macnn.com/articles/10/02/17/foxconn.said.to.have.special.status.in.china/.

See: *China Tech Factory Conditions Fuel Suicides*. AFP/Beijing. November 14, 2018. https://www.khaleejtimes.com/international/rest-of-asia/china-tech-factory-conditions-fuel-suicides.

See: *Apple – Supplier Responsibility*. Apple. http://images.apple.com/supplier responsibility/pdf/L418102A_SR_2010Report_FF.pdf.

29 *See*: More than 77% of India's wealth is concentrated in the hands of just 10% of its population – and it shows that its economic divide is only widening. BI India Bureau, October 23, 2018. www.businessinsider.in/more-than-77-of-indias-wealth-is-con centrated-in-the-hands-of-just-10-of-its-population-and-it-shows-that-its-economic-divide-is-only-widening/articleshow/66328504.cms. This article states in part: "With a total wealth of $6 trillion in mid-2018, India's 10% elites own 77.4% wealth. . . . Among the total adult population of 850 million, 91% people have wealth lower than $10,000. . . . The report points out the increasing economic divide in India, where poorest 60% are left out with 4.7% wealth in the nation."

See: Income inequality gets worse; India's top 1% bag 73% of the country's wealth, says Oxfam: In the period between 2006 and 2015, ordinary workers saw their incomes rise by an average of just 2% a year while billionaire wealth rose almost six times faster. *BusinessToday.in*, January 30, 2019 www.businesstoday.in/current/economy-politics/oxfam-india-wealth-report-income-inequality-richests-poor/story/268541.html.

30 *See*: Hook, L. & Reed, J. (October 24, 2018). Why the world's recycling system stopped working – China's refusal to become the west's dumping ground is forcing the world to face up to a waste crisis. *Financial Times* (UK). www.ft.com/content/360e2524-d71a-11e8-a854-33d6f82e62f8.

31 *See*: Malone & Jones (December 6, 2010) (supra).

See: Carlson (April 7, 2010) (supra).

See: *The Foxconn Suicides* (May 28, 2010) (supra).

See: Dean, J. & Tsai, T. (May 27, 2010) (supra).

32 *See*: *Environmental Auditing*. www.inc.com/encyclopedia/environmental-audit.html.

33 *See*: Clemente, J. (October 1, 2015). Cap-and-trade is fraught with fraud. *Forbes*. www.forbes.com/sites/judeclemente/2015/10/01/cap-and-trade-green-climate-fund-are-fraught-with-fraud/#5efb15f54940.

See: Haley, B. (March 13, 2017). Political manipulation could Derail Nova Scotia's cap-and-trade system. *Halifax Examiner* (Canadian Newspaper). www.halifaxexaminer.ca/environment/political-manipulation-could-derail-nova-scotias-cap-and-trade-system/.

See: Goldstein, L. (July 23, 2016). Call it cap-and-fraud. *Toronto Sun* (Canadian Newspaper). https://torontosun.com/2016/07/23/call-it-cap-and-fraud/wcm/7635fae3-866b-430c-97b9-24b212458188. This article stated in part: "A carbon credit entitles the bearer to emit one tonne of industrial carbon dioxide or equivalent, on the theory another emitter didn't. Since CO2 is a colourless, odourless gas, it's relatively easy to commit fraud. Interpol noted this can include: 'Fraudulent manipulation of measurements to claim more carbon credits from a project than were actually obtained; sale of carbon credits that either do not exist or belong to someone else; false or misleading claims with respect to the environmental or financial benefits of carbon market investments; exploitation of weak regulations in the carbon market to commit financial crimes, such as money laundering, securities fraud or tax fraud; computer hacking/phishing to steal carbon credits and personal information'. . . . The Stockholm Environment Institute reported last year that almost 75% (seventy five percent) of carbon credits generated by Russia and Ukraine could be fraudulent. There have been similar findings with regard to China, India and elsewhere. The public pays the cost because carbon pricing increases the price of most goods and service, since most are made using fossil fuel energy. And if a carbon credit is fraudulent, there's no lowering of emissions because of it."

34 *See*: Tang and Demmeritt (2018).

Bibliography

Acemoglu, D., Johnson, S. & Robinson, J. (2005). Institutions as a fundamental cause of long-run growth. Chapter in: Aghion, P. & Durlauf, S., eds., *Handbook of Economic Growth* (North-Holland, Amsterdam), Vol. 1A, pp. 385–472.

Acemoglu, D. & Restrepo, P. (2018). The race between man and machine: Implications of technology for growth, factor shares, and employment. *American Economic Review*, 108(6), 1488–1542.

Adam, H. & Galinsky, A. (2012). Enclothed cognition. *Journal of Experimental Social Psychology*, 48(4), 918–925.

Afridi, F., Li, S. & Ren, Y. (2015). Social identity and inequality: The impact of China's Hukou system. *Journal of Public Economics*, 123, 17–29.

Agarwal, S., Alok, S. et al. (2018). *Banking the Unbanked: What do 255 Million New Bank Accounts Reveal about Financial Access?* http://w3.bm.ust.hk/fina/2017symposium/paper/Sumit_JDY%20draft%20%20%20v17_November_12_final.pdf.

Agrawal, T. (2014). Educational inequality in rural and urban India. *International Journal of Educational Development*, 34, 11–19.

Albouy, D. & Zabek, M. (January 2016). *Housing Inequality*. NBER Working Paper No. 21916.

Aldabe, B., Anderson, R., Lyly-Yrjänäinen, M., Parent-Thirion, A., Vermeylen, G., Kelleher, C.C. & Niedhammer, I. (2011). Contribution of material, occupational, and psychosocial factors in the explanation of social inequalities in health in 28 countries in Europe. *Journal of Epidemiology & Community Health*, 65, 1123–1131.

Almås, I. & Kjelsrud, A. (2017). Rags and riches: Relative prices, non-homothetic preferences, and inequality in India. *World Development*, 97, 102–121.

Alonso-García, J. & Devolder, P. (2016). Optimal mix between pay-as-you-go and funding for DC pension schemes in an overlapping generations model. *Insurance: Mathematics and Economics*, 70, 224–236.

Anderlini, L., Gerardi, D. & Lagunoff, R. (2016). Auditing, disclosure, and verification in decentralized decision problems. *Journal of Economic Behavior & Organization*, 131A, 393–408.

Anderson, H., Chi, J. & Wang, Q. (2017). Political ties and VC exits: Evidence from China. *China Economic Review*, 44, 48–66.

André, Q., Carmon, Z. et al. (2018). Consumer choice and autonomy in the age of Artificial Intelligence and big data. *Customer Needs & Solutions*, 5(1–2), 28–37.

Antimiani, A., Costantini, V., Martini, C., Salvatici, L. & Tommasino, M.C. (2013). Assessing alternative solutions to carbon leakage. *Energy Economics*, 36, 299–311.

Apostolakis, G., Kraanen, F. & van Dijk, G. (2016). Examining pension beneficiaries' willingness to pay for a socially responsible and impact investment portfolio: A case study in the Dutch healthcare sector. *Journal of Behavioral and Experimental Finance*, 11, 27–43.

Araújo, T. & Mendes, V. (2009). Innovation and self-organization in a multi-agent model. *Advances in Complex Systems*, 12(2), 233–253. https://doi.org/10.1142/S0219525909002180.

Ashraf, B. (2017). Political institutions and bank risk-taking behavior. *Journal of Financial Stability*, 29, 13–35.

Asia Investor Group on Climate Change. (2017). *Connecting Commodities, Investors, Climate, and the Land – a Toolkit for Institutional Investors*. http://aigcc.net/wp-content/uploads/2017/10/IGCC-Sustainable-Land-Use.pdf.

Atkinson, A. (2015). *Inequality: What Can Be Done?* (Harvard University Press, Cambridge, MA).

Bagatella-Flores, N., Rodríguez-Achach, M., Coronel-Brizio, H.F. & Hernández-Montoya, A.R. (2015). Wealth distribution of simple exchange models coupled with extremal dynamics. *Physica-A*, 417, 168–175.

Bala, M. (March 2018). *GST in India: A Critical Review*. Conference on: *GST: Benefits and Impact on Indian Economy*. Haryana, India.

Beeghley, L. (2015). *Structure of Social Stratification in the United States* (Routledge, London).

Beer, J., Fisk, A. & Rogers, W. (2014). Toward a framework for levels of robot autonomy in human-robot interaction. *Journal of Human-Robot Interaction*, 3(2), 74–102.

Beetsma, R. & Romp, W. (2016). Intergenerational risk sharing. Chapter 6 in: *Handbook of the Economics of Population Aging*, Volume 1, pp. 211–380 (Elsevier, The Netherlands).

Bejan, A. & Errera, M. (2017). Wealth inequality: The physics basis. *Journal of Applied Physics*, 121(12), 124903.

Belz, T., von Hagen, D. & Steffens, C. (2019). Taxes and firm size: Political cost or political power? *Journal of Accounting Literature*, 42, 1–28.

Benhabib, J., Bisin, A. & Zhu, S. (2011). The distribution of wealth and fiscal policy in economies with finitely lived agents. *Econometrica*, 79, 123–157.

Bennett, G., Scharoun-Lee, M. & Tucker-Seeley, R. (2009). Will the public's health fall victim to the home foreclosure epidemic? *PLoS Med*, 6(6), e1000087. https://doi.org/10.1371/journal.pmed.1000087.

Berg, A., Buffie, E. & Zanna, L. (2016). Robots, growth, and inequality. *Finance & Development*, 32, 10–13.

Berman, Y., Ben-Jacob, E. & Shapira, Y. (2016). The dynamics of wealth inequality and the effect of income distribution. *PLoS One*, 11(4), e0154196.

Berman, Y., Shapira, Y. & Ben-Jacob, E. (2015). Modeling the origin and possible control of the wealth inequality surge. *PLOS One*, 10, e0130181.

Bernanke, B. & Olson, P. (2016). *China's Transparency Challenges*. Brookings Institution, USA. See www.brookings.edu/blog/ben-bernanke/2016/03/08/chinas-transparency-challenges.

Berthe, A. & Elie, L. (2015). Mechanisms explaining the impact of economic inequality on environmental deterioration. *Ecological Economics*, 116, 191–200.

Bhattacharjee, A., Shin, J., Subramanian, C. & Swaminathan, S. (2017). Healthcare investment and income inequality. *Journal of Health Economics*, 56, 163–177.

Bijoy, K. (2018). *Financial Inclusion in India and PMJDY: A Critical Review*. Proceedings of the First International Conference on Information Technology and Knowledge Management pp. 39–46. ISSN 2300-5963 ACSIS, Vol. 14. https://annals-csis.org/Volume_14/drp/pdf/32.pdf.

Bilala, U. & Kaufman, J. (2017). The theft of well-being: A comment on Zunzunegui et al. *Gaceta Sanitaria*, 31(5), 363–364.

Boghosian, B. (2014). Kinetics of wealth and the Pareto law. *Physical Review-E*, 89, 042804–042825.

Boghosian, B., Devitt-Lee, A. & Wang, H. (2016). *The Growth of Oligarchy in a Yard-Sale Model of Asset Exchange – A Logistic Equation for Wealth Condensation*. In Proceedings of the 1st International Conference on Complex Information Systems (COMPLEXIS 2016), 187–193.

Booker, K. (2018). Can clients of economically dependent auditors benefit from voluntary audit firm rotation? An experiment with lenders. *Research In Accounting Regulation*, 30, 63–67.

Bostrom, N. (2014). *Superintelligence: Paths, Dangers, Strategies* (Oxford, Oxford University Press).

Boubakri, N., El Ghoul, S. & Saffar, W. (2015). Firm growth and political institutions. *Journal of Multinational Financial Management*, 31, 104–125.

Brandau, M., Endenich, C., Trapp, R. & Hoffjan, A. (2013). Institutional drivers of conformity – Evidence for management accounting from Brazil and Germany. *International Business Review*, 22(2), 466–479.

Braveman, P. & Gottlieb, L. (2014). The social determinants of health: It's time to consider the causes of the causes. *Public Health Reports*, 129(1–2), 19–31.

Broeders, D. & Chen, A. (2010). Pension regulation and the market value of pension liabilities: A contingent claims analysis using Parisian options. *Journal of Banking & Finance*, 34(6), 1201–1214.

Brounen, D. & Eichholtz, P. (2005). Corporate real estate ownership implications: International performance evidence. *Journal of Real Estate Finance & Economics*, 30, 429–445.

Bushman, R. & Piotroski, J. (2006). Financial reporting incentives for conservative accounting: The influence of legal and political institutions. *Journal of Accounting and Economics*, 42(1–2), 107–148.

Cagetti, M. & De Nardi, M. (2008). Wealth inequality: Data and models. *Macroeconomic Dynamics*, 12, 285–313.

Calvano, E., Calzolari, G., Denicolò, V. & Pastorello, S. (February 2019). Artificial intelligence, algorithmic pricing, and collusion. *Vox*. https://voxeu.org/article/artificial-intelligence-algorithmic-pricing-and-collusion.

Calvo, E. & Williamson, J. (2008). Old-age pension reform and modernization pathways: Lessons for China from Latin America. *Journal of Aging Studies*, 22(1), 74–87.

Chatterjee, A., Chakrabarti, A., Ghosh, A., Chakraborti, A. & Nandi, T.K. (2016). Invariant features of spatial inequality in consumption: The case of India. *Physica A: Statistical Mechanics and its Applications*, 442, 169–181.

Chatterjee, A., Ghosh, A. & Chakrabarti, B. (2017). *Socio*-economic inequality: Relationship between Gini and Kolkata indices. *Physica A: Statistical Mechanics and its Applications*, 466, 583–595.

Chatterjee, A., Ghosh, A., Inoue, J. & Chakrabarti, B.K. (2015). Social inequality: From data to statistical physics modeling. *Journal of Physics: Conference Series*, 638, 012014.

Chaudhry, N., Yong, H. & Veld, C. (2017). Tax avoidance in response to a decline in the funding status of defined benefit pension plans. *Journal of International Financial Markets, Institutions and Money*, 48, 99–116.

Chen, D., Jiang, D., Liang, S. & Wang, F. (2011). Selective enforcement of regulation. *China Journal of Accounting Research*, 4(1–2), 9–27.

Chen, D., Li, J., Liang, S. & Wang, G. (2011). Macroeconomic control, political costs and earnings management: Evidence from Chinese listed real estate companies. *China Journal of Accounting Research*, 4(3), 91–106.

Chen, F. & Gao, G. (2006). Ownership structure, corporate governance, and fraud: Evidence from China. *Journal of Corporate Finance*, 12, 424–448.

Chen, H. & Jorgensen, B. (2018). Market exit through divestment – the effect of accounting bias on competition. *Management Science*, 64(1), 1–493.

Chen, Q., Kelly, K. & Salterio, S. (2012). Do changes in audit actions and attitudes consistent with increased auditor scepticism deter aggressive earnings management? An experimental investigation. *Accounting, Organizations & Society*, 37(2), 95–115.

Chen, W., Chen, X., Hseih, X. & Song, Z. (2019a). *A Forensic Examination of China's National Accounts*. BPEA Conference Draft, Spring 2019. Brooking Institute, USA. https://www.brookings.edu/bpea-articles/a-forensic-examination-of-chinas-national-accounts/; https://www.brookings.edu/wp-content/uploads/2019/03/BPEA-2019-Forensic-Analysis-China.pdf.

Chen, W., Chen, X., Hseih, C. & Song, Z. (2019b). *A Forensic Examination of China's National Accounts*. BPEA Conference Draft, Spring. Brooking Institute. www.brookings.edu/bpea-articles/a-forensic-examination-of-chinas-national-accounts/;www.brookings.edu/wp-content/uploads/2019/03/BPEA-2019-Forensic-Analysis-China.pdf.

Chen, X., Yao, T., Yu, T. & Zhang, T. (2014). Learning and incentive: A study on analyst response to pension underfunding. *Journal of Banking & Finance*, 45, 26–42.

Chen, Y., Ge, R. & Zolotoy, L. (2017). Do corporate pension plans affect audit pricing? *Journal of Contemporary Accounting & Economics*, 13(3), 322–337.

Cheng, L. & Leung, T. (2016). Government protection, political connection and management turnover in China. *International Review of Economics & Finance*, 45, 160–176.

Cigno, A. (2016). Conflict and cooperation within the family, and between the state and the family, in the provision of old-age security. Chapter 10 in: *Handbook of the Economics of Population Aging*, Volume 1, pp. 609–660 (Elsevier, The Netherlands).

Cingano, F. (2014). *Trends in Income Inequality and Its Impact on Economic Growth*. OECD Social, Employment and Migration Working Papers. dx.doi.org/10.1787/5jxrjncwxv6j-en.

Citi GPS (Citibank). (2016). *The Coming Pensions Crisis: Recommendations for Keeping the Global Pensions System Afloat*. www.agefi.fr/sites/agefi.fr/files/fichiers/2016/03/citi_retraite_hors_bilan_21_mars_1.pdf.

Condon, B. & Sinha, T. (2013). *The Role of Climate Change in Global Economic Governance* (Oxford University Press, Oxford).

Cotti, C. & Simon, D. (2018). The impact of stock market fluctuations on the mental and physical well-being of children. *Economic Inquiry*, 56(2), 1007–1027.

Cottie, C., Dunn, R. &Tefft, N. (2015). The Dow is killing me: Risky health behaviors and the stock market. *Health Economics*, 24(7), 803–821.

Cummings, M. (2017). *Artificial Intelligence and the Future of Warfare* (Chatham House, London, UK).

Demirel, P., Iatridis, K. & Kesidou, E. (2018). The impact of regulatory complexity upon self-regulation: Evidence from the adoption and certification of environmental management systems. *Journal of Environmental Management*, 207, 80–91.

Deng, Y. & Gyourko, J. (1999). *Real Estate Ownership by Non-Real Estate Firms: The Impact on Firm Returns*. www.usc.edu/schools/sppd/lusk/research/pdf/wp_1999_103.pdf.

Devitt-Lee, A., Wang, H., Li, J. & Boghosian, B. (2018). A nonstandard description of wealth concentration in large-scale economies. *SIAM Journal on Applied Mathematics*, 78(2), 996–1008.

Dietvorst, B., Simmons, J. & Massey, C. (2014). Algorithm aversion: People erroneously avoid algorithms after seeing them err. *Journal of Experimental Psychology: General*, 143(6), 1–13.

Dietvorst, B., Simmons, J. & Massey, C. (2016). Overcoming algorithm aversion: People will use imperfect algorithms if they can (even slightly) modify them. *Management Science*, 64(3), 1155–1170.

Dolls, M., Doerrenberg, P., Peichl, A. & Stichnoth, H. (2018). Do retirement savings increase in response to information about retirement and expected pensions? *Journal of Public Economics*, 158, 168–179.

Ebrahim, M., Mathur, I. & Gwilym, R. (2014). Integrating corporate ownership and pension fund structures: A general equilibrium approach. *Journal of Banking & Finance*, 49, 553–569.

Echeverri, M., Abadía-Barrero, C. & Palacios, C. (2017). Work-related illness, work-related accidents, and lack of social security in Colombia. *Social Science & Medicine*, 187, 118–125.

El Ghoul, S., Guedhami, O. & Pittman, J. (2016). Cross-country evidence on the importance of Big Four auditors to equity pricing: The mediating role of legal institutions. *Accounting, Organizations and Society*, 54, 60–81.

Elgar, F. & Aitken, N. (2011). Income inequality, trust and homicide in 33 countries. *European Journal of Public Health*, 21, 241–246.

Eliazar, I. (2016). Harnessing inequality. *Physics Reports*, 649, 1–30.

Elmer. (23 May 2017). *Poverty in the People's Republic of China*. Asian Development Bank. www.adb.org/countries/prc/poverty.

Ezrachi, A. & Stucke, M. (2015). *Artificial Intelligence and collusion: When computers inhibit competition*. Oxford Legal Studies Research Paper No. 18/2015, University of Tennessee Legal Studies Research Paper No. 267.

Falebita, O. & Koul, S. (2018). From developing to sustainable economy: A comparative assessment of India and Nigeria. *Environmental Development*, 25, 130–137.

Feng, J., He, L. & Sato, H. (2011). Public pension and household saving: Evidence from urban China. *Journal of Comparative Economics*, 39(4), 470–485.

Fernald, J., Malkin, I. & Spiegel, M. (March 2013). "*On the Reliability of Chinese Output Figures.*" FRBSF Economic Letter, No. 8, March 25, 2013. See www.frbsf.org/economic-research/publications/economic-letter/2013/march/reliability-chinese-output-figures.

Florişteanu, E. (2013). Repercussions of economic and social factors on pension systems. *Procedia Economics and Finance*, 6, 627–633.

Foltin, C. (2017). The role of federal regulation in state and local governments and the potential impact of new reforms: An assessment of the effectiveness of reporting, disclosure, and funding. *Research in Accounting Regulation*, 29(1), 19–29.

Freudenberg, C., Laub, N. & Sutor, T. (2018). Pension decrement rates across Europe – Are they too low? *The Journal of the Economics of Ageing*, 12, 35–45.

Frondel, M., Schmidt, C. & Vance, C. (2012). Emissions trading: Impact on electricity prices and energy-intensive industries. *Intereconomics*, 47(2), 104–111.

Fung, S., Raman, K. & Zhu, X. (2017). Does the PCAOB international inspection program improve audit quality for non-US-listed foreign clients? *Journal of Accounting and Economics*, 64(1), 15–36.

Furceri, D., Loungani, P. & Zdzienicka, A. (2018). The effects of monetary policy shocks on inequality. *Journal of International Money and Finance*, 85, 168–186.

Furman, J. & Seamans, R. (2018). *AI and the Economy*. NBER Working Paper Series, Cambridge, MA.

Gao, J. (2016). Bypass the lying mouths: How does the CCP tackle information distortion at local levels? *The China Quarterly*, 228, 950–969.

Gerrard, R., Hiabu, M., Kyriakou, I. & Perch Nielsen, J. (2019). Communication and personal selection of pension saver's financial risk. *European Journal of Operational Research*, 274(3), 1102–1111.

Ghatak, M. (2015). Theories of poverty traps and anti-poverty policies. *World Bank Economic Review*, 29(Suppl 1), S77–S105.

Glaeser, E. & Ponzetto, G. (2014). Shrouded costs of government: The political economy of state and local public pensions. *Journal of Public Economics*, 116, 89–105.

Goel, M. (2017). Inequality between and within skill groups: The curious case of India. *World Development*, 93, 153–176.

Gong, Y., Stinebrickner, T. & Stinebrickner, R. (2019). Uncertainty about future income: Initial beliefs and resolution during college. *Quantitative Economics*, 10(2).

Gordon, I. & Gallery, N. (2012). Assessing financial reporting comparability across institutional settings: The case of pension accounting. *The British Accounting Review*, 44(1), 11–20.

Goulder, L. & Stavins, R. (2011). Interactions between state and federal climate change policies. Chapter in: *The Design and Implementation of US Climate Policy* (University of Chicago Press, Chicago), pp. 109–121.

Graham, C. (2008). Fearful asymmetry: The consumption of accounting signs in the Algoma Steel pension bailout. *Accounting, Organizations and Society*, 33(7–8), 756–782.

Grubb, M., Sha, F., Spencer, T., Hughes, N., Zhang, Z. & Agnolucci, P. (2015). A review of Chinese CO2 emission projections to 2030: The role of economic structure and policy. *Climate Policy*, 15(1), S7–S39.

Gungoraydinoglu, A., Çolak, G. & Öztekin, O. (2017). Political environment, financial intermediation costs, and financing patterns. *Journal of Corporate Finance*, 44, 167–192.

Guojonsdottir, G., Kristjansson, M. & Olafsson, O. (2011). Immediate surge in female visits to the cardiac emergency department following the economic collapse in Iceland: An observational study. *Emergency Medicine Journal*, 29(9), 694–698.

Harrington, J. (2018). "Developing Competition Law for Collusion by Autonomous Price-Setting Agents". Working paper.

Hasmath, R. & MacDonald, A. (2018). Beyond special privileges: The discretionary treatment of ethnic minorities in China's welfare system. *Journal of Social Policy*, 47(2), 295–316.

He, G. (2016). Fiscal support and earnings management. *The International Journal of Accounting*, 51(1), 57–84.

Helm, D. (2009). EU climate-change policy – a critique. Chapter in: Helm, D. & Hepburn, C., eds., *The Economics and Politics of Climate Change* (Oxford University Press, Oxford).

Holz, C. (2004). China's Statistical System in Transition: Challenges, Data Problems, and Institutional Innovations. *Review of Income and Wealth*, 50(3), 381–409.

Holz, C. (2014). The quality of China's GDP statistics. *China Economic Review*, 30, 309–338.

Hook, L. & Reed, J. (October 24, 2018). Why the world's recycling system stopped working – China's refusal to become the West's Dumping ground is forcing the world to face up to a waste crisis. *Financial Times*. www.ft.com/content/360e2524-d71a-11e8-a854-33d6f82e62f8.

Houqe, M., Monem, R. & van Zijl, T. (2012). Government quality, auditor choice and adoption of IFRS: A cross country analysis. *Advances in Accounting*, 28(2), 307–316.

Hoynes, H. & Rothstein, J. (2019). *Universal Basic Income in the US and Advanced Countries*. NBER Working Paper Series.

Hughes, J. (2014). A strategic opening for a basic income guarantee in the global crisis being created by AI, robots, desktop manufacturing and biomedicine. *Journal of Evolution and Technology*, 24(1), 45–61.

Hwang, N. & Chang, J. (2010). Litigation environment and auditors' decisions to accept clients' aggressive reporting. *Journal of Accounting and Public Policy*, 29(3), 281–295.

IMF (2015). *Growing (un)equal: Fiscal Policy and Income: Inequality in China and BRIC+. Imf.org.* IMF, Washington, DC. www.imf.org/external/pubs/ft/wp/2015/wp1568.pdf.

Jacoby, J., Li, J. & Liu, M. (2016). Financial distress, political affiliation and earnings management: The case of politically affiliated private firms. *The European Journal of Finance*, 25, 508–523.

Jalaja, L. (2017). GST and its implications on Indian economy. *IOSR Journal of Business and Management*, 67–73. http://www.iosrjournals.org/iosr-jbm/papers/Conf.17037-2017/Volume-2/12.%2067-73.pdf.

Janssen, M., Manning, M. & Udiani, O. (2014). The effect of social preferences on the evolution of cooperation in public good games. *Advances in Complex Systems*, 17, No. 03–04, 1450015 (2014). https://doi.org/10.1142/S0219525914500155.

Johnson, J. & Taylor, E. (2019). The long run health consequences of rural-urban migration. *Quantitative Economics*, 10(2).

Josiah, J., Gough, O., Haslam, J. & Shah, N. (2014). Corporate reporting implication in migrating from defined benefit to defined contribution pension schemes: A focus on the UK. *Accounting Forum*, 38, 18–37.

Keane, M. & Thakur, R. (2018). Health care spending and hidden poverty in India. *Research in Economics*, 72(4), 435–451.

Kerr, S. & Duscha, V. (2014). Going to the source: Using an upstream point of regulation for energy in a national Chinese emissions trading system. *Energy & Environment*, 25(3–4), 593–612.

Khan, A. & Riskin, C. (2001). *Inequality and Poverty in China in the Age of Globalization* (Oxford University Press, Oxford).

Kleinman, G. & Palmon, D. (2009). Procedural instrumentality and audit group judgment: An exploration of the impact of cognitive fallibility and ability differences. *Group Decision & Negotiation*, 18(2), 147–168.

Knight, J., Li, S. & Song, L. (March 2004). *The Rural-Urban Divide and the Evolution of Political Economy in China.* www.peri.umass.edu/fileadmin/pdf/Knight_paper_griffin_conference.pdf.

Komiak, S. & Benbasat, I. (2006). The effects of personalization and familiarity on trust and adoption of recommendation agents. *Management Information Systems Quarterly*, 30(4), 941–960.

Konrad Adeneaur Stiftung. (2017). *Climate Report 2017–Private Sector and Climate Finance in the G20 Countries.* http://Www.Kas.De/Wf/Doc/Kas_49589-544-2-30.Pdf?170719090813.

Kopczuk, W. (2015). What do we know about the evolution of top wealth shares in the United States? *Journal of Economic Perspectives*, 29, 47–66. Norton, New York.

Kopp, M., Stauder, A., Purebl, G., Janszky, I. & Skrabski, Á. (2008). Work stress and mental health in a changing society. *European Journal of Public Health*, 18(3), 238–244.

Kosinski, M., Stillwell, D. & Graepel, T. (2013). Private traits and attributes are predictable from digital records of human behavior. *Proceedings of the National Academy of Sciences*, 110(15), 5802–5805.

Kreiger, J. & Higgins, D. (2002). Housing and health: Time again for public health action. *American Journal of Public Health*, 92(5), 758–768.

Kurtbegu, E. (2018). Replicating intergenerational longevity risk sharing in collective defined contribution pension plans using financial markets. *Insurance: Mathematics and Economics*, 78, 286–300.

Laswad, F. & Baskerville, R. (2007). An analysis of the value of cash flow statements of New Zealand pension schemes. *The British Accounting Review*, 39(4), 347–355.

Leimbach, M., Baumstark, L. & Luderer, G. (2015). The role of time preferences in explaining the long-term pattern of international trade. *Global Economy Journal*, 15(1), 83–106.

Leung, E., Paolacci, G. & Puntoni, S. (2018). Man versus machine: Resisting automation in identity-based consumer behavior. *Journal of Marketing Research*, 55(6), 818–831.

Lewellyn, K. & Bao, S. (2017). The role of national culture and corruption on managing earnings around the world. *Journal of World Business*, 52(6), 798–808.

Li, J. & Boghosian, B. (2017). Duality in an asset exchange model for wealth distribution. *Physica A: Statistical Mechanics and its Applications*, 497, 154–165.

Li, Z. & Wu, M. (2018). Education and welfare program compliance: Firm-level evidence from a pension reform in China. *China Economic Review*, 48, 1–13.

Lin, C., Chen, C. & Liu, T. (2014). Do stock prices drive people crazy? *Health Policy and Planning*, 30(2), 206–214.

Lin, H., Zhang, Y., Xu, Y., Liu, T., Xiao, J., Luo, Y., Xu, X. et al. (2013). Large daily stock variation is associated with cardiovascular mortality in two cities of Guangdong, China. *PloS One*, 8(7), e68417.

Lin, J. & Chen, B. (2011). Urbanization and urban-rural inequality in China: A new perspective from the government's development strategy. *Frontiers of Economics in China*, 6(1), 1–21.

Lin, S., Wang, C., Liu, T. & Chen, C. (2015). Stroke: A hidden danger of margin trading in stock markets. *Journal of Urban Health*, 92(5), 995–1006.

Lin, T., Lin, Y. & Tseng, W. (2016). Manufacturing suicide: The politics of a world factory. *Chinese Sociological Review*, 48(1), 1–32.

Ling, D., Naranjo, A. & Ryngert, M. (2012). Real estate ownership, leasing intensity, and value: Do stock returns reflect a firm's real estate holdings? *The Journal of Real Estate Finance and Economics*, 44(1), 184–202.

Liow, K. (1995). Property in corporate financial statements: The U.K. evidence. *Journal of Property Research*, 12, 13–28.

Liow, K. & Nappi-Choulet, I. (2008). A combined perspective of corporate real estate. *Journal of Corporate Real Estate*, 10(1), 54–67.

Liu, C. (November 2015). *How Does the Stock Market Affect Investor Sentiment? Evidence from Antidepressant Usage*. SSRN. https://ssrn.com/abstract=2691824 or http://dx.doi.org/10.2139/ssrn.2691824.

Liu, F., Zhang, J. & Zhu, J. (2016). How much can we trust China's investment statistics? *Journal of Chinese Economic and Business Studies*, 14(3), 215–228.

Logg, J., Minson, J. & Moore, D. (2019). Algorithm appreciation: People prefer algorithmic to human judgment. *Organizational Behavior and Human Decision Processes*, 151.

Lovely, M., Liang, Y. & Zhang, H. (2019). Economic geography and inequality in China: Did improved market access widen spatial wage differences? *China Economic Review*, 54(C), 306–323.

Lyu, C., Wang, K., Zhang, F. & Zhang, X. (2018). GDP management to meet or beat growth targets. *Journal of Accounting and Economics*, 66(1), 318–338.

Ma, B., Song, G., Zhang, L. & Sonnenfeld, D.A. (2014). Explaining sectoral discrepancies between national and provincial statistics in China. *China Economic Review*, 30, 353–369.

Ma, W., Chen, H., Jiang, L., Song, G. & Kan, H. (2011). Stock volatility as a risk factor for coronary heart disease death. *European Heart Journal*, 32(8), 1006–1011.

MacDonald, B. & Cairns, A. (2011). Three retirement decision models for defined contribution pension plan members: A simulation study. *Insurance: Mathematics and Economics*, 48(1), 1–18.

Manyika, J. & Bughin, J. (2018). *The Promise and Challenge of the Age of Artificial Intelligence* (McKinsey Global Institute, New York City, USA).

Manyika, J., Chui, M. et al. (2017). *A Future That Works: Automation, Employment, and Productivity* (Mckinsey Global Institute, New York City, USA).

Manyika, J., Lund, S. et al. (2017). *Jobs Lost, Jobs Gained: What the Future of Work Will Mean for Jobs, Skills, and Wages* (McKinsey Global Institute, New York City, USA).

Marquardt, C. & Zur, E. (2015). The role of accounting quality in the M&A market. *Management Science*, 61(3), 487–705.

Mathur, M. & Reichling, D. (2016). Navigating a social world with robot partners: A quantitative cartography of the Uncanny Valley. *Cognition*, 146(8), 22–32.

Mehta, A. & Hasan, R. (2012). The effects of trade and services liberalization on wage inequality in India. *International Review of Economics & Finance*, 23, 75–90.

Milanovic, B. (2016). *Global Inequality: A New Approach for the Age of Globalization* (Harvard University Press, Cambridge, MA).

Moloughney, B. (2004). *Housing and Population Health: The State of Current Research Knowledge*. Prepared for the Canadian Population Health Initiative, part of the Canadian Institute for Health Information, Canada Mortgage and Housing Corporation. https://secure.cihi.ca/free_products/HousingPopHealth_e.pdf.

Monjon, S. & Quirion, P. (2011). A border adjustment for the EU ETS: Reconciling WTO rules and capacity to tackle carbon leakage. *Climate Policy*, 11(5), 1212–1225.

Müller, V. & Bostrom, N. (2016). *Future progress in Artificial Intelligence: A survey of expert opinion*. Chapter in: Muelle, V., ed., *Fundamental Issues of Artificial Intelligence* (Springer International Publishing, Berlin), pp. 555–572.

Murray, C., Vos, T., Lozano, R., Naghavi, M., Flaxman, A.D., Michaud, C., Ezzati, M. et al. (2013). Disability-adjusted life years (DALYs) for 291 diseases and injuries in 21 regions, 1990–2010: A systematic analysis for the global burden of disease study 2010. *Lancet*, 380(9859), 2197–2223.

Nakajima, K. & Sasaki, T. (2010). Unfunded pension liabilities and stock returns. *Pacific-Basin Finance Journal*, 18(1), 47–63.

Nandi, A., Prescott, M.R., Cerdá, M., Vlahov, D., Tardiff, K.J. & Galea, S. (2012). Economic conditions and suicide rates in New York City. *American Journal of Epidemiology*, 175(6), 527–535.

Nettleton, S. (1998). Losing homes through mortgage possession: A "New" public health issue. *Critical Public Health*, 8(1).

Nguyen, C. (2016). Chinese restaurants are replacing waiters with robots. *Business Insider*, http://www.businessinsider.com/chinese-restaurant-robot-waiters-2016-7/.

Nwogugu, M. (2012). *Risk in the Global Real Estate Markets* (Wiley Finance, Hoboken, NJ, USA).

Nwogugu, M. (2015a). Failure of the Dodd-Frank act. *Journal of Financial Crime*, 22(4), 520–572.

Nwogugu, M. (2015b). Un-constitutionality of the Dodd-Frank act. *European Journal of Law Reform*, 17, 185–190.

Nwogugu, M. (2019). Implications for Decision Theory, Enforcement, Financial Stability and Systemic Risk. Chapter 13 in: Nwogugu, M. (2019). *Indices, Index Funds and ETFs: Exploring HCI, Nonlinear Risk and Homomorphisms* (Palgrave Macmillan, UK).

Ojha, V., Pradhan, B. & Ghosh, J. (2013). Growth, inequality and innovation: A CGE analysis of India. *Journal of Policy Modeling*, 35(6), 909–927.

Ongena, S. & Zalewska, A. (2018). Institutional and individual investors: Saving for old age. *Journal of Banking & Finance*, 92, 257–268.

Orlik, T. (2014). Reform at China's national bureau of statistics under Ma Jiantang 2008–2013. *China Economic Review*, 30, 304–308.

Osberg, L. (2015). *Economic Inequality in the United States* (Routledge, London).

Pang, T. & Duan, M. (2016). Cap setting and allowance allocation in China's emissions trading pilot programmes: Special issues and innovative solutions. *Climate Policy*, 16(7), 815–835.

Pesek, W. (July 29, 2019). *India's GDP Growth Figures Are Hard to Trust: Narendra Modi Needs to Ensure the Country's Statistics Are Accurate*. https://asia.nikkei.com/Opinion/India-s-GDP-growth-figures-are-hard-to-trust?utm_campaign=RN%20Free%20newsletter&utm_medium=opinion_newsletter_free&utm_source=NAR%20Newsletter&utm_content=article%20link.

Piketty, T. & Saez, E. (2014). Inequality in the long run. *Science*, 344, 838–843.

Platanakis, E. & Sutcliffe, C. (2016). Pension scheme redesign and wealth redistribution between the members and sponsor: The USS rule change in October 2011. *Insurance: Mathematics and Economics*, 69, 14–28.

Quick, R. & Schmidt, F. (2018). Do audit firm rotation, auditor retention, and joint audits matter? – An experimental investigation of bank directors' and institutional investors' perceptions. *Journal of Accounting Literature*, 41, 1–21.

Ratcliffe, A. & Taylor, K. (2015). Who cares about stock market booms and busts? Evidence from data on mental health. *Oxford Economic Papers*, 67(3), 826–845.

Rath, S., Yu, P. & Srinivas, S. (2018). Challenges of non-communicable diseases and sustainable development of China and India. *Acta Ecologica Sinica*, 38(2), 117–125.

Ravallion, M. & Chen, S. (2007). China's (Uneven) progress against poverty. *Journal of Development Economics*, 82(1), 1–42.

Rawski, T. (2001). What Is Happening to China's GDP Statistics?. *China Economic Review*, 12, 347–354.

Read, W. & Yezegel, A. (2018). Going-concern opinion decisions on bankrupt clients: Evidence of long-lasting auditor conservatism? *Advances in Accounting*, 40, 20–26.

Ribeiro, M. & Beetsma, R. (2008). The political economy of structural reforms under a deficit restriction. *Journal of Macroeconomics*, 30(1), 179–198.

Ritchie, H. & Roser, M. (2019). *Air Pollution*. https://ourworldindata.org/air-pollution.

Robertson, J. (2010). The effects of ingratiation and client incentive on auditor judgment. *Behavioral Research in Accounting*, 22(2), 69–86.

Romer, P. (1983). *Dynamic Competitive Equilibria with Externalities, Increasing Returns and Unbounded Growth*. Ph.D. Thesis at the University of Chicago.

Roulac, S. (2003). Corporate-owned real estate represents a substantial investment universe. *Journal of Real Estate Portfolio Management*, 9(2), 167–178.

Roy, A. & Pramanick, K. (2019). Analysing progress of sustainable development goal 6 in India: Past, present, and future. *Journal of Environmental Management*, 232, 1049–1065.

Sabonis-Helf, T. (2003). Catching air? Climate change policy in Russia, Ukraine and Kazakhstan. *Climate Policy*, 3(2), 159–170.

Salmi, A. & Heikkilä, K. (2015). Managing relationships with public officials – A case of foreign MNCs in Russia. *Industrial Marketing Management*, 49, 22–31.

Saxena, V. & Bhattacharya, P. (2018). Inequalities in LPG and electricity consumption in India: The role of caste, tribe, and religion. *Energy for Sustainable Development*, 42, 44–53.

Saygin, A., Chaminade, T. et al. (2012). The thing that should not be: Predictive coding and the Uncanny Valley in perceiving human and humanoid robot actions. *Social Cognitive and Affective Neuroscience*, 7(4), 413–422.

Scheffer, M., van Bavel, B., van de Leemput, I.A. & van Nes, E.H. (2017). Inequality in nature and society. *Proceedings of the National Academy of Sciences*, 114(50), 13154–13157.

Schneider, A. (2015). Does information about auditor switches affect investing decisions? *Research in Accounting Regulation*, 27(1), 39–44.

Schneider, A. (2018). Studies on the impact of accounting information and assurance on commercial lending judgments. *Journal of Accounting Literature*, 41, 63–74.

Schneider, L., Kollmuss, A. & Lazarus, M. (2015). Addressing the risk of double counting emission reductions under the UNFCCC. *Climatic Change*, 131(4), 473–486.

Schneider, M. & Yaşar, Y. (2016). Is inequality deadly and for whom? A Bayesian model averaging analysis. *The Social Science Journal*, 53(3), 357–370.

Schuetz, S. & Venkatesh, V. (2019). Blockchain, adoption, and financial inclusion in India: Research opportunities. *International Journal of Information Management*, in press.

Schutte, S., Chastang, J., Parent-Thirion, A., Vermeylen, G. & Niedhammer, I. (2014). Association between socio-demographic, psychosocial, material and occupational factors and self-reported health among workers in Europe. *Journal of Public Health*, 36, 194–204.

Schwalbe, U. (2018). *Algorithms, Machine Learning, and Collusion*. Working Paper.

Shah, S. & Narain, V. (2019). Re-framing India's "water crisis": An institutions and entitlements perspective. *Geoforum*, 101, 76–79.

Sham, H., Sing, T. & Tsai, I. (2009). Are there efficiency gains for larger Asian REITs? *Journal of Financial Management of Property and Construction*, 14(3), 231–247.

Shapiro, M., Rylant, R., de Lima, A., Vidaurri, A. & van de Werfhorst, H. (2017). Playing a rigged game: Inequality's effect on physiological stress responses. *Physiology & Behavior*, 180, 60–69.

Sheehan, S. (Feb. 22, 2017). China's Hukou Reforms and the Urbanization Challenge: China is speeding up hukou reform, but that won't be enough to solve the migrant worker problem. https://thediplomat.com/2017/02/chinas-hukou-reforms-and-the-urbanization-challenge/

Shi, K. & Ma, H. (2016). Evolution of trust in a dual-channel supply chain considering reciprocal altruistic behavior. *Advances in Complex Systems*, 19, No. 06–07, 1650014. https://doi.org/10.1142/S0219525916500144.

Sicular, T., Yue, X., Gustafsson, B. & Li, S. (2007). The urban-rural income gap and inequality in China. *Review of Income and Wealth*, 53(1), 93–126.

Sijm, J., Neuhoff, K. & Chen, Y. (2006). CO2 cost pass-through and windfall profits in the power sector. *Climate Policy*, 6(1), 49–72.

Sikka, P. & Hampton, M.P. (2005). The role of accountancy firms in tax avoidance: Some evidence and issues. *Accounting Forum*, 29(3), 325–343.

Smerlak, M. (2016). Thermodynamics of inequalities: From precariousness to economic stratification. *Physica-A: Statistical Mechanics & Applications*, 441, 40–50.

Srinidhi, B., Lim, C. & Hossain, M. (2009). Effects of country-level legal, extra-legal and political institutions on auditing: A cross-country analysis of the auditor specialization premium. *Journal of Contemporary Accounting & Economics*, 5(1), 34–46.

Staveley-O'Carroll, J. & Staveley-O'Carroll, O. (2017). Impact of pension system structure on international financial capital allocation. *European Economic Review*, 95, 1–22.

Stergiopoulos, V., Hwang, S.W., Gozdzik, A., Nisenbaum, R., Latimer, E., Rabouin, D.,
Adair, C.E. et al. (2015). Effect of scattered-site housing using rent supplements and
intensive case management on housing stability among homeless adults with mental illness: A randomized trial. *JAMA*, 313(9), 905–915.

Stiglitz, J. (2015). The origins of inequality, and policies to contain it. *National Tax Journal*, 68, 425–448.

Stone, P., Brooks, R. et al. (2016). Artificial Intelligence and Life in 2030, One Hundred
Year Study on Artificial Intelligence: Report of the 2015–2016 Study Panel.

Tambayong, L. (2011). Boolean Network and Simmelian Tie in the Co-Author Model: A
Study of Dynamics and Structure of a Strategic Alliance Model. *Advances in Complex
Systems*, 14(1), 1–12. https://doi.org/10.1142/S0219525911002901.

Tan, T. (2014). *China's Hukou System Furthers Its Educational Inequality*. https://future-
challenges.org/local/chinas-hukou-system-furthers-its-educational-inequality/.

Tang, S. & Demmeritt, D. (2018). Climate change and mandatory carbon reporting:
Impacts on business process and performance. *Business Strategy & The Environment*,
27(4), 437–455.

Tanuro, D. (2008). *Fundamental Inadequacies of Carbon Trading for the Struggle Against
Climate Change*. https://climateandcapitalism.com/2008/03/23/carbon-trading-an-
ecosocialist-critique/.

Tavoni, A., Dannenberg, A., Kallis, G. & Loschel, A. (2011). Inequality, communication,
and the avoidance of disastrous climate change in a public goods game. *Proceedings of
the National Academy of Sciences*, 108, 11825–11829.

Thomas, P. & Williams, P. (2009). Cash balance pension plans: A case of standard-setting
inadequacy. *Critical Perspectives on Accounting*, 20(2), 228–254.

Thorwaldsson, K. (Jan. 29, 2019). *Why Income Inequality Is Bad for the Climate*. https://
www.weforum.org/agenda/2019/01/income-inequality-is-bad-climate-change-action/.

Trotman, K., Bauer, T. & Humphreys, K. (2015). Group judgment and decision making in
auditing: Past and future research. *Accounting, Organizations and Society*, 47, 56–72.

Tuzel, S. (2010). Corporate real estate holdings and the cross-section of stock returns.
Review of Financial Studies, 23(6), 2268–2302.

Tynkkynen, N. (2014). *Russia and Global Climate Governance*. IFRI – Russia/NIS Center.
www.ifri.org.

Van Oort, F., Van Lenthe, F. & Mackenbach, J. (2005). Material, psychosocial, and behavioural factors in the explanation of educational inequalities in mortality in the Netherlands. *Journal of Epidemiology & Community Health*, 59, 214–220.

Vermeer, T., Styles, A. & Patton, T. (2012). Do local governments present required disclosures for defined benefit pension plans? *Journal of Accounting and Public Policy*, 31(1),
44–68.

Vian, T. & Crable, E. (2017). Corruption and the consequences for public health. *International Encyclopedia of Public Health* (Second Edition, 2017), 168–176.

Vitali, S., Glattfelder, J. & Battiston, S. (2011). The network of global corporate control.
PLoS One, 6, e25995.

Vlachou, A. & Pantelias, G. (2017). The EU's emissions trading system, part-2: A political
economy critique. *Capitalism Nature Socialism*, 28(3), 108–127.

Wang, B. & Xin, Q. (2011). Auditor choice and accruals patterns of cross-listed firm. *China
Journal of Accounting Research*, 4(4), 233–251.

Wang, X., Teng, F., Zhou, S. & Cai, B. (2017). Identifying the industrial sectors at risk of carbon leakage in China. *Climate Policy*, 17(4), 443–457.

Ward, P. (February 1, 2016). Transient poverty, poverty dynamics, and vulnerability to poverty: An empirical analysis using a balanced panel from rural China. *World Development*, 78, 541–553.

Weisbuch, G. & Louzoun,Y. (2013). Sustainable development and spatial in homogeneities. *Journal of Statistical Physics*, 151, 475–493.

Weishaar, S.E. (2014). *Linking Emissions Trading Schemes, Emissions Trading Design – A Critical Overview* (Edward Elgar, Cheltenham).

White, L. (2001). *Reducing the Barriers to International Trade in Accounting Services* (AEI Press). www.aei.org/press/reducing-the-barriers-to-international-trade-in-accounting-services/.

Whiteford, H., Ferrari, A., Degenhardt, L., Feigin, V. & Vos, T. (2015). The global burden of mental, neurological and substance use disorders: An analysis from the global burden of disease study 2010. *PLoS One*, 10(2), e0116820. www.ncbi.nlm.nih.gov/pmc/articles/PMC4320057/.

Williamson, J., Howling, S. & Maroto, M. (2006). The political economy of pension reform in Russia: Why partial privatization? *Journal of Aging Studies*, 20(2), 165–175.

Willmore, L. (2007). Universal pensions for developing countries. *World Development*, 35(1), 24–51.

World Bank GINI Index. (2015). data.worldbank.org/indicator/SI.POV.GINI/.

Wu, C., Hsu, H. & Haslam, J. (2016). Audit committees, non-audit services, and auditor reporting decisions prior to failure. *The British Accounting Review*, 48(2), 240–256.

Wu, H. (Jan. 2014). *"China's Growth and Productivity Performance Debate Revisited – Accounting for China's Sources of Growth with a New Data Set."* The Conference Board Economics Program Working Paper Series No. 14-01, January 2014. See www.conference-board.org/pdf_free/workingpapers/EPWP1401.pdf

Wu, X. & Li, J. (2017). Income inequality, economic growth, and subjective well-being: Evidence from China. *Research in Social Stratification and Mobility*, 52, 49–58.

Wu, Y., Kosinski, M. & Stillwell, D. (2015). Computer-based personality judgments are more accurate than those made by humans. *Proceedings of the National Academy of Sciences*, 112(4), 1036–1040.

Yakovenko, V. & Rosser, J. (2009). Colloquium: Statistical mechanics of money, wealth, and income. *Review of Modern Physics*, 81, 1703–1725.

Yeomans, M. (2015). What every manager should know about machine learning. *Harvard Business Review*.

Zacharias, A. & Vakulabharanam, V. (2011). Caste stratification and wealth inequality in India. *World Development*, 39(10), 1820–1833.

Zeng, Y., Weishaar, S. & Vedder, H. (2018). Electricity regulation in the Chinese national emissions trading scheme (ETS): Lessons for carbon leakage and linkage with the EU ETS. *Climate Policy*, 18(10), 1246–1259.

Zhang, B. & Dafoe, A. (2019). *Artificial Intelligence: American Attitudes and Trends.* Future of Humanity Institute, Oxford University, Oxford, UK.

Zhang, W. & Mauck, N. (2018). Government-affiliation, bilateral political relations and cross-border mergers: Evidence from China. *Pacific-Basin Finance Journal*, 51, 220–250.

Zunzunegui, M., Belanger, E., Benmarhnia, T., Gobbo, M., Otero, A., Béland, F., Zunzunegui, F. et al. (2017). Financial fraud and health: The case of Spain. *Gaceta Sanitaria*, 31(4), 313–319.

The list of top corporate scandals in the world that occurred without any insolvency (source: wikipedia – https://en.wikipedia. org/wiki/List_of_corporate_ collapses_and_scandals)

- *Australia and New Zealand Banking Group* (Australia; *https://en.wikipedia. org/wiki/Australia_and_New_Zealand_Banking_Group)* – scandal involving misleading file notes in the *Financial Ombudsman Service (Australia)* presented to the Victorian Supreme Court.
- *Australia and New Zealand Banking Group* (Australia; https://en.wikipedia. org/wiki/Australia_and_New_Zealand_Banking_Group) – alleged manipulation of the Australian benchmark interest rates. ANZ was being pursued by the *Australian Securities and Investments Commission*, which filed an originating process in the Federal Court of Australia against ANZ in March 2016.
- *BAE Systems* (USA; https://en.wikipedia.org/wiki/BAE_Systems#Corruption_ investigations) – bribery scandal related to the *Al-Yamamah arms deal* with Saudi Arabia.
- *Bristol-Myers Squibb* (USA; https://en.wikipedia.org/wiki/Bristol-Myers_ Squibb#Scandals_and_allegations) – accounting scandal.
- *Brown & Williamson* (USA; https://en.wikipedia.org/wiki/Bristol-Myers_ Squibb#Scandals_and_allegations) – for chemically enhancing the addictiveness of cigarettes, becoming the leading edge of the tobacco industry scandals of the 1990s, and eventually resulting in the *Tobacco Master Settlement Agreement* (*https://en.wikipedia.org/wiki/Tobacco_Master_Settlement_Agreement*).
- *Chevron-Texaco Lago Agrio oil field* (USA; https://en.wikipedia.org/wiki/ Lago_Agrio_oil_field) – pollution scandal.
- *Commonwealth Bank of Australia* (Australia; https://en.wikipedia.org/wiki/ Commonwealth_Bank) – facts un-covered that showed the insurance arm of the bank denied life insurance policy holders despite having legitimate claims, resulting in calls for a Royal Commission into the Australian insurance industry.
- *Commonwealth Bank of Australia* (Australia; https://en.wikipedia.org/wiki/ Commonwealth_Bank_Of_Australia) – the company provided un-suitable financial advice to a large number of customers between 2003 and 2012 and continuously delayed in providing compensation to the victims.
- *Compass Group* (https://en.wikipedia.org/wiki/Compass_Group#2005_ United_Nations_misconduct_incident) – the company bribed the United Nations in order to win business.

- *Corrib gas controversy* (Ireland; https://en.wikipedia.org/wiki/Corrib_gas_controversy) – Kilcommon, Erris, Co. Mayo, Ireland.
- *Deutsche Bank Libor scandal* (Germany; https://en.wikipedia.org/wiki/Libor_scandal) – Deutsche Bank engaged in LIBOR manipulation and agreed to a combined US$2.5 billion in fines.
- *Duke Energy* (USA; *https://en.wikipedia.org/wiki/Duke_Energy#Taxes*) – tax scandal.
- *El Paso Corporation* (USA; *https://en.wikipedia.org/wiki/El_Paso_Corp.#Price_fixing*) – price-fixing scandal.
- *Fannie Mae* (USA; https://en.wikipedia.org/wiki/Fannie_Mae#Accounting_controversy) – earnings management and under-reporting of profit.
- *FlowTex* (*https://en.wikipedia.org/wiki/FlowTex#Scandal*) – that was the largest corporate scandal in German history.
- *Global Crossing* (USA; *https://en.wikipedia.org/wiki/Global_Crossing*) – fraud.
- *Guinness share-trading fraud* (*https://en.wikipedia.org/wiki/Guinness_share-trading_fraud*) – share trading fraud.
- *Hafskip*'s collapse (*https://en.wikipedia.org/wiki/Hafskip*).
- *Halliburton* (USA – https://en.wikipedia.org/wiki/Halliburton) – the company was over-charging for government contracts.
- *Harken Energy Scandal* (USA; *https://en.wikipedia.org/wiki/Harken_Energy_Scandal*).
- *HealthSouth* (USA; https://en.wikipedia.org/wiki/HealthSouth) – reporting exaggerated earnings.
- *Homestore.com* (*https://en.wikipedia.org/wiki/Homestore.com*).
- *Kerr-McGee* (USA; *https://en.wikipedia.org/wiki/Karen_Silkwood*) – the *Karen Silkwood* case.
- *Kinney National Company* (https://en.wikipedia.org/wiki/Kinney_National_Company) – financial scandal.
- *Lernout & Hauspie* (https://en.wikipedia.org/wiki/Lernout_%26_Hauspie) – accounting fraud.
- *Lockheed bribery scandal* (USA; *https://en.wikipedia.org/wiki/Lockheed_bribery_scandals*) – bribery occurred in Germany, Japan, and Netherlands.
- *Livedoor* (https://en.wikipedia.org/wiki/Livedoor) scandal.
- *Marsh & Mclennan* (USA; *https://en.wikipedia.org/wiki/Marsh_%26_Mclennan*).
- *Merck Medicaid fraud* (USA; https://en.wikipedia.org/wiki/Merck_%26_Co.#Medicaid_overbilling) – investigation about Medicaid fraud..
- *Mirant* (https://en.wikipedia.org/wiki/Mirant).
- *Morrison-Knudsen* (USA; https://en.wikipedia.org/wiki/Morrison-Knudsen) – the scandal led to *William Agee*'s ouster.
- *Mutual-fund scandal (2003)* (https://en.wikipedia.org/wiki/Mutual-fund_scandal_(2003)).
- *Nestle* (https://en.wikipedia.org/wiki/Nestl%C3%A9).

- *Nugan Hand Bank* (*https://en.wikipedia.org/wiki/Nugan_Hand_Bank*).
- *Olympus scandal* (Japan; *https://en.wikipedia.org/wiki/Olympus_Scandal*) – scandal occurred in Japan.
- *Options backdating* (https://en.wikipedia.org/wiki/Options_backdating) – involving over one hundred companies.
- *Panama Papers* (*https://en.wikipedia.org/wiki/Panama_Papers*) – international leak of hundreds of thousands of confidential documents pertaining to bank accounts and companies owned by politicians, *High-net-worth individuals* and other people (some in off-shore tax havens). The focus was *Panama* law firm *Mossack Fonseca*.
- *Peregrine Systems* (USA; https://en.wikipedia.org/wiki/Peregrine_Systems) – its corporate executives were convicted of accounting fraud.
- *Phar-Mor* (USA; *https://en.wikipedia.org/wiki/Phar-Mor*) – the company lied to its shareholders; and its CEO was eventually sentenced to prison for fraud and the company eventually became bankrupt.
- *Qwest Communications* (USA; https://en.wikipedia.org/wiki/Qwest_Communications).
- *RadioShack* (USA; https://en.wikipedia.org/wiki/RadioShack) – CEO *David Edmondson* lied about attaining a B.A. degree from Pacific Coast Baptist College in *California*, USA.
- *Reliant Energy* (USA; https://en.wikipedia.org/wiki/Reliant_Energy).
- *Rite Aid* (USA) – accounting fraud.
- *Royal Dutch Shell* (Netherlands; https://en.wikipedia.org/wiki/Royal_Dutch_Shell) – company overstated its *oil reserves* twice; and it downgraded 3,900,000,000 barrels (620,000,000m^3), or about 20 percent of its total holdings.
- *S-Chips Scandals* (Singapore; https://en.wikipedia.org/wiki/S-Chips_Scandals).
- *Satyam Computers* (India; https://en.wikipedia.org/wiki/Satyam_Computers#Controversies).
- *7-Eleven* Australia (Australia; *https://en.wikipedia.org/wiki/7-Eleven*) – allegations of bullying tactics, underpayment of wages and entitlements.
- *Siemens Greek bribery scandal* (Germany; https://en.wikipedia.org/wiki/Siemens_Greek_bribery_scandal) – involving cases of bribery on behalf of *Siemens* towards the *Greek Government*.
- *Société Générale* (France; https://en.wikipedia.org/wiki/Soci%C3%A9t%C3%A9_G%C3%A9n%C3%A9rale) – derivatives trading scandal causing multi-billion Euros losses.
- *Southwest Airlines* (USA; https://en.wikipedia.org/wiki/Southwest_Airlines) – violations of safety regulations.
- *Tyco International* (USA; https://en.wikipedia.org/wiki/Tyco_International) – executive theft and prison sentences.
- *Union Carbide* (USA; *https://en.wikipedia.org/wiki/Union_Carbide*) – the *Bhopal disaster*.

- *ValuJet Airlines* (USA; https://en.wikipedia.org/wiki/ValuJet_Airlines) – loading live oxygen generators into cargo hold of passenger jet causing fatal crash.
- *Volkswagen emissions violations* (https://en.wikipedia.org/wiki/Volkswagen_ emissions_violations) – fraud in diesel motors pollution measurements.
- *David Wittig* (https://en.wikipedia.org/wiki/David_Wittig) – ”looting” scandals.
- *Xerox* (USA;   https://en.wikipedia.org/wiki/Xerox#Alleged_accounting_ irregularities) – alleged accounting irregularities.

Source: www.wikipedia.com – https://en.wikipedia.org/wiki/List_of_corporate_collapses_ and_scandals.

Appendix 3.2

List of major corporate collapses around the world
(source: wikipedia – https://en.wikipedia.org/wiki/
List_of_corporate_collapses_and_scandals)

Name	Headquarters	Date	Business	Causes
Danatbank	Germany	13-Jul-31	Banking	At the start of the Great Depression, after rumours about the solvency of the Norddeutsche Wollkämmerei & Kammgarnspinnerei, there was a bank run, and Danatbank was forced into insolvency.
Allied Crude Vegetable Oil Refining Corp	USA	16-Nov-63	Commodities	Commodities trader Tino De Angelis defrauded clients, including the Bank of America into thinking he was trading vegetable oil. He got loans and made money using the oil as collateral. He showed inspectors tankers of water, with a bit of oil on the surface. When the fraud was exposed, the business collapsed.
Herstatt Bank	Germany	26-Jun-74	Banking	Settlement risk – Counterparty banks did not receive their US Dollar payments, where Herstatt had received Deutsche Marks earlier, prior to its government-forced liquidation.
Carrian Group	Hong Kong (China)	1983	Real estate	Accounting fraud – an auditor was murdered, and an adviser committed suicide. That was the largest collapse in Hong Kong history.
Texaco	USA	13-Apr-87	Oil	After a legal battle with Pennzoil, whereby it was found to owe a debt of US$10.5 billion, Texaco went into bankruptcy. It was later resurrected and taken over by Chevron.

Qintex	Australia	1989	Real Estate	Qintex CEO Christopher Skase was found to have improperly used his position to obtain management fees prior to the US$1.5 billion collapse of Qintex including $700 million of unpaid debts. Skase absconded to the Spanish resort island of Majorca. Spain refused to extradite him for ten years during which time Skase became a citizen of Dominica.
Lincoln Savings and Loan Association	USA	1989	Banking	Financial institution that went bust following the *Keating Five* scandal.
Polly Peck	United Kingdom	30-Oct-90	Electronics, food, textiles	After a raid by the UK Serious Fraud Office in September 1990, the company's share price collapsed. The CEO Asil Nadir was convicted of stealing the company's money.
Bank of Credit and Commerce International	United Kingdom	5-Jul-91	Banking	Breach of US law, by owning another bank. Fraud, money laundering and larceny.
Nordbanken	Sweden	1991	Banking	After market de-regulation, there was a housing price bubble, and it burst. As part of a general rescue as the Swedish banking crisis unfolded, Nordbanken was nationalized for 64 billion kronor. It was later merged with Götabanken, which itself had to write off 37.3% of its creditors, and is now known as Nordea.
Barings Bank	United Kingdom	26-Feb-95	Banking	An employee in Singapore, Nick Leeson, traded futures, signed off on his own accounts and became increasingly indebted. The London directors were subsequently disqualified, as being unfit to run a company in *Re Barings plc* (No 5).
Bre-X	Canada	1997	Mining	After widespread reports that Bre-X had found a gold mine in Indonesia, the stories were found to be fraudulent.
Livent	Canada	Nov-98	Entertainment	In November 1998, Livent sought bankruptcy protection in the US and Canada, claiming a debt of $334 million. Garth Howard Drabinsky, co-founder of Livent, was convicted and sentenced to prison for fraud and forgery. A judgment was obtained against Deloitte & Touche LLP in respect of Deloitte's negligence in conducting the audit for Livent's 1997 fiscal year.

(Continued)

Continued

Name	Headquarters	Date	Business	Causes
Long-Term Capital Management	USA	23-Sep-98	Hedge fund	After purporting to have discovered a scientific method of calculating derivative prices, LTCM lost $4.6 billion in the first few months of 1998, and required state assistance to remain afloat.
Equitable Life Assurance Society	United Kingdom	8-Dec-00	Insurance	The insurance company's directors unlawfully used money from people holding guaranteed annuity rate policies to subsidize people with current annuity rate policies. After a House of Lords judgment in *Equitable Life Assurance Society v Hyman*, the Society closed. Though never technically insolvent, the UK government set up a compensation scheme for policyholders under the *Equitable Life (Payments) Act 2010*.
HIH Insurance	Australia	15-Mar-01	Insurance	In early 2000, after increases in the size of the business, it was determined that the insurance company's solvency was marginal, and a small asset price change could see the insurance company become insolvent. It did. Director Rodney Adler, CEO Ray Williams and others were sentenced to prison for fraudulent activity.
Pacific Gas and Electric Company	USA	6-Apr-01	Energy	After a change in regulation in California, the company determined it was unable to continue delivering power, and despite the California Public Utility Commission's efforts, it went into bankruptcy, leaving homes without energy. It emerged again in 2004.
Ore.Tel	Australia	29-May-01	Telecomms	After becoming one of the largest Australian public companies, losses of $290 million were reported, the share price crashed, and it entered into administration/insolvency. In the court case *ASIC vs. Rich*, the directors were found not to have been guilty of negligence.
WorldCom	USA	21-Jul-01	Telecomms	After falling share prices, and a failed share buy-back scheme, it was found that the directors had used fraudulent accounting methods to push up the stock price. Re-branded as MCI Inc., the company emerged from bankruptcy in 2004 and the assets were bought by Verizon.
Enron	USA	28-Nov-01	Energy	Enron's directors and executives fraudulently concealed large losses in Enron's projects; and some of them were sentenced to prison.

Company	Country	Date	Industry	Description
Chiquita Brands Int.	USA	28-Nov-01	Food	The company accumulated debts, after a series of accusations relating to breaches of labour and environmental standards. It entered a pre-packaged insolvency, and emerged with similar management in 2002.
Kmart	USA	22-Jan-02	Retail	After difficult competition, Kmart was put into Chapter 11 bankruptcy proceedings, but soon re-emerged.
Adelphia Communications	USA	13-Feb-02	Cable television	Internal corruption. Some of the Company's board members were sentenced to prison.
Arthur Andersen	USA	15-Jun-02	Accounting	A US court convicted Andersen of obstruction of justice by shredding documents related to the Enron scandal.
Parmalat	Italy	24-Dec-03	Food	The company's finance directors concealed its large debts.
MG Rover Group	United Kingdom	15-Apr-05	Automobiles	After diminishing demand, and getting a £6.5m loan from the UK government in April 2005, the company went into administration. After the loss of 30,000 jobs, Nanjing Automobile Group bought the company's assets.
Bayou Hedge Fund Group	USA	29-Sep-05	Hedge fund	Samuel Israel III defrauded his investors into thinking there were higher returns, and orchestrated fake audits. The US Commodity Futures Trading Commission filed a court complaint and the business was shut down after the company's board members were caught attempting to send $100 million into overseas bank accounts.
Refco	USA	17-Oct-05	Brokering	After becoming a public company in August 2005, it was revealed that Phillip R. Bennett, the company CEO and chairman, had concealed $430 million of bad debts. Its underwriters were Credit Suisse First Boston, Goldman Sachs, and Bank of America Corp. The company entered Chapter 11 and Bennett was sentenced to sixteen years in prison.
Bear Stearns	USA	14-Mar-08	Banking	Bear Stearns invested in the sub-prime mortgage market from 2003 after the US government had begun to deregulate consumer protection and derivatives trading. The business collapsed as more people began to be unable to meet mortgage obligations. After a stock price high of $172 per share, Bear Stearns was bought by JP Morgan for $2 per share on 16 March 2008, with a $29 billion loan facility guaranteed by the US Federal Reserve.

(Continued)

Continued

Name	Headquarters	Date	Business	Causes
Northern Rock	United Kingdom	22-Feb-08	Banking	Northern Rock had invested in the international markets for sub-prime mortgage debt, and as more and more people defaulted on their home loans in the US, Northern Rock's business collapsed. It triggered the first bank run in the UK since Overend, Gurney & Co in 1866, when it asked the UK government for assistance. Northern Rock was nationalized, and then sold to Virgin Money in 2012.
Lehman Brothers	USA	15-Sep-08	Banking	Lehman Brothers' financial strategy in from 2003 was to invest heavily in mortgage debt, in markets which were being de-regulated from consumer protection by the US government. Losses mounted, and Lehman Brothers was forced to file for Chapter 11 bankruptcy after the US government refused to extend a loan. The collapse triggered a global financial market meltdown. Barclays, Nomura and Bain Capital purchased Lehman's assets that were not encumbered/indebted.
AIG	USA	16-Sep-08	Insurance	Out of $441 billion worth of securities originally rated AAA, as the US sub-prime mortgage crisis unfolded, AIG found it held only $57.8 billion of these products. AIG was forced to take a 24-month credit facility from the US Federal Reserve Board.
Washington Mutual	USA	26-Sep-08	Banking	After the sub-prime mortgage crisis, there was a bank run on WaMu, and pressure from the FDIC forced the bank to close.
Royal Bank of Scotland Group (RBS)	United Kingdom	13-Oct-08	Banking	After the takeover of ABN-Amro, and the collapse of Lehman Bros, RBS found itself insolvent as the international credit market seized up. 58% of RBS's shares were purchased by the UK government.
ABN-Amro	Netherlands	Oct-08	Banking	After a takeover battle among Banco Santander, Fortis and RBS, ABN-Amro was split up and divided between the banking consortium. Fortis and RBS were found to be heavily indebted due to the sub-prime mortgage crisis. Fortis was split and the Dutch part of Fortis was taken under government ownership by The Netherlands, thus re-instating the company in ABN-AMRO. The Belgian part was taken over by BNP-Paribas. RBS was taken under government ownership by the UK.

Company	Country	Date	Industry	Description
Bernard L. Madoff Investment Securities LLC	USA	Dec-08	Securities	Madoff tricked investors out of $64.8 billion through the largest Ponzi scheme in history. Investors were paid returns out of their own money or that of other investors rather than from profits. Madoff told his sons about his scheme and they reported him to the US SEC. He was arrested the next day.
Bankwest	Australia	2008	Banking	Following the purchase of Bankwest by the Commonwealth Bank of Australia (CBA), there were calls for a royal commission specifically to investigate the conduct of the bank after allegations were made that the CBA engineered defaults of Bankwest customers in order to profit from clawback clauses under the purchase agreement.
Storm Financial	Australia	Jan-09	Financial services	Collapsed financial services business which cost thousands of persons their livelihoods.
Nortel	Canada	14-Jan-09	Telecomms	After the 2007–2008 financial crisis, and allegations of excessive executive pay, demand for this company' products dropped.
Anglo Irish Bank	Ireland	15-Jan-09	Banking	After the financial crisis of 2007–2008, the bank was forced to be nationalized by the Irish government.
Arcandor	Germany	9-Jun-09	Retail	After struggling to maintain business levels at its brand names Karstadt and KaDeWe, Arcandor sought help from the German government, and then filed for insolvency.
Schlecker	Germany	23-Jan-12	Retail	After continual losses mounting from 2011, Schlecker which had with 52,000 employees, was forced into insolvency, but continued to operate.
Dynegy	USA	6-Jul-12	Energy	After a series of attempted takeover bids, and a finding of fraud in a subsidiary's purchase of another subsidiary, Dynegy filed for Chapter 11 bankruptcy. It emerged from bankruptcy on 2 October 2012.

(Continued)

Continued

Name	Headquarters	Date	Business	Causes
China Medical Technologies (CMED)	Australia	27-Jul-12	Medical technology	In 2009, an anonymous letter alleging possible illegal and fraudulent activities by CMED's management since 2007 was sent to KPMG Hong Kong, then CMED's auditor, and the allegations were investigated by the law firm Paul Weiss Rifkind Wharton & Garrison. Since 27 July 2012, pursuant to an Order by the Grand Court of the Cayman Islands, CMED has been under the control of Joint Official Liquidators. Post-bankruptcy filing, CMED's liquidator probed an alleged $355 million insider fraud. In March 2017, the U.S. Department of Justice criminally indicted CMED's founder and CEO, as well as its former Chief Financial Officer, charging them with securities fraud and wire fraud conspiracy for stealing more than $400 million from investors as part of a seven-year scheme.
Banco Espírito Santo (BES)	Portugal	3-Aug-14	Banking	An audit performed in 2013 for a capital raise uncovered severe financial irregularities and the precarious financial situation of the bank. In July 2014, Salgado was replaced by economist Vitor Bento, who saw BES in an irrecoverable situation. Its good assets were bought by Novo Banco, a vehicle founded by Portugal's financial regulators for that purpose, on August 3, which hired Bento as CEO, while its toxic assets stayed in the "old" BES, whose banking license was revoked by the Portugese government.
Dick Smith (retailer)	Australia	5-Jan-16	Retail	On 5 January 2016, the retailer collapsed and was placed into receivership. McGrath Nicol were appointed as administrators by the company's board of directors and Ferrier Hodgson was appointed by the company's major creditors National Australia Bank (NAB) and HSBC Bank Australia.

Appendix 3.3

list of the top-100 most successful startups in the world (source: www.startupranking.com/top)

World Rank	Startup	SR Score	Description	Country	Country Rank
1	Airbnb	93,371	Vacation Rentals, Homes, Experiences & Places – Airbnb is a trusted online marketplace for people.	United States	1
2	Medium	93,040	Read, write and share stories that matter.	United States	2
3	Uber	92,995	Sign Up to Drive or Tap and Ride – Everyone's Private Driver.	United States	3
4	500px	92,725	The Premier Photography Community – We're the premier community for inspiring photographers.	Canada	1
5	Hootsuite	92,247	Social Media Management Dashboard – Hootsuite is a social relationship platform.	Canada	2
6	Giphy	92,086	Search and make GIFs – Animated GIF search. The first and largest GIF search platform.	United States	4
7	Quora	92,005	A place to share knowledge and to better understand – Quora connects you to everything you want to know.	United States	5
8	9GAG	91,850	Go Fun Yourself – 9GAG is your best source of fun.	Hong Kong/China	1
9	Canva	91,717	Amazingly Simple Graphic Design Software – Amazingly simple graphic design.	Australia	1
10	Slack	91,681	Where work happens – Slack – On a mission to make your working life simple.	United States	6
11	Prezi	91,614	Presentation Software – Online Presentation Tools.	Hungary	1
12	Buffer	91,422	A Smarter Way to Share on Social Media – Buffer is the easiest way to share the great links.	United States	7
13	Big Commerce	90,936	Ecommerce Software & Shopping Cart Platform.	Australia	2

(Continued)

Continued

World Rank	Startup	SR Score	Description	Country	Country Rank
14	Fiverr	90,819	Freelance Services Marketplace for Entrepreneurs.	Israel	1
15	WeTransfer	90,778	Cloud-based file transfer service.	Netherlands	1
16	Freelancer	90,764	Freelancer is the world's largest freelancing platform.	Australia	3
17	WeChat	90,599	Free messaging and calling app.	China	1
18	Stripe	90,372	Accept and manage online payments – Stripe is a suite of APIs that powers commerce.	United States	8
19	Freepik	90,078	Free vectors, photos and PSD Downloads.	Spain	1
20	Blockchain	90,071	Bitcoin Block Explorer – The world's most popular Bitcoin wallet!	United Kingdom	1
21	Duolingo	89,992	Learn Spanish, French and other languages for free.	Guatemala	1
22	Telegram	89,987	A new era of messaging – Telegram is the world's fastest and most secure messaging system.	Russia	1
23	Coinbase	89,925	BUY AND SELL DIGITAL CURRENCY – Coinbase is a digital wallet.	United States	9
24	IFTTT	89,918	Do more with the services you love.	United States	10
25	AngelList	89,874	Where the world meets startups – platform for startups.	United States	11
26	Teespring	89,810	Find something made for you.	United States	12
27	Nintendo	89,354	Nintendo is a Japanese multinational consumer electronics company that develops game consoles.	United States	13
28	Nginx	89,330	They learn, you earn – A high performance free open source web server.	United States	14
29	Philips Venture Capital Fund	89,052	Philips Venture Capital Fund is an Eindhoven-based venture capital fund that invests in technology startups worldwide.	Netherlands	2
30	Strava	89,051	Run and Cycling Tracking on a Social Network – Online network for athletes.	United States	15
31	GitLab	89,048	Code, test, and deploy together – GitLab is an open-source code collaboration platform.	Netherlands	3
32	Coursera	89,012	Free Online Courses From Top Universities.	United States	16
33	Base	88,884	Online shop easy creation for free.	Japan	1
34	Tokopedia	88,880	Tokopedia is an online marketplace.	Indonesia	1
35	SproutSocial	88,854	Powerful Social Media Software – Sprout Social is a social media management tool.	United States	17

#	Name	Value	Description	Country	
36	ZipRecruiter	88,759	Job Search – Millions of Jobs Hiring Near You.	United States	18
37	Treehouse	88,696	Start Learning for Free – Treehouse aims to be the best way to learn web design.	United States	19
38	TransferWise	88,639	Transfer Money Online, Send Money Abroad.	United Kingdom	2
39	About.me	88,562	Grow your audience and get more clients.	United States	20
40	Mapbox	88,535	The location platform for developers and designers.	United States	21
41	New Relic	88,534	Application Performance Management and Monitoring.	United States	22
42	Zapier	88,403	All-in-one web application integrations.	United States	23
43	Trustpilot	88,393	Experience the power of customer reviews.	Denmark	1
44	Gleam	88,271	Mobile fashion discovery and intelligence platform that brings engagement between style lovers and the industry to the next level.	Australia	4
45	Spreaker	88,133	Much more than Youtube for radio – Spreaker allows you to create your own online radio.	United States	24
46	Ecosia	88,094	Search the web to plant trees… – Ecosia is the search engine that plants trees!.	Germany	1
47	Hotjar	88,091	See how visitors are really using your website.	United States	25
48	CloudFlare	88,040	The Web Performance & Security Company.	United States	26
49	Bukalapak	87,998	Place of selling/buying.	Indonesia	2
50	Freshdesk	87,992	Customer support software and helpdesk solution – Freshdesk is a web 2.0 customer support software.	India	1
51	Unbounce	87,979	Landing Pages: Build Publish & Test Without I.T. – Unbounce is a self-serve hosted marketing tool.	Canada	3
52	DoorDash	87,894	DoorDash enables small businesses to provide its customers with local delivery services.	United States	27
53	Postmates	87,846	On-Demand Delivery – Postmates is transforming the way local goods move.	United States	28
54	Bol.com	87,816	Bol.com is an online retailer involved in providing books, entertainment, electronic devices, and toys for its clients.	Netherlands	4
55	Zomato	87,693	Delhi NCR Restaurants – Zomato helps you discover more places to eat.	India	2
56	Tokyo Otaku Mode	87,678	Destination for fans of Japanese pop culture – TokyoOtakuMode is all about sharing Japanese otaku.	Japan	2
57	Minube	87,629		Spain	2

(Continued)

Continued

World Rank	Startup	SR Score	Description	Country	Country Rank
58	Socialbakers	87,583	Social Media Marketing, Analytics & Performance.	Czechia	1
59	Mixpanel	87,572	Product analytics for mobile, web, and beyond.	United States	29
60	Designmodo	87,492	Web Design Blog and Shop – Design and Web Development Magazine.	United States	30
61	Twilio	87,491	APIs for Text Messaging, VoIP & Voice in the Cloud.	United States	31
62	Skillshare	87,465	A learning community for creators.	United States	32
63	DataCamp	87,456	DataCamp is a young team of data analytics enthusiasts that provide free interactive data science and statistics education to the world.	Belgium	1
64	ABS-CBN GLOBAL LTD.	87,415	ABS-CBN Global is a major commercial television network in the Philippines.	Philippines	1
65	ACT	87,308	ACT is an independent, non-profit organization that provides more than a hundred assessment, research, information, and program management.	United States	33
66	99designs	87,294	Logos, Web, Graphic Design & More – The #1 marketplace for graphic design.	Australia	5
67	Sellfy	87,204	Sell digital products, sell downloads.	Latvia	1
68	Zoosk	87,198	Online Dating Site – Dating Apps – Zoosk is the #1 dating app.	United States	34
69	Blibli	87,193	AppReal Double Deals Dekstop – Online retailer, Anywhere, Anytime Shopping.	Indonesia	3
70	Bank of Montreal (BMO)	87,088	Bank of Montreal, a financial services provider, offers retail banking, wealth management and investment banking products and solutions.	Canada	4
71	PeoplePerHour	87,079	Hire Freelancers Online & Find Freelance Work – PeoplePerHour is an online marketplace.	United Kingdom	3
72	Tictail	87,026	Buy and sell clothes, jewelry, art, fashion.	Sweden	1
73	App Annie	86,983	The App Analytics and App Data Industry Standard – Make better decisions with our app store data.	United States	35
74	Petco	86,869	Petco is a pet specialty retailer providing products, services and advice for pet owners.	United States	36

	Name	Description	Value	Country	Rank
75	Tinder	Find your match – Tinder is a mobile app that finds who likes you.	86,836	United States	37
76	Traveloka	Tiket Pesawat Murah – Traveloka.com is an Indonesian flight booking website.	86,820	Indonesia	4
77	CoSchedule	Content Marketing Editorial Calendar Software.	86,801	United States	38
78	LocalBitcoins	At LocalBitcoins.com, people from different countries can exchange their local currency to bitcoins.	86,795	Finland	1
79	Sticker Mule	Sticker Mule prints custom stickers for small businesses, startups, bloggers, artists, and companies.	86,793	United States	39
80	Musixmatch	The world's largest lyrics catalog.	86,755	Italy	1
81	ResearchGate	Share and discover research – ResearchGate was built by scientists, for scientists.	86,699	Germany	2
82	8tracks	Internet radio – Free music playlists.	86,667	United States	40
83	SSE Ventures	SSE Ventures is an entrepreneurial funding source for students on the Stanford campus.	86,637	United States	41
84	NationBuilder	SOFTWARE FOR LEADERS.	86,480	United States	42
85	Olacabs	Book a cab in India – Olacabs is India's largest online cab aggregator.	86,459	India	3
86	Toggl	Toggl offers an online time tracking software specifically designed for freelancers, graphic designers and consultants.	86,449	Estonia	1
87	Pearltrees	Organize all your interests – Pearltrees is the social curation community.	86,436	France	1
88	Babbel	Learn Spanish, French or Other Languages Online.	86,398	Germany	3
89	Help Scout	Simple Customer Service Software and Education.	86,393	United States	43
90	SendGrid	Marketing & Transactional Email Service – Email Delivery.	86,345	United States	44
91	Klarna	Klarna provides e-commerce payment solutions for merchants and shoppers.	86,325	Sweden	2
92	Truecaller	Phone Number Search – Truecaller is the world's largest collaborative phone number search system.	86,264	Sweden	3
93	Ameritrade	Ameritrade is a platform for online trading, investment Guidance for forex, stocks and mutual funds.	86,247	United States	45
94	Betterment	Betterment is a goal-based online investment company, delivering personalized financial advice paired with low fees and customer experience.	86,231	United States	46

(Continued)

Continued

World Rank	Startup	SR Score	Description	Country	Country Rank
95	ConvertKit	86,225	Email marketing for professional bloggers. – Email marketing for bloggers.	United States	47
96	Domo	86,178	Business Intelligence – Dashboards and Analytics.	United States	48
97	Kik	86,157	Kik lets you connect with friends.	Canada	5
98	Bayt.com	86,150	Bayt.com is an online recruitment website for the Gulf and Middle East regions.	United Arab Emirates	1
99	mytheresa.com	86,068	mytheresa.com is an online store that offers women's luxury and designer fashion products.	Germany	4
100	ThemeIsle	86,054	WordPress themes with a bang, so get yer guns ready! – ThemeIsle is a WordPress themes shop.	Romania	1

Source: www.startupranking.com/top (April 2018).

Appendix 3.4

list of the worst startup failures in the world – 2017 (source: www.cbinsights.com/research/biggest-startup-failures/)

Company Name	Total Announced Cash Raised By The Company (In Millions Of US Dollars)	Some Notable Investors	Country	Comments
Solyndra	$1,220.0	Redpoint Ventures; US Venture Partners;	USA	This solar energy company failed in 2018 and sold its businesses and licensed its copper indium gallium selenide (CIGS) technology. www.reuters.com/article/2011/08/31/us-solyndra-idUSTRE77U5K420110831; see Wikipedia comments: https://en.wikipedia.org/wiki/Solyndra;
Better Place	$950.0	VantagePoint Capital Partners; Lend Lease Ventures;	Israel	See: Noel, L. & Sovacool, B. (2016). Why Did Better Place Fail?: Range anxiety, interpretive flexibility, and electric vehicle promotion in Denmark and Israel. Energy Policy, 94, 377–386. Also see: http://venturebeat.com/2013/05/26/electric-car-company-better-place-shuts-down-after-burning-through-850m/; see Wikipedia comments: https://en.wikipedia.org/wiki/Better_Place_(company); www.fastcompany.com/3028159/a-broken-place-better-place; www.sciencedirect.com/science/article/pii/S0301421516301987;
Jawbone.	$929.8	Sequoia Capital; Khosla Ventures; Kleiner Perkins Caufield & Byers;	USA	The company had failed by July 2017, and it was a maker of a line of headsets, fitness trackers, and wireless speakers. see Wikipedia comments: https://en.wikipedia.org/wiki/Jawbone_(company);

(Continued)

Continued

Company Name	Total Announced Cash Raised By The Company (In Millions Of US Dollars)	Some Notable Investors	Country	Comments
Webvan Group	$780.0	Sequoia Capital; Softbank Capital;	USA	The company raised about $800 million of cash but didn't have sufficient demand but it had spent excessive cash on infrastructure. www.reuters.com/article/2011/08/31/us-solyndra-idUSTRE77U5K420110831; see Wikipedia comments: https://en.wikipedia.org/wiki/Webvan; https://yourstory.com/2014/09/webvan-e-tailer/;
Terralliance	$470.0	Kleiner Perkins Caufield & Byers; Goldman Sachs, DAG Ventures;	USA	Investors had invested an estimated total of about US$500 million in Terralliance, which never accomplished much. http://money.cnn.com/2010/03/26/news/companies/terralliance_tech_full.fortune/index.htm#full; http://archive.fortune.com/2010/03/26/news/companies/terralliance_tech_full.fortune/index.htm; www.cbsnews.com/news/how-terralliances-billion-dollar-bet-against-big-oil-failed/;
Amp'd Mobile.	$324.3	Highland Capital Partners; Columbia Capital, Redpoint Ventures;	USA	The company had very low cash, and Verizon had requested a court to stop Amp'd Mobile from providing costly airwaves that it couldn't afford. www.engadget.com/2007/07/20/ampd-in-death-throes-files-to-sell-off-assets/; see Wikipedia comments: https://en.wikipedia.org/wiki/Amp%27d_Mobile;
Caspian Networks.	$260.0	New Enterprise Associates; US Venture Partners;	USA	The company apparently thrived on fads such as "core routing" and then "P2P networking" and "net neutrality". www.lightreading.com/ethernet-ip/routers/caspian-closes-its-doors/d/d-id/632170; www.complex.com/pop-culture/2012/10/the-50-worst-internet-startup-fails-of-all-time/caspian; http://startupfundraising.com/10-expensive-startup-failures-history/;

Company	Amount	Country	Notes
Kozmo.com.	$256.2	USA	Oak Investment Partners; Flatiron Partners;	www.forbes.com/2001/04/12/0412topnews.html; see Wikipedia comments: https://en.wikipedia.org/wiki/Kozmo.com; https://techcrunch.com/2018/03/21/kozmo-com-is-back-from-the-dead-kind-of/;
KiOR.	$252.3	USA	Artis Capital Management; Khosla Ventures; Alberta Investment Management Corporation;	KiOR was rumoured to have made poor hiring decisions (too many Ph.Ds and few people with technical, operational experience). http://fortune.com/kior-vinod-khosla-clean-tech/; www.biofuelsdigest.com/bdigest/2016/05/17/kior-the-inside-true-story-of-a-company-gone-wrong/;
Mode Media.	$229.0	USA	Draper Fisher Jurvetson; Accel Partners; Greycroft Partners;	The consensus was that the company failed due to sub-optimal financial management. Mode Media's assets were later acquired by BrideClick. www.businessinsider.com/mode-media-glam-collapse-inside-story-2016-9; see Wikipedia comments: https://en.wikipedia.org/wiki/Mode_Media; https://techcrunch.com/2017/06/18/brideclick-acquires-mode-media/;
Aquion Energy.	$196.0	USA	CapX Partners; Constellation Technology Ventures; Bill Gates;	The company filed for bankruptcy and later emerged from bankruptcy proceedings with new owners. https://cleantechnica.com/2017/03/15/aquion-energy-files-chapter-11-bankruptcy/; see Wikipedia comments: https://en.wikipedia.org/wiki/Aquion_Energy; www.prnewswire.com/news-releases/aquion-energy-inc-emerges-from-chapter-11-bankruptcy-status-under-new-us-based-ownership-300492464.html;;
Quirky	$185.0	USA	Kleiner Perkins Caufield & Byers; Andreessen Horowitz; RRE Ventures;	On September 22, 2015, the company filed for Chapter 11 bankruptcy, and its assets were purchased by Q Holdings for $4.7 million. http://nymag.com/daily/intelligencer/2015/09/they-were-quirky.html; see Wikipedia comments: https://en.wikipedia.org/wiki/Quirky_(company); www.jason-stevens.com/2010/07/how-quirky-com-killed-my-dreams-of-becoming-an-inventor/;

(Continued)

Continued

Company Name	Total Announced Cash Raised By The Company (In Millions Of US Dollars)	Some Notable Investors	Country	Comments
Guvera.	$185.0	AMMA Private Investment	Australia	This Australian music streaming company privately raised $185 million before its $100 million IPO offering was blocked by the Australian Securities Exchange in 2017; and Guvera had make 45 amendments to its IPO prospectus after comments by the Australian Securities and Investments Commission. Guvera generated operating losses of A$81 million and had about A$1.2 million of revenues in FY2016. www.businessinsider.com.au/australian-streaming-startup-guvera-has-shut-down-after-taking-185-million-from-investors-2017–5; see Wikipedia comments: https://en.wikipedia.org/wiki/Guvera; www.afr.com/lifestyle/arts-and-entertainment/music/the-great-guvera-mystery-where-did-180-million-of-investors-money-go-20170524-gwbttm;
Powa Technologies.	$176.0	Otto Group; Wellington Management;	United Kingdom	The company spent more than $200 million, and was once valued at about $2.7 billion. www.ft.com/cms/s/0/db78778a-d727-11e5-829b-8564e7528e54.html#axzz40pbKitM6; see Wikipedia comments: https://en.wikipedia.org/wiki/Powa_Technologies; http://uk.businessinsider.com/inside-the-crash-of-londons-payment-unicorn-powa-technologies-2016-4?IR=T;
eToys.	$166.3	Bessemer Venture Partners, Sequoia Capital;	USA	www.nytimes.com/2001/02/06/technology/06ETOY.html; see Wikipedia comments: https://en.wikipedia.org/wiki/EToys.com; https://abcnews.go.com/Business/story?id=88548&page=1; www.reuters.com/article/us-goldmansachs-etoys-settlement/goldman-sachs-finally-ends-litigation-over-1999-etoys-ipo-idUSBRE98I0VL20130919;

Company	Amount	Country	Comments
Quixey	$164.0	USA	Alibaba Group; GGV Capital; Atlantic Bridge Capital;	After spending more than $130 million, Quixey shut down partly due to its inability to repay a loan provided its shareholder Alibaba. www.globalcorporateventuring.com/article.php/16602/quixey-closure-reportedly-due-to-alibaba-debt-deal?utm_medium=feed&utm_campaign=Feed%3A+GlobalCorporateVenturingArticles+%28Global+Corporate+Venturing+Articles%29; www.axios.com/behind-the-fall-of-quixey-2333564105.html; see Wikipedia comments: https://en.wikipedia.org/wiki/Quixey; www.axios.com/behind-the-fall-of-quixey-1513301224-05bad4bc-bae3-464a-b192-7dd9417b252b.html;
Drugstore.com.	$157.0	USA	Amazon, Kleiner Perkins Caufield & Byers, Maveron	www.chicagotribune.com/business/columnists/ct-rosenthal-walgreens-kills-drugstore-com-0802-biz-20160801-column.html; see Wikipedia comments: https://en.wikipedia.org/wiki/Drugstore.com;
Lilliputian Systems.	$150.0	USA	Kleiner Perkins, Atlas Venture, Intel Capital	Lilliputian Systems was spun-off from MIT (USA). www.betaboston.com/news/2014/07/31/lilliputian-systems-mit-spin-out-that-raised-150-million-runs-out-of-fuel/; www.xconomy.com/boston/2014/08/14/after-150m-spent-what-went-wrong-at-fuel-cell-startup-lilliputian/; www.forbes.com/forbes/welcome/?toURL=www.forbes.com/sites/michaelkanellos/2014/08/21/the-mit-curse-strikes-again-lilliputian-systems-runs-out-of-gas/&refURL=www.google.com.ng/&referrer=www.google.com.ng/;
Beepi	$147.7	USA	SAIC Motor; Redpoint Ventures; Foundation Capital; Gil Penchina;	The company benefited from the hype of transportation startups and marketplaces. In 2015, Beepi announced that it wanted to raise a "monster round" of $300 million at a $2 billion valuation. https://techcrunch.com/2017/02/16/car-startup-beepi-sold-for-parts-after-potential-exits-to-fair-and-then-dgdg-broke-down/.

(Continued)

Continued

Company Name	Total Announced Cash Raised By The Company (In Millions Of US Dollars)	Some Notable Investors	Country	Comments
Cereva Networks.	$137.0	Oak Investment Partners, North Bridge Venture Partners, Intel Capital, Goldman Sachs	USA	Due to shrinking corporate IT budgets and lower demand, the company shut down and laid off 140 employees. www.taborcommunications.com/dsstar/02/0709/104452.html; www.bizjournals.com/boston/blog/mass-high-tech/2002/06/cereva-networks-shuts-down.html; www.networkcomputing.com/data-centers/cereva-stalled-not-stopped/755248983;
Boo.com.	$135.0	Arts Alliance	USA	Boo.com over-spent on advertising and promotions, didn't innovate sufficiently, and kept out most of its target audience. www.ecommercetimes.com/story/3428.html; see Wikipedia comments: https://en.wikipedia.org/wiki/Boo.com; www.smartinsights.com/digital-marketing-strategy/online-marketing-mix/boo-com-case-study-a-classic-example-of-failed-ebusiness-strategy/;
AllAdvantage.com.	$133.5	Alloy Ventures, Walden Venture Capital.	USA	www.bizjournals.com/eastbay/stories/2001/01/29/daily29.html; see Wikipedia comments: https://en.wikipedia.org/wiki/AllAdvantage; www.bizjournals.com/sanfrancisco/stories/2001/01/29/daily35.html;
Pay By Touch.	$130.0	Mobius Venture Capital; Rembrandt Venture Partners;	USA	www.businessweek.com/stories/2007-12-06/battles-and-bids-over-pay-by-touchbusinessweek-business-news-stock-market-and-financial-advice; see Wikipedia comments: https://en.wikipedia.org/wiki/Pay_By_Touch; https://venturebeat.com/2007/11/12/pay-by-touch-in-trouble-founder-filing-for-bankruptcy/;

Company	Amount	Investors	Country	Notes
Rdio.	$117.0	Atomico, Mangrove Capital Partners	USA	Pandora acquired what was left of Rdio for $75 million. www.theverge.com/2015/11/17/9750890/rdio-shutdown-pandora; see Wikipedia comments: https://en.wikipedia.org/wiki/Rdio; www.theverge.com/2015/11/17/9750890/rdio-shutdown-pandora;
OnLive.	$116.5	Time Warner Investments; lauder Partners	USA	http://kotaku.com/onlive-the-first-big-streaming-games-service-is-dead-1695386223; www.theverge.com/2012/8/28/3274739/onlive-report;
RealNames Corporation.	$116.1	Draper Fisher Jurvetson, Clearstone Venture Partners	USA	The company owed Microsoft $25 million. http://searchenginewatch.com/article/2067393/RealNames-To-Close-After-Losing-Microsoft; articles.latimes.com/2002/may/14/business/fi-techbriefs14.4; www.computerworld.com/ … /realnames-calls-it-quits--blames-microsoft.html;
Coraid	$114.2	Azure Capital Partners, Menlo Ventures	USA	http://venturebeat.com/2015/04/21/data-center-storage-startup-coraid-is-now-officially-toast/; www.linkedin.com/pulse/coraid-back-brantley-coile; www.theregister.co.uk/2017/06/26/coraids_athenian_resurrection/;
Savaje Technologies.	$113.6	VantagePoint Venture Partners, RRE Ventures	USA	http://mobile.eweek.com/c/a/Application-Development/Savaje-Falls-on-Hard-Times/; see Wikipedia comments: https://en.wikipedia.org/wiki/Savaje;
Pets.com.	$110.0	Hummer Winblad Partners, Bowman Capital	USA	The company depended heavily on discounts, and was selling most of its products below cost. www.businessinsider.com/petscom-ceo-julie-wainwright-2011-2?IR=T;
COPAN Systems.	$108.3	Globespan Capital Partners, Austin Ventures	USA	COPAN filed for bankruptcy protection and Silicon Graphics International Corporation purchased its assets in bankruptcy. http://it.toolbox.com/blogs/storage-topics/the-unfortunate-demise-of-copan-systems-35721;

(Continued)

Continued

Company Name	Total Announced Cash Raised By The Company (In Millions Of US Dollars)	Some Notable Investors	Country	Comments
ChaCha.	$108.0	Vantage Point Capital Partners; Qualcomm Ventures; Rho Ventures.	USA	Chacha didn't generate adequate advertising revenue in 2016 and couldn't pay its debts. It sold its assets and its secured lender took over its bank accounts. www.ibj.com/articles/61651-chacha-unable-to-find-financial-answers-shuts-down-operations; https://en.wikipedia.org/wiki/ChaCha_(search_engine);
ACptix Technologies.	$107.5	Lehman Brothers; Kleiner Perkins Caufield & Byers; Clearstone Venture Partners	USA	www.lightreading.com/mobile/backhaul/exclusive-its-lights-out-for-aoptix/d/d-id/720915; www.corporationwiki.com/California/Campbell/aoptix-technologies-inc/4333 0288.aspx;
Calxeda.	$103.0	Battery Ventures, Flybridge Capital Partners	USA	www.theregister.co.uk/2013/12/19/calxeda_shutdown/; https://en.wikipedia.org/wiki/Calxeda;
Next Step Living	$100.4	Black Coral Capital, Braemar Energy Ventures, VantagePoint Capital Partners	USA	www.greentechmedia.com/articles/read/Next-Step-Living-Out-of-Cash-is-Shutting-Its-Doors-This-Week; boston.cbslocal.com/2016/03/18/i-team-boston-next-step-living-closes-massave/;
Juicero.	$99.8	Google Ventures; Kleiner Perkins Caufield & Byers, Thrive Capital	USA	The company collapsed due to excessive costs, poor media coverage and an ineffective product launch. www.bloomberg.com/news/features/2017-09-08/inside-juicero-s-demise-from-prized-startup-to-fire-sale; https://en.wikipedia.org/wiki/Juicero; www.theguardian.com/technology/2017/sep/01/juicero-silicon-valley-shutting-down;
DeNovis, Inc.	$98.6	Advanced Technology Ventures, UV Partners	USA	www.boston.com/business/technology/articles/2004/10/23/lexington_software_firm_shuts_down/; https://fail92fail.wordpress.com/tag/denovis-inc/;

Auctionata.	$97.3	German Startups Group, Bright Capital, e.ventures, Earlybird Venture Capital	Germany	https://news.artnet.com/market/auctionata-closes-insolvency-proceedings-874583; https://en.wikipedia.org/wiki/Auctionata; https://news.artnet.com/art-world/auctionata-insolvency-proceedings-822965;
Aereo.	$97.0	FirstMark Capital, Highland Capital Partners	USA	www.wired.com/2014/11/aereo-bankruptcy/; https://en.wikipedia.org/wiki/Aereo;
Beyond The Rack.	$95.5	Silicon Valley Bank, BDC Venture Capital, Highland Capital Partners	Canada	www.lightreading.com/mobile/backhaul/exclusive-its-lights-out-for-aoptix/d/d-id/720915; http://montrealgazette.com/business/local-business/what-went-wrong-with-montreals-beyond-the-rack;
Sonitus Medical.	$89.6	GE Capital; Aberdare Ventures; Novartis Venture Funds; RWI Ventures	USA	www.mddionline.com/blog/devicetalk/cms-coverage-decision-killed-my-80m-venture-backed-startup-04-02-15; www.hearingreview.com/2015/02/sonitus-medical-holds-auction-closing-doors/;
Canopy Financial.	$89.4	GGV Capital, Foundation Capital	USA	the US SEC filed a complaint against Canopy and it also declared bankruptcy and its officers were sentenced to jail. http://blogs.wsj.com/venturecapital/2009/11/30/embattled-canopy-financial-files-ch-11-bankruptcy-as-details-emerge/; www.sec.gov/litigation/complaints/2009/canopy113009.pdf; https://techcrunch.com/2009/11/24/canopy-financial-accused-of-serious-financial-fraud-investors-burned/;
Soapstone Networks	$87.2	Accel Partners, Oak Investment Partners	USA	http://clientadmin.lightreading.com/blog.asp?blog_sectionid=388&doc_id=179804&piddl_msgorder=asc; www.bloomberg.com/research/stocks/private/snapshot.asp?privcapId=25333;
Claria Corporation	$84.0	US Venture Partners, Crosslink Capital	USA	http://venturebeat.com/2008/10/06/controversial-ad-company-jellycloud-shuts-down-citing-industry-consolidation/

(Continued)

Continued

Company Name	Total Announced Cash Raised By The Company (In Millions Of US Dollars)	Some Notable Investors	Country	Comments
SunRocket	$79.2	Anthem Capital, BlueRun Ventures	USA	http://news.cnet.com/8301-10784_3-9745629-7.html; see wikipedia comments: https://en.wikipedia.org/wiki/SunRocket; www.cnet.com/news/sunrocket-closes-its-doors/;
38 Studios	$75.0	Rhode Island Economic Development Corporation	USA	www.bostonmagazine.com/2012/07/38-studios-end-game/; https://en.wikipedia.org/wiki/38_Studios; https://techraptor.net/content/project-copernicus-rise-fall-38-studios; www.wpri.com/news/eyewitness-news-investigates/qa-how-much-will-38-studios-cost-ri-taxpayers-when-all-is-said-and-done_20180314124518777/1044191311;
Beenz.com	$73.5	Gefinor Ventures, Apax Partners	England	http://news.cnet.com/2100-1017-271741.html; https://en.wikipedia.org/wiki/Beenz.com; www.theregister.co.uk/2001/08/16/beenz_is_dead_official/;
Veoh Networks	$70.8	Shelter Capital Partners, Spark Capital	USA	www.xconomy.com/san-diego/2010/02/11/shutdown-reported-at-veoh-networks-backed-by-bostons-spark-capital-and-other-vcs/; https://en.wikipedia.org/wiki/Veoh;
Dealstruck	$70.1	Community Investment Management, Brevet Capital Management, Trinity Ventures, Giles Raymond	USA	www.crowdfundinsider.com/2016/12/93348-finance-small-companies-still-broken/; www.valuepenguin.com/small-business/dealstruck-small-business-loan-review;
Nirvanix	$70.0	Valhalla Partners; Mission Ventures	USA	http://techcrunch.com/2013/09/27/its-official-the-nirvanix-cloud-storage-service-is-shutting-down/; https://en.wikipedia.org/wiki/Nirvanix; www.computerweekly.com/opinion/Nirvanix-failure-a-blow-to-the-cloud-storage-model;

Company	Amount	Country	Investors	Sources
Expand Networks	$69.0	Isreal	The Challenge Fund-Etgar; Tamir Fishman Ventures	www.globes.co.il/en/article.aspx?did=1000710763&fid=1725; https://en.wikipedia.org/wiki/Expand_Networks; www.riverbed.com/gb/press-releases/riverbed-purchases-assets-of-expand-networks.html;
Ecast	$66.8	USA	Crosslink Capital; Doll Capital	The company ran out of cash. www.vendingtimes.com/ME2/dirmod.asp?nm=Vending+Features&type=Publishing&mod=Publications%3A%3AArticle&tier=4&id=1FA76E9E03FA4C048872B380ABC0310E; https://en.wikipedia.org/wiki/Ecast,_Inc.;
Edgix	$65.0	USA	Venrock; Battery Ventures;	www.newsday.com/business/technology/queens-inc-edgix-to-close-lay-off-most-of-its-100-workers-1.309693; www.crunchbase.com/organization/edgix-corporation;
LOYAL3	$62.3	USA	Community Investment Management; Giles raymond; Brevet Capital Management; Trinity Ventures;	www.benzinga.com/fintech/17/04/9323918/discount-brokerage-loyal3-shutting-down?utm_source=feedburner&utm_medium=feed&utm_campaign=Feed%3A%20benzinga%20%28Benzinga%20News%20Feed%29; https://accessipos.com/death-loyal3/; www.valuewalk.com/2017/04/loyal3-brokerage-shut-may/;
Move Networks	$60.3	USA	Hummer Winblad Venture Partners, Steamboat Ventures	http://gigaom.com/2010/01/26/the-fall-of-move-networks/; www.prnewswire.com/news-releases/echostar-acquires-assets-of-move-networks-leader-in-adaptive-streaming-for-over-the-top-video-solutions-113018769.html;
Sprig	$56.6	USA	Greylock Partners, Social Capital and Sozo Ventures	www.pymnts.com/whats-hot-2/2017/sprig-couldnt-cut-it-in-food-delivery-space/; https://techcrunch.com/2017/05/26/on-demand-food-startup-sprig-is-shutting-down-today/;
DoubleTwist	$56.5	USA	Institutional Venture Partners, Boston Millennia Partners	www.bio-itworld.com/archive/050702/survivor_sidebar_252.html

(Continued)

Continued

Company Name	Total Announced Cash Raised By The Company (In Millions Of US Dollars)	Some Notable Investors	Country	Comments
TerraLUX	$55.5	Access Venture Partners, Emerald Technology Ventures	USA	www.denverpost.com/2017/08/15/terralux-sielo-longmont-shuts-down/
Sard 9	$55.4	Commonwealth Capital Ventures; Flybridge Capital Partners; General Catalyst;	USA	www.eenewsanalog.com/news/analog-devices-sand-9-buyer; https://en.wikipedia.org/wiki/Sand_9;
Akimbo	$54.7	Zone Ventures; Draper Fisher Jurvetson	USA	http://gigaom.com/2008/05/23/update-akimbo-skeleton-crew-looking-for-a-buyer/; https://venturebeat.com/2008/02/29/akimbo-failed-video-distribution-company-tries-again-raises-8m/; www.eetimes.com/document.asp?doc_id=1171591
Sequoia Communications	$54.0	Tallwood Ventures; BlueRun Ventures	USA	http://money.cnn.com/magazines/fsb/fsb_archive/2000/07/01/28696/index.htm
govWorks	$54.0	Tallwood Ventures, BlueRun Ventures	USA	
Hello	$52.8	Cherubic Ventures, Temasek Holdings	USA	http://fortune.com/2017/06/12/hello-sleep-tracking-shut-down/
PepperTap	$52.0	Innoven Capital, Sequoia Capital India	India	Indian online food/grocery retailer. http://techcircle.vccircle.com/2016/12/09/flawed-business-model-or-funding-crunch-what-led-to-startup-shutdowns/; www.techinasia.com/raising-us50-million-indias-largest-online-grocer-shut-shop; https://qz.com/669142/peppertaps-collapse-shows-everything-that-is-wrong-with-indias-young-internet-companies/;
Ka-hoo	$52.0	David Kowitz, Jonathan Feuer, Nick Gatfield	England	https://techcrunch.com/2016/11/08/uber-competitor-karhoo-shuts-down-after-blowing-through-250m/; www.ft.com/content/0bb3cba0-a69b-11e6-8898-79a99e2a4de6; https://techcrunch.com/2017/01/12/karhoo-rides-again-nissanrenault-buys-failed-on-demand-ride-startup/;

Company	Amount ($M)	Investors	Country	Sources / Notes
Flooz.com	$51.4	Oak Investment Partners, Maveron	USA	www.internetretailer.com/2001/08/28/flooz-finalizes-its-shut-down-amid-problems-with-fraud; https://en.wikipedia.org/wiki/Flooz.com;
Pearl Automation	$50.0	Accel Partners, Shasta Ventures, Venrock	USA	www.axios.com/automotive-startup-pearl-is-shutting-down-2448087174.html; https://en.wikipedia.org/wiki/Pearl_Automation; www.nytimes.com/2017/06/26/technology/pearl-automation-founded-by-apple-veterans-shuts-down.html;
Nanochip	$48.7	New Enterprise Associates, JK&B Capital	USA	http://blogs.wsj.com/venturecapital/2009/08/05/turning-out-the-lights-memory-chips-maker-nanochip/
Joost	$45.0	Sequoia Capital, Index Ventures	Netherlands	www.crainsnewyork.com/article/20090630/free/906309977; https://en.wikipedia.org/wiki/Joost;
Digg	$44.0	Highland Capital Partners, Greylock Partners	USA	www.theguardian.com/technology/2012/jul/13/digg-sold-for-500000; www.computerworld.com/article/2506833/web-apps/elgan--why-digg-failed.html;
Pixelon	$35.0	Advanced Equities	USA	In April 2018, it was discovered that "Paul Stanley" was the real name of Michael Fenne, the company's founder and former chairman; and that he had violated bail conditions after being convicted for stock-swindling and had been on Virginia's (USA state) most-wanted list of criminals for several years. www.wired.com/techbiz/media/news/2000/05/36243; https://en.wikipedia.org/wiki/Pixelon; www.nytimes.com/2000/04/15/technology/pixeloncom-founder-was-fugitive-from-virginia.html;

Source: Mike Nwogugu; www.cbinsights.com/research/biggest-startup-failures/.

List of all major financial crisis since the seventeenth century (source: https://en.wikipedia. org/wiki/Financial_crisis)

1 The crash of the *Tulip Mania Bubble* in the Netherlands in 1637 (*https:// en.wikipedia.org/wiki/Tulip_mania*).
2 The crashes of the *South Sea Bubble* (Great Britain) and the *Mississippi Bubble* (France) in 1720 (https://en.wikipedia.org/wiki/South_Sea_Bubble; *https://en.wikipedia.org/wiki/Mississippi_Bubble*).
3 The Financial Crisis of 1763 which started in Amsterdam and extended to Germany and Scandinavia (*https://en.wikipedia.org/wiki/ Amsterdam_banking_crisis_of_1763*).
4 The financial Crisis of 1772 (in London and Amsterdam): twenty important banks in London became bankrupt (*https://en.wikipedia.org/wiki/ Crisis_of_1772*).
5 France's financial and Debt Crisis of 1783–1788: France had incurred large debts for its involvement in the Seven Years' War (1756–1763) and the American Revolution (1775–1783).
6 The bank run of 1792 in the US: which was caused by the expansion of credit by the newly formed Bank of the United States (*https://en.wikipedia. org/wiki/Panic_of_1792*).
7 The crises and mass hysteria of 1796–1797 in Britain and the US: caused by land speculation bubble (*https://en.wikipedia.org/wiki/ Panic_of_1796%E2%80%931797*).
8 South Sea Bubble (1720) in the UK (*https://en.wikipedia.org/wiki/South_Sea_ Bubble*); and Mississippi Company (1720) (France) (*https://en.wikipedia. org/wiki/Mississippi_Company*).
9 The Great East Indian Bengal Bubble Crash of 1769 in India – the crash was caused by rapid over-valuation of East India Company (*https://en.wikipedia. org/wiki/Bengal_Bubble_of_1769*).
10 The economic crises and mass hysteria of 1785 in the United States.
11 The economic crises and mass hysteria of 1792 in the United States (*https:// en.wikipedia.org/wiki/Panic_of_1792*).
12 The crises and mass hysteria of 1796–1797 in Britain and United States. (*https://en.wikipedia.org/wiki/Panic_of_1796%E2%80%931797*).
13 The bankruptcy of the Danish government in 1813 (*https://en.wikipedia.org/ wiki/Danish_state_bankruptcy_of_1813*).

14 The Financial Crisis of 1818 in England which also affected the US – which reduced bank lending.

15 The economic recession and mass hysteria of 1819 in the USA – marked by bank failures and the USA's first boom-to-bust economic cycle (*https:// en.wikipedia.org/wiki/Panic_of_1819*).

16 The economic recession and mass hysteria of 1825 in Britain – wherein many British banks failed and Bank of England nearly failed (*https://en.wikipedia. org/wiki/Panic_of_1825*).

17 The economic recession and mass hysteria of 1837 in the USA – marked by bank failures and a subsequent 5-year depression (*https://en.wikipedia.org/ wiki/Panic_of_1837*).

18 Crises and mass hysteria of 1847 in Britain – marked by collapse of British financial markets and the end of the 1840s railroad boom (https:// en.wikipedia.org/wiki/Panic_of_1847; https://en.wikipedia.org/wiki/Railroad). Also see Bank Charter Act of 1844 (*https://en.wikipedia.org/wiki/ Bank_Charter_Act_1844*).

19 The economic recession of 1857 in the USA – marked by bank failures (*https://en.wikipedia.org/wiki/Panic_of_1857*).

20 The Overend Gurney crisis (international financial crises but primarily British) – defined by the failure of Overend, Gurney & Company in London (https://en.wikipedia.org/wiki/Panic_of_1866; *https://en.wikipedia.org/wiki/ Overend_Gurney_crisis*).

21 The Gold Panic of 1869 (*https://en.wikipedia.org/wiki/Black_Friday_(1869)*).

22 The USA economic recession and mass hysteria of 1873 – defined by bank failures and the five year "Long Depression" (https://en.wikipedia.org/wiki/ Panic_of_1873; *https://en.wikipedia.org/wiki/Long_Depression*).

23 The crises and mass hysteria of 1884 in the USA – affected New York banks (*https://en.wikipedia.org/wiki/Panic_of_1884*).

24 The Baring Crisis of 1890 – defined by the near-failure of a major London bank and the South American financial crises (*https://en.wikipedia.org/wiki/ Panic_of_1890*).

25 The economic recession and mass hysteria of 1893 in the USA – defined by failures of railroad overbuilding and bank failures (*https://en.wikipedia.org/ wiki/Panic_of_1893*).

26 The Australian banking crisis of 1893 (*https://en.wikipedia.org/wiki/ Australian_banking_crisis_of_1893*).

27 The 1896 acute economic depression in the United States – caused by lower silver reserves and perceptions of its effects on the gold standard (https://en. wikipedia.org/wiki/Panic_of_1896; https://en.wikipedia.org/wiki/Recession; *https://en.wikipedia.org/wiki/Gold_standard*).

28 The post-Napoleonic depression (post-1815) in England (*https://en.wikipedia. org/wiki/Post-Napoleonic_depression*).

29 The economic recession and mass hysteria of 1819 in the USA – marked by bank failures and the US's first boom-to-bust economic cycle (*https:// en.wikipedia.org/wiki/Panic_of_1819*).

30   The Great Depression of the British Agriculture industry during 1873–1896 (*https://en.wikipedia.org/wiki/Great_Depression_of_British_Agriculture*).

31   The Long Depression of 1873–1896 (*https://en.wikipedia.org/wiki/Long_Depression*).

32   The Australian banking crisis of 1893 (*https://en.wikipedia.org/wiki/Australian_banking_crisis_of_1893*).

33   US economic recession and mass hysteria of 1907 – marked by bank failures (*https://en.wikipedia.org/wiki/Panic_of_1907*).

34   The economic recession and mass hysteria of 1901 in the US – which started a tussle for the financial control of the Northern Pacific Railway (*https://en.wikipedia.org/wiki/Panic_of_1901*).

35   The crises and mass hysteria of 1910–1911 (*https://en.wikipedia.org/wiki/Panic_of_1910%E2%80%931911*).

36   The Shanghai rubber stock market crisis of 1910 (*https://en.wikipedia.org/wiki/Shanghai_rubber_stock_market_crisis*).

37   The US economic recession, depression and mass hysteria of 1920–21 after the end of World war One (*https://en.wikipedia.org/wiki/Depression_of_1920%E2%80%9321*).

38   The Wall Street Crash of 1929 and Great Depression of 1929–1939 in the US – which was the worst depression of modern history (https://en.wikipedia.org/wiki/Wall_Street_Crash_of_1929; *https://en.wikipedia.org/wiki/Great_Depression*).

39   The 1973 global oil crisis and the 1973 OPEC oil price shock – oil prices increased which caused the 1973–1974 stock market crash (https://en.wikipedia.org/wiki/1973_oil_crisis; *https://en.wikipedia.org/wiki/1973%E2%80%931974_stock_market_crash*).

40   The 1970s global energy crisis (*https://en.wikipedia.org/wiki/1970s_energy_crisis*).

41   The 1979 global energy crisis (*https://en.wikipedia.org/wiki/1979_energy_crisis*).

42   The secondary banking crisis of 1973–1975 in the UK (*https://en.wikipedia.org/wiki/Secondary_banking_crisis_of_1973%E2%80%931975*).

43   The Latin American debt crisis of late-1970s and early-1980s (*https://en.wikipedia.org/wiki/Latin_American_debt_crisis*).

44   The early 1980s economic recession (*https://en.wikipedia.org/wiki/Early_1980s_recession*).

45   The Chilean crisis of 1982 (https://en.wikipedia.org/wiki/Crisis_of_1982).

46   The bank stock crisis of 1983 in Isreal (*https://en.wikipedia.org/wiki/Bank_stock_crisis_(Israel_1983)*).

47   The Nigerian recession and structural adjustments programs of 1983–1986.

48   The Japanese asset price bubble of 1986–1992 – which collapsed in 1990 (*https://en.wikipedia.org/wiki/Japanese_asset_price_bubble*).

49   The stock market crash of 1987 in the USA (Black Monday) – one of the most significant declines of stock markets in history (*https://en.wikipedia.org/wiki/Black_Monday_(1987)*).

50   The US savings and loan (S&L) crisis of 1986–1995 – marked by the failures of 1,043 out of the approximately then-existing 3,234 S&L banks during 1986–1995 in the USA (*https://en.wikipedia.org/wiki/Savings_and_loan_crisis*).

51   The African sovereign debt crisis of 1980–1989.

52   The 1991 economic crisis in India.

53   The Scandinavian banking crisis of the early 1990s: Swedish and Finnish banking crises of 1990s (https://en.wikipedia.org/wiki/Economy_of_Sweden# Crisis_of_the_1990s; *https://en.wikipedia.org/wiki/Finnish_banking_crisis_ of_1990s*).

54   The early-1990s global economic recession (*https://en.wikipedia.org/wiki/ Early_1990s_recession*).

55   The speculative attacks on currencies in the European Exchange Rate Mechanism during 1992–1993 (https://en.wikipedia.org/wiki/Black_Wednesday; *https://en.wikipedia.org/wiki/European_Exchange_Rate_Mechanism*).

56   The Latin American debt crises of the 1990s.

57   The 1994–1995 economic and financial crisis in Mexico – marked by speculative attacks on the Mexican Peso and defaults of Mexican debt (*https:// en.wikipedia.org/wiki/1994_economic_crisis_in_Mexico*).

58   The economic crisis of 1991 in India (*https://en.wikipedia.org/wiki/1991_ India_economic_crisis*).

59   The 1997–1998 Asian financial crisis – marked by currency devaluations and banking crises in Asian countries (*https://en.wikipedia.org/wiki/1997_Asian_ financial_crisis*).

60   The 1998 financial crisis in Russia (*https://en.wikipedia.org/wiki/1998_ Russian_financial_crisis*).

61   The 1998–1999 financial crisis in Ecuador (*https://en.wikipedia.org/wiki/ 1998-99_Ecuador_financial_crisis*).

62   The Thailand financial crisis of 1997.

63   The economic crisis of 1999–2002 in Argentina (*https://en.wikipedia.org/ wiki/Argentine_economic_crisis_(1999%E2%80%932002)*).

64   The *Samba Effect of 1999* in Brazil (*https://en.wikipedia.org/wiki/Samba_effect*).

65   The Turkish economic crisis of 2000–2001 (*https://en.wikipedia.org/ wiki/2001_Turkish_economic_crisis*).

66   The early 2000s global recession (*https://en.wikipedia.org/wiki/ Early_2000s_recession*).

67   The crash of the technology/internet stock bubble in the US in 2000 – speculation about stock prices of internet companies (*https://en.wikipedia.org/ wiki/Dot-com_bubble*).

68   The Uruguay banking crisis of 2002 (*https://en.wikipedia.org/wiki/2002_ Uruguay_banking_crisis*).

69   The Venezuelan general strike of 2002–2003 (*https://en.wikipedia.org/wiki/ Venezuelan_general_strike_of_2002%E2%80%9303*).

70   The Global Financial Crisis and economic crises of 2007–2012 – which was caused in part by the subprime mortgage crises of 2006–2008 in the

USA. In many countries, government interventions (e.g. government bail-outs/bail-ins; new financial regulations; quantitative easing; etc.) didn't spur economic growth or lending volumes (*https://en.wikipedia.org/wiki/Late-2000s_financial_crisis*).

71   The late-2000s global economic recession (*https://en.wikipedia.org/wiki/Late-2000s_recession*).

72   The worldwide energy crisis and oil price bubble of 2003–2009 (*https://en.wikipedia.org/wiki/2000s_energy_crisis*).

73   The Thailand financial crisis of 2008.

74   The worldwide oil price bubble of 2013–2015.

75   The Subprime mortgage crisis of 2006–2010 in the USA (*https://en.wikipedia.org/wiki/Subprime_mortgage_crisis*).

76   The United States housing bubble and United States housing market correction of 2003–2011 (https://en.wikipedia.org/wiki/United_States_housing_bubble; *https://en.wikipedia.org/wiki/United_States_housing_market_correction*).

77   The Automotive industry crisis and government bailouts of 2008–2010 in the USA (*https://en.wikipedia.org/wiki/Automotive_industry_crisis_of_2008%E2%80%932010*).

78   The Icelandic financial crisis of 2008–2012 (*https://en.wikipedia.org/wiki/2008%E2%80%932012_Icelandic_financial_crisis*).

79   The 2008 financial crisis in Indonesia.

80   The Irish banking crisis of 2008–2010 (*https://en.wikipedia.org/wiki/2008%E2%80%932010_Irish_banking_crisis*).

81   The Russian financial crisis of 2008–2009 (*https://en.wikipedia.org/wiki/Russian_financial_crisis_of_2008%E2%80%932009*).

82   The Latvian financial crisis of 2008 (*https://en.wikipedia.org/wiki/2008_Latvian_financial_crisis*).

83   The Venezuelan banking crisis of 2009–2010 (*https://en.wikipedia.org/wiki/Venezuelan_banking_crisis_of_2009%E2%80%9310*).

84   The Venezuelan economic recession and financial crises of 2013-present (*https://en.wikipedia.org/wiki/Crisis_in_Bolivarian_Venezuela*; *https://en.wikipedia.org/w/index.php?title=2012-2017_Venezuela_crisis&action=edit&redlink=1*).

85   The Spanish financial crisis and sovereign debt crisis of 2008-present (*https://en.wikipedia.org/wiki/2008-16_Spanish_financial_crisis*).

86   The Mexican financial crisis of 2008.

87   The mass hysteria and financial crisis of 2008–2009 in South Korea.

88   The mass hysteria and financial crisis of 2008 in China.

89   The Nigerian banking crises and economic crises of 2007–2012 – marked by high bank NPL-rates, bank failures and excessive loan interest rates.

90   The European sovereign debt crisis of 2010–2018 (*https://en.wikipedia.org/wiki/2010_European_sovereign_debt_crisis*).

91   The Russian financial crisis of 2014–2015 – the rubble crisis (*https://en.wikipedia.org/wiki/2014_Russian_financial_crisis*).

92 The economic crisis of 2014–2017 in Argentina – marked by mass protests, economic recession and sovereign debt default.

93 The Nigerian currency/financial/economic crises of 2014–2018 – marked by the crash of the stock market in 2014–2015, 150%+ currency devaluation and economic recession.

94 Crashes of the Chinese stock markets during 2015 (https://en.wikipedia.org/wiki/2015_Chinese_stock_market_crash).

95 The crashes of global commodity prices during 2015–2017.

96 The Greek government-debt crisis of 2009–present (*https://en.wikipedia.org/wiki/Greek_government-debt_crisis*).

97 The Portuguese financial crisis of 2010–2014 (*https://en.wikipedia.org/wiki/2010-14_Portuguese_financial_crisis*).

98 The Ukrainian crisis of 2013–2014 (*https://en.wikipedia.org/wiki/Ukrainian_crisis*).

99 The Ukrainian/Crimea war and economic crises of 2016–2018.

100 The Brazilian economic crisis and mass hysteria of 2014–2017 – which was marked by popular mass protests, the jailing of two former Brazilian Presidents and radical changes in government (*https://en.wikipedia.org/wiki/2014-2017_Brazilian_economic_crisis*).

101 The 2013 financial crisis in Indonesia.

102 The Japan-South Korea trade dispute of 2018–present.

103 The Malaysian financial crisis, mass hysteria and 1MDB scandal of 2014–2018 which resulted in the re-election of a former President and the jailing of another former President of Malaysia.

104 The worldwide cryptocurrency mania, bubble and frauds of 2015-present.

105 The worldwide *"Sharing Economy"* mania, stock-bubble and frauds of 2014–present.

106 The USA housing bubble of 2016–2019

107 The United Nations, US and EU economic sanctions that were imposed on Russia, North Korea and Iran during 2010–2019.

108 The US–China trade disputes of 2018–present.

109 The economic crisis and debt crisis of 2017–2019 in India (excessive debt owed by companies which affected the growth of the Indian economy).

110 The economic, financial (peso) and political crisis and mass hysteria (of 2014–present) in Argentina

111 The 2014–2017 mass hysteria, political crisis and economic crisis in Brazil which resulted in the impeachment of President Dilma Rousseff and in widespread protests about the political system and the Brazilian economy.

112 The EU economic sanctions that were imposed on Belarus from 2016 to 2019.

113 The debt crisis (excessive debt especially in Chinese households and the private sector) of 2017–2019 in China.

114 The EU economic sanctions that were imposed on Egypt during 2015–2019.

115 The EU economic sanctions that were imposed on Democratic Republic of Congo during 2015–2018.

116   The mass hysteria, and socioeconomic and political crisis of 2012–present in Venezuela.

117   The mass hysteria and 2015–2018 economic recession and financial crisis in Japan.

118   The EU and US economic sanctions that were imposed on Iraq during 2009–2011.

4

Fintech-based disclosure and incentives-effects misconduct as macrofinancial and international political economy leakages: sustainable growth and financial stability[1]

This chapter:

i) Explains the common reasons for earnings management and some obvious ways to reduce earnings management.
ii) Explains why earnings management, insider trading, incentives-effects management and asset-quality management are significant macroeconomic "leakages" – in the sense that they reduce social welfare, distort and degrade policy making and policy effectiveness and can cause significant losses for governments, companies and households.
iii) Explains the usury and thus earnings management and asset-quality management inherent in asset securitization.
iv) Explains some macroeconomic effects of earnings management and asset-quality management; and accounting disclosures by banks.

USA statutes and case-law are used in this chapter because the US has the most advanced Usury, Structured Products and Asset Securitization laws and processes which have been copied by most countries.

4.1 Existing literature and reasons for earnings management

Zimmerman and Gontcharov (2006) summarized various reasons for earnings management. The motivation for earnings management are as follows:

a) Managerial self-interest derives from the following:

   i) Their behavioral motivations, e.g. reputation (see: Strong et al. [1987]; Elliott and Shaw [1988]; Dechow and Sloan [1991]; Pourciau [1993]; Francis et al. [1996]).
   ii) Job security (see: DeFond and Park [1997]).
   iii) Their short-term bonus contracts which are tied to reported accounting performance measures (see: Healy [1985]; Holthausen et al. [1995]; Koch and Wall [2000]).

    iv Management buy-out of publicly held shares (see: DeAngelo [1986]; Perry and Williams [1994]).

b) The second motivation is to maximize the interests of shareholders, which may occur at the expense of some other contracting party (see Francis [2001: 312]).

c) The academic literature shows that managers manipulate earnings for the following reasons among others:

    i) To increase their company's stock prices – see: Teoh et al. (1998a); Teoh et al. (1998b); and Erickson and Wang (1999).

    ii) To affect the values of equity based incentives and cash incentives that are issued by their companies.

    iii) To decrease the present value of taxes – see: Tse (1990); Hand (1993); and Kang (1993).

    iv) To convey private information – see: Jones (1991); Petroni (1992); Subramanyam (1996); and Key (1997).

    v) To reduce the likelihood of bond covenant violations – see: Watts and Zimmerman (1986); Smith and Warner (1979); Sweeney (1994); and DeFond and Jiambalvo (1994).

Some of the more obvious ways of reducing earnings management and asset-quality management are as follows:

i) Reducing or eliminating managerial discretion in the application of accounting rules.

ii) Requiring mandatory compliance with IFRS in all countries.

iii) Involving Central Banks and national securities regulatory agencies in the accounting standards legislation.

iv) Imposing harsher penalties for perpetrators of earnings management, asset-quality management and incentive-effects management.

As mentioned in Chapter 1 in this book, *Accounting Biases* and *Enforcement Patterns* can affect Industry Structure. *Accounting Biases* is relatively new line of research and has been studied from Behavioral Accounting, Management Science[2] and Operations Research[3] perspectives. Chen and Jorgensen (2018) noted that accounting Biases can affect competition and *Industry Structure* in various industries. Using a study of mergers/acquisitions, Marquardt and Zur (2015) found evidence that financial accounting quality is positively related to the efficiency of capital/resource allocation in economies.

4.1.1 Standardized contracts, earnings management and incentive-effects management in fintech environments, automated/digital contracting and networks-of-contracts

Earnings management, Asset-quality Management and Incentive-Effects Management typically occur and or are amplified within the context of, and often distort organizations, *Incentive-Mechanisms*, *Contracting-Frameworks*, *Networks-of-Contracts*, markets and benefits of Fintech. *Contract Theory* and *Mechanism Design Theory* have been jointly studied from various perspectives (and in Fintech Environments) including Economics/Finance, Operations Research, Mathematical Psychology, Computer Science, Game Theory and Applied Math – see: Hoppe and Schmitz (2018); Niederhoff and Kouvelis (2019); Hong, Wernz and Stillinger (2016); Wu, Zhao and Tang (2014); Li, Liu and Chen (2018); Lin and Chou (1990); Park and Kim (2014); Goetz et al. (2019); Fang and Yuan (2018); Madureira et al. (2014); Meneguzzi et al. (2012); Meneguzzi et al. (2011); Zohar and Rosenschein (2008); Terán, Aguilar and Cerrada (2017); and Wei et al. (2018). However, the models in most of these foregoing articles and literature are static, don't incorporate relevant variables; don't consider varying "states" and often complex "joint" effects of variables; and they don't consider Industrial Organization effects of contracts and *Incentive Mechanisms* – see: Nwogugu (2007b;c, 2008a;b, 2019a, 2019b, 2006).

Standardization of contracts can affect economic growth, Sustainability, *Inequality* and Economic Growth as noted by various academic researchers – see: Sussman (1999); Van Assche and Schwartz (2013); Patterson (2010), Engert and Hornuf (2018); Aguirre (2017); Ayotte and Bolton (2011); Baffi (2007; 2012); He, Xue and Zhou (2019); Vo et al. (2019); Sheng (2019); Eenmaa-Dimitrieva and Schmidt-Kessen (2019); Iossa and Martimort (2018); and Sprinkle, Williamson and Upton (2008). Sussman (1999) noted that ". . . The main implications of contract standardization are that (i) financial history matters in the growth process,(ii) early formation of the system may create a drag on economic growth and (iii) the effect may be non-monotonic because the system may be modernized at some point. . . ." Thus, given the proliferation of outsourcing contracts, procurement contracts, employee agreements, automated purchase orders, automated contracts and standardization of contracts, Earnings management, Asset-quality Management and Incentive-Effects Management have become major macroeconomic, macrofinancial and international political economy "leakages" in the sense that they: i) distort economic data and economic policy; and ii) amplify negative externalities, Systemic Risk, Financial Instability and Inequality.

4.2 Complexity in real life: Earnings Management, Incentive-Effects Management, Asset-Quality Management and structural changes

The literature on the relationship between Complexity and Structural Change is developed and includes Robert and Yoguel (2016); Cimoli, Pereima and Porcile (2016); Dosi and Virgillito (2017); Comim (2000); Heinrich and Dai (2016); Ciaschini, Pretaroli and Socci (2011); Brida, Anyul and Punzo (2003); and Cantwell and Santangelo (2006). Also see the comments and critiques in Nwogugu (2004b), Nwogugu (2005a, 2003), Colpan et al. (2007) and Nwogugu (2004a) (Jack-In-The-Box), and Nwogugu (2007a;b).

Earnings Management, Asset-Quality Management and Incentive-Effects Management can trigger or amplify structural changes in industries in several ways including the following:

i)   Companies tend to copy the earnings management and asset-quality management patterns and trade norms of competing firms. Such tendencies can lead to permanent and major changes in operating models, business models, organizational models, information systems, cash management and financial policies of a group of, or many companies in the industry which is in effect, a structural change.

ii) Corporate Governance Contagion (wherein firms hire board members and senior executives from, and copy the corporate governance practices and policies of their competitors) and associated permanent changes in firm's operations represent structural changes.

iii) The actual or perceived threat of Earnings management and asset quality management by competitors can compel a firm to invest more in innovation and new products/processes that are or cause structural changes in an industry.

iv) The actual or perceived threat of Earnings Management, Incentive-Effects Management and or Asset-Quality Management by competitors can trigger the enactment and or enforcement of government regulations, and issuance of new regulations by trade associations, which may be, or cause Structural Changes in an industry and *Multiplier Effects* in related/associated industries.

Structural changes can have significant effects on Financial Stability, and vice versa (actual or potential Financial Instability can cause industry relationships, norms, competition and regulations to change significantly). Also the rapidly increasing use of employee stock options (ESOs) (and equity-based incentives) among both US and foreign companies is a significant structural change that has major implications for managerial risk taking and Financial Stability. See: Nwogugu (2004b, 2015d, 2005a); Scazzieri (2009) and Schilirò (2012). Structural changes can have significant effects on Financial Stability, and vice versa (actual or potential Financial Instability can cause industry relationships, technology, organizational structures, norms, competition and regulations to change significantly).

Earnings management and asset-quality management have evolved into coordinated operations strategies of firms – rather than being one-off isolated incidents by one or a few managers at the firm. That is evident in the scope of reported earnings management, and the employees involved. The relationship between operations strategy and structural change is conjectured to be symbiotic, evolving and increasingly inter-dependent given globalization and the internet, but has not been sufficiently addressed in the finance, economics or operations management literature. Nwogugu (2015d) introduced the *Operations Strategy Model of Structural*

Change wherein structural change is caused primarily by changes in the operations strategies of a large dominant firm, or a group of firms. Nwogugu (2015d) also introduced other models of structural change. The *Operations Strategy Model of Structural Change* differs from the *Lewis Model of structural change* (introduced by US economist Arthur Lewis) which may have been confirmed in several Asian economies (e.g. India; China, Malaysia; etc.) during 1970–2018.

The rapidly increasing use of employee stock options (ESOs) and other equity-based incentives among both US and non-US companies is a significant structural change that has major implications for labor dynamics (e.g. employee motivation; prospects of unionization; etc.), intrapreneurship/entrepreneurship, technological progress, managers' risk taking and Financial Stability. The use of equity-based incentives is an element of corporate strategy. See the comments in Nwogugu (2004b, 2006); and Colpan et al. (2007).

Scazzieri (2009), Vu (2017) and Swiecki (2017) addressed various elements of structural change but they omitted relevant variables that are mentioned herein. One of the major problems is that there seems to be a Research–Practice gap in modeling of structural change; and models of structural change often don't include relevant variables, and the number/type of variables used seem to be constrained by the perceived availability of data. The foregoing discussion raises the following issues:

i)   The inclusion of corporate governance factors; operations strategy; specialized business structures (waves of strategic alliances; joint ventures; licensing; etc.); acquisitions/mergers of large companies; changes in regulation and or economic policy; organizational changes and political economy conditions in models of structural change.

ii) Whether and when one company can trigger structural changes in an industry by its strategy and or supply chain.

iii) Rapid and significant declines in stock prices of groups of companies in an industry represent a structural change. Stock prices are closely watched by employees, credit rating agencies, customers and suppliers and also affect the company's corporate reputation and credibility. Thus, such declines are likely to negatively affect employee morale; interest rates for new debt; terms of trade credit and demand from customers.

iv) The effects of the evolution of networks created by corporate governance contagion, strategic alliances (including licensing agreements, R&D agreements and distribution agreements) and joint ventures.

v)   The effects of actual acquisitions/mergers, the looming threat of mergers/acquisitions by large MNEs; associated earnings management and asset-quality management; and the effects of inefficient post-merger integration by MNEs on industry structure.

vi) In the literature, structural change is most often characterized by changes in sectoral employment and output shares but that is wrong or insufficient because it doesn't reflect the full dynamics.

vii) The evolution of credit chains in industries and associated earnings management and asset-quality management.

viii) The effects of bankruptcies of large dominant companies; and credit ratings and ratings transitions on industry structure; and vice versa; and associated earnings management and asset-quality management.

 ix) In structural change models, homogenous labor should not be the only primary factor of production.

See the comments in De Nicolò and Juvenal (2014); Ruttiman (2014); and Jovane, Seliger and Stock (2017).

4.3 Earnings management, incentive-effects management and asset-quality management nullify theories of IPO-decisions and theories of systemic risk and financial instability

Earnings management, incentive-effects management and asset-quality management contradict or nullify theories of IPO-decisions in Bancel and Mittoo (2001); Chemmanur and He (2011); Cumming and Johan (2013) and Humphery-Jenner and Suchard (2013); and theories of systemic risk and financial Instability in Haldane and May (2011); Liu and Tse (2012); Ma, Zhuang and Li (2011); Battiston and Glattfelder (2009); Li et al. (2014); Kuzubas, Ömercikoglu and Saltoglu (2014) and Elliott, Golub and Jackson (2014). See: Nwogugu (2014) and Nwogugu (2015b).

4.4 The omission of intangibles accounting regulations invalidates academic/practitioner studies of the crash-risk of financial markets

Many academic studies of the crash-risk of financial markets (i.e. debt, equity, commodity, derivatives and currency markets) completely omitted the issue of enforcement of accounting-regulations and Goodwill/Intangibles accounting rules (despite the fact that according to Salinas (2009) and other authors, during the last 15 years, Intangible assets accounted for 60–75 percent of the stock market capitalization values in most developed countries; and an increasing percentage of the stock market value in many developing countries such as South Korea Brazil; China/Hong Kong; Mexico; Thailand; Singapore; etc.).

The academic studies about the risks of market-crashes include Ascioglu et al. (2012); Bar-Yosef and Prencipe (2013); Eng and Lin (2012); An and Zhang (2013); Hutton, Marcus and Tehranian (2009); Francis, Hasan and Li (2014); Guo, Wang and Wu (2011); Kim and Zhang (2013); Kim, Li and Zhang (2011a;b); Kim and Zhang (2014); Pinegar and Ravichandran (2010); Zeitun and Tian (2007); and Lopes and Alencar (2010). Karpoff, Lee and Martin (2008a;b); Kim, Li and Zhang (2011a;b) and Kim and Zhang (2013, 2014) analyzed financial stability issues that arise from financial reporting opacity, earnings management (which affects incentives), tax avoidance and or asset-quality management (which affects incentives).

4.5 Some macroeconomic, financial stability and systemic risk effects of earnings management, asset-quality management, and incentive-effects management

Earnings Management, Incentive-Effects Management and Asset-Quality Management affects macroeconomic activity in many ways including but not limited to the following:

- i) Capital Allocations and investments by firms – Most in-house capital allocations by companies are based on financial statements. Thus, real earnings management and financial earnings management both have substantial effects on allocation and investment decisions at the division, subsidiary and corporate levels. Similarly, all forms of earnings management can affect performance evaluation standards especially for senior executives who are usually evaluated based on company-wide metrics.
- ii) Capital Allocation and investments by institutional investors (i.e. banks, family offices, foundations, pension funds, mutual funds, PE and VC funds; and insurance companies) – these entities constitute some of the most active determinants of allocations of capital to various industries and across economies.
- iii) The efficiency of capital allocation and investments by governments.
- iv) The nature of competition in industries – earnings management also affects the nature and extent of competition in industries. When firms take aggressive accounting positions, their immediate competitors are likely to respond by doing the same.
- v) The efficiency of capital allocations by households.
- vi) Pensions and pension deficits in all countries.
- vii) Capital expenditures.
- viii) Corporate taxation and tax avoidance.
- ix) Industry effects and network-effects – firms seem to follow disclosure practices of other firms. Firms that are suspected of perpetrating earnings management can have network effects.
- x) Distortion of monetary policy and fiscal policies.
- xi) Employee skills and training.
- xii) Effect on the efficiency of public policy.
- xiii) Effect on corporate credit ratings – that is, timing and accuracy.
- xiv) Effects on international capital flows, cross-border transaction and exchange rates.
- xv) Increased inflation.

Clearly earnings management, Incentive Effects Management and Asset-Quality Management increase financial instability and systemic-risk/contagion in asset markets. Karpoff, Lee and Martin (2008a;b); Kim, Li and Zhang (2011a;b) and Kim and Zhang (2013; 2014) analyzed financial stability and systemic risk issues that arise from financial reporting opacity, earnings management (which affects incentives), tax avoidance and or asset-quality management (which affects incentives). The findings of May and Boehme (May 2016) and Jin and Myers (2006) suggest the use of alternative measures of crash-risk and controlling for known determinants of crash-risk identified in prior studies – and in addition, these factors, multinational operations and the crash-risk factors mentioned in Kim, Li and Zhang (2011b) and Kim and Zhang (2013, 2014) should be included in asset pricing models.

Cichello and Kieschnick (2005); Nwogugu (2003); Melendy (2011); Claudiu (2013) and Nwogugu (2004a) analyzed corporate governance and strategy issues that can have financial instability and systemic risk effects. Pathak, Joshi and Ludhiyani (2010); García-Pérez, Yanes-Estévez and Oreja-Rodríguez(2014); and Grechuk and Zabarankin (2014) studied strategic decision-making – earnings management, asset-quality management and incentive-effects management appear to be corporate strategic decisions in many instances. Nwogugu (2007a;c;d) and Nwogugu (2009a;b) analyzed corporate transactions and Antitrust issues. See the comments about goodwill/intangibles accounting in Nwogugu (2015a;c) and Nwogugu (2007c), which also explains some asset pricing anomalies. Chandra and Thenmozhi (2017), Baker, Wurgler and Yuan (2012), and Cronqvist and Siegel (2014) analyzed behavioral asset pricing and investor sentiment.

Companies that perpetrate earnings management, and or asset-quality management and or incentive-effects management (the "*EAI Companies*") pose financial stability risks because: i) their operations affect tens of millions of people in their countries and around the world; ii) they provide critical goods and services and so any material bad news about them or any announcement or acknowledgment of their insolvency increases the probability of a sudden and material decline of their stock prices and bond prices, and the stock prices and perceived prospects of other related companies; iii) many companies and financial institutions directly or indirectly rely heavily on *EAI Companies*' services; iv) any technical insolvency or bankruptcy filing of an EAI Company may have a contagion effect on the credit ratings of companies that are perceived to be in the same sector or related industry sectors.

Many EAIs are important participants in global credit chains wherein they provide and also obtain trade credit (where such borrowing is partly based on their reputations and perceived solvency). Such credit chains have become a major source of capital for many companies and financial institutions, but they increase the probability of domino-effects in both the real and financial sectors. See comments in Boissay (2006). Many *EAI Companies* also have substantial debt; and any perceived insolvency and or business contraction of an EAI Company can trigger an industry-wide credit crunch and or hyperinflation for some products/

services in some countries. Contrary to the literature and as shown during the global financial crisis in 2008–2010, multinationals are not entirely immune from financial crises. *EAI Companies'* earnings management and reluctance to comply with accounting regulations is in line with the *"Bad News Hoarding"* theory in the literature – see Jin and Myers (2006) – which has spawned a new line of empirical research focused on identifying corporate activities and/or firm characteristics that cause or facilitate bad news hoarding and thus, predicts stock price crashes. Using a large sample of US headquartered firms during 1987–2011, May and Boehme (May 2016) found that multinational firms have greater stock price crash-risk than domestic firms; and that the difference in crash-risk between multinational and domestic firms is most acute among firms with weaker corporate governance mechanisms (i.e. weaker shareholder rights, less independent boards, and less stable institutional ownership).

Given the rapid increases in the types and volumes of strategic alliances and joint ventures (JVs) around the world during the last twenty years, just like swaps/derivatives, alliances/JVs create financial networks that increase interconnectedness of firms and the risk of domino-effects in both the real and financial sectors – and that is often omitted in financial stability analysis and in Sustainable Growth and asset pricing models.

In the US, the US FSOC may have hesitated to take over large *EAI Companies* (pursuant to the Dodd Frank Act's provisions) because of the reach and business impact of both companies and the possible information effects on financial markets and asset markets. See the comments in Nwogugu (2014) and Nwogugu (2015b).

A significant percentage (more than 30 percent) of the stock market values of some *EAI Companies* is in the form of Goodwill. First, that is an example of the inefficiency of current Goodwill/Intangibles accounting regulations – the accounting disclosure does not capture the true risk of *EAI Companies* assets. See comments about goodwill/intangibles accounting and Financial Stability in Nwogugu (2015a;d) and Nwogugu (2007). Second, it also poses a significant financial stability risk because: i) the accounting disclosure of goodwill does not capture the true risk of *EAI Companies* assets; ii) the lack of accounting classification of Intangibles (such as human capital; contracts; distribution/marketing rights; etc.) actually increases the probability that their stock price will suddenly decline substantially and that there will be significant differences of opinion about their Goodwill in general, and the possibility of existence of such identifiable intangible assets – all of which increases market volatility and volatility-spillovers.

The significant differences (distinct from goodwill) between the book and market values of tangible assets (such as real estate) can significantly increase: i) the risk of collapse of asset markets (such as real estate and the secondary markets for equipment parts); ii) disagreements among investors about equity values and hence, stock market volatility. These issues are not addressed properly by the current accounting model.

EBIs and cash incentives are the primary means by which perpetrators benefit from Earnings management, incentive-effects management and asset-quality management. Employee Stock Options (ESOs) and other equity-based incentives and associated Earnings management, incentive-effects management and asset-quality management can significantly increase disagreements among investors about the values of firms' human capital and equity; and the current accounting model (IASB/IFRS) increases such uncertainty and equity and bond volatility. ESOs are intangibles (as ruled by at least one US Federal Court of Appeals; and as stated in the business/economics literature) but are not governed by the goodwill/intangibles accounting regulations (IASB/IFRS). It is well established in the finance/economic literature that EBIs can affect employee morale and increase the propensity for managerial risk-taking, which in turn, can increase financial stability risks. See Nwogugu (2004b, 2006) and Kim, Li and Zhang (2011b).

The negative Financial Instability effects of Earnings management, incentive-effects management and asset-quality management include but are not limited to the following: i) over-valuation of shares (in domestic and foreign stock markets); and negative collateral effects on the stock prices of un-related companies – see Darrough, Huang and Zhao (2013); ii) the actual and perceived risk inherent in the use of shares of exchange-traded companies for foreign and domestic M&A transactions; iii) corporate governance contagion (wherein firms copy fraud and disclosure patterns from other firms; and firms increasingly share board members); iv) increased similarities in, and correlations between trading patterns of stocks in different markets; v) the use of shares of such cross-listed companies as collateral; viii) the significantly increased risk of collapse of the stock prices of companies that perpetrate Earnings management, incentive-effects management and or asset-quality management; ix) the government's or courts' rejection of transactions proposed by companies that perpetrate Earnings management, incentive-effects management and or asset-quality management, or the repudiation of their contracts by other companies can set off panic selling in stock markets which in turn, can cause sell-offs in stock markets in other countries.

Employee Stock Options and other equity-based incentives and associated Earnings management, incentive-effects management and asset-quality management can significantly increase disagreements among investors about the values of firms' human capital and equity; and the current accounting model (IASB/IFRS) increases such uncertainty and equity and bond volatility. ESOs are intangibles (as ruled by at least one US Federal Court of Appeals; and as stated in the business/economics literature) but are not governed by the goodwill/intangibles accounting regulations (IASB/IFRS). It is well established in the finance/economic literature that EBIs can affect employee morale and increase the propensity for managerial risk-taking, which in turn, can increase financial stability risks. See: Nwogugu (2004b, 2006) and Kim, Li and Zhang (2011b).

Nwogugu (2017) noted that the aggregation of all the errors and biases caused by the use of the NPV-IRR model and related approaches by individuals, companies and government agencies constitute a set of macroeconomic variables and are financial stability risks.

See the comments in Nwogugu (2004b, 2005a); Nwogugu (2007b); Nwogugu (2003) (Encompass Services); Fukao (1999); Francis, Hasan, and Li (2014); and Nwogugu (2004a) (Jack-In-The-Box). The Nwogugu (2007a) critique of bankruptcy prediction models and the Nwogugu (2007c) critique of corporate finance and Complex Systems theories also applies to the modeling of financial stability. The foregoing raises the following issues in the analysis of Financial Stability and Sustainable Growth:

i) The inclusion of *corporate governance contagion* (including earnings management contagion); patterns of equity-based incentives; structural changes; credit chains; earnings management and specialized business structures (waves of strategic alliances; joint ventures) in financial stability models.

ii) Many studies in the finance, management and economics literature have confirmed that corporate governance and corporate strategy factors affect stock prices, corporate bond prices, corporate growth, lenders' and suppliers' perceptions (credit chains), reputation; etc. McCahery, Sautner and Stark (2016) confirmed that when interacting with executives of investee companies (e.g. "Voice" or "Exit" options) institutional investors' preferences and criteria are mainly about corporate governance and corporate strategy.

iii) The negative effects of robo-trading (automated securities trading) and robo-advisers (automated financial advice) on asset prices, Sustainable Growth, Corporate Policies and monetary policy transmission.

iv) The effect of a company's number of shares-outstanding on a company's (and its competitors') stock prices. See: Nwogugu (2019c).

v) The negative impact of corporate earnings management, structural changes in industries, disclosure of equity-based incentives, and inefficient goodwill/intangibles accounting regulations on the values of corporate bonds, municipal bonds and treasury/government bonds (i.e. tax avoidance by companies) owned by the US Fed and other central banks is a major issue. The US Fed raised its benchmark interest rate in June 2017 (and additional rate increases were generally anticipated) even though inflation lagged the US Fed's target and unemployment among some demographics was high. As of mid-2017, the US Fed's assets were worth about 23 percent of US nominal GDP, which is similar to the 1930s after the Great Depression. The US Federal Reserve's (US Fed) balance sheet assets grew from about $0.7 Trillion in 2003 to about $4.5 trillion in mid-2017 primarily because beginning from 2009, the US Fed implemented *quantitative easing* (purchases of bonds, loans and securities) in order to lower interest rates. Other countries also implemented *quantitative easing* during that period. The last US recession began about 2008 but since 1945, the average economic cycle in the US has lasted for about seventy months (measured from trough-to-trough or peak-to-peak). Thus another recession may occur soon in the US, and when it happens, the US Fed's policy options will likely be severely restricted.

vi) The negative impact of corporate earnings management, structural changes in industries and inefficient goodwill/intangibles accounting regulations on banks' and insurers' willingness/propensity to provide loans and credit enhancement – which may lead to credit crunches.

vii) Whether firms' social capital and or technology products/initiatives enable them to avoid restrictions of financial regulations (such as the US FSOC's non-SIFI criteria) and or accounting regulations.

4.6 Some macroeconomic effects of accounting disclosures by banks and finance companies

Accounting regulations and the rule of law are generally very relevant to economic development. Researchers have noted the abuses of power by, and power clashes among the legislative, judicial and executive branches of both federal and state government in developing countries such as Nigeria. Researchers have also noted the effects of regulations and compliance on economic development. With regards to banks, the emerging markets countries are somewhat segmented – and the economic and non-economic *effects of* the banks' and finance companys' accounting disclosures in lower-tier Less Ddeveloped Countries (LDC) (e.g. Kenya; Sri Lanka; Vietnam; Nigeria; Mali; Venezuela; etc.) on economic development is conjectured to differ substantially from those of higher-tier LDCs (e.g. Thailand, Malaysia; Mexico, Brazil; etc.) in various ways.

Foreign investors often consider the credit quality, liquidity and solvency of banks and finance companies in addition to sovereign credit ratings before making investments in a foreign country – similarly some multinational companies consider these same factors before expanding into a foreign country.

In many developing countries, the accounting disclosures of banks and finance companies are clearly intended to obscure and hide their true liquidity and solvency and to facilitate capital raising by the banks. Such successful capital raising in the Eurobond markets has not been done recently by other industries in many African, MENA, Latin American and southeast Asian countries, and is closely watched as a primer for other industries. This situation has not occurred in other emerging markets countries such as Brazil, Mexico, India and Panama.

The accounting disclosures of LDC Banks and finance companies are more likely to affect the financing prospects of companies in other domestic industries than the impact of disclosures of the Foreign non-LDC Banks on their national economies. This is because LDC banks typically account for more than 65 percent of loans and lending activities in their countries, unlike in some developed countries where insurance companies, non-bank finance companies, hedge funds, government agencies, pension funds and leasing companies provide more loans (to companies, individuals and government agencies). Furthermore, in order to create effective short-term and long-term economic development, monetary policies and fiscal policies, the LDC government also analyzes the credit quality, accounting disclosures, asset size and lending-scope of local banks.

In many LDCs, some foreign investors (e.g. US banks) will provide loans to companies/individuals only if local LDC banks provide guarantees for such loans. Many non-LDC investors (e.g. the IFC; non-LDC bond-investors; non-LDC equity-investors; and some Chinese banks) have at some point, formally or informally decided to invest in LDC economies primarily or only by investing in LDC banks in these countries. Under the "*no-bank-liquidation and bank-bailout*" regimes and mentality that is prevalent in many LDCs and in the absence of third-party credit enhancements, such investments may be the safest approach. There is significant un-met demand for corporate/business loans in LDCs. Thus, the accounting disclosures, stock-price performance and credit ratings of LDC banks can have more impact on their nation's economic development, than the impact of accounting disclosures of non-LDC Banks on their nation's domestic economies.

In many LDCs, banks and bank holding companies are the best positioned financial institutions to foster economic development, and to reduce the size and impact of the "Informal Economy". LDC banks can provide zero-balance and low-cost bank accounts which will encourage the un-banked to participate in the financial system (savings; retirement products), and provide more capital for lending and investments. Insurance affiliates of bank holding companies can also help in reducing loan risks. Thus, the accounting disclosures of such banks are important.

Many international equity investors, international bond investors, private equity funds and "global macro" hedge funds analyze the credit quality, accounting disclosures, asset size and lending-scope of LDC banks as major investment criteria for investing in LDC bond markets or equity markets. Similarly, some multinational companies that want to enter new markets (countries) in LDCs or want to locate regional headquarters or locate plants/factories/warehouses and training/development/research centers analyze the credit quality, accounting disclosures, asset size and lending-scope of banks; and the availability of consumer credit and corporate credit; and corporate expenditures as major decision criteria. See the World Bank's chart of Bank NPLs (%) for various countries for 2009–2017 at https://data.worldbank.org/indicator/fb.ast.nper.zs. See the World Bank's chart of *Domestic credit provided by financial sector (% of GDP)* at http://data.worldbank.org/indicator/FS.AST.DOMS.GD.ZS/countries. See the World Bank's chart of Lending interest rate (%) at http://data.worldbank.org/indicator/FR.INR.LEND/countries. Due to regulatory and operational constraints, some non-LDC investors have at some point, formally or informally decided to invest in emerging markets primarily or only by investing in ADRs and GDRs issued by LDC companies. Similarly, some of such investors evaluate GDRs and ADRs of LDC issuers before investing directly in LDC stock markets. Generally, LDC companies receive much less coverage by research analysts than companies in other emerging markets. Many LDCs rely on foreign aid and foreign direct investment in order to manage their economies. Thus, the accounting disclosures of LDC GDR/ADR issuers have or can have much more impact on economic development and capital flows of LDCs, than those of companies in non-LDCs. Given that the economies of many LDCs are bank-oriented (rather than market-oriented), the accounting disclosures of LDC banks can have more impact on economic development, than the impact of foreign non-LDC banks on their national economies.

Prospective foreign investors that are considering making investments in LDCs (either FDI or purchases of loans and securities) may also check for the magnitude of protection of creditors' (and shareholders') rights, and the efficiency of procedures for loan recovery. One way of doing so is to review court cases filed by banks that want to recover loans; and banks' financial statements and public disclosures, as well as banks' loan-recovery costs.

Globally and in US dollars terms, cross-border capital inflows among countries have declined since 2006, due to government protectionist policies, the Global Financial Crisis, sustainability of economic growth in many countries, and concerns about the Balance Sheets of financial institutions and multinationals. Sustainable economic growth in many countries is often analyzed and framed within the context of availability of loans, and the liquidity and financial stability of banks and insurance companies.

According to Tirole (2012), Greece and Italy used accounting gimmicks (as noted by Eurostat, etc.) to facilitate their entry into, and continued membership of the European Union.

The government (state and federal) budgeting processes; government spending; corporate expenditures; strategic planning by large companies; investment decisions; and many other major decisions made by domestic entities are based partly or substantially on analysis of banks and their accounting disclosures; the stability of banks; availability of credit/loans from banks; and lending interest rates. Cornett, McNutt and Tehranian (2009); DeYoung, Peng and Yan (2013); Erkens, Hung and Matos (2012), analyzed earnings management and corporate governance at banks.

Earnings management and Opacity can also result in market crashes and significant illiquidity in markets. Kim and Zhang (2014); Kim and Zhang (2013); Kim, Li and Zhang (2011b); Kim, Li and Zhang (2011a); Hutton, Marcus and Tehranian (2009); An and Zhang (2013); Hutton, Marcus and Tehranian (2009); Ascioglu, Hegde, Krishnan and McDermott (2012); and Francis, Hasan and Li (2014), analyzed the relationships among opaque financial statements, earnings management and the trading patterns of stock prices on one hand, and the risk of stock market crashes.

4.7 The optimal characteristics of efficient regulations that govern earnings management, incentive-effects management and asset-quality management

Given the foregoing, the following are the necessary and sufficient characteristics of optimal regulations that govern earnings management and asset-quality management in most jurisdictions:

i) *Public Goods* – the statutes are public goods and their use-value is not affected or diminished by increase in the number of users
ii) *Regret Neutral* – does not increase or reduce Regret of managers/employees, investors and regulators.

iii) *Elicitation of Truthfulness* – truthfulness of parties that make accounting disclosures and can affect perceived incentive-effects.
iv) *Cost Effectiveness*.
v) *Self-Insurance* – the statutes must contain elements of self-insurance.
vi) *Combination Efficiency* – the combined applications of the statute and another un-related statute increases the efficiency of both statutes.

4.8 Some behavioral macroeconomic/ macrofinancial effects of insider trading

Around the world, Insider Trading is a major "channel" for managers and "Insiders" to benefit from long-term and or short-term Earnings Management, Asset Quality Management and Incentive Effects Management. The Macroeconomic/ Macrofinancial effects include but are not limited to the following:

i) Inflation – partly from windfall gains.
ii) Inefficient allocation of risk.
iii) Inefficient allocation of capital.
iv) Increased market volatility.
v) Loss of confidence in securities markets
vi) Inefficient price discovery.
vii) Difficulty in raising capital.
viii) Information asymmetry.
ix) Low compliance with disclosure regulations.
x) Low quality of corporate governance.
xi) Distortion and inefficiency of government policies.
xii) Increased inefficiency of taxation.
xiii) De-motivation of company employees.
xiv) Distortion of the "incentive effects" of EBIs. And cash incentives.
xv) Lack of confidence in capital markets.
xvi) Unjustified wealth transfers.

4.9 *Behavioral macroeconomics/macrofinance and complex adaptive systems*: some theories of the effects of asset securitization and structured products trusts/entities (and associated transactions) on economies and sustainable/ economic growth

As mentioned in Chapter 1, asset securitization products are a type of Structured Products. The Structured Products referred to in this section are those that involve Trusts and SPEs/SPVs. The following are new theories of Complex Adaptive Systems and the behavioral effects of asset securitization and Structured Products trusts/entities on the economy, market-participants, market mechanisms and on the effectiveness of the government's monetary policies – these issues are directly applicable in automated/Agent-based Asset Pricing, Sustainable Growth, Bankruptcy Prediction and Fraud Detection models.

4.9.1 The Deficit-Increase Effect

This hypothesis was introduced in Nwogugu (2008a;b). Securitization and Structured Products Vehicles can create government deficits and can increase the federal government's cost of borrowing. AAA-rated ABS/MBS/SP yields are typically greater than yields of government securities with the same maturity. Securitization and Structured Products entities divert capital away from the government bond market, and simultaneously provide AAA-rated bond alternatives in more variety, and hence reduce demand and liquidity in the government bond market and increase the government's cost of capital – this results in higher debt/interest payments by the government and lower volume of new-issue government bonds, and hence, greater government deficits. Hence, the Central Bank can improve fiscal policy and monetary policy by:

i)   Increasing/reducing taxes on banks' profits from securitization and structured products, and making such taxes vary with transaction volume.
ii) Taxing securitization and structured products transactions in which ABS or structured products' interest rates exceed a specified maximum.

Securitization and Structured Products entities can increase the demand for federal funds (Discount-Window loans to banks) – Discount-Window loans are often the cheapest source of capital for banks that want to purchase assets/loans for securitization and structured products. Hence, the Central Bank and federal government can improve the effectiveness of their monetary policies by:

i)   Limiting the possible uses of proceeds of *Discount-Window* loans.
ii)   Varying the Capital Reserve requirements for *Discount-Window* loans.
iii) Changing the duration/maturity of *Discount-Window* loans.
iv)   Linking the amount of *Discount-Window* loans to primary lending activity, Net Equity and the value of outstanding derivative products and structured products.

Securitization and Structured Products Entities reduce government tax revenues. Securitization (and Structured Products entities/trusts) can increase the government's operating expenditures in the following ways:

i)   Increased enforcement/litigation costs.
ii)   Increased costs of resolving Housing Inequality and Income Inequality.
iii) Unaffordable local transportation costs.
iv)   The Securitization of healthcare receivables (mostly Medicare and Medicaid which are government health insurance programs) has created substantial disincentives for healthcare providers to control/reduce healthcare costs.

4.9.2 The Secondary-Market Effect

This hypothesis was introduced in Nwogugu (2008a;b). Secondary securitization (where a financial institution purchases assets and then securitizes them) and some Structured Products vehicles encourages excessive leverage and improper capital structures in financial institutions (as exemplified by the problems at several US entities such as FNMA, Sallie Mae, and Freddie Mac at various times during 2000–2017). Hence, financial institutions have strong incentives to take on excess debt in order to purchase more loans/assets for securitization and Structured Products.

4.9.3 The Influence-Concentration Effect

This hypothesis was introduced in Nwogugu (2008a;b). In many countries, Asset Securitization and Structured Products transactions place too much control in the hands of a few powerful profit-seeking financial institutions (such as FNMA and Freddie Mac in the USA, and other financial institutions such as investment banks and commercial banks that have in-house or partner loan-conduit programs) whose policies/agenda may differ from the Federal Government's and or the Central Bank's agenda and policies.

4.9.4 The Capital Re-Allocation Theory

This hypothesis was introduced in Nwogugu (2008a;b). Asset Securitization effectively results in a reallocation of capital in financial systems, and this reallocation substantially interferes with the Federal Government's budgets and planning. This is because allocation of capital to one industry (by providing expansion capital) may create economic forces that effectively subvert the Federal Government's efforts in the same and or other industries.

4.9.5 The Information Diffusion Effect

This hypothesis was introduced in Nwogugu (2008a;b). The pre-transaction, post-transaction and post-default activities of all participants in securitizations and Structured Products transactions carry more information content, and hence has more impact on over-all interest rates (in all fixed income markets) and aggregate accounts, compared to the post-default activities of participants in traditional loan transactions (including loan syndications). Therefore, the Central Bank can improve the effectiveness of its monetary policy by:

i) Implementing and or varying regulations for disclosure of ABS.
ii) Establishing special capital-reserve requirements for defaulted ABS/MBS; and establishing PSA-based capital reserve requirements for ABS.
iii) Developing and implementing special procedures for ABS/MBS with relatively high default rates.

4.9.6 The ABS-Complexity Effect

This hypothesis was introduced in Nwogugu (2008a;b). As more assets are securitized, more ABS/MBS derivatives and Structured Products are created, which requires more monitoring and hedging/derivatives (hedging can be done in the currency, equity, debt, derivatives and commodity markets). This increased hedging and complexity:

i) Increases volatility in the debt, equity and commodity markets.
ii) Increases the cost of ABS/MBS to investors.
iii) Increases banks' propensity to take more risks.

4.9.7 The Segmentation Effect

This hypothesis was introduced in Nwogugu (2008a;b). Asset securitization and Structured Products vehicles can cause two types of segmentation effects which are as follows:

i) Banks and financial institutions become segmented by the size and sophistication of ABS/MBS and Structured Products transactions that they do. This segmentation is reflected in their credit ratings, perceived risk, types of clients, capital allocation to various transactions and trading patterns.
ii) The typical financial services company and its staff psychologically and physically segment its portfolio by type/class/PSA/duration of ABS/MBS and Structured Products – and this segmentation can become the conscious and unconscious basis for decision making, risk management and capital allocation.
iii) Asset securitization also causes segmentation in the valuation of fixed income securities and instruments – this results in increased emphasis on comparability, valuation within segments.

4.9.8 The Horizon-Substitution Effect

Asset securitization and Structured Products can cause sponsors/issuers to shift their horizons from the medium and long term to the short term. This is particularly true when proceeds of true sale securitizations and Structured Products transactions are greater than the present values of net spreads from the same transaction. Securitization and Structured products transactions can also cause their investors to shift their horizons and to become more sensitive to the time/yield tradeoff – this is partially attributable to payment patterns of ABS (interest-only and principle-only and associated ABS derivatives) and some Structured Products (e.g. those indexed to or based on short-term instruments or instruments that make relatively frequent payments). This hypothesis was introduced in Nwogugu (2008a;b).

4.9.9 The Knowledge-Volume-Scope Effect

This hypothesis was introduced in Nwogugu (2008a;b). As the sponsor or issuer gains more knowledge about sponsoring securitizations and Structured Products Entities transactions (and hedging/trading ABS/MBS and associated securities), the sponsor's/issuer's reach (number of asset classes securitized) will tend to increase irrespective of changes in transaction volume; and the transaction volume will tend to increase irrespective of yields (although with positive net spreads). The typical increase in the volume of securitizations and or Structured Products per sponsor/issuer over time is attributable to increased knowledge, and perceived profitability of current and future securitizations.

4.9.10 The Targeting Effect

Asset Securitization and Structured products transactions can cause a targeting effect in which the issuer/sponsor will seek to select and securitize only those loans/assets that will cause it to achieve targeted capital-reserve ratios, and or an absolute level of risk and or specific risk-weighted outstanding asset balances; and or credit ratings. This hypothesis was introduced in Nwogugu (2008a;b).

4.9.11 The Negative-Adverse-Selection Effect

Asset Securitization and Structured Product transactions can cause some sponsors/banks to securitize only their worst-performing assets – this is referred to as negative-adverse-selection effect, which is caused and or facilitated by the availability of mispriced third-party credit enhancement instruments (such as loan insurance, bond insurance, lease insurance, guarantees, swaps/caps/collars, etc.), true-sale securitizations, and insufficient regulation of ABS/MBS. This hypothesis was introduced in Nwogugu (2008a;b).

4.9.12 The Risk-Seeking Effect

This hypothesis was introduced in Nwogugu (2008a;b). Asset Securitization and Structured Products transactions can result in increases in banks' and financial companies' propensity to take risks because securitization provides a channel for disposing of mediocre and or marginally profitable assets/loans; and the components of true-sale securitization processes can be performed simultaneously in order to avoid the application of capital-reserve requirements.

4.9.13 The Central Bank Displacement Effect

This hypothesis was introduced in Nwogugu (2008a;b). The current large volumes of Asset Securitization and Structured Products in some countries effectively displace and weaken their Central Bank's monetary policy tools, primarily because the transactions return money to the capital markets for more lending activities and the interest rate, speed-of-return, form, magnitude and control of such "returned capital" is not primarily determined by the Central Bank.

4.9.14 The Capital Re-Allocation Theory

This hypothesis was introduced in Nwogugu (2008a;b). Asset Securitization and some Structured Products entity transactions effectively result in a reallocation of capital in financial systems, and this reallocation substantially interferes with the Federal Government's budgets and planning. This is because allocation of capital to one industry (by providing expansion capital) may create economic forces that effectively subvert the Federal Government's efforts in the same and or other industries. There is a finite pool of capital that can be invested in ABS. The allocation decisions are made by the investment banks and financial institutions that sponsor and issue ABS/MBS. The volume of capital allocated annually by the top ten commercial banks (loans) and the top ten financial institutions (loans, securities, commodities) in the United States far exceeds the US Government's annual budget. In the United States, securitization has not been very effective in allocating capital to society's needs. In the US healthcare, insurance, housing and transportation industries, prices remain unaffordable for many, capacity is often low, and operating costs remain high. Therefore, the Central Bank can better focus and improve monetary policy by:

i) Varying the capital-reserve requirements for loans not only by absolute/relative risk levels, but also based on industry, loan size, loan term/duration, loan purpose, and borrower location.
ii) Shifting the focus of monetary policy away from interest rates to aggregate macro accounts.
iii) Limiting the uses of discount-window loans.
iv) Changing the period of time that financial institutions are granted to comply with Central Bank monetary policies.
v) Enact laws that require mandatory separation of sponsor and servicer functions in securitizations.

4.10 Asset securitization and structured products vehicles transactions: some theories of harm and liability that can have macroeconomic/ macrofinancial and political effects

Nwogugu (2008a;b) introduced some theories that explain how securitization and some Structured Products vehicles transactions contravene the principles of US bankruptcy laws, and create both civil and criminal liability. The common factor among all these causes-of-action (and associated legal claims) is that the underlying misconduct have or can have adverse effects on national economies, political systems, Financial Stability and overall Social Welfare. The following are the theories:

i)   The *Illegal Wealth-Transfer Theory*.
ii)   The *Priority-Changing Effect*.
iii) The *Joint Venture Theory*
iv)   The *Information-Content Effect Theory*.
v)   The *Avoidance Effect*.
vi)   Intentional Misrepresentation and Deceit.

4.11 Asset securitization and some structured products vehicles transactions constitute violations of antitrust laws: a critique of *credit Suisse vs. billing* (US Supreme Court case)

The processes in asset securitization and some Structured Products entity transactions constitute violations of the Antitrust statutes which in turn has or can have negative Macroeconomic/Macrofinancial *Multiplier Effects* and *Spillover Effects* across economies. US Antitrust laws are used here because the US has the largest and deepest capital markets and the most-litigated and most-sophisticated antitrust laws and securities laws in the world. Here, Anti-trust misconduct is intertwined with, has systmbiotic relationships with and is treated as a type of Earnings Management and or Asset-Quality Management and or Incentive-Effects Management; and each such misconduct can have direct/indirect effects on corporate financial statements, managerial incentives/ compensation, corporate financial policies, "Internal Capital Markets" of Mul-tinational Corporations Sustainable Growth, Corporate Growth and govern-ment policies.

There has been substantial Antitrust litigation in the securities industry, but the US Supreme Court's rulings in *Credit Suisse vs. Billing*[4] was error because of the following reasons:

i)   Antitrust misconduct can be intertwined with securities operations. Contrary to the US Supreme Court's rulings, in *Credit Suisse vs. Billing*, the existing securities law framework in the US (and in many common-law countries) does not address all elements of Antitrust misconduct and is grossly inef-ficient and insufficient to address Antitrust misconduct. That is evidenced by the many documented failures of securities laws and securities litigation in the US (e.g. the rigging of government bond auctions (1960–present); insider trading; securities fraud; the LIBOR scandal; the global CDS scandal; the failure of asset securitization trusts and associated litigation (2006–2014); the worldwide Mutual Fund scandal or 2005–2008; etc.). Antitrust miscon-duct requires specialized statutes and analysis that are substantially different from those for securities law violations. Thus, there are constitutional law problems of *Substantive Due Process, Procedural Due Process* and *Equal Protection*. Many US states have their own securities laws, Antitrust Laws and unfair business practices laws (very similar to federal antitrust laws), and the insufficiency of federal and state securities laws to handle antitrust problems in the securities industry may result in violations of the *Interstate Commerce Clause* of the US Constitution.

ii)   Significant portions of the US federal securities laws were enacted during 1930–1960 when the structure of the US economy was substantially different, and telecommunications was much less developed (a significant portion of the securities industry is based on modern telecommunications). Since then, there have been many new economic/financial, social, political and technological developments that render that framework inefficient (and perhaps counter-productive). Furthermore, the Dodd Frank Act and most of the post-2005 financial regulations have not sufficiently addressed many of the Antitrust issues in asset securitization, Structured Products transactions and the securities industry in general (and the underlying related transactions in mortgages; consumer loans and pension assets/liabilities). See the comments in Nwogugu (2014, 2015b, 2015e), Dowd (2018), and Nitz (2018).

iii)   There are significant differences between the characteristics, objectives, efficiency and deterrence effect of the remedies and punishment/penalty schemes for antitrust and securities law violations; such that antitrust laws should be applied in the securities industries and should preclude securities laws where there is a conflict.

iv)   There are significant differences between the standards-of-proof, adjudication processes, compliance costs and transaction costs in antitrust cases and securities law cases, which are sufficient to justify the application of antitrust laws in securities industry contexts.

v)   In the US, many securities disputes are resolved by arbitration panels (FINRA and NYSE) that are directly or indirectly controlled and or influenced by the US securities industry. Second, the "self-regulation" of the US securities industry does not facilitate and reduces investor protection (from Antitrust misconduct). Thus, the existing securities law framework does not provide sufficient and constitutionally credible *Procedural Due Process* for individuals and litigants in antitrust cases in the securities industry.

vi)   It is reasonably inferable that the legislative intent of the US antitrust framework (a set of statutes and case-law) was that antitrust laws should be applied in all industries without exception.

vii)   The significant and long-term macroeconomic, microeconomic and macrofinancial effects of securities transactions and financial instruments are the type of problems/misconduct that Antitrust laws in general were designed to address.

ix)   The US Supreme Court's rulings in *Credit Suisse vs. Billings* was a major deviation from the US Supreme Court's precedent, and that created significant uncertainty and political costs (political lobbying; inefficient enforcement; etc.).

x)   In *Teamsters v. Daniel*, 439 U.S. 551, the US Supreme Court held that the *Employment Retirement Income Security Act of 1974* (ERISA) preempted the application of the Securities Acts to certain pension plans. Similar regulatory issues exist in this instance, which warrant the preemption of securities laws by Antitrust statutes.

Varney (2011)[5]; Markham (2010)[6]; Brunell (2012)[7]; Kahn (2008)[8]; Shelanski (2012, 2010); Brennan (2008); Sokol (2009) and Lee (2015) also critiqued the US Supreme Court's rulings in *Credit Suisse vs. Billing*.

Nwogugu (2008b) explained in detail the specific violations of, or theories of, liability for US antitrust laws that are inherent in asset securitization and or Structured Products Vehicles. The common factors among them are that they have or can have adverse effects, *Spillover Effects* and *Multiplier Effects* on national economies, financial stability and overall social welfare. The channels of transmission are conjectured here to include but are not limited to: international capital flows; corporate policies; internal capital markets of firms; central bank policies; government policies; etc.

The specific antitrust violations in asset securitization and Structured Products Vehicles transactions (in Nwogugu [2008b]) are summarized as follows:

i)   Market Concentration.
ii)   Market Integration.
iii) Syndicate Collusion.
iv)   Price Formation.
v)   Vertical foreclosure.
vi)   Tying.
vii) Price-fixing.
viii) Exclusive contracts.
ix)   Price Discrimination.
x)   Predatory Pricing
xi)   Rigging of Allocations.

4.12 Conclusion

Many academic researchers have formally noted the positive relationship between earnings management on one hand, and financial instability and systemic risk. However some other academic research has concluded that financial crisis increases the likelihood of earnings management – and thus the relationship between earnings management on one hand, and financial instability and systemic risk is likely to be symbiotic. However, asset-quality management and incentive-effects management have or can also have significant effects on economies, but haven't been studied in detail in the literature.

Notes

1 This chapter contains excerpts from Michael I. C. Nwogugu's articles that are cited as follows:

i)   Nwogugu, M. (2008a). Illegality of securitization, bankruptcy issues and theories of securitization. *Journal of International Banking Law & Regulation*, 23(7), 363–375.

ii)   Nwogugu, M. (2008b). Securitization is illegal: Racketeer influenced and corrupt organizations, usury, antitrust and tax issues. *Journal of International Banking Law & Regulation*, 23(6), 316–332.

2   *See*: Khan and Lo (2018); Chen and Jorgensen (2018); Kwon (2005); and Marquardt and Zur (2015).

3   *See*: Nan and Wen (2014).

4   *See*: *Credit Suisse Securities (USA) LLC vs. Billing*, 551 U.S. 264 (2007; US Supreme Court case).

5   *See*: Varney (2011) (". . . [T]here are about thirty federal statutes that exempt some conduct from antitrust entirely, that limit the applicability of antitrust laws to it, or that limit the penalties that can be assessed against it. . . .).

6   *See*: Markham (2010) ("[. . . The Court] regards antitrust litigation as frequently extortive, wasteful, unnecessary, and costly. Conversely, it seems to regard federal securities regulatory law a sounder public policy, notwithstanding the rather high-profile and catastrophic recent failures of that legal regime. . . .").

7   *See*: Brunell (2012) ("[T]he shift in the approach to immunity also appears to reflect a greater faith in regulators to achieve optimal outcomes and act as an 'effective steward of the antitrust function.'").

8   *See*: Kahn (2008) (". . . [T]he Court likely created even more uncertainty by deviating from its established precedents in [Trinko and Billing]. As a result, the lower courts' application of the doctrine is likely to become more unpredictable and, in light of the Supreme Court's apparent inclination to grant claims for implied immunity in Trinko and Billing, more sympathetic to regulated defendants.").

Bibliography

Almeida-Santos, P., Dani, A., Machado, A. & Krespi, N. (2013). Influence of family control in the practice of earnings management: The case of open Brazilian companies. *Management Research: Journal of the Iberoamerican Academy of Management*, 11(1), 77–99.

An, H. & Zhang, T. (2013). Stock price synchronicity, crash risk, and institutional investors. *Journal of Corporate Finance*, 21, 1–15.

Ascioglu, A., Hegde, S., Krishnan, G. & McDermott, J. (2012). Earnings management and market liquidity. *Review of Quant: Finance & Accounting*, 38, 257–274.

Baker, M., Wurgler, J. & Yuan, Y. (2012). Global, local, and contagious investor sentiment. *Journal of Financial Economics*, 104(2), 272–287.

Bancel, F. & Mittoo, C. (2001). European managerial perceptions of the net benefits of foreign stock listings. *European Financial Management*, 7(2), 213–236.

Bar-Yosef, S. & Prencipe, A. (2013). The impact of corporate governance and earnings management on stock market liquidity in a highly concentrated ownership capital market. *Journal of Accounting, Auditing and Finance*, 26, 199–227.

Battiston, S. & Glattfelder, J.B. (2009). Backbone of complex networks of corporations: The flow of control. *Physics Review-E*, 80, 036104.

Boissay, F. (2006). *Credit Chains and the Propagation of Financial Distress*. Working Paper Series #573. European Central Bank. www.ecb.europa.eu/pub/pdf/scpwps/ecbwp573.pdf?0c7b3859edb7d58a72b01309111c4b52.

Brennan, T. (2008). Essential facilities and trinko: Should antitrust and regulation be combined. *Federal Communications Law Journal*, 61, 133–143.

Brida, J., Anyul, M. & Punzo, L. (2003). Coding economic dynamics to represent regime dynamics. A teach-yourself exercise. *Structural Change* and *Economic Dynamics*, 14(2), 133–157.

Brunell, R. (2012). In regulators we trust: The Supreme Court's new approach to implied antitrust immunity. *Antitrust Law Journal*, 78, 279–299.

Cantwell, J. & Santangelo, G. (2006). The boundaries of firms in the new economy: M&As as a strategic tool toward corporate technological diversification. *Structural Change* and *Economic Dynamics*, 17(2), 174–199.

Cardoso, F., Martinez, A. & Teixeira, A. (2014). Free cash flow and earnings management in Brazil: The negative side of financial slack. *Global Journal of Management and Business Research: D – Accounting and Auditing*, 14(1).

Chandra, A. & Thenmozhi, M. (2017). Behavioural asset pricing: Review and synthesis. *Journal of Interdisciplinary Economics*, 24(1), 77–97.

Chemmanur, T.J. & He, J. (2011). IPO waves, product market competition, and the going public decision: Theory and evidence. *Journal of Financial Economics*, 101(2), 382–412.

Ciaschini, M., Pretaroli, R. & Socci, C. (2011). Balance, Manhattan norm and Euclidean distance of industrial policies for the US. *Structural Change* and *Economic Dynamics*, 22(3), 204–226.

Cichello, M. & Kieschnick, R. (2005). Product market competition, regulation, and financial contracts. *The Quarterly Review of Economics and Finance*, 45, 1–17.

Cimoli, M., Pereima, J. & Porcile, G. (2016). Introduction to the special issue SCED: *Complexity* and economic development. *Structural Change & Economic Dynamics*, 38, 1–2.

Claudiu, B. (2013). Formal representation of corporate governance principles and codes. *Procedia – Social and Behavioral Sciences*, 73, 744–750.

Colpan, A., Yoshikawa, T., Hikino, T. & Miyoshi, H. (2007). Japanese corporate governance: Structural change and financial performance. *Asian Business Management*, 6, 89–113.

Comim, F. (2000). The Santa Fe approach to complexity: A Marshallian evaluation. *Structural Change & Economic Dynamics*, 11(1–2), 25–43.

Cronqvist, H. & Siegel, S. (2014). The genetics of investment biases. *Journal of Financial Economics*, 113(2), 215–234.

Cumming, D. & Johan, S. (2013). Listing standards and fraud. *Managerial & Decision Economics*, 34(7–8), 451–470.

Darrough, M.N., Huang, R. & Zhao, S. (2013). *The Spillover Effect of Chinese Reverse Merger Frauds: Chinese or Reverse Merger?* Working Paper, Baruch College, CUNY, New York City.

Divya, V. (2014). Earnings management practices in India: A study of auditor's perception. *Journal of Financial Crime*, 21(1), 100–110.

Donaldson, J., Gershun, N. & Giannoni, M. (2012). Some unpleasant general equilibrium implications of executive incentive compensation contracts. *Journal of Theoretical Economics*, 148(1), 31–63.

Dosi, G. & Virgillito, M. (2017). In Order to stand up you must keep cycling: *Change* and coordination in complex evolving economies. *Structural Change* and *Economic Dynamics*, in press, accepted manuscript.

Dowd, K. (2018). *Asleep at the Wheel: The Prudential Regulation Authority and the Equity-Release Sector*. Report, Adam Smith Institute, UK.

Elliott, M., Golub, B. & Jackson, M.O. (2014). Financial networks and contagion. *American Economic Review*, 104, 3115–3153.

Eng, L. & Lin, Y. (2012). Accounting quality, earnings management and cross-listings: Evidence from China. *Rev. Pac. Basin Financial Markets*, 15(2).

Fang, X. & Yuan, F. (2018). The coordination and preference of supply chain contracts based on time-sensitivity promotional mechanism. *Journal of Management Science and Engineering*, 3(3), 158–178.

Francis, W., Hasan, I. & Li, L. (2014). *Abnormal Real Operations, Real Earnings Management, and Subsequent Crashes in Stock Prices*. Bank of Finland Research Discussion Papers #19. www.suomenpankki.fi/pdf/173785.pdf.

Fukao, M. (1999). *Japanese Financial Instability and Weakness in the Corporate Governance Structure* (OECD, Paris).

García-Pérez, A., Yanes-Estévez, V. & Oreja-Rodríguez, J. (2014). Strategic reference points, risk and strategic choices in small and medium-sized enterprises. *Journal of Business Economics and Management*, 21(3), 431–449.

Goetz, R., Yatsenko, Y., Hritonenko, N., Xabadia, A. & Abdulai, A. (2019). The dynamics of productive assets, contract duration and holdup. *Mathematical Social Sciences*, 97, 24–37.

Grechuk, B. & Zabarankin, M. (2014). Risk averse decision making under catastrophic risk. *European Journal of Operational Research*, 239(1), 166–176.

Guo, W., Wang, F. & Wu, H. (2011). Financial leverage and market volatility with diverse beliefs. *Economic Theory*, 47(2–3), 337–364.

Haldane, A.G. & May, R.M. (2011). Systemic risk in banking ecosystems. *Nature*, 469, 351–355.

Hill, C. (1996). Securitization: A low-cost sweetener for lemons. *Washington University Law Quarterly*, 74, 1061–1071.

Hong, S., Wernz, C. & Stillinger, J. (2016). Optimizing maintenance service contracts through mechanism design theory. *Applied Mathematical Modelling*, 40(21–22), 8849–8861.

Hoppe, E. & Schmitz, P. (2018). Hidden action and outcome contractibility: An experimental test of moral hazard theory. *Games & Economic Behavior*, 109, 544–564.

Humphery-Jenner, M. & Suchard, J. (2013). Foreign VCs and the internationalization of entrepreneurial companies: Evidence from China. *Journal of International Business Studies*, 44(6), 607–621.

Hutton, A., Marcus, A. & Tehranian, H. (2009). Opaque financial reports, R square, and crash risk. *Journal of Financial Economics*, 94, 67–86.

Iatridis, G. & Kadorinis, G. (2009). Earnings management and firm financial motives: A financial investigation of UK listed firms. *International Review of Financial Analysis*, 18(4), 164–173.

Jiang, H. & Habib, A. (2012). Split-share reform and earnings management: Evidence from China. *Advances in Accounting*, 28(1), 120–127.

Jin, L. & Myers, S. (2006). R^2 around the world: New theory and tests. *Journal of Financial Economics*, 79, 257–292.

Jovane, F., Seliger, G. & Stock, T. (2017). Competitive sustainable globalization general considerations and perspectives. *Procedia Manufacturing*, 8, 1–19.

Kahn, J. (2008). From *Borden* to *Billing*: Identifying a uniform approach to implied antitrust immunity from the Supreme Court's precedents. *Chicago Kent Law Review*, 83, 1439–1457.

Karpoff, J., Lee, D. & Martin, G. (2008a). The cost to firms of cooking the books. *Journal of Financial and Quantitative Analysis*, 43, 581–612.

Karpoff, J., Lee, D. & Martin, G. (2008b). The consequences to managers for cooking the books. *Journal of Financial Economics*, 88, 193–215.

Kelly, K. (2010). The effects of incentives on information exchange and decision quality in groups. *Behavioral Research in Accounting*, 22(1), 43–48.

Kim, J. & Zhang, L. (2013). Accounting conservatism and stock price crash risk: Firm-level evidence. *Contemporary Accounting Research*, 33(1), 412–441.

Kim, J. & Zhang, L. (2014). Financial reporting opacity and expected crash risk: Evidence from implied volatility smirks. *Contemporary Accounting Research*, 31(3), 851–875.

Kim, J.B., Li, Y. & Zhang, L. (2011a). Corporate tax avoidance and stock price crash risk: Firm-level analysis. *Journal of Financial Economics*, 100, 639–662.

Kim, J.B., Li, Y. & Zhang, L. (2011b). CFOs versus CEOs: Equity incentives and crashes. *Journal of Financial Economics*, 101, 713–730.

Kuzubas, T., Ömercikoglu, I. & Saltoglu, B. (2014). Network centrality measures and systemic risk: An application to the Turkish financial crisis. *Physica-A: Stat. Mech Appl.*, 405, 203–215.

Lee, M. (2015). The implied antitrust immunityanalysis of credit *Suisse vs. Billing*: A framework congress should apply to Mccarran-Ferguson Act repeal efforts. *Columbia Business Law Review*, 2015, 349–369.

Li, H., An, H., Gao, X., Huang, J. & Xu, Q. (2014). On the topological properties of the cross shareholding networks of listed companies in China: Taking shareholders' cross-shareholding relationships into account. *Physica-A*, 6, 80–88.

Li, W., Liu, Y. & Chen, Y. (2018). Modeling a two-stage supply contract problem in a hybrid uncertain environment. *Computers & Industrial Engineering*, 123, 289–302.

Lin, E. & Chou, M. (1990). Optimal contracts. *Applied Mathematics Letters*, 3(2), 65–68.

Liu, Q. & Zhou, J. (2007). Corporate governance and earnings management in the Chinese listed companies: A tunneling perspective. *Journal of Corporate Finance*, 13(5), 881–906.

Liu, X. & Tse, C. (2012). Dynamics of network of global stock market. *Accounting & Finance Research*, 1, 1–12.

Lopes, A. & Alencar, R. (2010). Disclosure and cost of equity capital in emerging markets: The Brazilian case. *The International Journal of Accounting*, 45(4), 443–464.

Ma, Y., Zhuang, X.T. & Li, L. (2011). Research on the relationships of the domestic mutual investment of China based on the cross-shareholding networks of the listed companies. *Physica-A*, 390, 749–759.

Madureira, A., Pereira, I., Pereira, P. & Abraham, A. (2014). Negotiation mechanism for self-organized scheduling system with collective intelligence. *Neurocomputing*, 132, 97–110.

Markham, J. (2010). The Supreme Court's new implied repeal doctrine: Expanding judicial power to rewrite legislation under the ballooning conception of "plain repugnancy". *Gonzaga Law Review*, 45, 437–439,

McCahery, J., Sautner, Z. & Starks, L. (2016). Behind the scenes: The corporate governance preferences of institutional investors. *Journal of Finance*, 71(6), 2905–2932.

Meneguzzi, F., Modgil, S., Oren, N., Miles, S., Luck, M. & Faci, N. (2012). Applying electronic contracting to the aerospace aftercare domain. *Engineering Applications of Artificial Intelligence*, 25, 1471–1487.

Niederhoff, J. & Kouvelis, P. (2019). Effective and necessary: Individual supplier behavior in revenue sharing and wholesale contracts. *European Journal of Operational Research*, 277(3), 1060–1071.

Nitz, L. (2018). Differential protection or uncontrolled marketing: CFPB reverse mortgage complaints across the states. *Innovation in Aging*, 2(Suppl 1), 319–320.

Nwogugu, M. (2003). Corporate governance, credit risk and legal reasoning: The case of Encompass Services Inc. *Managerial Auditing Journal*, 18(4), 270–291. Also published in *International Journal of Law & Management*, (47(1–2), 2–43, 2005), and reprinted in *ICFAI Journal of Financial Economics* (2004).

Nwogugu, M. (2004a). Corporate governance, risk and corporations law: The case of Jack-in-the-Box Inc. *Managerial Auditing Journal*, 19(1), 29–67. Also published in *International Journal of Law & Management* (November 2004), and reprinted in *ICFAI Journal of Financial Economics* (2004).

Nwogugu, M. (2004b). Legal, economic and behavioral issues in accounting for stock options. *Managerial Auditing Journal*, 19(9), 1078–1118.

Nwogugu, M. (2005a). Structural changes in the US retailing industry: Legal, economic and strategic implications for the US real estate sector. *International Journal of Law & Management*, 47(1–2).

Nwogugu, M. (2005b). Economic evolution and the constitutionality of REITs. *Corporate Control & Ownership* (2008).

Nwogugu, M. (2006). Employee stock options, production functions and game theory. *Applied Mathematics & Computation*, 181(1), 552–562.

Nwogugu, M. (2007a). Decision-making, risk and corporate governance: A critique of methodological issues in bankruptcy/recovery prediction models. *Applied Mathematics & Computation*, 185(1), 178–196.

Nwogugu, M. (2007b). Issues in disintermediation in the real estate brokerage industry. *Applied Mathematics & Computation*, 186(2), 1054–1064.

Nwogugu, M. (2007c). Some game theory and financial contracting issues in large corporate transactions. *Applied Mathematics & Computation*, 186(2), 1018–1030.

Nwogugu, M. (2007d). Some issues in securitization and disintermediation. *Applied Mathematics & Computation*, 186(2), 1031–1039.

Nwogugu, M. (2007e). Some securities law problems inherent in REITs. *Journal of International Banking Law & Regulation*, 22(11), 603–613.

Nwogugu, M. (2008a). Illegality of securitization, bankruptcy issues and theories of securitization. *Journal of International Banking Law & Regulation*, 23(7), 363–375.

Nwogugu, M. (2008b). Securitization is illegal: Racketeer influenced and corrupt organizations, usury, antitrust and tax issues. *Journal of International Banking Law & Regulation*, 23(6), 316–332.

Nwogugu, M. (2008c). Some corporate governance problems pertaining to REITs – Part one. *Journal of International Banking Law & Regulation*, 23(2), 71–85.

Nwogugu, M. (2008d). Some corporate governance problems pertaining to REITs – Part two. *Journal of International Banking Law & Regulation*, 23(3), 142–155.

Nwogugu, M. (2009a). On the choice between a strategic alliance and an M&A transaction. *International Journal of Mathematics, Game Theory & Algebra*, 17(5–6), 269–278.

Nwogugu, M. (2009b). Some new antitrust models. *International Journal of Mathematics, Game Theory & Algebra*, 17(5–6), 241–254.

Nwogugu, M. (2012). Un-constitutionality of asset securitization. Chapter in: Nwogugu, M., *Risk in the Global Real Estate Market* (John Wiley & Sons, USA).

Nwogugu, M. (2014). "Netting", the liquidity coverage ratio, and the US FSOC's non-SIFI criteria, and new recommendations. *Banking Law Journal*, 131(6), 416–420.

Nwogugu, M. (2015a). Goodwill/intangibles rules and earnings management. *European Journal of Law Reform*, 11(2).

Nwogugu, M. (2015b). Failure of the Dodd-Frank act. *Journal of Financial Crime*, 22(4), 520–572.

Nwogugu, M. (2015c). Real options, enforcement of and goodwill/intangibles rules and associated behavioral issues. *Journal of Money Laundering Control*, 18(3), 330–351.

Nwogugu, M. (2015d). *Complexity and Alternative Risk Premia: Some New Theories of Structural Change and Portfolio Decisions.* https://papers.ssrn.com/sol3/papers.cfm?abstract_id=3410631.

Nwogugu, M. (2015e). Un-Constitutionality of the Dodd-Frank Act. *European Journal of Law Reform*, 17, 185–190.

Nwogugu, M. (2017). Regret theory and asset pricing anomalies in incomplete markets with dynamic un-aggregated preferences. Chapter 3 in: Nwogugu, M., *Anomalies in Net Present Value, Returns and Polynomials, and Regret Theory in Decision-Making* (Palgrave Macmillan, London, UK).

Nwogugu, M. (2019a). Human computer interaction, incentive conflicts and methods for eliminating index arbitrage, index-related mutual fund arbitrage and ETF arbitrage. Chapter 9 in: Nwogugu, M., *Indices, Index Funds and ETFs HCI: Exploring HCI, Non-linear Risk and Homomorphisms* (Palgrave Macmillan, London, UK).

Nwogugu, M. (2019b). Economic policy, complex adaptive systems, human-computer interaction and managerial psychology: Popular-index ecosystems. Chapter 12 in: Nwogugu, M., *Indices, Index Funds and ETFs HCI: Exploring HCI, Nonlinear Risk and Homomorphisms* (Palgrave Macmillan, London, UK).

Nwogugu, M. (2019c). Complexity and some numerical algorithmic turning-point problems inherent in excessive outstanding shares. Chapter 15 in: Nwogugu, M., *Complex Systems, Multi-Sided Incentives and Risk Perception in Companies* (Palgrave Macmillan, London, UK).

Park, S. & Kim, J. (2014). A mathematical model for a capacity reservation contract. *Applied Mathematical Modelling*, 38(5–6), 1866–1880.

Peng, W., Wei, J. & Yang, Z. (2011). Tunneling or propping: Evidence from connected transactions in China. *Journal of Corporate Finance*, 17(2), 306–325.

Pinegar, J. & Ravichandran, R. (2010). Raising capital in emerging markets with restricted global depositary receipts. *Journal of Corporate Finance*, 16(5), 622–636.

Plank, T. (2004). The security of securitization and the future of security. *Cardozo Law Review*, 25, 1655–1660.

Robert, V. & Yoguel, G. (2016). *Complexity* paths in neo-schumpeterian evolutionary economics, *structural change* and development policies. *Structural Change & Economic Dynamics*, 38, 3–14.

Ruttiman, B. (2014). Modeling financial type 2b globalization and its repercussion on the real economy. *Procedia Economics & Finance*, 14, 534–543.

Saayman, A. (2003). *Securitization and Bank Liquidity in South Africa.* Working Paper, Potchefstroom University, South Africa.

Salinas, G. (2009). *The International Brand Valuation Manual* (1st ed., John Wiley & Sons, Ltd., Jersey City, NJ, USA).

Sarkar, J., Sarkar, S. & Sen, K. (2008). Board of directors and opportunistic earnings management: Evidence from India. *Journal of Accounting, Auditing and Finance*, 23(4).

Scazzieri, R. (2009). Structural economic dynamics: Looking back and forging ahead. *Economia Politica*, XXVI(3), 531–557.

Schilirò, D. (2012). *Structural Change and Models of Structural Analysis: Theories, Principles and Methods.* MPRA Working Paper, MPRA, Germany.

Schwarcz, S. (1999a). The inherent irrationality of judgment proofing. *Stanford Law Review*, 52, 1–20.

Schwarcz, S. (1999b). The impact on securitization of revised UCC article 9. *Kent Law Review*, 74, 947–957 (Revised Article-9 attempts to broaden its coverage to virtually all securitized assets).

Schwarcz, S. (2002). Enron and the use and abuse of special purpose entities in corporate structures. *University of Cincinnati Law Review*, 70, 1309–1329.

Segovia, J., Arnold, V. & Sutton, S. (2009). Do principles- vs. rules-based standards have a differential impact on U.S. auditors' decisions? In Arnold, V., ed., *Advances in Accounting Behavioral Research, Volume 12* (Emerald Group Publishing Limited, London, UK), pp. 61–84.

Shelanski, H. (2010). The case for rebalancing antitrust regulation *Michigan Law Review*, 109, 683–703.

Shelanski, H. (2012). Justice Breyer, Professor Kahn, and antitrust enforcement in regulated industries. *California Law Review*, 100(2), 487–517.

Siregar, S. & Utama, S. (2008). Type of earnings management and the effect of ownership structure, firm size, and corporate-governance practices: Evidence from Indonesia. *The International Journal of Accounting*, 43(1), 1–27.

Sokol, D. (2009). Limiting anticompetitive government interventions that benefit special interests. *George Mason Law Review*, 17, 119–129.

Stein, S., Gerding, E.H., Rogers, A.C., Larson, K. & Jennings, N.R. (2011). Algorithms and mechanisms for procuring services with uncertain durations using redundancy. *Artificial Intelligence*, 175(14–15), 2021–2060.

Swiecki, T. (2017). Determinants of structural change. *Review of Economic Dynamics*, 24, 95–131.

Terán, J., Aguilar, J. & Cerrada, M. (2017). Integration in industrial automation based on multi-agent systems using cultural algorithms for optimizing the coordination mechanisms. *Computers in Industry*, 91, 11–23.

Tirole, J. (2012). The euro crisis: Some reflexions on institutional reform. *Banque de France – Financial Stability Review*, 16, 225–230. https://www.imf.org/external/np/seminars/eng/2013/macro2/pdf/tirole1.pdf

Varney, C. (2011). Antitrust immunities. *Oregon Law Review*, 89, 775–795.

Vu, K. (2017). Structural change and economic growth: Empirical evidence and policy insights from Asian economies. *Structural Change and Economic Dynamics*, 41, 64–77.

Wei, W., Wang, J., Chen, X., Yang, J. & Min, X. (2018). Psychological contract model for knowledge collaboration in virtual community of practice: An analysis based on the game theory. *Applied Mathematics & Computation*, 329, 175–187.

Wu, Z., Zhao, R. & Tang, W. (2014). Optimal contracts for the agency problem with multiple uncertain information. *Knowledge-Based Systems*, 59, 161–172.

Yamazaki, K. (2005). *What makes Asset Securitization Inefficient?* Berkeley Electronic Press, Working Paper #603.

Zeitun, R. & Tian, G. (2007). Does ownership affect a firm's performance and default risk in Jordan? *Corporate Governance*, 7(1), 66–82.

Zimmerman, J. & Gontcharov, I. (2006). *Do Accounting Standards Influence the Level of Earnings Management? Evidence from Germany.* http://cosmic.rrz.uni-hamburg.de/webcat/hwwa/edok03/f10844g/ACCT041.pdf.

Zohar, A. & Rosenschein, J. (2008). Mechanisms for information elicitation. *Artificial Intelligence*, 172(16–17), 1917–1939.

Complex adaptive systems, sustainable growth and securities law: on *inequality, preferences+reasoning* and the optimal design of financial contracts

Optimal Financial Contracting and *Optimal Design of Financial Contracts* both have significant symbiotic relationships with Taxation, Human/Agent behaviors and Financial Statements, and typically occur in Complex Adaptive Systems and thus, they implicate Earnings Management, Asset-quality Management and Incentive-Effects Management. On the relationships among *Financial Development, Optimal Financial Contracting* and *Sustainable Growth*, see the comments in: Sabri (2011); Mirazizov, Radzhabova and Abdulaeva (2013); Snaije (2017); De Rato (Aug. 22, 2007); Guru and Yadav (2019); Guha-Khasnobis and Mavrotas (2008); Menyah, Nazlioglu and Wolde-Rufael (2014). *On Financial Development*, see the comments in Austin (2012); Song and Zhu (2018); Berger-Soucy, Garriott and Usche (Bank of Canada) (2018); Cheng, Massa and Zhang (2018); Silva (2003) and Moldogaziev and Luby (2016).

This chapter: i) explains why Mutual Funds, ARS (Auction-Rate Securities), "Structured Synthetic ETFs" (SSETFs) and Credit Default Swaps (CDS) are not "securities"; ii) summarizes the criteria for classification of debt and equity and explains why Mutual Funds and SSETFs are "hybrid" financial instruments (contract-Intangibles) and how "TARP/CPP Instruments" were mis-classified and failed (the TARP/CPP Instruments were issued by various entities as part of the US government's bailouts/bail-ins of financial institutions during the Global Financial Crisis); iii) explains why Mutual Funds, Structured Products and ARS can create significant problems – such as information asymmetry; exacerbation of agency problems; asset-quality management, earnings management; etc. – and are very much subject to human biases and group behaviors that can distort prices and liquidity (and they can have economic and psychological *Multiplier Effects* that *spill over* into other countries); iv) surveys the literature that shows how ARS contributed to the Euro Crisis, and recommends ways to improve the global ARS market; v) summarizes the Complex Adaptive Systems factors. These issues have significant implications for Market-Microstructure analysis, Financial Stability, Economic Policy, Portfolio Management and the optimal design of securities, Financial Instruments and debt contracts.

Auction-Rate Securities ("ARS"), Mutual Funds, Structured Synthetic ETFs (SSETFs), Structured Products and TARP/CPP Instruments (in the USA) are all based on, and are defined by financial contracts, and each can have substantial economic and psychological effects and "*Multiplier effects*" on productivity, *Inequality* and sustainable growth around the world primarily because these are directly and indirectly used to finance economic growth, households and corporate growth around the world but often in ways that amplify *Inequality* and reduce Sustainability. Thus Earnings Management, Incentive-Effects Management, Asset-Quality Management, corporate scandals and corporate financial distress (see the Appendices in Chapter 3 in this book), market-distortions, environmental pollution, household mis-allocations (of resources), inflation and financial instability that pertains to, or originates from these Financial Instruments can have substantial negative effects on government policy making, corporate policy making and Sustainability (i.e. economic/financial, social and environmental Sustainability).

Mutual Funds, SSETFs, ARS, TARP/CPP Instruments and Structured Products Vehicles are critical for economic growth and *Sustainability* and can have "*Multiplier Effects*" on other fixed-income/currency/equity markets, on financial institutions and on household economics for many reasons including but not limited to the following:

i)   Mutual Funds, SSETFs, ARS and Structured Products Vehicles essentially recycle capital in the economy, allocate capital in national economies and can be major influencers/determinants of the *Business Cycle*.

ii) Mutual Funds, SSETFs, ARS and Structured Products Vehicles serve as benchmarks for valuations, interest rates and firms' cost-of-capital. ARS and Structured Products yields/rates are used to price other fixed income instruments (bonds; notes; loans; mortgages; etc.). The borrowing costs of large/medium companies; financial institutions and government agencies are often based on ARS and Structured Products rates/yields.

iii) Mutual Funds, SSETFs, ARS and Structured Products Vehicles assets serve as collateral for loans (some of which are syndicated or securitized (and thus there are possibilities of *Domino Effects* and Systemic Risk); can serve as interest rate benchmarks; and can serve as inflation, currency exchange-rate and uncertainty hedges, and as stores-of-value and are also used in "spreads" and arbitrage in trading. Thus households' income/savings/consumption and Aggregate Investment are affected.

iv) Mutual Funds, SSETFs, ARS and Structured Products Vehicles transmit or can transmit economic, financial, political and psychological shocks and *Spillover Effects* (foreign investors purchase and sell them); and these Instruments can also affect human aspirations/motivation (and thus productivity), human perceptions of risk, investment horizons, uncertainty, perceptions of both individual and group achievement, and growth (both personal and macroeconomic).

v)   In many countries, significant *monetary policy* initiatives and strategies are implemented partially or wholly through ARS auctions (for example in the USA, the US Federal Reserve uses *Reverse ARS Auctions* to purchase

Treasury bonds in *Quantitative-Easing*) and Structured Products; and mixed (fiscal and monetary) policy interventions are executed through mechanisms such as the TARP/CPP Program. Similarly, significant *fiscal policy* initiatives and strategies are implemented partially or wholly through the taxation of income and capital gains from Mutual Funds, ARS, ETFs and Structured Products Vehicles.

vi) Mutual Funds, SSETFs, ARS, TARP/CPP Instruments and Structured Products Vehicles can cause and or transmit *Inequality* – and the "channels" include but are not limited to their financing terms, their associated securities brokerage commissions, the *Internal Markets* of firms, their Industrial Organization effects, their effects on households' economics, allocation-costs and decision making, etc. The significant *Housing Inequality, Income/Wealth Inequality* and *Social Inequality* caused by HAMP and HARP (part of the TARP/CPP Program in the US) is explained herein and below.

vii) Mutual Funds, SSETFs, ARS, Structured Products Vehicles and TARP/CPP-type government interventions can affect *Sustainability* and or *Inequality* and or *Financial Stability* through their financing terms, their financing function, their compliance with environmental regulations and CSR standards, and their direct/indirect effects on household dynamics/economics and quality-of-life – all of that can have negative *Multiplier Effects*.

viii) Mutual Funds, ARS and Structured Products Vehicles units are not securities, and they can be used for earnings management and asset-quality management by both issuers and investors; all of which can increase market volatility, systemic risk and crash-risk in markets. As explained herein and below, the legal classification of Mutual Funds, SSETFs, ARS, TARP/CPP Instruments and Structured Products Vehicles is critical and has important implications for a wide variety of issues, companies,investors, regulators and professionals and thus can have *Multiplier Effects* and *Spillover Effects*.

ix) Mutual Funds, SSETFs, ARS, TARP/CPP Instruments and Structured Products Vehicles can affect/influence the *Stock-Repurchase decisions* of multinational companies (MNCs), the efficiency of regulations, the *Compliance Decisions* of companies and regulators (as physical and psychological phenomena), and the "automated search-agents" that are used in executing *High-Frequency Trading*, all of which have had profound effects on modern stock, debt, commodities and currency markets, national economies and household economics/dynamics (in terms of savings, investment, expenditures, allocation of resources, risk-perception expectations, uncertainty, aspirations, etc.) around the world.

x) Individually and collectively, each of Mutual Funds, SSETFs, ARS, TARP/CPP Instruments and Structured Products Vehicles are *systems-of-systems* that can have evolving symbiotic relationships with each other and with other Macroeconomic/Macrofinancial factors.

xi) ARS, Structured Products and Mutual funds dynamics and associated *Noise* can cause or increase Systemic Risk and or Financial Instability, and can affect supply/demand, risk-perception, liquidity and contagion-risk in equity markets, CDS markets and or derivatives markets; can affect risk-perception, liquidity and contagion-risk in foreign exchange markets, Foreign Investment, Foreign Direct Investments and international trade.

The legal analysis in this chapter is done using USA statutes and case-law because the USA has the most litigated, comprehensive and sophisticated securities law framework which has been copied by many developed and developing countries[1]; and the US also has the largest and most sophisticated capital markets in the world.

5.1 Motivation and existing literature

The motivation for, and context of this chapter are varied, and the issues discussed apply to, or are applicable in various companies and countries (many foreign investors purchased ARS; ARS continue to be issued in various countries; some TARP/CPP Instruments issuers had extensive foreign operations; and Mutual Funds affected or could have affected both US and non-US investors). *First*, the Global Financial Crisis of 2007–2015 and many publicized earnings management scandals in the US, China, Japan, UK and Europe exposed significant weaknesses in Internal Controls, and the many problems inherent in complex financial instruments (such as Mutual Funds; ARS, CDS, TARP/CPP instruments and swaps/derivatives) and their direct and indirect impact on the economy and Corporate Governance standards in organizations. Many articles such as McConnell and Saretto (2010), Wantchinatimes.com (2015),[2] US Government Printing Office (Sept. 2008)[3] and Chang (June 16, 2013)[4] documented ARS Auction-Failures in China and the US. Pillai, Li and Huang (2015)[5] summarized the Chinese Treasury bond market. The *Mutual Fund scandal* of 2007–2009 in the US was documented by several researchers. Various academic researchers have also criticized CDS and Structured Products and Nwogugu (2008a,b) critiqued asset securitization (asset-backed securities and mortgage-backed securities). *Second*, the exponential growth of cross-border trade and investment during 1995–2018 subjected investors to conflicting and sometimes inadequate and inefficient regulations and corporate governance standards. *Third*, despite their inherent weaknesses, almost all Mutual Funds, Structured Products and ARS were sanctioned (and sometimes promoted) by Boards of Directors (BODs) and senior executives of banks and issuer-companies and government agencies (e.g. in China and the US); but both individual and institutional investors around the world are increasingly emphasizing the quality and implementation of corporate governance standards and Board Dynamics within companies as a major investment criteria. *Fourth*, given their inherent weaknesses, the issuance of Mutual Funds, CDS, Structured Products Vehicles or ARS represents psychological phenomena in group dynamics and decision-making which have not been addressed in the literature – this chapter introduces some theories about that. The behavioral issues implicit in the auctions, and the ownership of Mutual Funds and or ARS have not been studied fully in the literature. Specifically, the ownership of ARS and the associated auction-processes represent investor preferences that are very different from preferences predicted by CPT/PT/PT3 and related approaches. *Fifth*, there has been very little theoretical analysis of the legal status and legality of TARP/CPP Instruments, ARS and Mutual Funds; and the earnings-management and incentive-management effects of ARS. *Sixth*, during 1995–2019 and across the world, there were increases in shareholder activism, some of which was triggered by complex securities such as TARP/CPP Financial Instruments, Structured Products, ABS/MBS Trusts, Mutual Funds and ARS, and much of which was directed at or was handled by or was ultimately influenced by boards of directors (BODs). *Seventh*, on both retroactive and current bases, TARP/CPP Instruments, Structured Products, ABS/MBS Trusts, Mutual Funds and ARS are evidence of the failures of the Sarbanes-Oxley Act, the Dodd-Frank Act, the US FSOC's Non-Bank SIFI Criteria, Auditor Liability Allocation mechanisms and the US SEC's rules and similar regulations in other countries – all of which didn't sufficiently address or regulate those Financial Instruments. *Eighth*, the issue of whether Corporate Governance statutes (such as SOX) and the regulations for some Incentive Mechanisms (such as Mutual Funds, TARP/CPP Instruments and ARS) are Public Goods has not been addressed in the literature. *Ninth*, there has been evidence of, and controversy about manipulation, collusion and fraud in issuance of TARP/CPP Instruments, CDS trading, ARS auction processes and Mutual Fund markets around the world and especially in the US Treasury bond/bill auctions and CDS markets as indicated by various articles[6] and Milton (1964), Jegadeesh (1993) and Cornell and Shapiro (1989). Unfortunately many countries use similar auction methods for sales of their sovereign securities and so they probably suffer from the same problems. *Tenth*, as mentioned herein and above, Auction-Rate Securities ("ARS"), Mutual Funds, Structured Products and TARP/CPP Instruments (in the USA) have had and can have substantial economic, psychological and *Inequality* effects, *Spillover Effects* and "*Multiplier effects*" on productivity and sustainable growth around the world. Around the world, these Financial Instruments are used to finance many companies and government agencies that pollute the environment, cause climate change and foster *Compensation Inequality* (and gender-based pay-gaps), large and *increasing CEO Pay-Ratios* and *Social Inequality*. TARP/CPP Instruments also financed US-based financial services companies and operating companies that caused the same problems. The earnings management, asset-quality management and Incentive-Effects management that is encouraged, caused or amplified by those Financial Instruments can increase Inequality and reduce Sustainability. *Eleventh*, despite having invested about U$410 billion in US banks and companies during 2008–2014, the TARP/CPP Program failed as confirmed by many reports[7] (see: Calabrese, Degl'Innocenti and Angela Osmetti [2017], Black and Hazelwood [2013], Farruggioa, Michalak and Uhde [2013], Song and Uzmanoglu

[2016], and Semaan and Drake [2016]) and in other ways explained herein and below. The TARP/CPP Program was implemented by the US government to boost the US economy and to stabilize banks and some operating multinational companies. During the last fifty years, many countries have either implemented similar economic programs or bail-out/bail-in programs for their financial services companies and MNCs (see the list of economic/financial crisis in many countries in Appendices 3.1–3.5). *Twelfth,* the sizes and the resulting dynamics/perceptions of the Global Mutual Fund industry (more than US\$25 trillion of AUM in 2019), the global ARS market (more than US\$18 trillion *of outstanding Financial Instruments* in 2019) and the global Structured Products market are substantial and can have significant negative economic, psychological and political effects on national economies, governments and households. By addressing these issues, this chapter fills several gaps in, contributes to the literatures on international capital flows, *Inequality,* Complex Adaptive Systems, Optimal Financial Contracting, asset allocation, Financial Stability, asset pricing, Sustainable Growth, Securities Law and Enterprise Risk-Management.

As mentioned in Chapter 1, *Accounting Biases* is a relatively new line of research and has been studied from Behavioral Accounting, Management Science (see: Khan and Lo [2018], Chen and Jorgensen [2018], Kwon [2005] and Marquardt and Zur [2015]), Behavioral Operations Management and Operations Research (see: Nan and Wen [2014]) perspectives. Specific *Accounting Biases* were introduced in several chapters in this book, but in this chapter, the Accounting Biases pertain to earnings management, Incentive-effects Management and asset-quality management in the use of Mutual Funds, ARS, Structured Products and SSETFs. Chen and Jorgensen (2018) noted that *Accounting Biases* can affect competition and Industry Structure in various industries. Using a study of mergers/acquisitions, Marquardt and Zur (2015) found evidence that financial accounting quality is positively related to the efficient allocation of the economy's capital resources. *Enforcement Theory* has been analyzed from Operations Research, Political Philosophy and Law perspectives, and the associated literatures are cited in Chapter 2 in this book. *Enforcement Patterns* (e.g. enforcement of accounting regulations, commodities-trading regulations and securities laws; corporate laws; etc.) can also affect competition and Industry Structure in various industries because: i) they affect the nature of competition and collaboration among firms in industries; ii) they affect firms' allocations of resource and capital; iii) they affect product development, marketing and human resources decisions; iv) they affect the functioning, responsibilities and liability of boards of directors; v) they affect firms' perceived risk and liability-allocation in expected or existing disputes. Thus by extension, *Accounting Biases* and *Enforcement Patterns* can have both direct and indirect effects on economic growth and Sustainability.

As noted in Chapter 1 in this book, the Standardization of contracts can affect economic growth, Sustainability, Inequality and Economic Growth. In the realm of ARS, CDS and Investment Vehicles, various trade associations in many countries (such as FINRA, ISDA and ICMA in the US and the UK) have developed standardized contracts for swaps/derivatives, other Financial Instruments, securities brokers and securities brokerage customers.

As noted in Chapters 1 and 4 in this book, Earnings management, Asset-quality Management and Incentive-Effects Management typically occur and or are amplified within the context of, and often distort organizations, *Incentive-Mechanisms*, *Contracting-Frameworks*, *Networks-of-Contracts*, markets and the benefits of Fintech. *Contract Theory* and *Mechanism Design Theory* have been jointly studied from various perspectives including Economics/Finance, Operations Research, Mathematical Psychology, Computer Science, Game Theory and Applied Math.

5.1.1 A critique and survey of the literature on accounting disclosure, optimal financial contracting and industry structure

Accounting disclosure and *Optimal Financial Contracting* have a symbiotic and mutually dependent relationship. That is, *"Earnings Management Capacity"* (whether the Financial Instrument can be used for, or amplifies Earnings Management, Asset-Quality Management and or Incentive-Effects Management) and *"Disclosure Efficiency"* (whether accounting disclosure of the Financial Instrument captures its true risks/behavior; and or causes harmful human behaviors/biases) of Financial Instruments are key elements of the *"optimality"* of Financial Contracting.

"Optimal Financial Contracting" (and the optimal design of securities, financial instruments and debt contracts) is well discussed in the literature which includes the following: Noe and Nachman (1994); Nikolaev (2017); Bizjak, Kalpathy and Mihov (2018); Triantis (2013); DeMarzo and Duffie (1999); DeMarzo, Kremer and Skrzypacz (2005); Anantharaman (2014); Herbert (2018); Engert and Hornuf (2018); Dekker, Kawai and Sakaguchi (2018); Fizaine (2018); Eenmaa-Dimitrieva and Schmidt-Kessen (2019); Drozd and Serrano-Padia (2018); Martellini, Milhau & Tarelli (2018); DeMarzo and Fishman (2007); Roberts (2015); Colla, Ippolito and Li (2013); and Darrough and Deng (2018). The relationships among Financial Development, *Optimal Financial Contracting* and Sustainable Growth are discussed in Sabri (2011); Mirazizov, Radzhabova & Abdulaeva (2013); Snaije (2017); De Rato (Aug. 22, 2007); Guru and Yadav (2019); Guha-Khasnobis and Mavrotas (2008); Menyah, Nazlioglu and Wolde-Rufael (2014). The relationship between industry competition and economic growth on one hand, and Accounting Disclosure (and by extension, *Optimal Financial Contracting* and *Optimal Design of Financial Instruments*) is well documented – see: Darrough (1993); Board (March 2009); Ackert, Chruch and Sankar (2000); Heibatollah and Zhou (2009); Hwang and Kirby (2004); Kirby (2004); Liu, Jorion and Shi (2008); Naor (2006) and Pae (2002; 2000). However, most of these foregoing articles and their related literature are not entirely accurate and or are moot because: i) the empirical studies suffer from the *Reproducibility Crisis* discussed in Chapter 1

and other problems in empirical research; ii) most of the studies don't analyze the legal classification of financial instruments – that affects financial statements, risk perception, contracting capacity of firms, *Market Microstructure* and the efficiency of Financial Contracting (in terms of margin costs, transaction costs, repos, trading rules, etc.); iii) the studies don't discuss the Earnings Management, Incentive-Effects Management and Asset-Quality Management implications of these Financial Instruments; iv) most of the studies didn't discuss the Industrial Organization and or psychological effects of such Financial Instruments, earnings management and incentive-effects management – compare: Smith (2011).

On the regulation of investment funds, Structured Products, mutual funds and ETFs, see Pozen and Hamacher (2015); Lemke, Lins and Smith (2017); Lemke, Lins and McGuire (2017); Qu (2016) and Soklakov (June 2017; December 2016) – however, those materials didn't adequately analyze issues of classification (the legal status of financial instruments and the governing legal regime), economic and psychological costs, Industrial Organization effects and earnings management effects of Financial Instruments. The reality is that an accurate analysis of affected Market Microstructure or *Optimal Financial Contracting* cannot be done unless the issues of Accounting Disclosure and "Classification" (the legal status of financial instruments and the governing legal regime), costs, Industrial Organization effects and earnings management effects are first analyzed – as mentioned herein and below, these and other factors affect various costs, liabilities and evolving relationships. Nwogugu (2019a;b;c) analyzed some Industrial Organization effects, earnings management effects and associated Complexity costs of Indices, Index funds and ETFs. Nwogugu (2009a) analyzed the un-constitutionality of Asset Securitization (asset backed securities and mortgage backed securities). Nwogugu (2007c), Nwogugu (2014a) and Nwogugu (2008c;d) studied various securities law, corporate governance, earnings management and Industrial Organization problems inherent in Real Estate Investment Trusts (REITs) around the world. Nwogugu (2008a;b) and Nwogugu (2007a) studied various securities law, corporate governance, earnings management, Complexity costs and Industrial Organization problems inherent in asset securitization (asset-backed securities and mortgage-backed securities). Nwogugu (2006) analyzed dynamics and Complexity of, and the symbiotic relationship between Employee Stock Options (ESOs) and *Production Functions* – ARS, Structured Products, Mutual Funds and SSETFs may also affect *Production Functions*. Using US statutes and case-law, Nwogugu (2004) analyzed the legal classification of employee stock options (ESOs) and introduced new and more efficient ESOs. Nwogugu (2007b) analyzed Industrial Organization issues and developed new ESOs that can reduce un-warranted *"Wealth Transfers"* and earnings management in companies, which in turn can effect competition, Industry Structure and Sustainable Growth. Nwogugu (2007d) analyzed financial contracting problems that are inherent in corporate transactions (i.e. Mergers/Acquisitions, LBOs, etc.) and critiqued theories. Nwogugu (2009b) developed models of the choice between a Strategic Alliance and an M&A transaction. Nwogugu (2008e) analyzed contracting and decisions in commercial Real Estate leasing. Nwogugu (2008f) developed models of the choice between a Sale-Leaseback and Debt in a contracting framework.

5.2 Complex adaptive systems and the rule-of-law: *Preferences+Reasoning* and the inefficient design of financial contracts nullify (or reduce the applicability of) many utility preferences

The term *"Preferences+Reasoning"* in Artificial Intelligence" (AI) and Decision Theory is introduced in this book and is defined as the interactions and joint evolution of the *Preferences* and *Reasoning* of both Human Agents and Automated Agents in specific contexts, and constrained by regulations and mechanisms. In this context, the Preferences and Beliefs of Agents about the efficiency and classification of financial instruments has had significant effects on market dynamics, trading patterns and risk management and associated *Multiplier Effects*. See Zohar and Rosenschein (2008); Fang and Yuan (2018); Hong, Wernz and Stillinger (2016); Madureira, Pereira et al. (2014); Meneguzzi, Modgil et al. (2012); Stein, Gerding et al. (2011); Wu, Zhao and Tang (2014); Wei, Wang et al. (2018), Terán, Aguilar and Cerrada (2017), Janssen, Manning and Udiani (2014); Roos and Nau (2010); Zgonnikov and Lubashevsky (2014); Campion, Candeal et al. (2011); Lin and Druzdzel (1999); Wal (2017); Tsai, Lin and Wang (2009); and Niederhoff and Kouvelis (2019), all of which didn't address *Preferences+Reasoning*. On *Qualitative Reasoning* in AI, see: Forbus (2019); Halpern (2003) and Bredeweg and Struss (Winter 2003). The fact that in the US (and many countries), most trading of Financial Instruments is now algorithmic[8] means that much of the pre-2019 research on Market Microstructure, financial risk and Preferences in capital markets may be invalid or incomplete.

However, *Preferences+Reasoning* and the Inefficient Design of Financial Contracts nullify (or reduce the applicability/relevance of) most Utility Preferences in the Computer Science, Economics and Applied Math literatires – such as those discussed in Farahmand (2017); Boutilier, Caragiannis et al. (2012) and Abramowitz and Anshelevich (2018). This also partly because of the assumptions underlying such Preferences – such as Rationality, Complete Information, etc.

The International Political Economy, Constitutional Political Economy and *Regulatory Classification* issues that pertain to the classification of Debt and Equity, and regulatory regimes for Financial Instruments are critical and affect Accounting Disclosure, perceived risk, Financial Stability, allocation of capital/resources, international trade, market microstructure, Financial Contracting, worker motivation, executive compensation etc.

Complexity pertaining to these issues is or can be manifested in the following ways:

i) Nonlinearity in relation to rule-of-law development.
ii) Nonlinearity in the growth of markets.
iii) Self-organization of institutions and organizations – such as private and public enforcement groups; rule-making; etc.

iv)   Self-organization of traders, large customers and regulators.
v)   Change and theories of change.
vi)   Nonlinearity in relation to deadweight loses in the demand for, and enforcement of laws.
vii)   Nonlinearity in relation to compliance with statutes and enforcement of laws.
viii)   Complex Networks – traders; institutional investors; regulators; etc.
ix)   Network Effects.

The legal and economic environment and markets in which ARS, SSETFs, Structured Products, TARP/CPP Instruments and Mutual Funds function (defined by audit firms and audit clients, expectations, legislatures, political lobbying, regulations, regulators, financial institutions, capital markets, internet systems; etc.) is a complex adaptive system because it has some or all of the following attributes:

i)   The relations between the system and its environment are non-trivial and or nonlinear.
ii)   The system can be influenced by, or can adapt itself to its environment.
iii)   The system has feedback or memory, and can adapt itself according to its history or feedback.
iv)   The system is highly sensitive to initial conditions.
v)   The number of parts (and types of parts) in the system and the number of relations between the parts is non-trivial.

On *Complex Adaptive Systems* and Chaos, see the comments in: Andrews, Pritchett and Woolcock (2017); Byrne and Callaghan (2014); Bamberger, Vaessen and Raimondo (2016), Room (2011), Root (2013); Kuhlman and Mortveit (2014); LoPucki (1997); Melnik et al. (2013), Miklashevich (2003), Perc, Donnay and Helbing (2013), Post and Eisen (2000); Ruhl and Ruhl (1997); Williams and Arrigo (2002); Young (1997) and Arthur (1999).

5.2.1 The international constitutional political economy dilemma: the criteria for the classification of debt and equity

USA case-law and statutes/regulations are used in this chapter because the US has the most developed and most-litigated securities laws and commercial laws (which have been copied by many countries) and the US has the largest capital markets in the world; and the US has been at the forefront of the debate about debt-equity classification criteria and Optimal Financial Contracting.

The FASB (USA), IASB and the AICPA (American Institute of Certified Public Accountants) have issued various rules/standards for the classification of debt and equity in financial statements.[9] This chapter is based on US cases and statutes because the US has been on the forefront of the debate about debt-equity classification criteria. US case-law on the classification/characteristics of debt and equity is somewhat unsettled – different courts have enumerated different criteria for classification as debt or equity.[10]

In the US, there are at least five types of adjudicatory fora that have developed somewhat different criteria and standards for classifying instruments as debt or equity or hybrid. Although the black-letter rules promulgated by each of these fora may have some similarities, each forum has different standards of proof, different rules of evidence, and different rules of procedure and very different enforcement powers. These fora are as follows:

i)   US State appellate courts (state common law).[11]
ii) US Federal appellate courts (federal common law – mostly US Federal Circuit courts).[12]
iii) US Bankruptcy Courts ("common law" based on the US Bankruptcy Code).[13]
iv) State and federal administrative agencies ("common law" based on states and administrative laws). Federal agencies such as the US Internal Revenue Service, and the US Treasury Department, the US Tax Courts (based on the US Internal Revenue Code and Treasury regulations),[14] the US Securities & Exchange Commission, and the US Commodities & Futures Trading Commission (e.g. commodity-linked notes/debt) promulgate rules for the classification of instruments as debt/equity/hybrids/securities, and also adjudicate associated disputes. The enforcement and adjudication activities of these government agencies raises the constitutional law questions of the *Separation-of-Powers Doctrine, Procedural Due Process Doctrine*, the *Substantive Due Process Doctrine* and the *Equal Protection Doctrine*.
vi) The US Supreme Court[15] – the US Supreme Court has not ruled on many cases about this subject matter.

Also, FASB, GASB and IASB promulgate rules for the classification of instruments as debt/equity/hybrids/securities, raises the constitutional law questions of the Separation-of-Powers Doctrine, the Delegation Clause, the Substantive Due Process Doctrine and the Equal Protection Doctrine. Financial Accounting Standards Board (FASB) and Government Accounting Standards Board (GASB) in the USA are accounting trade associations that promulgate various "GAAP" that are used in financial reporting.[16] Due to activities/businesses of US entities, FAB and GASB have worldwide impact. The US SEC's rules are sometimes derived partly from FASB's accounting rules.

In addition to the foregoing, heavy political lobbying of IASB, courts (through independent briefs filed) and national governments significantly influence the enactment and enforcement of accounting regulations and associated statutes in many countries.

US courts have developed standards and criteria that are relevant to the characterization of an obligation as debt or equity for US federal income tax purposes.

204 *Complex adaptive systems*, sustainable growth and securities law

These standards are generally consistent with Section-385 of the US Internal Revenue Code.[17] See: Chan, Viswanat and Wong (2001). The factors are as follows:

- The label placed on the instrument by the parties.
- The presence of a maturity date.
- The source of payments.
- Whether the creditor has the right to enforce the payment of principal and interest.
- Whether the instrument gives the creditor the right to participate in the management of the debtor.
- Whether the rights of the creditor are subordinate to those of general creditors.
- The intent of the parties.
- Whether the debtor is thinly capitalized.
- Whether there is an identity of interests between the creditor and shareholders of the debtor.
- Whether there is an unconditional promise on the part of the debtor to pay a certain sum.
- The ability of the debtor to obtain loans from outside lenders.
- The reasonableness of interest rate and note terms.
- The absence of a sinking fund.
- The lack of security.

To determine whether a transfer is bona fide debt or equity, US courts now consider the thirteen factors established in *Lane*[84–2 USTC ¶9817][18]:

1) The names given to the certificates evidencing the indebtedness.
2) The presence or absence of a fixed maturity date.
3) The source of payments.
4) The right to enforce payment of principal and interest.
5) Participation in management flowing as a result.
6) The status of the contribution in relation to regular corporate creditors.
7) The intent of the parties.
8) "Thin" or adequate capitalization.
9) Identity of interest between creditor and stockholder.
10) Source of interest payments.
11) The corporation's ability to obtain loans from outside lending institutions.
12) The extent to which the advance was used to acquire capital assets.
13) The failure of the debtor to repay on the due date or to seek a postponement.
14) In addition, to be classified as debt, the expectation of repayment cannot depend solely on solely on the success of the company which borrowed the funds.

In Notice 94–47 (I.R.S. Notice 94–47, 1994–1 C.B. 357) the IRS set out familiar factors to distinguish debt from equity and added a few new ones to the mix including treatment by rating agencies and treatment for accounting purposes. The IRS Notice 94–47 factors are as follows:

i)   Whether there is an unconditional promise on the part of the issuer to pay a sum certain on demand or at a fixed maturity date that is in the reasonably foreseeable future.

ii)   Whether holders of the instruments possess the right to enforce the payment of principal and interest.

iii)   Whether the rights of the holders of the instruments are subordinate to the rights of general creditors.

iv)   Whether the instruments give the holders the right to participate in the management of the issuer.

v)   Whether the issuer is thinly capitalized.

vi)   Whether there is identity between the holders of the instruments and stockholders of the issuer.

vii)   The label placed on the instruments by the parties.

viii)   Whether the instruments are intended to be treated as debt or equity for non-tax purposes.

The *Disclosure Versus Recognition Debate* has been ongoing for quite a while and was analyzed in the following articles: Choudhary (2011); Yu (2013); Muller, Riedl and Sellhorn (2013); Michels (2013); Ang and Pinnuck (2010); Ahmed, Kilic and Lobo (2006); Ahmed, Goodwin and Sawyer (2006); Beattie, Goodacre and Thomson (2000) and Libby, Nelson and Hunton (2006).

5.2.2 Regulation under securities laws versus regulation under other statutes: international constitutional political economy considerations, and criteria for regulatory regimes

Given the uses and historical and outstanding volumes of ARS, SSETFs, Structured Products, Mutual Funds and TARP/CPP Instruments, the issue of whether or not these financial Instruments are securities; and the debate about the appropriate Regulatory Regime for them has critical and global implications in several dimensions including but not limited to the following:

i)   Investigation costs and enforcement costs; post-investigation litigation costs (private and public); and legal skills required.

ii)   Transaction costs and compliance costs.

iii)   *Deadweight Losses* in prices/pricing of financial instruments under a given Regulatory Regime.

iv)   *Deadweight Losses* in the demand/supply of enforcement and regulation under a given Regulatory Regime.

v)   The *Separation-of-Powers* and *Procedural/Substantive Due Process* (Constitutional Law) problems inherent in the concurrent legislative, adjudicatory and enforcement activities of regulatory agencies such as the US SEC – which were not fully or properly addressed in *Lucia vs. SEC*, 138 S. Ct. 2044 (US Supreme Court case) and other court cases.

vi)   Risk perceptions of both regulators and market participants.

vii)   The deterrence effects of the controlling regulatory scheme and associated penalties.

viii)   Political costs – the political will and *political capital* to restructure the government and to enact new legislation in order to properly regulate financial instruments and vehicles.

ix)   Allocation of capital by federal and or state governments, and Multinational Corporations.

x)   Sustainable economic growth – the ability to raise, deploy and manage capital/resources effectively; etc.; and Sustainability (economic, financial, social and environmental sustainability).

xi)   Credit ratings and leverage ratios of companies and banks; and the viability, stability and expansion of *Credit Chains*.

xii)   Financial Stability and Crash-risk in markets; and the cost-of-capital, access to capital and perceived bankruptcy risk of companies and government agencies.

xiii)   Some of the regulations that govern ARS, SSETFs and Mutual Funds are in some ways *Public Goods* – McCarter, Rockmann and Northcraft (2010) analyzed public goods whose eventual value is uncertain when contribution decisions are made; and the effects of outcome-variance on why individuals contribute and amounts they contribute to a public good (their research is applicable to analysis of Strategic Alliances and Statutes as public goods).

xiv)   The liability of secondary actors (e.g. lawyers, accountants, appraisers, service providers, etc.) for accounting fraud and securities fraud. See: *Stoneridge Investment Partners vs. Scientific-Atlanta*, 552 U.S. 148 (US Supreme Court case).

xv)   Antitrust issues – clearly the US Supreme Court's rulings *in Credit Suisse Securities (USA) LLC vs. Billing*, 551 U.S. 264 (that the securities markets are exempt from the scope of antitrust laws), were erroneous given past and ongoing anti-competitive misconduct in financial markets. Nwogugu (2008b) explained some of the antitrust misconduct that is intertwined with securities operations and securities law issues.

xvi)   Venue, choice-of-law and Jurisdictional issues – see: *Merrill Lynch, Pierce, Fenner & Smith Inc. vs. Manning*, 578 U.S. ___ (2016); and *Morrison vs. National Australia Bank Ltd.*, 561 U.S. 247 (2010) (US Supreme Court cases).

xvii)   Statute-of-Limitations issues – see: *Gabelli vs. SEC*, 568 U.S. 442 (2013) (US Supreme Court case).

xviii) Theories of fraud and the requirements for "*materiality*" in financial fraud cases – see: *TSC Industries, Inc. vs. Northway, Inc.*, 426 U.S. 438; and *Janus Capital Group., Inc. vs. First Derivative Traders*, 564 U.S. 135 (2011) (US Supreme Court cases).

xix) Disclosures presented to prospective investors by issuers – see: *Hagan vs. Khoja (Orexigen Therapeutics, Inc.)*, No. 18–1010; and *Omnicare Inc.*, 135 S.Ct. 1318 (2015) (US Supreme Court cases).

xx) The requirements for Class-Action lawsuits.

xxi) Trading rules in exchanges.

xxii) Margin costs; and the costs of repos and derivatives.

xxiii) *Arbitrage Efficiency* (whether the Financial Instrument can be used for, or amplifies harmful arbitrage under a given Regulatory Regime).

xxiv) "*Earnings Management Capacity*" (whether the Financial Instrument can be used for, or amplifies earnings management, Asset-Quality Management and or Incentive-Effects Management under a given Regulatory Regime).

xxv) "*Disclosure Efficiency*" (whether accounting disclosure of the Financial Instrument captures its true risks/behavior; and or causes harmful human behaviors/biases under a given Regulatory Regime).

xxvi) International capital flows and international trade.

xxvii) *Inequality Efficiency* (the extent to which the Financial Instrument causes or propagates any type of *Inequality* under a specific Regulatory Regime).

xxix) *Negative Externalities Efficiency* – the extent to which the Financial Instrument causes or propagates *Negative Externalities* (such as pollution, climate change, etc.) under a specific Regulatory Regime.

xxx) *Innovation Efficiency* (the extent to which the Financial Instrument will cause or influence incremental harmful financial or technological innovation under a specific Regulatory Regime – previous harmful innovations include high frequency trading, and some types of derivatives).

xxxi) *Regulatory Efficiency* (the extent to which the Financial Instrument reduces or increases investigation, compliance, transaction and enforcement costs under a specific Regulatory Regime).

xxxii) Standardization of contracts.

In most countries/jurisdictions, classification of Mutual Funds, Structured Products, SSETFs and or ARS as securities triggers compliance issues pertaining to securities registration requirements, broker-dealer registration requirements, securities fraud liability, and disclosure obligations; and hence has important operational, compliance, and profitability implications. Unfortunately, although Mutual Funds, SSETFs, and ARS are not securities, they are governed and regulated by securities laws in many countries. As written, the most reasonable interpretation is that Mutual Funds, SSETFs and ARS are hybrid intangibles and or commodities, but not corporate securities.[19]

The alternative regulatory regimes for SSETFs, Structured Products, CDS, Mutual Funds and ARS are as follows:

i)   Securities laws.
ii)   Commodities laws.
iii) Special hybrid "federal" statutes (that combine elements of securities laws and commodities laws).
iv)   Common law.
v)   "Federal" Financial Instruments laws.
vi)   Specialized regulations for each of ETFs, Mutual Funds, CDS, ARS and Structured Products.

In *SEC vs. Joiner*, the US Supreme Court noted that ". . . The test rather is what character the instrument is given in commerce by the terms of the offer, the plan of distribution, and the economic inducements held out to the prospect. In the enforcement of an act such as this it is not inappropriate that promoters' offerings be judged as being what they were represented to be . . ."

Some relevant criteria are as follows:

i)   The extent to which the regulatory scheme reduces *Deadweight Losses* both in trading of the financial instrument and in the demand for and supply of prosecution resources.
ii)   Effects on Transaction costs and hedging costs.
iii)   Psychological costs and effects.
iv)   "Substitutability" of financial instruments.
v)   Reduction of harmful arbitrage and volatility.
vi)   Standardization.
vii)   Propensity for earnings management.
viii) Industrial organization effects.
ix)   effects on costs of investigation and prosecution.
x)   Deterrence effects and perpetrators' assessed *probability-of-detection* and *probability-of-prosecution*.
xi)   Compliance with "*suitability*" requirements.
xii)   *Arbitrage Efficiency* (see above).
xiii) "*Earnings Management Capacity*" (see above).
xiv)   "*Disclosure Efficiency*" (see above).
xv)   International capital flows and international trade.
xvi)   Transaction costs and compliance costs.
xvii) *Deadweight Losses* in prices/pricing of financial instruments under a given Regulatory Regime.
xviii) *Deadweight Losses* in the demand/supply of enforcement and regulation under a given Regulatory Regime.
xix)   *Inequality Efficiency* (see above).
xx)   *Negative Externalities Efficiency* (see above).
xxi)   *Innovation Efficiency* (see above).

xxii) *Regulatory Efficiency* (see above).
xxiii) The other variables listed herein and above.

5.2.3 The case for special regulations; and regulation of ARS, CDS and investment vehicles as commodities and contract intangibles

There is a strong case for regulating Mutual Funds, ARS, Structured Products Vehicles and ETFs as non-securities and perhaps as commodities and Contract-Intangibles, and for creating special statutes for each of them. Some of the issues are as follows.

As interpreted by the US Supreme Court and US Federal Appellate Courts, the requirements for classification of a Financial Instrument as "securities" clearly are not met by Mutual funds, Structured Products Vehicles, ABS/MBS Trusts, ARS and some ETFs. Furthermore, the past and current statutory definitions[20] of "securities" and "futures" are grossly inadequate and perhaps misleading. With the advent and growing popularity of the Internet, disintermediation and many new financial products (i.e. ETFs, Structured Products, new derivatives; CDS; etc.), US securities laws have become increasingly and un-constitutionally vague and obsolete as applied – and the *Void-For-Vagueness doctrine* of constitutional law applies in the case of criminal securities law claims. See the comments in Hu and Morley (2018) about lack of proper statutory definition of "futures" and "securities". Kirk (2015) argued that the Dodd Frank Act changed the definition of "securities".

In *Board of Trade of the City of Chicago vs. Securities and Exchange Commission* (CA7; No. 98-2923; August 10, 1999; https://caselaw.findlaw.com/us-7th-circuit/1261082.html), the US Court of Appeals vacated a US SEC order that held that futures exchanges should not trade futures contracts that were based on the Dow Jones Utilities Average and the Dow Jones Transportation Average both of which are major stock Indices (i.e. the US SEC held that such contracts were not futures contracts). Many Mutual Funds and ETFs are functional equivalents of Indices and as mentioned herein, they have "Implicit Futures Contracts".

In *Board of Trade of City of Chicago*, 677 F.2d 1137 (CA7, 1982), the US Court of Appeals acknowledged that GNMAs are both "commodities" and "securities" (and noted that ". . . None of the parties suggests that GNMA's are not "legitimate" commodities. . . "); and that GNMA options/futures are not securities. GNMAs are structurally similar to ETFs, Mutual Funds and many Structured Products Vehicles. ARS are similar to a bundle of GNMA futures contracts.

A significant portion of US securities laws (and by extension, those of the many countries that copied US securities laws) were enacted during 1920–1960 which was a very different era (in terms of technology, transactions, regulation, capital flows and compliance). Some of the new and relevant events/changes are as follows:

1) The creation and rapid growth of CDS, new types of Swaps/derivatives, and new investment vehicles (such as hedge funds, ETFs and Structured Products Vehicles); and significant increases in the popularity of ETFs and Structured Products.

2) The Internet and the rapid growth of online news media and online social networks.

3) Changes in international capital flows and international trade; increased volumes of cross-border investment; and the rise of BRICS countries as technological, military and trade/economic powers.

4) Changes in Corporate Governance standards and regulations in many countries; and global convergence of accounting regulations, *Corporate Governance standards* and securities laws (many countries copied US laws and corporate governance standards) and *"Regulatory Contagion"* (wherein many countries copied US law/statutes during 1980–2019)

5) The rise of the US dollar (and since 2017, the decline of the US dollar) as the dominant currency in international trade and finance.

6) The significant growth of foreign operations of Multinational Corporations (MNCs) around the world which propagates *Corporate Governance Contagion, Regulatory Contagion* and often negative *Spillover Effects*.

7) Globalization, outsourcing, the movement of jobs to Mexico and Asia, and associated trade wars; each of which can cause/propagate *Corporate Governance Contagion, Regulatory Contagion* and often negative *Cross-border Spillover Effects*.

8) The occurrence of many economic/financial crisis and financial/earnings-management scandals around the world – see the Appendices in Chapter 3 in this book.

9) Structural Changes in many countries – the structures of many national economies have changed.

10) Changes in demography and the nature of investment needs of households.

11) High Frequency Trading.

12) Changes in the trading rules of financial and commodity exchanges.

13) Increased volumes of GDRs/ADRs and cross-listed shares around the world.

14) Changes in margin requirements, Repo-markets, trading rules and Market Microstructure around the world.

15) Technological advancements and changes in patterns of innovation.

16) The significant increases in volumes of Stock-Repurchases around the world; and changes in the capital structures and dividend policies of non-financial operating companies; and changes in their financing terms (terms for loans, trade credit, commercial paper, etc.).

17) As mentioned above, there are *Separation-of-Powers* and *Procedural/Substantive Due Process* (Constitutional Law) problems inherent in the concurrent legislative, adjudicatory and enforcement activities of regulatory agencies such as the US SEC and the US CFTC – which were not fully or properly addressed in *Lucia vs. SEC*, 138 S. Ct. 2044 (US Supreme Court case) and other court cases.

18) There has been rapid growth of joint ventures, franchising, distribution agreements, R&D partnerships and strategic alliances around the world, which expands the *"scope-of-the-firm"* and significantly changes the risk,

perceptions, solvency and profitability of operating companies (Mutual Funds, Structured Products Vehicles, Hedge Funds, ABS/MBS Trusts and ETFs are corporate entities that typically don't do such transactions and thus should be subject to different regulatory regimes). Advances in the *Theory-of-the-Firm* have further confirmed the operating and risk differences between operating companies on one hand and investment vehicles (e.g. Mutual Funds, Structured Products Vehicles, Hedge Funds, ABS/MBS Trusts and ETFs).

19) Increasingly, *Vertical Commonality* and *Horizontal Commonality* (in securities law) are applicable to only operating companies (and not to "investment vehicles") – due to competition and fee structures in the global securities industry; the structure and purposes of investment vehicles; regulation; etc. Note that in this context and for an investment manager, the criteria for evaluating *Vertical Commonality* should be the investment manager's *"Net Fees"* (and not *"Gross Fees"*). *Net Fees* is the sum of the *Base-Fee* and *Performance-Fee* minus applicable marketing costs and fund administration costs (i.e. *Gross Fees* minus direct fund expenses). In the case of pooled investments, many US judges/courts[21] erroneously used only the investment manager's Gross Fees as the criteria to determine whether *Vertical Commonality* exists and they didn't sufficiently differentiate between *"Base Fees"* (which are paid regardless of the fund's performance) and *"Performance Fees"* (which are paid only if the manager achieves specified investment returns or other benchmark).

20) The automation of finance and financial exchanges.

21) *"Regulatory Revolutions"* in some countries – for example, the enactment of the Dodd Frank Act and SOX in the US, and similar statutes in other countries; and the Indian government's de-monetization program of 2017–2018, and its implementation of the Goods and Services Tax (GST).

22) Beginning from the 1950s and until the present time, there have been academic articles about, and documented cases and prosecutions of fraud in ARS auctions process. ARS auctions represent less than 25 percent of capital raising processes for companies around the world.

23) During 1990–2018, more than 110 countries changed their national constitutions and many of them are similar to, or based on the US constitution.[22] See: Law and Versteeg (2012). Thus, similar Constitutional Political Economy problems can also occur in those countries. The regulation of Financial Instruments functions within the context of Constitutional Laws, and some countries have specialized Constitutional Courts.

24) The negative *Inequality* and Industrial Organization effects of Mutual Funds, ARS, ETFs and Structured Products Vehicles (some of which are discussed in Nwogugu [2019a;b]) can be significant and have become more visible.

25) *Gambling* occurs because: 1) the Index Products (ETFs, Index mutual funds, ETNs and Index Options/futures) sometimes create their own trading patterns, affect prices of underlying stocks/bonds/futures, and their price

dynamics contain Noise and are often un-related to the fundamental operations of the underlying companies; 2) CDS contracts are essentially bets on the underlying entities (companies or government entities) which don't receive any cash from the CDS contracts unless they are parties to such CDS contract; and 3) in the case of "Synthetic" ETFs, Structured Products Vehicles and Mutual Funds (constructed with only cash and swaps/derivatives), the underlying companies/entities don't receive any investment from such ETFs, Structured Products Vehicles and Mutual Funds which are essentially "baskets-of-bets"; and even when shares of ordinary (non-synthetic) investment vehicles are re-sold at increasing prices, the underlying firms/entities don't receive any of the incremental cash from such investment vehicles.

26) ETFs, Index Mutual Funds, Index Products and Indices are quickly replacing the "traditional intermediation" functions of traditional banks, securities-brokerages, real estate brokerages and finance companies (such "traditional intermediation" has been empirically shown to directly affect economic growth in several countries).

27) Clearly, "Self-regulation" by the securities industry is inefficient and has failed as evidenced by the number of arbitration claims and lawsuits against, and by the types of offences/misconduct perpetrated by securities professionals around the world.

The US FSOC's Non-Bank SIFI Criteria doesn't sufficiently address Mutual Funds, ABS/MBS Trusts, ETFs, ARS and Structured Products Vehicles, some of which are quite large and significant in terms of their assets (some ETFs' assets exceed US$80 billion), visibility, their use as Reference-Points and valuation benchmarks, and their market-impact. Nwogugu (2014b) critiqued the US FSOC's Non-Bank SIFI Criteria, and introduced more efficient criteria. As explained in Nwogugu (2014a), some of those Investment Vehicles can substantially increase Financial Instability and Systemic Risk. Similarly, sovereign ARS are quite significant in terms of market-size, visibility, their use as Reference-Points and valuation benchmarks, and their market-impact. Thus, companies and investment entities that own large amounts of ARS units, Mutual Fund units, ABS/MBS Trust units, ETF units and or Structured Products Vehicles units, or that issue large amounts of ARS, or Structured Products or ABS/MBS should also be under surveillance and US FSOC's jurisdiction.

As explained in Nwogugu (2019d), CDS are inefficient, unethical and have negative effects on markets and financial institutions. In addition, regulating CDS as securities will only compound these problems and increase systemic risk.

Under the current Regulatory Regimes in most countries, Mutual Funds, ABS/MBS Trusts, ARS, ETFs and Structured Products Vehicles can amplify the distortions, Financial Instability and Systemic Risk caused by "*Netting*". Nwogugu (2014b) critiqued the "*Netting*" of swaps/derivatives. Many ("synthetic") Mutual Funds, ETFs and Structured Products are constructed primarily with swaps/

derivatives and cash only; and derivatives are often used to hedge or arbitrage (e.g. spreads) those Investment Vehicles and ARS, and all such derivatives are usually *Netted.*

Most countries including the United States don't have a dedicated or efficient system of regulation for ETFs, Structured Products, ABS/MBS Trusts or ARS. The US SEC[23] proposed some new ETF regulations in 2018. Hu and Morley (2018), Grimm (2008) and McLaughlin (2008) argued for a new regulatory framework for ETFs, and Defusco, Ivanov and Karels (2011), Colon (2017), Petajisto (2017) and Broman (2016) analyzed market inefficiencies of ETFs but they didn't address the question of the appropriate *Regulatory Regime* for ETFs and the criteria for selecting such regime/framework. Around the world, ETFs and Mutual Funds now manage more than US$4 trillion and US$25 Trillion respectively; and more than US$5 Trillion and US$20 Trillion of Structured Products and ARS are outstanding respectively, and their risks impact and Industrial Organization effects can be significant. Thus ARS, Mutual Funds, asset securitizations and Structured Products also require specialized regulations. Hu and Morley (2018) stated in part: *"Despite their economic significance and distinctive risks, ETFs remain a regulatory backwater. The United States has neither a dedicated system of ETF regulation nor even a workable, comprehensive conception of what an ETF is. . . . Other regulatory constraints center on a process of discretionary review that generally allows the Securities and Exchange Commission ("SEC") to assess the merits of each proposed ETF on an ad hoc, individualized basis. This process of review is opaque and unfocused. It is also inconsistent over time, with the effect that older funds often operate under lighter regulation than newer ones. And because it has its roots in statutes originally designed for other kinds of vehicles, the regulation of ETFs fails to address the ETF's distinctive characteristics. Rooted in a disclosure system largely designed for mutual funds, the SEC's disclosure mandates for ETFs fail to comprehend the significance and complexities of the arbitrage mechanism and often require no public disclosure of major breakdowns in the mechanism's workings. . . . Seven of the ten most actively traded securities in the United States in 2016 were ETFs, and the trading volume of shares in the SPDR S&P 500 ETF ("SPY") exceeded the trading volume of shares in Apple. . . . As of September 30, 2017, each of the top fifteen holdings of Bridgewater Associates, the world's largest hedge fund, was an ETF. In January 2018, worldwide ETF assets reached $5 trillion."* Similarly, Nwogugu (2007c), Nwogugu (2014a) and Nwogugu (2008c;d) noted that the US and the many countries that copied US-style REIT statutes don't have clear or efficient regulatory frameworks and adequate corporate governance standards for REITs.

Mutual Funds, ARS and Structured Products Vehicles all have *"Implicit Arbitrage Mechanisms"* that are similar to that of ETFs which was mentioned by Hu and Morley (2018) – but the major differences are that there are no affiliated *"Authorized Participants"* in the case of Mutual Funds, ARS, ABS/MBS Trusts and Structured Products Vehicles; and in the case of ARS, some arbitrage usually occurs in the "When-Issued Market" before the ARS is auctioned. Those

"*Implicit Arbitrage Mechanisms*" are often exploited by independent traders/ investors. REITs also have an implicit Arbitrage Mechanism that arise from any of the following:

i) REIT shares usually trade at discounts of 5–30 percent discount to their NAV (Net Asset Values) – and that can be arbitraged by buying the REIT shares, and financing such purchase with a low-interest loan (interest rate is much lower than the REIT's dividend yield); or by arranging a swap to receive the excess of the REIT's dividend yield over the yield from an index of a port- folio of real estate; or by shorting REIT shares that have low NAV-discounts where such discounts may increase.

ii) REITs are usually statutorily required to pay-out 75–95 percent of their monthly/quarterly operating income (and some REITs' payout-rates are as much as 110–150 percent, and some borrow to finance such payouts). In this instance, the classic "Quarterly Dividend Arbitrage" methods can be used.

Hu (2018) argued for better regulation and disclosure standards for CDS (credit default swaps); Hu (2014) argued for better disclosure regulations and securities laws; and Nwogugu (2008a;b) argued for better and new regulations and disclo- sure standards for asset securitizations (ABS/MBS trusts); and Nwogugu (2007c), Nwogugu (2014a) and Nwogugu (2008c;d) argued for better regulation and dis- closure standards for REITs. The principles/theories and entity-governance issues they discussed also apply to ARS, Structured Products, Mutual Funds and ETFs. Also see the comments in Cheng, Massa and Zhang (2018) which have implica- tions for regulation.

Mutual Funds, ARS, Structured Products Vehicles and ETFs have the "*Mini- mum Level of Standardization*" that is sufficient to classify them as commodi- ties or *quasi-commodities* in terms of the demand for them, their use, and their "*Substitutability*" (i.e. the ability to substitute any Mutual Fund, ARS, Structured Products Vehicle or ETF unit with a similar unit while maintaining the same risk levels, investment-returns and investment objectives). These Financial Instru- ments are often traded in bulk, and ETFs and some Structured Products Vehicle units are traded on exchanges.

Mutual Funds, ARS, Structured Products Vehicles and ETFs have become commodities or quasi-commodities in terms of their risk profiles and operations which are very different from those of stocks, bonds and individual operating companies in industries, and from those of banks and insurance companies – and some issues are as follows:

1) The financing patterns and capital structures of Investment Vehicles (ETFs, Mutual Funds, Structured Products Vehicles and ABS/MBS Trusts) differ dramatically from those of operating companies. Operating companies typi- cally have perpetual/un-limited lives and raise debt and equity continuously throughout their existence and in various structures and from various sources

(e.g. common stock; bank loans; trade credit; taxes payable; commercial paper, bonds; notes; receivables financing; etc.). On the other hand, Investment Vehicles have relatively shorter lives (less than an average of twelve years, and some have stated lives) and typically raise money no more than twice (average) during their existence, and the money raised is usually in a maximum of two formats (ETF shares, Mutual Fund units or Structured Product units on one hand or margin loans) and usually from specific types of investors.

2) The ARS auction process and the risk profile and Industrial Organization effects of ARS differs significantly from other "normal" capital raising processes and Financial Instruments that are used by companies and government agencies, such that new and specialized regulations are required for ARS.

3) The corporate governance, decision-making and management of operating companies and Investment Vehicles (ETFs, Mutual Funds, Structured Products Vehicles and ABS/MBS Trusts) differ dramatically. Operating companies typically have a Board of Directors and an executive management team, and are required formally or morally to comply with corporate governance codes; and their decision-making is multi-tiered, dynamic and evolves over time. Investment Vehicles don't face similar pressure about corporate governance and most of the decisions are made by the portfolio managers or in the case of the Structured Products Vehicles and ABS/MBS Trusts, by the sponsors whose decisions are relatively static (conform to the stated investment objectives of the Investment vehicle).

4) The November 30, 2011 letter from US Senators Diane Feinstein and Carl Levin[24] to the US Commodities Futures Trading Commission (CFTC) about the need for the CFTC to regulate Mutual Funds that focus on investments in commodities and swaps/derivatives, explains some of the issues.

5) The proliferation of Financial Indices (as of 2019, there were more than three million indices compared to less than sixty thousand exchange-traded companies worldwide) and the use of Index Products (index futures, index options and Index swaps) to create Mutual Funds, ETFs and Structured Products will continue to increase the differences in risk profiles of operating companies in industry on one hand, and Mutual Funds, ETFs and Structured Products Vehicles on the other.

6) Similarly, the widespread and increasing use of exchange-traded Treasury bill/bond futures/options, commodity futures/options and currency futures/options to hedge ARS will continue to increase the differences in risk profiles and trading patterns of ARS on one hand, and non-ARS fixed income securities (bonds/notes and preferred stock) of operating companies in non-financial industries on the other.

A significant percentage of the outstanding volumes of Mutual Funds, Structured Products Vehicles and ETFs are "*synthetic*" (constructed with only cash, futures, options and swaps contracts) or are hedged with swaps/derivatives (i.e. interest rate, index, currency and commodities futures contracts; and futures-options contracts) or are simultaneously traded with swaps/derivatives in "spread" transactions. Many Mutual funds and ETFs that invest in debt, currencies and or equity use Index futures contracts, currency futures and or commodity futures contracts to hedge or to provide additional exposure or leverage. Thus, Mutual Funds, Structured Products Vehicles and ETFs have become more like, and are correlated to commodities futures or quasi-commodities and are less like securities in terms of their risk profile. During the last fifteen years, there was rapid growth of commodity-related Mutual Funds (that invest in futures contracts and commodity futures).

A significant percentage of the outstanding volumes of ARS are hedged with exchange-traded futures contracts (interest rate, currency, commodity and index futures), options and futures-options contracts; and or are traded in combination with exchange-traded commodity options and futures (e.g. spreads). The structure of ARS and associated periodic auctions can distort risk – that is, the ARS auction process can become detached from the underlying risk of the issuer due to conditions in the Repo-Market or the Pre-Sale Market, or just temporary demand-supply imbalances. There is an *implicit futures sub-market* in the ARS market, wherein: i) new ARS are traded in the *"When-Issued Market"* before they are officially auctioned; ii) customers place orders for ARS through their brokers, and their brokers' subsequent bids at associated ARS auctions are a function of such customer-orders; iii) some broker's bids are not affected by customer orders, but rather are influenced by market-manipulation and forward-looking arbitrage considerations; iv) because of severe illiquidity in some ARS markets, the only realistic opportunity to sell an ARS unit is during the next scheduled auction of that ARS tranche and thus, ARS units function as quasi-futures contracts; v) many sovereign ARS are used and traded like futures contracts (e.g. bond spreads) and for exposure and "leverage", and for hedging swaps contracts. There is an *implicit futures sub-market* in the Mutual Funds market, wherein unit holders can sell their units only at the end of each trading day, and only to the Mutual fund itself. There is an *implicit futures sub-market* in the SSETFs market and Structured Products market, wherein SSETFs and Structured Products are partly constructed with, and are hedged with futures contracts.

Given the comments in Hu and Morley (2018), Grimm (2008) and McLaughlin (2008), the US SEC's current regulation (statutes, processes and framework as of 2019) of ETFs, ABS/MBS Trusts and Structured Products Vehicles probably violates the *Procedural Due Process Clause, Substantive Due Process Clause, Right-to-Contract Clause, Interstate-Commerce* Clause (selective enforcement and approvals based on geographic location; and increase of transaction costs based on location of fund-sponsors), *Right-Of-Association Clause* and *Equal Protection Clause* of the US Constitution. Similar Constitutional Political Economy issues can occur in other countries whose constitutional laws are similar to the US Constitution. However, it is likely that due to the "political costs" of change, concerns about public opinion and successful political lobbying, many national governments have been reluctant to change the regulatory regimes for these Financial Instruments.

As explained in Chapter 4 in this book (the critique of *Credit Suisse vs. Billings*), the current securities law regulatory regime in the USA, cannot adequately handle specialized misconduct such as Antitrust and other unfair business practices. Given the comments in Hu and Morley (2018), Grimm (2008) and McLaughlin (2008), the US SEC has knowingly or un-knowingly evolved into an illegal antitrust facilitator that shapes competition through its non-uniform and discriminatory approval and regulatory processes.

Given the foregoing, it's reasonably inferable that the *Legislative Intent* of the 1933 Act and 1934 Act (US securities statutes), was that the term "investment" was to refer to only investments in operating companies/entities and some government agencies, but not investments in "Investment Vehicles" (such as Mutual Funds, Structured Products Vehicles, ABS/MBS Trusts and ETFs) or standardized and specialized products such as ARS.[25] See the comments in Selvers (1974). It's also reasonably inferable that *Legislative Intent* of the Investment Company Act of 1940 (the "1940 Act") and related statutes was to address only "Investment Vehicles" and more specifically, Mutual Funds (but not Structured Products Vehicles and ETFs)[26] – and the 1940 Act does not sufficiently define whether such vehicles are "securities". However, the term "investment" has been wrongly applied to analysis of the legal status of "investment vehicles".

In terms of size, an increasing number of Mutual Funds, Structured Products Vehicles and ETFs are as big as, or bigger than many mid-cap and large-cap operating companies when measured by assets and or market value and or Net Income. The risk profiles of Mutual Funds, Structured Products Vehicles and ETFs and their contributions to financial instability, systemic risk and sustainable growth can be quite different, and the linkages among them are evolving. In today's circumstances and for regulatory, Sustainability analysis and economic-policy purposes, it is critical to distinguish between: 1) investment vehicles (Mutual Funds, Structured Products Vehicles, ABS/MBS Trusts and ETFs); and 2) traditional operating companies; and iii) financial services companies (banks, insurance companies, finance companies, payments companies and transaction processing companies).

In some countries such as Canada, the regulations for Commodity Pools and Mutual Funds are converging or were proposed to converge;[27] and under the *Commodity Exchange Act* of 1974 and the *Commodity Futures Modernization Act of 2000* in the US, "*Commodity Pools*" are functional equivalents of Mutual Funds, ETFs and some Structured Products Vehicles.

The current *Regulatory Fragmentation* (various different statutes regulate Mutual Funds, ETFs, ARS, ABS/MBS Trusts and Structured Products) in many countries is sub-optimal and grossly inefficient, and can increase transaction costs, compliance costs, Regulatory Uncertainty, systemic risk and financial instability.

5.3 Mutual funds

Mutual Funds have been used in many developed and developing countries for more than forty years, and total Mutual Fund assets around the world now exceed

US$40 trillion. The major types of Mutual Funds are open-ended funds, unit investment trusts, closed-end funds and Synthetic Mutual Funds. As of 2018, the countries that had the largest mutual fund industries and their estimated Mutual Fund assets (in US dollars) were as follows: i) United States (greater than $18.9 trillion); ii) Luxembourg (> $3.5 trillion); iii) Ireland (> $2 trillion); iv) Germany (> $1.9 trillion); v) China (> $1.2 trillion); vi) Japan (> $1.3 trillion); vii) France (> $1.5 trillion); viii) United Kingdom (> $1.3 trillion); ix) Australia (> $1.4 trillion); and x) Brazil (> $1.1 trillion). Mutual Funds track (ordinary mutual funds or "OMFs") or mimic (synthetic mutual funds or "SMFs") an underlying portfolio of securities and or financial instruments. The primary purposes of a Mutual Fund unit are: i) to track and help derive a market value for the underlying portfolio assets; ii) to provide a basis for the Mutual Fund's periodic distributions (of cash and assets) and liquidating distribution. Thus in most cases, the Mutual Fund Unit does not represent an interest in the Mutual Fund's assets, but rather, represents only the right to cashflow/distributions from the Mutual fund. A Mutual Fund unit-holder can lose all of his/her investment depending on the value of the underlying portfolio.

There is evidence that Mutual Funds' holdings/portfolios affect or can affect earnings management and Incentive-Effects management by companies – see the comments in Dai, Kong and Wang (2013) and Chi, Yang and Young (2014).

In the United States, Mutual funds are regulated by many statutes at both the federal government and state government levels, but the main laws are: the Securities Act of 1933; the Securities and Exchange Act of 1934; the Revenue Act of 1936; the Investment Company Act of 1940; the Investment Advisers Act of 1940; The National Securities Markets Improvement Act of 1996. On regulation, see Pozen and Hamacher (2015); Lemke, Lins and Smith (2017) and Lemke, Lins and McGuire (2017).

Mutual Funds have had significant effects on Chinese, Indian, Japanese and Brazilian capital markets and economies because: i) China, Japan and Brazil were developing their equity markets which are based on US securities processes and regulations; and the Chinese (CSRC), Japanese, Indian and Brazilian securities regulatory agency) introduced Mutual Funds into their domestic markets (the US SEC's approval of Mutual Funds gave it perceived legitimacy); ii) mutual funds have invested in international securities – including those of China, Japan, India and Brazil; iii) Mutual Funds affect the amount of paid and deferred capital gains taxes and income taxes in the US and those four countries and the compensation of financial services employees; iv) the activities and investments of Mutual Funds could have changed the risk-taking propensity of executives of US companies that were either direct competitors of Chinese, Japanese and Brazilian manufacturers and or Indian IT companies, or US companies that had established manufacturing facilities in China (during 2000–2018, Chinese and Japanese exports of goods/services to the US, and their *Trade-Imbalances* with the US increased substantially).

The misclassification and improper regulation of Mutual Funds as securities presents regulatory and policy problems and whether such misclassification was done intentionally is a critical question that will determine liability.

Unlike swaps and most other derivatives, Mutual Funds are not measurable (and hence not reportable) until the Mutual Fund manager prices the units at the end of the trading day. See: FASB Statement # 123; FASB Statement # 123R, ; FASB Statement # 150; FASB Concepts Statement #6; IASB International Financial Reporting Standard #2 – Share Based Payment (February 204); FASB Exposure Draft: Proposed Statement Of Financial Accounting Standards – *"Accounting For Financial Instruments With Characteristics Of Liabilities, Equity Or Both"* (Norwalk, CT, October 2000); FASB Discussion Memorandum: *"Distinguishing Between Liability And Equity Instruments And Accounting For Instruments With Characteristics Of Both"* (Norwalk, CT, August 1990). The following factors are relevant considerations in analyzing Mutual Funds:

- In many instances, swaps/derivatives holders may not exercise their in-the-money options or futures.
- Options and futures holders and investors are not always rational when making decisions about exercising in-the-money positions.
- In many instances, the failure to exercise an option cannot be explained.
- The underlying swaps/derivatives in SMFs' contracts sometimes contain terms that are not reflected in Mutual Funds documents.

5.3.1 Some earnings management, asset-quality management and incentive-effects management problems inherent in the use of mutual funds

Earnings management, Incentive-Effects Management and asset-quality management problems at Mutual Funds (trading and harmful arbitrage; market timing; illegal sales practices and excessive fees; late trading; fictitious performance reporting; etc.) have been documented by several researchers such as: Carroll (2004); Baig, DeLisle and Zaynutdinova (2018); Luo (2014); Zitzewitz (2006); Goetzmann, Ivkovic and Rouwenhorst (2001); Choi and Kahan (2007); Frankel and Cunningham (2007); Houge and Wellman (2005); Frankel and Cunningham (2007); and Peterson (2010). Specific earning management, asset-quality management and *Incentive-Effects Management* problems at Mutual Funds include but are not limited to the following:

i) Falsification of the books and records of the Mutual Fund by the fund administrator or the fund manager – e.g. covering losses or creating fictitious performance.
ii) Misappropriation of the Mutual Fund's asset – by the fund manager or fund administrator.
iii) Investors can record "stale prices" of Mutual Funds.
iv) The Fund manager may intentionally use false or inflated asset prices to calculate the Mutual Fund's daily NAVs.

   v) The fund manager may engage in inappropriate investments solely to boost the fund management fees and or to reduce the Mutual Fund's operating expenses.

   vi) The fund manager may intentionally misclassify the risk, quality, liquidity and or dynamics of the fund's assets.

   vii) Investors can intentionally misclassify the risk, quality, liquidity, investment-intent (e.g. held-to-maturity asses versus trading securities) and or dynamics of the fund's assets. That can have balance sheet and income statement ramifications.

The behavioral problems that pertain to Mutual Funds include but are not limited to the following:

   i) Shirking, negligence and fraud by portfolio managers.

   ii) Collusion by portfolio managers – in portfolio selection and trading; and in structuring and pricing of derivatives; etc.

   iii) Collusion and fraud by fund administrators – in valuations of fund assets; in timing of dissemination of information; etc.

   iv) Group Think.

   v) Market Manipulation and Insider Trading – e.g. front running before stated rebalancing dates of mutual funds.

   vi) Fraudulent justification of the value of Mutual Fund Units.

   vii) Information Asymmetry.

   viii) Illegal Repricing/Backdating of swaps/derivatives trades in Mutual Funds' portfolios.

   ix) Agency problems.

   x) The conflicts-of-interest introduced in Nwogugu (2019a).

5.3.2 *Mutual funds are hybrids (not debt or equity): the US Tax court's and US bankruptcy court's perspectives*

The issue of whether Mutual Fund Units are debt or equity has implications in several dimensions. The relevant literature on classification/characteristics of debt and equity includes: Burilovich (December 2006); Burke (September 2006); Ryan, Herz et al. (2001); Brighton (2002); Harriton (1994); Whittington and Whittenburg (1980); Hopkins (1996); Magennis, Watts and Wright (1998); Dantzler (Jan. 2006). The US case law on the classification/characteristics of debt and equity is somewhat unsettled – different courts have enumerated different criteria for classification as debt or equity.[28] Under the different sets of criteria developed by different US courts (US Tax courts, US Bankruptcy courts and US civil courts) during the last thirty years, Mutual Fund units don't meet the requirements for classification as debt or equity; but they are contract intangibles. The Mutual Fund typically does not entitle the holder to any voting power, or direct ownership interest in the Mutual Fund corporate entity. In many cases, if the corporate entity is liquidated/dissolved, the Mutual Fund Unit-holder will be entitled to only the resulting cashflow, if any.

5.3.3 Mutual funds are hybrids (not debt or equity): the USA commercial law perspective

From a commercial law perspective, Guinn and Harvey [42:1140–1141][29] stated that there have not been any cases decided under the old or revised Article Nine of the Uniform Commercial Code (UCC) (USA) as to the proper classification of OTC derivatives (as mentioned, Mutual Funds are essentially interests in OTC derivatives). See: Ciro (2002); Hazen (1992); Bernstein (1992) and Hains (1997). Also, see the comments in Sobieski (1962); Armstrong (1962); and Howe and Jain (2004). Section 8–103 of the revised UCC (USA) describes rules for determining whether obligations/interests are securities or financial assets – and states that '*a share or similar equity interest issued by a corporation or business entity is a security*'. Since the sole purpose of the Mutual Fund status and Units is to track values of the underlying portfolio assets, the typical Mutual Fund does not have a '*business enterprise*' purpose and cannot be considered a business entity for the purposes of Article-8 of the UCC. Technically, Mutual Fund equity interests are not "issued" by Mutual Fund, as the term "issuance" is defined and used in federal and state securities laws – because the Mutual Fund Unit consists of the following components: i) the Mutual Fund shares; ii) the contract terms including fees, distributions and other costs. The "issuance" done by Mutual Funds is only of the Mutual Fund shares. Thus, Mutual Funds and exchange-traded options do not meet the requirements for classification as a security under Article Eight of the UCC (Sections 8–103, 8–102[a][15], and 8–102[9]), or UCC Article Nine. The "*economic substance*" test in Ciro (2002) is invalid, because derivative financial instruments are used to raise funds, and serve price discovery and risk management purposes, and in some instances, involve a transfer of the underlying asset (e.g. convertibles) or the functional equivalent of a transfer of economic benefits and obligations pertaining to the underlying asset.

Furthermore, the "*effective life*" of a typical Mutual Fund Unit is less than one month, because if at any time during the tax reporting period the Mutual Fund fails to comply with the applicable statutes (such as the Investment Company Act in the USA) and Tax Codes, it automatically and immediately loses its Mutual Fund status. Hence, the Mutual Fund Units cannot be classified as "securities".

The Mutual Fund equity interest can also be construed as bundle of futures contracts, where the "goods" to be delivered in the future (in continuous time) are the periodic cash distributions and the tax benefits that accrue from the Mutual Fund status. In this instance, and under *Board of Trade of City of Chicago*, the typical Mutual Fund Unit cannot be construed as a security.

5.3.4 Mutual funds are hybrids (not debt or equity): the US federal and state securities law perspectives

As mentioned, the issue of whether Mutual Fund Units are debt or equity has implications in several dimensions. Sections of the prospectus for various Mutual Funds provides the official definitions. As written, the most reasonable interpretation of the Mutual Fund offering documents, is that the Mutual Fund is a hybrid intangible, and not a corporate security.[30] The Mutual Fund is essentially a basket of OTC call options with the "strike price" being the joint/compound event defined as the strike price of the underlying/constituent assets, and compliance with all relevant federal laws.[31]

5.3.5 Mutual funds are not securities: the USA state securities law perspective

The *Cohn, Ivers & Co v. Gross*[32] court held that a call option was not a security, but was a general intangible, and the Court stated the following four conditions as requirements for classification of an option as a security: i) Issued in bearer or registered form; ii) is of a type commonly dealt in upon securities exchanges or markets or commonly recognized in any area in which it is issued or dealt in as a medium for investment; iii) Is either one of a class or series or by its terms, is divisible into a class or series of instruments; iv) Evidences a share, participation or other interest in property or in an enterprise or evidences an obligation of the issuer. Clearly, Mutual Funds are not issued in bearer/registered form. In most countries, Mutual Funds are not commonly traded on securities exchanges. The Mutual Fund unit does not evidence any share, participation or other interest in property or in an enterprise; but rather, represents only the right to a portion of the Mutual Fund's cashflows.

In addition to the foregoing four requirements developed in *Cohn Ivers*, some US federal appeals courts have required the existence of a *"common business enterprise"* as a requirement for classifying an interest as a security Mutual Funds does not meet this requirement because: i) as explained herein, there is no *Vertical Commonality*; and ii) the sole purpose of their existence isn't a "business enterprise" but rather, for tracking the market value of the underlying portfolio (it is reasonably inferable that the legislative intent of the state securities laws wasn't to classify a Mutual Fund as a "business enterprise").

Colt v. Fradkin[33] declined to follow *Cohn Ivers*, and sought to distinguish situations where: a) the holder of an option makes a contract to sell the option, and b) the owner or prospective owner of a security makes a contract to sell it at the option of a buyer. However, both situations are the same – if the option in the former is a general intangible, then the process of formation of the option (described in the latter) will also result in the same general intangible. In both situations, the underlying instrument represents a right created by contract. Note that the call options discussed in *Cohn Ivers* and in *Colt* were exchange-traded options (typically issued by exchanges), were not used to finance companies, did not represent title or equity, and were not instruments for the payment of money (because they were executory agreements that were contingent on conditions) and thus, are not very similar to Mutual Funds, which are not used to finance companies and are used for investment and standard risk-management. *"Performance"* in Mutual Fund Declarations of Trust or C-corporation bylaws differ from performance in exchange-traded call option agreements.

SMFs and OMFs are essentially *Gambling* because: i) in the case of SMFs, the underlying companies don't get any cash from the Mutual Fund; and in the case of OMFs, an underlying company may get cash only if the Mutual Fund purchases its shares or bonds in an IPO; ii) the Mutual Fund's underlying swaps/derivatives if any, are essentially bets on prices of assets and liabilities; iii) any increases in the values of Mutual Fund units don't accrue to the underlying companies.

The court's rulings in *Cohn Ivers* and *Colt* were partially erroneous with regard to the nature and purposes of stock options.

5.3.6 Mutual funds are not securities: the USA federal appellate and lower-court securities law perspective

From a US securities law perspective (at the US Courts of Appeals and US Federal District Courts), Mutual Funds are not securities.[34] 15 USC Section 78c(a) (10) (US securities laws) provides a definition of a security – and Mutual Funds don't comply with the requirements for classification as securities, which are described in *Board of Trade of City of Chicago*, 677 F2d 1137 (1982), for the following reasons. As mentioned here, SMFs and OMFs are essentially *gambling* because: i) in the case of SMFs, the underlying companies don't get any cash from the mutual fund; and in the case of OMFs, an underlying company may get cash only if the Mutual Fund purchases its shares or bonds in an IPO; ii) the Mutual Fund's underlying swaps/derivatives are essentially bets on prices of assets; iii) any increases in the values of Mutual Fund units don't accrue to the underlying companies.

Mutual Funds are not "investments in an operating business" per say (investors are essentially speculating and don't have an "investment" purpose of gaining from the company's business operations), but are intangibles that arise from contracts. Profits accrue to Mutual Fund unit-holders only from the changes in values of the Mutual Funds assets which are subject to significant *Market Noise*. The holder of the Mutual Fund unit does not assume personal risk of bankruptcy of the Mutual Fund. There is no *"Vertical Commonality"* at creation of the Mutual Fund because while the Mutual Fund sponsor/manger may lose money from Mutual Fund operations (administrative costs; compliance costs; marketing costs and management costs), the Mutual Fund unit-holder may gain from increases in the value of the Mutual Funds assets and cash balances. The existence and effectiveness of Mutual Funds often depends on compliance with tax laws, and as mentioned above, one of the main purposes of the Mutual Fund unit is to track and establish the market values of Mutual Fund assets and to serve as a basis for the payout of the Mutual Fund's distributions (and not to conduct operating business). The gains and losses from owning Mutual Fund units are not often proportional to the Mutual Fund-holder's contribution to both the Mutual Fund and the underlying companies (Mutual Fund unit gains depend on market fluctuations; estimated values of the underlying assets; the timing of exercises of underlying swaps/derivatives; the Mutual Fund's cash position and declaration of dividends).

5.3.7 Mutual funds are not securities: the US Supreme Court's perspective

From the US Supreme Court perspective,[35] Mutual Funds are not securities for the following reasons. *First*, the transactions and structures of Mutual Funds don't satisfy at least three of the four *original "Howey Tests"* under *SEC vs. Howey*, 328 U.S. 293 (1946), for the following reasons:

i) There is no *"expectation of profit"* because the purchase of Mutual Fund units is too speculative. Mutual Funds are a "derivative" of a "derivative (value is based on combined values of portfolio assets and mandatory compliance with specific regulations) but that didn't create *"Reference Dependence"* (Anchoring) because: 1) Mutual Fund unit-holders focus on, or are very likely to have focused on factors other than the underlying portfolio assets – such as *Market Noise*, general stock market trends, derivatives; CDS, macroeconomic trends; news releases; changes in regulation; etc.; 2) Mutual Fund unit-holders have almost no control over the patterns of exercise or sale/purchase of the underlying assets and swaps/derivatives in the Mutual Fund; and 3) it is very difficult for the average Mutual Fund unit-holder to predict the Mutual Fund manager's next moves. Just as in *United Housing v. Forman*, 421 U.S. 837, 852–53 (1975), the Mutual Fund unit purchased by the investors entitled them to the cashflows of the Mutual Funds. The investors had a desire to use or consume the item (Mutual Fund units) purchased. The Mutual Fund sponsor/manager promises benefits to Mutual Fund unit-holders in the form of money receivable in the future (distributions of cash and or assets) and merely referred to the benefits as "Mutual Fund units" while actually the benefit was not any kind of security at all – see *Foltz vs. US News*, 627 F. Supp. 1143 (D.DC.; 1986). *Bauman v. Bish*, 571 F. Supp. 1054, 1064 (N.D.W.Va.1983) held that an interest in an Employee Stock Ownership Plan ("ESOP") were not securities.

ii) For the Mutual Fund Units purchased by the investors, the *"investment"* test was not satisfied because their purchase of the Mutual Fund units made the Units similar to membership interests in mutual cooperative/insurance companies.[36] The purchase of Mutual Fund units does not involve any *"investment of money"* as defined by the courts – that is, the investment is not in an operating business, but is made in an environment where

Mutual fund returns are highly speculative and subject to *Market Noise* and thus are essentially *Gambling*. In the line of US Supreme Court cases that addressed the definition of securities, in most instances, the terms *"profits"*, *"Common Enterprise"* and *"conduct of business"* explicitly referred to the management of operating companies (and not investment vehicles).

iii) The typical Mutual Fund is not an operating company and does not result in *"'profits from the conduct of business"* as interpreted by the courts and in the traditional sense of commerce (management of operating companies but not Investment Vehicles) – the only positive results are indirect benefits which arise solely from changes in the values of the underlying Mutual Fund portfolio (and not from companies' business operations).

iv) There is no *Vertical Commonality* – the individual success of a Mutual Fund investor does not correlate with the success of the Mutual Fund sponsor/manager. Even when the Mutual Fund is performing well, the Mutual Fund issuer/sponsor/manager can still lose money due to low management fees and excessive marketing costs, administrative costs and compliance costs. Each Mutual Fund investors' return-on-investment is "unique" and depends on: 1) the prices at which each holder purchased his/her Mutual Fund unit; and 2) the fees charges to the unit-holder (which can vary across investors); 3) the timing of the investor's sale of the unit; 4) the timing of the sale or exercise of the underlying assets and or swaps/derivatives in the Mutual Fund portfolio; 5) changes in contract terms of underlying swaps/derivatives and or in regulations.

v) There is no *Horizontal Commonality* because there is no "market" for Mutual Fund units; and investors can sell Mutual Fund units only by redemption of the unit by the Mutual Fund; and as mentioned above, each investor's return is "unique".

vi) The typical Mutual Fund has a strictly contingent corporate status (contingent on compliance with various regulations and tax statutes).

vii) The *"efforts of others"* requirement is not satisfied because Mutual Fund Units can be (and is often) purchased by the Mutual Fund's managers/sponsors/issuers and employees; and by the managers/employees of the underlying companies whose stocks or bonds are included in the Mutual Fund or are indirectly being tracked by the Mutual Fund.

viii) In *SEC vs. Howey*, there were forty-two purchasers of the same type of alleged financial instrument, whereas in the case of Mutual Funds, groups of investor purchase at different prices.

Thus, Mutual Funds are not Investment Contracts. Investment contracts[37] are defined in section 2(1) of the 1933 Securities Act, 15 U.S.C. § 77b(1), and section 3(a)(10) of the Exchange Act, 15 U.S.C. § 78c(a)(10). Also see Gordon (2011). In *Securities and Exchange Commission vs. W. J. Howey Co.*,[38] the US Supreme Court established the main criteria for classification of a property as an investment contract: *"the test is whether the scheme involves an investment of money in a common enterprise with profits to come solely from the efforts of others"*.

Second, in *Marine Bank vs. Weaver*[39] and *International Brotherhood of Teamsters vs. Daniel*,[40] the US Supreme Court introduced the fifth and sixth "*Howey Tests*" which were the following: i) whether there is an alternative regulatory scheme that makes it un-necessary to apply federal securities law and US SEC jurisdiction; and ii) that "*for an instrument to be a security, the investor must risk loss*". In this instance, there are the common-law, insurance law, UCC and arbitration frameworks within which claims such as fraud and breach-of-contract can be asserted. The "risk-of-loss" requirement is hereby evaluated within the context of operating companies; and Mutual Funds differ from the contexts in both US Supreme Court cases and from what the US Supreme Court reasonably intended because purchasing Mutual Fund units is not a direct investment in an operating business.

Third, Mutual Funds are not securities and the US SEC doesn't have any jurisdiction because:

a) Where the Mutual Fund sales process results in a situation where the Mutual Fund sponsor/manager/issuer enters into privately negotiated "unique" contracts with one or more of such investors (in one-on-one, individually negotiated, face-to-face transactions for which the common law and equitable remedies are generally deemed adequate) then such mutual Fund units are not securities. Each such "unique" contract must be "different" in terms of the following: 1) price; 2) fees and loads; 3) other expenses. Thus, under *Marine Bank vs. Weaver*,[41] such Mutual Funds are not securities and the US SEC and state regulatory agencies do not have any jurisdiction.

b) In *Marine Bank vs. Weaver*, the US Supreme Court also introduced the "*Common Trading*" criteria for classifying financial instruments as securities – however, in the case of Mutual Funds, this additional requirement was not satisfied because:

   i)   the typical Mutual Fund does not have equivalent values to most Unit-holders (due to differences in purchase prices and fees; and the value and timing of sale/exercise of the underlying assets; and tax reasons); and

   ii) the Mutual Funds are not traded on public exchanges, and the only way for investors to sell their units is by redemption by the Mutual Fund.

Fourth, the Mutual Fund can be construed as loans (or the equivalent of Certificates of Deposit – see: *Marine Bank vs. Weaver*) that were not securities because of the following reasons and because the *Howey Tests* are not satisfied (and thus, the US SEC does not have any jurisdiction):

a) The typical Mutual Fund has quasi-mandatory redemption features (mandatory payment of periodic distributions and or right-of-redemption), which makes it more like contingent debt (or an equity-linked/market-linked Certificate-of-Deposit).

b) The typical Mutual Fund is similar to, and some have the same payoff-features as "Phantom Stock".

Fifth, in *Reeves vs. Ernst & Young*,[42] the US Supreme Court created the following four tests (based on the Exchange Act of 1934) for the existence of securities: i) whether the seller's purpose is to raise money for the general use of a "business enterprise" or to finance substantial investments, and the buyer is interested primarily in the profit the instrument is expected to generate; ii) whether there is *"common trading"* of the instrument for speculation or investment, iii) whether the investing public reasonably *expects* the instrument to be a security; iv) whether there is no other *alternate regulatory regime* that significantly reduces the risk of the instrument. Mutual Funds don't meet all four *Reeves Tests*, because Mutual Funds are not traded on public exchanges (no *common trading*); Mutual Funds are speculative; an investment in a Mutual Fund is not an investment in a traditional "business enterprise"; people don't expect Mutual Funds to be securities because they are not traded on public exchanges; and there are alternative risk-reducing regulatory regimes such as common-law, Commodities statutes and contract law.

Sixth, apart from the *Howey Tests*, the *Reeves Tests* and the *Marine Bank Criteria*, US Supreme Court cases have also looked at other criteria such as the marketing and the *"Plan of Distribution"* for the Financial Instruments and the *"Economic Incentives"* offered to "prospective investors" – all of which indicate that Mutual Funds are not securities. In the USA, the purchase and ownership of a Mutual Fund unit (MFU) incurs different fees such as the following (which are charged in addition to front-end and back-end Loads):

i)   Front-end Load (fee paid by investor when buying the unit) and or Back-end Load (fee paid when selling the unit) which can vary according to the distribution channel. Some Mutual funds don't charge any Loads.
ii) Redemption fee.
iii) Exchange fees.
iv) Purchase fee.
v)   Account fees.
vi) Shareholder service expenses that are not included in the 12b-1 fees, legal expenses, custodial expenses, record keeping, accounting expenses, transfer agent expense and other administrative expenses.

Thus, there is no *Horizontal Commonality* or *Vertical Commonality* (the fund sponsor or manager may incur a loss even when the fund is performing well). Each purchase of a Mutual Fund unit is a "unique" contract (among, the sponsor, the fund and the investor) whose explicit and implicit terms include: i) the above mentioned fees which for any fund, can vary across investors depending on the distribution channel; ii) applicable taxes which can vary across investors; iii) front-running and arbitrage of Mutual Funds; and iv) trading rules, exchange rules and usage-of-trade; v) associated *Multiplier Effects*.

5.4 Auction rate securities (ARS)

As mentioned above, ARS are used extensively around the world and finance governments, many companies and overall economic growth; and are used by investment funds, mutual funds, pension funds and insurance companies for investment management (that is ultimately related to economic growth). The dollar volume of outstanding instruments in the global Auction-Rate Securities ("ARS") market exceeded US$2 trillion in 2018, and can be divided into the following groups: i) the government Auction-Rate Securities ("GARS") market which consists of sovereign securities, federal government-agency securities, and government Reverse-Repos) – as explained in Bai, Fleming and Horan (2013) and Bloomberg (2015);[43] and ii) the municipal Auction-Rate Securities ("MARS") market which are securities issued by state governments (in the US, MARS constituted about 40 percent of the ARS market as of 2015); and iii) the Corporate Auction-Rate Securities ("CARS") which are corporate securities. The US CARS and MARS markets were hugely popular globally and grew to more than US$330 billion by 2017; and had many international investors. During 2000–2017, more than 40 percent of the US ARS market consisted of US tax-exempt municipal bonds. During 2000–2010, many US and non-US companies, closed end funds and small banks purchased US CARS from US issuers (in offerings managed by mostly US investment banks) purportedly for investment purposes, and subsequently incurred significant losses from such purchases. As of 2018, many large and medium companies (such as Apple; Microsoft; etc.) had substantial ARS portfolios which could be used for earnings management and asset quality management. Unfortunately, despite the obvious problems inherent in global ARS markets and associated lawsuits, many top executives of the top-ten Wall Street investment banks supported US CARS.[44] The US GARS market includes US Treasury securities which are sold through similar auctions processes as described by Malvey, Archibald and Flynn (2014). As of 2018, the Chinese government and Japanese government owned more than US$1.025 trillion and US$1.1 trillion worth of US treasury securities which accounted for a substantial portion of the government reserves of both countries. Thus, the issues discussed herein also have critical implications for Chinese and Japanese capital markets (that is, the occurrence of the same types of failures that harmed the US corporate and municipal ARS market in the US Treasuries markets or the Chinese Treasury bond market or the Japanese Treasury market can harm Chinese and or Japanese capital markets). Furthermore, empirical researchers have concluded that ARS sales/auction procedures were a cause or accelerator of the *Euro Crisis* of 2009–2015.

Also the problems in the ARS[45] market seem to have exacerbated both the subprime crisis of 2006–2009 in the US, and the EuroZone Crisis,[46] and has fostered contagion in EuroZone debt markets. Beetsma et al. (2013) noted that since 2007, secondary-market yields on Italian public debt increased in anticipation of auctions of new issues and declined after the auction, while no or a smaller such effect was present for German public debt; and there was some tendency of the yield movements to be larger when the demand for the new issue is smaller relative to its supply. Giuliodori, de Jong and Widijanto (2013) attributed that to the market-structure in which a small group of primary dealers require compensation for inventory risk and this compensation needs to be higher when market uncertainty is larger. Beetsma, Giuliodori, de Jong and Widijanto (2013) also found that the secondary-market behavior of series with a maturity close to the auctioned series, but for which there is no auction, is very similar to the secondary-market behavior of the auctioned series; and as such it is inferable that yield movements were based on the behavior of primary dealers with limited risk-bearing capacity. Lou et al. (2013) found that for the same series of bonds, the auction yield is always higher than the on-the-run bond yield, with a difference ranging from 0.8 basis points for the ten-year maturity, 1.4 basis points for the five-year maturity, and 2.5 basis points for the two-year maturity. While De Broeck and Guscina (Jan. 2011) argue that the Eurozone crisis compelled governments to change their funding (debt issuance) tactics, is reasonably inferable that government debt auctions transmitted contagion which in turn lead to changes in funding methods.

Alderson and Fraser (1993); D'Silva, Haley and Marshall (2008); Han and Li (Feb. 2008); Han and Li (2010); SVB Financial Group (August 15, 2007); Pan (June 30, 2006); Fichera (2011); and Johnston (Sept. 17, 2007) discussed various aspects of the ARS market. Securities Litigation & Consulting Group (2011) noted that the ARS market failed during the Global Financial Crisis because: i) broker-dealers supported auctions without proper disclosure of their holdings and bidding patterns; and that masked the liquidity and credit risk associated with ARS; ii) ARS prospectuses specified a "maximum rate" which effectively imposed a floor on ARS prices.

Melendy (2011) and Claudiu (2013) analyzed corporate governance issues. García-Pérez, Yanes-Estévez and Oreja-Rodríguez (2014) and Grechuk and Zabarankin (2014) studied strategic decision-making. Karpoff, Lee and Martin (2008a;b) analyzed the consequences of earnings management. Fichera (2011) critiqued ARS auctions processes and recommended ways to improve ARS auctions.

The classification of ARS as securities or non-securities can have significant effects on markets and households because of the following reasons. The classification affects the accounting classification of the equivalent of trillions of dollars of ARS globally (and related transactions in balance sheets and other financial statements). It affects the perceived liquidity and collateral values of ARS. The classification affects perception of risk and economic conditions because ARS often serve as benchmarks for loans and fixed income securities. In some jurisdictions/countries, it affects the capital reserve requirements of regulated companies that own ARS. The classification can affect the Repo-markets which are critical in many developed economies.

During the last 20 years, many lawsuits were filed against both ARS-issuers and investment banks about sales of ARS and associated misrepresentations. See: Austin (2012). During 2006–2019, various US government agencies filed lawsuits against investment banks and traders for manipulating government bond auctions.[47] Some lawsuits alleged that some investment banks sold ARS products as cash equivalents, but failed to disclose significant illiquidity risks and the extent of banks' support for ARS auctions. During 2011, Akamai Technologies, Inc. (a US tech company) sued Deustche Bank[48] in the US District Court for the District of Massachusetts to recover US$200 million of losses that Akamai sustained from buying Auction Rate Securities (ARS) pursuant to the advice of Deutsche Bank Securities (material misrepresentation or omission in violation of Section 10(b) of the 1934 Securities Exchange Act). In 2008, UBS[49] settled claims for litigation about ARS. Bear Stearns,[50] Merrill Lynch[51] and other investment banks were also sued by various parties for alleged misconduct pertaining to ARS. In 2010, a US federal bankruptcy judge approved a settlement wherein Citigroup Global Markets Inc.[52] agreed to repay US95.5 million to clients who purchased auction-rate securities and incurred losses. The ARS were sold by Citigroup to LandAmerica 1031 Exchange Services Inc., before the latter collapsed during 2008. The ARS had been valued at about $120 million. In 2008, the US SEC[53] filed securities fraud complaint in 2008 against two Credit Suisse brokers (Butler and Julian Tzolov) for engaging in a bait-and-switch sales of high risk ARS to foreign corporate customers that incurred losses. Butler was convicted of criminal charges for the unauthorized sale of more than US$1 billion in subprime-related ARS and he was sentenced to five years in prison (Butler appealed his sentence).

The problems inherent in ARS markets raise the following issues. *First*, the role and culpability of the BOD and corporate managers (who authorize and periodically review the type, amount and timing of the firm's purchases and sales of third-party securities and financial instruments). Should BODs approve such purchases? *Second*, the liability and culpability of the BOD and corporate managers who initiate and or approve the company's issuances of ARS and other high risk securities. *Third*, the liability and culpability of external auditors who misclassify such high risk securities (i.e. trading securities vs. available-for-sale securities vs. held-till-maturity securities). *Fourth*, the intentional use of ARS to manipulate and or misrepresent asset-quality in the balance sheet of corporate customers. *Fifth*, the intentional use of ARS to manipulate and or misrepresent earnings of corporate investors. *Sixth*, the intentional use of ARS to manipulate and or misrepresent earnings and balance sheets of ARS-issuers. *Seventh*, the need for third-party opinions of value and liquidity of ARS. *Eighth*, the use of ARS as collateral for loans, and the resultant systemic risk implications.

5.4.1 FINRA's ARS portfolio, and FINRA's failure to warn investors about the risks of investing in ARS

Ms. Mary Schapiro was formerly the Chairman of FINRA (a securities industry regulatory organization in the USA) immediately before she was appointed as the Chairperson of the US Securities & Exchange Commission (US SEC) in 2009. A 2008 article[54] noted that during 2008 (Ms. Schapiro's last year as FINRA's Chair-person):

i) FINRA failed to investigate or sanction Bernard Madoff and Robert Allen Stanford, who perpetrated two of the largest Ponzi schemes in US history (even though their investment companies were regulated by FINRA).

ii) FINRA failed to act against large FINRA members (Lehman Brothers, Bear Stearns and Merrill Lynch) in connection with their roles in the subprime mortgage securities scandals.

iii) FINRA failed to warn investors about *Auction Rate Securities* (ARS) problems after FINRA had liquidated its own ARS portfolio holdings during mid-2007, but before the ARS market "froze" (and there were numerous publicly available articles about the risks inherent in such "investments").

iv) FINRA suffered about US$700 million of losses in its ARS portfolio during Ms. Schapiro's tenure as Chairperson of FINRA.

Many US and foreign companies (that were regulated by the US SEC) owned substantial portfolios of ARS and ABS. As of 2014, Apple Inc., owned more than US$12 billion of ARS and ABS.

Ms. Schapiro's appointment as Chairperson of the US SEC created a conflict-of-interest because she had just resigned as Chairperson of FINRA immediately before she became SEC Chairperson. FINRA is an industry trade association that regulates the US securities brokerage industry and also lobbies the US government; and FINRA was regulated by the US SEC. FINRA's interests conflicted or could have conflicted with the US SEC's interests and objectives. Immediately after she stepped down from the position of Chairperson of the US SEC, Ms. Schapiro was appointed as a member of the BOD of General Electric which again was a major conflict-of-interest because GE is an exchange-traded company that is regulated by the US SEC. Less than five months after she stepped down from the US SEC, Ms. Schapiro joined Promontory Financial's office in Washington as a managing director in charge of its governance and markets practice (advising clients on risk management and compliance). To the extent that this position involved, appears to involve or will involve any type of lobbying of US legislators or other government entities, advocacy and or dealing with the US SEC, it's a major conflict-of-interest (appearances also matter). In January 2015, London Stock Exchange Group Plc announced that Mary Schapiro joined LSE's group BOD as a non-executive director. This was again a major conflict-of-interest because the LSE is a public stock exchange that is regulated by the UK government and some companies that are regulated by the US SEC are also listed in the LSE.

5.4.2 ARS are not securities: the US Supreme Court's perspective

From the US Supreme Court's perspective, ARS are not securities because of the following reasons. *First*, the transactions, auctions of ARS and structure of

ARS don't satisfy at least three of the four *original "Howey Tests"* under *SEC vs. Howey*, 328 U.S. 293 (1946), for the following reasons:

i) For many ARS customers that are not *primary dealers/brokers*, there is no or minimal *"expectation of profit"* because the investment in ARS is too speculative and this class of investors has almost no verifiable intentional influence (or has difficult-to-verify influence) on the auction process; and usually cannot predict auction outcomes which determine both ARS pricing and liquidity. *First*, most ARS were a "second-order derivative" or a "derivative" of a "derivative" (wherein the "underlying instrument" is the original right-to-receive a share of the ARS-Issuer's operating income or cashflow; and the "first derivative" is the ARS at the first auction; and the "second derivative" is the ARS at the second auction). Note that this process is different from *"Reference Dependence"* and there is no *"Anchoring"* because in ARS auctions, auction bidders usually focus on many factors other than the results of the prior auctions of that ARS – such as repo-markets trends (and solvency and capital of repo-market participants); yield-curves, and yields and total returns of other assets; macroeconomic data; trends in fixed income and currency derivatives markets; portfolio-level taxes; the relative liquidity of markets; relationships with other auction bidders; availability of hedging instruments; portfolio duration/Convexity; etc. *Second*, large volumes of ARS involve "Sequential-Auctions" wherein the primary-dealer purchases ARS in an auction and subsequently re-sells the ARS to customers in the functional equivalent of a *Dutch-Auction* or similar processes. There is no way to predict whether the next auction of an ARS will have active bidders (many ARS auctions have failed). For many classes of ARS, the only liquidity and sometimes the only opportunity to sell the ARS-Unit is during the next scheduled auction of that class of ARS. Just as in *United Housing v. Forman*, 421 U.S. 837, 852–53 (1975), for many classes of ARS, the ARS unit purchased by the investor entitled them to proceeds of future bidding in future ARS auctions if and when such bidding occurs.

ii) For the ARS-Units purchased by the investors, the *"investment"* test was not satisfied because their direct (bidding in auctions through a dealer) and or indirect (purchase from dealers) participation in the ARS auction Program made the ARS Units similar to membership interests in mutual cooperative/insurance companies.[55] Also the purchase of ARS units differs substantially from a "normal" investment in an operating company.

iii) There is no *Vertical Commonality or Horizontal Commonality* – There is no *Vertical Commonality* because while the ARS may be performing well, its issuer may be having operational problems; and the success of ARS investors doesn't always correlate with the success of the majority of shareholders of the ARS-issuer (typically, the ARS interest/dividends had to be paid regardless of the ARS-issuer's operating performance; and the process of determining the rates of interest/dividends were distant from the operating performance of the ARS-issuer). Each ARS-investor's return-on-investment from the ARS-units is "unique" and partly depends on: 1) the prices at which the ARS-holder purchased his/her ARS unit (only for "non-uniform price auctions"); 2) the timing and success of the next and future auctions of the same and similar classes of ARS (for some types of ARS, the only liquidity and opportunity to sell the ARS-unit is at the next auction of that class of ARS); 3) the trends in the associated repo-market for the subject class/type of ARS (including the nature/wealth/solvency of the primary-dealers and institutional investors who were party to such repo transactions) can make an ARS unit unique in terms of its prices and trading patterns both in the When-Issued Market and during and after its auction; and 4) the "*Specialness*" of each specific ARS unit makes it unique and determines its price at auction and after its auction/issuance. Bartolini et al. (2011) found that: i) repo spreads help explain a significant percentage of the yield spreads for short (money market) maturities; but on the contrary, GC repo-spreads had very little impact on determination of longer-term yield spreads; ii) rates on GC repos against Treasury collateral decline sharply relative to rates on GC repos against agency and mortgage-backed securities in periods of liquidity needs (such as year-ends, quarter-ends, holidays, etc.). Sundaresan (1994) found that that newly issued Treasury securities usually trade "*special*" in repo markets, and that the degree of *specialness* reflected auction-cycles of treasury securities. Jordan and Jordan (1997) found that the liquidity premium in newly issued Treasury securities reflects their "*specialness*" in repo markets; which is affected by *auction-tightness* and the percentage of the Treasury securities issue that is sold to primary-dealers and specifically, they noted that "*Duffie (1996) examines the theoretical impact of repo 'specials' on the prices of Treasury securities and concludes that, all else the same, an issue on special will carry a higher price than an otherwise identical issue. We examine this hypothesis and find strong evidence in support of it. We also examine whether the liquidity premium associated with 'on-the-run' issues is due to repo specialness and find evidence of a distinct effect. Finally, we investigate whether auction tightness and percentage awarded to dealers are related to subsequent specialness and find that both variables are generally significant.*" Krishnamurthy (2002) linked the spread between newly issued and old thirty-year Treasury bonds to the difference in repo market financing rates between the two bonds. Brunnermeir and Pedersen (2009) found that securities with identical cash flows can have substantially different margins because of differences in their current and future secondary market liquidity. There is no *Horizontal Commonality* because the individual success of each ARS-investor differed from, and did not correlate with either the success of other investors (who typically purchased the ARS at different prices in non-uniform-price auctions and or had severely limited and varying degrees of liquidity); and in both discriminatory and non-discriminatory

ARS auctions and for each specific ARS unit, the accepted winning bid was essentially a *"unique contract"* between the bidder and the ARS-issuer. The implicit and explicit terms of such contract include not only the ARS price, but also: 1) the delivery terms; 2) conditions and any related trades (of that ARS unit or tranche) in the *When-Issued Market* and or the associated Repo Market; 3) the *"Specialness"* of such specific ARS unit; 4); brokerage commissions charged to the ARS-holder; 5) processing and administrative fees and transaction taxes charged to the ARS-holder; 6) the Settlement Date for the purchase; 7) the viability of future periodic auctions of that ARS tranche. See Corradin and Maddaloni (2015) and the other articles cited above in this paragraph.

iv) ARS does not result in "profits" from the conduct of business in the traditional sense of commerce (i.e. the management of operating companies) – the only positive results are indirect benefits. In the line of US Supreme Court cases that addressed the definition of securities, in most instances, the terms *"profits"*, *"Common Enterprise"* and *"conduct of business"* explicitly referred to the management of operating companies (and not investment in specialized financial instruments that involve inefficient auctions).

v) The *"profits to come solely from the efforts of others"* requirement wasn't met because officers/employees of ARS-issuers, and the brokers/traders that bid in the issuer's ARS auctions sometimes purchase the issuer's ARS units.

vi) In *SEC vs. Howey*, there were many (forty-two) purchasers of the same type of alleged financial instrument. Similarly, in the case of non-uniform-price auctions of ARS, groups of investors purchased different instruments at different prices. Also, as explained herein, in the case of uniform-price auctions of ARS, groups of investors purchased different instruments at the same price.

vii) The ARS-investors had a desire to use or consume the item (ARS) purchased (by participating in the ARS auction). ARS grant benefits to ARS holders in the form of money receivable in the future and merely referred to the benefits as ARS while actually the benefit was not any kind of security at all – see *Foltz vs. US News*, 627 F. Supp. 1143 (D.DC.; 1986).

viii) *Bauman vs. Bish*, 571 F. Supp. 1054, 1064 (N.D.W.Va.1983) held that an interest in an Employee Stock Ownership Plan ("ESOP") were not securities.

Thus, ARS are not Investment Contracts. Investment contracts[56] are defined in section 2(1) of the 1933 Securities Act, 15 U.S.C. § 77b(1), and section 3(a)(10) of the Exchange Act, 15 U.S.C. § 78c(a)(10). Also see Gordon (2011). In *Securities and Exchange Commission vs. W. J. Howey Co.*[57] the Court established the main criteria for classification of a property as an investment contract: "the test is whether the scheme involves an investment of money in a common enterprise with profits to come solely from the efforts of others."

Second, in *Marine Bank vs. Weaver*[58] and *International Brotherhood of Teamsters vs. Daniel*,[59] the US Supreme Court introduced the fifth and sixth *"Howey*

Tests" which were the following: i) whether there is an alternative regulatory scheme that makes it un-necessary to apply federal securities law and US SEC jurisdiction; and ii) that "*for an instrument to be a security, the investor must risk loss*". In this instance, there are the common-law, UCC, insurance law and arbitration frameworks within which claims such as fraud can be asserted. The "risk-of-loss" requirement is hereby generally construed to refer to operating companies, and this context (issuance of ARS) differs from the contexts in both US Supreme Court cases and from what the US Supreme Court reasonably intended because: i) in the case of ARS issued by governments, the transaction is not a direct investment in an operating business and ii) in the case of ARS issued by companies, it differs substantially from "normal" investments in operating companies. Thus, ARS are not securities.

Third, under *Marine Bank vs. Weaver*,[60] ARS are not securities because:

i) The ARS auction process resulted in a situation where for each specific ARS unit, the ARS-issuer entered into privately negotiated "unique" "one-level" or "two-level" contracts with each successful bidder-investor (in one-on-one, individually negotiated transactions for which the common-law and equitable remedies are generally deemed adequate), and each such contract was different. A "*One-level Contract*" refers to when the investor buys ARS units directly from the issuer in an auction; while "*Two-level Contracts*" refers to when the investor buys ARS units from a primary dealer/broker that purchased the same in an ARS auction. The "uniqueness" arose because for any ARS issue/tranche, the value of each ARS contract differed in terms of the following: 1) the prices at which each ARS-holder purchased his/her ARS unit (only for "non-uniform price" or "discriminatory" auctions); 2) the timing and success of the next and future auctions of the same and similar classes of ARS (for some types of ARS, the only liquidity and opportunity to sell the ARS-unit was at the next auction of that class of ARS); 3) the trends in the associated repo-market for the subject class/type of ARS (including the nature/wealth/solvency of the primary-dealers and institutional investors who were party to such repo transactions). See the conclusions of Bartolini et al. (2011), Sundaresan (1994), Jordan and Jordan (1997), Krishnamurthy (2002) and Brunnermeir and Pedersen (2009) which are summarized above.

ii) In *Marine Bank vs. Weaver*, the US Supreme Court also introduced the "*common trading*" criteria for classifying financial instruments as securities – however, in the case of ARS, this additional test was not satisfied because:

1) As mentioned, at all times, each ARS-unit does not have equivalent values to most persons because of differences in the following factors: 1) the prices at which each ARS-holder purchased his/her ARS unit (only for "non-uniform price auctions"); 2) the timing and success of the next and future auctions of the same and similar classes of ARS (for some types of ARS, the only liquidity and opportunity to sell the ARS-unit

was at the next auction of the class of ARS); 3) the trends in the associated repo-market for the subject class/type of ARS (including the nature/wealth/solvency of the primary-dealers and institutional investors who were party to such repo transactions).

2)   The ARS are not traded on public exchanges. Most ARS are either not traded on public exchanges at all, or are traded only in inter-dealer markets (OTC).

Fourth, most of ARS are debt-type instruments (or the equivalent of Certificates of Deposit – see: *Marine Bank vs. Weaver*) that were not securities because of the following reasons and because the *Howey Tests* are not satisfied:

i)   Most ARS have quasi-mandatory redemption features, which made them more like debt (or an equity-linked Certificate-of-Deposit).

ii)   Most ARS are very similar to, and had the same payoff-features as: 1) a bond/loan or a Certificate-of-Deposit with a contingent principal repayment that depended on the success of the next auction for that specific class/type of instrument and on conditions in the repo-market; and a contingent interest/dividend repayment that depended on the credit quality of the ARS-issuer and the success of the next auction for that specific ARS, and the success of other auctions of other ARS issued by other entities (contagion effect); or 2) a zero-coupon bond/loan or a zero-coupon Certificate-of-Deposit with a contingent principal repayment that depended on the success of the next auction for that specific class/type of instrument and on conditions in the repo-market.

Fifth, ARS don't meet all four *Reeves*[61] *Tests*. ARS are not traded on public exchanges (no *common trading*); ARS are speculative; an investment in an ARS unit is not a traditional investment in a business enterprise; people don't expect ARS to be securities because most ARS are traded in OTC markets; and there are alternative risk-reducing regulatory regimes such as common-law, Commodities statutes and debtor-creditor statutes.

Sixth, apart from the *Howey Tests*, the *Reeves Tests* and the *Marine Bank Criteria*, US Supreme Court cases have also looked at other criteria such as the marketing and the "Plan of Distribution" for the financial instruments and the "Economic Incentives" offered to "prospective investors". In the case of ARS, most which are not traded on exchanges, the dynamics of the Repo Markets and When-issued Markets, arbitrage of ARS, the trading commissions, marketing/distribution, auctions, administration costs and associated *Multiplier Effects* and *Cross-border Spillover Effects* are critical, and all indicate that ARS are not securities.

5.4.3 ARS are not securities: the US federal appellate and lower-court securities law perspective

From a US securities law perspective (at the US Courts of Appeals and US District Courts), ARS are not securities[62] – and the above-mentioned arguments apply. 15 USC Section 78c(a)(10) (US securities laws) provides a definition of a security – and ARS don't comply with the requirements for classification as securities, which are described in *Board of Trade of City of Chicago*, 677 F2d 1137 (CA7; 1982), for the following reasons: i) ARS are not "investments" per say – ARS are too speculative and profits accrue to ARS-holders primarily from ARS interest/dividend payments and changes in ARS-values which are subject to Market Noise; ii) most ARS are not traded on exchanges; iii) investors don't have an "investment" purpose of gaining from an operating government-entity's/company's operations; iv) there is no "*Common Enterprise*" among the ARS-holders and the ARS-issuer – no *Vertical Commonality* or *Horizontal Commonality* as explained herein and v) the ARS-holder's gains and losses from owning ARS are usually not proportional to his/her pro-rata share of the gross amout of that ARS tranche/class that was sold/auctioned.

5.4.4 ARS are not securities: the USA state securities law perspective

The *Cohn, Ivers & Co. vs. Gross*[63] court held that a call option was not a security, but was a General Intangible, and the Court stated the following four conditions as requirements for classification of an option as a security: i) Issued in bearer or registered form; ii) is of a type commonly dealt in upon securities exchanges or markets or commonly recognized in any area in which it is issued or dealt in as a medium for investment; iii) is either one of a class or series or by its terms, is divisible into a class or series of instruments; iv) evidences a share, participation or other interest in property or in an enterprise or evidences an obligation of the issuer. Clearly, ARS are not issued in bearer/registered form. In most countries, ARS are not commonly traded on securities exchanges but rather, are traded in relatively opaque inter-dealer markets. The ARS unit (issued by companies and government entities) does not evidence any share, participation or other interest in property or in an enterprise; but rather, represents only the right to a portion of the ARS-issuer's cashflows. As mentioned, each set of ARS that is purchased in a primary discriminatory auction is essentially a privately negotiated unique contract that is not one of a class or series.

In addition to the foregoing four requirements developed in *Cohn Ivers*, some US federal appeals courts have required the existence of a "*common business enterprise*" as a requirement for classifying an interest as a security – ARS do not meet this requirement because as explained earlier, there is no *Vertical Commonality* or *Horizontal Commonality*.

Colt v. Fradkin[64] declined to follow *Cohn Ivers*, and sought to distinguish situations where: a) the holder of an option makes a contract to sell the option, and b) the owner or prospective owner of a security makes a contract to sell it at the option of a buyer. However, both situations are the same – if the option in the former is a general intangible, then the process of formation of the option (described in the latter) will also result in the same general intangible. In both situations, the underlying instrument represents a right created by contract. Note that the call options discussed in *Cohn Ivers* and in *Colt* were exchange-traded options (typically issued by exchanges), were not used to finance companies, did not represent title or equity, and were not instruments for the payment of money (because they were executory agreements that were contingent on conditions) and thus, are not very similar to Mutual Funds, which are not used to finance companies and are used for investment and standard risk-management. *"Performance"* in ARS markets differs from performance in exchange-traded call-option agreements.

The rulings in *Cohn Ivers* and *Colt* were partially erroneous with regard to the nature and purposes of stock options.

5.4.5 Auction rate securities (ARS) enabled ARS-issuers to perpetrate earnings management and asset-quality management

ARS facilitated or could have facilitated earnings management and asset-quality management by ARS-issuers in the following ways. *First,* because the Dutch Auctions[65] were used to sell ARS, under US GAAP and IFRS, ARS issuers had the managerial discretion to manipulate their balance sheets (create, increase or reduce accruals) and income statements. For a long time, and up to 2008 (and perhaps even after 2008), each time there was a successful ARS auction, the ARS yields typically changed and the carrying-values of ARS could be changed by both ARS-issuers and ARS-investors. Many ARS were issued under "shelf registrations" at the US SEC, which enabled issuers to move quickly to issue various classes of securities at the same time. Thus, ARS-issuers could simultaneously "repurchase" and issue very similar series/classes of ARS either simultaneously or during short periods of time in order to create or reduce accruals (balance sheets) and create gains or losses (income statements), and thus, perpetrate earnings management and asset-quality management. Because the yields on ARS were reset after each ARS-auction, ARS issuers could collude with investment banks and some investors that participated in these auctions, to manipulate the interest rate bids, and under US GAAP and IFRS, ARS-issuers could then manipulate the values of ARS liabilities in ARS-issuers' balance sheets. ARS-issuers could participate in these auctions solely to manipulate the interest-rate bids. *Second,* ARS sub-markets were often very illiquid when there were not enough auction bids. Under US GAAP and IFRS accounting standards, ARS-issuers had the managerial discretion to change the carrying values of ARS liabilities on their balance sheets based on prices that don't reflect true ARS values. It also allowed ARS issuers to collude among themselves (and with investment banks) to arrange for timed sales/purchases of ARS in order to realize false gains and losses on "callable" ARS. *Third,* because the true risks of many classes of ARS were grossly understated by ARS issuers (as confirmed by the subprime and ABS crisis in the US during 2005–2010), corporate issuers used ARS to perpetrate asset-quality management. Many of these issuers were high risk cities and companies that used the attraction of frequent yield resets through auctions to attract investors. The Dutch auctions[66] used to sell ARS often obfuscated the true risks of ARSs and their issuers.

5.4.6 Auction rate securities enabled ARS-investors to perpetrate earnings management and asset-quality management

ARS facilitated or could have facilitated earnings management and asset-quality management by ARS holders/investors in the following ways. *First*, under IFRS and US GAAP, ARS investors have the managerial discretion to move ARS among various balance sheet classifications of assets (i.e. trading securities vs. available-for-sale securities vs. held-to-maturity securities). Each such choice had its own Income Statement and balance sheet effects and facilitated the creation/ reduction of accruals and earnings management. Some ARS investors were treating ARS as cash-equivalents whereas by their very nature and relatively substantial illiquidity, ARS were not cash-equivalents because they were very risky (as confirmed by the crash of the ARS market in 2008). By 2005, Pricewaterhouse-Coopers and other major accounting firms stated that corporation should classify ARSs as "investments" rather than "cash equivalents" in their balance sheets. *Second*, because the yields on ARS were reset after each periodic (7, 14, 28, or 35 days) ARS-auction by the issuer, under US GAAP and IFRS, ARS investors had the managerial discretion to manipulate their balance sheets (create or reduce accruals) and income statements simply by holding ARS, or by simultaneously buying and selling ARS on or around the reset dates. Investment banks (that lead-managed initial offering of ARS) often participated in the auctions (and often saw participant's bids before they bid) primarily to provide liquidity to ARS-holders, and they could have colluded with ARS-investors to manipulate auction bids (and thus, the values of ARS). *Third*, because of the types of auctions that were used to sell ARS, under US GAAP and IFRS, ARS investors had the managerial discretion to manipulate their balance sheets (create or reduce accruals) and income statements. Some of these auctions resulted in the sales of the same class/series of securities at different prices to different investors during the same sale. Many ARS were issued under "shelf registrations" at the US SEC, which enables issuers to move quickly to issue different classes of securities at the same time. Thus, ARS investors could simultaneously purchase and sell very similar series/classes of ARS during short periods of time in order to perpetrate earnings management and asset-quality management.

Fourth, ARS sub-markets were often very illiquid and "normal" trading prices in those markets may not have reflected true asset values; while prices derived from "arranged" trading may provide false asset values. Under US GAAP and IFRS accounting standards, this allowed ARS investors to carry ARS on their balance sheets at values that were often much greater or much lower than their market values. It also allowed ARS investors to collude among themselves (and with investment banks) to arrange for timed sales/purchases of ARS in order to realize false gains and losses. For example, an investor could arrange for ARS sales at the end of the fiscal year at false prices in order to boost its reported income and or create accruals, and then repurchase the same ARS within a few months after the end of the fiscal year.

Fifth, because the true risks of many classes of ARS were grossly understated by ARS issuers (as confirmed by the subprime and ABS crisis in the US during 2005–2010), corporate investors used ARS to perpetrate asset-quality management. Many ARS issuers were high risk companies that used the attraction of frequent yield-resets through auctions to provide justification and compliance with the *"Prudent Man Rule"* and the *"Business Judgment Rule"* to corporate investors and professional institutional investors (e.g. funds; ETFs) who knew that their investment mandates would not have otherwise permitted them to invest in such securities. The auction methods used to sell ARS often obfuscated the true risks of ARSs and their issuers. *Sixth*, ARS permitted ARS investors to arbitrage by using margin loans to purchase ARS, and exploiting the differences between their cost-of-funds and the periodically reset yields of ARS. Thus, in some circumstances, the ARS reset yields were more of a function of the borrowing costs of the ARS-investors, rather than the credit risk of the ARS-issuers. *Seventh*, ARS sub-markets were often very illiquid. Under US GAAP and IFRS accounting standards, this allowed ARS investors to carry ARS on their books at values that were often much greater than their market values. It also allowed ARS investors to collude among themselves (and with investment banks) to arrange for timed sales/purchases of ARS in order to realize false gains and losses.

Eighth, valuation and accounting practices remains a controversial issue in the global ARS market, and many banks and investors have adopted wildly different models and accounting principles, all of which facilitates earnings management and asset-quality management. "Mark to market" accounting is the recommended principle. As of May 31, 2008, 402 exchange-traded companies owned ARSs; of which 185 had reported some wildly divergent impairment charges wherein discounts were 0–98 percent of par value. For example, during 2008–2009, Bristol-Myers Squibb, 3M, Citigroup and US Airways reported impairment charges for their ARS portfolios; IncrediMail, Ltd., recorded an impairment of 98 percent of face-value for its ARS; but Berkshire Hathaway didn't record any impairment charges for its $3.5+ billion holdings of ARS. As of 2008, Bank of America and other brokerage houses refused to assign values to their clients' ARS holdings; UBS AG presented clients with several different values for ARS; and Interactive Data Real Time Services discontinued the pricing of approximately 1,100 student-loan ARS on May 5, 2008.

5.4.7 Measures to reduce misconduct in the global ARS market

The Fichera (2011)[67] recommendations (for reducing misconduct in the ARS market) are grossly insufficient and they only scratch the surface of the huge ARS problems which have undermined the credibility of many government-issuers, investment banks and large corporate issuers of Asset Backed Securities (ABS) (many of which are ARS). Additional measures and reforms for the ARS market include but are not limited to the following (which are also applicable to auctions in general):

i) A securities regulatory agency (such as the US SEC and or FINRA) should establish a single set of rules, practices and disclosures for how auctions are conducted. The main argument is that there should be some leeway for experimentation and innovation in markets but within a strict framework that applies to all ARS auction methods.

ii) Impose substantial penalties on investment banks and brokers that engage in misconduct in sales and auctions of ARS.

iii) All ARS auctions should be non-uniform price (discriminatory) auctions and *Reverse-Dutch Auctions* in order to reduce collusion, and to increase competition in auction markets. Non-uniform/discriminatory auctions are more likely to provide less incentives and opportunities for collusion and fraud among ARS-issuers, bidders and investment banks primarily because of the following reasons:

1) Non-uniform price auctions are a better preference-revelation method, and uniform-price Dutch auctions create or can create a *race-to-the-bottom* mentality among market participants;

2) Not all bidders are "rational" and will always want the lowest clearing price – for various reasons including taxes (e.g. some bidders may prefer to get a higher tax basis in the ARS by buying at prices above the "clearing price"; or Rollover tax Relief provisions are more favorable if the bidder buys ARS at prices above the Clearing Price), relative-valuation of their other assets (e.g. the lower Clearing-Price may reduce or adversely affect the pricing and liquidity of the bidders' other ARS and non-ARS assets); etc.;

3) Discriminatory auctions are more likely to provide higher offering proceeds for ARS-issuers than uniform-price auctions;

4) Discriminatory auctions provide useful information about markets and bidders' preferences;

5) Uniform-price auctions are more likely to create substantial Regret among ARS-issuers and ARS-investors and primary dealers; and such Regret can significantly distort both future ARS auctions and related markets such as the Repo market;

6) Discriminatory auctions are less likely to create harmful volatility and illiquidity that arises from disparities of market-participants' estimates/forecasts of issuer-performance and market trends;

7) Discriminatory price auctions result or are more likely to result in less emphasis on investors' preferences and more investor consideration of ARS-issuers' preferences and operating performance. *Reverse Dutch Auctions* are more likely to compel bidders to focus on the credit quality of issuers (compared to regular Dutch Auctions).

Reverse Dutch Auctions are less likely to create a race-to-the-bottom mentality among auction bidders; and is less likely to create harmful volatility and illiquidity that arises from disparities of market-participants' estimates of issuer-performance and market trends. Compare comments in Sundaresan and Nyborg (1996), and Sundaresan (1994).

iv) Impose stringent limitations on participation of investment banks and ARS-issuers in ARS-auctions. For example, there should be specific monetary limits (either monetary limits or percentage limits) on the amount of ARS that can be purchased by primary dealers and the ARS-issuer in each ARS auction. For purposes of accounting/disclosure, taxation and regulation, a distinction should be made between new-issue ARS and repurchases of existing ARS by their issuers during ARS auctions. Primary dealers and ARS-issuers should not have pre-auction and post-auction access to auction bids submitted by their customers/bidders that are not primary dealers; and such customers should participate directly in ARS auctions and should be able to revise their bids at least once during each ARS-auction (perhaps through a dedicated website).

v) Impose stringent restrictions on the timing of issuances and repurchases of the same or similar classes of ARS by ARS-issuers and investment banks, in order to reduce arbitrage and earnings management.

vi) Implement new accounting rules for recording of ARS as assets or liabilities; and the associated creation/reduction of Balance Sheet accruals. The IFRS accounting rules for securities and investments should be drastically changed to reduce or eliminate managerial discretion in the classification and recording of investments and securities.

vii) There should be incentives to increase liquidity and transparency in ARS markets – e.g. persons that purchase ARS outside ARS-auctions can be granted tax credits; and persons that purchase ARS (outside ARS auctions) using proceeds of sales of other securities can be granted *rollover tax relief* (the investor's tax-basis is carried over to the ARS-unit, and his/her capital gain taxes will be deferred and payable only when the ARS-unit is sold); etc. Also ARS auctions should be restructured to enable investors to participate directly in the auctions instead of having to bid through brokers.

viii) There should be specific monetary limits (either monetary limits or percentage limits) on the amount of ARS that a primary dealer can re-sell to other primary dealers within 90–270 days after each ARS auction.

ix) All primary dealers/brokers, ARS-issuers and corporate ARS-purchasers should be required to publicly disclose their holdings and cost-basis of ARS and sales of ARS to primary dealers (and to update such disclosures weekly) – such disclosure can be made public on a government-maintained website.

5.5 Earnings management, asset-quality management and usury inherent in structured products vehicles and asset securitization

Structured Products (instruments and entities) are significant because they are widely used in many developed and developing countries to finance corporate growth and economic development, and for risk management and investment management (that is ultimately related to economic growth). The main types of generic Structured products[68] are: Credit-linked notes and deposits; Market-linked notes and deposits; Interest rate-linked notes and deposits; Hybrid-linked notes and deposits; Equity-linked notes and deposits; Constant proportion portfolio insurance (CPPI); FX and commodity-linked notes and deposits; and Constant proportion debt obligations (CPDOs). See: Qu (2016) and Soklakov (June 2017; December 2016).

A distinction is made here among the following types of Structured Products:

i) Structured Products Instruments – these are Structured Products that are issued directly by a wide range of companies (banks; companies in industry; insurance companies; etc.) and no special purpose vehicle is involved. Structured Products Instruments may be linked o currencies, commodities, the issuer's shares, other companies' shares, indices, etc.
ii) Structured Products Vehicles – these are special purpose vehicles that issue various types of financial products (not referred to as ABS or MBS).
iii) Asset Securitization – that refers to traditional securitization using special purpose entities that issue Asset Backed Securities (ABS) and Mortgage Backed Securities (MBS)

Asset securitization and many structured products are *incentive mechanisms* or have implicit incentives and are structurally and economically similar; but there are dichotomies in the accounting regulations and bankruptcy court rules/adjudication for Asset Securitization Vehicles and Structured Products Vehicles. Structured Products are special types of financial instruments that are issued by both financial and non-financial companies, but are usually targeted at specific investors that have defined risk preferences, return requirements, tax considerations and time horizons. Such transactions are sometimes combined with the sale or purchase of credit default swaps (CDS). Similarly, many traditional operating companies and financial services companies execute asset securitizations. Most structured products that involve the use of trusts and corporate entities are structurally, legally, economically and psychologically similar to asset securitizations.[69]

Structured Products vehicles (that involve trusts and corporate entities) also have the same or similar earning management, usury and legal problems as traditional asset securitization. Asset securitization and many types of Structured Products are both mechanisms and incentives because: i) they provide or can provide incentives to both the issuers' managers and investors (e.g. Contingent conversion rights; contingent performance rights; etc.); ii) they have payoff functions and economic and psychological effects that are similar to those of some EBIs; iii) similar to EBIs, they can be used for earnings management, asset-quality management and incentive-effects management.

Under IFRS/IASB accounting regulations, US GAAP and the accounting regulations of most countries, there are very different and perhaps conflicting accounting regulations for asset securitization entities (e.g. Trusts; LLCs; LLPs; etc.) and Structured Products entities (e.g. Trusts; LLCs; LLPs; etc.). Furthermore, in many countries, asset securitization entities (e.g. Trusts; LLCs; LLPs; etc.) and Structured Products entities (e.g. Trusts; LLCs; LLPs; etc.) are treated very differently in bankruptcy proceedings even though they are practically similar. This dichotomy is increasingly critical because: i) both the global asset securitization and Structured Products markets are large and growing rapidly and affect both the real and financial sectors of economies; ii) it creates opportunities for earnings management, reduces the comparability of financial statements; and increases the probability of divergent risk perceptions among investors (which can increase market volatility); iii) it has significant implications for economic growth, financial stability, systemic risk and public policy.

For an expalanation of the types of Structured Products and Securitization, see: Paškevicius and Sačilka (2010); and www.researchgate.net/publication/267225056_STruCTurEd_SECuriTiES_ANd_ThEir_dEvElOPMENT_iN_liThuANiA/figures?lo=1.

5.5.1 Earnings management

Asset Securitization and Structured Products Vehicles are popular mechanisms that are used around the world. Structured Products have grown exponentially during the last twenty years. As mentioned in Chapter 1 in this book, most structured products that involve the use of trusts and corporate entities are structurally, economically and psychologically similar to asset securitizations. The Structured Products analyzed herein are mostly those that were issued by special purpose "*Structured Products Vehicles*" (which sometimes resemble asset securitization entities). Structured Products Vehicles can have the same or similar earnings management and usury problems as traditional asset securitization. Structured Products and asset backed securities (ABS) are issued by both financial institutions and operating companies in industry. Piloto et al. (2016); Kim and Sohn (2013); An, Li and Yu (2013) and Liu, Ning and Davidson (2010) found that: i) earnings management increased before companies offered debt securities to the market; and or that ii) highly leveraged companies and more indebted companies are more likely to engage in earnings management.

Historically, Structured Products and asset securitizations were opaque (with regards to the sponsors' true intent, collateral-valuations and solvency) and these financial instruments were usually traded only in OTC markets. See: Friewald, Jankowitsch and Subrahmanyam (2017). Note that such opacity and the rampant use of dealer-quotes (for valuation of assets in Balance Sheets) facilitates earnings management and asset-quality management by both issuers and investors; and grossly distorts risk management. All of the foregoing reduce overall social welfare and the efficiency of allocation of capital/resources in national economies.

Nwogugu (2008a;b) noted that:

i) Under USA laws, asset securitization (as it pertains to asset-backed securities and mortgage-backed securities) is illegal because it violates Usury and antitrust statutes, and all "True-Sale", "disguised loan" and "assignment" securitizations are essentially tax-evasion schemes.

ii) In all "true-sale", "disguised loan" and "assignment" securitizations, the conflict of interest inherent in the sponsor also serving as the servicer, constitutes fraud and conversion.

iii) In all "true-sale", "disguised loan" and "assignment" securitizations where the SPV is a trust, the declaration of trust is void because it is for an illegal purpose.

iv) Off-balance-sheet treatment of ABS (both true-sale and assignment transactions) constitutes fraud; v) Asset Securitization constitutes a violation of Federal RICO statutes (in the USA);

vi) Securitization involves void contracts (illusory promises; no bargain; no mutuality; illegal subject matter; contravention of public policy).

Friewald, Jankowitsch and Subrahmanyam (2017)[70] noted the significant illiquidity in the structured products markets which also exists in the asset-backed securities (ABS) and mortgage-backed securities (MBS) markets. Note that such opacity and the rampant use of dealer-quotes facilitates: i) earnings management by dealers, issuers and investors; ii) allows dealers and investors to engage in fraudulent and illegal transactions that have the effect of boosting their assets, and or hiding losses and or reducing their perceived risk (e.g. temporarily "parking" assets at another firm; over-valuation/under-valuation of assets; etc.); iii) can amplify systemic risks and financial instability.

Indeed, many authors have illustrated the deficiencies inherent in securitization.[71] Schwarcz (2002) discussed earnings management inherent in securitization transactions executed by Enron which lead to its downfall and insolvency. Carlson (1998) and Lupica (2000) discussed how securitization evolved from efforts to circumvent the US bankruptcy Code and the earnings management implicit in such efforts. Carlson (1998), Janger (2002) and Lupica (2000) traced the history of asset securitization to direct and specific efforts/collaborations to avoid the impact of US bankruptcy laws. Klee and Butler (2002) and other authors have traced the history of securitization to attempts to handle the problem of non-performing debt.

Given the foregoing and the usury problems explained herein, most asset securitizations and Structured Products vehicles transactions constitute forms of earnings management, and or *Incentive-effects Management* and or "*Asset-Quality Management*" that can have substantial macroeconomic, public health and political economy effects.

5.5.2 Violations of usury statutes

Asset Securitization and some Structured Products Vehicles violate usury laws, because the resulting effective interest rate typically exceeds legally allowable rates (set by state usury laws). There is substantial disagreement (conflicts in case law holdings) among various US courts, and also within some judicial jurisdictions, about some issues and these conflicts have not been resolved by the US Supreme Court.[72] On these issues, even the cases for which the US Supreme Court denied *certiorari*, vary substantially in their holdings. The issues are as follows:

1) What constitutes usury.
2) What costs should be included when calculating the effective cost-of-funds.
3) What types of forebearance qualify for applicability of usury laws.
4) Conditions for preemption of state usury laws.

Where the securitization or structured products transaction is deemed an assignment of collateral, the effective cost-of-funds for the transaction is not the advertised interest cost (investor's coupon rate) of the asset-backed securities (ABS) but the sum of the following:

- i) *The Cost of Funds* – The greater of the sponsor's/originator's annual cost-of-equity (in percentages) or the percentage annual cash yield from the collateral (in a situation where the special purpose vehicle's (SPV) corporate documents expressly state that the excess spread should be paid to the sponsor, the excess spread should be subtracted from the resulting percentage). The excess spread is defined as the gross cash yield from the collateral, minus the interest paid to investors, minus the servicing expense (paid to the servicer), minus charge-offs (impaired collateral).
- ii) *The Amortized Value Difference* – The difference between the market value of the collateral, and the amount raised from the ABS offering (before bankers' fees), which is then amortized over the average life of the ABS bonds (at a discount rate equal to the US Treasury Bond of same maturity) and then expressed as percentage of the market value of the collateral. This difference can range from 10–30 percent of the market value of the collateral, and is highest where there is a senior/junior structure, and the junior/first-loss piece serves only as credit enhancement.
- iii) *Amortized Total Periodic Transaction Cost* – The *Pre-offering Transaction* costs are amortized over the average life of the ABS, a rate equal to the interest rate on an equivalent-term US treasury bond. The *Periodic Transaction* costs are then added to the amortized pre-offering transaction costs to obtain *Total Periodic Transaction Cost* which is expressed as a percentage of the value of the pledged collateral. The pre-offering transaction costs include external costs (underwriters' commissions/fees, filing fees, administrative costs, marketing costs, accountant's fees, legal fees, etc.) and internal costs incurred solely because of the securitization

transaction (costs incurred internally by the sponsor/originator – direct administrative costs, printing, etc.). The *Periodic Transaction Costs* include administrative costs, servicing fees, charge-off expenses and escrow costs.

- iv) *Foregone Capital Appreciation* – The foregone average annual appre-
  ciation/depreciation of the value of the collateral minus the interest rate on
  demand deposits, with the difference expressed as a percentage of the market
  value of the collateral.

The sum of these four elements is typically greater than state-law usury benchmark rates in US states.

Where the securitization is deemed a "true-sale", there is an implicit financing
cost which is typically usurious, because it is equal to the sum of the following:

- i) *Base Cost of Capital* – The greater of the sponsor's/originator's annual
  weighted-average-cost-of-capital, or the annual percentage yield from the
  collateral.
- ii) *The Amortized Total Periodic Transaction Cost* – The *Pre-securitization
  Transaction Costs* paid by the sponsor/originator and directly attributable to
  the offering is amortized over the life of the ABS, at a rate equal to the interest rate on an equivalent term US treasury bond, and the result (the "*Amortized Pre-securitization Costs*") is added to the *Periodic Transaction Costs*
  for only one period to obtain the *Total Periodic Transaction Cost*, which is
  then expressed as a percentage of the market value of the collateral is the
  Amortized Total Periodic Transaction Cost. The *Pre-Securitization Transaction Costs* include external costs (underwriters' commissions/fees, filing fees,
  administrative costs (escrow, transfer agent, etc.), marketing costs, accountant's fees, legal fees, etc.) and internal costs incurred solely because of the
  securitization transaction (costs incurred internally by the sponsor/origina-
  tor – direct administrative costs, printing, etc.). The *Periodic Transaction
  Costs* include servicing fees, administrative fees, and charge-off expenses.
- iii) *The Value Difference* – The difference between the market value of the
  collateral, and the amount raised from the ABS offering (before bankers'
  fees), is amortized over the average life of the ABS bonds and the result is
  then expressed as percentage of the market value of the collateral. This difference can range from 10–30 percent, and is highest where the senior/junior
  structure is used and the junior piece serves only as credit enhancement.
- iv) *Amortized Unrealized Losses* – Any unrealized loss in the carrying
  amount of the collateral, is amortized over the estimated average life of the
  ABS, and the result for one period is expressed as a percentage of the book
  value of the collateral. Most ABS collateral is recorded in financial statements at the lower-of-cost-or-market.
- v) *Foregone Capital Appreciation* – The foregone appreciation/depreciation
  of the value of the collateral minus the interest rate on demand deposits, with
  the difference expressed as a percentage of the market value of the collateral.

In the US, the sum of these five elements is typically greater that the US state-law usury benchmark interest rates.

5.5.3 The potentially harmful effects of structured products: the reverse-convertible bonds and the discount certificates that were issued based on Beiersdorf

During the last twenty years, there has been a proliferation of "Structured Products" that have been issued by third-parties ("*issuer-company*") that were often un-related to the "*subject-company*" (upon whose shares or assets the structured products are based). Beiersdorf is a German MNC that is listed on stock exchanges – and during 2010–2017, Beiesdorf perpetrated earnings management and asset-quality management and had corporate governance problems. See the comments in US SEC (Jan. 2015); FINRA (USA) (July 2011); Baker, Wurgler and Yuan (2012); Boehme and May (May 2016) and Beneta, Giannetti and Pissaris (2006). Such structured products can be harmful to:

i) Investors – for example, retail investors or institutional investors who don't fully understand the products or how to hedge them; or can't afford to hedge or who don't have ready access to hedging instruments;

ii) The subject-company (distinct from the issuer-company) – in terms of distortion/increases of its cost-of-capital; volatility of its stock prices and associated risk of crash of the stock price; harmful contagion effects; uncertainty; de-motivation of employees; devaluation of employee incentives; increased perceived bankruptcy risk; effects of publicity on the subject-company; etc. Many of the structured products favor the issuer-company and not the subject-company.

iii) The subject-company's shareholders.

In January 2017, Raiffeisen Centrobank AG (the "issuer-company") issued a nine-month reverse convertible bond that was based on Beiersdorf's ("subject-company") equity (the "BRCB"),[73] the terms of which were as follows.

In June 2017, Goldman Sachs ("issuer-company") issued one-year *Discount Certificates* that were based on Beiersdorf, the "subject-company" (the "BDC"). See the offering prospectus in German at: www.gs.de/en/documents/en-final_terms-de000gd5pre1-20170621060740.pdf. This was one of many structured products that are being issued by third parties based on the shares or assets of other companies.

Given Beiersdorf's corporate governance and earnings management problems (during 2010–2019), those reverse convertible bonds and the Discount Certificates were most probably not suitable for Beiersdorf's circumstances. It appears that that the combination of the BDC and the BRCB caused significant volatility in Beiersdorf's stock prices during 2017.

Table 5.1 Terms of the Beiersdorf Reverse Convertible Bonds.

ISIN	AT0000A1T448
WKN	RC0KDP
Public offer in:	Austria, Germany, Italy, Hungary, Poland, Czech Republic, Slovakia, Croatia, Romania, Slovenia
Underlying	Beiersdorf AG
Underlying price (delayed)	EUR 98.41
Chg. underlying in %	-0.22%
Underlying date/ time	35:10.0
Strike	EUR 82.00
Distance to strike	-
Max. return	-
Max. return p.a.	-
Interest rate total term	4.50%
Interest rate p.a.	6.75%
Accrued interest	Dirty (included in the price)
Starting value	EUR 81.71
No. of shares	12.19512
Country underlying	Germany
Issue date	Jan 20, 2017
Maturity date	Sep 20, 2017
Expected market trend	sideways, bullish
Tradeable unit/ nominal value	EUR 1,000
Listing	Vienna, Frankfurt, Stuttgart
Product classification	Investment Product without Capital Protection
Paid interest rate	4.50% on Sep 20, 2017
Spread	-
Spread homogenized	-
Spread	-
Issue price	100.00%
Initial valuation date	Jan 19, 2017
Final valuation date	Sep 15, 2017
Settlement method	Cash settlement/Physical delivery
Multiplier	12.19512
Product currency	EUR
Underlying currency	EUR
Taxation	Capital Gains Tax/Foreign Capital Gains Tax
Security type (Eusipa No.)	Reverse Convertible Bond (1220)

Source: www.rcb.at/en/produkt/stock/?ID_NOTATION=143111&ISIN=DE0005200000.

Between January 2017 (the issuance date of the BRCB) and June 2017 (the issuance date of the BDC), Beiersdorf's stock prices rose by about 20 percent; and then started decreasing in June 2017. Furthermore, Beiersdorf's stock prices declined substantially by more than 10 percent during the three months immediately before the September 2017 scheduled redemption of the BRCB; and then rose again substantially (by more than 10 percent) during the three months immediately after the September 2017 scheduled redemption date of the BRCB (see: www.rcb.at/

en/produkt/stock/?ID_NOTATION=143111&ISIN=DE0005200000). This significant volatility has information content (about investor's perceptions of Beiersdorf's solvency and corporate governance) and contravenes some asset pricing
and finance theories – for example, that bond redemptions should not have significant effects on the issuer's stock prices in some circumstances.

5.5.4 Structured products vehicles and structured products that are not listed on exchanges are not securities

From a US law perspective (i.e. The approaches/rulings of the US Federal Courts
of Appeals, US Federal District Courts, US state courts and the US Supreme
Court), and for the same reasons stated above (especially for Mutual Funds
and ARS), non-listed Structured Products are not securities[74] – and the above-
mentioned arguments apply. 15 USC Section 78c(a)(10) (US securities laws) provides a definition of a security and non-listed Structured Products don't comply
with the requirements for classification as securities, for the following reasons:
i) non-listed Structured Products are not "investments" per say – non-listed Structured Products are too speculative and profits accrue to holders primarily from
associated interest/dividend payments and capital appreciation which are subject
to Market Noise; ii) investors in non-listed Structured Products don't have an
"investment" purpose of gaining from an operating government-entity's/compa-
ny's operations; iii) non-listed Structured Products are not traded on exchanges;
iv) there is no *"Common Enterprise"* at issuance/auction of the non-listed Structured Products and iv) the holder's gains and losses from owning non-listed Structured Products are usually not proportional to his/her pro-rata share of the gross
amount of that non-listed Structured Products tranche/class that was sold.

5.6 Some securities law and debt-equity classification problems inherent in the US treasury's TARP/CPP Programs for US banks that were C-Corporations and S-Corporations (the "TARP/CPP Instruments")

This section addresses issues pertaining to the following:

i)   The evaluation of, and optimal design of interventions in Financial Crisis
     including cross-border issues in the management of economic/financial crisis.
ii) The optimal design of financial contracts.
iii) The costs and benefits of interventions for the real economy.
iv) Emergency lending facilities and capital purchases/injections in troubled
     institutions/companies.
v)   Actual and implicit Guarantees.
vi) Good-bank/bad-bank structures.
vii) Orderly liquidation/resolution.

viii) Economic and psychological thresholds for "Inefficient Continuance" of distressed companies.

ix) "Inefficient Continuance" in the context of corporate bankruptcy.

As a response to the credit crunch that worsened in 2007 and 2008, the US Congress enacted the Emergency Economic Stabilization Act of 2008[75] (the "EESA"); pursuant to which the US Treasury, the US Federal Reserve and the US FDIC developed and implemented several programs for various classes of persons including financial institutions, households and companies.[76] See: Cadwalader, Wickersham and Taft (April 23, 2009); A. M. Best (Stephanie McElroy & Rosemary Mirabella) (January 19, 2009); and Hunton and Williams (2009). As a result, the TARP/CPP Instruments program was launched by the US Treasury Department in 2008 in order to stabilize and boost the US economy by investing in US entities (mostly financial institutions). The US Treasury invested about US$420 billion during 2008–2014 through the TARP/CPP Program; and the list of TARP/CPP Program investee entities and the amounts they received is available at: https://www.treasury.gov/initiatives/finan cial-stability/TARP-Programs/bank-investment-programs/cap/Pages/cpp-results. aspx?Program=Capital+Purchase+Program.

More specifically, the TARP/CPP funds were used in the following ways:

1) On or around October 14, 2008, the US Treasury Department used $105 billion in TARP funds to launch the *Capital Purchase Program* wherein the U.S. government bought preferred stock of Bank of America/Merrill Lynch, Citigroup, Bank of New York Mellon, J.P. Morgan, Goldman Sachs, Wells Fargo, Morgan Stanley and State Street.

2) On or around November 23, 2008, the US Treasury invested an additional $20 billion in TARP funds in Citigroup. In return, Treasury received preferred stock with an 8 percent dividend.

3) On or around January 27, 2009, TARP invested $386 million of CPP funds in twenty three community banks.

4) On or around November 10, 2008, Treasury invested $40 billion of TARP Funds in AIG's preferred stock (which enabled AIG to avoid bankruptcy. On March 2, 2009, the US Treasury invested another $29.84 billion in AIG. Before these investments, the US Fed Federal Reserve had already loaned $112 billion to AIG.

5) From January 2009 to December 2014, the TARP/CPP Program used $80.7 billion to bailout the Big-Three US Auto Companies.

6) On or around November 23, 2008, the US Treasury loaned $20 billion of TARP Funds to the US Federal Reserve which it used to create the "Term Asset-Backed Securities Loan Facility" (TALF), which was loaned to the US Fed's member banks in order to increase those banks' lending volumes.

7) On or around February 18, 2009, the US Treasury launched the *Homeowner Affordability and Stability Plan* (HASP) wherein it allocated $75 billion in TARP

funds for assisting home owners to refinance or restructure their mortgages. The US Treasury also created the *Home Affordable Modification Program* (HAMP) and the *Home Affordable Refinance Program* (HARP). HASP, HAMP and HARP failed woefully as confirmed by several quarterly reports by the US Office of the Special Inspector General for the Troubled Asset Relief Program (SIGTARP).

As mentioned herein and above, the TARP/CPP program was not efficient and failed as confirmed by many reports[77] (see: Calabrese, Degl'Innocenti et al. (2017); Black and Hazelwood (2013); Farruggioa, Michalak and Uhde (2013); Song and Uzmanoglu (2016), and Semaan and Drake (2016)). Some of the specific failures of TARP/CPP Program were as follows:

i)   Many of the investee-banks didn't materially increase their lending volumes as expected – and so the major objective of providing expansion capital and boosting the US economy were not achieved.

ii) The compensation of bankers' at TARP/CPP investee-banks generally increased – the TARP/CPP investments increased bankers' and corporate executives' compensation and benefits without achieving the desired economic and social effects.

iii) The TARP/CPP Program resulted in "*Inefficient Continuance*" of banks and companies that should have instead filed for bankruptcy. That may also have affected the *Psychological Thresholds* for filing corporate bankruptcy.

iv) Many companies/banks and their executives/agents made formal fraudulent requests for TARP/CPP funds.

v)   Many of the participating/investee banks/companies were in much weaker financial positions after the TARP/CPP investment than before; and the perceived risk of the investee-banks didn't decline materially after they received TARP/CPP funds – as confirmed by their credit ratings, bond prices and CDS prices.

vi) TARP/CPP may have increased the costs-of-capital of, and perceived risk of other companies in the same industries as recipients of TARP/CPP investments (i.e. Credit Contagions and Spillovers).

vii) The financial contracts used in the TARP/CPP program were inefficient, costly (in terms of *Negative Externalities*) and were not designed to achieve or facilitate its objectives.

viii) As mentioned above, HASP, HAMP and HARP failed woefully (as confirmed by various reports by SIGTARP[78] and other entities and persons): 1) with associated consequences such as homelessness, foreclosures, mental health problems, divorces, etc.; 2) many of the restructured or refinance mortgages defaulted within eighteen months and many households lost their homes; 3) HAMP and HARP provided wrong incentives for banks and mortgage servicers, popularized Strategic Defaults and changed Risk Perception in the US residential real estate sector.

ix) As explained herein and below, the US Treasury Department mis-classified the TARP/CPP Financial Instruments (some debt were really equity and vice versa; and the warrants were debt) – which could have had *Negative Externalities* effects. During 2008 and 2009, the US Treasury implemented its purchase of certain "securities" of certain US banks that were designated as "S-Corporations" (hereafter, "S-Securities") and "C-Corporations" (hereafter, "C-Securities") under US state laws.[79] These investment programs were designed to provide capital to banks, stimulate lending and stabilize banks, many of whom had incurred loans losses. The C-Securities were designed to be "Preferred Stock" and many of the issuers were small and medium banks. The S-Securities were designed to be Senior Secured debt and most of the issuers were small regional or community banks. An analysis of these Financial Instrument indicates that:

1) The "S-Securities" (senior secured debt) that the US Treasury purchased from banks was really equity.
2) The "C-Securities" (Preferred Stock) that the US Treasury purchased from banks was really debt.
3) The Warrants that the US Treasury purchased from "C-Corporation" banks were really debt.
4) The Preferred Stock that FNMA and Freddie Mac sold to the US Treasury were debt.
5) Technically, the banks that were S-Corporations effectively lost their S-Corporation Status after the US Treasury's investment.
6) Technically, the investee banks that were C-Corporations lost their C-Corporation status after the investment by the US Treasury.

As mentioned herein and above, given the specific objectives, the legal classification of TARP/CPP Instruments had significant implications in several dimensions. This debt-equity "classification" problem had substantial implications for compliance with capital adequacy requirements for banks, solvency of banks and other financial institutions, and for maintenance of "S-Corporation" status under the US Internal Revenue Code. Whether these mis-classifications of financial instruments were intentional or not remains an issue that is critical for determining liability for earnings management and or incentive effects management. However, in most cases, the loss of S-Corporation or C-Corporation status were not reported or penalized or prosecuted.

x) All these foregoing factors increased or could have increased *Income/Wealth Inequality*, *Social Inequality* and *Housing Inequality*; and could have reduced Financial Stability, economic growth and Economic/Urban Sustainability. Such failures were caused primarily by the design of the TARP/CPP Financial Instruments.

5.6.1 Some of the continuing negative effects of the TARP/ CPP program

The reality is that even though the US Treasury Department recovered its last TARP/CPP investment in 2014 (the US Treasury Department invested about US$420 billion in TARP/CPP investments in US entities during 2008–2014), the economic, political, social and psychological *Multiplier Effects* and *Spillover Effects* of the TARP/CPP program continue to this day in various ways including but not limited to the following:

1) There continues to be Civil and criminal prosecutions of persons, banks and entities that tried to defraud the TARP/CPP Program (prosecutions by SIGTARP and other government agencies).
2) Long-term changes in the Internal Controls, "Internal Capital Markets", Capital Structures, Accounting Policies and lending policies of banks, insurance companies and finance companies (and some companies in industry that were financially or operationally distressed during 2005–2012) which were triggered by and maintained because of the TARP/CPP program and the Global Financial Crises.
3) Long-term changes in the executive compensation systems and recruitment priorities/policies of banks and finance companies which were triggered by and maintained because of the TARP/CPP program.
4) Long-term changes in the strategy, competitive benchmarking and corporate governance policies of banks and finance companies (and some companies in industry that were financially or operationally distressed during 2005–2012) which were triggered by and maintained because of the TARP/CPP program. By providing capital on specific terms, the TARP/CPP changed the nature of competition in the financial services industry where all-in cost-of-capital is critical.
5) Changes in risk perception and the metrics for evaluating and valuing companies.
6) The "stigma" and loss of Social Capital associated with companies that received TARP/CPP funds.
7) Long-term changes in measures implemented by banks and insurance companies to comply with capital requirements which were triggered by and maintained because of the TARP/CPP program.
8) The nature and objectives of political lobbying by financial services companies (which were triggered by and maintained because of the TARP/CPP program).
9) The research studies that are statutorily required by the Dodd–Frank Act had not been completed as of 2019.
10) Many of the foregoing factors seem to have spilled over among foreign investors that invest in the US, and to foreign countries where many TARP/ CPP investee-companies do business.

5.6.2 TARP/CPP program was or could have been perceived as "implicit guarantee" by the US government and or continuation of the "put-option" held by US banks

Some of the major problems were that:

i) Regardless of its legislative intent, the TARP/CPP instruments effectively functioned as, and or could have been perceived as an *Implicit Guarantee* provided by the US Treasury Department. That by itself could have had significant Contagion Effects and *Multiplier Effects* within and outside the US (given the volumes of international trade and capital flows).

ii) Regardless of its legislative intent, and regardless of the so called "no bailout" objectives of the Dodd–Frank Act, the TARP/CPP instruments effectively continued the perceived "Regulatory Put Option" that US banks have – i.e. that the US government will always intervene to help troubled banks. TARP/CPP contradicted the "no-bailout" objectives and legislative intent of the Dodd–Frank Act.

5.6.3 The structure of Fannie Mae, Freddie Mac and other government-sponsored enterprises

It is instructive to analyze several government-sponsored enterprises ("GSEs") in the US in order to better understand how federal regulation can affect corporate power and the evolution of corporate forms, hybrid corporations and quasi-government entities.[80] See the discussions in Reiss (2009); Reiss (2008); Moe and Kosar (2005) (Congressional Research Service); Carnell (2005); Jaffee (2006); Seiler (1999) and Wallison (2008).

The articles and materials in the footnotes herein describe the origins and recent changes at Fannie Mae and Freddie Mac. It is clear that both entities have been affected by government regulations.

The US government's Emergency Economic Stabilization Act of 2008 created the Troubled Asset Relief Program (TARP) whose objective was to purchase toxic assets and equity from financial institutions in order to stabile the US financial sector – and the Capital Purchase Program (CPP) was one such program. The Dodd–Frank Act of 2010 reduced the authorized TARP amount (including CPP) from $700 billion to $475 billion; and in October 2012, the US Congressional Budget Office (CBO) estimated total TARP disbursements would be $431 billion. The US Treasury sold its remaining holdings of Ally Financial in December 2014 and that ended the TARP which recovered funds totaling $441.7 billion from $426.4 billion invested, earning a $15.3 billion profit or an annualized rate of return of 0.6 percent.

Some differences between Fannie Mae and Freddie Mac on one hand, and on the other hand, the banks that participated in the US Treasury's CPP program are as follows:

1) Fannie Mae and Freddie Mac were incorporated in Washington DC, whose laws provide for government-sponsored entities as a form of corporate entity. In most US states, the state laws don't permit such entities.

2) Fannie Mae and Freddie Mac were expressly created by enabling federal legislation. On the contrary, the corporate form of the CPP investee banks were modified by the provisions of the EESA statutes – an unintended consequence of contentious federal legislation.

3) Fannie Mae and Freddie Mac were created to address the mortgage markets. The EESA addresses the entire US economy.

4) Fannie Mae and Freddie Mac have often enjoyed an "implied government guarantee" wherein most people erroneously believe that the obligations of both entities are guaranteed in part or whole by the US government.

5) Fannie Mae and Freddie Mac were taken over by a US government agency, due to their financial distress and the subprime loan problems that occurred in the US between 2007 and 2009.[81] The CPP investee-banks are independent.

6) The US Treasury also purchased Senior Preferred Stock and Warrants of Fannie Mae[82] and Freddie Mac.

5.6.4 The preferred stock that (C-corporation) banks sold to the US treasury department under the capital purchase program (CPP) during 2008–2014, was debt

The terms of the Senior Preferred Stock and the associated Stock Warrants that were developed by the US Treasury[83] are described in the footnotes. See: Humphreys (2007).[84] The terms of the Senior Preferred Stock were not negotiated, but rather were somewhat imposed on the banks. As part of the TARP/CPP program, beginning in October 2008, the US Treasury ("UST") purchased Senior Preferred Stock from many US banks. Under the various debt-equity classification criteria discussed earlier, the Senior Preferred Stock are debt instruments for the following reasons.

First, the Preferred Stock is senior to all other classes of the banks' Common Stock and some classes of Preferred Stock.

Second, for senior Preferred Stock that is issued by banks that are not subsidiaries of holding companies, the security will pay non-cumulative dividends at a rate of 5–9 percent per annum. Note that most of the issuers of the Senior Preferred Stock issued the Senior Preferred Stock with non-cumulative Dividends. Payment of non-cumulative dividends is indicative that the instrument is more like debt than equity. This term is a major criteria for classifying the security as debt or equity because it has a direct effect on the short-term solvency of the banks, and its ability to company with capital reserve requirements.[85] Furthermore, the holder of the non-cumulative Senior Preferred Stock does not share in the risks of the bank's operations.

Third, the fact that the Senior Preferred Stock is not mandatorily redeemable (has a perpetual life) is not a material criteria for classifying it as debt or equity or hybrid.[86] See comments in Polito (1998)[87] and other US federal appellate cases that have specifically found that a lack of a maturity date is not a material factor in determining whether an instrument is debt or equity. There are now many types debt that are continually refinanced upon maturity, such that they are "permanent capital". There are now various types of debt that have 40–50 year maturities, which is longer than the average life of most companies.[88] Many *"Trust Preferred Securities"* mature in more than forty years. Furthermore, in this instance, there is a reasonable expectation that the Senior Preferred Stock will be redeemed by the investee-banks because: a) its terms are relatively onerous, and b) its Dividend Rate is relatively high, c) there is, or can be a stigma attached to banks that participate in the CPP program, d) the terms of the Warrants (that were simultaneously issued by the investee banks) provide a significant incentive for the banks to redeem the Senior Preferred Stock before December 31, 2009.

The terms of the Senior Preferred Stock severely restrict Dividends for all classes of Common Stock and Preferred Stock. These restrictions are more than the typical restrictions imposed by terms of traditional Preferred Stock; and the net effect is that the restrictions function as a debt covenant. The key consideration is that other classes of Preferred Stock that are Pari-passu with or junior to the Senior Preferred Stock, may be mandatorily redeemable or may have non-cumulative Dividends, and other debt-like terms. Specifically, the restrictions on any increases in the Common Stock Dividend (not just payment) is in effect a "negative debt covenant". Such terms are typical in loan covenants and bond indentures.[89] In a study of 927 debt covenants, Paglia (2007)[90] found that more than 40 percent of the sample had this type of covenant.

Furthermore, the restriction on the repurchases of junior classes of Preferred Stock, and or classes of Preferred Stock that rank pari-passu with the Senior Preferred Stock, is a standard loan/debt covenant used in many loan/debt agreements; and it significantly affects the bank's capital structure. In a study of 927 debt covenants, Paglia (2007) found that about 14 percent of the sample had this type of covenant.

The terms of the Senior Preferred Stock require that the investee bank modify its benefits plans and executive compensation agreements for senior executives covered by EESA. This term is also essentially akin to a loan covenant. This term has a significant effect on the following: a) the motivation of employees, and b) the cost structure of banks. Hence, this is a major criterion in classifying the security as debt.

Like most types of debt, the Senior Preferred Stock does not have standard voting rights for typical matters that are submitted to a vote of the bank's Shareholders (except for some "class" voting rights). These same "Class voting rights" are often included in loan covenants and bond indentures. Hence, unlike most Shareholder's, the holders of the Senior Preferred Stock cannot have any meaningful influence on the bank's operations. This is indicative that the Senior Preferred Stock is really debt.

The amount of Senior Preferred Stock that the US Treasury invested in each investee bank was significant relative to the bank's equity.

The capital raised by the sale of the Senior Preferred Stock was typically not used by the investee bank in its operations, but was used to meet capital adequacy

requirements (most investee banks didn't increase their lending activities significantly after the US Treasury purchased the Senior Preferred Stock).

As a condition for purchasing the Senior Preferred Stock, the investee banks
also issued Stock Warrants to the US Treasury Department.

Some of the effects of the issuance of the Senior Preferred Stock on the Corporate Status of the "C-Corporation" Banks are discussed as follows. The net
"corporate status" effect of the issuance of the Senior Preferred Stock was that the
C-Corporations lost their status (or should have lost their status) as C-Corporations
and became government-controlled entities. In the US, all C-Corporations derive
their form, power and rights from state corporations laws. The following are some
critical issues:

1) *The EESA Preempts State Corporation Laws* – Given the US Supreme
   Court's preemption criteria/standards, and the new preemption criteria introduced in Nwogugu (2012), the EESA and related amendments that mandated
   the government bailout and the CPP program, effectively preempted state
   corporations laws. Thus, it can be argued that the combination of the legislative intent of EESA, the EESA preemption, the terms of the Senior Preferred
   Stock, and the implicit government control of the investee-company changed
   the corporate form (of the investee companies) created by and after the government bailout.
2) *Non-Compliance with State Corporations Laws* – Even if the EESA statutes are deemed not to preempt State Corporation laws, by the mere act
   of issuance of the Senior Preferred Stock, the C-Corp banks lost their
   C-Corporation status.
3) The EESA and the CPP Program invalidated the C-Corp investee-banks' Articles of Incorporation – the terms of the Senior Preferred Stock investment
   and the EESA clearly invalidated the investee-banks' Articles of Incorporation (which were similar for each state of incorporation).
4) The EESA and the CPP Program, and the Terms of the Senior Preferred Stock
   and Warrant effectively eliminated shareholders' voting rights for many
   important issues (such as executive compensation, employee benefits, dividends; redemption of preferred stock; repurchase of preferred stock; etc.).
5) The EESA and the CPP Program and the terms of the Senior Preferred Stock
   severely limited the powers of the Boards of Directors of the C-Corp Banks,
   and its general powers to conduct its business in the normal manner.

5.6.5 The warrants that (C-corporation) banks sold to the US treasury department in the capital purchase program (CPP) during 2008–2014, were debt

Under the various debt-equity classification criteria discussed herein and above,
the Warrants that the US Treasury purchased from the investee banks were akin to
one of the following types of "Imputed Debt":

a) Non-interest bearing (or Zero-coupon) equity-linked exchangeable debt – wherein the principal amount of the debt and the imputed interest are linked to the Share price of the investee-bank; and the principal amount can be exchanged for other securities of the investee-bank.

b) Non-interest bearing (or Zero-coupon) convertible-exchangeable debt with a variable principal amount (Face Value) – wherein the principal amount varies and depends on the Share Price; and the principal amount and any imputed interest can be either converted into Common Stock or exchanged for other securities.

The terms of the Warrants are described in the end-notes,[91] The banks sold the Warrants to the US Treasury as a condition for the sale of the Senior Preferred Stock.[92] Like most debt, the Warrants don't convey any voting rights. The Warrants don't grant any rights to Dividends or any periodic payments.

The *Imputed Interest* of the "Imputed Debt" is part of the difference between what the US Treasury paid for the Warrants (zero dollars) and the value of Warrants at maturity or exercise. Similarly, the *principal amount* of the "Imputed Debt" is variable and is part of the difference between what the US Treasury paid for the Warrants (zero dollars) and the value of Warrants at maturity or exercise (the difference between the Exercise Price and the Market Price of the bank's Common Stock).

The capital raised by issuance of the Warrant included both the Senior Preferred Stock and the future increases in the bank's stock price. Since most of the investee banks didn't increase their lending materially after the sale of the Senior Preferred Stock (and didn't apply a significant portion of the offering processed towards lending) the holders of the Senior Preferred Stock and Warrants were not materially exposed to the business risk of the investee banks.

The exercise price of the Warrant was to be reduced by 15 percent of the original exercise price on each six-month anniversary of the issue date of the warrants if the "consent" of the QFI stockholders (to increase the number of authorized Shares of the bank) had not been granted, subject to a maximum reduction of 45 percent of the original exercise price. This term is also a major indication that the Warrants are debt. This term is similar to a loan covenant that increases the principal amount of debt, if consent of the investee-bank's shareholders is required but is not granted. If shareholder consent is required but is not granted, then the US Treasury would not be able to exercise the Warrants, and would be compelled to exchange the Warrants for debt or other securities of the investee bank.

If the investee bank's Shares of Common Stock were no longer listed or traded on a national securities exchange or securities association, or if the bank did not obtain the consent of its stockholders (consent to request for authorization of more Shares of Common Stock for future issuance if the Warrants are exercised) within eighteen months after the issuance date of the Warrants, then the Warrants would become exchangeable, at the option of the US Treasury, for senior term debt or another economic instrument or security of the investee bank such that the US Treasury would be appropriately compensated for the value of the Warrant, as determined by the US Treasury. This term is highly indicative that the Warrants were either equity-linked debt or convertible debt. The investee banks' shareholders faced substantial dilution of their equity if the Warrants were exercised; and hence were likely to withhold their consent and prevent an increase of the number of authorized shares of the bank's Common Stock. There was a significant probability that the US Treasury would elect to exchange the Warrants for Senior Debt of the investee-banks, because it was likely or probable that shares of each investee bank would be temporarily or permanently suspended from trading on national securities exchanges. Many of the investee banks were either financially distressed, or a substantial portion of their loan portfolios were troubled. Furthermore, the US recession and the problems in the CMBS and US real estate sectors were having a contagion effect on share prices of US banks, many of which declined significantly during the Global Financial Crisis of 2007–2014.

The US Treasury's option to exchange the Warrants for debt or other securities of the investee bank was akin to a loan covenant that protected the US Treasury, and essentially reduced or even eliminated the US Treasury's exposure to both the investee bank's business operations and changes in its stock price.

If the US Treasury decided to exchange the Warrants for debt or other securities of the investee-bank, the US Treasury would have determined the value of the Warrant. Hence, the value of the Warrant would not be determined in an open market, or in an arms-length negotiation between the investee bank and the US Treasury. This term was essentially a loan covenant that granted the lender certain contingent valuation rights that effectively reduced or even eliminated the lender's exposure to the risks of the borrower's operations.

5.6.6 The "preferred stock" that Fnma and Freddie Mac sold to the US treasury department under the capital purchase program (CPP) during 2008–2014, was debt

Under the various debt-equity classification criteria discussed in Section-5.2.1, the Preferred Stock that FNMA and Freddie Mac sold to the US Treasury were debt. The net effect of this mis-classification was that it reduced FNMA's and Freddie Mac's solvency.

5.6.7 The "debt" that S-corporation banks sold to the US treasury department under the capital purchase program (CPP) during 2008–2014, was equity

Under the various debt-equity classification criteria discussed in Section-5.2.1 herein and above, the debt that S-corporation Banks sold to the US Treasury under the CPP program were equity.[93]

5.7 SSETFs

SSETFs are: i) "synthetic" ETFs (constructed with only cash, swaps and derivatives) that track listed options, options indices, indices or baskets-of-assets; or ii) Synthetic Long-Short ETFs that are constructed with Index Products and track the performance of indices or baskets-of-assets. Various ways of creating SSETFs are explained in Nwogugu (2019e). The SSETF can be construed as a basket of swaps/derivatives with the "strike price" of each derivative including compliance with all relevant federal laws.[94] As explained herein and contrary to existing practices, SSETFs are not securities and that has significant accounting, tax and regulatory consequences. SSETFs constitute *Gambling* and *bets* because: i) the underlying companies (who are indirectly tracked with swaps/derivatives) don't receive any investment from the SSETF; and ii) the underlying swaps/derivatives are affected by Market Noise and are bets on the directions of financial indices, market-segments and financial markets. In addition to the four requirements developed in *Cohn Ivers*, some US federal appeals courts have required the existence of a *common business enterprise* as a requirement for classifying an interest as a security – SSETFs units do not meet this requirement because the sole purpose of their existence is not a "business enterprise" but determining the market value of the SSETF and for allocating portions of the SSETFs cashflows.

The legal classification of SSETFs as securities or non-securities can have significant effects on markets because of the following reasons. The legal classification affects the accounting classification of the equivalent of billions of dollars of SSETFs globally (and related transactions in balance sheets and other financial statements). The legal classification affects the perceived liquidity and collateral values of ETFs in general. In some jurisdictions/countries, it affects the capital reserve requirements of regulated companies that own SSETF shares and equity interests. The classification can affect the Repo-markets which are critical in many developed economies.

In the following analysis, US case-law and US statutes/regulations are used for illustration because the US has the most advanced securities law system, and many countries have copied US securities laws and the US Constitution.

Under GAAP, debt, equity, assets and liabilities are typically recognized and or reported in financial statements once they become reasonably certain and or measurable. Each SSETF consists of a bundle of cash-settled Forward Contracts and or swaps and or options (with the imputed forward price being equal to the value of the portfolio at sale divided by the number of SSETF shares). Unlike swaps and most other derivatives, SSETFs are not truly measurable (and hence not reportable) until the underlying futures, swaps and option are exercised – while market values of swaps/derivatives may exist, they are not always correct and or arms-length transactions. See: FASB Statement # 123; FASB Statement # 123R; FASB Statement # 150; FASB Concepts Statement #6; IASB International Financial Reporting Standard #2 – Share Based Payment; FASB Exposure Draft: Proposed Statement of Financial Accounting Standards – "*Accounting*

For Financial Instruments with Characteristics of Liabilities, Equity or Both"
(Norwalk, CT, October 2000); FASB Discussion Memorandum: "*Distinguishing
Between Liability and Equity Instruments and Accounting for Instruments with
Characteristics of Both*" (Norwalk, CT, August 1990). The following factors are
relevant considerations in analyzing SSETFs:

•   In some instances, options and futures holders may not exercise their in-the-
    money rights.
•   Rollovers of options/futures contracts distorts tracking and SSETF values.
•   Hedging by the SSETF and associated costs distorts tracking and SSETF values.
•   SSETFs-holders, SSETFs managers and investors are not always rational
    when making decisions about exercising in-the-money rights.
•   In some cases, the swaps/derivatives (in SSETFs) contain terms that are not
    reflected or not permitted in the SSETF's governing documents or offering
    documents.

5.7.1 The US tax court's and US bankruptcy court's perspectives on the classification/characteristics of debt and equity

The relevant literature on classification/characteristics of debt and equity includes:
Burilovich (December 2006); Burke (September 2006); Ryan et al. (2001); Brighton
(2002); Harriton (1994); Whittington and Whittenburg (1980); Hopkins (1996);
Magennis, Watts and Wright (1998); Dantzler (Jan. 2006). The US case-law on the
classification/characteristics of debt and equity is somewhat unsettled – different
USA tax courts and bankruptcy courts have enumerated different criteria for the
classification as debt or equity[95] during the last thirty years. Under the different sets
of criteria, SSETFs don't meet the requirements for classification as debt or equity.
The SSETFs doe not entitle the holder to any voting power, or direct ownership
interest in the SSETF. The SSETF merely grants the holder the rights to dividends,
cash distributions and liquidation distributions of the SSETF. Under US Tax Court
and US Bankruptcy Court approaches, as written, the most reasonable interpretation is that the SSETF is a hybrid intangible, and not a corporate security.

SSETFs constitute *gambling* and *bets* because: i) the underlying companies (who
are indirectly tracked with swaps/derivatives) don't receive any investment from the
SSETF; and ii) the underlying swaps/derivatives are affected by Market Noise and
are bets on the directions of financial indices, market-segments and financial markets.

5.7.2 The US commercial law perspective on the classification/characteristics of debt and equity

From a commercial law perspective, Guinn & Harvey [42:1140–1141][96] state that
there have not been any cases decided under the old or revised Article Nine of the
UCC (Uniform Commercial Code) (USA code) as to the proper classification of

OTC derivatives (as mentioned, SSETFs are essentially interests in swaps/derivatives)[97]. Also, see the comments in Sobieski (1962); Armstrong (1962); and Howe and Jain (2004). Section 8–103 of the revised UCC describes rules for determining whether obligations/interests are securities or financial assets – and states that '*a share or similar equity interest issued by a corporation or business entity is a security*'. SSETFs and exchange-traded options do not meet the requirements for classification as a security under Article Eight of the UCC (Sections 8–103, 8–102[a][15], and 8–102[9]), or UCC Article Nine, because of the reasons mentioned in this paragraph. The "*Economic Substance*" test in Ciro (2002) is invalid, because derivative financial instruments are used to raise funds, and serve price discovery and risk management purposes, and in some instances, involve a transfer of the underlying asset (e.g. convertibles) or the functional equivalent of a transfer of economic benefits and obligations pertaining to the underlying asset.[98]

The SSETF equity interest can also be construed as a bundle of swaps/futures/options contracts, where the "good" to be delivered in the future (in continuous time) includes the tax benefits that accrue from status and structure of SSETFs. Thus, under *Board of Trade of City of Chicago*, the SSETFs interest cannot be construed as securities.

SSETFs constitute *gambling* and *bets* because: i) the underlying companies (that are indirectly tracked with swaps/derivatives) don't receive any investment from the SSETF; and ii) the underlying swaps/derivatives are affected by *Market Noise* and are bets on the "directional movements" of financial indices, market-segments and financial markets.

5.7.3 SSETFs are not securities: the US state securities law perspective

There may be a conflict between the principles of US federal district courts and appeals courts on one hand, and those of state courts. The relevant literature and US case-law on the USA State Securities Law Perspective were cited here. The *Cohn, Ivers & Co v. Gross*[99] court held that a call option was not a security, but was a general intangible, and the Court stated the following four conditions as requirements for classification of an option as a security: i) Issued in bearer or registered form; ii) is of a type commonly dealt in upon securities exchanges or markets or commonly recognized in any area in which it is issued or dealt in as a medium for investment; iii) Is either one of a class or series or by its terms, is divisible into a class or series of instruments; iv) Evidences a share, participation or other interest in property or in an enterprise or evidences an obligation of the issuer.

The following are arguments in support of SSETFs being securities. Clearly, SSETF units are issued in registered form. Most SSETFs are commonly traded on securities exchanges. The SSETF unit evidences a "participation" or other interest in the cashflows of the SSETF. As mentioned, in addition to the foregoing four requirements developed in *Cohn Ivers*, Some other federal appeals courts have required the existence of a common business enterprise as a requirement for classifying an interest as a security – SSETFs units do not meet this requirement because the sole purpose of their existence is not a "business enterprise" but determining the market value of the SSETF and for allocating portions of the SSETFs cashflows. In addition to the foregoing four requirements developed in *Cohn Ivers*, some federal appeals courts have required the existence of a *common business enterprise* as a requirement for classifying an interest as a security – SSETFs do not meet this requirement because the sole purpose of their existence is not "*business enterprise*" but tracking financial indices (and indirectly, the underlying stocks, bonds, commodities or currencies). SSETFs constitute *gambling* and *bets* because: i) the underlying companies (who are indirectly tracked with swaps/derivatives) don't receive any investment from the SSETF; and ii) the underlying swaps/derivatives are affected by Market Noise and are bets on the directions of financial indices, market-segments and financial markets.

The following are arguments against SSETFs being securities. Clearly, SSETF interests are not evidence of a share in the SSETF's assets (mostly cash and swaps/derivatives), but rather, are contract-rights that give the holder the right to a share of the SSETF's cashflow as determined by the SSETF's manager and corporate documents. The SSETFs do not evidence any share, participation or other interest in property or in an enterprise – rather, SSETF holders have only a "right" to dividends and cashflow from the SSETF. Clearly, SSETFs are not issued in bearer form. Some SSETFs are commonly traded on securities exchanges.

As mentioned, *Colt v. Fradkin*[100] declined to follow *Cohn Ivers*, and sought to distinguish situations where: a) the holder of an option makes a contract to sell the option, and b) the owner or prospective owner of a security makes a contract to sell it at the option of a buyer. However, both situations are the same – if the option in the former is a general intangible, then the process of formation of the option (described in the latter) will also result in the same general intangible. In both situations, the underlying instrument represents a right created by contract. Note that the call options discussed in *Cohn Ivers* and in *Colt* were exchange-traded options (typically issued by exchanges), were not used to finance companies, did not represent title or equity, and were not instruments for the payment of money (because they were executory agreements that were contingent on conditions) and thus, are very similar to SSETFs, which are not used to finance companies and are used for standard risk-management and to gain "exposure" to sectors. "*Performance*" in SSETFs' Declarations of Trust and C-corporation bylaws differ from performance in exchange-traded call option agreements.

The rulings in *Cohn Ivers* and *Colt* were partially erroneous with regard to the nature and purposes of stock options.

5.7.4 SSETFs are not securities: the US federal appellate and US district court securities law perspective

From a US securities law perspective (at the US Courts of Appeals and US District Courts), SSETFs are not securities.[101] 15 USC Section 78c(a)(10) (US securities laws) provides a definition of a security – and ESOARS don't comply with the requirements for classification as securities, which are described in *Board of Trade of City of Chicago*, 677 F2d 1137 (1982), for the following reasons. SSETFs constitute *gambling* and *bets* because: i) the underlying companies (who are indirectly tracked with swaps/derivatives) don't receive any investment from the SSETF; and ii) the underlying swaps/derivatives are significantly affected by *Market Noise* and are essentially bets on the directions of financial indices, market-segments and financial markets. SSETFs are not "investments" per say, but are intangibles that arise from contracts (and investors are essentially speculating and don't have an "investment" purpose of gaining from an operating company's business operations). Profits accrue to SSETFs-holders only from the changes in values of the underlying swaps/derivatives (in the SSETF) which are subject to *Market Noise*. In the case of SSETFs that invest in stock indices or bond indices, the holder of the SSETFs units does not directly assume risk of bankruptcy of the underlying companies. There is no *"Vertical Common Enterprise"* at creation of the SSETF – the sponsor/creator of the SSETF may not gain while the SSETF-units appreciate in value (or while the SSETF-holder uses it to successfully hedge its positions). The viability of the SSETF (for its creator/sponsor and investors) depends on compliance with tax laws, and the two main purposes of the SSETF-unit are to establish the market values of the SSETF (to serve as a "tracking instrument" for values of the underlying swap/derivative) and to serve as a basis for distribution of the SSETF's cashflows (and not to conduct operating business). The gains and losses from owning SSETF-units are not proportional to the SSETF-holder's contribution to the SSETF (SSETFs gains depend on market fluctuations; estimated values of the underlying swaps/derivatives; the timing of exercises of those swaps/derivatives; taxes; the SSETF's cash position and declaration of dividends).

5.7.5 SSETFs are not securities: the US Supreme Court's perspective

From the US Supreme Court perspective, SSETFs are also not securities for the following reasons. *First*, the transactions, and structure of SSETFs don't satisfy at least three of the four *original "Howey Tests"* under *SEC vs. Howey*, 328 U.S. 293 (1946), for the following reasons:

i)   For many SSETFs unit-holders, there is no or minimal *"expectation of profit"* because the SSETF is too speculative and constitutes Gambling – SSETFs contain relatively volatile swaps/derivatives that are subject to Market Noise. SSETFs holders have almost no verifiable intentional influence (or have difficult-to-verify influence) on the price dynamics of Swaps/derivatives in SSETFs process; and they usually cannot avoid *Market Noise* and fluctuations which determine both SSETFs pricing and liquidity. SSETFs constitute *Gambling* and *bets* because: i) the underlying companies (who are indirectly tracked with swaps/derivatives) don't receive any investment from the SSETF; and ii) the underlying swaps/derivatives are affected by Market Noise and are bets on the directions of financial indices, market-segments and financial markets. Most SSETFs are a "second-order derivative" or a "derivative" of a "derivative" (wherein the "underlying instrument" is the original right-to-receive cash/dividends of the SSETF; and the "first derivative" is the underlying swaps/derivatives and the "second derivative" is the SSETFs). That doesn't create "*Reference Dependence*" (Anchoring) because: 1) SSETFs-holders focused on, or were very likely to have focused on factors other than the underlying derivatives/swaps (which are opaque and their details are not disclosed) such as general stock market trends; exchange-traded stock options; macroeconomic trends; the issuer-company's news releases; changes in regulation; etc.; 2) SSETFs-holders had almost no control over the patterns of exercise of the underlying swaps/derivatives; and 3) it was very difficult for the average SSETFs-holder to predict when the SSETF manager would exercise the underlying swaps/derivatives. Just as in *United Housing v. Forman*, 421 U.S. 837, 852–53 (1975), the SSETFs unit purchased by the investors entitled them to proceeds of exercises/payments of the underlying swaps/derivatives in the SSETF. The investors had a desire to use or consume the item (SSETFs) purchased – by their purchase. SSETFs benefits to SSETFs-holders are in the form of money receivable in the future and merely referred to the benefits as SSETFs while actually the benefit was not any kind of security at all – see *Foltz vs. US News*, 627 F. Supp. 1143 (D.DC.; 1986). *Bauman v. Bish*, 571 F. Supp. 1054, 1064 (N.D.W.Va.1983) held that an interest in an Employee Stock Ownership Plan ("ESOP") were not securities.

ii) For the SSETFs Units purchased by the investors, the "*investment*" test was not satisfied because their participation in the SSETFs made the SSETFs Units similar to membership interests in mutual cooperative/insurance companies.[102] A purchase of a SSETF unit does not involve any "*investment of money*" in an operating business as defined by the courts and as intended by the US legislature.

iii) There is no *Vertical Commonality*[103] – the individual success of the SSETF investors does not correlate with the success of sponsor/originator of the SSETF – partly because of the SSETF management fees, fund administration costs, fund marketing costs, and the timing of purchases, maturities, exercises and rollovers of swaps/futures/options in the SSETF (the SSETF manager can incur losses even when SSETF investors make profits). Each SSETF-investor's return-on-investment from the SSETFs Units partly depends on: 1) the price at which each SSETF-holder purchased his/her SSETFs unit; and 2) the timing of the exercise of, and or payments from the underlying swaps/derivatives; 3) changes in purchases and maturity dates of the underlying swaps/derivatives in the SSETF; 4) market fluctuations; 5) the trends in the associated repo-market for the subject class/type of SSETF (including the nature/wealth/solvency of the primary-dealers and institutional investors who were party to such repo transactions). There is no "*Horizontal Commonality*" because: i) the "SSETF Contract" includes fees/loads (and not just only the SSETF), and a SSETF investor's returns can differ from those of other investors in the same SSETF investors depending on the sales channel through which he/she purchased the SSETF unit, and hence the applicable fees/Loads; and 2) the SSETF is created simply to track indices and baskets-of-securities (and indirectly, the underlying stocks, bonds, commodities or currencies) using swaps/derivatives.

iv)   The SSETFs are highly speculative and do not result in "*profits from the conduct of business*" in the traditional and legal sense of commerce as defined by the US Supreme Court (SSETFs are investment vehicles and not operating businesses) – the only positive results are indirect benefits which arise solely from changes Market Volatility and in the perceived/actual values of the underlying swaps/derivatives in the SSETFs, and not from a company's business operations.

v)   The "*efforts of others*" requirement is not satisfied because SSETF units can be purchased by the SSETF's managers, sponsors and employees, and by the managers/employees of the underlying companies whose stocks or bonds are indirectly being tracked by the SSETFs. In the line of US Supreme Court cases that addressed the definition of securities, in most instances, the terms "*profits*", "*Common Enterprise*" and "*conduct of business*" explicitly referred to the management of operating companies (and not Investment Vehicles).

vi)   The SSETFs is a *contingent* legal status – that is contingent on specific compliance with statutes and conditions.

vii) In *SEC vs. Howey*, there were forty-two purchasers of the same type of alleged financial instrument, whereas in the case of SSETFs, groups of investors purchased at different prices.

Gordon (2011) discussed some relevant issues. Thus, SSETFs are not Investment Contracts. Investment contracts[104] are defined in section 2(1) of the 1933 Securities Act, 15 U.S.C. § 77b(1), and section 3(a)(10) of the Exchange Act, 15 U.S.C. § 78c(a)(10). In *Securities and Exchange Commission vs. W. J. Howey Co.*,[105] the Court established the main criteria for classification of a property as an investment contract: "the test is whether the scheme involves an investment of money in a common enterprise with profits to come solely from the efforts of others".

Second, in *Marine Bank vs. Weaver*[106] and *International Brotherhood of Teamsters vs. Daniel*,[107] the US Supreme Court introduced the fifth and sixth "*Howey Tests*" which were the following: i) whether there is an alternative regulatory scheme that makes it un-necessary to apply federal securities law and US SEC jurisdiction; and ii) that "*for an instrument to be a security, the investor must risk loss*". In this instance, there are the common-law, UCC, insurance law and arbitration frameworks within which claims such as fraud can be asserted. With regards to the "risk-of-loss", this context differs from the contexts in both case US Supreme Court cases and from what the US Supreme Court reasonably intended because purchasing the SSETF units is not direct investment in any operating business.

Third, the SSETFs are not securities and the US SEC doesn't have any jurisdiction because in *Marine Bank vs. Weaver*, the US Supreme Court also introduced the "*common trading*" criteria for classifying financial instruments as securities. However, in the case of SSETFs, this additional test was not satisfied because although the SSETFs are traded on public exchanges, the SSETFs don't have equivalent values to most holders (differences in purchase prices, fees; and the value and timing of maturities, purchases and exercises of the underlying swaps/derivatives).

Fourth, the SSETFs were loans (or the equivalent of Certificates of Deposit – see: *Marine Bank vs. Weaver*) that were not securities because of the following reasons and because the *Howey Tests* are not satisfied (and thus, the US SEC does not have any jurisdiction):

i) The SSETFs have *quasi-mandatory redemption features* (mandatory payment of proceeds of the underlying swaps/derivatives), which made it more like contingent debt (or an equity-linked Certificate-of-Deposit).

ii) The SSETFs are very similar to, and have the same payoff-features as: 1) an equity-linked loan with contingent principal repayments that depends on the amount and timing of exercises of the underlying swaps/derivatives, and is settled with cash; and 2) "phantom Stock".

Fifth, SSETFs don't meet all four *Reeves*[108] *Tests*. SSETFs are speculative; an investment in a SSETF is not an investment in a business enterprise; people don't expect SSETFs to be securities because they are "synthetic" (constructed with only cash and swaps/derivatives); and there are alternative risk-reducing regulatory regimes such as common-law, Commodities statutes and debtor-creditor statutes.

Sixth, apart from the *Howey Tests*, the *Reeves Tests* and the *Marine Bank Criteria*, US Supreme Court cases have also looked at other criteria such as the marketing and the "Plan of Distribution" for the financial instruments and the "Economic Incentives" offered to "prospective investors" – all of which indicate that SSETFs are not securities. In the USA, the purchase and ownership of a SSETF unit incurs different fees such as the following:

i) Front-end Load (fee paid by investor when buying the unit) and or Back-end Load (fee paid when selling the unit) which can vary according to the distribution channel. Some ETFs don't charge any Loads.

ii) Exchange fees (for swapping ETF units).

iii) Purchase fee.

iv) Legal expenses, custodial expenses, record keeping, accounting expenses, transfer agent expense and other administrative expenses.

Thus, there is no *Horizontal Commonality* or *Vertical Commonality* (the SSETF sponsor or manager may incur a loss even when the SSETF is performing well). Each purchase of an SSETF unit is a "unique" contract (among, the sponsor, the SSETF and the investor) whose explicit and implicit terms include: i) the above mentioned fees which for any fund, can vary across investors; ii) applicable taxes which can vary across investors; iii) front-running and arbitrage of SSETFs; and iv) bid-ask spreads when selling the SSETF unit; v) trading rules and usage-of-trade; vi) associated *Multiplier Effects*.

5.8 CDS are not securities: a critique of Kirk (2015)

The US$8 trillion global CDS markets have been troubled for a long time.[109] Nwogugu (2019d) explained the many problems inherent in CDS, and the European Union has banned CDS contracts on sovereign Financial Instruments (most of which are ARS). Under the various theories and US Court cases stated above, CDS are not securities because:

i) For many CDS holders, there is no or minimal *"expectation of profit"* because the CDS is too speculative and constitutes Gambling: i) the underlying companies don't receive any investment from the CDS transaction; and ii) CDS represents a bet on credit quality; iii) he CDS do not result in *"profits from the conduct of business"* in the traditional and legal sense of commerce as defined by the US Supreme Court (CDS are quasi-insurance contracts and not operating businesses and are exposed to Market Noise) – the only positive results are indirect benefits which arise solely from changes Market Volatility and in the perceived/actual credit quality, and not from a company's business operations. There have been many reports and government investigations of manipulation of CDS markets and "Strategic Defaults" by underlying companies on whose debts CDS were written. Just as in *United Housing v. Forman*, 421 U.S. 837, 852–53 (1975), the CDS entitled the holder to proceeds of exercises/payments of the CDS.

ii) The *Howey* *"investment"* test was not satisfied because a purchase of CDS does not involve any *"investment of money"* in an operating business as defined by the courts and as intended by the US legislature.

iii) There is no *Vertical Commonality*[110] because the individual success of the CDS-buyer does not correlate with the success of CDS-seller. There is no *"Horizontal Commonality"* because although the CDS contracts are standardized, the CDS are not issued as a class, but rather are individual transactions usually between two parties.

iv) The *"efforts of others"* requirement is not satisfied because CDS can be purchased by the subject/underlying company and its managers and employees; and or by employees/shareholders of the CDS-seller.

v) CDS are not traded on public exchanges (they are traded only in OTC markets) – thus there isn't any *"common trading"*.

vi)   There are the common-law and arbitration frameworks within which claims
      such as fraud can be asserted; and so the *Fifth Howey Requirement* is not
      met. With regards to the "risk-of-loss", this CDS context substantially dif-
      fers from the contexts in both US Supreme Court cases (*Marine Bank* and
      International Brotherhood of Teamsters vs. Daniel) and from what the US
      Supreme Court reasonably intended because purchasing a CDS-contract is
      not a direct investment in the underlying operating company and thus the
      Sixth Howey Requirement is not met.
vii) There are alternative risk-reducing regulatory regimes such as insurance
      law, commodities statutes and debtor-creditor statutes.
viii) CDS don't meet all of the four *Reeves*[111] *Tests* because: 1) CDS are specula-
      tive (no reasonable expectation of profit); 2) a purchase of a CDS contract
      is not an investment in a "business enterprise", and the underlying com-
      pany doesn't get any money from the CDS transaction; 3) people don't
      expect CDS to be securities because of their structure and because they
      are traded only in the OTC market (and not on public exchanges); and
      4) there are alternative risk-reducing regulatory regimes such as insurance
      law, commodities statutes and debtor-creditor statutes.

The arguments by Kirk (2015) that CDS are securities under the *Investment Advisers Act of 1940* (henceforth, "IAA"; a US statute) are wrong for the following
reasons:

1) It is reasonably inferable that the IAA relies on the *1933 Act* and the *1934 Act* for
    the definition of "securities"; and that the *1933 Act* and *1934 Act* were expressly
    incorporated into IAA by reference (see Section 202(a)(3; 4; 7; 11; 21;27) of
    IAA), and they dominate/supersede the IAA on the issue of the definition of
    "securities". The scope of the IAA is much narrower than those of the *1933 Act*
    and the *1934 Act*. Thus, the Kirk (2015) heavy reliance on the IAA is wrong partly
    because the IAA (and its purported definition of "securities") expressly exempts:
    i) investment advisers whose clients all reside in the same state as the adviser's
    business office; ii) investment advisers who do not provide advice on securities
    that are listed on national exchanges (CDS are not listed on national exchanges);
    iii) investment advisers whose clients are insurance companies (many insurance
    companies purchase or sell CDS contracts); and iv) investment advisers who
    manage only private funds that own less than US$100 million obtained from
    US investors; v) any broker or dealer "whose performance of such [advisory]
    services is solely incidental to the conduct of his business as a broker or dealer
    and who receives no special compensation thereof"; vi) Banks, publishers, and
    advisers on financial instruments issued by government agencies.
2) The Kirk (2015) argument that by inserting the term "security-based swap"
    into the 1933 Act and the 1934 Act, the US Congress brought CDS under
    their regulatory regimes, is wrong. First, CDS and options don't involve any
    "swap" (exchange of payments or securities) in the traditional sense used

in financial terminology and in ISDA and ICMA standard agreements. The CDS is more like an option contract or insurance contract, wherein one party makes payment only if some "credit event" occurs. Thus, contrary to Kirk (2015: 242), the Dodd Frank Act[112] was wrong to have classified options (puts, calls, straddles) and CDS as swaps; and IAA (Section 202[a][18]) was wrong to have classified all options/straddle as securities. Many persons have argued that CDS are insurance contracts,[113] and for many years until about 2010, the Attorney General of New York state argued in many documents that CDS are insurance contracts. Second, in many cases, CDS contracts are written on bank loans (which are not "securities"). Third, as explained above, ARS are not securities and associated CDS are not securities (the European Union has banned CDS contracts on sovereign debt, most of which are ARS). Cox, Hillman and Langevoort (2009: 86–87) noted that swaps are not securities (with regards to registration and reporting requirements), but speculated that CDS may later be re-defined as securities.

3) Section 202(a)(29), of IAA states that " *'swap', 'swap dealer, and 'swap exe-cution facility' have the same meanings as in section-1a of the Commodity Exchange Act (7 U.S.C. 1a)"*.

4) Kirk (2015) admits that by enacting the Dodd Frank Act, "*Congress did not amend the Investment Advisers Act of 1940 ('Advisers Act') to include the term 'security-based swap,' nor did it similarly amend the Investment Com-pany Act of 1940"*; and that "*The term 'credit default swap' does not appear in the definition of 'security' under the Advisers Act"*; and that "*the term 'swap' does not appear in the Advisers Act's definition of 'security,' despite its inclusion in the Securities Act and the Exchange Act"*. Kirk (2015) admits that "*Congress chose not to insert 'security-based swap' in section 202(a) (18) of the Advisers Act, nor did it insert the term in section 2(a)(36) of the Investment Company Act of 1940"*.

5) The entire Kirk (2015) argument is based on two theories both of which are wrong and which are as follows: "*Accordingly, there are two theories rooted in the text of section 202(a)(18) which support defining certain CDSs as 'securities'. First, CDSs are the equivalent of an option, and are thus cov-ered by the options language of the statute. Alternatively, CDSs are evidences of indebtedness.*" First, *Board of Trade of City of Chicago v. SEC*, 677 F2d 1137 (1982) *cert. denied* 459 US 1026 (a US Supreme court case), ruled that GNMA options are not securities, and a CDS contract is very similar to a GNMA option contract. The US Second Circuit's ruling in *Caiola*[114] (that options on underlying securities are themselves securities) applies only to options that are listed on public exchanges (and not to OTC options). Thus, even if CDS are put options,[115] CDS are not listed on public exchanges, and thus are not securities. *Board of Trade of City of Chicago* is the controlling case and not *Caiola*. Second, under the definitions of debt stated earlier, a CDS is not evidence of any indebtedness because it is more like an option, and the CDS-writer is obliged to make a payment if and only if a specified

"credit event" occurs. Third, by alluding to CDS as either an option or debt, Kirk (2015) contradicts its prior assertion that CDS are "swaps". Thus, there is no evidence that US Congress believes that security-based CDSs are the equivalent of security-based options.

6) Hu (2018) argued for new regulations for CDS.

5.9 Evidence, and theories of sustainable growth, corporate governance, enterprise-risk and managerial psychology

The International Constitutional Political Economy, Corporate Governance and regulatory problems inherent in Mutual Funds, ARS, Structured Products, CDS, SSETFs and TARP/CPP Instruments are, or can be reasonably construed as evidence of the following:

i) The *Dynamic Coordination-Gaps Theory* – which refers to: 1) *Intra/Inter jurisdictional Coordination-Gaps* in enforcement of laws/statutes, which often increases enforcement and monitoring costs; and 2) *Coordination-Gaps* (strategy; compliance; incentives; policies; execution; human capital) among BODs, executive management teams, shareholders and regulators of the company; and or among Strategic-Alliance/JV partners.

ii) The *Sub-optimally Exercised Time-Varying Asymmetric Power Theory* – Sub-optimally Exercised Time-Varying Asymmetric Power among shareholders, BODs and executive management teams; and or among strategic-alliance/JV partners. Such Asymmetric Power is not necessarily bad (and can increase Social Welfare), but when it is exercised in sub-optimal ways or for meaningless purposes, it can reduce Social Welfare.

iii) The *Sub-optimal Investment Theory* – sub-optimal investment (cash; human capital; technology; etc.) in both corporate governance structures, Strategic Planning and competitive intelligence which eventually causes non-random repeating patterns of poor strategic decisions; and weakens incentive systems and compliance by employees. Such sub-optimal investment is typically not properly identified or effectively resolved by management and the BOD; and or there are communication gaps and inadequate execution directives between the BOD and management. Note that there is a difference between "*sub-optimal investment*" and "*inadequate investment*".

iv) Complex "*higher-order behaviors*" by BODs and executives, which degrade existing Corporate Governance statutes and measures. Bernard (1926b) distinguished between "Primary" and "Derivative" Attitudes and Ideals. Bernard (1936) analyzed conflicts between "Primary Group Attitudes" and "Derivative Group Ideals". "Hullian Theory" in psychology also distinguishes between "direct" and "derivative" human (individual and group) behaviors. Deck and Schlesinger (2014); Noussair, Trautmann and Kuilen (2013) and other articles have analyzed a few higher-order risk preferences.

v) *Incentive Mechanisms (e.g. Structured Products, SSETFs, ARS and Mutual Funds) and Statutes as Non-Public Goods (that may be created, diminished or amplified by Political Influence and Lobbying)* – the "use-value" and potency of Corporate Governance statutes ad mechanisms seem to, or can decline as more persons/companies use such statutes and mechanisms; and or when there is increasing complexity of the Strategy-spaces of many of the users of such statute/mechanism. Thus, Corporate Governance statutes (such as SOX) and mechanisms (such as Mutual Funds, SSETFs, Structured Products and ARS) are or can be *Non-Public Goods*. Similarly, the legality and potency of the announced or un-announced strategies or "mechanisms" or Strategic Alliances of large/medium companies (or groups of similar small companies) can decline as more persons/companies are subjected/exposed to such strategies, alliances and or mechanisms; and or when there is increasing complexity of the Strategy-spaces of many of such companies' customers and or suppliers. Thus, the strategies, mechanisms, Strategic Alliances and internal Corporate Governance principles of large multinational companies (or groups of similar small/medium companies) are or can be *Non-Public Goods*.

vi) The *Enforcement Leakages Theory* (enforcement deficiencies that may be caused or amplified by Political Influence And Lobbying) – such leakages occur when: 1) statutes don't require that regulators take preemptive or investigative action to forestall misconduct and or reduction of Social welfare; and or when existing statutes don't reduce or increase enforcement costs; 2) the enforcement statutes and or regulations distort the relationships among the firm and its external advisors and auditors.

vii) *Deadweight Losses* in the pricing, demand and supply of prosecutorial/ enforcement litigation (which may be caused or amplified by *Political Influence* and or *Lobbying*). Hines (1999) and Lind and Granqvist (2010) discussed Deadweight Losses.

viii) *Deadweight Losses* in the trading of the financial instruments.

ix) The *Selective Compliance Strategies Theory* – Among managers of some exchange-traded companies, there is generally low concern for compliance with, and low concern for Social Welfare issues that arise from regulations that don't require frequent reporting/filing; and the effect of quarterly financial reporting remains a dominant factor in both the operations, strategies and financial reporting of some exchange traded companies.

x) Compliance is or can be tempered by Aspirations and Career-Concerns.

xi) *Adverse Regulatory Entrenchment Theory* – there can be adverse effects of *Regulatory Entrenchment* – wherein the combination of a government agency's (e.g. US SEC's) rule-making, investigatory and enforcement powers (which is a delegation of the constitutionally mandated responsibilities of the US Congress) is a dominant factor in a market (e.g. the stock-market); often conflicts with the activities of similar government agencies (e.g. State securities regulatory agencies); can distort the market; provides opportunities for inefficient exercise of such powers, and is not appropriately reviewed by the legislature (e.g. the US Congress). All of these can increase Systemic Risk and Financial Instability.

xii) *Selective Enforcement* – of regulations/statutes by government regulatory agencies. That can be the result of deliberate government policies (as in China), bribery or political lobbying or Corporate Influence (i.e. the extensive influence and or Social Capital of multinational corporations or companies that are deemed critical for national security).

xiii) *Regulatory Capture* – wherein: 1) corporate lobbying is successful to the detriment of Social Welfare; 2) companies and their legal and or accounting advisors figure out ways to circumvent, denigrate, dampen or take advantage of regulations/statutes and or to influence regulators (in most cases to the detriment of social welfare).

xiv) *Regulatory Fragmentation* – wherein several government agencies directly/ indirectly and simultaneously regulate the same financial instruments and financial markets (in some countries, both at the state government and federal government levels) and: 1) laws/regulations that are intended to achieve the same or similar objectives are codified in different statutes that in some cases, may or often conflict; and or 2) enforcement efforts in both the public and private sectors are diffused; and or 3) government regulatory agencies have overlapping functions and or jurisdictions.

xv) *Regulatory Failures* (that may be caused or amplified by Political Influence and Lobbying) – the failures of the following statutes/regulations:

1) The *Sarbanes-Oxley Act* of 2002 (USA) and the *China SOX* (The *Basic Standard for Enterprise Internal Control*; caikuai [2008] No. 7, "Basic Standard") – these regulations should include more stringent accounting requirements, minimum corporate governance standards and greater civil penalties and monetary fines for non-compliance with accounting and or internal control rules.

2) *The Chinese CSRC's and the US SEC's regulations* – which should require more stringent monitoring of compliance with accounting regulations. The rule-making, enforcement and adjudicative functions of these regulatory agencies constitute violations of the Separation-of-Power principle Constitutional law.

3) *The regulation of credit rating agencies* (CRAs) – effective CRA regulations should eliminate all types of collusion; require mandatory ratings of all exchange-traded companies and some private companies (whose sales revenues exceed a specific amount) by at least four licensed credit rating agencies; and should provide adequate independence of CRAs in order to ensure objectivity and impartiality in credit rating.

4) The *Dodd-Frank Act* of 2010 (USA) and the US FSOC's "*Non-bank SIFI Criteria*" – efficient regulation would have required the early identification of a broader group of troubled and or non-compliant

companies (companies that don't comply with accounting and corporate governance standards but whose operations affect more than two million people/customers).

5) *Goodwill/Intangibles accounting regulations (IFRS/IASB)* – these should require mandatory write-downs of impaired intangibles; mandatory and post-acquisition classification of goodwill and other intangibles as identifiable intangibles; that goodwill should not exceed a specific percentage of a company's intangible assets; and government evaluation of companies whose intangible assets exceed a specific amount or a specific percentage of their total assets.

6) *US and Chinese securities laws* – which should require more stringent monitoring of compliance with accounting regulations; promote international coordination in enforcement and should make audit work-papers available to securities enforcement agencies of other countries.

7) *Auditor Liability-Allocation* mechanisms/rules in the US, China and other countries – which should be codified and allocate more liability to external auditors, the boards of directors and executives of auditee-companies.

8) *Auditor Work-Allocation* mechanisms/rules in the US, China and other countries – which should be codified and should reduce collusion and anti-competitive misconduct in the accounting/auditing and environmental auditing sectors.

9) *Chinese and US Bankruptcy laws* – which don't require preemptive intervention for most types of private and exchange-traded companies and medium and large companies whose operations affect many people and other companies.

Nwogugu (2015a), Nwogugu (2015b), Nwogugu (2015c); Nwogugu (2015d); Nwogugu (2010/2013); Papaikonomou (2010) and Nwogugu (2008) discussed these statutes and regulations. Young (Feb. 21, 2013) noted that the annual cost of regulations imposed by various US federal government agencies could be classified into various groups. Note that a portion of the above-mentioned regulatory costs can be attributed to *Regulatory Takings*. Nwogugu (2012) analyzed *Takings* theory and introduced new types of *Takings*. The factors that often discourage or preclude firms from filing lawsuits to challenge such *Takings* include but are not limited to the following: 1) fear of retaliation by regulators, and imposition of additional costly regulations; 2) lack of an organized industry-wide effort to curb Regulatory Takings; 3) perceived costs of litigation including the opportunity costs – on customers; stock prices; suppliers, employees; etc.; 4) the perceived influence of the Executive Branch of the US government on the judiciary (some federal judges were selected from, or had worked in the Executive Branch of the US federal government.

5.10 Conclusion

The implications of the foregoing are that: i) some of these financial instruments and processes promote earnings management, incentive-effects management and asset-quality management; and need to be significantly reformed and new legislation enacted; ii) new and more effective international corporate governance standards are required and should be incorporated into national accounting and securities statutes; iii) IFRS accounting standards have to be improved and made mandatory in all countries and the cross-border regulatory coordination and the enforcement of securities laws should be increased; iv) governments should implement internationally coordinated and tougher antitax-evasion statutes and enforcement methods; v) the cost and socio-economic and psychological impacts of regulations are a major factor that determines the extent, duration and evolution of compliance; vi) market microstructure analysis (of ARS, Structured Products, SSETFs and Mutual Funds) and the *optimal design of financial contracts* (i.e. the design of securities and debt contracts) cannot be done effectively or accurately unless issues such as "legal classification", earnings management and asset-quality management effects, costs and Industrial Organization effects of these financial instruments are first analyzed.

Notes

1 Law and Versteeg (2012) noted that the US Constitution is similar to those of many countries including the following countries: Albania, Armenia, Australia, Austria, Azerbaijan, Belgium, Bosnia and Herzegovina, Bulgaria, Canada, Croatia, the Czech Republic, Denmark, the Dominican Republic, El Salvador, Estonia, Fiji, Finland, France, Georgia, Germany, Greece, Honduras, Hungary, Iceland, Ireland, Italy, Japan, Jordan, Kazakhstan, Korea, Latvia, Lithuania, Luxembourg, Macedonia, Moldova, Mongolia, the Netherlands, the New Zealand, Nicaragua, Norway, the Philippines, Poland, Portugal, Romania, Singapore, the Slovak Republic, Slovenia, Spain, Sweden, Switzerland, Thailand, Tonga, Turkey, Ukraine, and the United kingdom; Antigua and Barbuda, Bahamas, Bahrain, Bangladesh, Barbados, Belize, Botswana, Brunei, Cyprus, Dominica, Gambia, Ghana, Grenada, Guyana, India, Israel, Jamaica, Kenya, Kiribati, Lesotho, Liberia, Malawi, Malaysia, Maldives, the Marshall Islands, the Federated States of Micronesia, Namibia, Nepal, Nigeria, Pakistan, Papua New Guinea, American Samoa, Saudi Arabia, Sierra Leone, the Solomon Islands, Somalia, South Africa, Sri Lanka, St. Kitts and Nevis, St. Lucia, St. Vincent and the Grenadines, Sudan, Swaziland, Tanzania, Trinidad and Tobago, Uganda, the United Arab Emirates, the United Kingdom, Vanuatu, Zambia and Zimbabwe.
2 *See*: Wantchinatimes.com (2015). *Liaoning Sees China's First Failed Local Bond Auction in Four Years*. Staff Reporter 2015–08–11 14:14 (GMT+8). www.wantchinatimes.com/news/content?id=20150811000047&cid=1203.
3 *See*: US Government Printing Office (September 18, 2008). *Auction Rate Securities Market: A Review of Problems and Potential Resolutions*. Hearing Before Committee on Financial Services, US House of Representatives, Washington, DC.
4 *See*: Chang, G. (June 16, 2013). Bad Omens in China: Banks default, debt auctions fail. *Forbes*. www.forbes.com/sites/gordonchang/2013/06/16/bad-omens-in-china-banks-default-debt-auctions-fail/.

5 *See*: Pillai, S., Li, L. & Huang, H. (2015) (Goldman Sachs Asset Management) (2015). *FAQ: China's Bond Market*. www.goldmansachs.com/gsam/glm/insights/market-insights/china-bond-market/china-bond-market.pdf.

6 *See*: Dugan, K. (June 9, 2015). *Justice Department Probes Banks for Rigging Treasury Market*. www.marketwatch.com/story/justice-department-probes-banks-for-rigging-treasury-market-2015-06-09.

   See: Moyer, L. (November 7, 2006). *Fed To Banks: Halt Bond Fraud*. www.forbes.com/forbes/welcome/.

7 *See*: US Government Accountability Office (2016). *Troubled Asset Relief Program: Capital Purchase Program Largely Has Wound Down*. www.gao.gov/assets/680/676954.pdf. This article states in part: "Most of the remaining CPP institutions have continued to exhibit signs of financial weakness. Specifically, nine of the sixteen institutions had negative returns on average assets (a common measure of profitability) in 2015. Also, six institutions had a lower return on assets in 2015 than they did at the end of 2011. Treasury officials stated that the remaining CPP firms generally had weaker capital levels and worse asset quality than firms that had exited the program. Also, nearly all the firms that are required to pay dividends have continued to miss payments. Treasury expects most remaining CPP institutions to exit through restructurings but has not set time frames for winding down the program. Over the past six years, repayment of Treasury's investment and Treasury's auction of CPP securities to interested investors were the primary means by which institutions exited CPP. Restructurings – the expected exit method for the remaining firms – allow institutions to negotiate terms for their investments and require institutions to raise new capital or merge with another institution. With this option, Treasury agrees to receive cash or other securities, typically at a discount. Treasury officials expect to rely primarily on restructurings because the overall financial condition of the remaining institutions makes full repayment unlikely."

8 *See*: *The Vast Majority f All Futures Trading Is Now Automated*. By Brian Merchant. April 26, 2019. https://www.gizmodo.com.au/2019/04/the-vast-majority-of-all-futures-trading-is-now-automated/.

   See: *80% of the Stock Market Is Now on Autopilot*. By Yun Li. June 29, 2019. https://www.cnbc.com/2019/06/28/80percent-of-the-stock-market-is-now-on-autopilot.html.

   See: *Robots Are Killing Off Wall Street's Traders*. By Laura French. October 29, 2014. https://www.worldfinance.com/markets/technology/robots-are-killing-off-wall-streets-traders.

   See: *Cracking The Street's New Math, Algorithmic Trades Are Sweeping the Stock Market*. http://www.businessweek.com/magazine/content/05_16/b3929113_mz020.htm.

   See: *The Future of Algorithmic Trading*. https://www.experfy.com/blog/the-future-of-algorithmic-trading.

   See: *The Growth and Future of Algorithmic Trading*. July 19, 2018. https://blog.quantinsti.com/growth-future-algorithmic-trading/.

   See: *Algorithmic Trading a "Prerequisite" for Surviving Tomorrow's Markets – With Technology, Data Sciences and Automated Trading Beginning to Play a Big Role, This Skill Is Fast Becoming a Prerequisite*. By Nitesh Khandelwal. Updated at February 17, 2019. https://www.business-standard.com/article/pf/algorithmic-trading-a-prerequisite-for-surviving-tomorrow-s-markets-119021601197_1.html.

   See: *The Quickening Evolution of Trading – in Charts: Automated Algorithms Are on the Rise, with High-Frequency Trading Volumes Picking Up*. By Robin Wigglesworth, April 11, 2017. https://www.ft.com/content/77827a4c-1dfc-11e7-a454-ab04428977f9.

   See: *"How Important Is Algorithmic Trading in the Retail Market? The Computerization of the Financial Markets Industry Began as Far Back as the Early 1970s and Program Trading Became Widely. . . ."* https://financefeeds.com/important-algorithmic-trading-retail-market/.

See: *Agent-Human Interactions in the Continuous Double Auction.* IBM T.J. Watson Research Center, August 2001. http://spider.sci.brooklyn.cuny.edu/~parsons/courses/840-spring-2005/notes/das.pdf.

See: *How to Build Robust Algorithmic Trading Strategies.* AlgorithmicTrading.net. https://algorithmictrading.net/project/robust-algorithmic-trading-strategies/.

See: Gjerstad and Dickhaut (January 1998); Technical Committee of the International Organization of Securities Commissions (July 2011); Shen and Yu (2014) and Shen (2017).

9 *See*: Financial Accounting Standards Board (November 2007). *Preliminary Views – Financial Instruments with Characteristics of Equity.*

See: FASB Statement No. 84, *Induced Conversions of Convertible Debt.*

See: FASB Statement No. 123 (revised 2004), *Share-Based Payment.*

See: FASB Statement No. 133, *Accounting for Derivative Instruments and Hedging Activities.*

See: FASB Statement No. 150, *Accounting for Certain Financial Instruments with Characteristics of both Liabilities and Equity.*

See: FASB Statement No. 155, *Accounting for Certain Hybrid Financial Instruments.*

See: APB Opinion No. 14, *Accounting for Convertible Debt and Debt Issued with Stock Purchase Warrants.*

See: APB Opinion No. 21, *Interest on Receivables and Payables.*

See: APB Opinion No. 26, Early Extinguishment of Debt.

See: AICPA Accounting Interpretation 1, —Debt Tendered to Exercise Warrants,‖ of Opinion 26

See: FSP FAS 150–1, *Issuer's Accounting for Freestanding Financial Instruments Composed of More Than One Option or Forward Contract Embodying Obligations under FASB Statement No. 150.*

See: FSP FAS 150–2, *Accounting for Mandatorily Redeemable Shares Requiring Redemption by Payment of an Amount That Differs from the Book Value of Those Shares under FASB Statement No. 150.*

See: FSP FAS 150–3, *Effective Date, Disclosures, and Transition for Mandatorily Redeemable Financial Instruments of Certain Nonpublic Entities and Certain Mandatorily Redeemable Non-controlling Interests under FASB Statement No. 150.*

See: FSP FAS 150–4, Issuers' *Accounting for Employee Stock Ownership Plans under FASB Statement No. 150.*

See: FSP FAS 150–5, *Issuer's Accounting under FASB Statement No. 150 for Free-standing Warrants and Other Similar Instruments on Shares That Are Redeemable.*

See: FSP EITF 00–19–2, *Accounting for Registration Payment Arrangements.*

See: EITF Issue No. 90–19, —Convertible Bonds with Issuer Option to Settle for Cash upon Conversion.

See: EITF Issue No. 96–19, —Debtor's Accounting for a Modification or Exchange of Debt Instruments.

See: EITF Issue No. 98–5, —Accounting for Convertible Securities with Beneficial Conversion Features or Contingently Adjustable Conversion Ratios.

See: EITF Issue No. 99–1, —Accounting for Debt Convertible into the Stock of a Consolidated Subsidiary.

See: EITF Issue No. 99–7, —Accounting for an Accelerated Share Repurchase Program.

See: EITF Issue No. 00–4, —Majority Owner's Accounting for a Transaction in the Shares of a Consolidated Subsidiary and a Derivative Indexed to the Minority Interest in That Subsidiary.

See: EITF Issue No. 00–6, —Accounting for Freestanding Derivative Financial Instruments Indexed to, and Potentially Settled in, the Stock of a Consolidated Subsidiary.

See: EITF Issue No. 00–19, —Accounting for Derivative Financial Instruments Indexed to, and Potentially Settled in, a Company's Own Stock.

See: EITF Issue No. 00–27, —Application of Issue No. 98–5 to Certain Convertible Instruments.

See: EITF Issue No. 01–6, —The Meaning of _Indexed to a Company's Own Stock.

See: EITF Issue No. 03–7, —Accounting for the Settlement of the Equity-Settled Portion of a Convertible Debt Instrument That Permits or Requires the Conversion Spread to Be Settled in Stock (Instrument C of Issue No. 90–19).

See: EITF Issue No. 05–1, —Accounting for the Conversion of an Instrument That Becomes Convertible upon the Issuer's Exercise of a Call Option.

See: EITF Issue No. 05–2, —The Meaning of _Conventional Convertible Debt Instrument' in Issue No. 00–19.

See: EITF Issue No. 06–6, —Debtor's Accounting for a Modification (or Exchange) of Convertible Debt Instruments.

See: EITF Issue No. 06–7, —Issuer's Accounting for a Previously Bifurcated Conversion Option in a Convertible Debt Instrument When the Conversion Option No Longer Meets the Bifurcation Criteria in FASB Statement No. 133.

See: ASR No. 268, *Presentation in Financial Statements of "Redeemable Preferred Stocks,"* and EITF Topic No. D-98, —Classification and Measurement of Redeemable Securities.

10 *See*: *Montclair Inc. v. Commissioner Of Internal Revenue*, 318 F2d 38 (CA5, 1963).

See: *Estate of Mixon v. US*, 464 F2d 394 (CA5, 1972).

See: J S Biritz Construction Co. v. Commissioner, 387 F2d 451 (CA8, 1967).

See: *Fin Hay Realty Co. v. US*, 398 F2d 694 (CA3, 1968).

See: *Trans Atlantic Co. v. Commissioner*, 469 F2d 1189 (CA3, 1972).

See: *In RE Autostyle Plastics Inc.*, 269 F3d 726 (CA6, 2000).

See: *In Re Hillsborough Holdings Corp.*, 176 BR 223 (MDFL, 1994).

See: *Meridian*, 132 F2d at 186 (___).

See: *Hubert Enterprises*, 125 TC No. 6 at 38.

See: *TIFD III-E*, 342 FSupp2d at 116 (_____).

See: *EPIC Associates*, 81 TCM at 1363.

Contrast: *Hubert Enterprises*, 125 TC No. 6 at 35, *quoting Stinnett's Pontiac Serv. Inc. v. Commissioner*, 730 F2d 634 (CA11, 1984).

See: *Indmar Products Co., Inc.*, 444 F3d 771 (6th Cir. 2006), rev'g TC Memo 2005–32.

See: *Roth Steel Tube Co.*, 800 F2d 625 (CA6, 1986).

See: *Gloucester Ice & Cold Storage Co.*, 298 F2d 183 (1st Cir. 1962).

See: *Estate of Travis Mixon*, 464 F2d 394 (5th Cir. 1972).

See: *Scriptomatic, Inc.*, 555 F2d 364 (3d Cir. 1977) (subordination).

See: *Alexander Jones*, 659 F2d 618 (5th Cir. 1981) (subordination).

See: *Alexander Jones*, 659 F2d 618 (5th Cir. 1981) (subordination).

See: *Universal Racquetball Rockville Centre Corp.*, TC Memo 1986–363.

See: *Midland Distributors, Inc.*, 481 F2d 730 (5th Cir. 1973) (subordination factor has been considered 'unimportant' when there are no other substantial creditors).

See: *Rudolph Hardman*, 827 F2d 1409 (9th Cir. 1987).

See: *Joseph Nachman*, TC Memo 1996–288.

See: *J.S. Biritz Construction Co.*, 387 F2d 451 (8th Cir. 1967).

See: *Donna Woolley v. Commissioner*, 61 TCM (CCH) 2225 (1991).

See: *Crawford Drug Stores v. US*, 220 F2d 292 (CA10, 1955).

See: Dantzler (Jan. 2006).

See: Magennis, Watts and Wright (1998); Hopkins (1996); Whittington and Whittenburg (1980); Brighton (2002); Ryan, Herz, et al. (2001); Burke (2006); and Burilovich (December 2006).

11 State common law cases include: *Prendergast v. Northern Virginia Regional Park Authority*, 227 Va. 190, 313 S.E.2d 399 (1984)(statute created implied contract). *Nelson County v. Loving*, 126 Va. 283, 299–300, 101 S.E. 406, 411 (1919)(statute created implied contract). *Nelson County v. Coleman*, 126 Va. 275, 279, 101 S.E. 413, 414 (1919). *Richmeade LP v. City of Richmond*, #031513, April 23, 2004 (Lacy J.; Circuit Court of Richmond). *J B Klein Iron & Foundry Co. v. Board Of County Comissioners Of Canadian County*, 61 P2d 1055 (1936). *US v. Great Falls Mfg. Co.*, 112 US 645. *US v. Lynah*, 188 US 445. *Great Falls Mfg. Co. v. Attorney General*, 124 US 581.

12 US Federal Circuit Court common law cases on classification of debt and equity include the following: *Gloucester Ice & Cold Storage Co.*, 298 F2d 183 (1st Cir. 1962). *Estate of Travis Mixon*, 464 F2d 394 (5th Cir. 1972). *Scriptomatic, Inc.*, 555 F2d 364 (3d Cir. 1977) (subordination). *Alexander Jones*, 659 F2d 618 (5th Cir. 1981)(subordination). *Midland Distributors, Inc.*, 481 F2d 730 (5th Cir. 1973) (subordination factor has been considered "unimportant" when there are no other substantial creditors). *Rudolph Hardman*, 827 F2d 1409 (9th Cir. 1987). *J.S. Biritz Construction Co.*, 387 F2d 451 (8th Cir. 1967). *Donna Woolley v. Commissioner*, 61 TCM (CCH) 2225 (1991).

See: R.A. Hardman, 827 F.2d 1409, 87–2 USTC ¶ 9523 (9th Cir. 1987) (listing 11 criteria for classification of instruments).

See: *Bauer v. Commissioner*, 748 F.2d 1365, 1367 (9th Cir. 1984).

See: *Smith v. Commissioner*, 370 F.2d 178, 180 (6th Cir. 1966).

See *Estate of Mixon v. United States*, 464 F.2d 394, 402–03 (5th Cir. 1972).

See: J & W Fence Supply Co. v. United States, 230 F.3d 896, 898 (2000). *Comdisco, Inc. v. United States*, 756 F.2d 569, 578 (7th Cir. 1985); *Sullivan v. United States*, 618 F.2d 1001, 1006–08 (3d Cir. 1980); *Sun Oil Co. v. Commissioner*, 562 F.2d 248 (3d Cir. 1977) (*cert. denied*) 436 U.S. 944 (1978); *Commissioner v. Danielson*, 378 F.2d 771, 775 (3d Cir. 1967); *Balthrope v. Commissioner*, 356 F.2d 28 (5th Cir. 1966); *Annabelle Candy Co. v. Commissioner*, 314 F.2d 1 (9th Cir. 1962); *Ullman v. Commissioner*, 264 F.2d 305 (2d Cir. 1959). With regard to substantive consolidation, see: *Reider v. FDIC* (In re Reider), 31 F.3d 1102, 1106–07 (11th Cir. 1994); *In Re Giller*, 962 F.2d 796, 798 (8th Cir. 1992); *Eastgroup Properties v. Southern Motel Assoc.*, 935 F.2d 245 (11th Cir. 1991); *In re Augie/Restivo Banking Co.*, 860 F.2d 515, 518 (2d Cir. 1988); *In re Auto-Train Corp.*, 810 F.2d 270 (D.C. Cir. 1987); *FMC Fin. Corp. v. Murphree*, 632 F.2d 413 (5th Cir. 1980); *Chemical Bank N.Y. Trust Co. v. Kheel*, 369 F.2d 845, 847 (2d Cir. 1966); *Anaconda Bldg. Materials Co. v. Newland*, 336 F.2d 624 (9th Cir. 1964). On classification of lease transactions as financings or loans, also see: *In re Fabricators, Inc.*, 924 F. 2d 1458, 1469 (5th Cir. 1991)); *Shawmut Bank Connecticut v. First Fidelity Bank* (In re Secured Equip. Trust of Eastern Air Lines, Inc.), 38 F.3d 86, 87 (2d Cir. 1994). The issue of preemption of state laws in the determination of whether a lease is a financing or a loan, is somewhat un-settled – *MNC Commercial Corp. v. Joseph T. Ryerson & Son, Inc.*, 882 F.2d 615, 619 (2d Cir. 1989); *Morton v. National Bank*, 866 F.2d 561, 563 (2d Cir. 1989); *In Re Harris Pine Mills*, 79 B.R. 919 (D. Or. 1987)(*affirmed*), 862 F.2d 217 (9th Cir. 1988); *International Trade Admin. v. Rensselaer Polytechnic Inst.*, 936 F.2d 744 (2d Cir. 1991)(federal law); *In re Moreggia & Sons, Inc.*, 852 F.2d 1179 (9th Cir. 1988)(federal law); *In Re PCH Assocs.*, 804 F.2d 193 (2d Cir. 1986).

13 US Bankruptcy Court cases on classification of instruments as debt or equity include: *In Re Hillsborough Holdings Corp.*, 176 BR 223 (MDFL, 1994). With regard to substantive consolidation, see: *Reider vs. FDIC* (In re Reider), 31 F.3d 1102, 1106–07 (11th Cir. 1994); *Central Claims Services vs. Eagle-Richer Indus. (In Re Eagle-Richer Indus.)*, 192 B.R. 903, 905–06 (Bankr. S.D. Ohio 1996); *In Re Standard Brand Paint Co.*, 154 B.R. 563 (Bankr. C.D. Cal. 1993); *In Re Crown Mach. & Welding, Inc.*, 100 B.R. 24 (Bankr. D. Mont. 1989); *In re DRW Property Co.*, 54 B.R. 489 (Bankr. N.D. Tex. 1985); *In re Snider Bros.*, 18 B.R. 230 (Bankr. D. Mass 1982); *In re Vecco Constr. Indus., Inc.*, 4 B.R. 407 (Bankr. E.D. Va. 1980). On classification of lease transactions

as financings or loans, also see: *Shawmut Bank Connecticut vs. First Fidelity Bank (In re Secured Equip. Trust of Eastern Air Lines, Inc.)*, 38 F.3d 86, 87 (2d Cir. 1994); *In re Best Products Co.*, 157 B.R. 222, 229–30, (Bankr. S.D.N.Y. 1993); *In re Wilcox*, 201 B.R. 334, 336–37 (Bankr. N.D.N.Y. 1996). The issue of preemption of state laws in the determination of whether a lease is a financing or a loan, is somewhat un-settled – see: *In Re Challa*, 186 B.R. 750, 755–756 (Bankr. M.D. Fla. 1995); *In Re Q-Masters, Inc.*, 135 B.R. 157, 159 (Bankr. S.D. Fla. 1991); *In Re Rosenshein*, 136 B.R. 368, 372 (Bankr. S.D.N.Y. 1992); *In Re Taylor*, 130 B.R. 849 (Bankr. E.D. Ark. 1991); *In Re Wingspread Corp.*, 116 B.R. 915 (Bankr. S.D.N.Y. 1990) (under state law, debtors' leases were financing agreements, and not true leases); *In Re Century Brass Prods., Inc.*, 95 B.R. 277, 279 (Bankr. C.D. Conn. 1989); *In Re Petroleum Products, Inc.*, 72 B.R. 739 (Bankr. D. Kan. 1987)(*affirmed*) 150 B.R. 270 (B.A.P. D. Kan. 1993); *In Re Harris Pine Mills*, 79 B.R. 919 (D. Or. 1987)(*affirmed*), 862 F.2d 217 (9th Cir. 1988); *City of Olathe vs. KAR Dev. Assocs. (In re KAR Dev. Assocs., L.P.)*, 180 B.R. 629, 637 (Bankr. D. Kan. 1995)(federal law preempts). *Barney's, Inc. vs. Isetan Co.*, 206 B.R. 328, 352 (Bankr. S.D.N.Y. 1997); *Hotel Syracuse, Inc. vs. City of Syracuse Indus. Dev. Agency*, 155 B.R. 824 (Bankr. N.D.N.Y. 1993); *In Re Tak Broad. Corp.*, 137 B.R. 728 (W.D. Wis. 1992); *In Re Starr*, 113 B.R. 481 (Bankr. S.D. Ill. 1990); *In Re MCorp Fin. Inc.*, 122 B.R. 49 (Bankr. S.D. Tex. 1990).

14 US Internal Revenue Service (IRS) and tax court cases on classification of debt and equity include the following: *Hubert Enterprises*, 125 TC No. 6 at 38. *TIFD III-E*, 342 F. Supp. 2d at 116 (____). *EPIC Associates*, 81 TCM at 1363. *Stinnett's Pontiac Serv. Inc. v. Commissioner*, 730 F.2d 634 (CA11, 1984). *Indmar Products Co., Inc.*, 444 F.3d 771 (6th Cir. 2006), *rev'g* TC Memo 2005–32. *Universal Racquetball Rockville Centre Corp.*, TC Memo 1986–363. *Joseph Nachman*, TC Memo 1996–288. *Donna Woolley v. Commissioner*, 61 TCM (CCH) 2225 (1991).
See: IRS Notice #94–47, 1994–1 CB 357 (listing eight factors but noting that no particular factor is conclusive and that the weight given any factor depends on all the facts and circumstances).
See: IRS Revenue Ruling #85–119, 1985–2 CB 60; Section 385(b)(1)–(5).
See: *R.A. Hardman*, 827 F.2d 1409, 87–2 USTC ¶ 9523 (9th Cir. 1987) (listing eleven criteria for classification of instruments).
See: R.W. Lease, TCM 1993–493 (listing thirteen criteria to be considered when classifying debt, equity or hybrids).
See: IRS Revenue Ruling #68–54, 1968–1 CB 69 (January 1, 1968) (listing eight factors to be considered when classifying debt or equity).
Some courts have used a fact-based approach and the "economic realities test" – see: *Lazisky*, 72 T.C. at 500–02; *Rich Hill Ins. Agency*, 58 T.C. at 617–19; *Transamerica Corp. v. United States*, 7 Cl. Ct. 441 (1985); *Torez v. Commissioner*, 88 T.C. 702, 721–27 (1987) (sale/leaseback); *Estate of Thomas v. Commissioner*, 84 T.C. 412, 436 (sale leaseback); Rev. Rul. 55–540, 1955–2 C.B. 39 (classification of a lease); Rev. Rul. 68–590, 1968–2 C.B. 66; Rev. Rul. 72–543, 1972–2 C.B. 87. See: US Treasury Regulation § 1.1245–1(a)(3) (as amended in 1997); Tech. Adv. Mem. 93–07–002 (Oct. 5, 1992); Tech. Adv. Mem. 93–38–002 (Sept. 24, 1993); *Illinois Power Co. v. Commissioner*, 87 T.C. 1417 (1986); *Grodt & McKay Realty, Inc. v. Commissioner*, 77 T.C. 1221 (1981); *Bolger v. Commissioner*, 59 T.C. 760, 767 n.4 (1973); *Bowen v. Commissioner*, 12 T.C. 446, 459 (1949); Rev. Rul. 55–540, 1955–2 C.B. 39. Some courts emphasize the intention of the parties – see: *Major v. Commissioner*, 76 T.C. 239, 246 (1981); *Lazisky v. Commissioner*, 72 T.C. 495, 500–02 (1979); *G.C. Servs. Corp. v. Commissioner*, 73 T.C. 406 (1979); *Lucas v. Commissioner*, 58 T.C. 1022, 1032 (1972); *Rich Hill Ins. Agency v. Commissioner*, 58 T.C. 610, 617–19 (1972). Rev. Rul. 83–98, 1983–2 C.B. 40; Revenue Ruling 85 119, 1985–2 C.B. 60; Revenue Ruling 68–54, 1968–1 C.B. 69; I.R.S. Notice 94–47, 1994–1 C.B. 357; Treas. Reg. § 301.7701–4(c).

15 *See*: *United Savings Assn. of Texas v. Timbers of Inwood Forest Associates*, Ltd., 484 U.S. 365, 370 -371 (1988) (refusing to treat "right to immediate foreclosure" as an "interest in property" under applicable non-bankruptcy law).

    Compare: *Gelfert vs. National City Bank of N.Y.*, 313 U.S., at 234 (____) ("The advantages of a forced sale" are not "a . . . property right" under the Constitution).

    See: *BFP vs. Resolution Trust Corp.*, ___ U.S. ___ (1994:14).

    See: *McDonald vs. Thompson*, 184 US 71 (1902).

    See: *Matteson vs. Dent*, 176 US 521. Carol v. Green, 92 US 509.

    See: *US vs. Great Falls Mfg. Co.*, 112 US 645.

    See: *US vs. Lynah*, 188 US 445.

    See: *Great Falls Mfg. Co. vs. Attorney General*, 124 US 581.

    See: *Commissioner vs. Duberstein*, 363 U.S. 278, 80 S.Ct. 1190, 4 L.Ed.2d 1218.

    Some courts have used a fact-based approach and the "economic realities test" – see: *Frank Lyon Co. vs. United States*, 435 U.S. 561, 572–73 (1978); *Helvering v. F. & R. Lazarus & Co.*, 308 U.S. 242 (1939); *Gregory vs. Helvering*, 293 U.S. 465 (1935); *Sun Oil Co. vs. Commissioner*, 562 F.2d 248 (3d Cir. 1977), *cert. denied*, 436 U.S. 944 (1978).

    With regard to *Substantive Consolidation*, see: *Consolidated Rock Prods. Co. vs. DuBois*, 31 U.S. 510 (1940); *BFP vs. Resolution Trust Corp.*, 511 U.S. 531 (1994)); *Barnhill vs. Johnson*, 503 U.S. 393 (1992); *Butner vs. United States*, 440 U.S. 48, 55 (1979).

16 The FASB rules on classification of instruments as debt or equity include the following:

    See: Financial Accounting Standards Board (November 2007). *Preliminary Views – Financial Instruments With Characteristics of Equity*.

    See: FASB Statement No. 84, *Induced Conversions of Convertible Debt*.

    See: FASB Statement No. 133, *Accounting for Derivative Instruments and Hedging Activities*.

    See: FASB Statement No. 150, *Accounting for Certain Financial Instruments with Characteristics of both Liabilities and Equity*.

    See: FASB Statement No. 155, *Accounting for Certain Hybrid Financial Instruments*.

    See: APB Opinion No. 14, *Accounting for Convertible Debt and Debt Issued with Stock Purchase Warrants*.

    See: AICPA Accounting Interpretation 1, —Debt Tendered to Exercise Warrants, of Opinion 26

    See: FSP FAS 150–1, *Issuer's Accounting for Freestanding Financial Instruments Composed of More Than One Option or Forward Contract Embodying Obligations under FASB Statement No. 150*.

    See: FSP FAS 150–2, *Accounting for Mandatorily Redeemable Shares Requiring Redemption by Payment of an Amount That Differs From the Book Value of Those Shares under FASB Statement No. 150*.

    See: FSP FAS 150–3, *Effective Date, Disclosures, and Transition for Mandatorily Redeemable Financial Instruments of Certain Nonpublic Entities and Certain Mandatorily Redeemable Non-controlling Interests under FASB Statement No. 150*.

    See: FSP FAS 150–5, *Issuer's Accounting under FASB Statement No. 150 for Freestanding Warrants and Other Similar Instruments on Shares That Are Redeemable*.

    See: EITF Issue No. 96–19, —Debtor's Accounting for a Modification or Exchange of Debt Instruments.

    See: EITF Issue No. 98–5 —Accounting for Convertible Securities with Beneficial Conversion Features or Contingently Adjustable Conversion Ratios.

    See: EITF Issue No. 00–27, —Application of Issue No. 98–5 to Certain Convertible Instruments.

    See: EITF Issue No. 05–1, —Accounting for the Conversion of an Instrument That Becomes Convertible upon the Issuer's Exercise of a Call Option.

    See: EITF Issue No. 05–2, —The Meaning of Conventional Convertible Debt Instrument' in Issue No. 00–19.

See: EITF Issue No. 06–6, —Debtor's Accounting for a Modification (or Exchange) of Convertible Debt Instruments.

See: EITF Issue No. 06–7, —Issuer's Accounting for a Previously Bifurcated Conversion Option in a Convertible Debt Instrument When the Conversion Option No Longer Meets the Bifurcation Criteria in FASB Statement No. 133.

See: ASR No. 268, *Presentation in Financial Statements of "Redeemable Preferred Stocks,"* and EITF Topic No. D-98, —Classification and Measurement of Redeemable Securities.

17 *See*: Estate Of Mixon, 464 F.2d 394 (US Ct. App. 5th Cir.).

See: Notice 94–47, 1994–1 CB 357 (listing 8 factors but noting that no particular factor is conclusive and that the weight given any factor depends on all the facts and circumstances);

See: Rev. Rul. 85–119, 1985–2 CB 60; Section 385(b)(1)-(5);

See: R.A. Hardman, 827 F.2d 1409, 87–2 USTC ¶ 9523 (9th Cir. 1987) (listing 11 criteria for classification of instruments);

See: R.W. Lease, TCM 1993–493 (listing 13 criteria to be considered);

See: Rev. Rul. 68–54, 1968–1 CB 69 (January 1, 1968) (listing 8 factors).

See: William T. Plumb, Jr., "The Federal Income Tax Significance of Corporate Debt: A Critical Analysis and a Proposal," 26 Tax L. Rev. 369 (1971) (seminal work discussing debt analysis).

See: Peaslee J & Nirenberg D (2001). *Federal Income Taxation of Securitization Transactions* (rev.ed. 2001) chs. 1–4 (providing an in-depth discussion of tax issues in asset-backed securitizations, including debt-equity characterization).

Non-tax administrative law cases on classification of instruments as debt or equity include:

Prendergast v. Northern Virginia Regional Park Authority, 227 Va. 190, 313 S.E.2d 399 (1984)(statute created implied contract). *Nelson County v. Loving*, 126 Va. 283, 299–300, 101 S.E. 406, 411 (1919)(statute created implied contract). *Nelson County v. Coleman*, 126 Va. 275, 279, 101 S.E. 413, 414 (1919). *Burns v. Bd. of Supervisors*, 218 Va. 625, 627, 238 S.E.2d 823, 825 (1977). See: *McDonald v. Thompson*, 184 US 71 (1902). *Matteson v. Dent*, 176 US 521. *Carol v. Green*, 92 US 509. *Richmeade LP v. City of Richmond*, #031513, April 23, 2004 (Lacy J.; Circuit Court of Richmond). *J B Klein Iron & Foundry Co. v. Board Of County Comissioners Of Canadian County*, 61 P2d 1055 (1936). *US v. Great Falls Mfg. Co.*, 112 US 645. *US v. Lynah*, 188 US 445. *Great Falls Mfg. Co. v. Attorney General*, 124 US 581.

18 *See*: www.icpas.org/hc-tax.aspx?id=2620.

See: Hubert Enter., Inc. & Subsidiaries v. Comm'r, 125 T.C. 72, 91 (2005).

19 *See*: *SEC vs. Life Partners*, 87 F3d 536 (CADC, 1996).

See: *First Financial Federal vs. E F Hutton Mortgage Corporation*, 834 F2d 685 (CA8, 1987).

See: *Revak vs. SEC Realty Corp.*, 18 F3d 81 (CA2, 1994).

See: *Banco Espanol De Credito vs. Security Pacific National Bank*, 973 F2d 51 (*cert. Den.*) 509 US 903.

See: *Perez-Rubio vs. Wyckoff*, 718 Fsupp 217 (1989).

See: *Developer's Mortgage Co. vs. Transohio Savings Bank*, 706 FSupp. 570 (1989).

See: *Matell vs. Maturat*, 862 F2d 720 (CA9, 1988).

See: *Giuffre Organization vs. Euromotor Sport Racing*, 141 F3d 1216 (CA7, 1998).

See: *Klaers v. St Peter*, 942 F2d 535 (CA8, 1991).

See: *Peeves vs. Teuscher*, 881 F2d 1495 (CA9, 1989).

See: *SEC vs. ETS Payphone*, 408 F3d 727 (CA11, 2005).

20 Hu and Morley (2018: 868; Footnote-91) stated in part: "Section-1 of the *Commodity Exchange Act* defines the word 'commodity' to include any good or article. 7 U.S.C. §1(a)(9) (2012). Note that although futures contracts on equity securities tend to be

defined as securities, rather than commodities, futures contracts on indexes of equity securities are commodities. Section 2(a)(1) of the Securities Act of 1933, for example, defines the term 'security' to include a future on a security but not a future on an index of securities. 15 U.S.C. §77b(a)(1) (2012)".

21 *See: In re J.P. Jeanneret Assocs.*, Inc., 769 F.Supp.2d 340, 360 (S.D.N.Y.2011); *Walther vs. Maricopa Intern. Inv. Corp.*, No. 97-cv-4816, 1998 WL 186736, at *7 (S.D.N.Y. Apr. 17, 1998); *Kaplan vs. Shapiro*, 655 F.Supp. 336, 341 (S.D.N.Y. 1987); *Lowenbraun vs. L.F. Rothschild, Unterberg, Towbin*, 685 F.Supp. 336, 341 (S.D.N.Y. 1988); *Savino vs. E.F. Hutton & Co., Inc.*, 507 F.Supp. 1225, 1238 (S.D.N.Y.1981); *SEC vs. Glenn W. Turner Enterprises, Inc.*, 474 F.2d 476 (9th Cir.1973); and *Brodt v. Bache & Co.*, 595 F.2d 459, 461 (9th Cir.1978).

22 Law and Versteeg (2012) noted that the US Constitution is similar to those of many countries.

23 *See*: US SEC (June 2018). *Exchange-Traded Funds, Securities Act Release No. 33–1051583, Fed. Reg. 37,332* (proposed July 31, 2018) (to be codified at 17 C.F.R. pts. 239, 270, 274). www.sec.gov/rules/proposed/2018/33-10515.pdf.

  See: Charles Schwab & Co., Inc. (August 17, 2015). *Comment Letter on Exchange-Traded Products*. www.sec.gov/comments/s7-11-15/s71115-28.pdf.

  See: Direxion Shares ETF Trust. (February 28, 2018). *Statement of Additional Information.* http://direxioninvestments.onlineprospectus.net/DirexionInvestments//DFEN/index.html?open=Statement%20of%20Additional%20Information.

  See: BlackRock, Inc. (August 11, 2015). Comment on exchange-traded products, release No.75165; File No. S7–11–15 at 12–13, 27; Ex.5. www.blackrock.com/corporate/en-at/literature/publication/sec-request-for-comment-exchange-traded-products-081115.pdf.

24 *See*: www.hsgac.senate.gov/imo/media/doc/Levin-Feinstein%20Comment%20Ltr%20to%20CFTC%20re%20Rule%204%205%20registration%20exemption%20(Nov%2030%202011).pdf

25 But see: *Reves v. Ernst & Young*, 494 U.S. 56, 61 (1990) (noting that "Congress' purpose in enacting the securities laws was to regulate investments, in whatever form they are made and by whatever name they are called").

26 Hu and Morley (2018: 868) stated in part "Note that although many funds regulated by the Investment company Act (ICA) (of 1940) are technically also subject to the 1933 Act and the Securities Exchange Act of 1934 ("1934 Act"), the ICA largely supplants the requirements of these two other statutes, mandating its own distinct forms of disclosure . . . Because a Commodity Pool ETF invests in commodity futures, rather than securities, its main regulatory statute is not the Investment company Act (of 1940), but the Commodity Exchange Act."

27 *See*: Katten Muchin Rosenman LLP. (September 2016). *Canada Proposes Commodity Pool Regulation Update.* www.lexology.com/library/detail.aspx?g=425d4564-2846-48f6-a4f7-7f22dfc4bbf0. This article stated in part "The Canadian Securities Administrators proposed amendments to existing rules that would move most of the existing Canadian regulatory framework related to commodity pools from a distinct regulation for CPOs to one applicable to all investment funds".

28 *See* the cases cited in Section 5.2.1. above.

29 *See*: Guinn and Harvey (42:1140–1141), *supra*.

30 *See: SEC Vs. Life Partners*, 87 F3d 536 (CADC, 1996); *First Financial Federal vs. E F Hutton Mortgage Corporation*, 834 F2d 685 (CA8, 1987); *Revak vs. SEC Realty Corp.*, 18 F3d 81 (CA2, 1994); *Banco Espanol De Credito vs. Security Pacific National Bank*, 973 F2d 51 (*cert. Den.*) 509 US 903; *Perez-Rubio vs. Wyckoff*, 718 Fsupp 217 (1989); *Developer's Mortgage Co. vs. Transohio Savings Bank*, 706 Fsupp 570 (1989); *Matell vs. Maturat*, 862 F2d 720 (CA9, 1988); *Giuffre Organization vs. Euromotor Sport Racing*, 141

F3d 1216 (CA7, 1998); *Klaers v. St Peter*, 942 F2d 535 (CA8, 1991); *Peeves v. Teuscher*, 881 F2d 1495 (CA9, 1989); *SEC vs. ETS Payphone*, 408 F3d 727 (CA11, 2005).

31 *See: Hackal v. Adler*, 650 NYS2d 792 (1996, AD); *Kodogiannis v. Mumford*, 535 NYS2d 494; *Metropolitan Transportation Authority v. Bruken Realty*, 501 NYS2d 306.

32 *See: Cohn, Ivers & Co v. Gross* (289 NYS2d 301).
     See: *Board Of Trade of City of Chicago v. SEC*, 677 F2d 1137 (1982) *cert den.* 459 US 1026 (GNMA options are not securities).

33 *See: Colt v. Fradkin*, 281 NE2d 213, 217 (paragraph 2).
     See: Hahn, A. (February 24, 2003). Goldman's dangerous REIT game: Firm now defending unpopular strategy it helped devise. *The Investment Dealers' Digest*, 7–8.

34 *See: Kaplan v. Shapiro*, 655 Fsupp 336 (SDNY, 1987); *Caiola vs. Citibank NA*, 137 Fsupp2d 362 (SDNY, 2001); *Perez-Rubio v. Wyckoff*, 718 Fsupp 217 (SDNY, 1989); *Mount Lucas Associates Inc. vs. M G Refining & Marketing Inc*, 682 NYS2d 14 (NYAD 1st Dept, 1998); *Tab Partnership v. Grantland Financial Corporation*, 866 Fsupp 807 (SDNY, 1994); *Tanuggi vs. Grolier Inc*, 471 FSupp 1209 (SDNY, 1981); *SEC vs. Energy Group Of America Inc.*, 459 Fsupp 1234 (SDNY; 1978); *Revak vs. SEC Realty*, 18 F3d 81 (CA2, 1994); *In Re Turley*, 172 F3d 671 (CA9, 1999); *Messer vs. E F Hutton*, 842 F2d 673 (CA11, 1988); *In Re National Mortgage Equity Corporation Mortgage Pool Certificate Securities Litigation*, 723 Fsupp 697, (C.D.Cal., 1989) (under certain conditions, MBS certificates are not securities); *Dryden v. Sunlife Assurance Co Of Canada*, 737 Fsupp 1058 (S.D.Ind., 1989)(*affirmed*) 909 F2d 1486 (dividends were return of excess premium rather than share of company's investment profits*); Procter & Gamble vs. Bankers Trust*, 925 Fsupp 1270 (SD Ohio, 1996); *In Re Schauer*, 62 BR 526 (D.Minn. 1986) (*appeal decided*) 835 F2d 1222 (patronage dividends are not securities); *First Citizens Federal Savings & Loan Association vs. Worthen Bank & Trust*, 919 F2d 510 (CA9, 1990) (note not security); *First Financial Federal Savings & Loan vs. E F Hutton*, 834 F2d 685 (CA8, 1987); *In Re Autostyle Plastics*, 216 BR 784 (WD Mich. 1997) (*opinion Supplemented*) 222 BR 812 (affirmed) 1999 WL 1005647 (loan participation); *In Re Okura & Co.*, 249 BR 596 (SDNY, 2000); *Chase Manhattan Bank v. Keystone Distributors*, 873 Fsupp 808 (SDNY, 1994) (right to receive reimbursement); *Hibiscus Associates vs. City Of Detroit*, 50 F3d 908 (CA7)(implicit option and securities issues in conversion of construction loan into permanent loan).

35 *See: Reves vs. Ernst & Young*, 494 US 56 (1990); *Landreth Timber vs. Landreth*, 471 US 681 (1985); *United Housing Found. vs. Forman*, 421 US 837 (1975).

36 *See: Global Van Lines, Inc.*, SEC No-Action Letter (October 2, 1979).
     See: Medical Device Mutual Assurance and Reinsurance Co., Ltd., US SEC No-Action Letter (August 31, 1979).
     See: Norcal Bowling Proprietors Mutual Insurance Co., Ltd., US SEC No-Action Letter (December5, 1983).
     See: Podiatric Assurance Co., SEC No-Action Letter (February 19, 1985).
     See: Medmarc Insurance Company Risk Retention Group, US SEC No-Action Letter (October 2, 1987).
     See: National Transport Assurance Alliance, Inc., US SEC No-Action Letter (February 22, 1989).
     See: Construction Trade Purchasing Group, Inc. and Construction Trades Insurance Company, US SEC No-Action Letter (October 1, 1993).

37 Also see the following cases: *United States v. Jones*, 712 F.2d 1316 (9th Cir.), *cert. denied*, 464 U.S. 986 (1983); *Mordaunt v. Incomco*, 686 F.2d 815 (9th Cir.1982), *cert. denied*, 469 U.S. 1115 (1985); *United States vs. McConney*, 728 F.2d 1195, 1202 (9th Cir.) (en banc), *cert. denied*, 469 U.S. 824 (1984); *Goodman v. Epstein*, 582 F.2d 388, 407 (7th Cir.1978), *cert. denied*, 440 U.S. 939 (1979); *Securities and Exchange Commission v. Aqua-Sonic Products Corp.*, 687 F.2d 577 (CA2), *cert.*

denied, 459 U.S. 1086 (1982); *Warfield vs. Alaniz*, 569 F. 3d 1015 (CA9, 2009) (investment contract); *S.E.C. vs. Merck. Capital, LLC*, 483 F.3d 747, 760 (CA11; 2007); *Endico vs. Fonte*, 485 F. Supp. 2d 411 (SD New York, 2007); *Uselton vs. Comm. Lovelace Motor Freight, Inc.*, 940 F.2d 564, 574 (10th Cir. 1991) ("[T]he 'investment' may take the form of 'goods and services,' or some other 'exchange of value'."); *Marini vs. Adamo*, 812 F. Supp. 2d 243 (ED New York, 2011); *U.S. vs. Zaslavskiy*, 17-cr-0647 (U.S. District Court for the Eastern District of New York); SEC v. Shavers, No. 4:13-CV-416, 2014 WL 4652121, at *1 (E.D. Tex. Sept. 18, 2014) (an investment of Bitcoin, complies with the first *Howey* test); *United States vs. Leonard*, 529 F.3d 83, 88 (2d Cir.2008).

    See: US Securities and Exchange Commission (SEC) (2017). *Report of Investigation Pursuant to Section 21(a) of the Securities Exchange Act of 1934: The DAO.* Release No. 81207, July 25, 2017. www.sec.gov/litigation/investreport/34-81207.pdf.

    See: Nick Szabo, Smart Contracts, 1994, www.virtualschool.edu/mon/Economics/SmartContracts.html.

    See: US SEC (Apr. 5, 2017). *Regulation Crowdfunding: A Small Entity Compliance Guide for Issuers.* www.sec.gov/info/smallbus/secg/rccomplianceguide-051316.htm;

    See: US SEC (May 2017). *Updated Investor Bulletin: Crowdfunding for Investors.* www.sec.gov/oiea/investor-alerts-bulletins/ib_crowdfunding-.html.

38 *Securities & Exchange Commission vs. W. J. Howey Co.*, 328 US 293 (1946).

39 *Marine Bank vs. Weaver*, 455 U.S. 551 (1982) (an individually negotiated profit-sharing agreement that did not involve multiple investors was not securities).

40 *International Brotherhood of Teamsters v. Daniel*, 439 U.S. 551 (1979).

41 *Marine Bank vs. Weaver*, supra.

42 *See*: *Reeves vs. Ernst & Young*, 494 U.S. 56, 67 (1990) (interpreting the Exchange Act).

43 *See*: Bloomberg News (February 25, 2015). *China Money Rates Fall As PBOC Unexpectedly Offers Reverse Repos.* www.bloomberg.com/news/articles/2015-02-26/china-money-rates-fall-as-pboc-unexpectedly-offers-reverse-repos.

44 *See*: Kumar, S. (May 8, 2008). Merrill's Thain backs auction-rate securities. *The Wall Street Journal*, May 8, 2008.

45 *See*: Van Brunt, D. (April 1, 2019). *The Bond Cartel.* https://compliancex.com/the-bond-cartel/.

46 *See*: Armitstead, L. (July 28, 2011). *Eurozone Crisis Fears Continue as Italy Forced to Pay Higher Rates to Borrow. The Telegraph* (UK). www.telegraph.co.uk/finance/financialcrisis/8667986/Eurozone-crisis-fears-continue-as-Italy-forced-to-pay-higher-rates-to-borrow.html.

    See: A complete disaster: Sovereign bond auction fizzles in Germany. *Spiegel Online.* www.spiegel.de/international/germany/a-complete-disaster-sovereign-bond-auction-fizzles-in-germany-a-799550.html.

    See: Charlton, E. (December 1, 2011). French bond yields decline most in 20 years, Spanish debt rises on auction. *Bloomberg.* www.bloomberg.com/news/2011-12-01/german-10-year-bonds-fall-as-crisis-optimism-curbs-safety-demand.html.

    See: Eurozone debt web: Who owes what to whom? *BBC News.* November 18, 2011. www.bbc.co.uk/news/business-15748696.

47 *See*: Dugan, K. (June 9, 2015). *Justice Department Probes Banks for Rigging Treasury Market.* www.marketwatch.com/story/justice-department-probes-banks-for-rigging-treasury-market-2015-06-09.

    See: Moyer, L. (November 7, 2006). *Fed To Banks: Halt Bond Fraud.* www.forbes.com/forbes/welcome/.

    See: Rennison, J. (September 28, 2015). *Investor Lawsuits Pile Up Claiming US Treasury Market Is Rigged.* www.ft.com/cms/s/0/43f0b014-6218-11e5-9846-de406ccb37f2.html.

48 *See*: Shepherd Smith Edwards & Kantas LTD LLP (March 2, 2011). *Akamai Technologies Inc.'s ARS Lawsuit Against Deutsche Bank Can Proceed*. www.institutionalin vestorsecuritiesblog.com/2011/03/akamai_technologies_incs_ars_l.html.
    See: *Akamai Technologies, Inc. and Akamai Securities Corp. v. Deutsche Bank AG* (US District of Massachusetts).
49 *See*: UBS (2008/2012). *Auction Rate Securities – Summary of Settlement Terms*. www. ubs.com/us/en/wealth/misc/auction-rate-securities-summary-of-settlement-terms-.html.
    See: Summons and complaint; *Cuomo vs. UBS Securities LLC, et al.*, case 650262–2008, filed July 24, 2008, in the Supreme Court of New York (New York County), p. 3. www.oag.state.ny.us/press/2008/july/ UBS.pdf.
50 *See*: SEC Administrative Proceeding File No. 3–12310, *In the Matter of Bear, Stearns & Co. Inc., et al.* (cease-and-desist order, May 31, 2006), www.sec.gov/litiga tion/admin/2006/33-8684.pdf.
51 *See*: Complaint, *In the Matter of Merrill Lynch, Pierce, Fenner & Smith, Inc.*, case 2008–0058, filed July 31, 2008, at the Office of the Secretary of the Commonwealth [of Massachusetts] Securities Division. www.sec.state.ma.us/sct/sctml2/ml_com plaint.pdf.
52 *See*: Shepherd Smith Edwards & Kantas LTD LLP (November 11, 2010). *Citigroup Global Markets to Pay Back US$95.5 Million Over ARS Sold to LandAmerica Exchange Fund*. www.institutionalinvestorsecuritiesblog.com/2010/11/citigroup_global_markets_to_pa_1.html.
53 *See*: Shepherd Smith Edwards & Kantas LTD LLP (February 12, 2011). *Credit Suisse Broker Previously Convicted for Selling High Risk ARS Is Barred from Future Securities Law Violations*. www.institutionalinvestorsecuritiesblog.com/2011/02/credit_suisse_broker_previousl.html.
54 *See*: *FINRA Board to Address Allegations of Schapiro Misconduct* (February 2010). www.senseoncents.com/2010/02/finra-board-to-address-allegations-of-schapiro-misconduct/#more-15966
55 *See*: *Global Van Lines, Inc.*, SEC No-Action Letter (October 2, 1979); *Medical Device Mutual Assurance and Reinsurance Co., Ltd.*, SEC No-Action Letter (August 31, 1979); *Norcal Bowling Proprietors Mutual Insurance Co.*, Ltd., SEC No-Action Letter (December 5, 1983); *Podiatric Assurance Co.*, SEC No-Action Letter (February 19, 1985); *Medmarc Insurance Company Risk Retention Group*, SEC No-Action Letter (October 2, 1987); *National Transport Assurance Alliance, Inc.*, SEC No-Action Letter (February 22, 1989); *Construction Trade Purchasing Group, Inc. and Construction Trades Insurance Company*, SEC No-Action Letter (October 1, 1993).
56 Also see the cases cited in Section-5.4.7 above.
57 *Securities and Exchange Commission v. W. J. Howey Co.*, 328 US 293 (1946).
58 *Marine Bank vs. Weaver*, 455 U.S. 551 (1982) (an individually negotiated profit-sharing agreement that did not involve multiple investors was not securities).
59 *International Brotherhood of Teamsters v. Daniel*, 439 U.S. 551 (1979).
60 *Marine Bank vs. Weaver*, supra.
61 *See*: *Reeves vs. Ernst & Young*, 494 U.S. 56, 67 (1990) (interpreting the Exchange Act).
62 *See* the cases cited in section 5.4.6 above.
63 *See*: *Cohn, Ivers & Co v. Gross* (289 NYS2d 301).
    See: *Board Of Trade of City of Chicago v. SEC*, 677 F2d 1137 (1982) *cert den.* 459 US 1026 (GNMA options are not securities).
64 *See*: *Colt v. Fradkin*, 281 NE2d 213, 217 (paragraph 2).
    See: Hahn, A. (February 24, 2003). Goldman's Dangerous REIT Game: Firm now defending unpopular strategy It Helped Devise. *The Investment Dealers' Digest*, pp. 7–8.
65 Austin (2012) stated in part "The broker/dealer and issuer choose an auction agent, typically a bank, to run the auctions. Investors wishing to hold ARSs submit bids in the

form of interest rates along with the amount of assets they wish to buy. . . . If bidders' requests are insufficient to take up the whole issue then the auction fails. The interest rate is then set by terms specified by the securitization contract, and investors holding a portion of the issue retain their stake. Because investors lacked a guaranteed option to sell ARS holdings back to issuers or broker/dealers, liquidity for those securities essentially depended on the success of auctions. After auction failures, investors holding ARSs may receive attractive interest rates, but may be unable to sell those holdings except at a high discount on a thin secondary market. . . . ARS auctions are typically sealed-bid, first-price auctions with multiple units, although some ARS broker/dealers see investors' bids before submitting their own. . . . Numerous internal emails quoted in court documents strongly imply that broker/dealers effectively set prices for many auctions at risk of failing. . . . Some broker/dealers held ARS inventories, acquired by their own bids, and for some auctions could, within limits, set interest rates that would balance needs of issuers against those of investors. ARS brokers/dealers that could see external bids before submitting their own, like market makers, had an important informational advantage that could in some cases produce trading profits".

66 *See*: Willis (May 2008). *Son Of Subprime: Auction Rate Securities Crisis*. www.willis. com/documents/publications/industries/Financial_Institutions/FI_Alert_0508_Son_of_ Subprime.pdf. This article stated in part *"When the credit markets are free-moving, you get a buoyant $330+ billion marketplace flush with liquidity for these relatively conservative investments. When a severe credit crunch hits, and investors – particularly the large investment banks – decline to bid on the securities, you get a frozen marketplace, asset write-downs and investor unrest. And then, of course, you get regulatory inquiries and lawsuits. . . . On a single day in late February (2008), 386 auctions of publicly offered bonds resulted in 258 failures, or 67%, according to data compiled by Bloomberg from four auction agents. . . . The system as it has evolved does not really involve buyers and sellers meeting and setting the interest rate via a true bidding process. Instead, Wall Street brokerage firms dominate the process by bidding with their own capital rather than facilitating a marketplace of buyers and sellers. And so, when the brokerage firms' capital dried up, the whole process screeched to a halt. . . . "Auction securities became a managed bidding system, not a true investor auction," said Joseph S. Fichera, chief executive of Saber Partners, a financial advisory firm. "The investor never knew how many investors there were, how often the brokerage firms were stepping in to make the system work, nor that the broker's support could stop all of a sudden.". . . . . At the end of 2006, institutional investors held about eighty percent (80%) of all auction-rate securities issues, according to Treasury Strategies, a consulting firm in Chicago. At the end of 2007, that portion had fallen to just thirty-percent (30%)."*

67 *See*: http://saberpartners.com/oped/saber_letter_msrb.html; and http://saberpartners. com/press/articlepages/ARS_04_12_10.html.
    See: http://saberpartners.com/management/bio-fichera.html; and www.saberpart ners.com/ARS.

68 *See*: Popper, N. (April 18, 2013). "Wall St. Redux: Arcane Names Hiding Big Risk". *New York Times*.

69 *See*: Mucciolo, C. (July 16, 2008). *Structured Products: The Bright Future of Securitization? – Securitization Has Gotten a Bad Reputation Lately. Indeed, Given the Current Dismal State of the CDO Market, You'd Think That They Might Taint the Entire Derivative, Structured Product Marketplace*. www.wealthmanagement.com/ data-amp-tools/structured-products-bright-future-securitization.
    See: LexisNexis. (2018). *Resolving Structured Products And Securitizations Disputes – Key Cases*. www.lexisnexis.com/uk/lexispsl/bankingandfinance/ document/391290/5NFT-NGY1-F185-S386-00000-00/Resolving_structured_ products_and_securitisations_disputes_key_cases.

See: the website for Hogan Lovells (www.hoganlovells.com/en/aof/derivatives-and-structured-products).

70 *See*: Friewald, Jankowitsch and Subrahmanyam (2017).

71 *See*: S. 420, 107th Cong. 912 (2001; USA).
    See: H.R. 333, 107th Cong. 912 (2001; USA).

72 See the following US Court cases: *Fogie vs. Thorn*, 95 F3d 645 (CA8, 1996) (*cert. den.*) 520 U.S. 1166; *Pollice vs. National Tax Funding LP*, 225 F3d 379 (CA3, 2000); *Najarro vs. SASI Intern. Ltd*, 904 F2d 1002 (CA5, 1990) (*cert. denied*) 498 U.S. 1048; *Video Trax vs. Nationsbank NA*, 33 Fsupp2d 1041 (S.D.Fla., 1998) (*affirmed*) 205 F3d 1358(*cert. den.*) 531 U.S. 822; *In Re Tammy Jewels*, 116 BR 290 (M.D.Fla., 1990); *ECE technologies vs. Cherrington Corp.*, 168 F3d 201 (CA5, 1999); *Colony Creek Ltd. vs. RTC*, 941 F2d 1323 (CA5, 1991) (*rehearing denied*); *Sterling Property Management vs. Texas Commerce Bank*, 32 F3d 964 (CA5, 1994); *Pearcy Marine vs. Acadian Offshore Services*, 832 F supp 192 (S.D.TX, 1993); *In Re Venture Mortgage Fund LP*, 245 BR 460 (SDNY, 2000); *In Re Donnay*, 184 BR 767 (D.Minn, 1995); *Johnson vs. Telecash Inc.*, 82 FSupp2d 264 (D. Del., 1999) (*reversed in part*) 225 F2d 366 (*cert. denied*) 531 US 1145; *Shelton vs. Mutual Savings & Loan Association*, 738 FSupp 50 (E.D.Mich., 1990); *S.E.C. vs. Elmas Trading Corporation*, 638 FSupp. 743 (D.Nevada, 1987) (*affirmed*) 865 F2d 265; contrast: *J2 Smoke Shop Inc. vs. American Commercial Capital Corp.*, 709 F Supp 422 (SDNY 1989) (cost of funds); *In Re Powderburst Corp.*, 154 BR 307 (E.D.Cal. 1993)(original issue discount); *In Re Wright*, 256 BR 626 (D.Mont., 2000) (difference between face amount and amount actually recovered or owed by debtor); *In Re MCCorhill Pub. Inc.*, 86 BR 283 (SDNY 1988); *In Re Marill Alarm Systems*, 81 BR 119 (S.D.Fla., 1987) (affirmed) 861 F2d 725; *In Re Dent*, 130 BR 623 (S.D.GA, 1991); *In Re Evans*, 130 BR 357 (S.D.GA, 1991); contrast: *In Re Cadillac Wildwood Development*, 138 BR 854 (W.D.Mich., 1992) (closing costs are interest costs); *In Re Brummer*, 147 BR 552 (D.Mont., 1992); *In Re Sunde*, 149 BR 552 (D.Minn., 1992); *Matter Of Worldwide Trucks*, 948 F2d 976 (CA5,1991) (agreement about applicable interest rate maybe established by course of conduct); *Lovick vs. Ritemoney Ltd*, 378 F3d 433 (CA5, 2004); *In Re Shulman Transport*, 744 F2d 293 (CA2, 1984); *Torelli vs. Esposito*, 461 NYS2d 299 (1983) (reversed) 483 NYS2d 204; *Reschke vs. Eadi*, 447 NYS2d 59 (NYAD4, 1981); *Elghanian vs. Elghanian*, 717 NYS2d 54 (NYAD1, 2000) (leave to appeal denied) 729 NYS2d 410 (there was no consideration in exchange for loan, and transaction violated usury laws); *Karas vs. Shur*, 592 NYS2d 779 (NYAD2, 1993); *Simsbury Fund vs. New St. Louis Associates*, 611 NYS2d 557 (NYAD1, 1994); *Rhee vs. Dahan*, 454 NYS2d 371 (NY.Sup., 1982); *Hamilton vs. HLT Check Exchange, LLP*, 987 F. Supp. 953 (E.D. Ky. 1997); *Turner vs. E-Z Check Cashing of Cookeville, TN, Inc.*, 35 F.Supp.2d 1042 (M.D. Tenn. 1999); *Hurt vs. Crystal Ice & Cold Storage Co.*, 286 S.W. 1055, 1056–57 (Ky. 1926); *Phanco vs. Dollar Financial Group*, Case No. CV99–1281 DDP (C.D. Cal., filed Feb. 8, 1999). *See*: Van Voris, B. (1999). Payday loans under scrutiny. *The National Law Journal* at B1.

73 See the prospectus for the Beiersdorf reverse convertible bonds at www.rcb.at/en/produkt/reverse/?ISIN=AT0000A1T448&file=file&hash=1b4a5d314b5b0af20b21892b78d26d8219dd7e21.

74 *See* the cases cited in section-5.4.6 above.

75 *See: The Emergency Economic Stabilization Act of 2008.* http://www.house.gov/finan cialservices/EESABill_section-by-section.pdf.
    Section 111(e) of the EESA, as amended by the American Recovery and Reinvestment Act on February 17, 2009, requires any entity that has received financial assistance under the Troubled Asset Relief Program (or "TARP") to permit an annual advisory shareholder vote to approve the compensation of executives, as disclosed

pursuant to the Commission's rules. This shareholder vote on executive compensation is non-binding and is required as long as obligations under the TARP remain outstanding. Section 111(e)(3) of the EESA directs the Commission to issue any required final rules not later than February 17, 2010.

76 *See*: US Treasury Department (2009). *United States Department of the Treasury Section 105(a) Troubled Assets Relief Program – Report to Congress for the Period February 1, 2009 to February 28, 2009.*

77 *See*: US Government Accountability Office (2016). *Troubled Asset Relief Program: Capital Purchase Program Largely Has Wound Down*. https://www.gao.gov/assets/680/676954.pdf.

78 *See*: "SIGTARP report reveals massive failure of HAMP – 'Massive lost opportunity for an emergency program'". July 29, 2015. By Brena Swanson. https://www.housingwire.com/articles/34609-sigtarp-report-reveals-massive-failure-of-hamp.

   See: "SIGTARP: HAMP's failure 'devastating', permanent mods flat in December". January 26, 2011. By Jon Prior. https://www.housingwire.com/articles/sigtarp-hamps-failure-devastating-permanent-mods-flat-december.

   See: "SIGTARP alleges Hardest Hit Fund failures – participating states spent only 22% of the funds in three years". October 29, 2013. By Kerri Ann Panchuk. https://www.housingwire.com/articles/27681-sigtarp-details-hardest-hit-fund-failures.

   See: "Obama program that hurt homeowners and helped big banks is ending". By David Dayen. December 28, 2015. https://theintercept.com/2015/12/28/obama-program-hurt-homeowners-and-helped-big-banks-now-its-dead/.

   See: SIGTARP (July 2015). *Quarterly Report to Congress – July 29, 2015*. https://www.sigtarp.gov/Quarterly%20Reports/July_29_2015_Report_to_Congress.pdf.

   See: SIGTARP (2018). *Congressional Justification for Appropriations and Annual Performance Report and Plan – FY 2018*. https://www.treasury.gov/about/budget-performance/CJ18/11.%20SIGTARP%20-%20FY%202018%20CJ.pdf.

79 *See*: US Treasury Department (2009). United States Department of the Treasury Section 105(a) Troubled Assets Relief Program – Report to Congress for the Period February 1, 2009 to February 28, 2009.

   See: A. M. Best (Stephanie McElroy & Rosemary Mirabella) (January 19, 2009). *Analyzing Securities Issued Under the US Treasury's Capital Purchase Program*. *See*: Hunton & Williams. *Term Sheet for TARP CPP Program from Private Companies*. http://www.hunton.com/files/tbl_s10News%5CFileUpload44%5C15799%5Ctarp_capital_purchase_program_term_sheet_for_privately_held_companies.pdf.

   See: *United States Department of the Treasury Tranche Report to Congress*; NOVEMBER 4, 2008. http://www.financialstability.gov/docs/TrancheReports/Tranche-Reportfinal.pdf).

80 *See*: www.fanniemae.com/faq/faq8.jhtml?p=FAQ (describing Fannie Mae as private company).

   See: Press Release, Freddie Mac (December 14, 2006). *Freddie Mac Announces Voluntary Delisting From NYSE Arca*.

   See: 12 U.S.C. 1716 (a USA statute).

   See: Federal Home Loan Banks website – www.fhlbanks.com/html/faq.html. In 1987, the US government created the Financing Corporation ("FICO"), to take on the obligations of the insolvent Federal Savings and Loan Insurance Corporation ("FSLIC").

   See: Competitive Equality Bank Act Of 1987, Pub. L. 100–86, Title III (codified at 12 U.S.C. § 1441(2006)). In 1989, the US Congress created the *Resolution Funding Corporation* to manage the S&L crisis. *See*: Financial Institutions Reform, Recovery and Enforcement Act (FIRREA) of 1989, Pub. L. No. 101–73, 103 Stat. 183 (establishing REFCO).

See: 12 U.S.C. § 1454(a)(2) (2006) (providing restrictions for Freddie Mac); *Ibid.* § 1717(b)(2) (providing restrictions for Fannie Mae).

See: Wallison, P.J. (2008), *Fannie and Freddie by Twilight*, FIN. SERVICES OUT-LOOK, p. 1 (Aug) (describing post-Act Fannie and Freddie as "explicitly government-backed entities").

See: Housing And Economic Recovery Act Of 2008 § 1101.

See: *Summary of The Housing And Economic Recovery Act Of 2008*. http://banking. senate.gov/public/_files/HousingandEconomicRecoveryActSummary.pdf.

81 *See*: *"Statement by Secretary Henry M. Paulson, Jr. on Treasury and Federal Housing Finance Agency Action to Protect Financial Markets and Taxpayers – September 7, 2008"*. www.treas.gov/press/releases/hp1129.htm.

82 See terms of FNMA Senior Preferred Stock - www.treas.gov/press/releases/reports/ seniorpreferredstockpurchaseagreementfnm1.pdf.

See: terms of FNMA Warrant - www.treas.gov/press/releases/reports/warrant fnm3.pdf.

See: FNMA Certificate - www.treas.gov/press/releases/reports/certificatefnm2.pdf.

See: The terms of Freddie Mac Senior Preferred Stock at: www.treas.gov/press/ releases/reports/seniorpreferredstockpurchaseagreementfrea.pdf.

See: Freddie Mac Certificate at: www.treas.gov/press/releases/reports/certificate freb.pdf.

See: The terms of Freddie Mac's Stock Warrants at: www.treas.gov/press/releases/ reports/warrantfrec.pdf.

See: AEI (USA). *"AEI - The Last Trillion Dollar Commitment"*.

83 *See*: Press Release, Federal Reserve Board, *Use of Cumulative Preferred Stock in Tier 1 Capital of Bank Holding Companies* (October 21, 1996) – www.federalreserve.gov/ boarddocs/press/bcreg/1996/19961021/default.htm.

See: United States Department Of The Treasury Tranch Report To Congress, November 4, 2008. http://news.lp.findlaw.com/hdocs/docs/2008-financial-crisis/20081104-bailout-tranche-report.pdf. This document contains a summary of the terms of the Senior Preferred Stock (purchased as part of the TARP Capital Purchase Program).

84 *See*: Humphreys (2007).

85 *See*: *Equitable Life Assurance Society*, 321 U.S. 560, 564 (1943) (finding that payments made at the company's discretion are indicative of dividends rather than interest).

See: *Talbot Mills*, 146 F.2d 809, 812 (1st Cir. 1944) (payments that are deferrable and discretionary not deductible as interest), *aff'd sub nom.*

See: *John Kelley Co.*, 326 U.S. 521 (1946); GCM 36136 (January 15, 1975) (stating that discretion in making payments is a key distinction between equity and debt).

See: *Richmond, Fredericksburg & Potomac R.R. Co.*, 528 F.2d 917 (4th Cir. 1975) (holding that guaranteed dividends paid to the holders of a railroad's guaranteed stock at the specified rate constituted deductible interest since such payments were attributable to the debt characteristics of the hybrid securities even through the excess amount paid to the holders was not deductible as interest since it was attributable to the equity characteristics of the securities).

86 *See*: *Curry vs. United States*, 396 F.2d 630 (CA5) (*cert. denied*) 393 U.S. 967 (1968).

See: Young, S. (Jan. 26, 2007). Tax Officials, Practitioners Discuss Trust Preferred Securities. *Tax Notes Today* (2007 TNT 18–7 January 26, 2007).

See: Polito, A. (1998). Useful fictions: Debt and equity classification in corporate tax law. *Arizona State Law Journal*, 30, 761–771.

See: Beale, L., Miller, D. & Wysocki, P. (July–August 2001). An overview of the U.S. federal income tax treatment of collateral debt obligation transactions. *Journal of Taxation of Financial Institutions*, 14(6), 27–57. www.cadwalader.com/assets/article/ Miller%20final_2001.pdf.

See: Campbell, L., Benchetrit, S. & Reinhold, R. (October 2006). *NAIC Regulatory Treatment of Hybrid Securities.* www.metrocorpcounsel.com/pdf/2006/October/18.pdf.
See: Humphreys, T. & Man, A. (November 2007). *Hybrid Capital – the US Tax Perspective.* Morrison & Foerster LLP. www.mofo.com/practice/docs/HybridCapital.pdf.
See: Bauer vs. Commissioner, 748 F.2d 1365, 1367 (9th Cir. 1984).
See: Smith vs. Commissioner, 370 F.2d 178, 180 (6th Cir. 1966).
See Estate of Mixon vs. United States, 464 F.2d 394, 402–03 (5th Cir. 1972).
See: J & W Fence Supply Co. vs. United States, 230 F.3d 896, 898 (2000).
See: Commissioner vs. Duberstein, 363 U.S. 278 (   ).
87 See: J & W Fence Supply Co. vs. United States, 230 F.3d 896, 898 (2000).
See: Cerand & Company, Incorporated vs. Commissioner of Internal Revenue Service, 254 F.3d 258 (D.C. Cir. 2001). http://bulk.resource.org/courts.gov/c/F3/254/254.F3d.258.99-1252.html.
See: Chan, K., Viswanath, V. & Wong, A. (2001). Century bonds: Debt or equity securities? *Journal of Applied Business Research*, 19(3), 89–93. www.cluteinstitute-onlinejournals.com/PDFs/2003165.pdf.
88 See: Chan, K. & Viswanath, P. (September 2002). *Century Bonds: Issuance Motivations and Debt Versus Equity Characteristics.* http://webpage.pace.edu/pviswanath/research/papers/kamchan_final_version_102303.pdf. (arguing that that 100-year debt should be treated as debt for federal tax purposes because it more resembles debt than equity particularly where the yield difference between an issuer's 100-year debt and its (or a similar issuer's) 30-year debt is relatively small).
See: Dillin vs. United States, 433 F.2d 1097, 1101 (5th Cir., 1970) (In *Dillin*, the demand notes in question were payable only when the issuer issued stock in an initial public offering).
89 See: Fitch IBCA (1999). *Loan Preserver – The Value of Covenants.* http://pages.stern.nyu.edu/~igiddy/articles/fitch_loan_covenants.pdf. According to Fitch IBCA, the typical covenants in loans and bonds include the following:

Financial Covenants:
– Maximum Total Debt/EBITDA.
– Maximum Total Senior Debt/EBITDA.
– Minimum Interest Coverage.
– Minimum Fixed-Charge Coverage.
– Minimum EBITDA.
– Minimum Net Worth.
– Minimum Current Ratio.

Negative Covenants:
– Limitation on Indebtedness.
– Limitation on Liens.
– Limitation on Contingent Obligations.
– Limitation on Sale of Assets.
– Limitation on Leases.
– Limitation on Dividends.
– Limitation on Capital Expenditures.
– Limitation on Transactions with Affiliates.
– Limitation on Sale/Leaseback.

Mandatory Prepayments:
– Excess Cash Flow Sweep.
– Asset Sale Sweep.
– Debt Issuance Sweep.
– Equity Issuance Sweep.

See: Paglia and Mullineaux (2006); Paglia (September 2007); Standard & Poors (Michael Silverberg & Anne Pedersen) (Nov 28, 2008); Francis (2009); and McKinnon & Hitt (Feb. 4, 2002).

90 *See:* Paglia (September 2007).

See: Fed. Exp. Corp. v. United States, 645 F. Supp. 1281 (W.D. Tenn.; 1986).

See: Plumb, W. (1971). The federal income tax significance of corporate debt: A critical analysis and a proposal. *Tax Law Review*, 26, 369–603 (". . . . . but if cumulative interest is unconditionally payable at maturity regardless of the sufficiency of earnings, the interim deferability of the payments, whether or not discretionary, should be given no adverse weight at all. . . . . .").

See: John Kelley Co. vs. Commissioner, 326 U.S. 521 (1946).

See: Crawford Drug Stores, Inc. vs. United States, 220 F.2d 292, 296 (10th Cir. 1955).

See: Tribune Publ'g Co. vs. Commissioner, 17 T.C. 1228, 1234 (1952).

91 *See*: United States Department Of The Treasury Tranch Report To Congress, NOVEMBER 4, 2008. http://news.lp.findlaw.com/hdocs/docs/2008-financial-crisis/20081104-bailout-tranche-report.pdf. This document contains a summary of the terms of the Warrants (issued as part of the TARP Capital Purchase Program.

92 *See*: Humphreys, T. (2007). *Tax Deductible Equity and Other Hybrids in the US – a Brief History and Current Developments* (Morrison & Foerster LLP). www.mofo.com/docs/pdf/TaxDeductibleHybrid.pdf.

93 The following are relevant US court cases:

See: Joseph M. Segel, 89 TC 816 (1987).

See: Motel Co., TCM 1963–174, 22 TCM (CCH) 825 (1963) (finding sufficient capital to support a debt characterization for a later unsecured note, when an earlier note was treated as a contribution).

See: Wrather, TCM 1955–104, 14 TCM (CCH) 345 (1955) (finding sufficient capital to support a debt characterization for certain general advances, where shareholder conceded that earlier advances to a corporation were in fact capital contributions).

See: Stratmore v. U.S., 292 F. Supp. 59, 63–64 (D.N.J. 1968), *rev'd on other grounds*, 420 F.2d 461 (CA3, 1969).

See: Danielson, 378 F.2d 771 (3rd Cir.), *cert. den.*, 389 U.S. 858 (1967)

See: Equitable Life Assurance Society, 321 U.S. 560, 564 (1943) (finding that payments made at the company's discretion are indicative of dividends rather than interest).

See: Talbot Mills, 146 F.2d 809, 812 (1st Cir. 1944) (payments that are deferrable and discretionary not deductible as interest), *aff'd sub nom.*

See: John Kelley Co., 326 U.S. 521 (1946); GCM 36136 (January 15, 1975) (stating that discretion in making payments is a key distinction between equity and debt).

See: Tomlinson v. The 1661 Corp., 377 F.2d 291, 294 (5th Cir. 1967) (debentures that paid cumulative interest held to be debt even though the corporation rarely, if ever, paid interest currently);

See: H.P. Hood & Sons, Inc., 141 F.2d 467, 470 (1st Cir. 1944) (instruments that were payable only out of net earnings but required payment of accumulated accrued interest were debt rather than equity);

See: First M&F Corp. v. U.S., 767 F. Supp. 792, 796 (N.D. Miss. 1991) (finding that since "the interest was cumulative [and therefore] was not lost forever . . . this factor weighs in favor of treating this as a debt relationship").

See: Federal Express Corp. v. United States, 645 F. Supp. 1281, 1290 (W.D. Tenn. 1986) (deferral of payments does not defeat a finding that such payments are interest).

See: GCM 36702 (reaffirmed in GCM 38133 (October 10, 1979)).

See: FSA 1999–9999–318 (suggesting that a purported loan with an equity kicker should be treated as an equity interest in a joint venture).

Compare facts: Rev. Rul. 83–51, 1983–1 CB 48 (March 28, 1983) (USA).
See: Farley Realty Corp. TCM 1959–93, *affirmed,* 279 F.2d 701 (2d Cir. 1960).
See: Ellinger, III vs. U.S., Court of Appeals, 11th Circuit, [2006–2 USTC ¶50,608].
See: Hubert Entertainment, Inc. & Subsidiaries vs. Commissioner, 125 T.C. 72, 91 (2005).

94   *See: Hackal vs. Adler*, 650 NYS2d 792 (1996, AD);
See: Kodogiannis vs. Mumford, 535 NYS2d 494; *Metropolitan Transportation Authority vs. Bruken Realty*, 501 NYS2d 306.

95   See the cases cited in Section 5.2.1 above.

96   Guinn & Harvey [42: 1140–1141], supra.

97   *See:* Ciro (supra).
See: Hazen (supra).
See: Bernstein (supra).
See: Hains (supra).

98   *See:* Bloomenthal (supra).

99   *See: Cohn, Ivers & Co v. Gross* (289 NYS2d 301).
See: Board of Trade of City of Chicago v. SEC, 677 F2d 1137 (1982) (*cert den.*) 459 US 1026 (GNMA options are not securities).

100 *See: Colt v. Fradkin*, 281 NE2d 213, 217 – paragraph 2.
See: Hahn, A. (February 24, 2003). Goldman's dangerous REIT game: Firm now defending unpopular strategy it helped devise. *The Investment Dealers' Digest*, 7–8.

101 *See* the cases cited in Section 5.4.6. above.

102 *See:* Global Van Lines, Inc., SEC No-Action Letter (October2, 1979); Medical Device Mutual Assurance and Reinsurance Co., Ltd., SEC No-Action Letter (August31, 1979); Norcal Bowling Proprietors Mutual Insurance Co., Ltd., SEC No-Action Letter (December5, 1983); Podiatric Assurance Co., SEC No-Action Letter (February 19, 1985); Medmarc Insurance Company Risk Retention Group, SEC No-Action Letter (October2, 1987); National Transport Assurance Alliance, Inc., SEC No-Action Letter (February 22, 1989); Construction Trade Purchasing Group, Inc. and Construction Trades Insurance Company, SEC No-Action Letter (October 1, 1993).

103 *See: Mordaunt vs. Incomco*, 686 F.2d 815 (9th Cir.; 1982).
See: *Revak vs. SEC Realty Corp.*, 18 F.3d 81, 88 (2d Cir.; 1994).
See: *SEC vs. Professional Associates*, 731 F.2d 349, 354 (6th Cir.; 1984).

104 Also see the cases cited in Section-5.4.7 above.

105 *Securities and Exchange Commission v. W. J. Howey Co.*, 328 US 293 (1946).

106 *Marine Bank vs. Weaver*, 455 U.S. 551 (1982) (an individually negotiated profit-sharing agreement that did not involve multiple investors was not securities).

107 *International Brotherhood of Teamsters v. Daniel*, 439 U.S. 551 (1979).

108 *See: Reeves vs. Ernst & Young*, 494 U.S. 56, 67 (1990) (interpreting the Exchange Act).

109 *See: "Wall Street looks for fix to shady credit default swap market amid Windstream bankruptcy"*. Finance by Wesley Brown. March 11, 2019. https://talkbusiness.net/2019/03/wall-street-looks-for-fix-to-shady-credit-default-swap-market-amid-windstream-bankruptcy/.
See: "Bloodsport on Wall Street: Hedge Funds Make Mayhem for Profit – In high-stakes battles over corporate debt, hedge funds may pressure companies to default. By Claire Boston and Davide Scigliuzzo. April 2019. www.bloomberg.com/news/articles/2019-04-18/bloodsport-on-wall-street-hedge-funds-make-mayhem-for-profit.
See: Hu, H. (February 24, 2019). *Reform the credit default swap market to rein in abuses – Windstream's fight with Aurelius highlights complexities of 'empty creditors'.* Financial Times. www.ft.com/content/1fcd2f34-2e14-11e9-80d2-7b637a9e1ba1.
See: Burne, K. (Oct. 1, 2015). Banks Finalize $1.86 Billion Credit-Swaps Settlement – Suit claimed banks conspired to prevent competition. *Wall Street Journal.* www.wsj.com/articles/wall-street-banks-in-credit-swaps-settlement-1443708335.

See: *In re: Credit Default Swaps Antitrust Litigation* (U.S. District Court for the Southern District of New York, No. 13-md-02476) (USA lawsuit about manipulation of the credit default swaps market by banks).

110 See: *Mordaunt vs. Incomco*, 686 F.2d 815 (CA9; 1982).
 See: *Revak vs. SEC Realty Corp.*, 18 F.3d 81, 88 (CA2; 1994).
 See: *SEC vs. Professional Associates*, 731 F.2d 349, 354 (CA6; 1984).
111 See: *Reeves vs. Ernst & Young*, 494 U.S. 56, 67 (1990) (interpreting the Exchange Act).
112 See: Dodd-Frank Wall Street Reform and Consumer Protection Act, Pub. L. No. 111–203, 721(a)(21), 124 Stat. 1376 (2010); 7 U.S.C. § 1a(47) (2012).
 See: Gramm-Leach-Bliley Act, Pub. L. No. 106–102, 113 Stat. 1338 (1999).
 Cf: 7 U.S.C. §1a(47)(B)(x) (2012) (excluding security-based swaps from the definition of "swap").
 See: "An Act to Clarify the Jurisdiction of the Securities and Exchange Commission and the Definition of security". Pub. L. No. 97–303, 96 Stat. 1409 (1982).
 See: H.R.REP.NO. 97–626(I) (1982), reprinted in 1982 U.S.C.C.A.N. 2780; H.R.REP.NO. 97–626(II) (1982), reprinted in 1982 U.S.C.C.A.N. 2792.
113 See: "Credit default swaps are insurance products. It's time we regulated them as such". By Barry Ritholtz. March 10, 2012. www.washingtonpost.com/business/credit-default-swaps-are-insurance-products-its-time-we-regulated-them-as-such/2012/03/05/gIQAAUo83R_story.html?utm_term=.174e68088d5f.
 See: Leisin, M., "Credit Swaps Investigated by U.S. Justice Department (update 3)". Bloomberg.com Online, 14 July 2009.
 See: "Soros Says Default Swaps Should be Outlawed". *New York Times* Online Dealbook, 12 June 2009.
114 See: *Caiola vs. Citibank, N.A., N.Y.*, 295 F.3d 312, 325–27 (CA2; 2002).
115 See: Section 721 of the Dodd Frank Act. Dodd-Frank Wall Street Reform and Consumer Protection Act, Pub. L. No. 111–203, §721(a)(47), 124 Stat. 1376, 1666 (2010) § 721(a)(47).

Bibliography

Abeysekera, I. (2003). Political economy of accounting in intellectual capital reporting. *The European Journal of Management and Public Policy*, 2(1), 65–79.

Abramowitz, B. & Anshelevich, E. (2018). *Utilitarians Without Utilities: Maximizing Social Welfare for Graph Problems Using Only Ordinal Preferences.* https://arxiv.org/pdf/1711.10588.pdf.

Ackert, L., Chruch, B. & Sankar, M. (2000). Voluntary disclosure under imperfect competition: Experimental evidence. *International Journal of Industrial Organization*, 18, 81–105.

Ahmed, K., Goodwin, A. & Sawyer, K. (2006). Recognition versus disclosure: The case of land and buildings' revaluations. *Pacific Accounting Review*, 17, 4–33.

Alderson, M. & Fraser, D. (1993). Financial innovations and excesses revisited: The case of auction rate preferred stock. *Financial Management*, 22(2).

A. M. Best (Stephanie McElroy & Rosemary Mirabella) (Jantrary 19, 2009). *Analyzing Securities Issued Under the US Treasury's Capital Purchase Program* (A. M. Best, Oldwick, NJ, USA).

An, Z., Li, D. & Yu, J. (2013). *Earnings management, capital structure and the role of institutional environments.* Financial Research Network Research Paper. SSRN: http://ssrn.com/abstract=2207804 ou http://dx.doi.org/10.2139/ssrn.2207804.

Anantharaman, D. (2014). Inside debt and the design of corporate debt contracts. *Management Science*, 60(5), 1083–1350.

Andrews, M., Pritchett, L. & Woolcock, M. (2017). *Building State Capability: Evidence, Analysis, Action* (Oxford Scholarship Online, Oxford, UK).

Ang, H. & Pinnuck, M. (2010). *Do Investors Value Disclosed Versus Recognised Employee Share Options Differently?* In AFAANZ 2010: Accounting and Finance Association of Australia and New Zealand Annual Conference, AFAANZ, [Christchurch, New Zealand], pp. 1–40.

Armstrong, O. (1962). State securities regulation of real estate investment trusts: An Attorney's viewpoint. *Virginia Law Review*, 48(6), 1082–1103.

Arthur, W. (1999). Complexity and the economy. *Science*, 284, 107–109.

Austin, A. (July 2012). *Auction-Rate Securities*. US Congressional Research Service, Washington, DC. www.fas.org/sgp/crs/misc/RL34672.pdf.

Badia, F., Dicuonzo, G. et al (2019). Integrated reporting in action: Mobilizing intellectual capital to improve management and governance practices. *Journal of Management and Governance*, 23(2), 299–320.

Baffi, E. (2007). *The Economics of Standard Form Contracts* (Università degli Studi "Roma Tre" – Faculty of Law", Italy).

Bai, J., Fleming, M. & Horan, C. (2013). *The Microstructure of China's Government Bond Market*. Staff Report No. 622. US Federal Reserve Bank of New York. www.new yorkfed.org/research/staff_reports/sr622.pdf.

Baig, A., DeLisle, J. & Zaynutdinova, G. (2018). *Passive Ownership and Earnings Manipulation*. 9th Conference on Financial Markets and Corporate Governance (FMCG) 2018. SSRN: https://ssrn.com/abstract=3101874 or http://dx.doi.org/10.2139/ssrn.3101874.

Baker, M., Wurgler, J. & Yuan, Y. (2012). Global, local, and contagious investor sentiment. *Journal of Financial Economics*, 104(2), 272–287.

Bamberger, M., Vaessen, J. & Raimondo, E. (2016). *Dealing with Complexity in Development Evaluation: A Practical Approach* (Sage Publications, London, UK).

Bargeron, L., Lehn, M. & Zutter, C. (2010). Sarbanes-Oxley and corporate risk taking. *Journal of Accounting & Economics*, 49, 34–52.

Bartolini, L., Hilton, S., Sundaresan, S. & Tonetti, C. (2011). Collateral values by asset class: Evidence from primary securities dealers. *Review of Financial Studies*, 24(1), 248–278.

Beattie, V., Goodacre, A. & Thomson, S. (2000). Recognition versus disclosure: An investigation of the impact on equity risk using UK operating lease disclosures. *Journal of Business Finance & Accounting*, 27, 1185–1224.

Beneta, B.A., Giannetti, A. & Pissaris, S. (2006). Gains from structured product markets: The case of Reverse Exchangeable Securities (RES). *Journal of Banking & Finance*, 30(1), 111–132.

Bergemann, D. & Morris, S. (2005). Robust mechanism design. *Econometrica*, 73(6), 1771–1813.

Berger-Soucy, L., Garriott, C. & Usche, A. (Bank of Canada) (2018). *Government of Canada Fixed-Income Market Ecology*. Bank of Canada Staff Discussion Paper 2018–2010.

Bernard, L. (1926a). *Primary and Derivative Groups*. Chapter *26* in *An Introduction to Social Psychology* (New York: Henry Holt and Co.), pp. 411–425. www.brocku.ca/ MeadProject/Bernard/1926/1926_26.html.

Bernard, L. (1926b). *Primary and Derivative Attitudes and Ideals*. Chapter 27 in *An Introduction to Social Psychology* (New York; Henry Holt and Co., 425–437). www.brocku. ca/MeadProject/Bernard/1926/1926_27.html.

Bernard, L. (1936). The conflict between primary group attitudes and derivative group ideals in modern society. *American Journal of Sociology*, 41(5), 611–623.

Bernstein, L. (1992). Opting out of the legal system: Extralegal contractual relations in the diamond industry. *Journal of Legal Studies*, 21, 115–130. Reprinted in part in Barnett, R. (1995), *Contracts: Theory and Doctrine* (Little, Brown, Boston, MA).

Bikhchandani, S. & Huang, C. (2011). *The Treasury Bill Auction and the When-Issued Market: Some Evidence* (Nabu Press, Charleston, SC, USA).

Bizjak, J., Kalpathy, S. & Mihov, V. (2018). Performance contingencies in CEO equity awards and debt contracting. *The Accounting Review*, in press.

Black, L. & Hazelwood, L. (2013). The effect of TARP on bank risk-taking. *Journal of Financial Stability*, 9(4), 790–803.

Board, O. (March 2009). Competition and disclosure. *Journal of Industrial Economics*, 57(1), 197–213.

Boczko, T. (2000). A critique on the classification of contemporary accounting: Towards a political economy of classification – the search for ownership. *Critical Perspectives on Accounting*, 11, 131–153.

Boehme, R. & May, A. (May 2016). Multinational corporations and stock price crash risk. *International Journal of Finance & Banking Studies*, 5(4), 39–44. www.ssbfnet.com/ ojs/index.php/ijfbs/article/view/593.

Boutilier, C., Caragiannis, I. et al. (2012). *Optimal Social Choice Functions: A Utilitarian View*. Conference Paper. EC'12, June 4–8, 2012, Valencia, Spain. http://procaccia.info/ papers/optvoting.ec12.pdf.

Bredeweg, B. & Struss, P. (Winter 2003). Current topics in qualitative reasoning. *AI Magazine*, pp. 13–17.

Brighton, J. (2002). Capital contribution or a loan? *American Bankruptcy Institute Journal*, 21(1), 42–45.

Broman, M. (2016). Liquidity, style investing and excess co-movement of exchange-traded fund returns. *Journal of Financial Markets*, 30, 27–35.

Burilovich, L. (December 2006). Planning techniques to avoid the reclassification of shareholder debt as equity. *The Tax Strategist*, 1.

Burke, J. (September 2006). Debt vs. Equity: The saga continues. *Tax Adviser*, 507–509.

Byrne, D. & Callaghan, G. (2014). *Complexity Theory and The Social Sciences: The State of The Art* (Routledge, London, UK).

Cadwalader, Wickersham & Taft (April 23, 2009). *Treasury, Federal Reserve and FDIC Credit and Liquidity Programs*. www.cadwalader.com/assets/client_friend/042309_ Treasury,_Federal_Reserve,_FDIC.pdf.

Calabrese, R., Degl'Innocenti, M. & Angela Osmetti, S. (2017). The effectiveness of TARP-CPP on the US banking industry: A new copula-based approach. *European Journal of Operational Research*, 256(23), 1029–1037.

Cammack, E. (1991). Evidence on bidding strategies and the information contained in Treasury bill auctions. *Journal of Political Economy*, 9, 100–130.

Campion, M., Candeal, J., et al. (2011). Aggregation of Preferences in Crisp and Fuzzy Settings: Functional Equations Leading to Possibility Results. *International Journal of Uncertainty, Fuzziness and Knowledge-Based Systems*, 19(1), 89–114.

Carnell, R. (2005). Handling the failure of a government-sponsored enterprise. *Washington Law Review*, 80, 565–570.

Carroll, B. (December 1, 2004). The mutual fund trading scandals: Implications for CPAs and their clients. *Journal of Accountancy*. www.journalofaccountancy.com/issues/2004/ dec/themutualfundtradingscandals.html.

Chan, K., Viswanat, V. & Wong, A. (2001). Century bonds: Debt or equity securities? *Journal of Applied Business Research*, 19(3), 89–93. www.cluteinstitute-onlinejournals. com/PDFs/2003165.pdf.

Chance, D. (2009). Liquidity and employee options: An empirical examination of the Microsoft experience. *Journal of Corporate Finance*, 15(4), 469–487.

Chen, H. & Jorgensen, B. (2018). Market exit through divestment – the effect of accounting bias on competition. *Management Science*, 64(1), 1–493.

Cheng, S., Massa, M. & Zhang, H. (2018). The unexpected activeness of passive investors: A worldwide analysis of ETFs. *The Review of Asset Pricing Studies, in press*.

Chi, J., Yang, J. & Young, M. (2014). Mutual funds' holdings and listed firms' earnings management: Evidence from China. *Journal of Multinational Financial Management*, 28, 62–78.

Choi, S. & Kahan, M. (2007). The market penalty for mutual fund scandals. *Boston University Law Review*, 87, 1021–1057.

Choudhary, P. (2011). Evidence on differences between recognition and disclosure: A comparison f inputs to estimate fair values of employee stock options. *Journal of Accounting and Economics*, 51(1–2), 77–94.

Ciro, T. (2002). The regulation of equity derivatives: Functional rhetoric vs economic substance. *Corporate & Securities Law Journal*, 20(5), 276–288.

Claudiu, B. (2013). Formal representation of corporate governance principles and codes. *Procedia – Social and Behavioral Sciences*, 73, 744–750.

Colla, P., Ippolito, F. & Li, K. (2013). Debt specialization. *The Journal of Finance*, 68(5), 2117–2141.

Colon, J. (2017). The great ETF tax swindle: The taxation of in-kind redemptions. *Pennsylvania State Law Review*, 122, 20–30.

Cornell, D. & Shapiro, A. (1989). The mispricing of U.S. Treasury bonds: A case study. *Review of Financial Studies*, 2, 297–310.

Corradin, S. & Maddaloni, A. (2015). *The Importance of Being Special: Repo Markets During the Crisis*. European Central Bank. www.greta.it/sovereign/sovereign2/ papers/02_Corradin.pdf.

Cox, J., Hillman, R. & Langevoort, D. (2009). *Securities Regulation: Cases and Materials* (Wolters Kluwer, The Netherlands).

Crew, M. & Kleindorfer, P. (2000). A Critique of the Theory of Incentive Regulation: Implications for the Design of Performance Based Regulation for Postal Service. *Topics in Regulatory Economics and Policy*, 38, 37–66.

D'Silva, A., Haley, G. & Marshall, D. (November 2008). Explaining the decline in the auction rate securities market. *Chicago Fed Letter* (USA).

Dai, Y., Kong, D. & Wang, L. (2013). Information asymmetry, mutual funds and earnings management: Evidence from China. *China Journal of Accounting Research*, 6(3), 187–209.

Dantzler, W. (January 2006). Debt vs. Equity in the partnership context. *Tax Notes*, 497–504.

Darrough, M. (1993). Disclosure policy and competition: Cournot vs. Bertrand. *The Accounting Review*, 68, 534–561.

Darrough, M. & Deng, M. (2018). The role of accounting information in optimal debt contracts with informed lenders. *The Accounting Review, in press*.

Debt Management Office of Nigeria (2015). *Nigerian Treasury Bills Auction Results for November 04, 2015*. www.dmo.gov.ng/arnews.php.

Deck, C. & Schlesinger, H. (2014). Consistency of higher order risk preferences. *Econometrica*, 82(5), 1913–1943.

Defusco, R., Ivanov, S. & Karels, G. (2011). The exchange traded funds' pricing deviation: Analysis and forecasts. *Journal of Economics & Finance*, 35, 181–191.

Dekker, H., Kawai, T. & Sakaguchi, J. (2018). Contracting abroad: A comparative analysis of contract design in host and home country outsourcing relations. *Management Accounting Research*, 40, 47–61.

DeMarzo, P. & Duffie, D. (1999). A liquidity-based model of security design. *Econometrica*, 67(1), 65–100.

DeMarzo, P. & Fishman, M. (2007). Optimal long-term financial contracting. *The Review of Financial Studies*, 20(6), 2079–2128.

DeMarzo, P., Kremer, I. & Skrzypacz, A. (2005). Bidding with securities: Auctions and security design. *American Economic Review*, 95(4), 936–959.

De Rato, R. (Aug. 22, 2007). *Economic Growth and Financial Market Development: A Strengthening Integration.* Speech by Rodrigo de Rato, Managing Director of the International Monetary Fund. https://www.imf.org/en/News/Articles/2015/09/28/04/53/sp082207.

Dey, A. (2010). The chilling effect of Sarbanes-Oxley: A discussion of Sarbanes-Oxley and corporate risk taking. *Journal of Accounting and Economics*, 49, 53–57.

Ding, R., Li, J. & Wu, Z. (2018). Government affiliation, real earnings management, and firm performance: The case of privately held firms. *Journal of Business Research*, 83(C), 138–150.

Drozd, L. & Serrano-Padia, R. (2018). Financial contracting with enforcement externalities. *Journal of Economic Theory*, 178, 153–189.

Eenmaa-Dimitrieva, H. & Schmidt-Kessen, M. (2019). Creating markets in no-trust environments: The law and economics of smart contracts. *Computer Law & Security Review*, 35(1), 69–88.

Engert, A. & Hornuf, L. (2018). Market standards in financial contracting: The Euro's effect on debt securities. *Journal of International Money and Finance*, 85, 145–162.

Fang, X. & Yuan, F. (2018). The coordination and preference of supply chain contracts based on time-sensitivity promotional mechanism. *Journal of Management Science and Engineering*, 3(3), 158–178.

Farahmand, F. (2017). Decision and experienced utility: Computational applications in privacy decision making. *IEEE Security & Privacy*, 15, 68–72. https://www.computer.org/csdl/magazine/sp/2017/06/msp2017060068/13rRUILc8dJ

Farruggioa, C., Michalak, T. & Uhde, A. (2013). The light and dark side of TARP. *Journal of Banking & Finance*, 37(7), 2586–2604.

Fichera, J. (2011). *Auction Rate Securities Need Reform, Not Just Redemption.* http://saberpartners.com/oped/Ars_Market_Analysis_And_Recommendation_5-31-11.pdf.

FINRA (USA). (July 2011). *Reverse Convertibles – Complex Investment Vehicles.* www.finra.org/investors/alerts/reverse-convertibles-complex-investment-vehicles.

Fizaine, F. (2018). Toward generalization of futures contracts for raw materials: A probabilistic answer applied to metal markets. *Resources Policy*, 59, 379–388.

Forbus, K. (2019). *Qualitative Representations: How People Reason and Learn About the Continuous World* (MIT Press, Boston, MA, USA).

Francis, J. (2009). Covenants in US public debt agreements. *Accounting & Finance*, 29(2), 31–45.

Frankel, T. & Cunningham, L. (2007). The mysterious ways of mutual funds: Market timing. *Annual Review of Financial and Banking Law*, 25, 235–293.

French, J., Spyker, D. & O'Connor, N. (2014). *Magnum P.I. – Getting to the Bottom of IRS and SEC Risks in Equity Compensation.* www.scu.edu/business/cepi/symposiums/2014/upload/3B_Magnum_PI.pdf.

Friewald, N., Jankowitsch, R. & Subrahmanyam, M. (2017). Transparency and liquidity in the structured product market. *Review of Asset Pricing Studies*, 7(2), 316–326.

García-Pérez, A., Yanes-Estévez, V. & Oreja-Rodríguez, J. (2014). Strategic reference points, risk and strategic choices in small and medium-sized enterprises. *Journal of Business Economics and Management*, 21(3), 431–449.

Gjerstad, S. & Dickhaut, J. (January 1998). Price formation in double auctions. *Games and Economic Behavior*, 22(1), 1–29.

Glachant, M. (1998). The Use of Regulatory Mechanism Design in Environmental Policy: A Theoretical Critique. published in: F. Duchin, S. Faucheux, J. Gowdy, I. Nicolai, eds., *Firms and Sustainability* (Edward Elgar Publishers, 1998). http://www.cerna.ensmp.fr/Documents/MG-inFaucheux.pdf.

Goetzmann, W., Ivkovic, Z. & Rouwenhorst, G. (2001). Day trading international mutual funds: Evidence and policy solutions. *Journal of Financial & Quantitative Analysis*, 36, 287–309.

Gordon, J. (2011). Defining a common enterprise in investment contracts. *Ohio State Law Journal*, 72(1), 59–69. http://moritzlaw.osu.edu/lawjournal/issues/volume72/number1/gordon.pdf.

Grechuk, B. & Zabarankin, M. (2014). Risk averse decision making under catastrophic risk. *European Journal of Operational Research*, 239(1), 166–176.

Grimm, D. (2008). A process of natural correction: Arbitrage and the regulation of exchange-traded funds under the investment company act. *University of Pennsylvania Journal of Business Law*, 11, 95–105.

Gross, C., Königsgruber, R. et al. (2016). The financial reporting consequences of proximity to political power. *Journal of Accounting and Public Policy*, 35(6), 609–634.

Guha-Khasnobis, B. & Mavrotas, G. (2008). *Financial Development, Institutions, Growth and Poverty Reduction* (Palgrave Macmillan, New York).Guru, B. & Yadav, I. (2019). Financial development and economic growth: Panel evidence from BRICS. *Journal of Economics, Finance and Administrative Science.* https://doi.org/10.1108/JEFAS-12-2017-0125.

Hains, M. (1997). *The Re-Characterization of Futures Contracts.* Unpublished PhD thesis, University of Sydney, Sydney, Australia.

Halpern, J. (2003). *Reasoning about Uncertainty* (MIT Press, Boston, MA, USA).

Han, S. & Li, D. (February 2008). *Liquidity Crisis, Runs, and Security Design: Lessons from the Collapse of the Auction Rate Securities Market.* Federal Reserve Board (USA), February 15.

Han, S. & Li, D. (2010). *The Fragility of Discretionary Liquidity Provision – Lessons from the Collapse of the Auction Rate Securities Market.* Finance and Economics Discussion Series: Divisions of Research & Statistics and Monetary Affairs; Federal Reserve Board, Washington, DC. www.federalreserve.gov/pubs/feds/2010/201050/201050pap.pdf.

Harriton, D. (1994). Distinguishing between equity and debt in the new financial environment. *Tax Law Review*, 49, 499–506.

Hazen, T. (1992). Rational investments, speculation or gambling? Derivatives securities and financial futures and their effect on the underlying capital markets. *Northwestern University Law Review*, 86, 987–990.

Heibatollah, S. & Zhou, H. (2009). The economic consequences of increased disclosure: Evidence from cross-listings of Chinese firms. *Journal of International Financial Management & Accounting*, 19(1), 1–27.

Herbert, B. (2018). Moral hazard and the optimality of debt. *The Review of Economic Studies*, 85(4), 2214–2252.

Hong, S., Wernz, C. & Stillinger, J. (2016). Optimizing maintenance service contracts through mechanism design theory. *Applied Mathematical Modelling*, 40(21–22), 8849–8861.

Houge, T. & Wellman, J. (2005). Fallout from the mutual fund trading scandal. *Journal of Business Ethics*, 62, 129–139.

Hu, H. (2014). Disclosure universes and modes of information: Banks, innovation, and divergent regulatory questions. *Yale Journal on Regulation*, 31, 565–626.

Hu, H. (2018). Corporate distress, credit default swaps, and defaults: Information and traditional, contingent, and empty creditors. *Brooklyn Journal of Corporate, Financial & Commercial Law*, 13, 5–32.

Hu, H. & Morley, J. (2018). A regulatory framework for exchange-traded funds. *Southern California Law Review*, 91, 839–941.

Hwang, Y. & Kirby, A.J. (2004). Competitive effects of disclosure in a strategic entry model. *Review of Accounting Studies*, 5(1), 57–85.

Jaffee, D. (2006). Reining in Fannie Mae and Freddie Mac. *Regulation*, 29(3), 22–25.

Janger, E. (2002). Muddy rules for securitizations. *Fordham Journal of Corporate & Financial Law*, 7, 301–316.

Janssen, M., Manning, M. & Udiani, O. (2014). The Effect of Social Preferences on the Evolution of Cooperation in Public Good Games. *Advances in Complex Systems*, 17, No. 03–04, 1450015 (2014). https://doi.org/10.1142/S0219525914500155.

Jegadeesh, N. (1993). Treasury auction bids and the Salomon squeeze. *Journal of Finance*, 48, 1403–1419.

Johnston, M. (September 17, 2007). Firms caught in money lockup – failed auctions make cash stashes illiquid: As much as $6 billion tied up. *Financial Week*. www.financial week.com/apps/pbcs.dll/article?AID=/20070917/REG/70914033.

Jordan, B. & Jordan, S. (1997). Special repo rates: An empirical analysis. *Journal of Finance*, 52, 2051–2072.

Karpoff, J., Lee, D. & Martin, G. (2008a). The cost to firms of cooking the books. *Journal of Financial and Quantitative Analysis*, 43, 581–612.

Karpoff, J., Lee, D. & Martin, G. (2008b). The consequences to managers for cooking the books. *Journal of Financial Economics*, 88, 193–215.

Khan, U. & Lo, A. (2018). Bank lending standards and borrower accounting conservatism. *Management Science*, in press.

Kim, J. & Sohn, B. (2013). Real earnings management and cost of capital. *Journal of Accounting and Public Policy*, 32(6), 518–543.

Kirby, A. (2004). The product market opportunity loss of mandated disclosure. *Information Economics & Policy*, 16, 553–577.

Kirk, T. (2015). Superior supererogation: Why credit default swaps are securities under the investment advisers act of 1940. *William & Mary Business Law Review*, 6, 237–257. https://scholarship.law.wm.edu/wmblr/vol6/iss1/7

Klee, K. & Butler, B. (2002). Asset-backed securitization, special purpose vehicles and other securitization issues. *Uniform Commercial Code Law Journal*, 35(2), 23–67.

Krishnamurthy, A. (2002). The bond/old-bond spread. *Journal of Financial Economics*, 66, 463–506.

Kuhlman, C. & Mortveit, H. (2014). Attractor stability in non-uniform Boolean networks. *Theoretical Computer Science*, 559, 20–33.

Kwag, S. & Stephens, A. (2009). Investor reaction to earnings management. *Managerial Finance*, 36(1), 44–56.

Kwon, Y. (2005). Accounting conservatism and managerial incentives. *Management Science*, 51(11), 1593–1732.

Law, D. & Versteeg, M. (2012). The declining influence of the united states constitution. *NYU Law Review*, 87, 762–826. www.nyulawreview.org/sites/default/files/pdf/NYULawReview-87-3-Law-Versteeg_0.pdf.

Lemke, T., Lins, G. & McGuire, J. (2017). *Regulation of Exchange-Traded Funds* (Matthew Bender; ISBN 978-0-7698-9131-6).

Lemke, T., Lins, G. & Smith, T. (2017). *Regulation of Investment Companies* (Matthew Bender; ISBN 978-0-8205-2005-6).

Libby, R., Nelson, W. & Hunton, J. (2006). Recognition vs. Disclosure, auditor tolerance for mis-statement, and the reliability of stock-compensation and lease information. *Journal of Accounting Research*, 44, 533–560.

Lin, Y. & Druzdzel, M. (1999). Relevance-Based Incremental Belief Updating in Bayesian Networks. *International Journal of Pattern Recognition and Artificial Intelligence*, 13(2), 285–295.

Liu, Y., Ning, Y. & Davidson, W. (2010). Earnings management surrounding new debt issues. *The Financial Review*, 45, 659–681.

Liu, Z., Jorion, P. & Shi, C. (2008). Informational effects of regulation FD: Evidence from rating agencies. *Journal of Financial Economics*, 76(2), 309–330.

LoPucki, L.M. (1997). The systems approach to law. *Cornell Law Review*, 82, 479–483.

Luo, R. (2014). Operational risk, fund performance and investors protection: Evidence from China. *Journal of Business and Financial Affairs*, 3, 116.

Lupica, L. (2000). Circumvention of the bankruptcy process: The statutory institutionalization of securitization. *Connecticut Law Review*, 33, 199–210.

Madureira, A., Pereira, I., Pereira, P. & Abraham, A. (2014). Negotiation mechanism for self-organized scheduling system with collective intelligence. *Neurocomputing*, 132, 97–110.

Malvey, P., Archibald, C. & Flynn, S. (2014). *Uniform-Price Auctions: Evaluation of the Treasury Experience*. Office of Market Finance, U.S. Treasury, Washington, DC. 20220. www.treasury.gov/resource-center/fin-mkts/Documents/final.pdf.

Marquardt, C. & Zur, E. (2015). The role of accounting quality in the M&A market. *Management Science*, 61(3), 487–705.

Martellini, L., Milhau, V. & Tarelli, A. (2018). Capital structure decisions and the optimal design of corporate market debt programs. *Journal of Corporate Finance*, 49, 141–167.

McCarter, M., Rockmann, K. & Northcraft, G. (2010). Is it even worth it? The effect of loss prospects in the outcome distribution of a public goods dilemma. *Organizational Behavior and Human Decision Processes*, 111(1), 1–12.

McConnell, J. & Saretto, A. (2010). Auction failures and the market for auction rate securities. *Journal of Financial Economics*, 97, 451–469.

McKinnon, J. & Hitt, G. (February 4, 2002). How treasury lost in battle to quash a dubious security – instrument issued by Enron and others can be used as both debt and equity – win for flotilla of lobbyists. *Wall Street Journal*, at A1.

McLaughlin, T. (2008). Eyes wide shut: Exchange traded funds, index arbitrage, and the need for change. *Review of Banking & Finance*, 22, 597–610.

Melendy, S. (2011). Monitoring legal compliance: The growth of compliance committees. *Accounting Perspectives*, 10(4).

Melnik, S., Ward, J., Gleeson, J. & Porter, M. (2013). Multi-stage complex contagions. *Chaos*, 23, 013124. http://dx.doi.org/10.1063/1.4790836.

Meneguzzi, F., Modgil, S., Oren, N., Miles, S., Luck, M. & Faci, N. (2012). Applying electronic contracting to the aerospace aftercare domain. *Engineering Applications of Artificial Intelligence*, 25, 1471–1487.

Menyah, K., Nazlioglu, S. & Wolde-Rufael, Y. (2014). Financial development, trade openness and economic growth in African countries: New insights from a panel causality approach. *Economic Modelling*, 37, 386–394.

Michels, J. (2013). *Disclosure versus Recognition: Inferences from Subsequent Events*. Working paper, University of Pennsylvania, USA.

Miklashevich, I. (2003). Mathematical representation of social systems: Uncertainty and optimization of social system evolution. *Non Linear Phenomena In Complex Systems*, 6(2), 678–686.

Milton, F. (1964). Comment on collusion in the auction market for treasury bills. *Journal of Political Economy*, 72, 513–514.

Mirazizov, A., Radzhabova, I. & Abdulaeva, M. (2013). The effectiveness of financial and monetary instruments of sustainable development in Tajikistan's economy and ways of improving them. *Journal of Internet Banking and Commerce*. http://www.icommercecentral. com/open-access/the-effectiveness-of-financial-and-monetary-instruments-of-sustainable-development-in-tajikistans-economy-and-ways-of-improving-them.php?aid=83749.

Moe, R. & Kosar, K. (May 18, 2005). (Congressional Research Service). *The Quasi Government: Hybrid Organizations with Both Government and Private Sector Legal Characteristics*, p. 11, Cong. Research Serv., CRS Report for Congress; Order Code RL30533.

Moldogaziev, T. & Luby, M. (2016). Too close for comfort: Does the intensity of municipal advisor and underwriter relationship impact bond borrowing costs? *Public Budgeting & Finance*, 36(3), 69–93.

Muller, M.A., Riedl, E. & Sellhorn, T. (2013). *Recognition Versus Disclosure of Fair Values*. Working paper. Available at SSRN: http://ssrn.com/abstract=2362362.

Nan, L. & Wen, X. (2014). Financing and investment efficiency, information quality, and accounting biases. *Operations Research*, 60(9), 2111–2380.

Naor, N. (2006). Reporting on financial derivatives – a law and economics perspective. *European Journal of Law & Economics*, 21(3), 285–314.

Niederhoff, J. & Kouvelis, P. (2019). Effective and necessary: Individual supplier behavior in revenue sharing and wholesale contracts. *European Journal of Operational Research*, 277(3), 1060–1071.

Nikolaev, V. (2017). Scope for renegotiation in private debt contracts. *Journal of Accounting and Economics*, 65(2), 270–301.

Noe, T. & Nachman, D. (1994). Optimal design of securities under asymmetric information. *Review of Financial Studies*, 7(1), 1–44.

Noussair, C., Trautmann, S. & Kuilen, G. (2013). Higher order risk attitudes, demographics and saving. *Review of Economic Studies*, 81(1), 325–355.

Nwogugu, M. (2003). Decision-making under uncertainty: A critique of options pricing models. *Journal of Derivatives & Hedge funds* (now part of *Journal of Asset Management*), 9(2), 164–178.

Nwogugu, M. (2004). Legal, economic and behavioral issues in accounting for stock options. *Managerial Auditing Journal*, 19(9), 1078–1118.

Nwogugu, M. (2006). Employee stock options, production functions and game theory. *Applied Mathematics & Computation*, 181(1), 552–562.

Nwogugu, M. (2007a). Some issues in securitization and disintermediation. *Applied Mathematics & Computation*, 186(2), 1031–1039.

Nwogugu, M. (2007b). Equity-based incentives: Wealth transfers, disruption costs and new models. *Corporate Control Ownership & Control*, 5(1), 292–304.

Nwogugu, M. (2007c). Some securities law problems inherent in REITs. *Journal of International Banking Law & Regulation*, 22(11), 594–602.

Nwogugu, M. (2007d). Some game theory and financial contracting issues in corporate transactions. *Applied Mathematics & Computation*, 186(2), 1018–1030.

Nwogugu, M. (2008). The efficiency of sarbanes-oxley act: Willingness to comply and agency problems. *Corporate Control & Ownership*, 5(1), 449–454.

Nwogugu, M. (2008a). Illegality of securitization, bankruptcy issues and theories of securitization. *Journal of International Banking Law & Regulation*, 23(7), 363–375.

Nwogugu, M. (2008b). Securitization is illegal: Racketeer influenced and corrupt organizations, usury, antitrust and tax issues. *Journal of International Banking Law & Regulation*, 23(6), 316–332.

Nwogugu, M. (2008c). Some corporate governance problems pertaining to REITs – part one. *Journal of International Banking Law & Regulation*, 23(2), 71–89.

Nwogugu, M. (2008d). Some corporate governance problems pertaining to REITs – part two. *Journal of International Banking Law & Regulation*, 23(3), 142–162.

Nwogugu, M. (2008e). Decisions in commercial real estate leasing in the real estate sector. *Corporate Ownership & Control*, 5(3). An earlier version of this article was published in the *Proceedings of the Pre-Conference Meetings (2007) On Risk Management and Engineering Management 2007*, by RiskChina Research Center, University of Toronto, Canada.

Nwogugu, M. (2008f). On the choice between a sale-leaseback and debt. *Corporate Ownership & Control*, 5(4), 326–329.

Nwogugu, M. (2009). Economic policy and the constitutionality of asset securitization. *International Company & Commercial Law Review*, 20(7), 245–254.

Nwogugu, M. (2009b). On the choice between a strategic alliance and an M&A transaction. *International Journal of Mathematics, Game Theory & Algebra*, 17(5/6), 269–278.

Nwogugu, M. (2010/2012). *A Critique of Options-Based Indices and CDS Indices*. www.ssrn.com.

Nwogugu, M. (2010/2013). *Problems Inherent in the Compensation and Business Models of Credit Rating Agencies*. www.ssrn.com.

Nwogugu, M. (2013). Decision-making, sub-additive recursive "matching noise and biases in risk-weighted index calculation methods in in-complete markets with partially observable multi-attribute preferences. *Discrete Mathematics, Algorithms & Applications*, 05(3), 1350020.

Nwogugu, M. (2014a). REIT shares/interests are derivatives instruments: And REITs are SIFIs. *Pratt's Journal of Bankruptcy Law*, 10(3), 242–246.

Nwogugu, M. (2014b). "Netting", the liquidity coverage ratio: And the US FSOC's non-SIFI criteria, and new recommendations. *Banking Law Journal*, 131(6), 416–420.

Nwogugu, M. (2014c). *Conflicts of Interest: And the Existence of Anti-Compliance Coordination and Un-Cooperative Cartels Among Nigerian Financial Services Companies*. www.ssrn.com.

Nwogugu, M. (2015a). Goodwill/intangibles rules and earnings management. *European Journal of Law Reform*, 17(1).

Nwogugu, M. (2015b). Failure of the Dodd-frank act. *Journal of Financial Crime*, 22(4), 520–572.

Nwogugu, M. (2015c). Un-constitutionality of the Dodd-Frank act. *European Journal of Law Reform*, 17, 185–190.

Nwogugu, M. (2015d). Real options, enforcement of and goodwill/intangibles rules and associated behavioral issues. *Journal of Money Laundering Control*, 18(3), 330–351.

Nwogugu, M. (2019a). Human computer interaction, incentive conflicts and methods for eliminating index arbitrage, index-related mutual fund arbitrage and ETF arbitrage. Chapter 9 in: Nwogugu, M. (2019), *Indices, Index Funds and ETFs HCI: Exploring HCI, Nonlinear Risk and Homomorphisms* (Palgrave Macmillan, London, UK).

Nwogugu, M. (2019b). Financial indices, joint ventures and strategic alliances invalidate cumulative prospect theory, third-generation prospect theory, related approaches and intertemporal asset pricing theory: HCI and three new decision models. Chapter 11 in: Nwogugu, M. (2019), *Indices, Index Funds and ETFs HCI: Exploring HCI, Nonlinear Risk and Homomorphisms* (Palgrave Macmillan, London, UK).

Nwogugu, M. (2019c). Economic policy, complex adaptive systems, human-computer interaction and managerial psychology: Popular-index ecosystems. Chapter 12 in: Nwogugu, M. (2019), *Indices, Index Funds and ETFs HCI: Exploring HCI, Nonlinear Risk and Homomorphisms* (Palgrave Macmillan, London, UK).

Nwogugu, M. (2019d). A critique of Credit Default Swap (CDS) indices. Chapter 3 in: Nwogugu, M. (2019), *Indices, Index Funds and ETFs HCI: Exploring HCI, Nonlinear Risk and Homomorphisms*" (Palgrave Macmillan, London, UK).

Nwogugu, M. (2019e). Anomalies in Taylor series, and tracking errors and homomorphisms in the returns of leveraged/inverse ETFs and synthetic ETFs/funds. Chapter 7 in: Nwogugu, M. (2019), *Indices, Index Funds and ETFs HCI: Exploring HCI, Nonlinear Risk and Homomorphisms* (Palgrave Macmillan, London, UK).

Nyborg, K., Sundaresan, S. & Rydqvist, K. (2005). Bidder behavior in multiunit auctions: Evidence from Swedish treasury auctions. *Journal of Political Economy*, 78(3), 997–1021.

Pae, S. (2000). Information sharing in the presence of preemptive incentives: Economic consequences of mandatory disclosure. *Review of Accounting Studies*, 5(4), 331–350.

Pae, S. (2002). Optimal disclosure policy in oligopoly markets. *Journal of Accounting Research*, 40(3), 901–932.

Paglia, J. (September 2007). An overview of covenants in large commercial bank loans. *The RMA Journal*. www.exceptioncomplete.com/PDF/4993.pdf.

Paglia, J. & Mullineaux, D. (2006). An empirical exploration of financial covenants in large bank loans. *Banks & Bank Systems*, 1, 103–122.

Pan, P. (June 30, 2006). *True Colors of an 'Auction' Market: What the SEC Unveiled in the Auction Rate Securities Market*. Capital Advisors Group, Credit Commentary.

Papaikonomou, V. (2010). Credit rating agencies and global financial crisis: Need for a paradigm shift in financial market regulation. *Studies in Economics and Finance*, 27, 161–174.

Paškevicius, A. & Sačilka, O. (2010). *Structured Securities and Their Development in Lithuania*. DOI: 10.15388/Ekon.2010.0.965. www.researchgate.net/publication/267225056_STruCTurEd_SECuriTiES_ANd_ThEir_dEvElOPMENT_iN_liThuANiA/figures?lo=1.

Patterson, M. (2010). Standardization of standard-form contracts: Competition and contract implications. *William and Mary Law Review*, 52(2), 327–340.

Perc, M., Donnay, K. & Helbing, D. (2013). Understanding recurrent crime as system-immanent collective behavior. *PLoS One*, 8(10), e76063.

Petajisto, A. (2017). Inefficiencies in the pricing of exchange-traded funds. *Financial Analysts Journal*, First Quarter, 24–33.

Peterson, A. (2010). Skimming the profit pool: The American mutual fund scandals and the risk for Japan. *Asian Journal of Criminology*, 5(2), 109–121.

Piloto, B., Sincerre, B., Sampaio, J., Famá, R. & dos Santos, J. O. (2016). Debt issues and earnings management. *Revista Contabilidade & Finanças*, 27. DOI: 10.1590/1808-057x201601660.

Post, D. & Eisen, M. (2000). How long is the coastline of the law? Thoughts on the fractal nature of legal systems. *Journal of Legal Studies*, 29, 545–555.

Pozen, R. & Hamacher, T. (2015). *The Fund Industry: How Your Money is Managed* (2nd ed., Wiley Finance, Hoboken, NJ; ISBN 978-1118929940).

Qu, D. (2016). *Manufacturing and Managing Customer-Driven Derivatives* (Wiley; ISBN 978-1-118-63262-8).

Reiss, D. (2008). The federal government's implied guarantee of Fannie Mae and Freddie Mac's obligations: Uncle Sam will pick up the tab. *Georgia Law Review*, 42, 1019–1029.

Reiss, D. (2009). The role of the Fannie Mae/Freddie Mac duopoly in the American housing market. *Journal of Financial Regulation & Compliance*, 17(3), 336–348.

Roberts, M. (2015). The role of dynamic renegotiation and asymmetric information in financial contracting. *Journal of Financial Economics*, 116, 61–68.

Room, G. (2011). *Complexity, Institutions, and Public Policy* (Edward Elgar, Northampton, MA, USA).

Roos, P. & Nau, D. (2010). Risk Preference and Sequential Choice in Evolutionary Games. *Advances in Complex Systems*, 13(4), 559–578. https://doi.org/10.1142/S0219525910002682.

Root, H. (2013). *Dynamics Among Nations* (MIT Press, Boston, MA, USA).

Ruhl, J. & Ruhl, H. (1997). The arrow of the law in modern administrative states: Using complexity theory to reveal the diminishing returns and increasing risks the burgeoning of law poses to society. *University of California Davis Law Review*, 30, 405–426 (explaining the various kinds of attractors).

Sabri, N. (2011). The role of financial instruments in economic development of Mediterranean countries. *International Review of Applied Financial Issues and Economics*, 3(3), 504–512.

Schwarcz, S. (2002). Enron and the use and abuse of special purpose entities in corporate structures. *University of Cincinnati Law Review*, 70, 1309–1329.

Securities Litigation & Consulting Group (2011). *Auction Rate Securities*. www.slcg.com/pdf/workingpapers/SLCG-ARS%20Paper.pdf.

Selvers, J. (1974). Investment contracts: Expanding effective securities regulations. *St. John's Law Review*, 48(3). https://scholarship.law.stjohns.edu/lawreview/vol48/iss3/8.

Semaan, E. & Drake, P. (2016). TARP and the long-term perception of risk. *Journal of Banking & Finance*, 68, 216–235.

Shen, J. (2017). *Hybrid IS-VWAP Dynamic Algorithmic Trading via LQR*. http://papers.ssrn.com/sol3/papers.cfm?abstract_id=2984297.

Shen, J. & Yu, J. (2014). *Styled Algorithmic Trading and the MV-MVP Style*. http://papers.ssrn.com/sol3/papers.cfm?abstract_id=2507002.

Silva, A. (2003). Bidding strategies in Brazilian treasury auctions. *Revista Brasileira de Finanças*, 1(1), 113–161.

Simon, D. (1994). Markups, quantity risk and bidding strategies at treasury coupon auctions. *Journal of Financial Economics*, 35, 43–62.

Smith, A. (2011). An experimental study of exclusive contracts. *International Journal of Industrial Organization*, 29(1), 4–13.

Snaije, B. (2017). Can finance and credit enable economic growth and democracy? Chapter in: Luciani, G. (ed.), *Combining Economic and Political Development: The Experience of MENA*. International Development Policy series 7 (Geneva, Graduate Institute Publications, Boston, Brill-Nijhoff), pp. 132–143.

Sobieski, J. (1962). State securities regulation of real estate investment trust: The midwest position. *Virginia Law Review*, 48(6), 1082–1103.

Soklakov, A. (December 2016). Elasticity theory of structuring. *Risk*, 81–86.

Soklakov, A. (June 2017). *Why Quantitative Structuring?* SSRN: https://ssrn.com/abstract= 2639383 or http://dx.doi.org/10.2139/ssrn.2639383.

Song, W. & Uzmanoglu, C. (2016). TARP announcement, bank health, and borrowers' credit risk. *Journal of Financial Stability*, 22, 22–32.

Song, Z. & Zhu, H. (2018). Quantitative easing auctions of treasury bonds. *Journal of Financial Economics*, 128(1), 103–124.

Sprinkle, G., Williamson, M. & Upton, D. (2008). The effort and risk-taking effects of budget-based contracts. *Accounting, Organizations and Society*, 33, 436–452.

Stein, S., Gerding, E.H., Rogers, A.C., Larson, K. & Jennings, N.R. (2011). Algorithms and mechanisms for procuring services with uncertain durations using redundancy. *Artificial Intelligence*, 175(14–15), 2021–2060.

Sun, B. (2009). *Asset Returns with Earnings Management*. Board of Governors of the Federal Reserve System, USA. International Finance Discussion Papers, Number 988. https://pdfs.semanticscholar.org/aa00/39e86ed742989269bb10d460f95d36c767b9.pdf.

Sussman, O. (1999). Economic growth with standardized contracts. *European Economic Review*, 43, 1797–1818.

SVB Financial Group (August 15, 2007). *Auction Rate Securities: Know the Risks and Rewards*. www.svbassetmanagement.com/pdfs/AuctionRateSecurities0907.pdf.

Technical Committee of the International Organization of Securities Commissions (July 2011), *Regulatory Issues Raised by the Impact of Technological Changes on Market Integrity and Efficiency*. IOSCO Technical Committee. http://www.iosco.org/library/pubdocs/pdf/IOSCOPD354.pdf.

Terán, J., Aguilar, J. & Cerrada, M. (2017). Integration in industrial automation based on multi-agent systems using cultural algorithms for optimizing the coordination mechanisms. *Computers in Industry*, 91, 11–23.

Triantis, G. (2013). Exploring the limits of contract design in debt financing. *University of Pennsylvania Law Review*, 161, 2014–2044.

Tsai, C., Lin, Y. & Wang, Y. (2009). Discovering Stock Trading Preferences by Self-Organizing Maps and Decision Trees. *International Journal on Artificial Intelligence Tools*, 18(4), 603–611.

US SEC (January 2015). *Investor Bulletin: Structured Notes*. www.sec.gov/oiea/investor-alerts-bulletins/ib_structurednotes.html.

Van Assche, A. & Schwartz, G. (2013). Contracting institutions and ownership structure in international joint ventures. *Journal of Development Economics*, 103, 124–132.

Veganzones, D. & Severin, E. (June 3, 2017). *The Impact of Earnings Management on Bankruptcy Prediction Models: An Empirical Research*. Available at SSRN: https://ssrn.com/abstract=2980144 or http://dx.doi.org/10.2139/ssrn.2980144.

Wall, F. (2017). Learning to Incentivize in Different Modes of Coordination. *Advances in Complex Systems*, 20, No. 02–03, 1750003. https://doi.org/10.1142/S0219525917500035.

Wei, W., Wang, J., Chen, X., Yang, J. & Min, X. (2018). Psychological contract model for knowledge collaboration in virtual community of practice: An analysis based on the game theory. *Applied Mathematics & Computation*, 329, 175–187.

Whittington, R. & Whittenburg, G. (1980). Judicial classification of debt versus equity. *Accounting Review*, 55(3), 409–418.

Williams, C. & Arrigo, B. (2002). *Law, Psychology and Justice: Chaos Theory and New (Dis)Order* (State University of New York Press, Albany).

Wu, Z., Zhao, R. & Tang, W. (2014). Optimal contracts for the agency problem with multiple uncertain information. *Knowledge-Based Systems*, 59, 161–172.

Young, T. (1997). The ABCs of crime: Attractors, bifurcations and chaotic dynamics. In Milanovic, D. (ed.), *Chaos, Criminology and Social Justice: The New Orderly (Dis)Order* (Praeger Publishers, Westport, CT, USA).

Yu, K. (2013). Does recognition versus disclosure affect value relevance? Evidence from pension accounting. *The Accounting Review*, 88, 1095–1127.

Zambon, S., Marasca, S. & Chiucchi, M. (2019). Special issue on The role of intellectual capital and integrated reporting in management and governance: A performative perspective. *Journal of Management and Governance*, 23(2), 291–297.

Zgonnikov, A. & Lubashevsky, I. (2014). Unstable Dynamics of Adaptation in Unknown Environment Due to Novelty Seeking. *Advances in Complex Systems*, 17, No. 03–04, 1450013. https://doi.org/10.1142/S0219525914500131.

Zitzewitz, E. (2006). How widespread was late trading in mutual funds? *American Economic Review*, 96, 284–289.

Zohar, A. & Rosenschein, J. (2008). Mechanisms for information elicitation. *Artificial Intelligence*, 172(16–17), 1917–1939.

6

Mechanism design theory, public health and *Preferences+Beliefs*: behavioral biases and structural-effects inherent in REITs, "RECs" and "PICs"*

This chapter: i) introduces some behavioral biases and *structural effects* inherent in the operations of REITs (real estate investment trusts), "Property-Intensive Companies" ("PICs"; operating companies outside the real estate industry and which own substantial real estate, property-lease interests and or mortgages such as hotel-chains, restaurant chains; nursing home chains; movie theatre chains; finance companies; banks; etc.) and "non-REIT real estate companies" ("RECs"; non-REIT companies and mortgage companies in the global real estate industry) around the world; and ii) summarizes some Earnings Management, Incentive-Effects Management and Asset-Quality Management (collectively, *"Disclosure Misconduct"*) problems, and public health issues that sometime implicate Corporate Governance within REITs, RECs and PICs. Some of the behavioral biases and Structural Effects introduced herein can cause or amplify Earnings Management, Incentive-Effects Management and Asset-Quality Management.

For purposes of this chapter, companies that own substantial real estate are divided into the following groups:

1) REITs.
2) "RECs" are Non-REITs that are corporate entities that own substantial real estate. RECs include: 1) companies that own real estate which are used primarily for their own operations; and 2) companies that own substantial real estate most of which is leased to third parties.
3) "Property-Intensive Companies" ("PICs") are operating companies outside the real estate industry and which own substantial real estate and property-lease interests (that are used for their own operations), and or mortgages – such as hotel-chains, restaurant chains; nursing home chains; movie theatre chains, finance companies, banks, etc.

This chapter uses US statutes and processes because the US has the most advanced and the most-litigated corporate, securities and real estate laws (which have been copied by other countries). During 1970–2019, more than fifty countries introduced new REIT statutes that are the same as, or are very similar to US REIT statutes. Many companies and countries have also copied the operations processes and corporate structures of US-style RECs (e.g. real estate C-corporations, LLPs and LLCs) and PICs. Similarly, in many countries, many PICs are franchisee companies that use US-style franchise agreements and franchise-networks. In the US, REITs are defined by various statutes such as Section 856/857 of the Internal Revenue Code, the REIT Modernization Act of 1999, and the American Job Creation Act of 2005 and other statutes (collectively, the "REIT Codes").

On the relationships among real estate, Sustainability and Economic Growth, see the comments in: Bouchouicha and Ftiti (2012); Chui and Chau (2005); Zhang, Wang and Zhu (2012); Hong (2014); Coulson and Kim (2000); Wigren and Wilhelmsson (2007); Kauskale and Geipele (2016); International Monetary Fund (2016); Lim (2018); Cargill and Pingle (2019); Xue (2012); Zheng and Walsh (2019); Loutskina and Strahan (2015); Liu, Wang and Zhang (2019) and Warren (2010). Although REITs are flawed (see Nwogugu (2008a;b), and Nwogugu (2007d;2014)), REITs and RECs are relevant for economic growth and Sustainability for many reasons including but not limited to the following:

i)   REITs and RECs recycle capital, increase financial flows in the Global Economy and are major influencers/determinants of the *Business Cycle*. See the comment in Combes, Kinda et al. (2019). REITs and RECs can affect economic activity through their construction, financing, mortgage, redevelopment and renovation activities (which creates jobs and purchases of goods/services) and their dividend-policies; and through their acquisitions of newly constructed real estate and land (which provides developers/owners with cash for new construction/renovations) and the capital gains taxes and income taxes associated with their activities/transactions.

ii) REITs and RECs can transmit economic, financial, political and psychological shocks, Spillover Effects (they have foreign investors); *Inequality*, Fiscal Policy and Monetary Policy and thus can affect Financial Stability and or Systemic Risk. See Nwogugu (2014). The possible transmission "channels" include but are not limited to their compensation and hiring practices; their financing/borrowing terms; their dividend policies; the taxation of REITs and their investors; their property management agreements and practices; terms of their lease contracts; their real estate commissions; their construction/renovation costs and activities; their purchasing policies; etc.

iii) REITs and RECs serve as inflation, currency exchange-rate, income and uncertainty hedges; and as stores-of-value; and are also used in "spreads" and arbitrage in trading; and as benchmarks for valuations and firms' cost-of-capital; and their assets serve as collateral for loans, some of which are syndicated or securitized (and raises issues of *Domino Effects* and Financial Stability risks).

iv) REITs and RECs can affect households' economics, quality-of-life *Sustainability* (economic, social, urban and environmental Sustainability), human Aspirations, and human (individual and group) perceptions of risk, investment horizons, Uncertainty, Achievement, economic conditions, personal Growth and macroeconomic Growth. The possible transmission "channels" include REITs'/RECs' compensation and hiring practices; their financing/

borrowing terms; their property management and waste-disposal practices; the terms of their lease contracts; their real estate commissions; their waste-disposal practices; their construction/renovation activities and costs; their purchasing policies; etc.

v) Some of REITs' and RECs' property management and waste disposal practices, and some of the biases and Structural Effects introduced herein can result in Public Health problems.

6.1 Existing literature

Most existing academic literature are tangentially related to the issue of earnings management, asset-quality management, incentive-effects management and accounting distortions inherent in the operations of REITs, RECs and PICs – and extremely few academic articles address the inherent behavioral/psychology issues specific to these entities.

Bradley, Capozza and Seguin (1998) found that REITs' dividend payouts are lower for REITs that have more volatile cash-flow; where volatility is measured by leverage, size and property-level diversification. Li, Sun and Ong (2006) stated that REITs' stock splits are a signal of future cash flows, and that stock-splits and dividends are information substitutes. Roychowdhury (2006) found that managers manipulate real activities (such as price discounts; overproduction; reduction of discretionary expenditures, etc.) in order to avoid reporting annual losses. Gunny (2005) found that increased reported income via real earnings management activities, have significant negative impacts on future operating performance. Ooi (2001) found that real estate companies smooth dividend payout ratios in order to minimize having to reduce future dividends, and the dividend payout is a function of a firm's total assets and leverage ratio. Hanlon (2005) found that investors typically perceive large positive differences between the "book" and "tax" assets and income/expenses as a "red flag" and such differences are related to lower persistence of future earnings. Lev and Nissim (2004) stated that tax-to-book income ratio predicts subsequent five-year earnings changes. Manzon and Plesko (2002) analyzed the demand for tax-advantaged financing and investing activities (which typically generate timing and permanent differences, and also noise in the estimation of financial and tax income) and found that financial statement measures of income have become less representative of taxable income. Erickson, Hanlon and Maydew (2004), examined a sample of firms that were accused of fraudulently overstating their earnings, and found that these firms typically overpay taxes in the process of inflating their earnings. Kato, Kunimura and Yoshida (2002) found that Japanese banks manipulate earnings in order to maintain stable dividends and not contravene the statutory limit of 40 percent of net income. Gong, Louis and Sun (2007) stated that firms that repurchase their shares will experience post-purchase long-term abnormal returns, which is caused in part by pre-repurchase downward earnings management; and the extent of post-repurchase earnings management increases with the percentage of the company's equity that is repurchased. Ghosh and Sirmans (2006) show that dividend payouts are influenced by managerial performance, ownership as well as corporate governance. Ayers, Jiang and Laplante (2006) found that the relative information content of taxable income to book income is greater for firms that have low earnings quality, and thus, "taxable income" provides investors with an alternative performance measure. Chen, Dhaliwal and Trombley (2007), found that both earnings management and tax planning are related to the informativeness of book income and taxable income. Badertscher, Phillips, Pincus and Olhoft Rego (2006) found that companies tend to engage in earnings management activities that do not have current income tax consequences. Wang and D'Souza (2006) analyzed the relationship between a firm's flexibility in engaging in accruals earnings management and R&D investment choices; and found that managers are more (less) likely to cut R&D when accounting flexibility is low (high), and that managers prefer the use of accrual to real earnings management given ample accounting flexibility. Teoh, Wong and Rao (1998), and Teoh, Welch and Wong (1998a) found that after their IPOs, firms that have high current earnings and abnormal accruals, subsequently have poor long-run earnings in the next three years, after which there is a reversal of abnormal accruals. Teoh, Welch and Wong (1998b) found that seasoned equity issuers that change their discretionary accruals in order to report higher net income before a public stock offering have lower post-issue long-run abnormal stock returns. However, many of the empirical studies in the foregoing articles suffer from the methodological problems discussed in Nwogugu (2007c), and many of the balance sheet and income statement accounts (e.g. Current Assets, Net Income, Total Assets, etc.) used in models for identifying earnings management are also inappropriate as discussed in Nwogugu (2007c).

Earnings management, Asset-quality Management and Incentive-Effects Management typically occur and or are amplified within the context of, and often distort organizations, *Incentive-Mechanisms*, *Contracting-Frameworks*, *Networks-of-Contracts*, markets and benefits of Fintech. *Contract Theory* and *Mechanism Design Theory* have been jointly studied from various perspectives including Economics/Finance, Operations Research, Mathematical Psychology, Computer Science, Game Theory and Applied Math – see: Hoppe and Schmitz (2018); Niederhoff and Kouvelis (2019); Hong, Wernz and Stillinger (2016); Wu, Zhao and Tang (2014); Li, Liu and Chen (2018); Lin and Chou (1990); Park and Kim (2014); Goetz et al. (2019); Fang and Yuan (2018); Madureira et al. (2014); Meneguzzi et al. (2012); Meneguzzi et al. (2011); Zohar and Rosenschein (2008); Terán, Aguilar and Cerrada (2017); and Wei et al. (2018). However, the models in most of these foregoing articles and literature are static, don't incorporate relevant variables; don't consider varying "states" and often complex "joint" effects of variables; and they don't consider Industrial Organization effects of contracts/mechanisms – see Nwogugu (2007a;b), Nwogugu (2019a;b) and Nwogugu (2006).

6.2 Public health

When aggregated at the national economy level, the behavioral biases, *Structural Effects* and earnings management possibilities introduced in this chapter combine to create complex systems, and macroeconomic and macrofinance indicators (which are hereby referred to as the *"Behavioral Bias Indicators"*). These indicators have not been properly recognized or analyzed in the economics/finance, public health, political economy, behavioral operations research or psychology literatures and are not tracked. Niamir et al. (2018); Nakagawa, Oiwa and Takeda (2012); Korniotis and Kumar (1993); Acquier, Daudigeos and Pinkse (2017); Schnellenbach and Schubert (2015); Pennings and Wansink (2004); and Rosenbaum et al. (2012) concluded or implied that human biases can affect national economies, although the links they established or theorized were indirect and they didn't discuss the issue of *Behavioral Bias Indicators*.

Also, when aggregated at the national or regional economy level, the behavioral biases and the extensive earnings management possibilities/opportunities introduced in this chapter can become public health risks as explained in Chapter 1 in this book. The major public health risks are as follows:

i) Mental health problems (e.g. depression; substance abuse; schizophrenia; irritability; violent tendencies; Attention Deficit Disorders; anxiety; phobias; etc.) which can cause or morph into other illnesses such as obesity, hypertension, diabetes, vascular problems; kidney disease, heart disease, etc.

ii) Adverse changes in diet and reductions of activity and physical exercise, any of which can cause a variety of illnesses such as obesity, kidney disease, liver disease, etc.

As mentioned in Chapter 1, *Accounting Biases* is a relatively new line of research and has been studied from Behavioral Accounting, Management Science (see: Khan and Lo [2018]; Chen and Jorgensen [2018]; Kwon [2005]; and Marquardt and Zur [2015]), Behavioral Operations Management and Operations Research (see: Nan and Wen [2014]) perspectives. Specific *Accounting Biases* were introduced in several chapters in this book. Chen and Jorgensen (2018) noted that *Accounting Biases* can affect competition and Industry Structure in various industries – and by extension, can affect Public Health. Several chapters in this book introduce *Accounting Biases*. Using a study of mergers/acquisitions, Marquardt and Zur (2015) found evidence that financial accounting quality is positively related to the efficient allocation of the economy's capital resources. *Enforcement Theory* has been analyzed from Operations Research, Political Philosophy and Law perspectives, and the associated literatures are cited in Chapter 2 in this book. *Enforcement Patterns* (e.g. enforcement of accounting regulations, commodities-trading regulations and securities laws; corporate laws; etc.) can also affect Public Health, competition and Industry Structure in various industries because: i) they affect the nature of competition and collaboration among firms in industries; ii) they affect firms' allocations of resource and capital; ii) they affect product development, marketing and human resources decisions; v) they affect the functioning, responsibilities and liability of boards of directors; v) they affect firms' perceived risk and liability-allocation in expected or existing disputes; vi) they affect human physiological and mental responses to stressors, risks, volatility, events and changes. Thus by extension, *Accounting Biases* and *Enforcement Patterns* can have both direct and indirect effects on economic growth and Sustainability.

6.3 Technology disruption in real estate

On the significant and evolving relationships among Artificial Intelligence, Fintech, Sustainable Growth and *Inequality*, see the discussion and cited articles in Chapter 3 in this book. Artificial Intelligence and Fintech have fundamentally changed the nature, values and efficiency of real estate and mortgages around the world. The disrupting software/technology include but are not limited to the following: *Sharing Economy* software firms (e.g. Airbnb; HomeAway; ShareDesk; LiquidSpace), inventory management software (e.g. Primaseller; NetSuite; RAM), Enterprise Resource Planning software (e.g. SAP; Microsoft Dynamics; etc.), online retailing platforms (e.g. Amazon, Alibaba, Ebay, Rakuten.co.jp; Kakaku.com; Yahoo Japan! Shopping), Real Estate Websites (e.g. Zillow; Trulia; Yahoo Homes; Fangjia.com; youtx.com; mayi.com), online social networks and news portals (e.g. Yahoo Finance; Aol.com; Facebook; Wechat; Weibo; Bloomberg; Toudou Youku), online search portals (e.g. Google; Baidu Tieba), online Multiple Listing Systems (MLS), mortgage/loan application/servicing software (e.g. Calyx; Interhyp), property appraisal software (HouseCanary; ValueLink; SFREP), AI/ML and real estate data (e.g. Mashvisor), automated online contracting software, online banking and ATMs, Augumented-Realty/Virtual-Reality software, Mobilephones, HVAC/Building-Management software (e.g. ThermoGRID; mHelpDesk; Shinryo), customer-service software and online work-collaboration software (for virtual teams – Zoho Projects; Asana; LiquidPlanner; Freshdesk; Salesforce Essentials; Zoho Desk), consumer social-credit-score systems in China (e.g. Alibaba's Sesame Credit), consumer financial credit scoring systems (e.g. FICO in the US), entertainment/gaming software. The disruption of brokerage services, real estate and mortgages has occurred or may occur in several dimensions (such as demand; valuation; obsolescence; re-use and adaptability; efficiency; energy costs; building code compliance; transaction costs; psychological utility/disutility; rapid information dissemination and *"Contagion"*; standardization of contracts and processes; human resources; etc.). See the comments in Nwogugu (2019d;e;f).

6.4 Behavioral Biases and *Structural Effects:* *Preferences+Beliefs*

The Behavioral Biases and *Structural Effects* hypotheses introduced in this section are intended to help researchers develop better mathematical models of, and public-policies for related phenomena. *Structural Effects* are effects that occur primarily because of regulations, institutions and contracts. See the *Structural Effects* and behavioral biases in Nwogugu (2008a;b) and Nwogugu (2009).

The term "*Preferences+Beliefs*" in Artificial Intelligence" (AI) is introduced here in this book and it refers to the interactions and joint evolution of the *Preferences+Beliefs* of both Human Agents and Automated Agent in specific contexts, and constrained by regulations and mechanisms. See Zohar and Rosenschein (2008); Fang and Yuan (2018); Hong, Wernz and Stillinger (2016); Madureira et al. (2014); Meneguzzi et al. (2012); Stein et al. (2011); Wu, Zhao and Tang (2014); Wei et al. (2018), Terán, Aguilar and Cerrada (2017); Edmonds (2012); Pfeffer & Carley (2013); Lekeas (2013); Ko & Zhijian (2012); Gomez-Serrano & Boudec (2012); Weiler (2003); and Niederhoff and Kouvelis (2019), all of which didn't address *Preferences+Beliefs*.

Some of the *Preferences* introduced in this chapter differ from, and may contradict the utility preferences in the Economics, Computer Science and Applied Math literatures. See: Farahmand, (2017), Boutilier et al. (2012), Abramowitz and Anshelevich (2018).

6.4.1 Proposition-1: The Debt-Value Differential Effect

Debt-Value Differential Effect, is conjectured here to refer to a situation wherein the Book Values of REIT's/REC's debt differs significantly from the Market Values of its debt (both short-term debt and long term debt. This *Debt-Value Differential Effect* is also present in non-real estate companies. The *Debt-Value Differential Effect* is often not reflected in prices of REIT Beneficial Interests and REC shares, and is often not disclosed by REITs/RECs in their financial statements, although the information is critical to investors and lenders. The *Debt-Value Differential Effect* may also be a major reason why the beneficial interests of public REITs often trade at significant discounts or premia to NAV. REITs/RECs typically don't report changes in the carrying values of their debt.

The book values and market values of a corporate entity's debt can differ due to various reasons including the following:

1) The changing default risk (where debt is used for the purchase or construction) of the underlying real estate.
2) Changes in credit qualities of tenants – this refers to changes in credit ratings of commercial tenants; and in the case of multifamily properties, changes in "aggregate average" credit scores (e.g. FICO in the US) of neighborhoods.
3) Changes in tenants' Willingness-to-Pay-rents – for both financially stable and financially distressed entities. Some tenants who can afford to pay rents may not be willing to pay such rent in the hope that they can negotiate better terms with the landlord, or that the landlord will defer eviction proceedings, or that they can obtain free rent and then vacate the property.
4) The differences between the average/portfolio Modified-Duration of the entity's debt, and the Modified Duration of the entity's assets.
5) The landlord may be party to long-term capital leases, the terms of which may not be fully disclosed in financial statements or public filings.

6) The landlord may have issued Preferred Stock with contingent terms or conversion rights or unusual features which may complicate the valuation of the debt. Such Preferred Stock may rank pari-passu with some of its debt or may grant Preferred Stock holders certain rights that may decrease the value of its debt – such as the right to elect Board Members; the right to increased participating Dividends; the right to exchange the Preferred Stock into certain forms of senior Debt; etc.

7) The entity may have contingent liabilities such as guarantees and liens – which may not be disclosed or fully disclosed in its Balance Sheets or public government filings.

8) The entity may have under-funded pension obligations and employee benefits obligations.

9) There may be substantial differences between the book and market values of the entity's assets, which in turn, will affect the recovery values of the entity's debt.

10) The REIT's de-REITing risk is unique to REITs, and reduces the value of REITs' debt.

11) The terms of the REIT's Property Management Agreements (which are often not disclosed) may increase or reduce the differences between the book value and market values of the REITs debt and or assets.

12) The entity may be a party to swaps/forward/options transactions – which may not be disclosed or may be partially disclosed in its financial statements.

13) The entity may be party to off-balance sheet leases.

14) The entity's Accounts Payables may be "guaranteed" such that it has super priority over its long-term debt or short-term debt.

15) The entity may have un-disclosed tax payables/liabilities.

This *Debt-Value Differential Effect* is typically not incorporated into REIT valuation models, but may cause increased volatility (due to activities of sophisticated investors), particularly in times of increasing or declining interest rates. REITs that borrow debt typically don't recognize or disclose any gains from declines of their debt.

The *Debt Value Differential Effect* can be confirmed by the following:

i)   A valuation of the REIT's or company's debt using YTMs of comparable debt.

ii)   A valuation of the REIT's or company's debt using CDS-adjusted interest rates.

6.4.2 Proposition-2: The Capital Expenditure (Capex) Effect

See the full explanation in Nwogugu (2019c). The use of the REIT/REC formats is conjectured to cause the following:

i)   The Capex costs for the property typically increases after the REIT/REC acquires the property. REIT/RECs typically outsource CapEx decisions to property managers. The quarterly rate of increase in the REIT/REC's CapEx account (Balance Sheet) is greater than the rate of increase in the REIT/REC's property (Balance Sheet) account.

ii) The REIT/REC's property portfolio incurs significant Capex costs in each fiscal quarter – this is typically a substantial minimum percentage of the PP&E account in each quarter.

iii) The REIT/REC's quarterly/annual portfolio CapEx cost always exceeds the REIT/REC's Cash Flow From Operations, and the REIT/REC funds the difference by borrowing substantial debt or issuing equity interests.

iv) The REIT/REC's significant CapEx costs are often not related to the age of the REIT/REC's properties (and in some instances, is not related to the size of the REIT/REC's property portfolio – measured in square meters).

Presumably, REITs can easily amend their acquisition criteria so that they purchase only commercial properties that have relatively minimal budgeted or actual CapEx. Indeed this would be the expected action given REIT/RECs'/RECs' emphasis on Dividends, and their cash constraints. REIT/RECs have substantial negotiating power in commercial real estate markets and are exposed to many commercial properties that are available for sale because brokers know that REIT/RECs are "credible" and have access to capital. Thus, REIT/RECs have substantial choice and discretion in terms of timing of the transaction and number of properties available for purchase. The *Capital Expenditure Effect* occurs in all segments of the REIT/REC industry and is not related to, and is not affected by the average tenure and or average remaining tenure (remaining lease duration) of the REIT/RECs' tenants at each property. In most instances, REIT/RECs cannot and don't raise rents during the first few years after they acquire a property (REIT/RECs often seek buildings whose rents are at the high end of the market) and thus, the REIT/RECs' high CapEx costs have not been justified by increases in rents.

The typical components of CapEx include leasing commissions, tenant improvements and direct capital expenditures – however, in many markets, leasing commissions (paid to brokers) have declined partly due to Fintech, and REIT/RECs and their property managers have in-house real estate brokers.

The typical REIT/REC's delegation of the primary CapEx decisions to the property manager is suspect given the critical cash flow implications of REIT/RECs' CapEx costs. Here, for the REIT/REC, delegation achieves the purposes of legal protection, and justification.

Hence, the sudden and significant post-acquisition increases in CapEx costs and "continuous" high Capex costs at many REIT/RECs, constitutes either an "operations surprise" or a "managed fraud". Given the predictable nature of REIT/RECs CapEx costs, and the fact that this pattern of Capex changes occurs in all segments of the REIT/REC industry, such changes in Capex costs are more likely to involve fraud or misconduct. On the other hand, a REIT/REC's knowing purchase of a commercial property that is known to have historically relatively very high CapEx costs, either constitutes a breach of fiduciary duty, or gross mis-management.

The *Capital Expenditure Effect* is prevalent in Property-Intensive Companies and REITs and is evident in the following:

i)   A comparison of commercial buildings' Capex costs before and after the REIT acquires the property.

ii)   The statistical relationship between the quarterly rate of increase in the REIT's CapEx account (Balance Sheet), and the rate of increase in the REIT's property (Balance Sheet) account.

iii) The statistical relationship between the REITs' Cumulative Capex costs, and the sum of the REIT's property (Balance Sheet) account and Accumulated Depreciation Account.

iv)   The statistical relationship between the REITs' Cumulative Capex costs, and the average age of the REIT's property portfolio (weighted by square meters and ages of the buildings).

v)   The REIT's Capex costs in each fiscal quarter as a percentage of the REIT's Property & Plant account (balance Sheet).

vi)   The statistical relationship between the difference between REIT's quarterly/annual portfolio CapEx cost and the REIT's Cash Flow From Operations, and the on the other hand, the REIT funds the difference by borrowing substantial debt or issuing equity interests.

vii) The statistical relationship between the quarterly or monthly weighted average remaining tenure (remaining lease term) of the REITs' tenants at each building and the REIT's quarterly CapEx costs (or the REIT's cumulative CapEx costs) incurred for the associated building.

viii) The statistical relationship between the cumulative CapEx and the lease-up/lease-expiration schedule for each property owned by a REIT.

The result is that managers tend to misclassify operating expenses as Capex in order to boost FFO.

6.4.3 Proposition-3: The Deferred Tax Asset/Liability Bias

See the full explanation in Nwogugu (2019c). In most jurisdictions, REITs report *Deferred Tax Assets* and *Deferred Tax Liabilities* in their Balance Sheets and Income Statements, even though REITs are not taxable entities.[1] See: Nwogugu (2015a). In the US, although REITs are exempt from federal taxes, they are usually subject to state taxes but can deduct the Dividends-paid. However, US REITs (and some foreign REITs) still calculate their Deferred Tax Assets/Liabilities for both federal and state taxes as if the REITs were subject to federal taxes – and thus, such REIT's Deferred Tax Asset/Liability accounts are either error or are grossly overstated.

Given that property transactions are more likely to cause timing-differences than other assets, Property-Intensive Companies (PICs) are more likely to report

Deferred Tax Assets/Liabilities in their financial statements than regular companies (e.g. LLPs).

6.4.4 Proposition-4: The Goodwill Disclosure Bias

The *Goodwill Disclosure Bias* – wherein the PIC/REC/REIT is hereby conjectured to be more likely (than ordinary companies) to grossly under-report its property-related Goodwill in its Balance Sheets and Income Statements.[2]

Under the IASB/IFRS and US GAAP rules, real estate is an asset that is used in day to day operations of PICs/REITs/RECs – much like equipment and fixtures are used in regular companies. However, when some REITs/RECs/PICs purchase real estate, they typically don't record any Goodwill or Negative Goodwill for the difference between the purchase price and FMV of the real estate – the implicit assumption is that the purchase price is the FMV of the real estate, but that isn't always the case. In many instances, the Appraised value of commercial real estate differs from the purchase price and any such difference is Goodwill or Negative Goodwill. The key issue is that the Appraised Value (by a third party licensed Appraiser) is the most relevant indicator of value; and there are many reasons why the Purchase Price may differ from the Appraised value – such as: a) ability to negotiate, b) buyer's and seller's preferences and prior relationship, c) delegation, d) perceived fairness, e) framing, f) multiple and shifting reference points of value, for example, seller is satisfied once the offer price exceeds one or more temporary specific reference points, g) access to financing, h) time considerations, etc.

In PLR 200823014, the US Internal Revenue Service confirmed that Goodwill should be recorded for purchases of real estate assets (and the same accounting/tax treatment applies in other countries).[3]

The *Goodwill Disclosure Bias* is attributable to several factors. First, some REIT/REC/PIC staff/officers may not associate Goodwill with real estate transactions – Goodwill is typically associated with M&A. Second, there can be disagreements about an asset's Fair market Value. Third, reporting Goodwill in Balance Sheets is likely to create negative controversy about REITs', RECs' and or PICs' management capabilities, and hence their fiduciary duties – this has implications for the REIT's/REC's/PIC's and its manager's social capital and Reputation.

The *Goodwill Disclosure Bias* can be confirmed by the following:

i)   A comparison of the differences between the Appraised Value and Sale Price of real estate purchased and sold by REITs/RECs/PICs; and the changes in the periodic (i.e. quarterly) Goodwill accounts and Impaired-Goodwill accounts of these entities.

ii) The statistical relationship between the excess (negative or positive) of the Market-Value (based on a weighted-average from comparable transactions) over the Sale/Purchase Price of real estate purchased and sold by REITs/RECs/PICs (i.e. Negative-Goodwill and Goodwill and Impaired Goodwill) on one hand, and on the other hand, similar data for non-REITs/RECs/PICs.

iii) A comparison of the differences between the Appraised Value and Sale Price of real estate purchased by REITs/RECs/PICs and periodic changes in their Goodwill accounts on one hand, and similar data for non-REIT/REC/PIC companies.

6.4.5 Proposition-5: The Stable Paid-In-Capital Effect

This was discussed in Nwogugu (2019c). During 2000–2017, the Paid In Capital account of many exchange-traded US, European and Asian PICs/REITs seemed relatively stable and didn't vary much from year-to-year or from quarter to quarter (more stable than those of non-REITs, non-RECs and non-PICs).

6.4.6 Proposition-6: The Current Assets Effect

This was discussed in Nwogugu (2019c). During 1995–2017, the Current Assets of many exchange-traded US, European and Asian RECs/PICs/REITs varied substantially from year-to-year or from quarter to quarter (more volatile than the Current Assets of non-REITs, non-RECs and non-PICs).

6.4.7 Proposition-7: The Cash Distortion Effect

During 2002–2017 (and unlike non-REITs/RECs/PICs), in the financial statements of many exchange-traded US, Canadian, West-European and Asian REITs/RECs, the annual/quarterly changes in Accounts payables and Accounts Receivables (A/R) in the Cash Flow Statement, didn't match the changes in those accounts in their Balance Sheets for the same period. See O'Brien and Folta (2009). The *Cash Distortion Effect* can be attributed to the following reasons:

i)   REITs/RECs may not be good cash managers, they issue debt and equity more frequently; and their "restatements" are relatively frequent
ii) There may have been problems in calculating Bad Debt (un-collectible A/R).

6.4.8 Proposition-8: The Under-Stated Accounts Receivables Bias

During 2002–2017, many exchange-traded US and Asian PICs/REITs understated their property-related Accounts Receivables (A/R). Technically, for each tenant, the REIT should record A/R that is the lower of the net rent for 12 months or for the remaining lease term, whichever is shorter (however, most REITs record A/R that is about 6–12 percent of the annual rental income). This is because the REIT has provided the product to the tenant – the tenant occupies the property and hence, the REIT as landlord has completed almost everything that is required for occupancy and has earned the future rents. The REIT cannot just evict the tenant without a court proceeding that usually takes three–fifteen months. Even when commercial or residential tenants vacate a leased space, in most instances, they remain legally liable for rent for the space. Leasing companies that lease all types of equipment recognize lease receivables.

In an operating lease, the lessor/REIT/RECI credits the Rent Revenue account and simultaneously debits either cash or Rent Receivable accounts. The REIT/RECI/landlord also records depreciation expense during the life of the asset.[4]

REITs are more likely to understate their A/R than non-REIT real estate companies. This is because REITs want to reduce or manage expectations of: i) prospective sellers of properties who may equate substantial A/R to greater willingness to pay higher prices for property; and ii) current and prospective shareholders who may view greater A/R as indications of greater potential Dividends – and may become disappointed when such A/R is not "converted" into Dividends.

REITs may also want to avoid getting bad operational efficiency ratios (which are used to evaluate credit quality and investment potential) such as Days Sales Outstanding (DSO) and A/R Turnover Ratio. The key issue is that REITs' A/R is very different from the A/R of traditional companies. A significant percentage of any A/R that is recorded in the Balance Sheet of a traditional company is collected within ninety days. On the other hand, REITs' A/R is typically collected evenly each month over twelve months (or the remaining lease term if less than twelve months) after the balance sheet. Hence, REITs' DSO ratio will typically be much greater than those of traditional companies if calculated accurately.

Under-stating REITs' A/R weakens their perceived credit quality. REITs are very concerned about their credit quality because they depend on external debt financing. Hence, such understatement of A/R by REIT's implies that they are more concerned about the foregoing expectations of property sellers and investors, than REITs are concerned about rating analysts' beliefs.

The *Understated A/R Bias* can be confirmed by comparing the Accounts Receivables/Property Income ratio for REITs, non-REIT real estate companies and ordinary companies.

6.4.9 Proposition-9: The Long-Term Debt Illusion

The *Long-term Debt Illusion* was explained in detail in Nwogugu (2019c). REITs/RECs finance most of their property acquisitions with Long-term Debt (LTD) which often constitutes a significant portion of the REIT's total capital. However, although most of the LTD consist of property-level mortgages that are collateralized by individual properties, these mortgages are economically and psychologically medium-term loans. PICs/REITs can manipulate earnings and cash flows by selecting the amount, timing and terms of loan-refinancing.

6.4.10 Proposition-10: The Write-Down Aversion Effect

Some exchange-traded US REITs, Asian REITs and some European REITs and some US RECs did not write-off the losses (declines in the market values of their real estate) in their portfolios which occurred between 2004 and 2010. Such write-downs will typically affect their balance sheets and Income Statements. Under GAAP and IASB standards, real estate and loans are typically reported on a lower-of-cost-or market. In the case of REITs, some of their assets declined in value by 30–60 percent between 2004 and 2008 – and given that commercial real estate has estimated life of twenty–thirty-five years, the REITs that incurred such losses should have written them down.

REITs/RECs are more likely to be averse to write-downs of commercial real estate, compared to non-REIT real estate companies, because of the following reasons:

i) REITs are subject to Asset tests (REIT qualification test).

ii) The potential information content of such write-offs can be more detrimental to the market prices of the REIT/REC shares/interests, than to shares of a non-REIT/REC.

iii) The REITs/REC executive compensation scheme is more closely tied to the values of the owned-property portfolio, than the compensations scheme of non-REITs/RECs.

iv) The write-down will have a significant effect on the REIT/REC's Depreciation expense – which typically reduces the REIT/REC's taxable income.

v) REITs/RECIs are sometimes valued or evaluated based on their "*Net Asset Values*" (NAV) which depends on the book values of their real estate.

vi) In many countries and because of mandatory or contractual dividend payouts, REITs/RECIs are heavily dependent on loans/mortgages to fund their operations. Such loans/mortgages are sometimes based wholly or partially on the REITs/RECI's assets (which are used as actual or implied collateral). The ability to obtain such loans/mortgages depend on REITs/RECIs' credit ratings which can be negatively affected by such asset writedowns.

vii) Asset writedowns by REITs/RECIs can significantly affect price discovery in real estate markets and mortgages markets – partly because it implicates issues of "*financial credibility*" and or "*operational credibility*" of REITs/RECIs as local/regional "buyer-groups" and or "Seller-groups".

viii) Asset writedowns by REITs/RECIs can significantly affect the compensation/incentives (which are sometimes partly dependent on asset growth and NAV) of their midlevel and senior executives of REITs/RECIs – and raises the issues of employee motivation and effort.

ix) Some investors equate or link REITs'/RECIs' dividend growth and absolute dividends to their NAVs and or Total Assets.

6.4.11 Proposition-11: The Re-Statement/Re-Classification Bias

The *Re-Statement/Re-Classification Bias* was discussed in Nwogugu (2019c). Based on their conduct, frequent restatements and Accounting Disclosures during 2000–2018, Exchange-traded REITs were much more likely than RECs/PICs (and RECs/PICs were much more likely than ordinary companies), to re-state or re-classify their annual or quarterly audited financial statements. Such restatements and re-classifications usually occurred within three years after the original financial statements were issued.

6.4.12 Proposition-12: The Negative Free-Cash-Flow Effect

The *Negative Free-Cash-Flow Effect* was discussed in Nwogugu (2019c). The use of the REIT format causes most REITs to generate negative Free Cash Flow (FCF).

6.4.13 Proposition-13: The Mis-Stated Depreciation Bias

Many REITs and regulated-RECs under-state or over-state their Depreciation expense (for property, plant and equipment) in order to manipulate their "Taxable Income" and or "FFO". The mandatory REIT Dividend Payout is based on the REITs' "Taxable Income" and not their FFO or Net Income, and there are often substantial divergencies among the REIT's Taxable Income, Net Income and FFO. However, the standard approach has been to value REITs based on their FFOs.

6.4.14 Proposition-14: The Dividend Debt Effect

As explained in Nwogugu (2008),[5] the REIT Dividend payout requirement creates statutory short-term debt, which most REITs don't disclose in their financial statements. Ideally and given fundamental accounting principles, REITs and RECs should disclose the present value of estimated Dividends for the next twelve months, as a Current Liability in their Balance Sheets.

6.4.15 Proposition-15: The Mis-Classified Leasing Commissions and Tenant Improvements

REITs, RECs and PICs can easily mis-classify all or parts of their Lease Commissions expenses and or Tenant Improvements (e.g. as maintenance; bonuses; professional services; "other operating expenses"; etc.). The IFRS/IASB and US FASB accounting standards don't provide sufficient guidance or mandatory classification rules for such expenses. The reality is that for REITs, RECs and PICs, and for all leases (especially in the case of leases that last for more than one year), Leasing Commissions or Tenant Improvements provide benefits (or create costs) that affect these entities for more than one year (including brand equity; etc.), and thus should be capitalized.

6.4.16 Proposition-16: The Over-Stated Liquidity Effect

In many instances, REITs', PICs' and some regulated-RECs' short-term liquidity is grossly over-stated for several reasons most of which are attributable to GAAP and IFRS models. The overstatement arises from the following: i) many such entities don't create accounting reserves for their mandatory dividend payments, commission payments or rent-payments or taxes that are due within the next nine months; ii) some of these entities don't create sufficient accounting reserves for lease credit-losses and unexpected but probable tenant vacancies (e.g. financial distress of tenants); iv) the GAAP accounting model.

6.4.17 Proposition-17: The Bad Debt Bias

Based on the author's review of their financial statements, US REITs are more likely to create and use a Bad Debt Account than RECs (non-REIT real estate companies) and ordinary companies. REITs' bad debt arises from tenants that don't pay rent. In most corporate entities, management has the discretion to change/manipulate the Bad Debt valuation account depending on its estimates of collectability of un-paid rent. The Bad Debt Accounts affects the calculation of the REITs' FFO and their mandatory quarterly Dividend Payout.

6.4.18 Proposition-18: The Fair Value Accounting Effect

REITs have more incentives to (and are more likely to) manipulate the fair value estimates of their real estate than non-REIT real estate companies which in turn are more likely to manipulate the fair value estimates of their real estate than non-REIT non-REC companies. Under IFRS rules, any adjustments to the fair values of REITs' underlying real estate, must be recorded in their Income Statements. This is critical for REIT's because they are valued based on their Income Statements, Dividend Payout Ratios and FFO.

Most of these fair value changes are justified and reinforced with third-party appraisals. In most cases, REIT's senior management select external appraisers and decide their compensation. The selection process is typically not transparent and does not involve any type of bidding or competitive selection mechanism. Hence, REITs' management can directly or indirectly influence not only appraisals of their own REIT's real estate, but also valuations of other REITs' real estate. Real estate appraisers are typically "local" consultants – they focus on one market or region and sometimes focus on one or a few types of real estate. Within each market or region, there is a finite number of properties. Hence, real estate appraisers are subject to a *Reputation Effect*, and are heavily dependent on repeat business from customers. Furthermore, in many real estate markets, *Appraiser Turnover* for various end-users is low, and many entities that retain real estate appraisers (such as banks and REITs) don't implement "rotation" of appraisers (maximum-duration contracts for real estate appraisers). Under these circumstances, it is reasonably inferable that real estate appraisers are likely to "negotiate" property appraisals instead of providing independent un-biased appraisals.

6.4.19 Proposition-19: The Equity Dilution Bias

REITs and some non-taxable PICs (such as LLPs and LLCs) have more incentive to (and thus are more likely to) issue new ownership interests at prices that are dilutive compared to ordinary companies. REITs need external financing because they don't retain internally generated cash flow (because of mandatory dividend payout). Furthermore, many REITs and real estate LLPs/LLCs are highly leveraged. In an environment characterized by reduced lending, low volumes of ABS issuances, and a recession, many REITs whose debts were and are maturing are compelled to issue REIT interests at substantial discounts to market value. Thus, REITs and such LLPs/LLCs often issue equity at prices that represent 10–35 percent dilution of equity of existing shareholders. This trend is indicative of "hidden crashes" of the REIT market in the US and certain countries – which happened in 2009 in the US and although the US government didn't expressly bail out REITs, the financially distressed REITs were bailed out by investment banks that underwrote offerings of REIT interests at deep discounts during 2009. The situation in Japan in 2009 was similar except that the Japanese government expressly considered granting loans to Japanese REITs. The prices of these distressed equity offerings by REITs and LLPs/LLCs are set by their senior management and investment bankers, and may not represent their true value.

Such equity dilution constitutes earnings management, asset quality management and incentive effects management because it is used by REIT/LLP/LLC senior management and investment bankers to manipulate incentive compensation packages and their investors' perceptions of the condition and future prospects of REITs – primarily by manipulating popular valuation metrics. Hence, such equity dilution is also an accounting distortion, because it enables the REIT/LLP/LLC to manipulate key and popular valuation metrics such as the following:

i)   FFO per share – the reduction of interest payments may increase the FFO per share. But the REIT's asset base (real estate) remains constant.
ii) NAV per share. The REIT's NAV/Share will typically change.
iii) Total Assets per share
iv) Cash per share.
v)   Dividend Payout ratio – after dilution, the stock price declines and the Dividend payout ratio may increase.
vi) Debt/capital ratio – the proceeds of the offerings are typically used to reduce long-term debt. However, the REIT's real estate asset base remains constant and continues to generate the same cash flow.

6.4.20 Proposition-20: The Management Fee Manipulation Bias

In many countries, Property Management Fees and performance fees (paid to property managers) that are usually based on periodic Total Assets and or Gross Income or Operating Income can be manipulated – by real earnings management or accrual-based earnings management. Property Managers are subject to relatively low supervision, and have very strong incentives to manipulate operating results.

6.4.21 Proposition-21: Under-Reported Security Deposits

In many countries, REITs and some RECs typically don't report tenants' security deposits as liabilities.

6.4.22 Proposition-22: The Return-Of-Capital Non-Disclosure Bias

In many countries, REITs' dividends are often greater than their Net Income and FFO, and hence in many instances, more than 40 percent of public (exchange traded) REITs' Dividends consist of a return-of-capital. However, such REITs often don't disclose such return-of-capital to investors in their financial statements, because: i) any such disclosure will damage the REIT's Dividend Reputation (reputation for paying relatively large dividends and high dividend payout ratios) and reduce its ability to raise equity from investors; ii) such disclosure may contravene corporate law statutes that restrict REITs to paying dividends only from their Retained Earnings.

6.4.23 Proposition-23: The Preferred Stock Bias

There is no standard treatment for dividends of Preferred Stock that are issued by REITs and some RECs. In some countries, some REITs typically deduct "Preferred Stock" dividends before calculating their Pretax Income, and some don't.

In some countries: i) REITs and non-REIT real estate companies are more likely to issue shares of Preferred Stock before issuing substantial company-level un-secured debt; ii) REITs and non-REIT real estate companies are more likely to issue shares of Preferred Stock before issuing dilutive common stock. The usual variables include the entity's sector in the real estate industry, its profitability and Dividend Payout Rate; etc.

Separately, Kallberg and Liu (2010) noted that: i) a REIT is more likely to issue equity when its price-to-net asset value ratio is high – i.e. REITs issue equity in public markets when the cost of equity capital is lower in the public market than in the private market; ii) REITs are more likely to issue equity after experiencing large price increases; iii) REITs are less likely to issue debt when proxies for expected bankruptcy costs are high.

6.5 Some corporate governance and organizational psychology problems pertaining to REITs, RECs and PICs[6]

This section summarizes some Corporate Governance problems that implicate Earnings Management and organizational psychology within REITs, RECs and PICs.

Under US laws, the REIT is a tax overlay defined in Sections 856–860 of the US Internal Revenue Code ("IRC Section 856"), the REIT Modernization Act of 1999 (the "RMA"), and the American Job Creation Act (the "AJCA"); collectively, hereafter referred to as the "REIT Statutes". Unfortunately, US-style REITs have been implemented in various countries, despite many corporate governance problems inherent in REITs.[7] The following are hypothesis of some governance problems inherent in REITs.

6.5.1 Taxable REIT Subsidiaries ("TRS") are not justified; REITs can circumvent the RMA/AJCA 10 percent asset test and the 20 percent asset test

This was discussed in Nwogugu (2008a;b). The AJCA and the REIT Modernization Act of 1999 ("RMA") expressly permit "Taxable REIT Subsidiaries" ("TRS") that can engage in business activities that are not permitted for REITs. The use of TRSs enables REITs to effectively avoid other IRC Section 856, AJCA and RMA limitations on their activities,[8] and hence defeats some of the purpose of REITs. More specifically, there can be abuses by the shifting of taxable income and deductions from the TRS (typically a taxable corporation) to the REIT and vice versa.

6.5.2 REITs can use derivatives to circumvent the statutory REIT-qualification income-tests and the asset tests; and PICs/RECs can use derivatives to circumvent private contractual income and asset tests

In the US, IRC Section 856, the RMA and the AJCA have not provided sufficient guidance on REITs' use of Derivatives. Before the AJCA was enacted, if a REIT used a derivative instrument to hedge debt incurred or to be incurred to acquire or carry "real estate assets", any periodic income or gain from the disposition of that derivative contract generally constituted qualifying income for purposes of the 95 percent gross income test, but not the 75 percent gross income test. The AJCA amended this rule and states that REIT income (including gain from the sale or disposition of such derivative contract) that is attributable to a hedging transaction that is properly identified in accordance with IRC Section 1221(a)(7),[9] does not constitute gross income for purposes of the 95 percent gross-income-test (i.e. as opposed to being qualifying income), to the extent that the transaction hedges debt incurred or to be incurred by the REIT to acquire or carry real estate assets. Section 1221(a)(7), among other things, requires a hedging transaction to be clearly identified on the REIT's books and records.[10]

The term "Hedge" is not sufficiently defined in IRC Section 1221 and Section 856/RMA/AJCA (US statutes) – such that it is difficult to distinguish between REIT swaps/derivatives that are for hedging, and those that are for investment.

Furthermore, Section 856, RMA and AJCA do not provide any dollar limits on the notional amount of derivatives transactions that REITs can undertake in any time period.

REITs can circumvent the REIT-qualification Asset Tests and Income Tests by using derivatives.

6.5.3 The non-standardization and inadequate regulation of management agreements is highly detrimental to REITs/RECs/PICs and can facilitate earnings management and asset-quality management

This issue was discussed in more detail in Nwogugu (2008a;b). Many REITs/ RECs/PICs retain third-party companies to manage their properties; and such arrangements are formalized with management agreements.[11] There are no standard terms of Management Agreements, and much of the terms are negotiated between both parties, often without any competitive bidding process. The Management Agreement is a critical element of profitability, asset maintenance, efficiency, value creation and solvency for the REIT/REC/PIC. Thus, the lack of standardization and or regulation of Property Management Agreements creates substantial opportunities for fraud, illegal wealth transfers to property managers, collusion with management, and errors/mis-statements in financial reporting.[12] Management Agreements are critical to financial reporting and disclosure because the agreement states terms and conditions for incurring ordinary expenses and capital expenses, and what types of costs are capitalized or expensed in each period, and who is financially responsible for certain types of expenses, and when/ how revenues are collected.

Management Agreements greatly expand the boundaries and scope of the real estate entity. The third-party property managers effectively take on the role of managers in the REIT and function as subsidiaries of the REIT/REC/PIC, and often have more meaningful control of assets than the REIT/REC/PIC managers.[13]

The use of Management Agreements increases the risk of insider-trading violations. For example, many real estate companies and REIT/RECs typically contract with one–three third-party property managers. In cases where a property management company manages more than 40 percent of a publicly traded REIT/REC's portfolio of properties, that property management company has access to substantial relevant information that can affect the prices of the REIT/REC's Beneficial Interests, and can take actions that can increase or reduce the volatility of the REIT/ REC share price; but this property management company is not subject to the same securities law standards and Sarbanes-Oxley standards as the REIT/REC's managers, officer, diREIT/RECtors and employees. This relationship and significant influence of third-party property management companies is more critical because REIT/ RECs are typically evaluated based on their dividends and quality of properties.

Hence, given the legal/economic/psychological importance of Property Management Agreements, any proposed Management Agreement that covers a significant percentage of the company's or REIT/REC's properties (e.g. more than 20 percent of the entity's properties) should be approved by a vote of the entity's shareholders or the REIT/REC/PIC's beneficiaries, before becoming effective.

Non-standardization and lack of minimal regulation of Management Agreements causes several problems[14] including but not limited to the following:

i) *Information Asymmetry* – greater information asymmetry between REIT/REC managers and the property manager, between REIT/REC beneficiaries and REIT/REC's officers, between investors in stock exchanges and REIT/REC officers, between regulators (SEC, etc.) and REIT/REC property managers, and between lenders and REIT/REC officers.

ii) *Reputation Effects* – the Management Agreement inefficiently transfers responsibility for the company's or the REIT/REC's reputation and Social Capital to the Property Manager.

iii) Increased *Shirking* by property managers.

iv) Inefficient *Shift of Compliance Burden* – to the property manager, without providing for adequately penalizing the property manager for non-compliance.

v) *Moral Hazard.*

v) *Knowledge Effects and Problems.*

vi) Reduced *Property Manager Motivation.*

vii) *The Free Rider Problem.*

viii) Significant *Negative Externalities.*

ix) Increased *Dispute Resolution Costs.*

x) *Non-Compliance with Trust Laws.*

6.5.4 Many real estate sale-leaseback transactions are usurious or potentially usurious

The *Effective Interest Rates* implicit in some real estate sale-leaseback transactions exceed statutory Usury limits[15] in some countries (even without classifying and including directly related transaction costs such as closing costs, administrative costs, insurance costs, due diligence costs, etc., as financing costs). However, because some real estate sale-leaseback transactions are not treated as loans in some cases, usury laws are not applied – this is an error. The trend in the accounting and tax area (as evidenced by several proposed regulations[16] – some of which are described in footnotes in this article), is to treat all real estate leases as capital leases (financing leases).

In many sale-leaseback transactions, REITs/REC/PICs are the buyer-lessors, and hence, are in the position of the "lender", where the sale-leaseback transaction is deemed a financing for accounting and or tax purposes. REITs/PICs/RECs typically don't disclose the Effective Interest Rates implicit in their sale-leaseback transactions. Unfortunately in the USA, most state usury laws don't expressly include REIT sale-leaseback transactions in the categories of financing transactions covered by usury laws – and the associated legislative histories of such state statutes don't indicate any legislative intent that such usury laws should be applied to REIT sale-leaseback transactions.

6.5.5 Debt can be used to manipulate the cost structure and dividends of REITs/REC/PICs

Nwogugu (2008a;b) noted that under the present REIT qualification rules in the US and many countries, REIT management and trustees can use debt to manipulate REITs' accounting income (upon which REIT dividends are based) and REITs' cost structure – more so than in traditional limited liability corporations and partnerships. Similarly, the boards of directors of RECs and PICs can manipulate their cost structure, taxable income and accounting income using debt (loans and mortgages).

6.5.6 The Sarbanes–Oxley Act (USA) (and similar statutes in other countries) does not address many issues pertaining to real estate operations and REITs

While competitive bidding is critical to many operations and processes in REITs and property management companies, SOX does not contain specific requirements and standards for bidding or for REITs. SOX does not provide sufficient standards for valuation of real estate – valuation methods, time-frames, etc.[17] SOX provides relatively vague guidelines on environmental issues and hazardous waste disposal. SOX has increased the scrutiny of structured leases and off balance sheet financing in general – by external counsel, external accountants and internal auditing teams. This trend has increased the financing costs of such transactions, and associated insurance costs.

SOX requires increased disclosure of use of non-GAAP accounting measures. FFO is a widely used non-GAAP measure in the REIT industry. There is no standard method of calculating FFO, even though NAREIT[18] has issued a White Paper[19] about the calculation of FFO. This lack of standardization increases information asymmetry, and also increases investors' monitoring costs and transaction costs.

While SOX prohibits insider loans, the AJCA permits REITs to provide business loans to its "insiders". REITs outsource most of their critical operations such as property management and renovations/construction. However, s.404 of SOX requires that the REIT file internal control reports, and also review and obtain reports on internal controls of its contractors. The process of obtaining adequate documentation of a contractor's internal controls is critical, but executives seldom include clear requirements about internal control performance in service contracts, and also typically don't fail to establish the contractual right to perform internal control audits or request an SAS 70 or equivalent report.

6.5.7 The accounting for synthetic leases is incorrect: a proposed new accounting regime for synthetic leases

The present accounting methods and disclosure for synthetic lease transactions is inaccurate, because it does not reflect economic reality and the risks/obligations of the parties involved.[20] REITs and their taxable subsidiaries are typically the lessor/sponsor in synthetic lease transactions. Under the present accounting regime for synthetic leases, such transactions are off-balance-sheet. The US Internal Revenue Code doesn't provide adequate guidelines for the treatment of a synthetic leasing transaction as a lease or a financing transaction, but US courts and the IRS have applied a fact-based analysis to determine whether the substance of the transaction matches its form and the express intent of the parties.[21] Clearly, the special purpose entities in synthetic lease transactions should be consolidated, and synthetic lease transactions should be disclosed in financial statements.

A proposed new accounting regime for synthetic lease transactions is as follows:

i) The Special Purpose Entity (SPE) must be consolidated in the REIT's/entity's financial statements. This is because the REIT/sponsor typically has operating and/or voting "control" of the SPE, and owns all or most of its equity.

ii) The value of the property should be reported as an asset, and if the transaction terms permit, any depreciation should be deducted.

iii) The outstanding balance of the acquisition loan or construction loan (presumably secured by the property) should be reported as a liability in the REIT's/sponsor's balance sheet.

iv) The lessee's promise to indemnify the lessor at the end of the lease term for any loss of property value should be reported in the REIT's/sponsor's balance sheet as a long-term asset, and also reported in the shareholder's equity in the balance sheet. This amount will increase as the property value declines, and vice versa (but typically cannot exceed 85 percent of the property value).

v) The lessee's right to any increase in property value at lease expiration should be reported as a long-term liability in the REIT's/sponsor's balance sheet, and as a reserve on the asset side of its balance sheet. This amount will increase as the property value increases, and vice versa.

6.5.8 The Income-Focus Effect

REITs (and some PICs) attract investors that focus on dividends and value REIT/PIC shares/interests based on dividend payouts. This provides a very strong incentive for REITs'/PICs' management to engage in earnings management and asset-quality management; and to increase dividends in order to boost the prices of REIT Beneficial Interests (indeed, during 1995–2019 and around the world, many REITs' dividend payout rates were typically 110–190 percent of REIT accounting earnings). Increasing dividends results in increased need for external financing, mostly in the form of debt, which increases the REIT's bankruptcy risk – issuing equity is more likely to dilute management's equity and lower share prices.

6.5.9 The Compensation-Structure Effect

Nwogugu (2008b) noted that: i) executive compensation systems of most exchange-traded REITs (and also PICs) are inefficient, and compensate management for stock market variations that often don't have any relationship to operations and performance; ii) the REIT structure is a negative constraint on executive compensation, associated incentives and capital budgeting; and the executive compensation systems for REIT managers (cash and stock options) can result in sub-optimal decisions by managers. That can encourage REIT/PIC managers to engage in earnings management, Incentive-effects management and asset-quality management. Unlike internet or biotech companies, the REIT's operations are much more stable and predictable, and are much less risky, but there are much fewer ways to increase value. Given this "stable state", the REIT's FFO, earnings, depreciation are relatively stable and are very inappropriate performance measures. The more appropriate performance measures include: 1) project selection; 2) quality, efficiency and profitability of management agreements; 3) acquisition "fit"; 4) reduction of cost of capital; 5) quality of tenant relations; 6) quality of disclosure.

6.5.10 Invalid stock option plans and employee stock purchase plans

Nwogugu (2008b) noted that many REITs' stock option plans and employee stock purchase plans are null and void.

6.5.11 REITs and PICs have inherent accounting problems and are not transparent

Nwogugu (2008b): i) reiterated that REITs are unconstitutional, and are essentially non-existent entities, and are not securities; and ii) suggested implementation of rules in order to eliminate the accounting anomaly caused by depreciation charges; iii) noted that the present accounting model for REITs and PICs is grossly inaccurate because it doesn't reflect proper usage of assets or true values of assets, it grants management too much discretion in classification of expenses, and hence causes unnecessary volatility in the stock market; iv) REIT ownership concentration rules provide strong incentives for management to manage earnings by creating reserves, capitalizing costs, increasing depreciation expense, etc.; v) property depreciation charges distort the financial statements (financial condition) of REITs and most corporations that own or lease substantial real estate – in most instances, depreciation charges have no meaningful relationship to the intensity of usage of the property, and to the actual physical deterioration. Most properties can last for 70–90 years with average maintenance.

As noted in Nwogugu (2008b), REITs/PICs lack transparency in many aspects to the detriment of REIT/PIC Beneficiaries and investors and which encourage REIT/PIC management to engage in earnings management and or asset-quality management.

6.5.12 Corporate control problems

Nwogugu (2008b) noted that there were corporate control problems in REITs – and some of them can provide opportunities for excessive managerial power, managerial misconduct and earnings management.

6.5.13 Divestitures and spin-offs of REITs/RECs may be ultra vires and some may be fraudulent

Nwogugu (2008b) noted that under US laws, some divestitures and spinoffs of REITs may be illegal. Furthermore, companies that engage in such transactions do so to offload troubled real estate and or mortgages, often at inflated prices and with inadequate disclosures of problems.

6.5.14 Under the corporate opportunities doctrine, the use of REITs provides more opportunities for misconduct and conflicts of interest (compared to C-corporations, Llcs and partnerships)

As noted in Nwogugu (2008b), where REITs are used, there are more opportunities for fraud and conflict of interest problems that trigger the *Corporate Opportunities Doctrine* – hence REIT managers are more likely to convert its opportunities for their own benefit.

6.5.15 D&O (directors and officers) insurance policies

Nwogugu (2008b) noted that REITs' D&O Policies were not efficient. Separately, inefficient D&O Policies can provide substantial opportunities for REIT/PIC management to engage in earnings management and or asset-quality management.

6.6 Conclusion

There are numerous economic psychology and social psychology issues inherent in the formation and use of REITs/PICs/RECs, many of which have not been properly addressed in the existing literature. Existing REIT statutes have substantial and often negative influences on the economic decisions of employees, shareholders and management of REITs. It is evident that the structure of REITs/

RECs and relevant defining laws have to be modified substantially to eliminate these problems. In all jurisdictions, Synthetic REITs can be far more efficient and beneficial to the overall economy than the traditional REIT.

Notes

* This Chapter contains excerpts from Michael I. C. Nwogugu's articles which are cited as follows:

  i) Nwogugu, M. (2008a). Some Corporate Governance Problems Pertaining To REITs – Part One. *Journal of International Banking Law & Regulation*, 23(2), 71–85.
 ii) Nwogugu, M. (2008b). Some Corporate Governance Problems Pertaining To REITs – Part Two. *Journal of International Banking Law & Regulation*, 23(3), 142–155.
iii) Nwogugu, M. (Revised 2009). *Earnings Management and Accounting Distortions in REIT's and Companies That Own Substantial Commercial Real Estate*. Available at: https://www.ssrn.com/abstract=1515517; https://papers.ssrn.com/sol3/papers.cfm?abstract_id=1515517.

1 *See*: Pricewaterhouse Coopers. (2009). *Investment property and Accounting for Deferred Tax under IAS-12*.
   See: Alston & Bird (January 7, 2009). *2008 REIT Tax Developments – the Year in Review*.
2 *See*: Dunse, Hutchison & Goodacre (2004); Bens (2006); Duangploy, Shelton & Omer (2005); Lander & Reinstein (2003); Sevin & Schroeder & Bhamornsiri (2007); Zang (2008).
3 *See*: Pricewaterhouse Coopers (2009). *Investment property and Accounting for Deferred Tax under IAS-12*.
   See: Alston & Bird (January 7, 2009). *2008 REIT Tax Developments – the Year in Review*.
   See: Nwogugu (2015a).
4 *See*: IASB – *Leases*. www.iasb.org/Current+Projects/IASB+Projects/Leases/Leases.htm.
   See: *IASB discussion paper* (March 2009). www.iasb.org/Current+Projects/IASB+Projects/Leases/Leases.htm.
   See: FASB Project Update – Joint Project of FASB And IASB (2009). www.fasb.org/project/leases.shtml. www.fasb.org/draft/DP_Leases.pdf.
5 *See*: Nwogugu, M. (2008a). Some corporate governance problems pertaining to REITs – part one. *Journal of International Banking Law & Regulation*, 23(2), 71–89.
   See: Nwogugu, M. (2008b). Some corporate governance problems pertaining to REITs – part two. *Journal of International Banking Law & Regulation*, 23(3), 142–162.
6 This section contains excerpts from the author's articles that were published in *Journal of International Banking Law & Regulation* during 2008.
7 *See*: Anonymous. (April 2005). "China to make real estate trusts official"; "Korea Lifts Restriction To Breathe Life Into REITs"; "Romanian modernizers stop short of REIT law"; "Taiwan looks to build on success of Fubon No 1". "How US Tax Rules Make REIT Status Uncertain." *International Financial Law Review*, 1.See: Anonymous. (2003). REITs: Success in Hong Kong depends on flexible regulation. *International Financial Law Review*, 13.
   See: Starkman, D. (2005). The 8 governance issues that matter most. Real Estate Portfolio. www.nareit.com/portfoliomag/05julaug/feat1.shtml.
   See: Linklaters (January 2007). Germany: Germany Introduces REITs – with a Major Defect?
   See: Lachner, C. & Von Heppe, R. (2007). The introduction of real estate investment trusts in Germany. *German Law Journal*, 8(1), 133–1242.

See: London Stock Exchange. (2007). Listing a UK REIT on the London Stock Exchange – the Listing Rules.

See: UK – H. M Treasury (March 2005). UK real estate investment trusts: A discussion paper.

See: Hahn, A. (February 24, 2003). Goldman's dangerous REIT game: Firm now defending unpopular strategy it helped devise. *The Investment Dealers' Digest*, 7–8.

8 The following publicly traded lodging REITs created taxable REIT subsidiaries ("TRS") and have transferred the leases of some or all of their properties to the TRSs which in turn, have each entered management agreements with third-party management companies – Humphrey Hospitality Trust, Ashford Hospitality Trust, Boykin Lodging Co., Equity Inns, FelCor Lodging Trust, MeriStar Hospitality Corp., Hersha Hospitality Trust, Highland Hospitality Corp., LaSalle Hotel Properties, Host Marriott Corp., and Innkeepers USA Trust. ILM II Senior Living Inc., (http://edgar.secdata base.com/948/91205799007589/filing-main.htm) and ILM Senior Living Inc. (https://www.nasdaq.com/markets/ipos/filing.ashx?filingid=1158737), both of which were US senior-living REITs, leased their properties to two affiliated operating REITs named ILM II Lease Corporation, and ILM I Lease Corporation respectively, each of which in turn, then entered into management agreements with third-party property management companies.

See: City Of Tulsa v. Davis, 376 P2d 282 (1962). *City Of Holderville v. Moore*, 293 P2d 363 (1956). *City Of Magnum v. Garrett*, 200 Okl. 274.

Compare the RMA and AJCA provisions on TRSs with the following state statutes pertaining to "piercing the corporate veil": North Dakota Cent. Code sec. 10–32–29(3); Illinois Rev. Stat. Ch. 805, para. 180/10; Colorado Rev. Stat. 7–80–107; California Corp. Code sec. 1710(b); Wisconsin Stat. Ann. Sec. 183.0304(2); and Minnesota Stat. Sec. 322b.303(s).

9 Section 1221 of the US Internal Revenue Code.

10 *See:* www.lw.com/Resources.aspx?page=ClientAlertDetail&publication=1114.

See: Horng and Wei (1999).

11 *See:* Capozza and Seguin (2000); Capozza and Seguin (2003); and Downs and Guner (1999).

12 *See:* http://caselaw.lp.findlaw.com/cgi-bin/getcase.pl?court=11th&navby=case&no=9914962MAN;

See: *Fleischhauer v. Feltner,* 879 F.2d 1290 (6th Cir.1989).

On management agreements, see: www.secinfo.com/d14D5a.13S1r.6.htm; www.secinfo.com/d1488v.11ct.b.htm;

See: Damodaran, John and Liu (1997); Capozza and Seguin (2000); Starkman (2005); Linklaters (January 2007); and Lachner and Von Heppe (2007).

13 See: Cunningham (2002); Capozza and Seguin (2000)(supra); Sagalyn (1996) (supra); Capozza and Seguin (1999); Devaney and Weber (2005); Campbell and Sirmans (2002)(supra); Pagliari, Scherer and Monopoli (2003); Brown and Riddioug (2003); RIC (2005)(supra). Brady and Conlin (2004); Damodaran, John and Liu (1997); Topuz, Darrat and Shelor (2005). Scordato (2004).

14 See: Einhorn (1997). Epstein, Staudt and Wiedenbeck (_____). Garmaise and Moskowitz (2003).

15 On Usury, see the following US court cases: *Fogie v. Thorn*, 95 F3d 645 (CA8, 1996) (*cert. den.*) 520 US 1166; *Pollice v. National Tax Funding LP*, 225 F3d 379 (CA3, 2000); *Najarro v. SASI Intern. Ltd*, 904 F2d 1002 (CA5, 1990)(*cert. den.*) 498 US 1048; *Video Trax v. Nationsbank NA*, 33 Fsupp2d 1041 (S.D.Fla., 1998)(*affirmed*) 205 F3d 1358(*cert. den.*) 531 US 822; *In Re Tammy Jewels*, 116 BR 290 (M.D.Fla., 1990); *ECE Technologies v. Cherrington Corp.*, 168 F3d 201 (CA5, 1999); *Colony Creek Ltd. v. RTC*, 941 F2d 1323 (CA5, 1991)(*rehearing denied*); *Sterling Property Management v. Texas Commerce Bank*, 32 F3d 964 (CA5, 1994); *Pearcy Marine v. Acadian*

Offshore Services, 832 Fsupp 192 (S.D.TX, 1993); *In Re Venture Mortgage Fund LP*, 245 BR 460 (SDNY, 2000); *In Re Donnay*, 184 BR 767 (D.Minn, 1995); *Johnson v. Telecash Inc.*, 82 FSupp2d 264 (D.Del., 1999)(*reversed in part*) 225 F2d 366 (*cert. denied*) 531 US 1145; *Shelton v. Mutual Savings & Loan Asssociation*, 738 FSupp 50 (E.D.Mich., 1990); *S.E.C. v. Elmas Trading Corporation*, 638 FSupp 743 (D.Nevada, 1987)(*affirmed*) 865 F2d 265; contrast: *J2 Smoke Shop Inc. v. American Commercial Capital Corp.*, 709 FSupp 422 (SDNY 1989)(cost of funds); *In Re Powderburst Corp.*, 154 BR 307 (E.D.Cal. 1993)(original issue discount); *In Re Wright*, 256 BR 626 (D.Mont., 2000)(difference between face amount and amount actually recovered or owed by debtor); *In Re MCCorhill Pub. Inc.*, 86 BR 283 (SDNY 1988); *In Re Marill Alarm Systems*, 81 BR 119 (S.D.Fla., 1987)(*affirmed*) 861 F2d 725; *In Re Dent*, 130 BR 623 (S.D.GA, 1991); *In Re Evans*, 130 BR 357 (S.D.GA, 1991); contrast: *In Re Cadillac Wildwood Development*, 138 BR 854 (W.D.Mich., 1992)(closing costs are interest costs); *In Re Brummer*, 147 BR 552 (D.Mont., 1992); *In Re Sunde*, 149 BR 552 (D.Minn., 1992); *Matter Of Worldwide Trucks*, 948 F2d 976 (CA5,1991)(agreement about applicable interest rate maybe established by course of conduct); *Lovick v. Ritemoney Ltd*, 378 F3d 433 (CA5, 2004); *In Re Shulman Transport*, 744 F2d 293 (CA2, 1984); *Torelli v. Esposito*, 461 NYS2d 299 (1983)(*reversed*) 483 NYS2d 204; *Reschke v. Eadi*, 447 NYS2d 59 (NYAD4, 1981); *Elghanian v. Elghanian*, 717 NYS2d 54(NYAD1, 2000)(*leave to appeal denied*) 729 NYS2d 410 (there was no consideration in exchange for loan, and transaction violated usury laws); *Karas v. Shur*, 592 NYS2d 779 (NYAD2, 1993); *Simsbury Fund v. New St. Louis Associates*, 611 NYS2d 557 (NYAD1, 1994); *Rhee v. Dahan*, 454 NYS2d 371 (NY.Sup., 1982); *Hamilton v. HLT Check Exchange, LLP*, 987 F. Supp. 953 (E.D. Ky. 1997); *Turner v. E-Z Check Cashing of Cookeville, TN, Inc.*, 35 F.Supp.2d 1042 (M.D. Tenn. 1999); *Hurt v. Crystal Ice & Cold Storage Co.*, 286 S.W. 1055, 1056–57 (Ky. 1926); *Phanco v. Dollar Financial Group.*, Case No. CV99–1281 DDP (C.D. Cal., filed Feb. 8, 1999).
See: Van Voris, B. (May 17, 1999) 'Payday' loans under scrutiny. *The National Law Journal*, page B1.

16 *See*: Berman (July/August 2005); US Securities & Exchange Commission(June 2005); FASB (2005); Graff (2001); Murray (2001); Shilling, Eppli and Chun (2006); Maydew (May 2005); Sandler (Feb. 2005); Elayan, Meyer and Li (2006); and Holland and Knight (2003).
See: Murray, J. (2001). *Off Balance Sheet Financing: Synthetic Leases*. (citing cases). First American Title Insurance Company. www.firstam.com/content.cfm?id=4320.
See: *Unocal Corp. v. Kaabipour*, 177 F.3d 755 (9th Cir. 1999).
Some courts have used a fact-based approach and the "economic realities test" – see: *Lazisky*, 72 T.C. at 500–02; *Rich Hill Ins. Agency*, 58 T.C. at 617–19; *Transamerica Corp. v. United States*, 7 Cl. Ct. 441 (1985); *Torez v. Commissioner*, 88 T.C. 702, 721–27 (1987) (sale/leaseback); *Estate of Thomas v. Commissioner*, 84 T.C. 412, 436 (sale leaseback); Rev. Rul. 55–540, 1955–2 C.B. 39 (classification of a lease); Rev. Rul. 68–590, 1968–2 C.B. 66; Rev. Rul. 72–543, 1972–2 C.B. 87. See: Treas. Reg. § 1.1245–1(a)(3) (as amended in 1997); Tech. Adv. Mem. 93–07–002 (Oct. 5, 1992); Tech. Adv. Mem. 93–38–002 (Sept. 24, 1993); *Frank Lyon Co. v. United States*, 435 U.S. 561, 572–73 (1978); *Helvering v. F. & R. Lazarus & Co.*, 308 U.S. 242 (1939); *Gregory v. Helvering*, 293 U.S. 465 (1935); *Comdisco, Inc. v. United States*, 756 F.2d 569, 578 (7th Cir. 1985); *Sullivan v. United States*, 618 F.2d 1001, 1006–08 (3d Cir. 1980); *Sun Oil Co. v. Commissioner*, 562 F.2d 248 (3d Cir. 1977), *cert. denied*, 436 U.S. 944 (1978); *Commissioner v. Danielson*, 378 F.2d 771, 775 (3d Cir. 1967); *Sullivan v. United States*, 461 F. Supp. 1040 (W.D. Pa. 1978); *Illinois Power Co. v. Commissioner*, 87 T.C. 1417 (1986); *Grodt & McKay Realty, Inc. v. Commissioner*, 77 T.C. 1221 (1981); *Bolger v. Commissioner*, 59 T.C. 760, 767 n.4 (1973); *Bowen v. Commissioner*, 12 T.C. 446, 459 (1949); Rev. Rul. 55–540, 1955–2 C.B. 39. Other courts have required the party

requesting recharacterization to show that the parties intended a different allocation for tax purposes other than the allocation provided in the contract – see: *Balthrope v. Commissioner*, 356 F.2d 28 (5th Cir. 1966); *Annabelle Candy Co. v. Commissioner*, 314 F.2d 1 (9th Cir. 1962); *Ullman v. Commissioner*, 244 F.2d 305 (2d Cir. 1959). Some courts emphasize the intention of the parties – see: *Major v. Commissioner*, 76 T.C. 239, 246 (1981); *Lazisky v. Commissioner*, 72 T.C. 495, 500–02 (1979); *G.C. Servs. Corp. v. Commissioner*, 73 T.C. 406 (1979); *Lucas v. Commissioner*, 58 T.C. 1022, 1032 (1972); *Rich Hill Ins. Agency v. Commissioner*, 58 T.C. 610, 617–19 (1972).

17 See: Weiss, S. & Knotts, S. Start off right with your D&O application. *Directors & Boards*. www.hklaw.com\content\whitepapers\D&Oapplication.pdf.

18 *National Century Financial Enterprises v Gulf Insurance Co* (Bankr. S.D. Ohio January 10, 2005).

19 See www.nareit.org/policy/government/index.cfm; www.nareit.org/policy/government/ridea.cfm [Accessed November 25, 2007].

20 See: Keeler, M. (March 2006). Leasing and SOX compliance. www.gtnews.com/article/6294.cfm.

See: Berman, M. (July–August 2005). SEC report calls for overhaul of lease accounting. *Equipment Leasing Today*.

See: US Securities & Exchange Commission. (June 2005). Report and recommendations pursuant to section 401[c] of the Sarbanes Oxley act of 2002 on arrangement with off-balance sheet implications, special purpose entities and transparency of filings by issuers.

See: FASB (2005). *FASB Response to SEC Study on Arrangements with Off-Balance Sheet Implications, Special Purpose Entities and Transparency of Filing by Issuers* (Financial Accounting Standards Board).

See Bosco, B. (November 2006). *How Will Accounting Rules Impact Off Balance Sheet Leases?*

See Boyce, G.R. (January 13, 2000). Synthetic lease: The hard facts. *New York Law Journal*, 5, 5–10; See FASB. (2003). *Interpretation No.46, Consolidation of Variable Interest Entities* (Financial Accounting Standards Board); See Graff, R. (2001). Off-balance sheet corporate finance with synthetic leases: Shortcomings and how to avoid them with synthetic debt. *Journal of Real Estate Review*, 22(213), 213–240; See Harris, T. (May 2002). Synthetic leases, off balance sheet financing: Are they legitimate tools for the leasing business? *Equipment Leasing*; See Murray, J.C. (2001). Synthetic leases: Bankruptcy proofing the lessee's option to purchase. *Commercial Law Journal*, 106(221), 221–241; See Nesvold, J. (1999). What are you trying to hide? Synthetic leases financial disclosure and the information mosaic. *Stanford Journal of Law, Business and Finance* 83, 83–98; See Weidner, D. (Spring 2000). Synthetic leases: Structured finance, financial accounting and tax ownership. *Journal of Corporation La*, 445, 445–470; See Tunick, B. (March 2002). Many worries for synthetic leases: Loans may be disguised but even bankruptcy can't avoid them. *Investment Dealer's Digest*, 18; See Shilling, J., Eppli, M. & Chun, G. (2006). Percentage retail leases and FASB's off-balance sheet financing standards; See Maydew, E. (May 2005). Discussion of firms' off balance sheet and hybrid debt financing: Evidence from their book-tax reporting differences, 43(2) *Journal of Accounting Research*, 283, 283–293; See Sandler, G. (February 2005). Real estate finance leases: On or off balance sheet? *Real Estate Finance* 21(5), 3, 3–9; See Campbell, R. White-Huckins, N. & Sirmans, C. (2006). Domestic and international equity REIT joint ventures: Structuring corporate options. *Journal of Real Estate Finance and Economics*, 32(275), 275–288.

See Elayan, F., Meyer, T. & Li, J. (2006). Evidence from tax exempt firms on motives for participating in sale leaseback transactions. *Journal of Real Estate Research*, 28(4), 381, 381–391.

See www.syntheticdebt.com/accounting_reform_SyntheticLeases.pdf; www.synthe
ticdebt.com/syntheticdebt_dslobstb.pdf;   www.hklaw.com/Publications/Newsletters.
asp?IssueID=357&Article=1997 [Accessed November 25, 2007]. See FASB Interpretation No.46, Consolidation of Variable Interest Entities and Interpretation of
ARB No.51 (FIN 46). See Holland & Knight. What is the Future for the Synthetic
Leasing of Real Property Under the New Rules Issued by FASB and the SEC? www.
hklaw.com/Publications/Newsletters.asp?IssueID=357&Article=1997 [Accessed
November 25, 2007], s.401(a) of the Sarbanes-Oxley Act of 2002. On or around January 27, 2003, the US Securities & Exchange Commission promulgated rules requiring
the following: (1) disclosure of off-balance-sheet arrangements in registration statements, annual reports, and proxy or information statements that are required to include
financial statements for fiscal years ending on or after June 15, 2003, and (2) a table
of material contractual obligations in financial statements and reports for fiscal years
ending on or after December 15, 2003.

21 See Murray, J. (2001). *Off-Balance-Sheet Financing: Synthetic Leases.* (citing cases)
(First American Title Insurance Company). www.firstam.com/content.cfm?id=4320
[Accessed November 25, 2007]. *Unocal Corp v Kaabipour* (9th Cir. 1999) 177 F.3d
755. Some courts have used a fact-based approach and the "economic realities test" –
see *Lazisky* 72 T.C. at 500–502; *Rich Hill Ins. Agency,* 58 T.C. at 617–619; *Transamerica Corp v United States* (1985) 7 Cl. Ct. 441; *Torez v Commissioner* (1987) 88 T.C.
702, 721–727 (sale/leaseback); *Estate of Thomas v Commissioner* 84 T.C. 412, 436
(sale leaseback); Rev. Rul. 55–540, 1955–2 C.B. 39 (classification of a lease); Rev.
Rul. 68–590, 1968–2 C.B. 66; Rev. Rul. 72–543, 1972–2 C.B. 87. See Treas. Reg. §
1.1245–1(a)(3) (as amended in 1997); Tech. Adv. Mem. 93–07–002 (October 5, 1992);
Tech. Adv. Mem. 93–38–002 (September 24, 1993); *Frank Lyon Co v United States*
(1978) 435 U.S. 561, 572–573; *Helvering v F. & R. Lazarus & Co* (1939) 308 U.S.
242; *Gregory v Helvering* (1935) 293 U.S. 465; *Comdisco, Inc v United States* (7th
Cir. 1985) 756 F.2d 569, 578; *Sullivan v United States* (3d Cir. 1980) 618 F.2d 1001,
1006–1008; *Sun Oil Co v Commissioner* (3d Cir. 1977) 562 F.2d 248, *cert. denied,*
(1978) 436 U.S. 944; *Commissioner v Danielson* (3d Cir. 1967) 378 F.2d 771, 775;
Sullivan v United States (W.D. Pa. 1978) 461 F. Supp. 1040; *Illinois Power Co v Commissioner* (1986) 87 T.C. 1417; *Grodt & McKay Realty, Inc v Commissioner* (1981)
77 T.C. 1221; *Bolger v Commissioner* (1973), 59 T.C. 760, 767 n.4; *Bowen vs. Commissioner* (1949), 12 T.C. 446, 459; Rev. Rul. 55–540, 1955–2 C.B. 39. Other courts
have required the party requesting recharacterisation to show that the parties intended
a different allocation for tax purposes other than the allocation provided in the contract – see *Balthrope v Commissioner* (5th Cir. 1966) 356 F.2d 28; *Annabelle Candy
Co. vs. Commissioner* (9th Cir., 1962) 314 F.2d 1; *Ullman vs. Commissioner* (2nd Cir.,
1959) 244 F.2d 305. Some courts emphasise the intention of the parties – see *Major
vs. Commissioner* (1981), 76 T.C. 239, 246; *Lazisky vs. Commissioner* (1979), 72 T.C.
495, 500–502; *G.C. Servs. Corp. vs. Commissioner* (1979) 73 T.C. 406; *Lucas v Commissioner* (1972) 58 T.C. 1022, 1032; *Rich Hill Ins. Agency v Commissioner* (1972), 58
T.C. 610, 617–619. With regard to substantive consolidation, see *Consolidated Rock
Prods. Co. vs. DuBois* (1940), 31 U.S. 510; *Reider vs. FDIC* (In re Reider) (11th Cir.,
1994), 31 F.3d 1102, 1106–1107; *In Re Giller* (8th Cir. 1992), 962 F.2d 796, 798;
Eastgroup Properties vs. Southern Motel Assoc (11th Cir. 1991), 935 F.2d 245; *In re
Augie/Restivo Banking Co* (2nd Cir., 1988) 860 F.2d 515, 518; *In re Auto-Train Corp.*
(D.C. Cir. 1987) 810 F.2d 270; *FMC Fin. Corp. vs. Murphree* (5th Cir. 1980) 632
F.2d 413; *Chemical Bank N.Y. Trust Co. vs. Kheel* (2nd Cir. 1966) 369 F.2d 845, 847;
Anaconda Bldg Materials Co. vs. Newland (9th Cir., 1964) 336 F.2d 624; *Fish vs. East*
(10th Cir. 1940) 114 F.2d 177; *Central Claims Servs. vs. Eagle-Richer Indus (In re
Eagle-Richer Indus)* (Bankr. S.D. Ohio 1996) 192 B.R. 903, 905–906; *In re Standard
Brand Paint Co* (Bankr. C.D. Cal. 1993) 154 B.R. 563; *In re Crown Mach. & Welding,*

Inc. (Bankr. D. Mont. 1989)100 B.R. 24; *In re DRW Property Co* (Bankr. N.D. Tex. 1985) 54 B.R. 489; *In re Snider Bros.* (Bankr. D. Mass 1982) 18 B.R. 230; *In re Vecco Constr Indus, Inc* (Bankr. E.D. Va. 1980) 4 B.R. 407. Some courts have held that as a corporation becomes insolvent, its directors owe a fiduciary duty to its creditors – see *In re Andreuccetti* (7th Cir. 1992) 975 F.2d 413, 421; *Clarkson Co vs. Shaheen* (2nd Cir.1981) 660 F.2d 506, 512; *In Re Kingston Square Assocs.*, No.96B44962 (TLB), 1997 Bankr. LEXIS 1514, at *75 (Bankr. S.D.N.Y. September 24, 1997); *Geyer vs. Ingersoll Publications Co.* (Del. Ch. 1992) 621 A.2d 784, 787–789; *Credit Lyonnais Bank, Nederland, N.V. vs. Pathe Communications Corp.* (Del. Ch. Dec. 30, 1991) Civ. A. No.12150, 1991 WL 277613; *Tampa Waterworks Co. vs. Wood* (Fla. 1929)121 So. 789; *Francis vs. United Jersey Bank* (N.J. 1981) 432 A.2d 814. On classification of lease transactions as financings or loans, also see *United States vs. Colorado Invesco, Inc.* (D. Colo., 1995) 902 F. Supp. 1339, 1342 (quoting *In re Fabricators, Inc* (5th Cir. 1991) 924 F. 2d 1458, 1469); *Shawmut Bank Connecticut vs. First Fidelity Bank* (In re Secured Equip. Trust of Eastern Air Lines, Inc) (2nd Cir., 1994) 38 F.3d 86, 87; *In re Best Products Co.* (Bankr. S.D.N.Y. 1993)157 B.R. 222, 229–230; *In re Wilcox* (Bankr. N.D.N.Y. 1996) 201 B.R. 334, 336–337. On options-to-purchase and clogging the equity of redemption, see *Humble Oil & Ref Co vs. Doerr* (N.J. Super. Ch. Div. 1973) 303 A.2d 898; *Barr vs. Granahan* (Wis. 1949) 38 N.W.2d 705; *Getty Petroleum vs. Giordano* (D.N.J., May 19, 1988) No.87–3165 1988 U.S. Dist. LEXIS 4567, at *1; *Blackwell Ford, Inc. vs. Calhoun* (Mich. Ct. App. 1996) 555 N.W.2d 856; *McArthur vs. North Palm Beach Utils* (Fla. 1967) 202 So. 2d 181; *Coursey vs. Fairchild* (Okla. 1967) 436 P. 2d 35; *Hopping vs. Baldridge* (Okla. 1928) 246 P. 469; *Lincoln Mortgage Investors*, 659 P. 2d at 928. The issue of pre-emption of state laws in the determination of whether a lease is a financing or a loan, is somewhat un-settled – see *In re Challa* (Bankr. M.D. Fla. 1995)186 B.R. 750, 755–756; *In re Q-Masters, Inc* (Bankr. S.D. Fla. 1991) 135 B.R. 157, 159; *BFP vs. Resolution Trust Corp* (1994) 511 U.S. 531; *Barnhill vs. Johnson* (1992) 503 U.S. 393; *Butner vs. United States* (1979) 440 U.S. 48, 55; *MNC Commercial Corp vs. Joseph T. Ryerson & Son, Inc* (2nd Cir. 1989) 882 F.2d 615, 619; *Morton vs. National Bank* (2nd Cir. 1989) 866 F.2d 561, 563; *In re Rosenshein* (Bankr. S.D.N.Y. 1992)136 B.R. 368, 372; *In re Taylor* (Bankr. E.D. Ark. 1991)130 B.R. 849; *In re Wingspread Corp* (Bankr. S.D.N.Y. 1990)116 B.R. 915 (under state law, debtors' leases were financing agreements, and not true leases); *In re Century Brass Prods., Inc.* (Bankr. C.D. Conn. 1989) 95 B.R. 277, 279; *In Re Petroleum Products Inc.* (Bankr. D. Kan. 1987) 72 B.R. 739 (affirmed), 150 B.R. 270 (B.A.P. D. Kan. 1993); *In Re Harris Pine Mills* (D. Or. 1987) 79 B.R. 919 (*affirmed*), 862 F.2d 217 (9th Cir. 1988); H.R. REP. NO.95–595, at 314 (1978), reprinted in 1978 U.S.C.C.A.N. 5963, 6271; S. REP. No.95–989, at 24 (1978), reprinted in 1978 U.S.C.C.A.N. 5787, 5812; *City of Olathe vs. KAR Dev. Assocs (In re KAR Dev. Assocs, L.P.)*, 180 B.R. 629, 637 (Bankr. D. Kan. 1995)(federal law preempts); *International Trade Admin v Rensselaer Polytechnic Inst* (2nd Cir. 1991) 936 F.2d 744 (federal law); *In re Moreggia & Sons, Inc.* (9th Cir. 1988) 852 F.2d 1179 (federal law); *In Re PCH Assocs.* (2nd Cir. 1986) 804 F.2d 193; *Barney's, Inc. vs. Isetan Co.* (Bankr. S.D.N.Y. 1997) 206 B.R. 328, 352; *Hotel Syracuse, Inc. vs. City of Syracuse Indus. Dev. Agency* (Bankr. N.D.N.Y. 1993) 155 B.R. 824; *In Re Tak Broad. Corp.* (W.D. Wis. 1992)137 B.R. 728; *In Re Starr* (Bankr. S.D. Ill. 1990)113 B.R. 481; *In Re MCorp Fin Inc* (Bankr. S.D. Tex. 1990)122 B.R. 49. On title insurance issues, see *Transamerica Title Ins. Co. vs. Alaska Fed. Sav. & Loan Assoc.* (9th Cir.; 1987) 833 F.2d 775, 776; *Ticor Title Ins. Co. vs. FFCA/IIP 1988 Property Co.* (N.D. Ind.; 1995) 898 F.Supp. 633, 640–641; *Bank of Miami Beach vs. Lawyers' Title Guar. Fund* (Fla. Dist. Ct. App.; 1968) 214 So.2d 95 (*cert. dismissed*) 239 So.2d 97, 99 (Fla. 1970); *Goode vs. Federal Title & Ins. Corp.* (Fla. Dist. Ct. App.; 1964)162 So.2d 249, 270; *Bidart vs. American Title Ins. Co.* (Nev. 1987) 734 P. 2d 732, 734; *Gerrold* *vs. Penn Title Ins. Co.* (N.J. Super. Ct., App. Div.; 1994) 637 A.2d 1293, 1295; *Title Ins. Corp. vs. Wagner* (N.J. Super. Ct.; Ch. Div. 1981) 431 A.2d 179, 182.

Bibliography

Abramowitz, B. & Anshelevich, E. (2018). *Utilitarians Without Utilities: Maximizing Social Welfare for Graph Problems Using Only Ordinal Preferences.* Working Paper, Rensselaer Polytechnic Institute, Troy, NY, USA. https://arxiv.org/pdf/1711.10588.pdf.

Banas, L. & Block, J. (2002). Caveat member: Courts begin to "pierce the entity veil," imposing personal liability on all members. *Michigan Real Property Review*, 29, 15–30.

Bens, D. (2006). Discussion of accounting discretion in fair value estimates: An examination of SFAS-142 goodwill impairments. *Journal of Accounting Research*, 44(2), 298–296.

Berman, M. (July–August 2005). SEC report calls for overhaul of lease accounting. *Equipment Leasing Today.*

Bouchouicha, R. & Ftiti, Z. (2012). Real estate markets and macroeconomy: A dynamic coherence framework. *Economic Modelling*, 29(5), 1820–1829.

Boutilier, C., Caragiannis, I. et al. (2012). *Optimal Social Choice Functions: A Utilitarian View.* Conference Paper. EC'12, June 4–8, 2012, Valencia, Spain. http://procaccia.info/papers/optvoting.ec12.pdf.

Brady, P. & Conlin, M. (2004). The performance of REIT-owned properties and the impact of REIT market power. *Journal of Real Estate Finance & Economics*, 28(1), 81–91.

Brigham, C. (2001). Comment: Just how limited is the Illinois limited liability company? *Illinois University Law Journal*, 26, 53–73.

Brown, D. (2000). Liquidity and liquidation: Evidence from REITs. *Journal of Finance*, 55, 469–479.

Brown, D. & Riddioug, T. (2003). Financing choice and liability structure of real estate investment trusts. *Real Estate Economics*, 31(3), 313–346.

Campbell, R., White-Huckins, N. & Sirmans, C. (2006). Domestic and international equity REIT joint ventures: Structuring corporate options. *Journal of Real Estate Finance and Economics*, 32(275), 275–288.

Cannon, S. & Vogt, S. (1995). REITs and their management: An analysis of organization structure, performance and management compensation. *Journal of Real Estate Research*, 10, 297–317.

Capozza, D. & Seguin, P. (1999). Focus, transparency, and value: The REIT evidence. *Real Estate Economics*, 27, 587–619.

Capozza, D. & Seguin, P. (2000). Debt, agency and management contracts in REITs: The external advisor puzzle. *Journal of Real Estate Finance & Economics*, 20, 91–116.

Capozza, S. & Seguin, P. (2001). Debt without taxes: Capital structure of REITs. *Real Estate Finance*, 18, 38–47.

Capozza, D. & Seguin, P. (2003). Inside ownership, risk sharing and Tobin's (/-Ratios: Evidence from REITs. *Real Estate Economics*, 31, 367–404.

Cargill, T. & Pingle, M. (2019). Federal reserve policy and housing: A goal too far. *Economic Analysis and Policy*, 62, 150–158.

Chui, L. & Chau, K. (2005). An empirical study of the relationship between economic growth, real estate prices and real estate investments in Hong Kong. *Surveying and Built Environment*, 16(2), 19–32.

Combes, J., Kinda, T. et al. (2019). Financial flows and economic growth in developing countries. *Economic Modelling*, in press.

Coulson, N. & Kim, M. (2000). Residential investment, non-residential investment and GDP. *Real Estate Economics*, 28, 233–247.

Cunningham, L. (2002). Behavioral finance and investor governance. *Washington & Lee Law Review*, 59(3), 767–837.

Damodaran, A., John, K. & Liu, C. (1997). The determinants of organizational form changes: Evidence and implications from real estate. *Journal of Financial Economics*, 45(2), 169–192.

Devaney, M. & Weber, W. (2005). Efficiency, scale economies, and the risk/return performance of real estate investment trusts. *Journal of Real Estate Finance and Economics*, 31(3), 301–317.

Downs, D. & Guner, Z.N. (1999). Is the information deficiency in real estate evident in public market trading? *Real Estate Economics*, 27(3), 517–541.

Duangploy, O., Shelton, M. & Omer, K. (2005). The value relevance of goodwill impairment loss. *Bank Accounting & Finance*, 18(5), 23–28.

Dunse, N., Hutchison, N. & Goodacre, A. (2004). Trade-related valuations and the treatment of goodwill. *Journal of Property Investment & Finance*, 22(3), 236–258.

Edmonds, B. (2012). Modeling Belief Change In A Population Using Explanatory Coherence. *Advances in Complex Systems*, 15(6), 1250085. https://doi.org/10.1142/S0219525912500853.

Einhorn, D. (1997). Unintended advantage: Equity REITS Vs. Taxable real estate companies. *Tax Lawyer*, 51, 203–213.

Elayan, F., Meyer, T. & Li, J. (2006). Evidence from tax exempt firms on motives for participating in sale leaseback transactions. *Journal of Real Estate Research*, 28(4), 381–391.

Epstein, L., Staudt, N. & Wiedenbeck, P. (2003). Judging statutes: Thoughts on statutory interpretation and notes for a project on the internal revenue code. *Washington University Journal of Law And Policy*, 13, 305–315.

Evans, L. & Quigley, N. (1995). Shareholder liability regimes, principal-agent relationships and banking industry performance. *Journal of law & Economics*, 38(2), 497–520.

Fang, X. & Yuan, F. (2018). The coordination and preference of supply chain contracts based on time-sensitivity promotional mechanism. *Journal of Management Science and Engineering*, 3(3), 158–178.

Farahmand, F. (2017). Decision and experienced utility: Computational applications in privacy decision making. *IEEE Security & Privacy*, 15, 68–72. https://www.computer.org/csdl/magazine/sp/2017/06/msp2017060068/13rRUILc8dJ

FASB (2005). *FASB Response o SEC Study on Arrangements with Off-Balance Sheet Implications, Special Purpose Entities and Transparency of Filing by Issuers*. Financial Accounting Standards Board.

Garmaise, M. & Moskowitz, T. (2003). Confronting information assymetry: Evidence from real estate markets. *Review of Financial Studies*, 17(2), 405–437.

Goetz, R., Yatsenko, Y., Hritonenko, N., Xabadia, A. & Abdulai, A. (2019). The dynamics of productive assets, contract duration and holdup. *Mathematical Social Sciences*, 97, 24–37.

Gomez-Serrano, J. & Boudec, J. (2012). Comment On "Mixing Beliefs Among Interacting Agents." *Advances in Complex Systems*, 15(7), 1250028. https://doi.org/10.1142/S0219525912500282

Graff, R. (2000). Off-balance sheet corporate finance with synthetic leases: Shortcomings and how to avoid them with synthetic debt. *Journal of Real Estate Review*, 21(3), 213–240.

Graff, R. (2001). Off-balance sheet corporate finance with synthetic leases: Shortcomings and how to avoid them with synthetic debt. *Journal of Real Estate Review*, 22, 213–240.

Harris, T. (May 2002). Synthetic leases, off balance sheet financing: Are they legitimate tools for the leasing business? *Equipment Leasing*.

Hong, L. (2014). The dynamic relationship between real estate investment and economic growth: Evidence from prefecture city panel data in China. *IERI Procedia*, 7, 2–7.

Hong, S., Wernz, C. & Stillinger, J. (2016). Optimizing maintenance service contracts through mechanism design theory. *Applied Mathematical Modelling*, 40(21–22), 8849–8861.

Hoppe, E. & Schmitz, P. (2018). Hidden action and outcome contractibility: An experimental test of moral hazard theory. *Games & Economic Behavior*, 109, 544–564.

Horng, Y. & Wei, P. (1999). An empirical study of derivatives use in the REIT industry. *Real Estate Economics*, 27, 561–586.

Huss, R. (2001). Revamping veil piercing for all limited liability entities: Forcing the common law doctrine into the statutory age. *Cincinnati Law Review*, 70, 95–115.

International Monetary Fund (2016). Time for a Supply-Side Boost? Macroeconomic Effects of Labor and Product Market Reforms in Advanced Economies. *World Economic Outlook*, Chapter 3, April, Washington.

Kallberg, J. G. & Liu, C. H. (2010). An analysis of REIT security issuance decisions. *Real Estate Economics*,38(1), 91–120.

Kauskale, L. & Geipele, I. (2016). Economic and social sustainability of real estate market and problems of economic development – A historical overview. *Baltic Journal of Real Estate Economics and Construction Management*, 4, 6–31.

Ko, J. & Zhijian, H. (2012). Persistence of Beliefs in an Investment Experiment. *Quarterly Journal of Finance*, 2(1), 1250005. https://doi.org/10.1142/S201013921250005X.

Lachner, C. & Von Heppe, R. (2007). The introduction of real estate investment trusts in Germany. *German Law Journal*, 8(1), 133–1242.

Lander, H. & Reinstein, A. (2003). Models to measure goodwill impairment. *International Advances in Economic Research*, 9(3), 227–232.

Lekeas, P. (2013). Coalitional Beliefs in Cournot Oligopoly TU Games. *International Game Theory Review*, 15(1), 1350004. https://doi.org/10.1142/S0219198913500047.

Li, W., Liu, Y. & Chen, Y. (2018). Modeling a two-stage supply contract problem in a hybrid uncertain environment. *Computers & Industrial Engineering*, 123, 289–302.

Lim, T. (2018). Growth, financial development, and housing booms. *Economic Modelling*, 69, 91–102.

Lin, E. & Chou, M. (1990). Optimal contracts. *Applied Mathematics Letters*, 3(2), 65–68.

Linklaters (January 2007). *Germany: Germany Introduces REITs – with a Major Defect?* (Linklaters, London, UK).

Liu, L., Wang, Q. & Zhang, A. (2019). The impact of housing price on non-housing consumption of the Chinese households: A general equilibrium analysis. *The North American Journal of Economics and Finance*, 49, 152–164.

Loutskina, E. & Strahan, P. (2015). Financial integration, housing, and economic volatility. *Journal of Financial Economics*, 115(1), 25–41.

Madureira, A., Pereira, I., Pereira, P. & Abraham, A. (2014). Negotiation mechanism for self-organized scheduling system with collective intelligence. *Neurocomputing*, 132, 97–110.

Maydew, E. (May 2005). Discussion of firms' off balance sheet and hybrid debt financing: Evidence from their book-tax reporting differences. *Journal of Accounting Research*, 43(2), 283–293.

Mendelson, N. (2002). A control based approach to shareholder liability for corporate torts. *Columbia Law Review*, 102, 1203–1223.

Meneguzzi, F., Modgil, S., Oren, N., Miles, S., Luck, M. & Faci, N. (2012). Applying electronic contracting to the aerospace aftercare domain. *Engineering Applications of Artificial Intelligence*, 25, 1471–1487.

Murphy, D. (1998). Holding company liability for debts of its subsidiaries: Corporate governance implications. *Bond Law Review*, 10(2), 241–251.

Murray, J.C. (2001). Synthetic leases: Bankruptcy proofing the lessee's option to purchase. *Commercial Law Journal*, 106, 221–241.

Nesvold, J. (1999). What are you trying to hide? Synthetic leases financial disclosure and the information mosaic. *Stanford Journal of Law, Business and Finance*, 83, 83–98.

Niederhoff, J. & Kouvelis, P. (2019). Effective and necessary: Individual supplier behavior in revenue sharing and wholesale contracts. *European Journal of Operational Research*, 277(3), 1060–1071.

Nwogugu, M. (2006). Employee stock options, production functions and game theory. *Applied Mathematics & Computation*, 181(1), 552–562.

Nwogugu, M. (2007a). Issues in disintermediation in the real estate brokerage industry. *Applied Mathematics & Computation*, 186(2), 1054–1064.

Nwogugu, M. (2007b). Some issues in securitization and disintermediation. *Applied Mathematics & Computation*, 186(2), 1031–1039.

Nwogugu, M. (2007c). Decision-making, risk and corporate governance: A critique of bankruptcy/recovery prediction models. *Applied Mathematics & Computation*, 185(1), 178–196.

Nwogugu, M. (2007d). Some securities law problems inherent in REITs. *Journal of International Banking Law & Regulation*, 22(11), 594–602.

Nwogugu, M. (2008a). Some corporate governance problems pertaining to REITs – part one. *Journal of International Banking Law & Regulation*, 23(2), 71–85.

Nwogugu, M. (2008b). Some corporate governance problems pertaining to REITs – part two. *Journal of International Banking Law & Regulation*, 23(3), 142–155.

Nwogugu, M. (Revised 2009). *Earnings Management and Accounting Distortions in REITs and Companies That Own Substantial Commercial Real Estate*. Available at: https://www. ssrn.com/abstract=1515517; https://papers.ssrn.com/sol3/papers.cfm?abstract_id=1515517.

Nwogugu, M. (2014). REIT shares/interests are derivatives instruments: And REITs are SIFIs. *Pratt's Journal of Bankruptcy Law*, 10(3), 242–246.

Nwogugu, M. (2015a). Goodwill/intangibles rules, earnings management and associated behavioral issues. *European Journal of Law Reform*. www.ssrn.com.

Nwogugu, M. (2019a). Human computer interaction, incentive conflicts and methods for eliminating index arbitrage, index-related mutual fund arbitrage and ETF arbitrage. Chapter 9 in: Nwogugu, M. (2019), *Indices, Index Funds and ETFs HCI: Exploring HCI, Nonlinear Risk and Homomorphisms* (Palgrave Macmillan, London, UK).

Nwogugu, M. (2019b). Economic policy, complex adaptive systems, human-computer interaction and managerial psychology: Popular-index ecosystems. Chapter 12 in: Nwogugu, M. (2019), *Indices, Index Funds and ETFs HCI: Exploring HCI, Nonlinear Risk and Homomorphisms* (Palgrave Macmillan, London, UK).

Nwogugu, M. (2019c). Group decision-making and belief-systems In REITs and "RECs": Theories of financial stability,antitrust, games and complex systems. Chapter 3 in:

Nwogugu, M. (forthcoming 2019), *Complex Systems, Multi-Sided Incentives And Risk Perception in Companies* (Palgrave Macmillan, London, UK).

Nwogugu, M. (Revised 2019d). *Fintech and Network Economics in Real Estate: REWs and MLS As Policy Transmission Mechanisms, 'Portfolio Screens' and 'Portfolio Frames'.* Working Paper. https://papers.ssrn.com/sol3/papers.cfm?abstract_id=3410637.

Nwogugu, M. (Revised 2019e). *Value-Drivers and Some Principal-Agent Conflicts in Commercial Real Estate Portfolios: A Company-Level and Market-Level Analysis.* Working Paper. https://papers.ssrn.com/sol3/papers.cfm?abstract_id=3410641.

Nwogugu, M. (Revised 2019f). *Alternative-Risk Premia and Value-Drivers in the Sharing Economy (and Digital Currencies).* Working Paper. https://papers.ssrn.com/sol3/papers.cfm?abstract_id=3410634.

Pagliari, J., Scherer, K. & Monopoli, R. (September 2003). Public versus private real estate equities: A risk-return comparison. *Journal of Portfolio Management*, Special Real Estate Issue, 101–111.

Park, S. & Kim, J. (2014). A mathematical model for a capacity reservation contract. *Applied Mathematical Modelling*, 38(5–6), 1866–1880.

Pfeffer, J. & Carley, K. (2013). The Importance of Local Clusters for the Diffusion of Opinions and Beliefs in Interpersonal Communication Networks. *International Journal of Innovation and Technology Management*, 10(5), 1340022. https://doi.org/10.1142/S0219877013400221.

Rogge, S. (2001). Casenote: Hollowell v. Orleans regional hospital: Piercing the corporate veil of a Louisiana limited liability company and successor liability. *Loyola Law Review*, 47, 923–933.

Sandler, G. (February 2005). Real estate finance leases: On or off balance sheet? *Real Estate Finance*, 21(5), 3, 3–9.

Scordato, M. (2004). Evidentiary surrogacy and risk allocation: Understanding imputed knowledge and notice in modern agency law. *Fordham Journal of Corporate and Financial Law*, 10(1), 129–166.

Sevin, S., Schroeder, R. & Bhamornsiri, S. (2007). Transparent financial disclosure and SFAS No. 142. *Managerial Auditing Journal*, 22(7), 674–687.

Shilling, J., Eppli, M. & Chun, G. (2006). *Percentage Retail Leases and FASB's Off-Balance Sheet Financing Standards.* Wisconsin-Madison CULER working papers 97-02, University of Wisconsin Center for Urban Land Economic Research. USA.

Starkman, D. (2005). The eight governance issues that matter most. Real Estate Portfolio. www.nareit.com/portfoliomag/05julaug/feat1.shtml.

Stein, S., Gerding, E.H., Rogers, A.C., Larson, K. & Jennings, N.R. (2011). Algorithms and mechanisms for procuring services with uncertain durations using redundancy. *Artificial Intelligence*, 175(14–15), 2021–2060.

Terán, J., Aguilar, J. & Cerrada, M. (2017). Integration in industrial automation based on multi-agent systems using cultural algorithms for optimizing the coordination mechanisms. *Computers in Industry*, 91, 11–23.

Topuz, J., Darrat, A.F. & Shelor, R.M. (2005). Technical, allocative and scale efficiencies of REITs: An empirical inquiry. *Journal of Business Finance & Accounting*, 32(9/10), 1961–1971.

Tunick, B. (March 18, 2002). Many worries for synthetic leases: Loans may be disguised but even bankruptcy can't avoid them. *Investment Dealer's Digest*,

US Securities & Exchange Commission (June 2005). Report and recommendations pursuant to section 401[c] of the Sarbanes–Oxley Act of 2002 on arrangement with off-balance sheet implications, special purpose entities and transparency of filings by issuers.

Warren, C. (2010). Measures of environmentally sustainable development and their effect on property asset value: An Australian perspective. *Property Management*, 28(2), 68–79.

Wei, W., Wang, J., Chen, X., Yang, J. & Min, X. (2018). Psychological contract model for knowledge collaboration in virtual community of practice: An analysis based on the game theory. *Applied Mathematics & Computation*, 329, 175–187.

Weidner, D. (Spring 2000). Synthetic leases: Structured finance, financial accounting and tax ownership. *Journal of Corporation Law*, 445–470.

Weiler, T. (2003). Approximation of Belief Functions. *International Journal of Uncertainty, Fuzziness and Knowledge-Based Systems*, 11(6), 749–777.

Wigren, R. & Wilhelmsson, M. (2007). Construction investments and economic growth in Western Europe. *Journal of Policy Modelling*, 29(3), 439–451.

Wu, Z., Zhao, R. & Tang, W. (2014). Optimal contracts for the agency problem with multiple uncertain information. *Knowledge-Based Systems*, 59, 161–172.

Xue, J. (2012). Potentials for decoupling housing-related environmental impacts from economic growth. *Environmental Development*, 4, 18–35.

Zang, Y. (2008). Discretionary behavior with respect to the adoption of SFAS no. 142 and the behavior of security prices. *Review of Accounting & Finance*, 7(1), 38–68.

Zhang, J., Wang, J. & Zhu, A. (2012). The relationship between real estate investment and economic growth in China: A threshold effect. *Annals of Regional Science*, 48, 123–134.

Zheng, W. & Walsh, P. (2019). Economic growth, urbanization and energy consumption – A provincial level analysis of China. *Energy Economics*, 80, 153–162.

Zohar, A. & Rosenschein, J. (2008). Mechanisms for information elicitation. *Artificial Intelligence*, 172(16–17), 1917–1939.

7

The *Global Intangibles+Digital Economy*, sustainability and public health: on *Preferences+Beliefs* and intangibles accounting regulations as fintech-driven incentive mechanisms[1]

While Intangible assets account for 60–75 percent of the market capitalization value in most developed stock markets around the world, the US GAAP and IFRS Goodwill and Intangibles accounting regulations (ASC 805 – Business Combinations; ASC 350 – Goodwill and Intangible Assets; IFRS 3R – *Business Combinations*; *and* IAS 38 – accounting for Intangible Assets) are inefficient and create potentially harmful psychological biases. These accounting regulations are used and their effects are propagated primarily within the context of *Contract Theory* (i.e. employment agreements; Equity-Based Incentives; M&A agreements; procurement contracts; licensing agreements; strategic alliance agreements; brokerage contracts; etc.) and *Fintech/Insurtech Environments* around the world (e.g. portfolio management systems; trading systems; financial management systems; financial advisory "apps"; insurance platforms; etc.). These accounting regulations are also *Incentive Mechanisms* because they simultaneously affect the behaviors and payoff-functions of various persons (e.g. shareholders, managers, traders, funds, etc.). These regulations facilitate earnings management, reduce competition within industries and are likely to increase the incidence of fraud and misconduct. This article introduces a new Goodwill/intangibles disclosure/accounting model that can reduce the incidence of fraud, information asymmetry, moral hazard, adverse selection and inaccuracy; and also introduces new economic psychological theories that can explain fraud, misconduct and non-compliance arising from the implementation of the Goodwill/Intangibles Accounting rules.

Generally, the critiques and theories introduced in this chapter are intended to help researchers develop better public policies for, and mathematical models of related phenomena.

Intangibles accounting regulations and the values of Intangible Assets around the world are driven by, experienced through, enforced through and effected through various types of fintech including but not limited to: trading systems; automated financial exchanges; Financial Management software; accounting software; Enterprise Resource Planning software; mobile phones; online work collaboration software; online payment systems; online banking software; fintech news portals; etc.

7.1 Existing literature

The symbiotic and evolving relationships among Intangible Assets Accounting Regulations, Intangible Assets and *Sustainable Growth* is discussed in: Zhang (2017); Robbins (2016); Marrocu, Paci and Pontis (2012); Suriñach and Moreno (2011); Corrado et al. (2012); UKCES (UK) (2011); Jona-Lasinio and Meliciani (2018); Jorgenson, Landefeld and Schreyer (eds.) (2014); Corrado, Haskel et al. (2018); OECD (2013); Jona-Lasinio, Manzocchi and Meliciani (2016); McGrattan (2017); Corrado, Hulten and Sichel (2009); Ahn, Duval and Sever (Dec. 2018); Haskel and Westlake (May 2018), Badia et al. (2019); Zambon, Marasca and Chiucchi (2019) and Haskel and Westlake (2017). The consensus is that Intangible Assets affect economic growth; and the inaccurate measurement of Intangible assets affects management decisions, business cycles and the formulation and implementation of economic policy and public policy. However, those foregoing articles and books don't address the behavioral aspects of both Intangibles Assets and associated accounting regulations which can have macroeconomic effects.

Earnings Management, Asset-Quality Management and Incentive-Effects Management typically occur and or are amplified within the context of, and often distort organizations, *Incentive-Mechanisms*, *Contracting-Frameworks*, *Networks-of-Contracts*, markets and the benefits of Fintech. Similarly, Accounting Regulations, Intangible Assets and the Digital Economy function in the context of contracts, Fintech and Incentive Mechanisms. *Contract Theory* and *Mechanism Design Theory* have been jointly studied from various perspectives including Economics/Finance, Operations Research, Mathematical Psychology, Computer Science, Game Theory and Applied Math – see: Hoppe and Schmitz (2018); Niederhoff and Kouvelis (2019); Hong, Wernz and Stillinger (2016); Wu, Zhao and Tang (2014); Li, Liu and Chen (2018); Lin and Chou (1990); Park and Kim (2014); Goetz et al. (2019); Fang & Yuan (2018); Madureira et al. (2014); Meneguzzi, Modgil et al. (2012); Meneguzzi, Modgil, Oren et al. (2011); Zohar and Rosenschein (2008); Terán, Aguilar and Cerrada (2017) and Wei et al. (2018). However, the models in most of these foregoing articles and literature are static, don't incorporate relevant variables; don't consider varying "states" and often complex "joint" effects of variables; and they don't consider Industrial Organization effects of contracts/mechanisms – see Nwogugu (2007b); Nwogugu (2019a;b) and Nwogugu (2006b).

Nwogugu (2015) critiqued Intangibles accounting regulations. See: Nwogugu (2003) and Leung and Cooper (2003) – the series of transactions done by Encompass Services illustrates various reasons for changing the disclosure rules for Goodwill and Intangibles.

There remains significant contention about Intangibles impairment and required testing and accuracy of Intangibles accounting. Lhaopadchan (2010); Uzma (2011); Nichita (2019); Smalt and McComb (2016); Aicha, Hamdani and Benziane (2020); Black and Zyla (2018); Jeny, Paugam and Astolfi (2019); Henning, Shaw and Stock (2011); Nwogugu (2015); PriceWaterhouse (May 2018);

Price (2019); ICAEW (2017) critiqued the Intangibles/Goodwill accounting regulation; and noted that there is substantial information content in identification and reporting of goodwill impairments and in the selection of goodwill amortization periods; and that the Goodwill/Intangibles Rules cause and or facilitate both "Accrual-based Earnings Management" and "Real Activities Earnings Management". Martins (2011) and Nwogugu (2010, 2015) noted that the Goodwill/Accounting Rules can cause substantial litigation. The Altshuler and Grubert (2010) analysis of formula apportionment noted that: a) income shifting has two main sources, which are the excess returns attributable to intangibles and debt; b) a major goal of income division systems is preserving neutrality between arm's length and related party transactions; c) the shifting of income from intangibles assets like patents and trademarks to low tax countries is a major source of profitability differences across high and low tax countries and d) formula apportionment (FA) has no clear advantage over separate accounts (SA). However, many of the foregoing empirical studies suffer from the methodological problems discussed in Nwogugu (2007a) and in Chapter 1 in this book.

The gaps and omissions in the existing Intangibles/Goodwill literature include analysis of the behavioral effects of ASC 805 & 350; and an accounting model for Goodwill/Intangibles that can reduce information asymmetry, Public Health risks and the propensity for fraud.

7.2 Preferences+Beliefs and intangibles accounting regulations nullify or reduce the applicability of most utility preferences

The term "*Preferences+Beliefs*" in Artificial Intelligence (AI) is introduced here and it refers to the interactions and evolution of the Beliefs and Preferences of both Human Agents and Automated Agents in specific contexts and associated revisions/reversals – that of course includes biases and applicable known "*Structural Effects*". When aggregated at the national economy level, behavioral biases such as those introduced in this chapter create a class of Complex Systems, AI, macroeconomic and macrofinance indicators which are hereby referred to as the "*Behavioral Bias Indicators*". These "*Behavioral Bias Indicators*" are also Incentive Mechanisms because by themselves, they affect the Preferences/Beliefs/Behaviors of Agents and their payoff functions. These indicators have not been properly recognized in the economics/finance, public health, political economy, behavioral operations research or psychology literatures and are not tracked. Niamir et al. (2018); Nakagawa, Oiwa and Takeda (2012); Korniotis and Kumar (1993); Acquier, Daudigeos and Pinkse (2017); Schnellenbach and Schubert (2015); Pennings and Wansink (2004) and Rosenbaum et al. (2012) concluded or implied that human biases can affect national economies, although the links they established or theorized were indirect and they didn't discuss the issues of *Preferences+Beliefs* and *Behavioral Bias Indicators*.

However, both *Preferences+Beliefs* and the opacity of financial statements and inefficiency caused by Intangible-Asset Accounting Regulations (as explained in Nwogugu [2015]) nullify or reduce the applicability/relevance of most Utility Preferences in the Economics, Computer Science and Applied Math literatures – such as those discussed in Farahmand, (2017); Boutilier et al. (2012) and Abramowitz and Anshelevich (2018).

7.3 Public health

When aggregated at the national or regional economy level, the behavioral biases and the extensive earnings management possibilities/opportunities introduced in this chapter can become Public Health risks as explained in Chapter 2 in this book. The major risk is that of mental health problems (e.g. depression; substance abuse; schizophrenia; irritability; violent tendencies; Attention Deficit Disorders; anxiety; phobias; etc.) which can cause or morph into other illnesses such as Obesity, Hypertension, Strokes, Diabetes, vascular problems; Kidney diseases, Heart diseases, etc.

Nandi et al. (2012), Ma et al. (2011), Guojonsdottir, Kristjansson and Olafsson (2011) noted that sudden increases/decreases in the volatility of stocks, or a noticeable change in overall regional or national economic conditions can cause severe illness and public health problems. The Goodwill/Intangibles Rules constitute a substantial public health risk because they can cause mental health problems (e.g. depression, substance abuse, anxiety, phobias, etc.), strokes or cardiac arrest due to the following reasons:

i)   Application of the Goodwill/Intangibles Rules can result in greater-than-normal creation of balance sheet accruals (in terms of both the number and size of accruals), and also greater-than-normal periodic changes in the values of accruals; all of which can substantially increases the volatility of stock prices of a company and its competitors in the industry. The criteria for creation of many of these accruals don't differentiate between temporary and permanent changes in values of the Intangibles, and many accruals can be changed at any time during the fiscal year, and the net result can be substantially increased volatility of stock prices – a firm's reputation or brand equity can significantly deteriorate in a matter of hours or days. Similarly, the Goodwill/Intangibles Rules can result in manipulation of asset impairments which affects the income statement, and thus, can increase stock price volatility.

ii) The Goodwill/Intangibles Rules can substantially change and distort National Income Accounting data (e.g. Corporate Income; corporate taxes; values of intangibles; etc.) which in turn changes the government's and private sector estimates of economic conditions of regions and countries, which can cause emotional distress. For example, when there are substantial expensing of impairments of Intangible Assets, reported Corporate Profits will decline, and companies will tend to shrink their activities (e.g. reduce the hiring of new employees, and corporate investment), which in turn will tend to increase emotional distress and depression among the population. Nakamura (2010) found that the economic theory and practice underlying measurement of Intangible Assets remains controversial and incomplete.

iii)   The *Goodwill/Intangibles accounting regulations* can cause significant re-allocation of investments/capital by the government and or private sector investors and or foreign investors.

iv)   In the present era, the *Goodwill/Intangibles accounting regulations* can reduce the attractiveness of Intangible assets from various perspectives – such as credit (difficult to value and monitor), collateral (low recovery value), etc.

v)   According to Salinas (2009) and other authors,[2] during the last twenty years, Intangible assets accounted for more than 60 percent of the stock market capitalization values in most developed countries (stock market capitalization of the major stock indices in the world); and by extension, an increasing percentage of the stock market value in many developing countries (such as South Korea, Brazil, China/Hong-Kong, Mexico, Thailand, Singapore). Thus, changes in the disclosed values of Intangible assets can affect individual and group psychology.

As mentioned in Chapter 1 in this book, *Accounting Biases* is a relatively new line of research and has been studied from Behavioral Accounting, Management Science (see: Khan and Lo [2018]; Chen and Jorgensen [2018]; Kwon [2005]; and Marquardt and Zur [2015]), Behavioral Operations Management and Operations Research (see: Nan and Wen [2014]) perspectives. Specific *Accounting Biases* were introduced in several chapters in this book. Chen and Jorgensen (2018) noted that *Accounting Biases* can affect competition and Industry Structure in various industries – and by extension, can affect Public Health. Using a study of mergers/acquisitions, Marquardt and Zur (2015) found evidence that financial accounting quality is positively related to the efficient allocation of the economy's capital resources. *Enforcement Theory* has been analyzed from Operations Research, Political Philosophy and Law perspectives, and the associated literatures are cited in Chapter 2 in this book. *Enforcement Patterns* (e.g. enforcement of accounting regulations, commodities-trading regulations and securities laws; corporate laws; etc.) can also affect competition and Industry Structure in various industries because: i) they affect the nature of competition and collaboration among firms in industries; ii) they affect firms' allocations of resource and capital; ii) they affect product development, marketing and human resources decisions; v) they affect the functioning, responsibilities and liability of boards of directors; v) they affect firms' perceived risk and liability-allocation in expected or existing disputes; vi) they can affect human physiological and mental responses to perceptions, risk, stressors, events and changes – and eventually, medical costs. Thus, by extension, *Accounting Biases* and *Enforcement Patterns* can have both direct and indirect effects on economic growth and Sustainability.

7.4 The intangibles/goodwill accounting regulations

The main differences between IASB/IFRS and US/GAAP FASB accounting regulations for Intangible/Goodwill were noted in various articles such as Nwogugu (2015), Deloitte (2009), Price Waterhouse (2010) and Ernst and Young (2010) (Available at: (www.ey.com/Publication/vwLUAssets/IFRS_vs_US_GAAP_ Basics_March_2010/$FILE/IFRS_vs_US_GAAP_Basics_March_2010.pdf).

7.4.1 ASC 850 and ASC 350 (formerly SFAS 141R & 142); and petitioners' objections to the implementation of SFAS 141, 141R & 142

During June 2001, the Financial Accounting Standards Board (FASB, United States) introduced two accounting standards: SFAS #141, Accounting for Business Combinations (http://72.3.243.42/pdf/fas141r.pdf) and SFAS #142, Accounting for Goodwill and Intangible Assets. Under these two standards, the pooling-of-interests accounting method for business combinations was been eliminated. SFAS #141R (http://72.3.243.42/pdf/fas141r.pdf) became effective on December 15, 2008, and completely replaced SFAS 141. SFAS 141R/142 replaced APB 16 & 17. In 2008, FASB issued a guideline named FSP FAS 141(R)-1, *Accounting for Assets Acquired and Liabilities Assumed in a Business Combination That Arise from Contingencies*.[3] This guidance will be effective for business combinations in the first annual reporting period beginning after December 15, 2008. The new guidance will:

*   Apply to contingent assets and liabilities (as defined in FAS-5, *Accounting for Contingencies*) acquired in business combinations.
*   States that when the fair value of a contingent asset or liability can be determined as of the acquisition date, it must be reported on the financial statements.
*   States that even when fair value cannot be determined, if it is probable that a contingent asset or liability existed as of the acquisition date *and* the value can be estimated using existing FAS 5 standards and literature, the estimate must be recorded in the financial statements.
*   States that where either the existence of a contingent asset or liability is not probable at the acquisition date (or even if probable, the value cannot be estimated), no asset or liability need be recorded in the financial statements.

During 2009, SFAS 141R and SFAS 142 were renamed *Accounting Standards Codification* 805 and *Accounting Standards Codification* 350 respectively.

Under ASC 805/350, companies must use purchase accounting, and cannot amortize Goodwill. Any recorded Goodwill will be subject to periodic reviews for impairment. Under ASC 805/350, acquiring firms are required to record

352 Global Intangibles+Digital Economy, sustainability and public health

Goodwill whenever the purchase price of an entity/asset exceeds the fair market value ("FMV") of the entity/asset. Instead of amortizing Goodwill on a regular basis, companies can retain Goodwill on their Balance Sheets but are required to perform annual impairment tests, and in any reporting period that the Goodwill become impaired, it must be amortized. Under ASC 805/350, a business combination is defined broadly to include most types of corporate change of control, and thus, most merger and acquisition transactions will be recorded using ACS 805 purchase price allocation methods.

Under ASC 805/350, the required periodic asset valuation and measurement of Goodwill impairment is done in a two-stage process. Testing for Goodwill impairment will require firms to identify Reporting Units, allocate purchase prices of past acquisitions with existing Goodwill to the assets and liabilities of Reporting Units, and identify and separate other Intangible assets from Goodwill. ACS 350 defines a Reporting Unit as the same level as an Operating Segment or one level below an Operating Segment. The Financial Accounting Standards Board ("FASB") considers a Reporting Unit as one level below an Operating Segment under the following conditions:

i)   Management evaluates the performance of one or more components of an Operating Segment at a level below the Operating Segment.
ii) There is discrete financial information about the component; and the component's economic characteristics are different from those of the other components of the Operating Segment.

When the Financial Accounting Standards Board (FASB; US) was about to enact SFAS 141R and SFAS 142 (now ASC 805 & 350), many financial statement users objected and petitioned the FASB. Lewis, Lippitt and Mastracchio (2001), and Corporate Executive Board (2002) explained some of these objections which were as follows.

Petitioners stated that the principle of not amortizing Goodwill on a regular basis contrasts with the IASB standards which allows some forms of pooling. Petitioners were also concerned that some parties may begin to push for non-amortization of Intangibles that have the same characteristics as Goodwill, such as acquired brands, purchased credit card relationships, and excess reorganization values for bankrupt entities. SFAS 141R/142 (ASC 805 & 350) treats Negative Goodwill as an extraordinary gain provision for non-apportioned Negative Goodwill, and many Petitioners suggested that Negative Goodwill should be recorded as an Intangible liability and amortized to non-interest income over some reasonable period.

While SFAS 141R/142 (ACS 805 & 350) requires the apportionment of Goodwill at the level of divisions or Reporting Units – some Petitioners indicated that Goodwill should be allocated at the level of SFAS 131 reporting units.

Many Petitioners expressed concern about the reliability of the methods for testing for impairment of Goodwill, and some questioned whether Goodwill is a wasting or non-wasting asset. Under the FASB rules, Goodwill write-downs are not reversible, and thus for example, a temporary fluctuation of interest rates could cause a permanent impairment of Goodwill, where the present value method is used to calculate asset values and Goodwill impairment – this type of Goodwill impairment does not reflect economic reality. Second, it can be difficult to estimate the market values of patents, trademarks, and brands. Third, the FMV of other identifiable intangible assets can't be measured with sufficient reliability to isolate the value of the Goodwill residual amount. SFAS 142 (ASC 350) requires that the Fair Market Value of the reporting unit be assigned to all assets in order to determine the residual value of the unit's Goodwill, but this may result in the manipulation of Reporting Units in efforts to protect Goodwill.

Some Petitioners stated that any impairment of Goodwill that is measured at the initial impairment review should be treated as a change in accounting principle under APB-20 (*Accounting Changes*), which will result in a different impairment standard from what is required under SFAS-121 (*Accounting for the Impairment of Long-Lived Assets and for Long-Lived Assets to be Disposed of*). The FASB standards permitted APB 20 treatment.

Under SFAS 141R/142 (ASC 805 & 350), Reporting Units that receive Goodwill allocations will be subject to periodic Goodwill impairment reviews. This will provide strong incentives to management to arbitrarily allocate Goodwill based upon a Reporting Unit's ability to support specific elements of the company's future operations. Furthermore, a finding of "unimpaired valuation of Goodwill" may result in the creation of artificial "Goodwill support Divisions", created solely to receive and maintain acquired Goodwill.

Under SFAS 141R/142 (ASC 805 & 350), companies have substantial incentives to allocate acquired Goodwill to Reporting Units that have significant unrecorded Goodwill, rather than Reporting Units that are most likely to benefit from the acquired Goodwill. Under SFAS 141R/142, only identified assets are used in allocating the fair market value of a Reporting Unit to which Goodwill has been allocated, and thus, any unidentified assets (such as advertising, research and development, gain contingencies, and other assets whose capitalization is prohibited) that contribute to the company's market value will be included as a portion of the value ascribed to Goodwill. Hence, it will be very difficult to distinguish the separate value of acquired-Goodwill from this collection of unidentified assets (which contribute to overall financial performance); and impossible to separate the value of said unidentified assets from internally developed Goodwill. Thus, under SFAS 141R/142 (ASC 805 & 350), unrecognized-Goodwill can shield acquired-Goodwill from accounting impairment, because un-recognized-Goodwill will or can increase the expected present value of future cash flows that will be generated by the company without increasing the market value of the company's recorded assets.

Petitioners stated that under SFAS 141R/142 (ASC 805 & 350), companies can manipulate transfer pricing mechanisms and corporate reorganizations in order to create and or enhance "Goodwill havens" within large and complex organizations. The Goodwill/Intangible Rules facilitate and provide substantial incentive for "Real Activities" earnings management and income-shifting through transfer pricing that pertains to both Intangibles and Goodwill. Bartelsman and Beetsma (2003), OECD (2010), Silberzstein (2011), Dischinger& Riedel (2011), Wills (1999), McDonald (2008), and Lipsey (2010) addressed some of the basic issues that pertain to earnings management from transfer pricing of intangibles/Goodwill costs. Lipsey (2010) posited that as more intangible assets are used in production, the location of production by multinational firms and the associated allocation of product costs becomes increasingly ambiguous; partly because within the firm, these Intangible assets have no clear geographical location, but only a nominal location determined by the firm's tax or legal strategies. These location ambiguities, and the resulting tax distortions are sometimes substantial.

SFAS 121 and SFAS 142 had different standards for testing Goodwill impairment – SFAS 121 uses undiscounted future cash flows as a gross measure of impairment, while SFAS 142 uses present values of future cash flows as a measure of Goodwill impairment, and thus, there are now different impairment standards for different types of assets. An SFAS-121 review is one of the remaining triggers for an intra-period Goodwill impairment review. There can be Goodwill write-downs caused exclusively by SFAS-121 reviews, although other assets might not be written down because of the nature of its impairment test; and this creates significant inconsistency. Hence, in order to maintain consistency, SFAS 142 should supersede SFAS 121 or vice versa.

SFAS 142 does not address the Deferred-Tax issue that arises from not amortizing tax-deductible Goodwill. Some users/petitioners stated that if Goodwill has an indefinite life, rather than just different amortization schedules for book and tax purposes, then "permanent difference" treatment will be appropriate.

A 2005 survey conducted by The American Business Conference, Grant Thornton, LLP, and the NASDAQ Stock Market, Inc., asked CFOs how they would handle the valuation provisions of SFAS 142. Fifty-seven percent of CFOs said that they'd be likely or almost certain to use third parties for valuation, and 71 percent of the CFOs indicated that they will use third parties when testing for impairment.

Petitioners expressed concern that Goodwill-related valuation and testing will impose additional compliance costs on companies, and yield only minimal benefits. FASB permits shortcut calculations if the Goodwill in a Reporting Unit substantially exceeded the impairment threshold in the previous year and circumstances pertaining to the collection of net assets in the current year have not changed significantly.

Many credit unions and mutual banks are not-for-profit entities but are subject to SFAS 141R/142. When these entities merge with similar entities, typically, no consideration is exchanged. Since there is no purchase price, and no acquiring entity in many of these combinations, one entity's net assets must be treated as Negative Goodwill recorded at the market value of the assets, which will contravene FASB's transparency objective.

Petitioners and practitioners raised the issue of SFAS 141's and 142's effect on compliance with the mandatory capital requirements for banks that were created pursuant to Title 12 of the U.S. Code (USC). These institutions must perform periodic checks of their mandatory minimum capital while complying with FASB standards for reporting their financial position and performance. Goodwill is treated as a special item in the USC calculations, and indefinite capitalization of Goodwill (under GAAP) may adversely distort the minimum capital requirements, and simultaneous compliance with the SFAS and the USC can cause suboptimal capital management strategies.

Some Practitioners noted that SFAS 141/142 required that the market values of all of a Reporting Unit's identifiable assets be established in order to adjust the value of its goodwill residual; but US GAAP does not permit the restatement of these other, tangible, identifiable assets to their market values, presumably because of the inherent subjectivity of such restatements. They also noted that approach has questionable benefits to financial services industry users (of financial statements) and potential high cost to the reporting entities.

7.4.2 IASB-38 and IFRS-3R

IASB-38 governs disclosure for Intangible Assets. IASB-38 applies to financial assets, mineral rights, intangibles from insurance contracts; and intangibles that arise from other IASB rules. IASB-38 does not apply to Goodwill.

Under IASB-38, Intangibles are defined as assets that are identifiable (separable; arises from contractual or legal rights), and have future earning power (revenues or reduced costs) and are controlled by the company (power to obtain benefits). Under IASB-38 Intangibles arise from only five sources or types of transactions which are: a separate purchase; or an exchange of assets; or a government grant; or a business combination; or is internally generated. Under IASB-38, Intangibles are to be recognized only if the cost of the Intangible can be measured reliably; and the Intangible has probable future economic benefits. If not recognized as Intangible, the cost of the asset is expensed.

Under IASB 38, some costs must be expensed, and these include: Startup costs; Training Costs; Internally generated Goodwill; Research costs; Development costs for which commercial feasibility has not been established; Relocation costs; Advertising and promotion costs; Internally generated Brands, mastheads, and customer lists.

With regard to measurement of the Intangible asset after the acquisition, the firm must choose between the Revaluation Model or Cost Model. Under the Cost Model, intangibles are carried at cost less amortization or impairment. Under the Revaluation Model, Intangibles may be carried at re-valued cost less impairment or amortization, if FMV can be determined from an active market. Under IASB-38, there are different treatments for assets that have finite lives or indefinite lives. For finite-life Intangible assets, the asset must be amortized by straight line method or according to the pattern of actual use; and the Amortization period should be reviewed annually; and the Intangible Asset should be assessed for impairment under IAS-36. For Indefinite Life Intangible Assets, there is no amortization.

Under IASB-38, internally generated Intangibles are not recognized as Assets; and the following must be disclosed about recognized Intangible Assets: i) Useful life; carrying value; amortization period; ii) Accumulated Amortization and impairment losses; iii) Basis for finite/infinite life; iv) Restricted Intangibles; v) Revalued Intangibles; vi) R&D costs that were expensed; vii) Description of material intangibles; viii) Reconciliation of changes in beginning and ending balances of Intangibles.

IFRS-3R (Business Combinations) was enacted by the IASB, and cover business combinations and Goodwill. Under IFRS-3R, all combinations must be accounted for using the Purchase Method – however, under IAS 22, the Pooling Method is allowed "where acquiror cannot be identified". Under IFRS-3R, Purchase Price Allocation is by Residual Method – the Purchase Price is allocated to acquired assets and liabilities, and residual is Goodwill or Negative Goodwill. Purchased Intangibles are recognized separately if: a) the Intangible is controlled by acquiror, b) the Intangible has future earning power, c) the FMV of the Intangible can be estimated easily, and d) the Intangible is separately identifiable.

Under IFRS-3R, Goodwill is recognized as asset and is measured at cost. IFRS-3R prohibits the amortization of Goodwill that is acquired in a business combination. Under IFRS-3R, Goodwill should be assessed annually for impairment under IAS-36; and Negative Goodwill should be expensed immediately (in the accounting period that the business combination occurred). The required Disclosure under IFRS-3R includes information that is sufficient to assess business combinations during reporting period; and after Balance Sheet date but before the combinations; and information that is sufficient to asses carrying value of Goodwill.

7.5 Earnings management, asset-quality management, incentive-effects management and misstatements under the goodwill/intangibles rules

Acquirors and acquirees have substantial discretion in interpretation of the Goodwill/Intangibles Rules, and some problems inherent in the implementation of these accounting rules are described as follows.

7.5.1 Improper definition of "Reporting Unit"

SFAS 142's definition of a Reporting Unit (SFAS 142, paragraphs 30 & 31) is not sufficiently specific, and creates opportunities (before or after a transaction), for the acquirer and or acquiree to change the size, asset-base and structure of Reporting Units in order to get more favorable accounting treatment.

7.5.2 Lack of specificity for the criteria for assignment of assets and liabilities to Reporting-Units/CGUs

SFAS 142 is not sufficiently specific in defining the criteria for assignment of assets and liabilities to Reporting Units (SFAS 142, paragraphs 32–36). Thus, management can arbitrarily assign assets and liabilities to Reporting Units in order to obtain specific and or different accounting treatments. Management can use major outsourcing agreements (typically signed at the corporate level), to real-locate assets and liabilities to manage earnings and reported cash flow. In large companies, management can use transfer-pricing and corporate reorganizations to create and enhance Goodwill "havens" in Reporting Units and Operating Units. Management can use overhead allocation to substantially reallocate assets and liabilities. Under ASC 350, management can manage earnings by allocating low values to acquired assets and correspondingly high values to Goodwill; and by creating a provision for future rationalization costs and using it to inflate reported Goodwill. Management can also manipulate earnings by using different/alternative words (such as trademarks, brands, licenses, titles, trade-area rights, concessions, etc.) to describe acquired Intangibles and or new internally generated intangibles, and applying very different write-down criteria; and by avoiding the creation of both Goodwill and share-premium, when structuring business combinations.

7.5.3 Insufficient triggers for impairment testing

The seven stated conditions (Paragraph 28 of ASC 350) that can trigger an intra-period impairment test for any tangible or intangible asset, don't include critical issues such as a significant changes in government regulations, or a significant technological breakthrough that affects products or services; or specific standards or severity levels for evaluation – for example, the magnitude of a change that will justify an interim impairment test; and or the type/scope/intensity of competition that is "unanticipated".

7.5.4 No standard assumptions for FMV of goodwill/ intangibles; use of internal estimates

In many instances, it is not possible to determine the accurate Fair Market Value of Intangible assets with sufficient accuracy to isolate the value of the Goodwill residual amount. It may not be possible to distinguish acquired-Goodwill from internally developed Goodwill, and from unidentified assets (which contribute to firm performance). Unrecognized Goodwill can increase the value of an asset without increasing its FMV, and thus, under ASC 350 and IFRS-3R, management can use un-recognized Goodwill to eliminate impairment of acquired Goodwill.

Since companies are permitted to use their own assumptions, rather than "marketplace" estimates to determine FMV of Goodwill, companies can manipulate earnings and asset values. A slight change in the assumptions used in valuation can significantly affect estimated FMVs. Under ASC 350 and IFRS-3R, Goodwill write-downs are not reversible, and thus, a temporary change in assumptions can cause a permanent impairment of goodwill; and the estimated useful life of an identifiable intangible asset (especially those that have indefinite lives) can sub-stantially affect an entity's financial statements.

7.5.5 Substantial incentives for mis-allocation of goodwill; and for manipulation of reporting-units/CGUs

Under ASC 350 and IFRS 3R, companies have strong economic and behavioral incentives to allocate acquired Goodwill into Reporting Units (ASC 350) or Cash generating Units ("CGU"; IFRS 3R; IAS 36) that have significant unrecorded goodwill rather than Reporting Units that are most likely to benefit from the acquired Goodwill. Also, companies now have substantial incentives to manipulate the definition of Reporting Units or CGUs in order to obtain desired accounting and tax results.

7.5.6 ASC-121 and ASC-350 have different standards for testing goodwill impairment for different assets – and ASC 350 does not supersede ASC 121

ASC 350 uses present values of cash flows, while ASC 121 uses undiscounted future cash flows as a gross measure of Goodwill impairment. There could be Goodwill write-downs solely due to ASC 121 reviews, although other assets might not be written down because of the nature of ASC 121's impairment test.

7.5.7 Newly identified unrecorded intangibles are not recorded in the financial statements

Under ASC 350, any newly identified un-recorded Intangibles are not recorded in the financial statements, regardless of FMV calculations of assets and liabilities made in the impairment testing process. Thus, there is an issue of accuracy, identification and representation.

7.5.8 Limitations on intra-period impairment testing

ASC 350 and IAS-36 (IAS-36.12) list circumstances under which intra-period testing (distinct from year-end testing) of Goodwill of a Reporting-Unit/CGU is mandatory, but do not include the following types of triggers: a) cancellation of critical contracts (e.g. outsourcing, payments systems; data processing; third-party marketing; etc.), b) material changes in management, c) changes in insurance coverage; d) specific types of corporate reorganizations and dollar amount thresholds; e) specific types of changes in corporate control (ownership interests; membership of board of directors; contingent rights, etc.) that may affect the value of the company's equity and or assets, e) labor problems and changes in union agreements, f) changes in transfer pricing policies; g) changes in effectiveness of marketing strategies/programs; h) changes in the quality of human capital and or automated operations systems (distinct from obsolescence); i) changes in the value of business-location; etc. Thus, there remains substantial management discretion about Impairment testing that can result in earnings management. IFRS Impairment testing can be done at any time.

7.5.9 Avoidance of impairment tests

Under ASC 350 and IFRS 3R, after the initial impairment test, a subsequent impairment test is not necessary under certain conditions (e.g. Paragraphs 27–28 of ASC 350). Thus, management can completely avoid ASC 350 and IFRS 3R annual and or intra-period Goodwill impairment tests.

7.5.10 Bargain purchases and negative goodwill

ASC 805 defines a *bargain purchase* as a business combination in which the total acquisition-date fair market value of the identifiable net assets acquired exceeds the fair market value of the consideration transferred plus any non-controlling interest in the acquiree, and ASC 805 requires the acquirer to recognize that excess in earnings is a gain attributable to the acquirer. Although IFRS 3R does not use "negative Goodwill", IFRS requires that any Negative Goodwill be immediately recognized in income. This is erroneous because there are circumstances where Negative Goodwill is not intentional (did not arise from arms length bargaining), and or is beyond the control of the acquirer – and the treatment of Negative Goodwill under US GAAP and IFRS reduces incentives to undertake acquisitions/combinations, and provide substantial incentives for companies to mis-state estimated values of assets, rather than being penalized by taxation of taxable gains. See: Ketz (2004); Comiskey and Mulford (2008).

7.5.11 ASC 805 and IFRS3R don't apply to joint ventures and strategic alliances

ASC 805 and IFRS3R do not apply to joint ventures and Strategic Alliances, and this is a significant error. In many instances, one party to a joint venture typically has a controlling interest (more than 51 percent) in the JV entity, and typically has options to acquire more equity interests in the JV entity. The JV entity is akin to an acquired subsidiary, because typically, at least one party to the JV Agreement has some operating control over the JV entity. Similarly, the JV entity is akin to a company that is acquired in a multiple-step acquisition. Many strategic alliances have the same or similar economic substance and economic benefits of a merger or acquisition, but without the attendant post-merger integration problems or transaction costs. Often companies choose strategic alliances because of the implicit flexibility and termination-option, and because it is sometimes a first step toward a merger or acquisition. JVs and alliances often create the same types of Intangibles that arise solely and directly from acquisitions (such as Goodwill and Brand Equity). Hence, the Goodwill/Intangible Rules should apply to joint ventures and strategic alliances. Yeow, Yeo and Liu (2003). Nwogugu (2009). ASC 805 and IFRS 3R provides substantial incentives for companies to classify business combinations as joint ventures or strategic alliances and thus, avoid compliance with both accounting regulations – that is:

i) Companies can use joint ventures to create synthetic mergers and acquisitions and thus avoid compliance with the Goodwill/Intangibles Rules – wherein the Acquiror company and the target company contribute most of or their critical assets (recorded in the JV's books at book value or at market value) to, and assign most of their staff to a separate joint venture entity, and then conduct most of their business through the joint venture entity.

ii) Companies can use joint ventures or strategic alliances to amend the size/scope/location/assets/revenues of "Reporting Units" (ASC 805) and "cash generating units" (IFRS-3R); eliminate Reporting-Units/CGUs; and or re-shuffle assets among Reporting Units/CGUs in order to avoid compliance with the Goodwill/Intangibles Rules, or in order to re-allocate Goodwill and intangibles.

iii) Companies can use Strategic alliances to create synthetic mergers and acquisitions and thus avoid compliance with the Goodwill/Intangibles Rules – wherein the Acquiror company and the target company will provide services to each other and or share resources or jointly perform activities as if they had been combined, and then record the costs at book value (synthetic merger) or at market value (synthetic acquisition).

7.5.12 ASC 805 and IFRS-3R don't apply to "non-business entities", and "strategic business real estate"

ASC 805 and IFRS-3R does not apply to the acquisition of an asset or a group of assets that does not constitute a "business".[4] This rule is not well defined in ASC 805 and IFRS-3R; and provides substantial management discretion in the classification of assets, and significant incentives for companies to mis-classify assets and or re-shuffle assets in order to avoid compliance with Goodwill/Intangibles Rules. Furthermore, non-qualifying assets can become qualifying assets once they are combined with other third-party assets. Hence, and on the contrary, the key criteria should be: i) what happens to the asset or group of assets when it is combined with the prospective acquiror's assets or human capital or other resources – if such combination results in a "business" that is organized with a profit objective, then ASC 805 and IFRS-3R should apply; and if not, then ASC 805 and IFRS-3R should not apply; and ii) the revenue generating potential of the asset in various contexts.

ASC 805 and IFRS 3R do not apply to the acquisition of cash-generating strategic business real estate[5] that creates brand equity and other intangibles for the company; and by itself, has unique business value – such limitation is an error. Such strategic business real estate are critical core revenue-generating assets in industries where location, accessibility, physical design/layout, size or visual appeal of commercial buildings are important for generating revenues, such as hotels/lodging; retailing; restaurants; professional sports; leisure; etc.

7.5.13 ASC 805 and IFRS-3R do not apply to affiliated companies (entities under common control)

ASC 805 and IFRS-3R do not apply to a combination between entities or businesses under common control – which is an error. It is important to maintain consistency and comparability among companies and within conglomerates; particularly where allocation of costs and Goodwill requires the demarcation of Reporting-Units/CGUs. Companies regularly spin-off subsidiaries, and the compensation and cost allocation systems of subsidiaries are often based on reported financial statements of such subsidiaries. Thus, ASC-805 and IFRS-3R should also apply to all combinations between entities or businesses under common control.

7.5.14 The use of fair market values in acquisitions provides opportunities for earnings management

ASC 805 requires an acquirer to recognize the assets acquired, the liabilities assumed, and any non-controlling interest in the acquiree at the acquisition date, measured at their fair market values (FMV) as of that date, with limited exceptions specified in the Statement. However, this provides an opportunity to manipulate the amounts allocated to assets and liabilities. A more realistic approach will be to allocate the purchase price to assets based on a greater-of-cost-or-FMV rule, which will ensure that companies will not mis-allocate too much of the purchase price to Goodwill (which does not have to be amortized, unlike some assets that must be depreciated). See: Hitz (2007); Huefner and Largay (2004); Institute of Chartered Accountants in England and Wales (ICAEW) (October 2007); Nurnberg (2006); Sevin and Schroeder (2005); Skinner (2008); Churyk (2005); Beatty and Weber (2006); Benston (2008).

7.5.15 Accounting treatment of transaction costs (for mergers and acquisitions) provided opportunities for earnings management

Unlike ASC 141, ASC 805 and IFRS-3R require that transactions costs (M&A fees, etc.) be recognized separately from the acquisition, and be expensed in the period incurred. Applicable transaction costs include: a) professional M&A fees – which are typically success fees (and in a few instances, are hourly billing rates), b) direct administrative costs; c) fees for permits and registrations; d) legal fees, e) fees for due diligence; f) post-merger/acquisition integration costs; and g) restructuring costs. Restructuring costs in business combinations are not expensed only if the target company was part of or committed to the restructuring plan before the acquisition. This provision is likely to create agency problems and significant information asymmetry in business combinations, because management and M&A advisors will have substantial incentives to manipulate transaction costs in order to reduce the impact of the acquisition on reported earnings and cash flow. Hence, management is more likely to: a) use contingent fees, contractually deferred fees, equity compensation; b) re-classify and transaction costs (such as direct adminis-trative costs, and post-transaction integration costs) as ordinary expenses; or shift transaction-related costs to future periods; or capitalize what should be treated as transaction costs. The rule about treatment of transaction costs is not useful or accurate for companies that are in the business of acquiring other companies, or execute many partnerships, acquisitions and JVs. The benefits of acquisitions typically continue for several reporting periods, and many acquisition costs are directly related to acquisitions. Hence, the direct costs associated with JVs, merg-ers and acquisitions should be included in the purchase price.

7.5.16 Multi-step acquisitions

In multi-step acquisitions, ASC 805 requires the acquirer to recognize the identifi-able assets and liabilities, as well as the non-controlling interest in the acquiree, at the full amounts of their fair values (or other amounts determined in accordance with this Statement). Under ASC 141, an entity that acquired another entity in a series of purchases (a step acquisition) identified the cost of each investment, the fair market value of the underlying identifiable net assets acquired, and the Good-will for each step. Application of ASC 141 resulted in recognizing and measur-ing assets and liabilities in a step acquisition at a blend of historical costs and fair values. Both ASC 805 and ASC 141 are likely to provide opportunities for companies to mis-state and or manipulate asset values and hence, a more accurate approach is to allocate the purchase price (to all assets, liabilities and prior non-controlling equity interests) based on a "greater-of-cost-or-FMV" rule, which will ensure that companies will not mis-allocate too much of the purchase price to Goodwill (which does not have to be amortized, unlike some assets that must be depreciated). See: Hitz (2007); Huefner and Largay (2004); Institute of Chartered Accountants in England and Wales (ICAEW) (October 2007); Nurnberg (2006); Sevin and Schroeder (2005); Skinner (2008); Churyk (2005); Beatty and Weber (2006); Benston (2008).

7.5.17 Contractual contingencies

Unlike ASC 141, ASC 805 and IFRS-3R require that an acquirer recognize acquired assets and assumed liabilities that arise from *contractual contingencies* as of the acquisition date, measured at their fair market values as of the acquisition date. This rule is likely to provide opportunities for companies to mis-state and or manipulate the values of contingencies. A more accurate approach is to record contractual contingencies based on a "greater-of-cost-or-FMV" rule, where the cost is the forecasted expense to fulfil the company's obligations under the contract. This rule will ensure that companies will not mis-allocate too much or too little of the purchase price to Goodwill (which does not have to be amortized, unlike some assets that must be depreciated) or to the contractual contingency. See: Hitz (2007); Huefner and Largay (2004); Institute of Chartered Accountants in England and Wales (ICAEW) (October 2007); Nurnberg (2006); Sevin and Schroeder (2005); Skinner (2008); Churyk (2005); Beatty and Weber (2006); Benston (2008).

7.5.18 Deferred taxes

ASC 805 amends FASB ASC #109 (*Accounting for Income Taxes*) to require the acquirer to recognize changes in the amount of its deferred tax benefits that are recognizable because of a business combination either in income from continuing operations in the period of the combination or directly in contributed capital, depending on the circumstances. (Such changes arise through the increase or reduction of the acquirer's valuation allowance on its previously existing deferred tax assets because of the business combination.) Previously, ASC #109 required a reduction of the acquirer's valuation allowance because of a business combination to be recognized through a corresponding reduction to goodwill or certain non-current assets or an increase in so-called negative goodwill. Thus the Goodwill/Intangibles Rules provides incentives for earnings management.

Furthermore, ASC 805 and IFRS 3R don't facilitate differentiation between traditional Goodwill and Goodwill that originates from deferred taxes – and this causes or can cause significant mis-interpretation of the subject company's risk and asset quality, particularly when such deferred taxes are substantial.

7.5.19 Leases

Under ASC 805 and IFRS, regardless of whether the Acquiree-company is the lessee or the lessor, the Acquiror-company shall determine whether the terms of each of an Acquiree's operating leases are favorable or unfavorable compared with the market terms of leases of the same or similar items at the acquisition date (but this does not apply to capital leases). The Acquiror-company shall recognize an intangible asset if the terms of an operating lease are favorable relative to market terms and a liability if the terms are unfavorable relative to market terms. However, this provision introduces substantial subjectivity in valuations of leases that is likely to result in manipulation of earnings; and the same standards should also apply to both operating leases and capital leases, for uniformity. Many securities analysts and credit analysts treat operating leases as capital leases.

Companies can completely avoid compliance with the Goodwill/Intangibles Rules by structuring an acquisition as a lease agreement wherein the Acquiror company will lease all or most of the assets of the target-company, and then hire the employees of the target-company. This problem an occur because the GAAP and IFRS are not sufficiently specific about the differences between a sale and a lease; and sometimes, the GAAP/IFRS standards differ from the tax rules. To avoid such circumvention of accounting rules, in addition to the existing lease-classification criteria (i.e. lease term; whether present value of lease payments exceeds 90 percent of current value); option to purchase the lased asset; etc.), the Goodwill/Intangibles Rules must specify the criteria that distinguish a sale from a lease – such as the following: a) the leased asset as a percentage of the tangible and intangible total assets of the company – the greater this percentage is, the more likely the transaction is a disguised acquisition; b) continuity of business operations – if the lessee continues the same business with the same assets, then it is more likely to be a disguised acquisition; c) the importance of the leased asset to the target-company's or acquiror's business (regardless of the book value or market value of the asset; d) the lease term – the greater the lease term exceeds 60 percent of the useful life of the asset, the more likely the transaction is a disguised acquisition.

Leases also generate intangible assets such as: i) Leasehold interests – which are created by below-market lease payments; and ii) Location – which are created when the firm leases space at a location that gives it substantial visibility, competitive advantages, proximity, and or substantially increases the firm's brand Equity; iii) the option to renew a lease or to purchase the property at expiration of the lease; iv) The option to change the designated use of the property.

However, the Goodwill/Intangibles rules don't address these types of "real property intangibles" which are somewhat different from all other Intangibles and are much more difficult to distinguish from Goodwill.

The use of the same lease classification criteria (i.e. operating leases versus capital leases) for both tangible and intangible assets is an error, and facilitates earnings management because both types of assets differ substantially in terms of: a) useful life of the asset; b) the appropriate discount rate (intangible assets are generally much more risky and have lower recovery rates (i.e. the liquidation values as a percentage of market value is lower than for tangible assets.

7.5.20 Earnouts

Earnouts are typically used to reduce the risk of over-payment in acquisitions – which is often caused by a combination of information asymmetry, agency problems, mis-aligned incentives, regulation, availability of acquisition financing; inaccurate estimates of human capital; technological obsolence and other factors. The treatment of Earnouts under ASC 805 and IFRS-3R reduces firms' propensity to structure acquisitions as Earnouts; and can increase the volatility of their shares' prices; and also provides opportunities for earnings management. DeAngelo et al. (1996), and Barth et al. (1999) noted that investors pay a premium for predictable earnings. The Goodwill/Intangibles Rules require recognition of the Earnout liability at FMV; and any gain or loss from periodic re-measurement of the Earnout liability must be reported in the income statement. However, Under ASC 805, Earnouts are not subject to re-measurement and recognition of gains/losses if: a) the earnout is paid by the issuance of a fixed number of the acquirer's shares, and b) the performance benchmark for the Earnout is based solely on the future performance of the firm. The earnings management issues are as follows:

i)   Management has substantial discretion in the estimation of the Earnout liability amount, which becomes one more accrual that is subject to manipulation.
ii) Companies can avoid compliance with the Earnout rules by structuring the acquisition transaction as a joint venture or strategic alliance. For example, the target company will contribute its assets to the JV entity, and the Acquiror will contribute management staff, and the JV agreement will state that the target company will be paid a percentage of the JV entity's cash flow, or pre-tax income or sales revenues. Similarly, the acquisition can be structured as a strategic alliance wherein the target-company will render services to, or share resources with the acquirer company, in exchange for a share of acquiror's revenues, cash flow, pre-tax income, etc.
iii) Companies can avoid compliance with the Goodwill/Intangibles Rules for Earnouts by structuring an acquisition as a cash-out recapitalization that is effected by issuing "Participating debt" to the selling-shareholders wherein subject to usury laws, the company will pay the debt-holder a share of the target-company's operating cash flow, Net Income, or sales revenues, and such payments will contain elements of both principal repayment and interest.

7.5.21 The effect of goodwill/intangibles rules on investors' valuation of debt

Because the Goodwill/Intangibles Rules require the creation and maintenance of various types of accruals (e.g. for goodwill; Earnouts; contingent liabilities; etc.) for which management has substantial discretion; and for periodic re-measurement of balance sheet items, these rules provide substantial incentives and opportunities for investors' to manipulate the recorded values of debt of investee-companies that own substantial Goodwill/Intangibles (especially manipulation by banks, insurance companies and investment companies that own such debt). One good approach to limit such manipulation of investment values is to infuse dollar limits into accounting treatments in order to account for the often significant differences in the nature of the investee-companies' industries; large and small firms; investors' holding periods; etc.

7.5.22 The effect of goodwill/intangibles rules on the target-company's shareholder's classification of acquisition securities

While securities (such as bonds; convertible preferred stock, warrants, etc.) and non-security "Interests" as sometimes issued as payment for acquisitions (hereafter, "Acquisition-Consideration"), the Goodwill/Intangible Rules don't account for the differences among the accounting classifications of such Acquisition Consideration by the recipients (i.e. shareholders of the target company) who have the option of classifying the received Acquisition consideration as trading securities, or available-for-sale securities or as "held-to-maturity" securities. Such accounting classifications provide opportunities for earnings management by the target-company's shareholders; and can have substantial economic and psychological effects on perceived fairness of the acquisition, and the recipients' future valuation of such Acquisition Consideration, and the recipient's perceived riskiness.

7.5.23 Compliance with debt covenants

The Goodwill/Intangibles Rules has created two types of huge schisms that have substantial effects on companies' propensity, ability and or willingness to comply with debt covenants; and the schisms are summarized as follows:

i)   Between profitable and un-profitable companies – Under the Goodwill/ Intangibles Rules, profitable companies have much more earnings management opportunities because they can create tax shields and can afford "Big Bath" earnings management (perennially un-profitable companies are more likely to incur lasting declines in their stock prices and or credit ratings by engaging in Big Bath earnings management).
ii) Between large and small companies – All else held constant, large companies that can create more and larger accruals as a result of the Goodwill/ Intangibles Rules have much more opportunities to manage earnings than small companies.

The Goodwill/Intangibles Rules makes it much easier for firms to circumvent debt covenants and bond indentures because: a) more accruals are permitted and managers have substantial discretion about the calculation of the values of such accruals; b) management has greater flexibility to manipulate interest coverage ratios – by timing goodwill/intangibles impairment or earnout-liability impairments, and by selective/discriminatory impairment decisions; c) management has greater discretion to manipulate tangible-net-worth and tangible assets – by reconfiguring Reporting-Units/CGUs, and by timing goodwill/intangibles impairments and by selective capitalization of costs; d) companies that generate Pretax Income have more opportunities to generate tax shields.

7.5.24 Effects of substantial new debt

The Goodwill/Intangibles Accounting Rules don't apply to significant new debt (e.g. debt whose face value is greater than 50 percent of the Fair Market Value of the borrower's total assets or equity) even though such new debt can provide the same or similar economic effects and validation of Goodwill/Intangibles values as a regular acquisition of all the equity or assets of a company. The net effects are that: a) companies that have substantial valuable intangibles remain under-valued and find it more difficult to raise capital; b) companies that issue such debt can benefit from interest tax shields (that will not obtain otherwise) and intangibles impairment tax shields; c) companies can improve their asset-based financial ratios by not having to write-up assets to FMV; d) some companies can circumvent the Goodwill/Intangibles Rules by structuring and disguising an acquisition as a recapitalization – that is, by issuing medium- or long-term debt that has a terminal or mandatory conversion feature.

7.5.25 Lack of goal congruence of the goodwill/intangibles accounting rules and reorganization statutes

In some jurisdictions, the goals of the Reorganization Statutes (such as sections 354, 355, 356 & 368 of the US Internal Revenue tax Code) and the Goodwill/Intangibles Accounting Rules appear to diverge substantially. For example, in the US, the wording and legislative intent of the Reorganization Laws seem to be more oriented toward the classification of transactions, rather than reflection of the economics and psychological effects of disclosure of the underlying transactions.

While the market values, book values and the liquidation values of Goodwill and Intangibles change drastically as the typical firm enters different states (i.e. recapitalization; exchange offer; financial distress; restructuring, prepackaged bankruptcy, regular bankruptcy; etc.), the Goodwill/Intangibles Rules don't account for, or reflect the significant economic consequences of these changes in values. For firms that are financially distressed or are in bankruptcy proceedings or are effecting some types of reorganizations, the values of the Goodwill/Intangibles decline substantially, but the downward Goodwill/intangibles impairment tests and adjustments carry negative information content about the firm's future prospects, which causes further decline of the firm's asset values. The Goodwill/Intangibles Rules don't distinguish between short-term and long-term impairments of intangible assets although such distinctions are critical in financial distress or bankruptcy.

Within the context of financial distress, and under the Goodwill/Intangibles Rules, it can be very difficult to identify that portion of Goodwill that is closely associated with the firm's financial or operational distress – this creates opportunities for earnings management.

Within the context of prepackaged bankruptcies, exchange offers and plans of reorganization, all else held constant, the changes in the values of the firm's debt and some types of Preferred Stock will affect the values of the firm's intangibles/goodwill. Within the context of prepackaged bankruptcies, exchange offers and plans of reorganization, all else held constant, what was once Goodwill is likely to decline to zero and evolve into Negative Goodwill which may subsequently evolve back into regular Goodwill as the firm's financial stability and earning power improves. but the Goodwill/Intangible Rules don't provide detailed guidance about how to make adjustments for such changes.

7.5.26 Non-controlling interests (minority investments)

The Goodwill/Intangibles Rules don't apply to significant Non-Controlling Interests (acquisition of 20–49 percent of the target-company's equity or assets without operating control of the target-company), even though these investments provide the same or similar economic effects and validation of Goodwill and intangibles values as a regular acquisition of all the equity or assets of a company. The net effects are that: a) some companies can circumvent the Goodwill/Intangibles Rules by structuring the acquisition as a Non-controlling Interest, while maintaining control of the target-company by placing their trusted persons in middle/senior management, but without obvious control of the board of directors of the target-company; b) companies can improve their asset-based financial ratios by not having to write-up assets to FMV, while benefiting from the earnings-increasing and cash-increasing effects of the quasi-acquisition; c) Investor-acquiror companies that are generating operating losses.

7.6 Economic psychology and behavioral issues

Other than the above-mentioned issues raised by the users/petitioners in industry and academia, there are several relevant behavioral and psychological considerations that directly influence the incidence of fraud and misconduct.

7.6.1 The Risk-Judgment Effect

See a full discussion in Chapter 5 in Nwogugu (2019c). ASC 805/350 and pre-ASC 805/350 Goodwill accounting rules complicate the analysis of the "risk" of Goodwill and Intangibles as a whole, or its components – because under these regulations, a) Goodwill and many Intangibles remain opaque and cannot be meaningfully analyzed, b) Goodwill/Intangibles amortization methods often have no relationship to true changes in asset values, c) Goodwill/Intangibles impairment tests are arbitrary and can be biased. Thus, the opacity of Goodwill creates substantial information asymmetry and psychological effects (such as greater perceived risk; more group think; more "herding behavior"; difficulty in comprehension of risk, short-sighted behavior, and increased propensity of non-compliance).

7.6.2 The Replication Bias

Under ASC 805/350 and IFRS-3R, companies can effectively use the Purchase Method to replicate the Pooling Method (for accounting for combinations) by making the Purchase Price exactly equal to the book value of the assets and liabilities of the of the company that is being purchased; and by using other means to ensure that Goodwill is not created from the transaction (for example, by assigning values to, and specifically identifying all Intangibles). This *Replication Bias* negates the objectives of ASC 805 and IFRS-3R and can lead to increased propensity for fraud and misconduct.

Also, Under the Goodwill/Intangibles Rules, and as explained earlier, companies can use joint ventures and strategic alliances to replicate mergers and acquisitions of companies, and thereby avoid compliance with the Goodwill/Intangibles Rules.

7.6.3 The Tax-Shield Bias

Amortized or expensed (based on annual impairment tests) Goodwill/Intangibles produce tax-shields, and thus, the limitations on the expensing/amortization of Goodwill/Intangibles that are caused by application of ASC 350 and IASB-38 reduces the subject company's reported and actual Operating Cash Flow (by increasing taxable income). Hence, in periods of intense competition and low profitability, and or financial distress, ASC 805/350 and IASB-38 provide significant incentives for companies to record Goodwill/Intangibles impairments in order to reduce their taxable income, generate tax-shields and increase their Operating Cash flows. Hake (2004); Hayn and Hughes (2006) and Nurnberg (2006) discussed some of the distorting effects of acquisitions and dispositions.

7.6.4 The Illusion Effects – "real activities" earnings management, and accounting for product development costs and selling/general/administrative costs

See a full discussion in Chapter 5 in Nwogugu (2019c). ASC 805 and IFRS-3R permit only post-acquisition recognition of specific intangibles related to marketing (brand-name, brand equity, etc.), customers (e.g. Customer lists; etc.), contracts, technology (e.g. Patents; software; databases), but do not permit pre-acquisition recognition of internally generated marketing related Intangibles. As illustrated in Mosca and Viscolani (2004), Rodov and Leliaert (2002), Lim and Dallimore (2004), Tollington (2006), Australian Taxation Office (2011), Robinson and Sansing (2008), Lipsey (2010), and Flesher, Thompson and Hoskins (August 1991); under current accounting rules in most jurisdictions, "Goodwill" and "Brand Equity" consist of "quasi recoveries" of substantial portions, what is now classified as Marketing Expenses in Income Statements of companies; and marketing expenses create Intangible Assets because Sales and Marketing expenses create multi-period revenues, earning power and brand equity (such intangibles are typically not recognized until the company is acquired or merged; and thus, there can be substantial divergencies between book-values and market-values of companies).

7.6.5 The Constrained Entrepreneurship/Intrapreneurship Effect

See a full discussion in Chapter 5 in Nwogugu (2019c). As illustrated in Mosca and Viscolani (2004), Hölzl (2005); Kramer et al. (2011), and Robinson and Sansing (2008), the early stages of venture formation and growth involves many costs and elements of what is now classified as Goodwill and Intangibles. However, under the Goodwill/Intangibles Rules (US GAAP and IFRS rules), most startup costs and development costs are expensed and in most cases, create operating losses. Hence, ASC 805/350, IASB-38 and IFRS-3R discourage acquisitions and mergers of emerging growth companies (particularly those companies in the technology, healthcare, business services sectors), where elements of Goodwill/Intangibles account for a substantial portion of firms' value and or assets.

7.6.6 The Reduced Comparability Effect

See a full discussion in Chapter 5 in Nwogugu (2019c). ASC 805/350 don't enhance or improve the comparability of financial statements across industries because Goodwill can be allocated at below ASC 131/805 Reporting Units; and under ASC 805/350 and IFRS-3R, there are no standard criteria for impairment tests of Goodwill that will result in uniform comparable financial statements across industries.

7.7 Incorporating intangible assets and *industry evolution* into models of bankruptcy prediction, economic growth, earnings management and asset pricing

See the comments herein and above about *Preferences*. Most Earnings Management models, Asset Pricing models and Bankruptcy Prediction models are grossly inaccurate because they don't adequately incorporate *Industry Evolution, Accounting Biases* and the fact that Intangible Assets account for more than 60 percent of the stock-market capitalization in many developed and some developing countries. Relatively, very few but an increasing number of research studies have incorporated Intangible Assets into Asset Pricing models, or Growth models, Earnings Management models or Bankruptcy Prediction models – see Nwogugu (2017c; 2006a), Li and Liu (2012) and Berk, Stanton, and Zechner (2010). On *Industry Evolution*, see: Caballero and Pindyck (1996) and Corrado, Hulten and Sichel (2009). Iazzolino and Laise (2013) critiqued the VAIC which is used to evaluate the usefulness and efficiency of Intellectual Capital. See the discussion about Intangible Assets and the UIWD in Nwogugu (2017c). Rauh and Sufi (2010) noted that firms' asset tangibility is a critical determinant for Corporate Policies and corporate Debt Capacity. Separately, Cenciarelli, Greco and Allegrini (2018), Lev and Gu (2016), Massaro, Dumay and Bagnoli (2015) and Dženopoljac, Janoševic and Bontis (2016), concluded that Intangible Assets (and specifically, Intellectual Capital) affect the financial and operating performance of companies.

The Arthur (1999); Nwogugu (2013) (theorems about variance/covariance); Taleb (2009); Nwogugu (2007a;b;c) and Nwogugu (2017a;b;c;d) critiques (i.e. biases in investment returns; asset pricing errors; WTAL; framing effects;

intertemporal substitution; invalidity of regressions, Risk Aversion and Loss Aversion; etc.) also apply to Asset Pricing models, Bankruptcy Prediction models, Growth models and AI/Machine-Learning models.

The *"Market Value"* of Intangibles Assets is usually *Noisy*, and for purposes of this section/chapter it is the excess, if any, of the firm's market value over the book value of its tangible assets. Intangible Assets and Industry Evolution can be incorporated into Asset Pricing models, Growth models, Fraud-Identification models and Bankruptcy Prediction models in several ways but note the above-mentioned critiques (especially those about anomalies in investment returns and regressions) and the critiques of empirical methods in Chapter 1 in this book. Some of the methods are as follows:

i)   Using *Debt Capacity* (in the presence of Intangible Assets) as a model variable. See: Falato, Kadyrzhanova and Sim (2014). That will require calculating the periodic changes in *Debt Capacity* that is attributable to the firms' Intangible Assets.

ii)   Use of *"Behavioral Ratios"* and *"Bankruptcy Scores"* – see: Nwogugu (2006a).

iii) Eliminating the use of regressions – see Nwogugu (2007c).

iv)   Using *Machine Learning* and *Artificial Intelligence* – see: Chaudhuri and Ghosh (2017); Nwogugu (2006a) and Nwogugu (2007a;b;c).

v)   Using periodic changes in the absolute market values of firms' Intangible Assets as a model variable. See: Corrado & Hulten (2010).

vi)   Using periodic R&D Expenses and "R&D Intensity", or using periodic *Aggregate Investment* or *Corporate Investment* in both tangible Assets and Intangible Assets as model variables – ie. both the *Adjustment Cost Effect* of intangible investment and the *Investment-specific Technological Change Effect*. See: Li and Liu (2012) and Chan, Lakonishok and Sougiannis (2001).

vii) Using the volumes/money-value/timing of technology Strategic Alliances and or Joint Ventures as model variables. There are now databases of such transactions in North America, Europe and East Asia.

viii) Using advertising expenditiures and or SG&A (selling, general and administrative expenses) and or *Brand Value* as model variables – see Vitorino (2014); Ptok, Jindal and Reinartz (2018) and Belo et al. (2019).

ix)   Using measures of *"Organizational Capital"* and or non-accounting measures of Firm Effiency (in the presence of Intangible Assets) as model variables. See: Eisfeldt and Papanikolaou (2013), Ptok, Jindal and Reinartz (2018) and Gourio and Rudanko (2014).

x)   Using measures of "Innovativeness" as model variables – see: Berzkalne and Zelgalve (2013) and Lin (2012).

xi)   Using measures of Human Capital and or Knowledge as model variables – eg. Changes in values/awards/balances/exercises of employee stock options; or changes in Unemployment and Labor metrics as model variables etc. See: Belo et al. (2019), Belo et al. (2017), Ai and Kiku (2013), Belo et al. (2017).

xii) Using *Disclosure Quality* and *Enforcement Patterns*, Intangibe Asset Impair-
ments/write-downs and related accounting restatements as model variables
(enforcement of accounting rules and securities laws) as model variables.

Generally, its likely that the abovementioned variables will have signifcant
serial auto-correlation and or cross-sectional multi-collinearity among the individual variables and appropriate adjustments should be made. The use of Intangibles Assets as variables in asset pricing and bankruptcy prediction models
sometimes requires the use of *Production Functions* of the types mentioned in Li
and Liu (2012) and Nwogugu (2016).

7.8 Conclusion

The changes in the US economy and global economy raises very critical economic,
accounting and public policy issues that have certainly not been sufficiently analyzed in existing literature, and have not been addressed by existing Goodwill and
Intangibles disclosure laws/rules. These rules have significant implications for
banks, investors and financial institutions, particularly in an era where intangibles
constitute more than 30 percent of the asset values of many private and publicly
traded companies. Goodwill and Intangibles disclosure laws/rules creates some
incentives for misconduct; and are likely to increase enforcement costs and compliance costs. There is a significant need for better enforcement and amendments
of Goodwill and Intangibles disclosure rules.

Notes

1 This article contains excerpts from Michael I. C. Nwogugu's article that is cited as:
Nwogugu, M. (2015). Goodwill/intangibles rules and earnings management. *European
Journal of Law Reform*, 17(1).
2 *See*: Ballow, J., Thomas R. & Roos G. (Accenture) (2004). *Future Value: The $7 Tril-
lion Challe*nge. www.accenture.com/SiteCollectionDocuments/PDF/manage.pdf. Noting that "Nearly sixty percent of the aggregate value of the US stock market is based
on investor expectations of future growth. And because this future value tends to be
concentrated in industries and companies that are built on intangible assets, it is critical
to find better ways to recognize, report and manage these assets".
    See: Hulten, C. (2008). *Intangible Capital and the "Market to Book Value" Puzzle.*
www.conference-board.org/pdf_free/workingpapers/E-0029-08-WP.pdf. The conference Board – Economics Program Working Paper Series. Also see: http://raw.rutgers.
edu/docs/intangibles/Papers/Intangible%20Capital%20and%20the%20Market%20
to%20Book%20ValuePuzzle.pdf.
    See: Hassett, K. & Shapiro, R. (2012). *What Ideas Are Worth: The Value of Intellectual
Capital and Intangible Assets in the American Economy.* www.sonecon.com/docs/stud-
ies/Value_of_Intellectual_Capital_in_American_Economy.pdf. (noting that "The value
of the intangible assets – which includes intellectual capital plus economic competencies – in the U.S. economy totals an estimated $14.5 trillion in 2011. . . . The ten industries
whose intellectual capital represents at least fifty percent of their market value – the ten
most intellectual-capital intensive industries – are media; telecommunications services;

automobiles and components; household and personal products; food, beverages and tobacco; commercial and professional services; software and services; healthcare equipment and services; pharmaceuticals, biotech and life sciences; and consumer services.").

See: Bond, S. & Cummins, J. *The Stock Market and Investment in the New Economy: Some Tangible Facts and Intangible Fictions.* www.brookings.edu/~/media/Projects/ BPEA/Spring%202000/2000a_bpea_bond.PDF.

See: OCEAN TOMO (2015). *2015 Annual Study of Intangible Asset Market Value.* https://www.oceantomo.com/blog/2015/03-05-ocean-tomo-2015-intangible-asset-market-value/ (noting that as of 2015, Intangible Assets accounted for about 87 percent of the stock market values of S&P 500 companies).

3 See: FASB Staff Position 141(R)-1, "Accounting for Assets Acquired and Liabilities Assumed in a Business Combination That Arises from Contingencies" (Apr. 1, 2009) ("FSP 141R-1"). www.fasb.org/pdf/fsp_fas141r-1.pdf.

See: *www.gibsondunn.com/publications/Pages/FASBVotestoIssueNewGuidanceon KeyFinancialReportingTopics.aspx.*

4 See: Ernst & Young. (January 2011). IFRS for real estate: Current issues and financial statements survey. www.ey.com/Publication/vwLUAssets/IFRS_for_Real_Estate_2011/$FILE/IFRS_for_Real_Estate_2011.pdf.

See: PriceWaterhouse (2017). *Applying IFRS for the Real Estate Industry.* https:// www.pwc.com/gx/en/audit-services/ifrs/publications/applying-ifrs-for-the-real-estate-industry.pdf.

See: KPMG (2019). *IFRS for Real Estate.* https://home.kpmg/lu/en/home/insights/ 2018/01/ifrs-for-real-estate.html.

5 See: Ernst & Young. (January 2011) (supra).

Bibliography

Abramowitz, B. & Anshelevich, E. (2018). *Utilitarians Without Utilities: Maximizing Social Welfare for Graph Problems Using Only Ordinal Preferences.* https://arxiv.org/ pdf/1711.10588.pdf.

Acquier, A., Daudigeos, T. & Pinkse, J. (2017). Promises and paradoxes of the sharing economy: An organizing framework. *Technological Forecasting & Social Change,* 125, 1–10.

Ahn, J., Duval, R. & Sever, C. (Dec. 2018). *Macroeconomic Policy, Product Market Competition, and Growth: The Intangible Investment Channel.* Working Paper. USA.

Ai, H. & Kiku, D. (2013). Growth to value: Option exercise and the cross section of equity returns. *Journal of Financial Economics,* 107(2), 325–349.

Aicha, D., Hamdani, Z. & Benziane, A. (2020). The economics of intangible assets: From just value-to-value creation. Book Chapter in: Kantola, J., Barath, T. & Nazir, S. (Eds.), *Advances in Human Factors, Business Management and Leadership* (Springer, Germany).

Altshuler, R. & Grubert, H. (December 2010). Formula apportionment: Is it better than the current system and are there better alternatives? *National Tax Journal,* 63(4), 1145–1184. ftp://snde.rutgers.edu/Rutgers/wp/2011-23.pdf

Arthur, W.B. (1999). Complexity and the economy. *Science,* 284, 107–109.

Australian Accounting Standards Board (July 2004). AASB-3: *Business Combinations* (July 2004); AASB-136: *Impairment of Assets* (July 2004); Australian Accounting Standards Board; AASB-1013: *Accounting for Goodwill* (July 2004).

Australian Taxation Office (Australian Government) (March 2011). *International Transfer Pricing – Marketing Intangibles.* www.ato.gov.au/corporate/content.aspx?doc=/ content/68495.htm

Badia, F., Dicuonzo, G., et al. (2019). Integrated reporting in action: Mobilizing intellectual capital to improve management and governance practices. *Journal of Management and Governance*, 23(2), 299–320.

Banegil, P. & Galvan, S. (2007). Intangible measurement guidelines: A comparative study in Europe. *Journal of Intellectual Capital*, 8(2), 92–204.

Bartelsman, E. & Beetsma, R. (2003). "Why pay more? Corporate tax avoidance through transfer pricing in OECD Countries. *Journal of Public Economics*, 87(9–10), 2225–2252.

Belo, F., Gala, V. et al. (2019). *Decomposing Firm Value*. Available at SSRN: https://ssrn.com/abstract=3104993 or http://dx.doi.org/10.2139/ssrn.3104993.

Belo, F., Li, J. et al. (2017). Labor-force heterogeneity and asset prices: The importance of skilled labor. *The Review of Financial Studies*, 30(10), 3669–3709.

Benston, G. (2008). The shortcomings of fair-value accounting described in SFAS 157. *Journal of Accounting & Public Policy*, 27(2), 101–194.

Berk, J.B., Stanton, R. & Zechner, J. (2010). Human capital, bankruptcy, and capital structure. *The Journal of Finance*, 65(3), 891–926.

Berzkalne, I. & Zelgalve, E. (2013). Innovation and company value: Evidence from the Baltic countries. *Regional Formation and Innovation Studies*, 11(3).

Black, E. & Zyla, M. (2018). Recognizing intangible assets. Book Chapter in: Black, E. & Zyla, M. (2018), *Accounting for Goodwill and Other Intangible Assets* (Wiley, Jersey City, NJ, USA).

Boutilier, C., Caragiannis, I. et al. (2012). *Optimal Social Choice Functions: A Utilitarian View*. Conference Paper. EC'12, June 4–8, 2012, Valencia, Spain. http://procaccia.info/papers/optvoting.ec12.pdf.

Bryer, L. & Lebson, S. (2003). *Intellectual Property Assets in Mergers & Acquisitions*. www.wipo.int/sme/en/documents/pdf/mergers.pdf.

Bugeja, M. & Gallery, N. (2006). Is older goodwill value relevant? *Accounting & Finance*, 46(4), 519–535.

Caballero, R. & Pindyck, R. (1996). Uncertainty, investment and industry evolution. *International Economic Review*, 37(3), 641–662.

Cain, M., Denis, D. & Denis, D. (2011). Earnouts: A study of financial contracting in acquisition agreements. *Journal of Accounting and Economics*, 51(2011), 151–170.

Cenciarelli, V., Greco, G. & Allegrini, M. (2018). Does intellectual capital help predict bankruptcy?. *Journal of Intellectual Capital*, 19(2), 321–337.

Chan, L., Lakonishok, J. & Sougiannis, T. (2001). The stock market valuation of research and development expenditures. *The Journal of Finance*, 56(6), 2431–2456.

Chau, K., Leung, A., Yiu, C. & Wong, S. (2009). Estimating the value of enhancement effects of refurbishment. *Facilities*, 21(1/2), 13–19.

Chaudhuri, A. & Ghosh, S. (2017). *Bankruptcy Prediction through Soft Computing Based Deep Learning Technique* (Springer, Germany).

Chen, H. & Jorgensen, B. (2018). Market exit through divestment – the effect of accounting bias on competition. *Management Science*, 64(1), 1–493.

Cleaver, K. & Ormrod, P. (1994). The economic circumstances surrounding the decision to capitalize brands – a comment. *British Journal of Management*, 5, 303–306.

Corporate Executive Board (Working Council for CFOs) (2002). *Key Findings – Accounting for Goodwill*. www.m-cam.com/downloads/01012002.pdf.

Corrado, C., Haskel, J., et al. (2012). *Intangible Capital and Growth in Advanced Economies: Measurement Methods and Comparative Results*. Institute for the Study of Labor, Bonn, Germany. IZA DP No. 6733. http://repec.iza.org/dp6733.pdf.

Corrado, C., Haskel, J., et al. (2018). Intangible investment in the EU and US before and since the Great Recession and its contribution to productivity growth. *Journal of Infrastructure, Policy & Development*, forthcoming.

Corrado, C. & Hulten, C. (2010). How do you measure a technological revolution? *American Economic Review*, 100(2), 99–104.

Corrado, C., Hulten, C. & Sichel, D. (April 2006). Intangible capital and economic growth. *US Federal Reserve Board: Finance and Economics Discussion Series: 2006–24*. www.federalreserve.gov/Pubs/feds/2006/200624/index.html.

Corrado, C., Hulten, C. & Sichel, D. (2009). Intangible capital and US economic growth. *Review of Income & Wealth*, 55, 661–685.

Cumming, D., Siegel, D.S. & Wright, M. (2007). Private equity, leveraged buyouts, and governance. *Journal of Corporate Finance*, 13, 439–460.

Cuny, C. & Talmore, E. (2007). A theory of private equity turnarounds. *Journal of Corporate Finance*, 13, 629–646.

D'Arcy, A. (2006). *De Facto Accounting Harmonization Versus National Context – Goodwill Accounting in Germany and Japan*. www.unifr.ch/controlling/kolloquium/.

DeAngelo, H., DeAngelo, L. & Wruck, K. (2002). Asset liquidity, debt covenants and managerial discretion in financial distress: The collapse of L.A. gear. *Journal of Financial Economics*, 64, 3–34.

Deloitte (2009). *A Roadmap to Accounting for Business Combinations and Related Topics*. www.iasplus.com/dttpubs/0912buscombroadmap.pdf.

Desai, C. & Savickas, R. (2010). On the causes of volatility effects of conglomerate breakups. *Journal of Corporate Finance*, 16, 554–571.

Desai, M., Dyck, A. & Zingales, L. (2007). Theft and taxes. *Journal of Financial Economics*, 84(3), 591–623.

Dischinger, M. & Riedel, N. (2011). Corporate taxes and the location of intangible assets within multinational firms. *Journal of Public Economics*, 95(7–8), 691–707.

Duangploy, O., Shelton, M. & Omer, K. (2005). The value relevance of goodwill impairment loss. *Bank Accounting & Finance*, 18(5), 23–28.

Dženopoljac, V., Janoševic, S. & Bontis, N. (2016). Intellectual capital and financial performance in the Serbian ICT industry. *Journal of Intellectual Capital*, 17(2), 373–396.

Eisfeldt, A. & Papanikolaou, D. (2013). Organization capital and the cross-section of expected returns. *The Journal of Finance*, 68(4), 1365–1406.

Falato, A., Kadyrzhanova, D. & Sim, J. (2014). *Rising Intangible Capital, Shrinking Debt Capacity, and the U.S. Corporate Savings Glut*. Working Paper, Federal Reserve Board of Governors, USA.

Fang, X. & Yuan, F. (2018). The coordination and preference of supply chain contracts based on time-sensitivity promotional mechanism. *Journal of Management Science and Engineering*, 3(3), 158–178.

Farahmand, F. (2017). Decision and experienced utility: Computational applications in privacy decision making. IEEE Security & Privacy, 15, 68–72. https://www.computer.org/csdl/magazine/sp/2017/06/msp2017060068/13rRUILc8dJ

Financial Accounting Standards Board (FASB) (2001). *Statement of Financial Accounting Standards No. 142: Goodwill and Other Intangible Assets. Statement of Financial Accounting Standards No. 141R – Business Combinations* (FASB, Stamford, CT).

Goetz, R., Yatsenko, Y., Hritonenko, N., Xabadia, A. & Abdulai, A. (2019). The dynamics of productive assets, contract duration and holdup. *Mathematical Social Sciences*, 97, 24–37.

Goodwin, J. & Ahmed, K. (2006). Longitudinal value relevance of earnings and intangible assets: Evidence from Australian firms. *Journal of International Accounting, Auditing and Taxation*, 15(1), 72–91.

Gourio, F. & Rudanko, L. (2014). Customer Capital. *The Review of Economic Studies*, 81(3), 1102–1136.

Griffin, W. & Lev, A. (September 2007). *Tax Aspects of Corporate Mergers and Acquisitions* (Davis, Malm & D'Agostine P.C.).

Gu, Z. & Hao, X. (2011). Wealth effects of the creditor in mergers: Evidence from Chinese listed companies. Chapter in: Wu, D., ed., *Quantitative Financial Risk Management, Computational Risk Management*. DOI: 10.1007/978-3-642-19339-2_16, # (Springer-Verlag Berlin Heidelberg, Germany).

Guo, S., Hotchkiss, E. & Song, W. (2011). Do buyouts (Still) create value? *The Journal of Finance*, 66(2), 479–517.

Guojonsdottir, G., Kristjansson, M. & Olafsson, O. (2011). Immediate surge in female visits to the cardiac emergency department following the economic collapse in Iceland: An observational study. *Emergency Medicine Journal*, 29(9), 694–698.

Haskel, J. & Westlake, S. (May 2018). Productivity and secular stagnation in the intangible economy. VOX. https://voxeu.org/article/productivity-and-secular-stagnation-intangible-economy.

Henning, S., Shaw, W. & Stock, T. (2011). The Amount and Timing of Goodwill Write-Offs and Revaluations: Evidence from U.S. and U.K. Firms. *Review Of Quantitative Finance & Accounting*, 23(2), 99–121.

Hibbert, A., Daigler, R. & Dupoyet, B. (2008). A behavioral explanation for the negative assymetric return-volatility relation. *Journal of Banking & Finance*, 32, 2254–2266.

Hitz, J. (2007). The decision usefulness of fair value accounting – a theoretical perspective. *European Accounting Review*, 16(2), 323–362.

Hölzl, W. (2005). Tangible and intangible sunk costs and the entry and exit of firms in a small open economy: The case of Austria. *Applied Economics*, 37(21), 2429–2443.

Hong, S., Wernz, C. & Stillinger, J. (2016). Optimizing maintenance service contracts through mechanism design theory. *Applied Mathematical Modelling*, 40(21–22), 8849–8861.

Hoppe, E. & Schmitz, P. (2018). Hidden action and outcome contractibility: An experimental test of moral hazard theory. *Games & Economic Behavior*, 109, 544–564.

Huefner, R. & Largay, J. (2004). *The Effect of the New Goodwill Accounting Rule on Financial Statements* (A Publication of the New York State Society of CPAs, New York City, USA).

Iazzolino, G. & Laise, D. (2013). Value added intellectual coefficient (VAIC) A methodological and critical review. *Journal of Intellectual Capital*, 14(4), 547–563.

ICAEW (2017). *Intangible Assets: The Achilles heel of financial reporting*. https://ion.icaew.com/talkaccountancy/b/weblog/posts/intangible-assets-the-achilles-heel-of-financial-reporting.

Institute of Chartered Accountants in England and Wales (ICAEW) (October 2007). *EU Implementation of IFRS and the fair Value Directive: A Report for the European Commission*. http://ec.europa.eu/internal_market/accounting/docs/studies/2007-eu_imple mentation_of_ifrs.pdf.

International Accounting Standards Board (IASB) (2004). *Intangible Assets*. International Accounting Standards #38 (IASB, London).

Jain, A., Kini, O. & Shenoy, J. (2011). Vertical divestitures through equity carve-outs and spin-offs: A product markets perspective. *Journal of Financial Economics*, 100, 594–615.

Jarboe, K. (2007). *Athena Alliance Report: Measuring Intangibles: A Summary of Recent Activity*. www.athenaalliance.org/apapers/MeasuringIntangibles.htm.

Jeny, A., Paugam, L. & Astolfi, P. (2019). The usefulness of intangible assets' disclosure for financial analysts: Insights from Purchase Price Allocation conditional on deal quality. *Comptabilite Controle Audit*, forthcoming.

Jerman, M. & Manzin, M. (2008). Accounting treatment of goodwill in IFRS and US GAAP. *Organizacija*, 41(6), 218–224.

Jona-Lasinio, C. & Meliciani, V. (2018). Productivity Growth and International Competitiveness: Does Intangible Capital Matter? *Intereconomics: Review of European Economic Policy*, 53(2), 58–62.

Jones, S. (2011). Does the capitalization of intangible assets increase the predictability of corporate failure? *Accounting Horizons*, 25(1), 41–70.

Jorgenson, D., Landefeld, J. & Schreyer, P. (eds) (2014). *Measuring Economic Sustainability and Progress* (University of Chicago Press, Chicago, USA).

Khan, U. & Lo, A. (2018). Bank lending standards and borrower accounting conservatism. *Management Science*, in press.

Kind, H., Midelfart, K. & Schjelderup, G. (2005). Corporate tax systems, multinational enterprises, and economic integration. *Journal of International Economics*, 65(2), 507–521.

Klier, D. (2009). *Managing Diversified Portfolios: What Multi-Business Firms Can Learn from Private Equity*. Springer Series in Contributions to Management Science (Springer, Germany).

Korniotis, V. & Kumar, A. (1993). Do behavioral biases adversely affect the economy? *Review of Financial Studies*, 24(5), 1513–1559.

Kosaka, H. (2004). Japanese managerial behavior in strategic planning case analyses in global business contexts. *Journal of Business Research*, 57, 291–296.

Kramer, J., Marinelli, E., Iammarino, S. & Diez, J. (2011). Intangible assets as drivers of innovation: Empirical evidence on multinational enterprises in German and UK regional systems of innovation. *Technovation*, 31(9), 447–458.

Kwon, Y. (2005). Accounting conservatism and managerial incentives. *Management Science*, 51(11), 1593–1732.

Lander, H. & Reinstein, A. (2003). Models to measure goodwill impairment. *International Advances in Economic Research*, 9(3), 227–232.

Leary, T. (2000). *The Significance of Variety in Antitrust Analysis*. www.ftc.gov/speeches/leary/atljva4.shtm.

Lev, B. & Gu, F. (2016). *The End of Accounting and the Path Forward for Investors and Managers* (John Wiley & Sons, Hoboken, NJ).

Lewis, E., Lippitt, J. & Mastracchio, N. (2001). User's comments about SFAS 141 and 142 on business combinations and goodwill. *The CPA Journal*.

Lhaopadchan, S. (2010). Fair value accounting and intangible assets. *Journal of Financial Regulation and Compliance*, 18(2), 120–130.

Li, E. & Liu, L. (2012). *Intangible Assets and Cross-Sectional Stock Returns: Evidence from Structural Estimation*. https://pdfs.semanticscholar.org/d069/ae2fcf9d6947fb5b2d-869bd8f05c9a4cefa0.pdf.

Li, W., Liu, Y. & Chen, Y. (2018). Modeling a two-stage supply contract problem in a hybrid uncertain environment. *Computers & Industrial Engineering*, 123, 289–302.

Li, Z., Shroff, P., Venkataraman, P. & Zhagng, X. (2011). Causes and consequences of goodwill impairment losses. *Review of Accounting Studies*, 16(4), 745–778.

Lin, E. & Chou, M. (1990). Optimal contracts. *Applied Mathematics Letters*, 3(2), 65–68.

Lin, X. (2012). Endogenous technological progress and the cross-section of stock returns. *Journal of Financial Economics*, 103(2), 411–427.

Lipsey, R. (2010). Measuring the location of production in a world of intangible productive assets, FDI, and intra-firm trade. *Review of Income and Wealth*, 56(1), S99–S110.

Ma, W., Chen, H., Jiang, L., Song, G. & Kan, H. (2011). Stock volatility as a risk factor for coronary heart disease death. *European Heart Journal*, 32(8), 1006–1011.

Madureira, A., Pereira, I., Pereira, P. & Abraham, A. (2014). Negotiation mechanism for self-organized scheduling system with collective intelligence. *Neurocomputing*, 132, 97–110.

Marquardt, C. & Zur, E. (2015). The role of accounting quality in the M&A market. *Management Science*, 61(3), 487–705.

Márquez-Ramos, L. (2008). *The Effect of IFRS Adoption on Trade and Foreign Direct Investments*. International Trade and Finance Association, Working Paper 19.

Marrocu, E., Paci, R. & Pontis, M. (2012). Intangible capital and firms' productivity. *Industrial & Corporate Change*, 21, 377–402.

Martinez-Jerez, A. (2008). Governance and merger accounting: Evidence from stock price reactions to purchase versus pooling. *European Accounting Review*, 17(1), 5–35.

Martins, A. (2011). Impairment of goodwill and its fiscal treatment: More trouble for the Portuguese firms and tax courts? *European Journal of Management*, 11(1).

Massaro, M., Dumay, J. & Bagnoli, C. (2015). Where there is a will there is a way: IC, strategic intent, diversification and firm performance. *Journal of Intellectual Capital*, 16(34), 90–517.

McDonald, M. (2008). *Income Shifting from Transfer Pricing: Further Evidence from Tax Return Data*. OTA Technical Working Paper #2. Office of Tax Analysis (OTA), US Department of the Treasury, USA. www.transferpricing.com/pdf/Income%20Shifting.pdf.

McGrattan, E. (2017). *Intangible Capital and Measured Productivity*. NBER Working Paper No. 23233, USA. Available at: https://www.nber.org/papers/w23233.

Meneguzzi, F., Modgil, S., Oren, N., et al. (2011). Algorithms and mechanisms for procuring services with uncertain durations using redundancy. *Artificial Intelligence*, 175(14–15), 2021–2060.

Meneguzzi, F., Modgil, S., Oren, N., Miles, S., Luck, M. & Faci, N. (2012). Applying electronic contracting to the aerospace aftercare domain. *Engineering Applications of Artificial Intelligence*, 25, 1471–1487.

Nakagawa, R., Oiwa, H. & Takeda, F. (2012). The economic impact of herd behavior in the Japanese loan market. *Pacific-Basin Finance Journal*, 20(4), 600–613.

Nakamura, L. (March 2005). *Advertising, Intangible Assets and Un-Priced Entertainment*. Working Paper, Federal Reserve Bank of Philadelphia. www.fep.up.pt/conferences/earie2005/cd_rom/Session%20II/II.H/Nakamura.pdf.

Nakamura, L. (2010). Intangible Assets and National Income Accounting. *Review of Income and Wealth*, 56(1), S135–S155. Also www.philadelphiafed.org/research-and-data/publications/working-papers/2008/wp08-23.pdf.

Nan, L. & Wen, X. (2014). Financing and investment efficiency, information quality, and accounting biases. *Operations Research*, 60(9), 2111–2380.

Nandi, A., Marta, R., Cerdá, M., Vlahov, D., Tardiff, K.J. & Galea, S. (2012). Economic conditions and suicide rates in New York City. *American Journal of Epidemiology*, 175(6), 527–535.

Niamir, L., Filatova, T., Voinov, A. & Bressers, H. (2018). Transition to low-carbon economy: Assessing cumulative impacts of individual behavioral changes. *Energy Policy*, 118, 325–345.

Nichita, E. (2019). Intangible assets – insights from a literature review. *Accounting and Management Information Systems*, 18(1), 4–8.

Niederhoff, J. & Kouvelis, P. (2019). Effective and necessary: Individual supplier behavior in revenue sharing and wholesale contracts. *European Journal of Operational Research*, 277(3), 1060–1071.

Nurnberg, H. (2006). The distorting effects of acquisitions and dispositions on net operating cash flow. *Accounting Forum*, 30(3), 209–226.

Nwogugu, M. (2003). Corporate governance, legal reasoning and credit risk: The case of encompass services Inc. *Managerial Auditing Journal*, 18(4), 270–291.

Nwogugu, M. (2006b). Employee stock options, production functions and game theory. *Applied Mathematics & Computation*, 181(1), 552–562.

Nwogugu, M. (2007a). Issues in disintermediation in the real estate brokerage industry. *Applied Mathematics & Computation*, 186(2), 1054–1064.

Nwogugu, M. (2007b). Some issues in securitization and disintermediation. *Applied Mathematics & Computation*, 186(2), 1031–1039.

Nwogugu, M. (2007c). Decision-making, risk and corporate governance: A critique of bankruptcy/recovery prediction models. *Applied Mathematics & Computation*, 185(1), 178–196.

Nwogugu, M. (2006a). Decision-making, risk and corporate governance: New dynamic models/algorithms and optimization for bankruptcy decisions. *Applied Mathematics & Computation*, 179(1), 386–401.

Nwogugu, M. (2006b). Decision-making, risk and corporate governance: New dynamic models/algorithms and optimization for bankruptcy decisions. *Applied Mathematics & Computation*, 179(1), 386–401.

Nwogugu, M. (2007a). Decision-making, risk and corporate governance: A critique of methodological issues in bankruptcy/recovery prediction models. *Applied Mathematics & Computation*, 185(1), 178–196.

Nwogugu, M. (2007b). Some game theory and financial contracting issues in large corporate transactions. *Applied Mathematics & Computation*, 186(2), 1018–1030.

Nwogugu, M. (2009). On the choice between a strategic alliance and an M&A transaction. *International Journal of Mathematics, Game Theory & Algebra*, 17(5/6).

Nwogugu, M. (2010). Real options, enforcement of goodwill/intangibles rules and associated behavioral issues. Working Paper. www.srn.com.

Nwogugu, M. (2013). Decision-making, sub-additive recursive matching noise and biases in risk-weighted index calculation methods in in-complete markets with partially observable multi-attribute preferences. *Discrete Mathematics, Algorithms & Applications*, 05, 1350020.

Nwogugu, M. (2015). Real options, enforcement of goodwill/intangibles rules and associated behavioral issues. *Journal of Money Laundering Control*, 18(3), 330–351.

Nwogugu, M. (2016). "Economic psychology issues inherent in illegal online filesharing by individuals and institutions and illegal online fileSharing as production systems". Book-chapter in: Nwogugu, M. (2016). *Illegal Online Filesharing, Decision Analysis, and the Pricing of Digital Goods* (CRC Press, New York City, USA).

Nwogugu, M. (2017a). "The historical and current concepts of 'plain' interest rates, forward rates and discount rates are or can be misleading". Chapter 6 in *Anomalies in Net Present Value, Returns and Polynomials: and Regret Theory In Decision-Making* (Palgrave Macmillan, London, UK).

Nwogugu, M. (2017b). "Some biases and evolutionary homomorphisms implicit in the calculation of returns". Chapter 8 in *Anomalies in Net Present Value, Returns and Polynomials and Regret Theory in Decision-Making* (Palgrave Macmillan, London, UK).

Nwogugu, M. (2017c). "Regret theory and asset pricing anomalies in incomplete markets with dynamic unaggregated preferences". Chapter 3 in *Anomalies In Net Present Value, Returns and Polynomials; and Regret Theory In Decision-Making* (Palgrave Macmillan, London, UK).

Nwogugu, M. (2017d). "Spatio-temporal framing anomalies in the NPV-IRR model and related approaches; and regret theory". Chapter 2 in *Anomalies in Net Present Value, Returns and Polynomials; and Regret Theory in Decision-Making* (Palgrave Macmillan, London, UK).

Nwogugu, M. (2019a). Human computer interaction, incentive conflicts and methods for eliminating index arbitrage, index-related mutual fund arbitrage and ETF arbitrage. Chapter 9 in: Nwogugu, M. (2019), *Indices, Index Funds and ETFs HCI: Exploring HCI, Nonlinear Risk and Homomorphisms* (Palgrave Macmillan, London, UK).

Nwogugu, M. (2019b). *Economic Policy, Complex Adaptive Systems, Human-Computer Interaction and Managerial Psychology: Popular-Index Ecosystems*. Chapter 12 in: Nwogugu, M. (2019), *Indices, Index Funds and ETFs HCI: Exploring HCI, Nonlinear Risk and Homomorphisms* (Palgrave Macmillan, London, UK).

Nwogugu, M. (2019c). *Complex Systems, Multi-Sided Incentives And Risk Perception In Organizations* (forthcoming; Palgrave Macmillan, London, UK).

OECD (2013). *Supporting Investment in Knowledge Capital, Growth and Innovation* (OECD Publishing, Paris).

Price, C. (2019). *The Knowledge Economy, Intangible Assets and Public Wealth.* https://oecdonthelevel.com/2019/06/12/the-knowledge-economy-intangible-assets-and-public-wealth/.

PriceWaterhouse (May 2018). *Accounting Treatment of Intangible Assets with a View to Financial Reporting Requirements Under the Future European Public Sector Accounting Standards (EPSAS).* https://circabc.europa.eu/sd/a/725ae06f-0a27-426d-a1af-880859336184/Issue%20paper%20on%20accounting%20treatment%20of%20intangible%20assets%20.pdf.

OECD (2010). "Special considerations for intangible property", and Chapter IX – "Transfer pricing aspects of business restructurings". In OECD Transfer Pricing Guidelines for Multinational Enterprises and Tax Administrations 2010, OECD Publishing.

Oliveira, L., Rodrigues, L. & Criag, R. (2010). Intangible assets and value relevance: Evidence from the Portuguese stock exchange. *British Accounting Review*, 42(2), 241–252.

Park, S. & Kim, J. (2014). A mathematical model for a capacity reservation contract. *Applied Mathematical Modelling*, 38(5–6), 1866–1880.

Pennings, J. & Wansink, B. (2004). Channel contract behavior: The role of risk attitudes, risk perceptions, and channel members' market structures. *The Journal of Business*, 77(4), 697–724.

Pricewaterhouse Coopers (November 2007). *Similarities and Differences: A Comparison of IFRS, US GAAP and Indian GAAP.* http://petrofed.winwinhosting.net/upload/S&D.pdf.

Pricewaterhouse Coopers (2010). *A Global Guide to Accounting for Business Combinations and Noncontrolling Interests Application of the U.S. GAAP and IFRS Standards.* www.pwc.com/en_US/us/issues/business-combinations/assets/accounting-business-combinations-nci.pdf.

Ptok, A., Jindal, R. & Reinartz, W. (2018). Selling, general, and administrative expense (SGA)-based metrics in marketing: Conceptual and measurement challenges. *Journal of the Academy of Marketing Science*, 46(6), 987–1011.

Ratnatunga, J., Gray, N. & Balachandran, K. (2004). CEVITA™: The valuation and reporting of strategic capabilities. *Management Accounting Research*, 15(1), 1–105.

Rauh, J & Sufi, A. (2010). Capital structure and debt structure. *the Review of Financial Studies*, 23(12), 4242–4280.

Renneboog, R. & Szilagyi, P. (2008). Corporate restructuring and bondholder wealth. *European Financial Management*, 14(4), 792–819.

Robbins, C. (2016). Using New Growth Theory to Sharpen the Focus on People and Places in Innovation Measurement. Blue Sky Forum, Informing Science and Innovation Policies, Towards the Next Generation of Data and Indicators. Available at: www.oecd.org/sti/124%20-%20Focusing_on_People_and_Places_Robbins.pdf.

Robinson, L. & Sansing, R. (2008). The effect of "invisible" tax preferences on investment and tax preference measures. *Journal of Accounting and Economics*, 46(2–3), 389–404.

Rodov, I. & Leliaert, P. (2002). FiMIAM: Financial method of intangible assets measurement. *Journal of Intellectual Capital*, 3(3), 323–336.

Rosenbaum, S., Billinger, S., Stieglitz, N., Djumanov, A. & Atykhanov, Y. (2012). Market economies and pro-social behavior: Experimental evidence from Central Asia. *The Journal of Socio-Economics*, 41(1), 64–71.

Salinas, G. (2009). *The International Brand Valuation Manual* (1st ed., John Wiley & Sons, Ltd., Jersey City, NJ, USA).

Schnellenbach, J. & Schubert, C. (2015). Behavioral political economy: A survey. *European Journal of Political Economy*, 40B, 395–417.

Seetharaman, A., Sreenivasan, J. & Sudha, R. & Yee, T. (2006). Managing impairment of goodwill. *Journal of Intellectual Capital*, 7(3), 338–353.

Silberzstein, C. (2011). Transfer pricing aspects of intangibles: The OECD project. *Transfer Pricing International Journal. BNA.* www.oecd.org/dataoecd/26/40/48594010.pdf.

Siegel, P. & Borgia, C. (2007). The measurement and recognition of intangible assets. *Journal OF Business & Public Affairs*, 1(1). www.scientificjournals.org/journals2007/articles/1006.htm.

Skinner, D. (2008). Discussion of "the implications of unverifiable fair-value accounting: Evidence from the political economy of goodwill accounting". *Journal of Accounting and Economics*, 45(2–3), 282–288.

Smalt, S. & McComb, M. (2016). Accounting for internally generated intangible assets. *Journal of International Accounting Auditing and Taxation*, 4(1).

Stein, S., Gerding, E.H., Rogers, A.C., Larson, K. & Jennings, N.R. (2011). Algorithms and mechanisms for procuring services with uncertain durations using redundancy. *Artificial Intelligence*, 175(14–15), 2021–2060.

Suriñach, J. & Moreno, R. (2011). The Role of Intangible Assets in the Regional Economic Growth. *Investigaciones Regionales – Journal of Regional Research* (Asociación Española de Ciencia Regional), 20, 165–193.

Swartz, L. (2011). *Multiple-Step Acquisitions: Dancing the Tax-Free Tango* (Cadwalader, Wickersham & Taft, New York City, USA).

Szymanski, S. & Valetti, T. (2005). Parallel trade, price discrimination, investment and price caps. *Economic Policy*, 20(44), 705–749.

Taleb, N. (2009). Finiteness of variance is irrelevant in the practice of quantitative finance. *Complexity*, 14(3), 66–76.

Taylor, W. (2011). *The International Taxation of Goodwill and Other Intangibles.* Working Paper. www.ibdt.com.br/material/arquivos/Biblioteca/Willard%20B.%20Taylor.pdf.

Teece, D. (2006). Reflections on the Hymer thesis and the multinational enterprise. *International Business Review*, 15(2), 124–139.

Terán, J., Aguilar, J. & Cerrada, M. (2017). Integration in industrial automation based on multi-agent systems using cultural algorithms for optimizing the coordination mechanisms. *Computers in Industry*, 91, 11–23.

Tollington, T. (2006). UK goodwill and intangible asset structuration: The FRS10 rule creation cycle. *Critical Perspectives in Accounting*, 17(6), 703–844.

Uzma, S. (2011). Challenges of reporting intangible assets in financial statements. *The IUP Journal of Accounting Research & Audit Practices*, X(4), 29–33.

Vitorino, M. (2014). Understanding the effect of advertising on stock returns and firm value: Theory and evidence from a structural model. *Management Science*, 60(1). https://doi.org/10.1287/mnsc.2013.1748.

Walker, D. (March 2006). Financial accounting and corporate behavior. Working Paper Series (#06–05), Law & Economics, Boston University Law School, USA.

Wei, W., Wang, J., Chen, X., Yang, J. & Min, X. (2018). Psychological contract model for knowledge collaboration in virtual community of practice: An analysis based on the game theory. *Applied Mathematics & Computation*, 329, 175–187.

Weiss, L. & Wruck, K. (1998). Information problems, conflicts of interest, and asset stripping: Chapter 11's failure in the case of eastern airlines. *Journal of Financial Economics*, 48, 55–97.

Wills, M. (1999). The tax treatment of intangibles in the context of transfer pricing. *Revenue Law Journal*, 9(1). http://epublications.bond.edu.au/rlj/vol9/iss1/2.

Wright, M., Bacon, N. & Amess, K. (2009). The impact of private equity and buyouts on employment, remuneration, and other HRM practices. *Journal of Industrial Relations*, 51, 501–516.

Wright, M., Kitamura, M. & Hoskisson, R. (2003). Management buy-outs and restructuring Japanese corporations. *Long Range Planning*, 36, 355–374.

Wruck, K. (1989). Equity ownership concentration and firm value: Evidence from private equity financings *Journal of Financial Economics*, 23, 3–28.

Wruck, K. (1990). Financial distress, reorganization, and organizational efficiency. *Journal of Financial Economics*, 27, 419–444. Reprinted in Altman, E., ed. (1992), *Bankruptcy and Distressed Restructurings: Analytical Issues and Investment Opportunities* (Business One Irwin Publishers).

Wruck, K. (1991). What really went wrong at Revco? *Journal of Applied Corporate Finance*, 79–92. Reprinted in *The New Corporate Finance: Where Theory Meets Practice*, 1993, edited by Donald Chew (McGraw Hill).

Wruck, K. & Baker, G. (1989). Organizational changes and value creation in leveraged buyouts: The case of O.M. Scott & Sons company. *Journal of Financial Economics*, 25, 163–190. Reprinted in Kanter, R., Stein, B. & Jick, T., eds. (1992), *The Challenge of Organizational Change* (Free Press, New York), pp. 349–365.

Wruck, K. & Baker, G. (1991). Lessons from a middle market LBO: The case of O.M. Scott. *Journal of Applied Corporate Finance*, 46–58. Reprinted in *The New Corporate Finance: Where Theory Meets Practice*, 1993, edited by Donald Chew (McGraw Hill).

Wruck, K., Kaplan, S. & Mitchell, M. (2000). A clinical exploration of value creation and destruction in acquisitions: Organization design, incentives and internal capital markets. Chapter in: Kaplan, S., ed., *Productivity of Mergers and Acquisitions* (National Bureau of Economic Research, Conference Volume). Downloadable at http://papers.ssrn.com/sol3/paper.taf?ABSTRACT_ID=10995.

Wruck, K., Warner, J. & Watts. R. (1988). Stock prices and top management changes. *Journal of Financial Economics*, 20(8), 461–492.

Wu, Z., Zhao, R. & Tang, W. (2014). Optimal contracts for the agency problem with multiple uncertain information. *Knowledge-Based Systems*, 59, 161–172.

Yeow, C., Yeo, F. & Liu, C. (2003). Information asymmetry and accounting disclosures for joint ventures. *The International Journal of Accounting*, 38(1), 23–39.

Zambon, S., Marasca, S. & Chiucchi, M. (2019). Special issue on "The role of intellectual capital and integrated reporting in management and governance: a performative perspective". *Journal of Management and Governance*, 23(2), 291–297.

Zang, Y. (2008). Discretionary behavior with respect to the adoption of SFAS no. 142 and the behavior of security prices. *Review of Accounting & Finance*, 7(1), 38–68.

Zhang, L. (2017). The Investment CAPM. Forthcoming in European Financial Management. http://theinvestmentcapm.com/InvCAPM2017March.pdf.

Zohar, A. & Rosenschein, J. (2008). Mechanisms for information elicitation. *Artificial Intelligence*, 172(16–17), 1917–1939.

8

Economic policy, sustainability and fintech-driven decisions: Chinese VIEs and Chinese reverse-merger companies contradict mechanism-design theory, contract theory and asset-pricing theory

Chinese VIEs (Variable Interest Entities) and Chinese Reverse-Merger Companies (CRMs) were structured vehicles that were used to infuse foreign capital into the Chinese economy and especially its media, technology and telecom sectors. The Chinese VIEs (Variable Interest Entities) and Chinese Reverse-Merger Companies (CRMs) cross-listed their shares in foreign stock markets such as the US, Canada and Singapore stock markets (typically as American Depository Receipts or as global Depositary Receipts), and are hereafter referred to as "SinoCos". The securities fraud, asset-quality management and earnings management perpetrated by SinoCos such as Alibaba and Baidu seemed to be a major corporate objective and an integral part of their organizational strategies, and has systemic risk and financial stability implications. This chapter: i) explains the context of, and securities fraud and earnings management perpetrated by, and litigation against some of the SinoCos; ii) illustrates why Sarbanes-Oxley Act (USA); the US FSOC's "Non-Bank SIFI Criteria"; the Dodd-Frank Act (USA); Fair-Value accounting regulations (both FASB, and IASB/IFRS standards); Auditor-liability allocation mechanisms; the US Bankruptcy statutes; and the US and Chinese securities regulations and enforcement efforts have been and remain ineffective; iii) illustrates the interactions of, and sometimes symbiotic relationships among managerial psychology, systemic risk, Enterprise-Risk and litigation strategies (both the government/prosecutor's and the defendant-company's strategies) on one hand, and investors' psychology, efficient price-discovery, and "under-investment" in Corporate Governance by government agencies and individual firms; iv) explains why the internal corporate governance principles/standards of SinoCos and Alibaba are non-Public Goods; v) introduces new theories – such as the *Governance-Strategy Gap Theory*; and the *Mass Truncated Evolving Cognition Theory*; vi) explains how fintech amplified or could have amplified the effects of the SinoCos misconduct, and how gaps in the development of fintech may have delayed regulators' responses; vii) explains why some theories of IPOs and decision-making and *Third-generation Prospect Theory*, *Cumulative Prospect Theory* and *Prospect Theory* and related methods in the literature, are not entirely correct; viii) explains why the SinoCos and their misconduct represent significant financial stability risks, systemic risks and asset-pricing anomalies.

At various times between 2010 and 2019, the SinoCos had a total market-capitalization of between US$720 billion and US$1,600 billion.[1] As of 2018, at least 200 Chinese VIEs and at least 150 reverse-merger Chinese companies had been listed in US stock exchanges. From details of lawsuits and US SEC investigations and Chinese government's investigations in China, senior executives of many SinoCos and Chinese government-owned entities seemed to be actively involved in the SinoCos' earnings management and accounting fraud. Apparently, Chinese companies that were cross-listed in Singapore, Canada and other jurisdictions also perpetrated similar earnings management and asset-quality management. Each SinoCo either cross-listed its shares in US stock markets; or executed a reverse-merger wherein it merged into, and acquired an exchange-traded "shell" company listed in US stock markets; or cross-listed its shares in the US using an ADR/GDR;[2] or cross-listed by using a Chinese *"Variable-Interest Entity"* (VIE) (which has only rights to the profits of the associated Chinese company but not any economic interest in such Chinese company).[3] See: Johnson (2015); Cadwalader (Aug. 10, 2011); Ziegler (2016); Eales (2015); and Hopkins, Lang and Zhao (2016). VIEs have been found to be illegal by Chinese courts; and as explained herein, VIEs amount to earnings management and asset-quality management.

The motivation for, and context of this chapter is somewhat varied and begins with the Global Financial Crisis which exposed significant weaknesses in Corporate Governance standards in multinational organizations, and strategic decision-making by Boards of Directors. *First*, there is the exponential growth of cross-listings of companies (stock exchanges) and cross-border trade during 1995–2015 caused the growth of the numbers and sizes of cross-listed companies that are often subject to conflicting corporate governance and labor standards. Both individual and institutional investors around the world are increasingly emphasizing the quality and implementation of corporate governance standards and Board Dynamics within companies as major investment criteria. *Second*, as of 2014/2015, Alibaba was one of the largest companies in the world (by stock market value) and China was the second largest economy in the world; and Alibaba and other cross-listed Chinese (China-based) companies and Chinese reverse-merger companies had generated significant controversy about their poor corporate governance and their actual systemic risk and financial instability effects which in turn, have become public policy issues in other countries but have not been addressed sufficiently. Alibaba once had a stock market value of about US$168 billion, but during 2015, Alibaba's stock price crashed and Alibaba lost about US$140 billion of stock market value. Other researchers such as Wang (2014); Darrough, Huang and Zhao (2012); Chen et al. (Nov. 2015); Lee, Li and Zhang (2012); Chen, Li and Wu (2010) and Chen, Lin and Lin (2012) have proffered similar reasons for securities fraud by Chinese companies that executed reverse-mergers in US stock markets – but they haven't analyzed VIEs and the managerial psychology, and systemic risk and financial instability issues. During 1995–2015 and across the world, there were increases in shareholder activism (and associated litigation), much of which was directed at, or was handled by, or was ultimately influenced by regulators and BODs of large multinationals such as Alibaba or cross-listed companies such as the SinoCos. *Third*, the misconduct of Alibaba's and the SinoCos' senior executives and Boards of Directors (BODs) constitute psychological, financial stability, Enterprise-risk and systemic risk phenomena which have not been addressed fully in the literature–and this chapter develops some theories. *Fourth*, the pattern of misconduct of the SinoCos' senior executives and Boards of Directors ("BODs) cannot be explained by Prospect Theory (PT), Cumulative Prospect Theory (CPT) or Third-generation Prospect Theory (PT3), and contradicts theories and empirical results in the literature and thus has implications for asset pricing. *Fifth*, Woolford (2013) noted that South African BODs have difficulties in evaluating enterprise risk; and their BOD members are subject to a high degree of cognitive bias and source dependence when facing risk and uncertainty; and that Prospect Theory couldn't fully describe BODs' responses to Enterprise-Risk. *Sixth*, the pattern of behaviors and misconduct of the SinoCos' senior executives and Boards of Directors cannot be explained by the *Porter Model* type competitive analysis which is basic and perhaps insufficient given comments in Nwogugu (2005a;b). *Seventh*, the existing literature doesn't address the issue of whether the internal corporate governance principles/standards and compliance quality of reverse-merger companies and cross-listed companies such as the SinoCos and Alibaba are non-Public Goods given the broad geographical scope of their operations, the possibility of Financial Instability and actual/perceived effects on foreign investors. *Eighth*, fintech and gaps in regulation and development of fintech seems to have amplified the SinoCos' misconduct. *Ninth*, researchers such as Güçbilmez (2014) and Güçbilmez (2015) have studied IPOs in China and Hong Kong but have completely omitted the *Chinese Reverse-merger Phenomenon* and the *Chinese VIE Phenomenon* (which are the functional equivalents of an IPO), and the managerial psychology, Systemic Risk and securities-fraud issues associated with such transactions. Specifically, the finding in Güçbilmez (2014) of the existence of a separating equilibrium wherein small profitable firms choose ChiNext and large Chinese firms backed by foreign venture capital prefer to execute IPOs in US stock exchanges, is strongly contradicted by the SinoCos' behaviors, reverse-merger patterns and VIEs. *Tenth*, the Chinese Reverse-merger Phenomenon and the Chinese VIE Phenomenon contradict elements of *Mechanism Design Theory*, *Contract Theory* and *Asset-Pricing Theory*. By addressing these issues, this chapter fills several gaps in, and contributes to the Managerial Psychology, Financial Stability, Contract Theory, Mechanism Design Theory, Asset Pricing, Systemic Risk, Complex Adaptive Systems, Corporate Governance and Entrepreneurship literatures.

8.1 Existing literature

There is virtually no analysis of managerial psychology, Systemic Risk and enterprise-risk implications inherent in patterns of misconduct in the financing and operations of the SinoCos in the literature (most of the few articles are descriptive). Barber (2013), Wang (2014); Darrough, Huang and Zhao (2012); Chen et al. (Nov. 2015); Lee, Li and Zhang (2012); Chen, Li and Wu (2010), Chen, Lin and Lin (2012), Norris (May 26, 2011)[4] and Sovereign Advisers (Globalsecuritieswatch.org) (2013)[5] commented on the wave of domestic and foreign securities frauds by Chinese companies and SinoCos during 2000–2015 but they didn't address the psychology, financial stability and systemic risk issues. Ziegler (2016), Eales (2015) and Johnson (2015) discussed the invalidity of Chinese VIEs.

Pathak, Joshi and Ludhiyani (2010), Bliss, Pottera and Schwarz (2012), García-Pérez, Yanes-Estévez and Oreja-Rodríguez (2014), Grechuk and Zabarankin (2014) analyzed strategic decision-making in organizations. Nwogugu (2003; 2004a;b), Claudiu (2013), Melendy and Huefner (2011), Arena et al. (2010); Bowman (1984); Dickinson (2001); Donaldson (2012); Engau and Hoffman (2011); Jankowicz and Hisrich (1990) and Ku (2012) analyzed corporate governance, enterprise risk and strategy issues. Schwenk (1984) developed theories about enterprise risk and BODs.

Karpoff, Lee and Martin (2008a) and Karpoff, Lee and Martin (2008b) analyzed the consequences of earnings management to firms and managers.

McCarter, Rockmann and Northcraft (2010) analyzed public goods whose eventual value is uncertain when contribution decisions are made; and the effects of outcome-variance on why individuals contribute and amounts they contribute to a public good (their research is applicable to analysis of Strategic Alliances and Statutes as public goods). Dey (2010) and Bargeron Lehn and Zutter (2010) studied the effects of Sarbanes–Oxley on corporate risk taking – some researchers have noted that compliance with SOX has often resulted in lower corporate investment.

For obvious reasons, Nwogugu (2003); Melendy and Huefner (2011); Claudiu (2013); Arena et al. (2010); Bowman (1984); Dickinson (2001); Donaldson (2012); Engau and Hoffman (2011); Jankowicz and Hisrich (1990); and Nwogugu (2004a;b) analyzed corporate governance, policy, strategy and Enterprise-Risk issues. Schwenk (1984) developed theories about enterprise risk and BODs.

The responses of executive managers and BODs to enterprise-risk in the events that unfolded in companies analyzed in Nwogugu (2004a) and Nwogugu (2003) cannot be explained by Prospect Theory (PT), Cumulative Prospect Theory (CPT), Third-generation Prospect Theory (PT3); or the "*Remoteness From Reality Risk*" ("RFR"; which was developed in Woolford [2013] and Beasley et al. [2010]), or the "*Risk Readiness Index*" ("RRI"; which was developed in Woolford [2013] from the "Repertory Grid" in Alexander et al. [2010]).

8.1.1 The Chinese reverse-merger phenomenon and the Chinese VIE phenomenon contradict elements of contract theory and mechanism design theory

Earnings management, Asset-quality Management and Incentive-Effects Management typically occur and or are amplified within the context of, and often distort organizations, markets, *Incentive-Mechanisms*, *Contracting-Frameworks* and *Networks-of-Contracts*. However, *Contract Theory* and *Mechanism Design Theory* have been studied from various perspectives including Economics/Finance, Operations Research, Mathematical Psychology, Computer Science, Game Theory and Applied Math – see: Hoppe and Schmitz (2018); Niederhoff and Kouvelis (2019); Hong, Wernz and Stillinger (2016); Nwogugu (2007b, 2006b); Wu, Zhao and Tang (2014); Li, Liu and Chen (2018); Lin and Chou (1990); Park and Kim (2014); Goetz et al. (2019); Fang and Yuan (2018); Madureira et al. (2014); Meneguzzi et al. (2012); Meneguzzi et al. (2011); Zohar and Rosenschein (2008); Terán, Aguilar and Cerrada (2017); and Wei, Wang et al. (2018).

The *Chinese Reverse-merger Phenomena* and the *Chinese VIE Phenomena* contradict elements of *Contract Theory* and *Mechanism Design Theory* that pertain to the following: i) utility, ii) Moral Hazard, iii) principal–agent relationships; iv) effects of Observability; v) Belief-revisions (scope; timing; contagion; etc.); vi) macro effects of contracting; vii) the *Revelation Principle*, viii) Incentive Compatibility; ix) Implementability; etc.

Contract Theory is implicit in, but doesn't necessarily dominate Prospect Theory, Cumulative Prospect Theory and Third Generation Prospect Theory, and as explained here, PT/CPT/PT³ cannot explain the *Chinese Reverse-merger Company Phenomena* and the *Chinese VIE Phenomena*.

8.2 Sustainability (economic, social, environmental and urban sustainability)

The SinoCos sold and caused the purchases of huge volumes of products around the world each year (many of which were manufactured under questionable circumstances in developing countries – many of the factories violated labor and environmental regulations). The SinoCos and many of the companies that sell products through the SinoCos operated factories in many countries where labor, emissions and environmental degradation standards/regulations are much weaker than those in developed countries. Many of the products sold by or through the SinoCos (and the products used in processing them) are not really biodegradable – it takes hundreds of years for them to decompose, and their reactions with other elements in the environment could have produced toxic substances. As of 2017, the SinoCos didn't have any comprehensive global waste disposal, environmental remediation and labor policies for those products.

The SinoCos caused or facilitated the sales and use of products, services and equipment that use significant amounts of energy that was generated from fossil fuels (the SinoCos significantly increased the *carbon footprints* of households, companies and governments), and yet during 2001–2007, the SinoCos didn't have any programs to generate clean energy for mass consumption, or to significantly reduce energy consumed by the products/services that they sell directly or indirectly, or cause the purchases of (including ancillary and complementary products that are manufactured and sold by other companies).

The SinoCos's earnings management and asset-quality management and their other corporate governance problems had or could have had "*governance contagion effects*" both in the technology industry and in other industries which in turn, can cause or increase systemic risk and financial instability (and also increase firms' cost-of-capital and perceived risk), all of which could have reduced economic/financial sustainability. The corporate governance, strategy, operations research and corporate finance literatures indicate that in many countries, many large and medium -ized companies hire senior executives and board members from, and copy the corporate governance policies and operational strategies of their competitors. The SinoCos were also financial stability risks, given their assets, industry and scope of operations.

Thus legally, the SinoCos may be partly liable for the foregoing problems based on tort law (contribution; Product Liability) and or criminal law. Governments should consider creating "*national sustainability funds*" that will be funded by contributions from companies such as the SinoCos, and will be used to solve sustainability problems.

The financial distress or failure of groups of SinoCos could have caused or increased systemic risk and financial instability in markets; and negative effects in the global technology industry.

The SinoCos were a key element of the global digital economy. The SinoCos' GVCs (global value chains) were extensive and supported many local and multinational companies.

The SinoCos were part of the "backbone" of social and urban sustainability because they sold consumer products/services, other products and information infrastructure that carry the urban social networks, services, digital products, critical information, news and entertainment that support and facilitate urban systems, urban life and human perceptions of cities/towns/environments, other human beings and risk.

The SinoCos are one of a relatively new class of "*hybrid evolving multinational LDC companies*" (HEMLCs) which is characterized by the following: i) they are based in developing countries and are listed on both developed and developing country stock exchanges and operate in many countries; ii) they or the companies that sell products through their platform, do a significant portion of their manufacturing in developing and under-developed countries, and a significant portion of their assets are in emerging markets companies (e.g. machinery/equipment; cash; brand equity; outsourcing contracts; human capital; customer relationships; etc.); iii) they generate a substantial portion of their annual revenues from developing countries; iv) they are "functionally" emerging markets companies – in terms of culture, corporate governance and processes; v) they have caused or facilitated global structural changes in their industries or industry segments, and or their reactions to structural changes have been a major determinant of their operating performance; vi) their global value chains (GVCs) are "hybrid" because they involve third-party companies/processes/contracts, and effective control can be an issue (their GVCs fuse companies); vii) their operations are or can be significantly affected by international trade policies, economic sanctions and geopolitical risk; viii) their operations and businesses are evolving and are vital to many economies.

8.3 The evolution of the SinoCos; and theories of risk and corporate governance: the SinoCos' misconduct was facilitated by, and grossly amplified by fintech, gaps in the development of fintech, and improper regulation of fintech

The typical pattern was that each SinoCo was created by entrepreneurs in China and the fraud was initially organized in China; and the SinoCos and the Chinese securities brokers got local Chinese indigenes to invest in the SinoCo. The SinoCo was then listed in the US (NASDAQ or NYSE) via a "reverse-merger" into an exchange-traded shell company or as a VIE (in most cases as a way for investors to "exit"). In some instances the SinoCo was also cross-listed in other countries such as Singapore and Canada in addition to the US. The SinoCo would typically continue to perpetrate fraud and the fraudsters would sell their shares before the fraud is discovered and the stock-prices of the SinoCo subsequently crashes. See: www.bloomberg.com/news/2011-08-18/chinese-protest-5-billion-losses-tied-to-u-s-reverse-mergers.html. The use of cross-listed IPOs and reverse-mergers by companies driven by entrepreneurs has also become a public-policy issue in China, US, Europe and other countries. In the US and Canada, many reverse-mergers (which enabled private companies to trade their shares in stock markets quicker and with much lower listing costs compared to traditional IPOs) have been associated with fraud and investigations by government agencies. Alibaba and many of the SinoCos were built by entrepreneurs and had VC firms and local (Chinese) individuals as investors and then used cross-listed IPOs and reverse-mergers as "exits" for some investors (in contrast to using such transactions to raise expansion capital). In 2011, the Bloomberg index of US-listed Chinese reverse-merger stocks declined by more than 60 percent YTD, which represented a loss of approximately $15 billion in market-value. *See*: www.bloomberg.com/quote/CHINARTO:IND. See the Bloomberg chart showing Chinese reverse-merger companies listed on US stock exchanges at: www.bloomberg.com/news/2011-06-22/table-of-chinese-reverse-merger-companies-listed-on-u-s-stockexchanges.html. These issues obviously have negative implications for capital formation for startups, the motivation and aspirations of entrepreneurs; Systemic Risk and Financial Instability, and the risk preferences of angel investors and entrepreneurs.

The Corporate Governance, financial and Strategy problems of the SinoCos and the simultaneous crashes of the Shanghai Stock Market and the Shenzhen Stock Market in 2015 are, or can be reasonably construed to be evidence of the following which also shaped the evolution of the SinoCos:

i) The *Dynamic Coordination-Gaps Theory* – which refers to: 1) *Intra/Inter jurisdictional Coordination-Gaps* in enforcement of laws/statutes, which often increases enforcement and monitoring costs; and 2) *Coordination-Gaps* among BODs, executive management teams, shareholders and regulators of the company; and or among Strategic-Alliance/JV partners.

ii) The *Sub-optimal Investment Theory* – sub-optimal investment (cash; human capital; technology; etc.) in both corporate governance structures, Strategic Planning and competitive intelligence which eventually causes non-random repeating patterns of poor strategic decisions and low corporate governance; and weakens incentive systems and compliance by employees. Such sub-optimal investment is typically not properly identified or effectively resolved by management and the BOD; and or there are communication gaps and inadequate execution directives between the BOD and management. Note that there is a difference between *"sub-optimal investment"* and *"inadequate investment"*.

iii) *Corporate Governance Statutes and Corporations' Strategies/Mechanisms/ Alliances as Non-Public Goods (that may be created, diminished or amplified by Political Influence and Lobbying)* – the "use-value" and potency of Corporate Governance statutes ad mechanisms seem to, or can decline as more persons/companies use such statutes and mechanisms; and or when there is increasing complexity of the Strategy-spaces of many of the users of such statute/mechanism. Thus, Corporate Governance statutes (such as SOX) and mechanisms are or can be *Non-Public Goods*. Similarly, the legality and potency of the announced or un-announced strategies or "mechanisms" or Strategic Alliances of large/medium companies (or groups of similar small companies) can decline as more persons/companies are subjected/exposed to such strategies, alliances and or mechanisms; and or when there is increasing complexity of the Strategy-spaces of many of such companies' customers and or suppliers. Thus, the strategies, mechanisms, Strategic Alliances and internal Corporate Governance principles of large multinational companies (or groups of similar small/medium companies) are or can be *Non-Public Goods*.

iv) There are adverse effects of *Managerial Entrenchment*; *BOD Entrenchment*; and *Quasi-managerial Entrenchment* (managers' philosophies and methods are entrenched by BOD reliance, long-term transactions; Policies & procedures; organizational culture and fear of change).

Fintech and the inadequate regulation of fintech facilitated and amplified the Sino-Cos' misconduct in the following ways. First, Reverse-mergers into public shells rely on the fintech of stock exchanges. The ways that the trading systems quote stock prices, the accuracy of price updates/quotes, and the duration between price-updates; and the news that the trading system carries, all affect the viability of reverse-mergers and VIEs in stock markets.

Second, the earnings management and differential reporting of SinoCos (filing of different financial reports to the US SEC and Chinese regulators) can be attributed to ineffective fintech and gaps in fintech development and inadequate regulation of fintech. That is, ideally there should be a single online platform for cross-listed companies around the world to file IASB/IFRS-compliant financial statements, and such a platform should be accessible to securities regulators in all countries who should be required to review such financial statements for fraud and misstatements, given the potential systemic risks and financial instability risks of such accounting disclosures.

Third, Fintech shaped the way that retail investors reacted to the SinoCos' misconduct during 2010–2017. Many of the retail investors in China and the US often got news and financial data through fintech companies that provide content and or online trading and or online research. The reactions of these retail investors indicate that: 1) excessive and perhaps un-warranted consumer trust was placed on fintech companies that provide online content, online research and or online trading; 2) in the internet age, retail investors expectations are largely influenced by such fintech companies; 3) such fintech companies encourage and amplify self-help by retail investors and thus reduce or can reduce the influence, trading activities and profits of retail securities brokers; 4) the liability regimes (for allocating liability in securities law disputes) needs to be changed.

Fourth, fintech companies that provide online trading and or investment research have significant incentives to create and sustain stock-price bubbles and crashes, and to delay updates of stock prices in their online trading systems (and to take positions against their customers when stock prices are declining) because they can earn huge profits from doing so.

Fifth, Fintech may have shaped the way that regulators reacted to the SinoCos' misconduct during 2000–2017. It can be argued that regulators in China and the US were slow to react to and prosecute the erring SinoCos. As mentioned, fintech companies that provide online information and or trading can create speculation and stock price bubbles. It seems that regulators relied on the accuracy of such fintech companies. Such fintech companies also add or provide a false aura of legitimacy to erring SinoCos. Should such fintech companies have any legal liability for carrying misleading information?

Another critical issue is that many of the SinoCos were fintech companies[6] that originated in China. Thus, the SinoCos' fraud and misconduct in the US, China, Canada and Singapore has had a symbiotic relationship with the fintech ecosystem in China (i.e. the development, financing and expansion of Chinese fintech companies). Because of the high valuation multiples often assigned to Chinese fintech, VR and gaming companies, many non-finance and non-fintech companies and manufacturing companies sometimes acquired fintech or VR or gaming companies and repositioned themselves solely in order to get high stock valuation multiples. The reverse-merger and VIE structures may have accelerated the development of the Chinese fintech sector because more fintech companies were able to use both mechanisms to "exit" and to raise capital.

Alibaba is a type of *second generation fintech* company and hosts various types of fintech companies in its platform. Alibaba is henceforth referred to as both:

i)   A "*Private/Restricted Leveraged Fintech*" which is characterized by the following: 1) the fintech app is developed by a separate party ("developer') and is available only or primarily through a third party platform ("provider"); 2) consumers don't have direct access to the fintech developer – and in most instances customer service is provided by the platform-provider; 3) consumers can offer very limited feedback to the developer; 4) in most instances, revenues paid by the app are initially paid to the platform providers who then makes payments to the developer; 5) the platforms are two-sided platforms; 6) the platform "finances" apps developers directly or indirectly (by reducing or eliminating their marketing/sales, distribution, and or administration expenses) – thus the term *Private/Restricted Leveraged Fintech* applies to both fintech and non-fintech apps developers.

ii)   A *"Public Leveraged Fintech"* which is characterized by the following: 1) the fintech app is developed by a separate party ("developer') and is available only or primarily through a third party platform ("provider"); 2) consumers may or may not have direct access to the fintech developer – and customer service is provided by the platform-provider or the developer; 3) consumers can offer regular or limited feedback to the developer; 4) revenues generated by the app are initially paid to either the developer or to the provider (who then makes payments to the developer); 5) the platforms are two-sided platforms; 6) the platform "finances" apps developers directly or indirectly (by reducing or eliminating their marketing/sales, distribution, and or administration expenses).

Given the wild global popularity of fintech and technology companies and the relatively good long-term performance of their stock-prices (and associated investor expectations), it is conjectured here that: i) the global dominance of Alibaba as a fintech facilitator of financing and trade transactions has helped to dampen the severity of its misconduct; and has reduced regulators' willingness and ability to prosecute Alibaba; and that has had a "spillover effect" that protects other erring SinoCos that are technology companies; ii) the position of some SinoCos as fintech or technology companies has reduced regulators' willingness and ability to prosecute them; and that has had a "spillover effect" that protects other erring SinoCos that are not technology companies. This phenomenon is henceforth referred to as the *"Tech Expectations & Social-Capital Syndrome"*.

8.4   Chinese VIEs and Chinese reverse-merger companies (CRMS) are types of fraud, earnings management and asset-quality management; and they distort the cost-of-capital of firms in their industry sectors

As of 2015–2017, more than 40 percent of the SinoCos were Chinese VIEs. See comments in: Cadwalader (USA) (Aug. 10, 2011); Xianwu and Lihui (2012); Eales (2015); Liu (2016); Ma (2013); Chen & Co. Law Firm; Hopkins, Lang and Zhao (2016); Chen (2011) and Schindelheim (2012). The three main financial and legal risks inherent in the Chinese VIE[7] structure are that the Peoples Republic of China (PRC) government may declare the VIE illegal; second, the underlying contracts for VIEs may be deemed unenforceable under PRC law; and third, there may be selective enforcement of regulations which is common in china.

The Chinese VIEs structure is a type of fraud because foreign investors (that is, US investors in the "*wholly foreign owned company*" (WFOC) that enters into contracts with, and lends money to the Chinese VIE company) have effectively been significantly misled about the legal and accounting risks inherent in the Chinese VIE structure. There is inherent and clear intent in such misrepresentation because the Chinese companies that use VIEs and their investment banks and lawyers knew or should have known about the significant risks inherent in VIEs; and public disclosures of such risks in filings of WFOCs have been generally inadequate. While Ziegler (2016) noted that the VIE structure is illegal, most of the prospectuses of investor-owned companies associated with Chinese VIEs (WFOCs), apparently don't fully disclose the risks inherent in the VIE structure. The VIE investors suffered harm because the VIE structure is very likely to negatively affect the trading and market values of the WFOC/PWFOC shares.

The Chinese VIE structure is a form of earnings management and asset-quality management because of the following reasons. Ziegler (2016) noted that the VIE structure is illegal. The "*wholly foreign owned company*" (WFOC) that enters into contracts with, and lends money to the Chinese VIE company essentially overstates the value of the WFOC's assets which consists only of debt and contract rights to cashflow/dividends (and so does the WFOC's foreign parent company – the "PWFOC") – all of which are uncertain due to significant legal risks. The Chinese VIE structure mis-represents the viability and liquidity of the WFOC's and the Chinese VIE's assets. The actual value and disclosure of the WFOC-VIE contracts can be easily manipulated by the PWFOC's or WFOC's or the VIE's management. There is a significant difference between accounting recognitions and disclosures by the Chinese VIE and the WFOC such that the WFOC's financial statements and notes are or can be misleading – that is, the PWFOC/WFOC does not recognize transactions or make all the accounting adjustments and disclosures that the Chinese VIE company does (changes in accruals; etc.). The US SEC does not compel the WFOCs to disclose instances of corruption by, and investigations of the Chinese VIE company. The PWFOC and the WFOC typically don't disclose (and are not required to disclose) the debt and loan-covenants and the general accounting irregularities of the associated Chinese VIE company. Under US GAAP[8] and IASB accounting standards, the WFOC (or the PWFOC) is required to consolidate the Chinese VIE in its accounts where the WFOC is the VIE's primary beneficiary or has implicit or explicit voting control but in most instances, that doesn't happen – see: FASB (2017); Gillis and Lowry (2014); Wang (2012) and PriceWaterhouse (2015).

Generally, reverse-mergers in the US are legal and common. Chinese Reverse-merger companies that are listed in US markets (CRMs) are formed by the acquisition of a US listed shell-company (USC) by a China-based company (CBC). The problems inherent in the Chinese reverse-mergers are as follows:

1) The CBC can transfer its assets to the USC at inflated values.
2) In the merger, the allocation of Intangibles/Goodwill may not be accurate.

3) In some cases, the recorded sales revenues of the CBC are inflated immediately before and after the reverse-merger.

4) In some cases, the CBC's liabilities are often not stated in full immediately before and after the reverse-merger.

5) The Chinese government's investigations of, and third-party lawsuits against the CBC are often not disclosed in full in the CRM's books.

6) Some CRMs report different accounting data to Chinese securities regulatory agencies and to the US SEC.

7) Some CRMs don't expense the full costs of arranging the reverse-merger, as required by US GAAP and IFRS.

8) In many cases, the CBCs enter into reverse-merger transactions with the intent of perpetrating fraud, earning management and asset-quality management.

9) The Chinese reverse-mergers are often executed to avoid both the US SEC's scrutiny of IPOs and the listing requirements of Chinese stock exchanges and securities regulatory agencies.

10) During 2005–2017, the US Public Company Accounting Oversight Board (PCAOB) and the US SEC were prevented by Chinese government regulators from getting access to Chinese reverse-merger companies' audit workpapers. Thus, it is reasonably inferable that the Chinese government was complicit in, and supported the earnings management and asset-quality management perpetrated by the Chinese reverse-merger companies. If Chinese CRMs truly have nothing to hide, then why won't the Chinese government permit access to their external auditors' work papers?

11) Many of the Chinese auditing firms that bear the name of the big-four audit firms are actually strategic alliances or joint ventures between a big-four audit firm and a local audit firm. Thus the quality controls usually associated with a big-four audit firm are not in place in local offices of big-four audit firms in China (which audit the Chinese reverse-merger companies).

Zhu et al. (2015) and many other articles have confirmed that there has been significant accrual-based and real activity earnings management by Chinese reverse-merger companies.

8.5 Some SinoCos that perpetrated fraud, earnings management, asset-quality management and incentive-effects management

8.5.1 Alibaba[9]

As of 2015–2017, Alibaba was one of the largest companies in the world (by stock market value) and was once valued at US$168 billion, although it lost about US$140 billion of stock market value during 2015. During 2014–2015, some researchers and investment analysts raised questions about Alibaba's disclosure and accounting practices, and implied or alleged that Alibaba had been perpetrating earnings management, asset-quality management and incentive-effects management. During September 2015, Laing (2015)[10] (a *Forbes* article) alleged that Alibaba had been perpetrating earnings management and asset-quality management.

In response, Alibaba (Jim Wilson, SVP of International Corporate Affairs at Alibaba)[11] countered and denied most of the charges of misconduct. See Egan (2016),[12] Weiczner (2015),[13] Hempton (2015)[14] and McKenna (2015),[15] all of which expressed significant skepticism and doubts about Alibaba's financial statements and accounting disclosures. Guo and Hu (2012) reported that there was fraud in Alibaba's B2B business operations.

In 2014, Alibaba announced that there were potential accounting problems at its then recently acquired film division (Alibaba Pictures Group) which may have not have fully complied with accounting requirements and may have under-reported losses. In May 2016, Alibaba announced that it was being investigated by the US SEC[16] about: i) how Alibaba accounts for companies in which it owns stakes or has some say in the operations (affiliated companies), including a logistics venture; ii) how Alibaba treats related-party transactions; iii) how Alibaba accounts for *Singles Day*, a one-day shopping event in China that Alibaba says gave it the world record for most online sales volume in a day.

Apart from Alibaba's accounting irregularities, other researchers and regulators have complained about the illegality of Alibaba's "*Variable Interest Entity*" (VIE) structure[17] which is opaque and can facilitate fraud; and a similar VIE has been deemed to be illegal by Chinese courts. See: Johnson (2015) and Ziegler (2016). As noted earlier, Chinese VIEs are forms of fraud, earnings management and asset-quality management.

The combination of alleged fraud and earnings management by Alibaba and its VIE structure can increase systemic risks and Financial instability in US and or Chinese stock markets, given the size and influence of Alibaba's business operations, and its market value and its listing in both Chinese and US markets.

8.5.2 Chinese state-owned companies that were listed on NASDAQ and NYSE-Euronext failed to disclose defaulted sovereign debt

An October 2007 letter from Sovereign Advisors to the US SEC noted that Chinese State-Owned Companies Listed on NASDAQ and NYSE Euronext failed to disclose defaulted Sovereign Debt. The letter claimed that American persons purchased Chinese government bonds issue before 1949 which matured in 1960; but in 1987, China repaid British holders of the same bonds but has refused to repay US holders of the same bonds. The letter also noted that most Chinese companies that are listed in the US failed to disclose the risk of repudiation of debts by both the Chinese government and Chinese companies. See: www.globalse curitieswatch.org/Complaint_Filed_with_NYSE_and_NASDAQ.pdf. Sovereign Advisors noted that the US SEC didn't respond to that letter.

8.5.3 Other erring Chinese companies

Other erring Chinese companies that perpetrated fraud include Baidu[18]; Longtop Financial[19,20,21,22]; China Huishan Dairy Holdings Co.; Tianhe Chemicals Group Ltd.; China Forestry Holdings Co.; Sino-Forest Corporation[23,24]; China-Biotics[25]; China Expert Technology ("CXTI")[26] (see: http://seekingalpha.com/article/47467-china-expert-technology-return-to-priortrading-range-unlikely).

China Media Express Holdings Inc. ("CCME")[27,28,29] (see: www.zerohedge.com/article/presenting-global-hunters-humiliating-february-17-maintain-buy-report-ccme). According to Sovereign Advisers (Globalsecuritieswatch.org) (2013),[30] the SinoCos that have been alleged or confirmed to have perpetrated securities fraud and earnings management included but were not limited to the following (and most were technology companies): Advanced Battery Technologies Inc.; Advanced Refractive Technologies Inc.; AgFeed Industries Inc.; Bodisen Biotech Inc.; Chaoda Modern Agriculture; China Agritech Inc.; China-Biotics; China Century Dragon Media; China Changjiang Mining & New Energy Co.; China Education Alliance; China Electric Motor; China Finance; China Green Agriculture; China Integrated Energy Inc.; China Intelligent Lighting and Electronics Inc.; China Marine Food Group Ltd.; China MediaExpress Holdings Inc.; China Medical Express Holdings; China Natural Gas Inc./Xi'an Xilan Natural Gas Co.; China Ritar Power; China Sky One Medical Inc.; China Yingxia International; Deer Consumer Products; Digital Youth Network Corp.; Duoyuan Global Water Inc.; Duoyuan Printing; Focus Media Holding Ltd.; Gulf Resources, Inc.; Harbin Electric Inc.; Heli Electronics Corp.; HiEnergy Technologies Inc.; Jiangbo Pharmaceuticals; Keyuan Petrochemicals; Lihua International Inc.; L&L Energy Inc.; NIVS IntelliMedia Technology Group Inc.; Orient Paper Inc.; Puda Coal Inc.; RINO International Corp.; Shengda-Tech Inc.; Silvercorp Metals Inc.; Sino Clean Energy, Inc.; Sinotech Energy Ltd.; SkyPeople Fruit Juice, Inc.; Skystar Bio-Pharmaceutical Co.; Spreadtrum Communications, Inc.; Subaye, Inc.; Universal Travel Group; Wonder Auto Technology Inc.; Yongue International; and Yuhe International.

The following link shows lists of other (more than 110) erring Chinese companies that were cross-listed outside China and the US: http://chinastockfraud.blogspot.com.ng/2013/11/china-stock-fraud.html.

8.6 Some of the negative effects of the SinoCos' misconduct on US, Chinese and other investors[31]

According to Sovereign Advisers (www.Globalsecuritieswatch.org) (2013), the securities fraud and earnings management by Alibaba and the SinoCos harmed many major US institutional investors including but not limited to the following: Wellington Management (which reportedly held an 8 percent stake in China Biotics, 5 percent stake in Jiangbo Pharmaceuticals, 3.7 percent stake in Yuhe International, 2.2 percent stake in Puda Coal, and an 800,000 share position in China Electric Motor); C.V. Starr (which held a 15 percent stake in CCME);

Paulson & Co. (which realized over a half-billion dollar loss on its thirty-five million share, 14 percent equity position in SinoForest); Carlyle (which held in excess of a 20 percent stake in China Agritech); Glickenhaus & Co. (1.6 percent stake in China Agritech); Maverick Capital (10 percent stake in Longtop Financial Technologies); Tiger Global Management (4.6 percent stake in Longtop Financial Technologies and equity positions in both Duoyuan Global Water and Duoyuan Printing); Citadel Advisors (Focus Media); Prudential (Focus Media); UBS Global Asset Management and UBS Strategy Fund (Focus Media); Fidelity Management (Focus Media); Fred Alger Management (Focus Media); Baillie Gifford & Co. (Focus Media); BNY Mellon Asset Management (Spreadtrum Communications); Fidelity Investments (Longtop Financial Technologies and Spreadtrum Communications); HSBC Global Asset Management (U.K.) Limited (Spreadtrum Communications); Morgan Stanley (Spreadtrum Communications); CIBC Asset Management (Spreadtrum Communications); Charles Schwab Investment Management (Spectrum Communications); Baring Asset Management (Asia) Limited (Spectrum Communications); the State of Wisconsin Investment Board (Spreadtrum Communications);Citadel Investment Group (Spreadtrum Communications); SAC Capital Advisors (Spreadtrum Communications); and Amaranth Advisors LLC (China Natural Gas). At the end of Q3–2014,Viking Global Investors had a $1 billion stake in Alibaba (with 11.4 million shares); Soros Fund Management owned more than four million shares and Paulson & Co. nearly two million shares of Alibaba; and other hedge funds that owned Alibaba's equity included Omega Advisors, Jana Partners, Moore Capital Management, Third Point, Appaloosa Management, and Tiger Management.

Chinese investors also suffered substantial economic losses and psychological trauma because they invested in these SinoCos and other erring Chinese companies.[32]

It is conjectured here that the misconduct of the SinoCos: i) introduced significant elements of uncertainty, Financial Instability and Systemic Risk in the market for stocks and bonds of US and Chinese technology companies and Chinese companies in general; ii) caused *Deadweight Losses* in trading of the shares of US companies; iii) encouraged greater insider trading, and shorting by executives/ managers. To the extent that there is "demand" and "supply" for the prosecution of securities fraud, the ineffective regulatory framework in the US and China could have caused Deadweight Losses in the supply and demand of enforcement of statutes, and *Deadweight Losses* in the pricing, demand and supply of prosecutorial/enforcement litigation (which may be caused or amplified by Political Influence and Lobbying). Hines (1999) and Lind and Granqvist (2010) discussed Deadweight Losses.

8.7 Some macroeconomic/macrofinancial and complex adaptive systems issues

The SinoCo's misconduct increased or could have substantially increased systemic risk and financial instability in various markets. Kim, Li and Zhang (2011a;b) and

Kim and Zhang (2013, 2014) analyzed stock price crash-risk that arises from various sources.

8.7.1 Systemic risk

The negative Systemic Risk effects of the SinoCos' misconduct include but are not limited to the following: i) the SinoCo's misconduct increased or could have increased the interconnectedness of US and Chinese stock markets in ways that exacerbate systemic risk; and the decline of the stock price of a SinoCo usually had negative effects on stock prices of un-related companies – see Darrough, Huang and Zhao (2013); ii) risks inherent in the use of shares of exchange-traded Chinese companies for foreign and domestic M&A transactions; iii) the percentage of equity of cross-listed companies owned by US institutional investors; iv) the leverage of cross-listed companies; v) the effects of short-positions in shares of cross-listed companies, and the increased risk of crashes of segments of the stock market; vi) corporate governance contagion (wherein firms copy fraud and disclosure patterns from other firms; and firms increasingly share board members), and vii) increased similarities in, and correlations between trading patterns of stocks in US and Chinese equity markets; viii) the perceived risk of actual rejection of VIEs by the Chinese government or Chinese courts or the repudiation of VIE contracts by Chinese companies and the Peoples Republic of China (PRC) government's continuing failure or refusal to resolve the VIE question substantially increases volatility and systemic risk; ix) the actual rejection of VIEs by the Chinese government or Chinese courts or the repudiation of VIE contracts by Chinese companies can set off panic selling in US and Chinese stock markets which in turn can cause sell-offs in stock markets in other countries.

8.7.2 IPO decisions

The SinoCos' misconduct contradicts or doesn't entirely concur with theories of IPO-decisions in Bancel and Mittoo (2001); Chemmanur and He (2011); Cumming and Johan (2013) and Humphery-Jenner and Suchard (2013).

8.7.3 Financial stability

The misconduct by the SinoCos contradicts or doesn't entirely concur with theories of systemic risk and financial Instability in Haldane and May (2011); Liu and Tse (2012); Ma, Zhuang and Li (2011); Battiston and Glattfelder (2009); Li et al. (2014); Kuzubas, Ömercikoglu and Saltoglu (2014) and Elliott, Golub and Jackson (2014). See: Nwogugu (2014b) and Nwogugu (2015b).

Karpoff, Lee and Martin (2008a;b); Kim, Li and Zhang (2011a;b) and Kim and Zhang (2013, 2014) analyzed financial stability issues that arise from financial reporting opacity, earnings management (which affects incentives), tax avoidance and or asset-quality management (which affects incentives).

The negative Financial Instability effects of the SinoCos' misconduct include but are not limited to the following: i) over-valuation of shares (in the US and Chinese stock markets); and the fact that the decline of the stock price of a SinoCo usually had negative effects on stock prices of un-related companies – see Darrough, Huang and Zhao (2013); ii) the actual and perceived risk inherent in the use of shares of exchange-traded SinoCos and Chinese companies for foreign and domestic M&A transactions; iii) corporate governance contagion (wherein firms copy fraud and disclosure patterns from other firms; and firms increasingly share board members); iv) increased similarities in, and correlations between trading patterns of stocks in US and Chinese equity markets; v) the use of shares of such cross-listed companies as collateral; viii) the significantly increased risk of collapse of the stock prices of SinoCos and listed Chinese companies; ix) the rejection of VIEs by the Chinese government or Chinese courts or the repudiation of VIE contracts by Chinese companies can set off panic selling in US and Chinese stock markets which in turn, can cause sell-offs in stock markets in other countries.

More specifically, Alibaba and the SinoCos are substantial financial stability risks due to their operations, financing and accounting disclosures; and because of the following reasons. See: Nwogugu (2015a;b). Any sudden drop or collapse of the stock prices of Alibaba and or the larger SinoCos could or would have had a significant and negative effect on not only the stock prices of internet/technology companies around the world, but also the stock prices of S&P-500 companies, logistics companies, retailers, electronics parts suppliers and manufacturing companies and their credit ratings. Any announced or perceived financial distress of Alibaba and or a large SinoCo would have likely had a negative effect on the many companies that it hosts and also the credit ratings of many internet/technology companies around the world, and on the stock prices of S&P-500 companies, logistics companies, electronics parts suppliers and manufacturing companies regardless of whether or not they supply products/parts to Alibaba's corporate clients. In Alibaba's business model, Alibaba essentially finances or props most of its corporate customers by reducing their customer acquisition costs and providing them with much needed visibility and logistics. Alibaba's annual revenues, profits and assets are among the largest in the world. Products sold through Alibaba affect more than one billion people around the world. Alibaba's ecosystem involves many companies and more than one million products.

Alibaba and some SinoCos are important participants in global credit chains wherein they provide and also obtain trade credit (where in each case, such borrowing is partly based on their reputation and perceived solvency). Such credit chains have become a major source of capital for many companies and financial institutions, but they increase the probability of domino-effects in both the real and financial sectors. See comments in Boissay (2006). Alibaba also has substantial debt; and any perceived insolvency and or business contraction of Alibaba can trigger an industry-wide credit crunch and or hyperinflation for some products/ services in some countries. Contrary to the literature and as shown during the global financial crisis in 2008–2010, multinationals are not entirely immune from financial crises. Alibaba's and the SinoCos' earnings management and reluctance to comply with accounting regulations is in line with the "*Bad News Hoarding and Stock-price Crashes*" theory in the literature – see Jin and Myers (2006) which has spawned a new line of empirical research focused on identifying corporate activities and/or firm characteristics that cause or facilitate bad news hoarding and thus, predicts stock price crashes. Using a large sample of US headquartered firms during 1987–2011, Boehme and May (May 2016) found that multinational firms have greater stock price crash-risk than domestic firms; and that the difference in crash-risk between multinational and domestic firms is most acute among firms with weaker corporate governance mechanisms (i.e. weaker shareholder rights, less independent boards, and less stable institutional ownership).

Given the rapid increases in the types and volumes of strategic alliances and joint ventures (JVs) around the world during the last twenty years, like swaps/ derivatives, alliances/JVs create financial networks that increase interconnectedness and the risk of *domino-effects* in both the real and financial sectors – and that is often omitted in both financial stability analysis and asset pricing models.

A significant percentage (more than 30 percent) of the stock prices of Alibaba and some SinoCos was Goodwill. First, that is an example of the inefficiency of current IFRS/IASB Goodwill/Intangibles accounting regulations – the accounting disclosure does not capture the true risk of those companies' assets. See the comments about goodwill/intangibles accounting and Financial Stability in Nwogugu (2015a;d) and Nwogugu (2007c). Second, it also poses a significant financial stability risk because: i) the accounting disclosure of goodwill does not capture the true risk of those companies' assets; ii) the lack of accounting classification of Intangibles (such as human capital; technology; marketing rights; contracts; etc.) actually increases the probability that their stock-prices will decline and there will be differences of opinion about their Goodwill/intangibles in general, and the possibility of existence of such identifiable intangible assets – all of which increases market volatility and volatility-spillovers.

The significant differences (distinct from Goodwill) between the book and market values of tangible assets (such as real estate) can significantly increase: i) the risk of collapse of asset markets (such as real estate and the secondary markets for equipment parts); ii) disagreements among investors about equity values and hence, stock market volatility. These issues are not addressed properly by the current accounting model.

Employee Stock Options (ESOs) and other equity-based incentives (EBIs) can significantly increase disagreements among investors about the values of firms' human capital and equity; and the current accounting model (IASB/IFRS) increases such uncertainty and equity and bond volatility. ESOs are intangibles (as ruled by at least one US Federal Court of Appeals; and as stated in the business/ economics literature) but are not governed by the goodwill/intangibles accounting regulations (IASB/IFRS). It is well established in the finance/economic literature that EBIs can affect employee morale and increase the propensity for managerial risk-taking, which in turn, can increase financial stability risks. See: Nwogugu (2004b, 2006b) and Kim, Li and Zhang (2011b).

Nwogugu (2017) noted that the aggregation of all the errors and biases caused by the use of the NPV-IRR model and related approaches by companies and government agencies constitute a macroeconomic variable and are a financial stability risk.

See the comments in Nwogugu (2004b), Nwogugu (2005a); Nwogugu (2007b); Nwogugu (2003) (Encompass Services); Fukao (1999); Francis, Hasan, and Li (2014); and Nwogugu (2004a) (Jack-In-The-Box). The Nwogugu (2006a) critique of bankruptcy prediction models and the Nwogugu (2007c) critique of corporate finance theories also applies to Machine Learning and the modeling of financial stability, Asset Pricing and Corporate Financial Distress.

The foregoing raises the following issues in the analysis of Financial Stability:

i)   The inclusion of *corporate governance contagion* (including earnings management contagion); patterns of equity-based incentives; structural changes; credit chains; earnings management and specialized business structures (waves of strategic alliances; joint ventures) in financial stability models.

ii) Many studies in the finance, management and economics literature have confirmed that corporate governance and corporate strategy factors affect stock prices, corporate bond prices, lenders' perceptions, suppliers' perceptions (credit chains) and corporate reputation. McCahery, Sautner and Stark (2016) confirmed that when interacting with executives of investee companies (e.g. "Voice" or "Exit" options) institutional investors' preferences and criteria are mainly about corporate governance and corporate strategy.

iii) The negative effects of robo-trading (automated securities trading) and robo-advisers (automated financial advice) on asset prices and monetary policy transmission.

iv) The effect of a company's number of shares-outstanding on a company's (and its competitors') stock prices. See Nwogugu (2015f).

v)   The negative impact of corporate earnings management, structural changes in industries, disclosure of equity-based incentives, and inefficient goodwill/intangibles accounting regulations on the values of corporate bonds, municipal bonds and treasury/government bonds (i.e. tax avoidance by companies) owned by the US Fed and other central banks is a major issue. The US Fed raised its benchmark interest rate in June 2017 (and additional rate increases were generally anticipated) even though inflation lagged the US Fed's target and unemployment among some demographics was high. As of mid-2017, the US Fed's assets were worth about 23 percent of US nominal GDP, which is similar to the 1930s after the Great Depression. The US Federal Reserve's (US Fed) balance sheet assets grew from about $0.7 Trillion in 2003 to about $4.5 trillion in mid-2017 primarily because beginning from 2009, the US Fed implemented *quantitative easing* (purchases of bonds, loans and securities) in order to lower interest rates. Other countries also implemented *quantitative easing* during that period. The last US recession began about 2008 but since 1945, the average economic cycle in the US has lasted for about seventy months (measured from trough-to-trough or peak-to-peak).

Thus another recession may occur soon in the US, and when it happens, the US Fed's policy options will likely be severely restricted.

vi) The negative impact of corporate earnings management, structural changes in industries and inefficient goodwill/intangibles accounting regulations on banks' and insurers' willingness/propensity to provide loans and credit enhancement – which may lead to credit crunches.

vii) Whether firms' social capital and or technology products/initiatives enable them to avoid restrictions of financial regulations (such as the US FSOC's non-SIFI criteria).

As mentioned herein, the relationship between structural changes and Financial Instability is symbiotic.

8.7.4 Structural changes

The industries in which Alibaba and some of the SinoCos (e.g. technology; internet; environmental services; etc.) competed experienced significant structural changes during 2010–2016 and in ways that are not easily detectable by traditional econometric models. In some instances, Alibaba's or the SinoCos' strategic moves were or precipitated a structural change (e.g. mass cross-listings in foreign stock exchanges and corporate governance contagion in technology companies; earnings management by groups of SinoCos that were technology companies; the collective litigation strategies of the SinoCos; technological progress through new products; etc.). One interesting observation is that structural changes can have significant effects on Financial Stability, and vice versa (actual or potential Financial Instability can cause industry relationships, norms, competition and regulations to change significantly). Also the rapidly increasing use of employee stock options (ESOs) (and equity-based incentives) by companies around the world is a significant structural change that has major implications for managerial risk taking and Financial Stability. See Nwogugu (2004b), Nwogugu (2005a; 2006b); Scazzieri (2009) and Schilirò (2012).

Structural changes can have significant effects on Financial Stability, and vice versa (actual or potential Financial Instability can cause industry relationships, technology, organizational structures, norms, competition and regulations to change significantly). Furthermore, the structural changes in the global retailing and the global financial services industry affected this industry, and vice versa.

The relationship between operations strategy and structural change is conjectured to be symbiotic, evolving and increasingly inter-dependent given globalization and the internet, but has not been sufficiently addressed in the finance, economics or operations management literature. Nwogugu (revised 2018) introduced the *Operations Strategy Model of Structural Change* wherein structural change is caused primarily by changes in the operations strategies of a large dominant firm, or a group of firms. Nwogugu (revised 2018) also introduced other models of structural change. The *Operations Strategy Model of Structural Change* differs from the Lewis Model of structural change (introduced by US economist Arthur Lewis) which may have been confirmed in several Asian economies (e.g. India; China, Malaysia; etc.) during 1970–2005.

The rapidly increasing use of employee stock options (ESOs) and other equity-based incentives among both US and non-US companies is a significant structural change that has major implications for labor dynamics (e.g. employee motivation; prospects of unionization; etc.), intrapreneurship/entrepreneurship, technological progress, managers' risk taking and Financial Stability. The use of equity-based incentives is an element of corporate strategy. See the comments in Nwogugu (2004b, 2006b); and Colpan et al. (2007).

See the comments and critiques in Nwogugu (2004b, 2005a, 2007b, 2007a, 2007c); Nwogugu (2003) (Encompass Services); Colpan et al. (2007); and Nwogugu (2004a) (Jack-In-The-Box).

The literature on the relationship between complexity and structural change is developed and includes Robert and Yoguel (2016); Cimoli, Pereima and Porcile (2016); Dosi and Virgillito (2017); Comim (2000); Heinrich and Dai (2016); Ciaschini, Pretaroli and Socci (2011) and Brida, Anyul and Punzo (2003); Scazzieri (2009); Vu (2017); Ruttiman (2014); Gabardo, Pereima and Einloft (2017) and Swiecki (2017) addressed various elements of structural change but those articles often omit relevant variables that are mentioned herein. There seems to be a Research-Practice gap in modeling of structural change; which often doesn't include relevant variables, and the number/type of variables used seem to be constrained by the perceived availability of data. The foregoing raises the following issues:

i) The inclusion of corporate governance factors; operations strategy; specialized business structures (waves of strategic alliances; joint ventures; licensing; etc.); acquisitions/mergers of large companies; changes in regulation and or economic policy; organizational changes and political economy conditions in models of structural change.

ii) Whether and when one company can trigger structural changes in an industry by its strategy and or supply chain.

iii) Rapid and significant declines in stock prices of groups of companies in an industry represent a structural change. Stock prices are closely watched by employees, credit rating agencies, customers and suppliers and also affect the company's corporate reputation and credibility. Thus, such declines are likely to negatively affect employee morale; interest rates for new debt; terms of trade credit and demand from customers.

iv) The effects of the evolution of networks created by strategic alliances (including licensing agreements, R&D agreements and distribution agreements) and joint ventures.

v) The effects of actual acquisitions/mergers, the looming threat of mergers/acquisitions by large MNEs; and the effects of inefficient post-merger integration by MNEs on industry structure.

vi) In the literature, structural change is most often characterized by changes in sectoral employment and output shares but that is wrong or insufficient because it doesn't reflect the full dynamics.

vii) The evolution of credit chains in industries.

viii) The effects of bankruptcies of large dominant companies; and credit ratings and ratings transitions on industry structure; and vice versa.

ix) In structural change models, homogenous labor should not be the only primary factor of production.

The changes in the economies of some Asian countries (e.g. India, Malaysia; etc.) and the Chinese economy during 1980–2018 indicate that the *Lewis Model of Structural Change* (introduced by US economist Arthur Lewis) may have been correct and that those countries may have used the Lewis Model.

The relationship between firms' operational strategy and business processes on one hand, and globalization has often been neglected in theoretical and empirical studies of globalization, structural changes and operations management. Clearly, the operational strategies and business processes of some multinationals (MNEs) are sometimes structural changes and have or can have global effects in terms of competition, efficiency, profits, human capital; technological progress; outsourcing; regulation; etc.

Alibaba, Baidu and the SinoCos have been both beneficiaries and victims of globalization. A non-trivial portion of their problems can be attributed to both financial, labor and economic globalization which have not delivered many touted benefits.

•   With the growth of MNEs and the advent of global "robo-traders" (automated securities trading systems) and internet-based financial news, it appears that the effectiveness of monetary policies has declined and or is declining.

See comments in De Nicolò and Juvenal (2014); Ruttiman (2014), and Jovane, Seliger and Stock (2017).

8.7.5 Recursive time-varying regulatory failures, regulatory-capture and regulatory-fragmentation that can have significant negative macroeconomic, psychological and political effects

Alibaba's and the SinoCos' problems are evidence of the following failures and failed regulations:

1) The *Sarbanes–Oxley Act* of 2002 (USA) and *China SOX* (The *Basic Standard for Enterprise Internal Control*; caikuai [2008] No. 7, "Basic Standard"). These regulations should include more comprehensive BOD governance standards; more stringent accounting requirements, minimum corporate governance standards and greater civil penalties and monetary

fines for non-compliance with BOD governance standards, accounting and or internal control rules.

2) The *Dodd–Frank Act* of 2010 (USA) and the US FSOC's "*Non-bank SIFI Criteria*" – an efficient regulation would have required the early identification of a broader group of troubled and or non-compliant companies (companies that don't comply with accounting and corporate governance standards but whose operations affect more than two million people/customers).

3) *Goodwill/Intangibles accounting regulations (IFRS/IASB)* – these should require mandatory write-downs of impaired intangibles; mandatory and post-acquisition classification of goodwill and other intangibles as identifiable intangibles; that goodwill should not exceed a specific percentage of a company's intangible assets; and government evaluation of companies whose intangible assets exceed a specific amount or a specific percentage of their total assets.

4) *The regulations of the US SEC and the Chinese securities regulatory agency* – which should require more stringent monitoring of compliance with accounting regulations. The combined rule-making, enforcement and adjudicative functions of each of these two agencies constitute violations of the *Separation-of-Powers* principle.

5) The regulation of credit rating agencies (CRAs) – effective CRA regulations should require mandatory ratings of all exchange-traded companies and some private companies (whose sales revenues exceed a specific amount) by at least four licensed credit rating agencies; and should provide adequate independence of CRAs in order to ensure objectivity and impartiality in credit rating.

6) *Auditor Liability-Allocation* mechanisms/rules in China and the US – which should be codified and allocate more liability to external auditors, the boards of directors and executives of auditee-companies.

7) *US and Chinese Bankruptcy laws* – which don't require preemptive intervention for most types of private and exchange-traded companies and medium and large companies whose operations affect many people and other companies.

8) *US and Chinese securities laws* – which should require more stringent monitoring of compliance with accounting regulations.

9) *Regulatory Capture* – wherein: i) corporate lobbying is successful to the detriment of Social Welfare; ii) companies and their legal and or accounting advisors figure out ways to circumvent, denigrate, dampen or take advantage of regulations/statutes and or to influence regulators (in most cases to the detriment of social welfare).

10) *Regulatory Fragmentation* – wherein: i) laws/regulations that are intended to achieve the same or similar objectives are codified in different statutes that in some cases, may or often conflict; and or ii) enforcement efforts in both the public and private sectors are diffused; and or iii) government regulatory agencies have overlapping functions and or jurisdictions.

11) *Adverse Regulatory Entrenchment Theory* – there can be adverse effects of *Regulatory Entrenchment* wherein the combination of a government agency's (e.g. US SEC's) rule-making, investigatory and enforcement powers (which is a delegation of the constitutionally mandated responsibilities of the US Congress) is a dominant factor in the stock-market; often conflicts with the activities of similar government agencies (e.g. State securities regulatory agencies, and the US Attorneys' offices); can distort the market; provides opportunities for inefficient exercise of such powers, and is not appropriately reviewed by the US Congress. All of these can increase Systemic Risk and Financial Instability.

12) *Enforcement Leakages* (*that may be caused or amplified by Political Influence and Lobbying*) – such leakages occur when: 1) statutes don't require that regulators take preemptive or investigative action to forestall misconduct and or reduction of Social welfare; and or when existing statutes don't reduce or increase enforcement costs; 2) the enforcement statutes and or regulations distort the relationships among the firm and its external advisors and auditors.

Nwogugu (2015a), Nwogugu (2015b), Nwogugu (2015c); Nwogugu (2015d); Nwogugu (2010/2013); Papaikonomou (2010) and Nwogugu (2008) discussed these statutes and regulations. Young (Feb. 21, 2013) noted that the annual cost of regulations imposed by various US federal government agencies could be classified into various groups.[33] Note that a portion of the above-mentioned regulatory costs can be attributed to *Regulatory Takings*. Nwogugu (2012) analyzed *Takings* theory and introduced new types of *Takings*. The factors that often discourage or preclude firms from filing lawsuits to challenge such *Takings* include but are not limited to the following: i) fear of retaliation by regulators, and imposition of additional costly regulations; ii) lack of an organized industry-wide effort to curb Regulatory Takings; iii) perceived costs of litigation including the opportunity costs – on customers; stock prices; suppliers, employees; etc.; iv) the perceived influence of the Executive Branch of the US government on the judiciary (some federal judges were selected from, or had worked in the Executive Branch of the US federal government. Compliance is or can be tempered by aspirations and career concerns.

8.8 Public health implications: some new theories of human and organizational behavior, strategy and financial stability

That the SinoCos were able to deceive so many professional investors, fund-managers and regulators in the US, Europe, Japan and China for such long periods of time is a psychological and Systemic Risk phenomenon that is henceforth referred to as the *Mass Truncated Evolving Cognition Theory* wherein: i) the cognitive capabilities of large groups of un-related people often in different locations (separated by time, opportunity-sets, wealth and distance) are impaired or changed due to dependence on actual or perceived government capabilities, or use of fintech, or interventions and institutions such as external audits and securities enforcement agencies (this trend/behavior was also evident in the reactions of Chinese investors to announcements by the Chinese government after the Summer 2015 crash of the Chinese stock market); ii) the individual and group cognitions among these populations (connected by a group of third-party actions) about a specific set of third-party actions evolve at different rates over successive equal units of time; iii) the changes in cognition are or can be linked to emotions and are highly sensitive to public announcements and government policies; iv) individual and group truncation can be drastically affected (truncated) by "shocks" such as the public announcement of government policies.

The earnings management and fraud by these SinoCos seemed to be integral parts of the SinoCo's corporate strategies (as confirmed by their behaviors, public communications and responses to government investigations). Also the SinoCo's litigation strategies were similar and bizzare – after any investigation or lawsuit was launched, many SinoCos would typically deny any wrongdoing, incur litigation costs and then suddenly stop litigating or settle or disappear from the US. These behaviors constituted a psychological and Systemic Risk phenomena which is henceforth referred to as the *Governance-Strategy Gap Theory*. That is, managers' individual and group *Governance-Strategy Gap* can be consciously or un-consciously selective; and is often consciously selective and is wider in entrepreneurial firms and on some corporate governance matters. Within the context of systemic risk, the *Governance-Strategy Gap* refers to the magnitude of divergence between a person's or group's compliance with corporate governance standards and it/his/her development and implementation of legal strategies that facilitate or improve business operations, profits and corporate governance. The *Governance-Strategy Gap Theory* was evident in some Hong Kong companies during the crashes of the Chinese stock markets in Summer 2015.

The apparently voluntary and coordinated non-compliance (with accounting rules) by so many SinoCos during the same period of time (2009–2015) and in the same pattern of behavior seems to be part of an emerging trend (that began in 1998–2002) of informal un-documented *"Non-compliance Strategic Alliances"* (non-compliance cartels) among companies in emerging markets countries where the weaknesses of institutions, activities of "Oligarchs", political influence and government intervention affected stock markets and increased Systemic Risk. During 1998–2012, there were instances of such un-documented *non-compliance Strategic Alliances* among companies in Russia and the emigration of Russian business owners to London and other parts of Europe. It is conjectured that in such "alliances", companies and their executives voluntarily agree not to comply with government regulations for various reasons or for no reason. One of their motivations or expectations may be that the resultant enforcement burden on the government would reduce overall enforcement and perhaps lead to the enactment of more lenient states/regulations. Nwogugu (2014a) discussed such un-documented non-compliance Strategic Alliances among financial services companies in Nigeria.

The earnings management and fraud by these SinoCos are evidence of Complex *"higher-order behaviors"* by: 1) BODs and executives, which degrade existing Corporate Governance statutes and measures; and 2) government agencies which degrade international market regulation standards, impose Takings on private persons without adequate compensation and distort expectations that are based on usage-of-trade. Bernard (1926b) distinguished between "Primary" and "Derivative" Attitudes and Ideals. Bernard (1936) analyzed conflicts between "Primary Group Attitudes" and "Derivative Group Ideals". "Hullian Theory" in psychology also distinguishes between "direct" and "derivative" human (individual and group) behaviors. Deck and Schlesinger (2014); Noussair, Trautmann and Kuilen (2013) and other articles have analyzed a few higher-order risk preferences.

The *Selective Compliance Strategies Theory* – Among managers of some exchange-traded companies, there is generally low concern for compliance with, and for Social Welfare issues that arise from regulations that don't require frequent reporting/filing; and the effect of quarterly financial reporting remains a dominant factor in both the operations, strategies and financial reporting of some exchange traded companies. This risk attitude can increase Systemic Risk and Financial Instability.

Sub-Optimal Litigation Strategies can increase Systemic Risk, and can adversely affect company's stock prices, employees, customers and suppliers. Instead of admitting guilt, some of the erring SinoCos chose to engage in litigation in the US or China which caused adverse information effects on the shares of tech companies. Corporate Litigation Strategies are an important aspect of overall Corporate Strategy. Corporate Litigation Strategies are or can be influenced by 1) human biases; 2) knowledge deficits; 3) internal communication deficits; 4) internal controls; 5) internal or external collusion (intentional or un-intentional); 6) criminal misconduct; 7) external pressures (such as meeting analysts' EPS estimates or shareholders' demand for greater dividends); 8) difficulties in either assessing the markets' technology needs and or in incorporating strategy into innovation processes and development of technology; 9) economic and psychological costs of innovation, strategy development and implementation; 10) impact of innovation and strategy development on managers' compensation and career progress; 11) managers' perception of apprehension; 12) availability of insurance; 13) managers' perceived impact of guilty pleas or settlements or court awards on their career prospects; 14) the company's financial condition and access to capital; 15) perceived impact of litigation on customers and suppliers.

The earnings management and fraud by these SinoCos are evidence of *Sub-optimally Exercised Time-Varying Asymmetric Power Theory* – among shareholders, BODs and executive management teams; external auditors and investment banks. Such Asymmetric Power is not necessarily bad (and can increase Social Welfare), but when it is exercised in sub-optimal ways or for meaningless purposes, it can reduce Social Welfare. It is obvious that were instances of asymmetric power between each SinoCo on one hand, and its external auditors and investment banks.

8.9 Neoclassical and behavioral asset pricing anomalies, and some asset-pricing implications of corporate policies

Alibaba's and the SincoCos' misconduct contradicted various theories in the literature (about IPO Decisions; selection of Auditors; corporate fraud, and *Third-Generation Prospect Theory*).

Wang (2014) concluded that Chinese companies that executed Reverse-mergers in US markets significantly preferred non-Big Four audit firms; and among the 228 firms in the Wang (2014) sample, 180 of them were connected through linked directors; and 48 firms were "isolated" of which, 41.67 percent were delisted by May 2013, and 35.42 percent were involuntarily delisted. The Wang (2014) finding that shared-directors among such Chinese reverse-merger companies in the US were a major cause of fraud by such companies is not entirely correct because Wang (2014) cannot prove active coercion by "common directors" – offending SinoCos may have learnt about patterns of misconduct just by reading the news or by talking with their external auditors. Offending SinoCos may have simply decided to perpetrate fraud as a core business strategy and or in response to socio-economic conditions in China and perceived less-stringent regulations (about IPO pricing and listing requirements) in the US.

The misconducts by the SinoCos contradict or don't entirely concur with theories of IPO-decisions in Bancel and Mittoo (2001); Chemmanur and He (2011); Cumming and Johan (2013) and Humphery-Jenner and Suchard (2013) or with theories of systemic risk and financial Instability in Haldane and May (2011); Liu and Tse (2012); Ma, Zhuang and Li (2011); Battiston and Glattfelder (2009); Li et al. (2014); Kuzubas, Ömercikoglu and Saltoglu (2014); and Elliott, Golub and Jackson (2014).

The SinoCos' misconduct and the findings and theories in this chapter also contradict the theories in the following series of articles on corporate fraud in IPOs (and impliedly, Financial Instability and Systemic Risk). Wang, Winton and Yu (2010) concluded that Fraud propensity increases with the level of investor beliefs about industry prospects but decreases when beliefs are extremely high; and that fraud is affected by monitoring by investors and short-term executive compensation, both of which vary with investor beliefs about industry prospects; and that monitoring incentives of investors and underwriters differ. On the contrary and as shown by the SinoCos, corporate fraud occurred despite professional investor monitoring; and despite investors' beliefs about the tech industry prospects; and the monitoring incentives of investors and underwriters are aligned whereas in this case underwriter reputation and or investor reputation are at risk. Dyck, Morse and Zingales (2010) concluded that fraud detection does not rely on standard corporate governance actors (investors, SEC, and auditors), but rather takes several traditional and non-traditional players (employees, media, and industry regulators), and that such patterns could be attributed to differences in access to information, as well as monetary and reputational incentives, while reputational incentives in general are weak. On the contrary and as indicated by the case of the SinoCos, fraud was detected primarily by standard corporate governance actors (investors, SEC, and auditors), and the reputational incentives of the hedge funds that invested in the SinoCos were a major factor. Fang, Huang and Karpoff (2015) concluded that short selling (or the prospect of short selling), curbs earnings management, helps detect fraud, and improves price efficiency. On the contrary despite short selling of some SinoCos, other SinoCos continued their earnings management.

The SinoCos' misconduct and the findings and theories in this chapter also contradict the theories in the following series of articles on issuer-underwriter relationships in IPOs (and impliedly, Financial Instability and Systemic Risk). Corwin and Schultz (2005) analyzed the underwriting syndicates for 1,638 IPOs during 1997–2002 and found evidence of information production by syndicate members. This Information-Production Hypothesis is strongly contradicted by the post-IPO performance and earnings management of the SinoCos. Syndication that did not necessarily improve information production, and the relatively large syndicates for the IPOs of some SinoCos didn't uncover the pre-IPO earnings management by the SincoCos. Das, Guo and Zhang (2006) noted that analysts' choice of covering a company contains information about their true underlying expectation of future firm prospects; and that in the three years after initial analyst coverage, IPOs with high residual coverage had significantly better return and operating performance than those with low residual coverage. This hypothesis is or can be directly contradicted by the performance of the SinoCos after their IPO or cross-listings in the US.

Fama and French (1992, p. 427) stated that book leverage predicts returns with a negative sign, while market leverage predicts returns with a positive sign, all of which reflects the *book-to-market effect* – this argument is clearly wrong and historically, the differences between the book and market values of corporate liabilities have been relatively very small compared to equities and real estate. As confirmed by Zhang (2017), Fama and French (1992) stated that the difference between the one-period-ahead expected return and the internal rate of return is not important; but Fama and French (1992) derived the relationships among investment, book-to-market and profitability only with the internal rate of return. That is inherently inconsistent, and as stated in Nwogugu (2017), the IRR is wrong.

The quality of accounting disclosure by companies remains a major issue. The text in the form-10Ks and Form-10Qs (filed at the US SEC) of many companies don't change much from year to year in terms of content, style and issues discussed; and the financial statements presented. Cohen, Malloy and Nguyen (2016) found that changes to the language of financial reports affect firms' future returns: a portfolio that shorts "changers" and buys "non-changers" earns up to 188 basis points per month (over 22 percent per year) in abnormal returns in the future. They noted that such reporting changes are concentrated in the management discussion (MD&A) section; and that changes in language referring to the executive (CEO and CFO) team, or regarding litigation, are especially informative for future returns.

The articles that specifically address the impact of earnings management and inaccurate accounting disclosures on asset pricing include but are not limited to the following: Francis, Hasan and Li (2014); Sun (June 2011); Du (Aug. 2016); Marinovic (2013); and Teoh, Welch and Wong (1998). However, most of the articles don't fully address the following issues: i) investors' cognition (the extent to which investors recognize earnings management and or react to rumors of earnings management and then subsequently discount stock prices); ii) the effects of managers' incentives and compensation.

Chan, Kensinger, Keown and Martin (1997); Bodnaruk, Massa and Simonov (2013); and Nwogugu (2016;2019c) analyzed strategic alliances.

The foregoing and the SinoCo's misconduct (which were corporate policies) have obvious implications for asset pricing in terms of the following:

i) The risk premia of growing technology and fintech companies.

ii) Valuation of the equity of the SinoCos and the impact of reverse-mergers and VIEs.

iii) The development of factor models.

iv) The inclusion of corporate governance; manager' policies about goodwill/intangibles accounting; specialized business structures (reverse-mergers; VIEs; etc.); accounting disclosure risk; auditor-risk; and compliance-risk in asset pricing models.

v) The effects of structural changes in industries and collateral impact on related industries.

vi) The differences between the book and market values of tangible assets (such as real estate) can distort asset pricing models.

vii) The effects of Employee stock options (ESOs) and equity-based incentives which are intangibles and a major element of human capital, and affect managerial risk-taking.

viii) Managers' cognition and Framing Effects in corporate transactions (i.e. IPOs; dividend; acquisitions; asset dispositions; etc.).

ix) As explained in Nwogugu (2007a), many of the accounting-based variables used in asset pricing studies (such as ROE; ROA; EPS; etc.) are misleading and inaccurate.

x) The Nwogugu (2007a) critique of bankruptcy prediction models and the Nwogugu (2007c) critique of finance theories also applies to asset pricing. See the comments in Nwogugu (2004b), Nwogugu (2006b) (employee stock options); Nwogugu (2005a); Nwogugu (2003) (Encompass Services); and Nwogugu (2004a) (Jack-In-The-Box).

xi) Many studies in the finance, management and economics literature have confirmed that corporate governance factors affect stock prices, corporate bond prices and corporate reputation. McCahery, Sautner and Stark (2016) confirmed that when interacting with executives of investee companies (e.g. "Voice" or "Exit" options) institutional investors' preferences and criteria are mainly about corporate governance and corporate strategy.

xii)   In the modern asset-pricing literature (post-1995), the NPV-IRR model and discounting are major foundations in both theoretical and empirical studies. It is well established in the finance/economics and corporate strategy literature that the corporate decisions made by many (if not most) companies about their transactions were most probably wholly or partly based on the NPV-IRR model or related approaches. As explained in Nwogugu (2017), the NPV-IRR model and related approaches, and the *consumption-investment-savings-production* paradigm of asset pricing are all wrong.

xiii)   Political economy conditions affect companies and should be included in asset-pricing models.

xiv)   The effects of structural changes in industries and collateral impact on related industries should be reflected in asset-pricing models.

xv)   Nwogugu (2016) explained some of the effects of strategic alliances.

xvi)   Investors' cognition and whether investors can detect earnings management; and how investors react to rumors of earnings management.

xvii)   The effect of the number of shares outstanding on a company's (and its competitors') stock prices. See: Nwogugu (2019d).

xviii)   The impact of earnings management and asset-quality management on asset pricing.

xix)   The effects of robo-trading and robo-advisers on asset prices and monetary policies.

xx)   The effects of Dividend payments and share repurchases.

xxi)   Nwogugu (2012) addressed issues in asset pricing in real estate (i.e. estimation of housing-demand and house-price models).

See comments about goodwill/intangibles in Nwogugu (2015a, 2015d) and Nwogugu (2007c) which also explains some asset-pricing anomalies. Chandra and Thenmozhi (2017), Baker, Wurgler and Yuan (2012), and Cronqvist and Siegel (2014) analyzed behavioral asset pricing and investor sentiment. The findings of Boehme and May (May 2016) and Jin and Myers (2006) suggest the use of alternative measures of crashrisk and controlling for known determinants of crash-risk identified in prior studies – and in addition, these factors, multinational operations and the crash-risk factors mentioned in Kim, Li and Zhang (2011b) and Kim and Zhang (2013; 2014) should be included in asset-pricing models. Clearly, both the time-varying risk premia in their stock prices and investor sentiments affected the SinoCos' corporate policies – for example, the SinoCos cross-listed their shares in the US and Canada when they felt they had enough investor support/interest in China and the US; and their decisions to engage in earnings management and fraud can be partly attributed to their estimates of continuing investor interest in their companies. More importantly, during 2011–2016, the prices of shares of many SinoCos were anomalies because they didn't reflect the risks inherent in their operations, compliance with regulations, accounting disclosures and future prospects. Traditional asset-pricing models would not have captured such risks.

Part of the problem are the following conjectured behavioral anomalies: i) investors tend to include a premium in the stock prices of exchange-traded technology companies regardless of their operating performance, compliance-risk and accounting disclosure risk simply because of their listing, product/services breadth and industry; and ii) investors are more likely to have positive expectations and assign positive future prospects to exchange traded technology companies, than to exchange traded non-technology companies; iii) investors' excessive reliance on corporate financial statements (especially financial statements prepared by the big-four accounting firms) and on compliance by exchange-traded companies, and such reliance sometimes increases as the size and perceived influence of the company increases; iv) investors are more reluctant to assign discounts to stock prices of exchange-traded technology companies suspected of misconduct or earnings management, than to similarly situated non-technology companies; v) there is a reputation effect wherein in some markets, some types of institutional investors and or advisors serve as "credibility investors" and their continuous association with a company can provide valuation support for its securities; vi) the social capital generated by companies because of their multinational operations and being in the technology industry may increase their appeal to investors, and may reduce regulators' willingness to prosecute them for offenses; vii) investors are more likely to under-value goodwill/intangibles in smaller companies and for under-performing companies than for larger companies, technology companies and over-performing companies.

Woolford (2013) noted that corporate governance statutes (such as SOX in the US) require BODs to manage enterprise risk and BODs' behavior toward risk is linked to their degree of regulatory compliance with such statutes. Woolford (2013) also noted that South African BODs have difficulties in evaluating enterprise risk; and their BOD members are subject to a high degree of cognitive bias and source dependence when facing risk and uncertainty; and that Prospect Theory couldn't fully describe BODs' responses to Enterprise-Risk. Woolford (2013) identified the following: i) a "behavioral form of moral hazard" wherein BODs that implemented Enterprise-Risk measures develop a sense of overconfidence and believe that such measures will automatically and fully protect the company; ii) the "Common/Variable Characteristics of Risk' hypothesis" wherein Boards appear to possess a common set of behavioral characteristics which govern the way they manage their risk, and the extent of which is directly linked to the level of risk-readiness of the Board, iii) the "Reality Drift phenomenon" wherein BODs may gradually lose touch with key aspects of their businesses through a process of cognitive bias and false and inadequate information. Dey (2010) and Bargeron Lehn and Zutter (2010) studied the effects of Sarbanes-Oxley on corporate risk taking – some researchers have noted that compliance with SOX has often resulted in lower corporate investment.

On the contrary, Wen (2010) analyzed the effects of corporate capital investment by using the value-function of cumulative prospect theory (Kahneman and

Tversky, 1992) and data from 685 listed Taiwanese companies, between 2001 and 2006 (they used firm performance as a reference point, and used the change in annual capital investment as a proxy for the value function). Wen (2010) observed there were "biased" behaviors of risk aversion relating to capital investment when firms faced gains; and risk seeking relating to capital investment when firms faced losses; and loss aversion which is predicted by Prospect Theory; and that when corporate governance factors were introduced, the degree of risk aversion in the "domain-of-gains" is further reduced, and similarly, in the loss domain, levels of risk seeking are diminished in the "domain-of-losses".

The pattern of behaviors and misconduct of the SinoCos' senior executives and Boards of Directors cannot be explained by the Porter-type competitive analysis which is considered basic and perhaps insufficient given comments in Nwogugu (2005a) and Nwogugu (2005b).

The pattern of misconduct of the SinoCos' senior executives and Boards of Directors ("BODs) cannot be explained by Prospect Theory (PT), Cumulative Prospect Theory (CPT) and Third-generation Prospect Theory (PT³). Some of the SinoCos were unprofitable while others were profitable when they perpetrated the securities fraud and earnings management; and their behaviors in the domains of gains and losses contradicted PT/CPT/PT3.

Various researchers have developed CPT-based and PT-based asset pricing models and portfolio management models. He and Zhou (2011); Jin and Zhou (2013); Zou and Zagst (2017); Yang and Liu (2018); Chau and Rasonyi (2017); Bernard and Ghossoub (2010), Pirvu and Schulze (2012 and; Liu et al. (2014); Grishina, Lucas and Date (2016); Liu, Shu and Zhang (2014), Li (2014) and Davies and Satchell (2004) claimed that they developed investment portfolios and strategies that were purportedly based on Cumulative Prospect Theory (CPT) or Prospect Theory (PT). Baele et al. (2018); Solnik and Zuo (2012); Bonomo, Garcia, Meddahi and Tédongap (2011); Lia and Yang (2013); Yang (2010); Barberis and Huang (2008); Hung and Wang (2005); De Giorgi, Hens and Mayer (2007); Yogo (2008) and Barberis, Huang and Santos (2001) stated that they developed asset pricing models that are based on PT or CPT preferences. The analysis and theories in all these foregoing articles are invalidated by the critiques of CPT/PT/PT³ which are mentioned in this book and by Nwogugu (2005a;b); Nwogugu (2006c) and Nwogugu (2019b). Schmidt, Starmer and Sugden (2008) introduced *Third Generation Prospect Theory*. Rieger and Bui (2011) developed alternative specifications for Prospect Theory ("PT"), and noted that in financial markets where the majority of participants are PT-maximizers, the classic PT value function (v) results in non-existence of equilibria; and the problem can be solved by using exponential value functions. Neilson and Stowe (2002) and Nwogugu (2006d) critiqued CPT and found that CPT is an extension of Expected Utility Theory; and their results (and Nwogugu (2005d) which are cited in Nwogugu [2006c]) contradict findings in Bleichrodt et al. (2013) and Wakker (2001). Schmidt (2003) critiqued CPT, and re-defined reference-dependence in CPT.

As noted by Schmidt, Starmer and Sugden (2008): ". . . PT³ has three key features: reference dependence, decision weights and uncertain reference points (i.e. reference points that can be lotteries). The first two features are the common characteristics of different versions of prospect theory, including the original (or first-generation) version (Kahneman and Tversky [1979]) and the later cumulative (or second-generation) versions featuring rank-dependent decision weights (e.g. Starmer and Sugden [1989]; Luce and Fishburn [1991]; Tversky and Kahneman [1992]; Wakker and Tversky [1993]). Variants of cumulative prospect theory are increasingly widely applied in both theoretical and empirical work (recent examples are Davies and Satchell [2004]; Trepel, Fox and Poldrack [2005]; Wu, Zhang and Abdellaoui [2005]; Baucells and Heukamp [2006]; Schmidt and Zank [2008]) and some have argued that such theories may be serious contenders for replacing expected utility theory at least for specific purposes (see Camerer, 1989). . . ." The SinoCos and their management teams didn't seem to have any positive or negative *Reference Points*, and were not subject to *Anchoring* or the *Reflection Effect*, or the "*Certainty Effect*"; *Reference-Dependence*; *Preference-Reversals*; *decision-weighting*, or the "*Isolation Effect*" and their preferences don't match the "*S-curve*" all of which form the basis for PT/CPT/PT[3]. Probabilistic Insurance as defined in PT/CPT and as re-defined in Nwogugu (2005d;e) would not have been very useful for hedging the types of risks presented by the misconduct of the SinoCos. The SinoCos' misconduct and the findings and theories in this article contradict the findings in many articles about PT/CPT. Ljungqvist and Wilhelm (2005) developed a behavioral measure of the IPO decision-maker's satisfaction with the underwriter's performance and concluded that IPO firms were less likely to switch underwriters when their model indicated they were satisfied with the IPO underwriter's performance. The SinoCos described herein switched underwriters. Chang, Solomon and Westerfield (2015) concluded that increasing investors' cognitive dissonance results in both a larger disposition effect in stocks and a larger reverse-disposition effect in funds; and that increasing the salience of delegation increases the reverse-disposition effect in funds. On the contrary, the investors in many hedge funds (some of which were similar to mutual funds) that lost money as a result of misconduct by the SinoCos didn't display the reverse-disposition effect. In the Barberis and Xiong (2009) experiment on prospect theory, the annual gain/loss model often didn't predict a disposition effect; unlike the realized gain/loss model. This finding can be partly contradicted by looking at how investors (hedge funds and mutual funds) reacted after they realized losses due to fraud by the SinoCos as a group were popularized.

8.10 Conclusion

Clearly, given the foregoing regulatory failures and sub-optimal enforcement efforts that have been both ineffective and welfare-reducing, and the foregoing regulations/statutes should be amended. The implications of findings in this chapter are as follows. Corporate governance deficiencies (in both compliance and enforcement) can increase Systemic Risk; and Alibaba and many Chinese companies should conduct internal revamping of their Corporate Governance principles/standards and implementation methods. New and more effective international corporate governance standards are required and should be incorporated into national accounting and securities statutes. IFRS accounting standards have to be improved and made mandatory in all countries. Governments should implement internationally coordinated and tougher antitax-evasion statutes and enforcement methods. Governments should implement internationally coordinated and tougher statutes for cross-border listing and cross-border reverse-mergers and cross border IPOs and associated enforcement methods. The cost and socio-economic and psychological impacts of regulations are major factors that determine or can affect the extent, duration and evolution of compliance. The misconduct and Securities Fraud by the SinoCos had the potential to cause significant systemic risk in the US and China – some of the SinoCos' shares were cross-listed in both China and US (NASDAQ; NYSE; Shanghai). The SinoCos' misconduct affected many families and investors in the US and China, and could have had substantial multiplier effects (such as uncertainty; reduced trust; depression; mis-evaluation of risk; unwarranted risk-aversion; etc.). The present securities enforcement systems in the US and China (as of 2010–2016) make it very expensive for prosecutors (and even private citizens) to successfully file claims against such erring companies in any fora (e.g. court; arbitration; etc.) – in many cases the Chinese companies disappeared from the US and Chinese authorities were not cooperative when US tried to investigate or prosecute these companies in China. Auditor liability-allocation systems, criteria and principles have to be changed drastically. Finally, CPT/PT/PT[3] are invalid.

Notes

1   *See:* Zhang, J. (July 24, 2011). *Investing in Chinese ADRs Is Not as Simple as Following IBD's Checklist.* http://seekingalpha.com/article/281328-investing-in-chinese-adrs-is-not-as-simple-as-following-ibds-checklist. This article noted that: "Currently there are over 300 Chinese companies with a combined market capitalization of approximately $900 billion listed in the major North American stock exchanges. Almost all of them are listed in the US, with about 40 companies – with a combined market cap of $15 billion – listed in Canada's TSX and TSX Venture Exchanges." Ang, Jiang and Wu (2012) noted that of all Chinese companies listed in US, only 29 went public via an IPO of ordinary shares, 116 went public via IPO of ADRs and 122 via reverse-merger; and market capitalization of these China-based companies listed in US markets reached $320 billion by the end of June, 2011.
2   *See:* Fink, J. (December 7, 2012). *Chinese ADRs, Accounting Fraud, and Delisting Risk.* www.investingdaily.com/15971/chinese-adrs--fraud-and-delisting-risk/.
       See: Morgan, J. P. (June 2014). *The Investment Landscape for Chinese ADRs.* www.jpmorgan.com/jpmpdf/1320676276731.pdf.
3   *See:* US Senator Bob Casey's 2014 letter to Ms. Mary-Jo White, Chairperson of the US SEC. https://dealbook.nytimes.com/2014/09/17/on-eve-of-alibabas-i-p-o-senator-urges-s-e-c-to-look-at-risks-in-some-chinese-offerings/?_r=0.
4   *See:* Norris, F. (May 26, 2011). *The Audacity of Chinese Frauds.* www.nytimes.com/2011/05/27/business/27norris.html?pagewanted=all&_r=0.
5   *See:* Sovereign Advisers (Globalsecuritieswatch.org) (2013). *Exchange-Listed Chinese Company Fraud.* www.globalsecuritieswatch.org/Chinese_investment_bank_

alleged_operate_fraud_school_creating_fake_Chinese_companies_listing_on_overseas_exchanges.pdf.

6 *See*: Ren, S. (May 11, 2016). China cracks down on speculative M&A in FinTech, VR, gaming, films. *Barron's*. www.barrons.com/articles/china-cracks-down-on-speculative-m-as-in-fintech-vr-gaming-films-1462949776.

7 *See*: Melloy, J. (July 8, 2015). *China Crash Underscores Risk for US investors*. www.cnbc.com/2015/07/08/china-crash-underscores-risk-for-us-investors.html.
   See: PriceWaterhouse. (2015). *Consolidation and Equity Method of Accounting – 2015 Edition*. www.pwc.com/us/en/cfodirect/publications/accounting-guides/consolidation-framework-equity-method-accounting-vie-guide.html.

8 *See*: FASB. (2017). Financial accounting standards board interpretation No. 46: *Consolidation of Variable Interest Entities*.
   See: *FASB Issues Guidance to Improve Financial Reporting for SPEs, Off-Balance Sheet Structures and Similar Entities*. (FASB News Release, January 2013). www.fasb.org/news/nr011703.shtml.
   See: Steel, J. (May 2012). *Variable Interest Entities (VIEs), Qihoo 360 and China'*. Hedge Fund Consulting and Short Equity Research. www.shortzilla.com/variable-interest-entities-vie-qihoo-360-and-china.

9 *See:* De la Merced, M. (September 17, 2014). *On Eve of Alibaba's I.P.O., Senator Urges S.E.C. to Look at Risks in Some Chinese Offerings*. https://dealbook.nytimes.com/2014/09/17/on-eve-of-alibabas-i-p-o-senator-urges-s-e-c-to-look-at-risks-in-some-chinese-offerings/?_r=0.

10 *See*: Laing, J. (2015). *Alibaba: Why It Could Fall 50% Further – The Chinese Internet giant's stock has been plunging amid an array of problems. Expect more trouble ahead*. www.barrons.com/articles/alibaba-why-it-could-fall-50-further-1442036618?mod=trending_now_1.

11 *See*: Alibaba Group. (September 14, 2015). *Alibaba Responds to Barron's Story*. www.alizila.com/alibaba-responds-barrons-story.
   See: Mozur, P. (2016). *Alibaba Faces U.S. Accounting Inquiry*. https://www.nytimes.com/2016/05/26/business/dealbook/alibaba-faces-us-accounting-inquiry.html?_r=0.
   See: "Alibaba Investors Will Buy a Risky Corporate Structure". *Dealbook*. By Steven Davidoff Solomon. May 6, 2014. https://dealbook.nytimes.com/2014/05/06/i-p-o-revives-debate-over-a-chinese-structure/. This article noted that ". . . the (VIE) structure may be illegal under Chinese law since it conveniently circumvents those prohibitions on foreign investment. There is precedent for such a finding. In a letter to Baidu questioning the effectiveness of such a structure, the (US) Securities and Exchange Commission noted that a ruling in late 2012 by the Supreme People's Court of China invalidated a V.I.E. structure used by Minsheng Bank. . . ."

12 *See*: Egan, M. (May 25, 2016*). Famous Shortseller Thinks Alibaba Is Shady*. http://money.cnn.com/2016/05/13/investing/jim-chanos-alibaba-shady-china/

13 *See*: Weiczner, J. (September 18, 2015). *Here's Why One Hedge Fund Manager Thinks Alibaba Could Be a Big Fraud*. http://fortune.com/2015/09/18/alibaba-faking-numbers-hedge-fund/.

14 *See*: Hempton, J. (September 15, 2015). *Job Interview Questions: The Size and Scope of Alibaba*. http://brontecapital.blogspot.com.ng/2015/09/job-interview-questions-size-and-scope.html

15 *See*: McKenna, F. (September 15, 2015). *Can We Trust Alibaba's Numbers? Auditor Has Never Faced U.S. Regulatory Scrutiny*. www.marketwatch.com/story/can-we-trust-alibabas-numbers-auditor-has-never-faced-us-regulatory-scrutiny-2015–09–15.

16 *See*: Mozur, P. (2016). *Alibaba Faces U.S. Accounting Inquiry*. www.nytimes.com/2016/05/26/business/dealbook/alibaba-faces-us-accounting-inquiry.html?_r=0.

17 *See*: "Alibaba Investors Will Buy a Risky Corporate Structure". *Dealbook*. By Steven Davidoff Solomon. May 6, 2014. https://dealbook.nytimes.com/2014/05/06/i-p-o-revives-debate-over-a-chinese-structure/. This article noted that "the (VIE) structure may be illegal under Chinese law since it conveniently circumvents those prohibitions on foreign investment. There is precedent for such a finding. In a letter to Baidu questioning the effectiveness of such a structure, the (US) Securities and Exchange Commission noted that a ruling in late 2012 by the Supreme People's Court of China invalidated a V.I.E. structure used by Minsheng Bank."
     See: US Senator Bob Casey's 2014 letter to Ms. M. White, Chairperson of the US SEC. https://dealbook.nytimes.com/2014/09/17/on-eve-of-alibabas-i-p-o-senator-urges-s-e-c-to-look-at-risks-in-some-chinese-offerings/?_r=0.
     See: Johnson (2015).
18 *See*: Oster, S. & Lawrence, D. (December 15, 2013). Baidu forced to add warnings as regulators focus on China stocks. *Bloomberg*. www.bloomberg.com/news/articles/2013-12-15/baidu-forced-to-add-warnings-as-regulators-focus-on-china-stocks.
19 *See*: White, F. (May 23, 2011). *Longtop Financial: The $1 Billion Chinese Accounting Disaster Whose Accountant Just Resigned.* www.businessinsider.com/deloitte-longtop-financial-resigns-2011-5.
20 See: www.businessinsider.com/china-stock-fraud-longtop-banks-complicit-2011-5.
     See: Hempton (Bronte Capital) (May 20, 2011).
21 *See*: *SEC Charges China-Based Longtop Financial Technologies for Deficient Filings – For Immediate Release – 2011–241.* Washington, DC, November 10, 2011.
     See: Gillis, P. *Longtop Financial Technologies Case Study – Accounting fraud in China.* Peking University's Guanghua School of Management. www.paulgillis.org/longtop_financial_technolog.pdf.
     See: Gillis, P. *Citron reports on Longtop Financial (NYSE:LFT).* www.paulgillis.org/citronresearchcom__citron.pdf.
     See: Gillis, P. *Auditing cash in China.* www.chinaaccountingblog.com/weblog/auditing-cash-in-china.html. Peking University's Guanghua School of Management.
     See: Norris, F. (May 26, 2011). *The Audacity of Chinese Frauds.* www.nytimes.com/2011/05/27/business/27norris.html?pagewanted=all&_r=0.
22 *See*: "US, Chinese regulators make peace over Longtop". Chris Dodd. January 29, 2014. www.financeasia.com/News/370799,us-chinese-regulators-make-peace-over-longtop.aspx.
23 *See*: Durden, T. (June 2011). *Paulson Flagship Fund Loses More Than Half of "Assets Under Management" In 2011.* www.zerohedge.com/news/paulson-flagship-fund-loses-more-half-aum-2011.
24 *See*: Durden, T. (June 2011). *John Paulson Loses Half a Billion in Under 24 Hours.* www.zerohedge.com/article/john-paulson-loses-half-billion-under-24-hours.
     See: Durden, T. (June 2011). *Paulson Dumps All Sino-Forest Holdings: $750 Million+ Realized Loss.* www.zerohedge.com/article/paulson-dumps-all-sino-forest-holdings-750-million-realized-loss.
25 *See*: http://chinesecompanyanalyst.com/2010/09/10/china-biotics-an-investigation-of-its-alleged-store-base/.
26 *See*: *China Expert Technology, Inc. Securities Litigation.* http://securities.stanford.edu/filings-case.html?id=103882.
     See: *Rosen Law Firm, P.A. Announces Proposed Class Action Settlement on Behalf of Purchasers of Common Stock of China Expert Technology, Inc.* www.bloomberg.com/research/stocks/private/snapshot.asp?privcapId=8983116.
     See: China Briefing. (November 2011). *Chinese State Secrecy Laws Being Pulled Apart Under Audit Stresses.* www.china-briefing.com/news/2011/11/28/chinese-state-secrecy-laws-being-pulled-apart-under-audit-stresses.html#more-14845.

27 *See*: Durden, T. (2011). *Presenting Global Hunter's Humiliating February 17 "Maintain Buy" Report On CCME*. www.zerohedge.com/article/presenting-global-hunters-humiliating-february-17-maintain-buy-report-ccme

28 *See*: Muddy Waters LLC. (2011). *CCME: Taking the Short Bus to Profits*. http://d.muddywatersresearch.com/wp-content/uploads/2011/02/CCME_MW_020311.pdf.

29 See: Muddy Waters LLC (2011).

30 *See*: Sovriegn Advisers (Globalsecuritieswatch.org). (2013). *Exchange-Listed Chinese Company Fraud*. www.globalsecuritieswatch.org/Chinese_investment_bank_alleged_operate_fraud_school_creating_fake_Chinese_companies_listing_on_overseas_exchanges.pdf.

31 See: Eden S. (June 23, 2013). Bigtime investors lose big on China. *TheStreet.com*, June 23, 2011). www.thestreet.com/story/11163573/1/bigtime-investors-lose-big-on-china.html.

See: "China's Reverse-Merger Candidates Plunge on Regulatory Scrutiny". By Fox Hu and Kana Nishizawa. May 8, 2016. www.bloomberg.com/news/articles/2016-05-09/china-s-reverse-merger-candidates-plunge-on-regulatory-scrutiny.

See: www.zerohedge.com/news/fmcn-halted-over-60-down.

See: www.zerohedge.com/news/thestreet-fmcn-8-hours-ago-upgrading-neutral-buy.

See: www.globalsecuritieswatch.org/Complaint_Filed_with_NYSE_and_NAS DAQ.pdf.

See: http://absaroka.com/.

See: http://brontecapital.blogspot.com/. Bronte Capital's website.

See: http://citronresearch.com/. Citron Research's website.

See: http://glaucusresearch.com/. Glaucus Research's website.

See: http://kerrisdalecap.com/. Kerrisdale Capital is an investment management firm that specializes in identifying fraudulent U.S.-listed Chinese companies, and it achieved a 400%+ total return in 2011 by shorting Nasdaq-listed Chinese companies.

See: http://buyersstrike.wordpress.com/.

See: www.muddywatersresearch.com/.

See: Most Profitable Q1 Investing Strategy? Identifying And Shorting Chinese Frauds. By Tyler Durden; May 17, 2011. www.zerohedge.com/article/most-profitable-q1-investing-strategy-identifying-and-shorting-chinese-frauds.

See: Muddy Waters LLC. (April 10, 2012). *The Fraud School, RINO and FSIN (Fraud University)*. www.muddywatersresearch.com/wp-content/uploads/2012/04/MW_FraudSchool_20120410.pdf. See:
The report is also accessible at: www.scribd.com/doc/88760273/MW-Fraud School-20120410.

See: Caines, J. (April 2012). Unmasking the disaster of 'China concept'. *Fortune Today*. www.webcitation.org/67AfP8FO7.

See: "Chinese Companies Go To Fraud School". by Matthew Robertson, *Epoch Times* (April 24, 2012). www.theepochtimes.com/n2/china-news/chinese-companies-go-to-fraud-school-226634.html.

See: www.zamansky.com/blog/2012/03/chinese-fraud-hiding-in-plain-sight.html.

See: www.chiefcapital.com.hk/english/.

See: Stansberry's Investment Advisory (December 2011). *The Corruption of America*.

32 *See*: *"Family Values in the Emerging Market Ruling Class."* The article is accessible at: http://brontecapital.blogspot.com/2011/02/family-values-in-emerging-market-ruling.html

See: Cookson, E. (June 5, 2011). China foreign listings dogged by scandal. *Financial Times* (UK).

33 Group-F5 (Greater Than $100 billion per year):

- Environmental Protection Agency (EPA): $353 billion
- *Health & Human services (HHS)*: $184.8 billion
- *FCC and Telecom Regulation*: $142 billion
- *Department of Labor*: $116.3 billion
- *Financial Regulation (several agencies)*: $102.5 billion

Group-F4 ($10 billion – $100 billion per year):

- *Department of Transportation*: $61.8 billion
- *Department of Homeland Security (DHS)*: $55.32 billion

Group-F3 ($5 billion – $10 billion per year):

- *Energy Department*: $9.809 billion
- *US Department of Agriculture (USDA)*: $9.05 billion
- *Department of the Interior*: $5.2 billion

Group-F2 ($1 billion – $5 billion per year):

- *Department of Education*: $3.302 billion
- *Housing & Urban Development (HUD)*: $1.827 billion
- *Department of Commerce*: $1.801 billion
- *Department of the Treasury*: $1.32 billion
- *Department of Justice*: $1.25 billion

Group-F1 (Less Than $1 billion per year):

- *U.S. Access Board (ATBCB)*: $851 million
- *Nuclear Regulatory Commission*: $414 million
- *FERC*: $336 million
- *CPSC*: $193 million
- Equal Employment Opportunity Commission (EEOC): $121 million

Source: Wayne Crews, *"Tip of the Costberg"*; working paper.

Bibliography

Ang, J., Jiang, Z. & Wu, C. (2012). *Good Apples, Bad Apples: Sorting Among Chinese Companies Traded in the U.S.* Working Paper. https://editorialexpress.com/cgi-bin/conference/download.cgi?db_name=cicf2013&paper_id=358.

Arena, M., Arnaboldi, M. & Azzone, G. (2010). The organizational dynamics of enterprise risk management. *Accounting, Organizations and Society*, 659–675.

Baele, L., Driessen, J. et al. (2018). Cumulative prospect theory, option returns, and the variance premium. *The Review of Financial Studies*, 3, 229–257.

Baker, M., Wurgler, J. & Yuan, Y. (2012). Global, local and contagious investor sentiment. *Journal of Financial Economics*, 104(2), 272–287.

Bancel, F. & Mittoo, C. (2001). European managerial perceptions of the net benefits of foreign stock listings. *European Financial Management*, 7(2), 213–236.

Barber, P. (2013). Bull in the China market: The gap between investor expectations and auditor liability for Chinese financial statement frauds. *Duke Journal of Comparative & International Law*, 24, 349–359. http://scholarship.law.duke.edu/cgi/viewcontent.cgi?article=1402&context=djcil.

Barberis, N. & Huang, M. (2008). Stocks as lotteries: The implications of probability weighting for security prices. *American Economic Review*, 98(5), 2066–2100.

Barberis, N., Huang, M. & Santos, T. (2001). Prospect theory and asset prices. *The Quarterly Journal of Economics*, 116(1), 1–53.

Barberis, N. & Xiong, W. (2009). What drives the disposition effect? An analysis of a long-standing preference-based explanation. *Journal of Finance*, 64(2), 751–784.

Bargeron, L., Lehn, M. & Zutter, C. (2010). Sarbanes-Oxley and corporate risk taking. *Journal of Accounting and Economics*, 49, 34–52.

Battiston, S. & Glattfelder, J.B. (2009). Backbone of complex networks of corporations: The flow of control. *Physics Review-E*, 80, 036104.

Bernard, L. (1926a). Primary and derivative groups. Chapter 26 in: *An Introduction to Social Psychology* (Henry Holt and Co., New York), pp. 411–425. www.brocku.ca/MeadProject/Bernard/1926/1926_26.html.

Bernard, L. (1926b). Primary and derivative attitudes and ideals. Chapter 27 in: *An Introduction to Social Psychology* (Henry Holt and Co., New York), pp. 425–437). www.brocku.ca/MeadProject/Bernard/1926/1926_27.html.

Bernard, L. (1936). The conflict between primary group attitudes and derivative group ideals in modern society. *American Journal of Sociology*, 41(5), 611–623.

Bernard, C. & Ghossoub, M. (2010). Static portfolio choice under cumulative prospect theory. *Mathematics and Financial Economics*, 2, 77–306.

Bliss, R., Pottera, M. & Schwarz, C. (2012). Decision making and risk aversion in the cash cab. *Journal of Economic Behavior & Organization*, 84(1), 163–173.

Bodnaruk, A., Massa, M. & Simonov, A. (2013). Alliances and corporate governance. *Journal of Financial Economics*, 107(3), 671–693.

Boehme, R. & May, A. (May 2016). Multinational corporations and stock price crash risk. *International Journal of Finance & Banking Studies*, 5(4), 39–44. www.ssbfnet.com/ojs/index.php/ijfbs/article/view/593.

Boissay, F. (2006). *Credit Chains and the Propagation of Financial Distress*. Working Paper Series #573. European Central Bank. www.ecb.europa.eu/pub/pdf/scpwps/ecbwp573.pdf?0c7b3859edb7d58a72b01309111c4b52.

Bonomo, M., Garcia, R., Meddahi, N. & Tédongap, R. (2011). Generalized disappointment aversion, long-run volatility risk, and asset prices. *Review of Financial Studies*, 24(1), 82–122.

Bowman, E.H. (1984). Content analysis of annual reports for corporate strategy and risk. *Interfaces*, 14, 61–72.

Brida, J., Anyul, M. & Punzo, L. (2003). Coding economic dynamics to represent regime dynamics. A teach-yourself exercise. *Structural Change and EconomicDynamics*, 14(2), 133–157.

Cadwalader. (August 10, 2011). *Understanding the VIE Structure: Necessary Elements for Success and the Legal Risks Involved*. www.cadwalader.com/resources/clients-friends-memos/understanding-the-vie-structure-necessary-elements-for-success-and-the-legal-risks-in-volved.

Chan, S., Kensinger, J., Keown, A. & Martin, J. (1997). Do strategic alliances create value? *Journal of Financial Economics*, 46, 199–221.

Chandra, A. & Thenmozhi, M. (2017). Behavioural asset pricing: Review and synthesis. *Journal of Interdisciplinary Economics*, 24(1), 77–97.

Chang, T., Solomon, D. & Westerfield, M. (2015). Looking for someone to blame: Delegation, cognitive dissonance, and the disposition effect. *Journal of Finance*, 71(1), 267–302.

Chau, H. & Rasonyi, M. (2017). Skorohod's representation theorem and optimal strategies for markets with frictions. https://arxiv.org/pdf/1606.07311.pdf.

Chemmanur, T.J. & He, J. (2011). IPO waves, product market competition, and the going public decision: Theory and evidence. *Journal of Financial Economics*, 101(2), 382–412.

Chen & Co. Law Firm. *In Focus: Variable Interest Entities (VIEs)-Part I*. www.ey.com/Publication/vwLUAssets/EY-vie-report-english/$FILE/EY-vies-english.pdf.

Chen, D. (2011). Selective enforcement of regulation. *China Journal of Accounting Research*, 4, 9.

Chen, K., Cheng, Q., Lin, Y., Lin, Y. & Xiao, X. (November 2015). Financial reporting quality of Chinese reverse merger firms: The reverse merger effect or the weak country effect? *Accounting Review*, 91(5), 1363–1390.

Chen, K., Li, G. & Wu, L. (2010). Price discovery for segmented us-listed Chinese stocks: Location or market quality? *Journal of Business Finance & Accounting*, 37(1–2), 242–269.

Chen, K., Lin, Y. & Lin, Y. (2012). *Does Foreign Company's Shortcut to Wall Street Cut Short their Earnings Quality? Evidence from Chinese Reverse Mergers*. Working Paper.

Ciaschini, M., Pretaroli, R. & Socci, C. (2011). Balance, Manhattan norm and Euclidean distance of industrial policies for the US. *Structural Change and Economic Dynamics*, 22(3), 204–226.

Cimoli, M., Pereima, J. & Porcile, G. (2016). Introduction to the special issue SCED: Complexity and economic development. *Structural Change & Economic Dynamics*, 38, 1–2.

Claudiu, B. (2013). Formal representation of corporate governance principles and codes. *Procedia – Social and Behavioral Sciences*, 73, 744–750.

Cohen, L., Malloy, C. & Nguyen, Q. (2016). *Lazy Prices*. Working paper. SSRN. https://ssrn.com/abstract=1658471 or http://dx.doi.org/10.2139/ssrn.1658471.

Colpan, A., Yoshikawa, T., Hikino, T. & Miyoshi, H. (2007). Japanese corporate governance: Structural change and financial performance. *Asian Business Management*, 6, 89–113.

Comim, F. (2000). The Santa Fe approach to complexity: A Marshallian evaluation. *Structural Change & Economic Dynamics*, 11(1–2), 25–43.

Corwin, S. & Schultz, P. (2005). The role of IPO underwriting syndicates: Pricing, information production, and underwriter competition. *Journal of Finance*, 60(1), 443–486.

Cronqvist, H. & Siegel, S. (2014). The genetics of investment biases. *Journal of Financial Economics*, 113(2), 215–234.

Cumming, D. & Johan, S. (2013). Listing standards and fraud. *Managerial & Decision Economics*, 34(7–8), 451–470.

Darrough, M.N., Huang, R. & Zhao, S. (2013). *The Spillover Effect of Chinese Reverse Merger Frauds: Chinese or Reverse Merger?* Working Paper, Baruch College, CUNY, New York City, USA.

Das, S., Guo, R. & Zhang, H. (2006). Analysts' selective coverage and subsequent performance of newly public firms. *Journal of Finance*, 61(3), 1159–1185.

Davies, G. & Satchell, S. (2004). *Continuous Cumulative Prospect Theory and Individual Asset Allocation*. Cambridge Working Paper in Economics #467. Cambridge University, UK.

Dbouk, B. & Zaarour, I. (2017). Towards a machine learning approach for earnings manipulation detection. *Asian Journal of Business and Accounting*, 10(2), 215–220.

De Giorgi, E., Hens, T. & Mayer, J. (2007). Computational aspects of prospect theory with asset pricing applications. *Computational Economics*, 29(3–4), 267–281.

De Nicolò, G. & Juvenal, L. (2014). Financial integration, globalization, and real activity. *Journal of Financial Stability*, 10, 65–75.

Deck, C. & Schlesinger, H. (2014). Consistency of higher order risk preferences. *Econometrica*, 82(5), 1913–1943.

Dey, A. (2010). The chilling effect of Sarbanes-Oxley: A discussion of Sarbanes-Oxley and corporate risk taking. *Journal of Accounting and Economics*, 49, 53–57.

Dickinson, G. (2001). Enterprise risk management: Its origins and conceptual foundation. *The Geneva Papers on Risk and Insurance*, 26(3), 360–366.

Dikmen, B. & Kukkocaoglu, G. (2010). The detection of earnings manipulation: The three-phase cutting plane algorithm using mathematical program-ming. *Journal of Forecasting*, 29(5), 442–466.

Donaldson, T. (2012). The epistemic fault line in corporate governance. *Academy of Management Review*, 37(2), 256–271.

Dosi, G. & Virgillito, M. (2017). In order to stand up you must keep cycling: Change and coordination in complex evolving economies. *Structural Change And Economic Dynamics*, in press, accepted manuscript.

Drabkova, Z. (2016). Models of detection of manipulated financial statements as part of the internal control system of the entity. *ACRN Oxford Journal of Finance and Risk Perspectives*, 5(1), 227–235.

Du, K. (August 2016). *Investor Expectations, Earnings Management, and Asset Prices*. Working paper, Pennsylvania State University, USA. SSRN. https://ssrn.com/abstract=2852553.

Dyck, A., Morse, A. & Zingales, L. (2010). Who blows the whistle on corporate fraud? *Journal of Finance*, 65(6), 2213–2253.

Eales, J. (2015). The future of Chinese Foreign investments: An exploration of the Perils and consequences of investing in variable interest entities. *Kent Student Law Review*, 2.

Elliott, M., Golub, B. & Jackson, M.O. (2014). Financial networks and contagion. *American Economic Review*, 104, 3115–3153.

Engau, C. & Hoffman, V.F. (2011). Strategising in an unpredictable climate: Exploring corporate strategies to cope with regulatory uncertainty. *Long Range Planning*, 44(1), 42–63.

Evans, G. & Honkapohja, S. (2003). Expectations and the stability problem for optimal monetary policies. *Review of Economic Studies*, 70, 807–824.

Fama, E. & French, K. (1992). The cross-section of expected stock returns. *Journal of Finance*, 47, 427–465.

Fang, V., Huang, A. & Karpoff, J. (2015). Short selling and earnings management: A controlled experiment. *Journal of Finance*.

Fang, X. & Yuan, F. (2018). The coordination and preference of supply chain contracts based on time-sensitivity promotional mechanism. *Journal of Management Science and Engineering*, 3(3), 158–178.

Francis, W., Hasan, I. & Li, L. (2014). *Abnormal Real Operations, Real Earnings Management, and Subsequent Crashes in Stock Prices*. Bank of Finland Research Discussion Papers #19. www.suomenpankki.fi/pdf/173785.pdf.

Fukao, M. (1999). *Japanese Financial Instability and Weakness in the Corporate Governance Structure* (OECD, Paris).

Gabardo, F., Pereima, J. & Einloft, P. (2017). The incorporation of structural change into growth theory: A historical appraisal. *Economia*, in Press, uncorrected proof, available online June 3, 2017.

García-Pérez, A., Yanes-Estévez, V. & Oreja-Rodríguez, J. (2014). Strategic reference points, risk and strategic choices in small and medium-sized enterprises. *Journal of Business Economics and Management*, 21(3), 431–449.

Gillis, P. & Lowry, M. (2014). Son of Enron: Investors weigh the risks of Chinese variable interest entities. *Journal of Applied Corporate Finance*, 26(3).

Goetz, R., Yatsenko, Y., Hritonenkoc, N., Xabadia, A. & Abdulai, A. (2019). The dynamics of productive assets, contract duration and holdup. *Mathematical Social Sciences*, 97, 24–37.

Grechuk, B. & Zabarankin, M. (2014). Risk averse decision making under catastrophic risk. *European Journal of Operational Research*, 239(1), 166–176.

Grishina, N., Lucas, C. & Date, P. (2017). Prospect theory–based portfolio optimization: An empirical study and analysis using intelligent algorithms. *Quantitative Finance*, 17(3), 353–367.

Güçbilmez, U. (2014). Why do some Chinese technology firms avoid ChiNext and go public in the US? *International Review of Financial Analysis*, 36, 179–194.

Güçbilmez, U. (2015). IPO waves in China and Hong Kong. *International Review of Financial Analysis*, 40, 14–26.

Guo, C. & Hu, X. (2012). Rogue insiders, signature loopholes, and fraud rings: Lessons learned by a Chinese B2B mogul. *International Journal of Accounting & Information Management*, 20(4), 348–362.

Haldane, A.G. & May, R.M. (2011). Systemic risk in banking ecosystems. *Nature*, 469, 351–355.

He, X. & Zhou, X. (2011). Portfolio choice under cumulative prospect theory: An analytical treatment. *Management Science*, 57(2), 315–331.

Heinrich, T. & Dai, S. (2016). Diversity of firm sizes, complexity, and industry structure in the Chinese economy. *Structural Change And Economic Dynamics*, 37, 90–106.

Hempton, J. (Bronte Capital) (May 20, 2011). *Longtop Financial: Lessons in the Morphology of Sin, Loss of Virginity, and Your 17-Year Old Daughter*. www.businessinsider.com/john-hempton-longtop-financial-2011-5. Also see www.brontecapital.com/files/sma/Client_Letter_201105.pdf.

Hines, J.R. (1999). Three sides of Harberger Triangles. *Journal of Economic Perspectives*, 13(2), 167–188.

Hong, S., Wernz, C. & Stillinger, J. (2016). Optimizing maintenance service contracts through mechanism design theory. *Applied Mathematical Modelling*, 40(21–22), 8849–8861.

Hopkins, J., Lang, M. & Zhao, D. (2016). *When Enron Met Alibaba: The Rise of VIEs in China*. Working Paper, University of Virginia, USA. www.darden.virginia.edu/uploaded Files/Darden_Web/Content/Faculty_Research/Seminars_and_Conferences/HLZ--3_25_complete.pdf.

Hoppe, E. & Schmitz, P. (2018). Hidden action and outcome contractibility: An experimental test of moral hazard theory. *Games & Economic Behavior*, 109, 544–564.

Humphery-Jenner, M. & Suchard, J. (2013). Foreign VCs and the internationalization of entrepreneurial companies: Evidence from China. *Journal of International Business Studies*, 44(6), 607–621.

Hung, M. & Wang, J. (2005). Asset prices under prospect theory and habit formation. *Review of Pacific Basin Financial Markets and Policies*, 8(1), 1–29.

Ikenberry, D., Lakonishok, J. & Vermaelen, T. (1995). Market under-reaction to open market share repurchases. *Journal of Financial Economics*, 39, 181–208.

Jankowicz, A.D. & Hisrich, R.D. (1990). Intuition in venture capital decisions: An exploratory study using a new technique. *Journal of Business Venturing*, 5(1), 49–62.

Jin, H. & Zhou, X. (2013). Greed, leverage, and potential losses: A prospect theory perspective. *Mathematical Finance*, 23(1), 122–142.

Jin, L. & Myers, S. (2006). R^2 around the world: New theory and tests. *Journal of Financial Economics*, 79, 257–292.

Johnson, A. (2015). Variable interest entities: Alibaba's regulatory work-around to China's Foreign investment restrictions. *Loyola University Chicago International Law Review*, 12(2), 249–229. http://lawecommons.luc.edu/cgi/viewcontent.cgi?article=1181&context=lucilr.

Jovane, F., Seliger, G. & Stock, T. (2017). Competitive sustainable globalization general considerations and perspectives. *Procedia Manufacturing*, 8, 1–19.

Karpoff, J., Lee, D.S. & Martin, G. (2008a). The cost to firms of cooking the books. *Journal of Financial and Quantitative Analysis*, 43, 581–612.

Karpoff, J., Lee, D.S. & Martin, G. (2008b). The consequences to managers for cooking the books. *Journal of Financial Economics*, 88, 193–215.

Kim, J.B., Li, Y. & Zhang, L. (2011a). Corporate tax avoidance and stock price crash risk: Firm-level analysis. *Journal of Financial Economics*, 100, 639–662.

Kim, J.B., Li, Y. & Zhang, L. (2011b). CFOs versus CEOs: Equity incentives and crashes. *Journal of Financial Economics*, 101, 713–730.

Kim, J.B. & Zhang, L. (2013). Accounting conservatism and stock price crash risk: Firm-level evidence. *Contemporary Accounting Research*, 33(1), 412–441.

Kim, J.B. & Zhang, L. (2014). Financial reporting opacity and expected crash risk: Evidence from implied volatility smirks. *Contemporary Accounting Research*, 31(3), 851–875.

Ku, E. (2012). China's internal control and audit regulatory framework. *China Briefing*. www.china-briefing.com/news/2012/03/09/chinas-internal-control-and-audit-regulatory-framework.html.

Kuzubas, T., Ömercikoglu, I. & Saltoglu, B. (2014). Network centrality measures and systemic risk: An application to the Turkish financial crisis. *Physica A: Statistical Mechanics and its Applications*, 405, 203–215.

Lee, C., Li, K. & Zhang, R. (2012). *Shell Games: Are Chinese Reverse Merger Firms Inherently Toxic?* Working Paper.

Li, E., Livdan, D. & Zhang, L. (2009). Anomalies. *The Review of Financial Studies*, 22(11), 4302–4331.

Li, H., An, H., Gao, X., Huang, J. & Xu, Q. (2014). On the topological properties of the cross shareholding networks of listed companies in China: Taking shareholders' cross-shareholding relationships into account. *Physica-A*, 6, 80–88.

Li, L. (2014). The optimal portfolio selection model under –expectation. *Abstract & Applied Analysis*, Article ID 426036, 2014. doi:10.1155/2014/426036.

Li, W., Liu, Y. & Chen, Y. (2018). Modeling a two-stage supply contract problem in a hybrid uncertain environment. *Computers & Industrial Engineering*, 123, 289–302.

Lia, Y. & Yang, L. (2013). Prospect theory, the disposition effect and asset prices. *Journal of Financial Economics*, 107(3), 715–739.

Lin, E. & Chou, M. (1990). Optimal contracts. *Applied Mathematics Letters*, 3(2), 65–68.

Lind, H. & Granqvist, R. (2010). A note on the concept of excess burden. *Economic Analysis and Policy*, 40, 63–73.

Liu, X. & Tse, C. (2012). Dynamics of network of global stock market. *Accounting & Finance Research*, 1, 1–12.

Liu, Y., Nacher, J., Martino, M. et al. (2014). Prospect theory for online financial trading. *PLoS One*. 2014, 9(10), e109458. http://www.ncbi.nlm.nih.gov/pmc/articles/PMC4198126/.

Liu, Y., Shu, P. & Zhang, Y. (2014). Risk decision analysis in emergency response: A method based on cumulative prospect theory. *Computers & Operations Research*, 42, 75–82.

Liu, Z. (2016). Basic corporate governance pattern in variable interest entities. *Emory Corporate Governance and Accountability Review*, 3, 2064–2071. http://law.emory.edu/ecgar/_documents/volumes/3/3/perspectives/liu.pdf

Ljungqvist, A. & Wilhelm, W. (2005). Does prospect theory explain IPO market behavior? *Journal of Finance*, 60(4), 1759–1790.

Ma, M. (2013). The perils and prospects of China's variable interest entities: Unraveling the murky rules and the institutional challenges posed. *Hong Kong Law Journal*, 43, 1061–1064.

Ma, Y., Zhuang, X.T. & Li, L. (2011). Research on the relationships of the domestic mutual investment of China based on the cross-shareholding networks of the listed companies. *Physica-A*, 390, 749–759.

Madureira, A., Pereira, I., Pereira, P. & Abraham, A. (2014). Negotiation mechanism for self-organized scheduling system with collective intelligence. *Neurocomputing*, 132, 97–110.

Marinovic, I. (2013). Internal control system, earnings quality and the dynamics of financial reporting. *The RAND Journal of Economics*, 44, 145–167.

McCahery, J., Sautner, Z. & Starks, L. (2016). Behind the scenes: The corporate governance preferences of institutional investors. *Journal of Finance*, 71(6), 2905–2932.

McCarter, M., Rockmann, K. & Northcraft, G. (2010). Is it even worth it? The effect of loss prospects in the outcome distribution of a public goods dilemma. *Organizational Behavior and Human Decision Processes*, 111(1), 1–12.

Melendy, S. & Huefner, R. (2011). Monitoring legal compliance: The growth of compliance committees. *Accounting Perspectives*, 10(4).

Meneguzzi, F., Modgil, S., Oren, N., Miles, S., Luck, M. & Faci, N. (2012). Applying electronic contracting to the aerospace aftercare domain. *Engineering Applications of Artificial Intelligence*, 25, 1471–1487.

Muddy Waters LLC (2011). *CCME: Taking the Short Bus to Profits*. http://d.muddywatersresearch.com/wp-content/uploads/2011/02/CCME_MW_020311.pdf.

Neilson, W. & Stowe, J. (2002). A further examination of cumulative prospect theory parameterizations. *Journal of Risk and Uncertainty*, 24(1), 31–46.

Niederhoff, J. & Kouvelis, P. (2019). Effective and necessary: Individual supplier behavior in revenue sharing and wholesale contracts. *European Journal of Operational Research*, 277(3), 1060–1071.

Noussair, C.N., Trautmann, S. & Kuilen, G. (2013). Higher order risk attitudes, demographics and saving. *Review of Economic Studies*, 81(1), 325–355.

Nwogugu, M. (2003). Corporate governance, credit risk and legal reasoning: The case of encompass services, Inc. *Managerial Auditing Journal*, 18(4), 270–291. Also published in *International Journal of Law & Management*, (47(1/2): 2–43, 2005), and reprinted in *ICFAI Journal of Financial Economics* (2004).

Nwogugu, M. (2004a). Corporate governance, risk and corporations law: The case of jack-in-the-box, Inc. *Managerial Auditing Journal*, 19(1), 29–67. Also published in *International Journal of Law & Management* (November 2004), and reprinted in *ICFAI Journal of Financial Economics* (2004).

Nwogugu, M. (2004b). Legal, economic and behavioral issues in accounting for stock options. *Managerial Auditing Journal*, 19(9), 1078–1118.

Nwogugu, M. (2005a). Structural changes in the US retailing industry: Legal, economic and strategic implications for the US real estate sector. *International Journal of Law & Management*, 47(1/2).

Nwogugu, M. (2005b). Legal, economic and corporate strategy issues in housing in the 'new' economy: An over view of the New York Tri-state area. *International Journal of Law & Management*, 47(1/2).

Nwogugu, M. (2005c). Structural changes in the US retailing industry: Legal, economic and strategic implications for the US real estate sector. *International Journal of Law & Management*, 47(1/2).

Nwogugu, M. (2005d). Towards multifactor models of decision making and risk: Critique of prospect theory and related approaches, part one. *Journal of Risk Finance*, 6(2), 150–162.

Nwogugu, M. (2005e). Towards multifactor models of decision making and risk: Critique of prospect theory and related approaches, part one. *Journal of Risk Finance*, 6(2), 150–162.

Nwogugu, M. (2005f). The legal, economic and corporate strategy issues of housing in the new economy. *International Journal of Law & Management*, 47(1/2).

Nwogugu, M. (2006a). Decision-making, risk and corporate governance: New dynamic models/algorithms and optimization for bankruptcy decisions. *Applied Mathematics & Computation*, 179(1), 386–401.

Nwogugu, M. (2006b). Employee stock options, production functions and game theory. *Applied Mathematics & Computation*, 181(1), 552–562.

Nwogugu, M. (2006c). A further critique of cumulative prospect theory and related approaches. *Applied Mathematics & Computation*, 179(2), 451–465.

Nwogugu, M. (2007a). Decision-making, risk and corporate governance: A critique of methodological issues in bankruptcy/recovery prediction models. *Applied Mathematics & Computation*, 185(1), 178–196.

Nwogugu, M. (2007b). Issues in disintermediation in the real estate brokerage industry. *Applied Mathematics & Computation*, 186(2), 1054–1064.

Nwogugu, M. (2007c). Some game theory and financial contracting issues in large corporate transactions. *Applied Mathematics & Computation*, 186(2), 1018–1030.

Nwogugu, M. (2007d). Some issues in securitization and disintermediation. *Applied Mathematics & Computation*, 186(2), 1031–1039.

Nwogugu, M. (2008). The efficiency of Sarbanes-Oxley act: Willingness to comply and agency problems. *Corporate Control Ownership & Control*, 5(1), 449–454.

Nwogugu, M. (2010/2013). *Problems Inherent in the Compensation and Business Models of Credit Rating Agencies*. www.ssrn.com.

Nwogugu, M. (2012). *Risk in Global Real Estate Market* (John Wiley & Sons, Jersey City, NJ, USA).

Nwogugu, M. (2014a). *Conflicts of Interest: And the Existence of Anti-Compliance Coordination and Un-Cooperative Cartels Among Financial Services Companies*. www.ssrn.com.

Nwogugu, M. (2014b). "Netting", the liquidity coverage ratio: And the US FSOC's non-SIFI criteria, and new recommendations. *Banking Law Journal*, 131(6), 416–420.

Nwogugu, M. (2015a). Goodwill/intangibles rules and earnings management. *European Journal of Law Reform*, 17(1).

Nwogugu, M. (2015b). Failure of the Dodd-Frank act. *Journal of Financial Crime*, 22(4), 520–572.

Nwogugu, M. (2015c). Un-constitutionality of the Dodd-Frank act. *European Journal of Law Reform.*, 17, 185–190.

Nwogugu, M. (2015d). Real options, enforcement of goodwill/intangibles rules and associated behavioral issues. *Journal of Money Laundering Control*, 18(3), 330–351.

Nwogugu, M. (2016). *Stock-Indices and Strategic Alliances as Evidence of the Invalidity of Third-Generation Prospect Theory, Related Approaches and Intertemporal Asset Pricing Theory: Three New Decision Models.* Working paper. www.ssrn.com.

Nwogugu, M. (2017). *Anomalies in Net Present Value, Returns and Polynomials: And Regret in Decision-Making* (Palgrave Macmillan, London, UK).

Nwogugu, M. (Revised 2018). *Complexity and Alternative Risk Premia: Some New Theories of Structural Change and Portfolio Decisions.* Available at www.ssrn.com. https://posei don01.ssrn.com/delivery.php?ID= 7290010221140110170920990820240280940260060140010840490301250920181180680641060890991220241270990300440440140001191181100640990210290630580101011200281090200800860220190150960931261181140651221271221050840160730871251160880101250010800680210761113006&EXT=pdf.

Nwogugu, M. (2019a). *Complex Systems, Multi-Sided Incentives and Risk Perception in Companies* (Palgrave Macmillan, UK).

Nwogugu, M. (2019b). "Perception-based decisions and optimal financial contracting: Auctions, strategic alliances and a critique of third generation prospect theory". Chapter 4 in: Nwogugu, M. (2019), *Complex Systems, Multi-Sided Incentives and Risk Perception in Companies* (Palgrave Macmillan, UK).

Nwogugu, M. (2019c). "Financial indices, joint ventures and strategic alliances invalidate cumulative prospect theory, third generation prospect theory, related approaches and intertemporal asset pricing theory: HCI and three new decision models". Chapter 11 in: Nwogugu, M. (2019), *Indices, Index Funds and ETFs: Exploring HCI, Nonlinear Risk and Homomorphisms* (Palgrave Macmillan, UK).

Nwogugu, M. (2019d). "Complexity and some numerical *algorithmic turning-point* problems inherent in excessive outstanding shares". Chapter 15 in: Nwogugu, M. (2019), *Complex Systems, Multi-Sided Incentives and Risk Perception in Companies* (Palgrave Macmillan, UK).

Papaikonomou, V. (2010). Credit rating agencies and global financial crisis: Need for a paradigm shift in financial market regulation. *Studies in Economics and Finance*, 27, 161–174.

Park, S. & Kim, J. (2014). A mathematical model for a capacity reservation contract. *Applied Mathematical Modelling*, 38(5–6), 1866–1880.

Pathak, R., Joshi, S. & Ludhiyani, A. (2010). Strategic decision-making and game theoretic approach for the commercialization of nanotechnology. *Intellectual Economics*, 2, 47–56.

Pirvu, T. A. & Schulze, K. (2012). Multi-stock portfolio optimization under prospect theory. *Mathematics and Financial Economics*, 6(4), 337–362.

PriceWaterhouse (2015). *Consolidation and Equity Method of Accounting – 2015 Edition.* www.pwc.com/us/en/cfodirect/publications/accounting-guides/consolidation-frame work-equity-method-accounting-vie-guide.html.

Rieger, M. & Bui, T. (2011). Too risk-averse for prospect theory? *Modern Economy*, 2.

Robert, V. & Yoguel, G. (2016). Complexity paths in neo-Schumpeterian evolutionary economics, structural change and development policies. *Structural Change and Economic Dynamics*, 38, 3–14.

Ruttiman, B. (2014). Modeling financial Type-2b globalization and its repercussion on the real economy. *Procedia Economics & Finance*, 14, 534–543. Scazzieri, R. (2009). Structural economic dynamics: Looking back and forging ahead. *Economia Politica*, XXVI(3), 531–557.

Schilirò, D. (2012). *Structural Change and Models of Structural Analysis: Theories, Principles and Methods.* MPRA Working Paper, MPRA, Germany.

Schindelheim, D. (2012). Variable interest entity structures in the People's Republic of China: Is uncertainty for foreign investors part of China's economic plan? *Cardozo Journal of International & Comparative Law*, 21, 195–232.

Schmidt, S., Starmer, C. & Sugden, R. (2008). Third generation prospect theory. *Journal of Risk and Uncertainty*, 36, 203–223.

Schmidt, U. (2003). Reference dependence in cumulative prospect theory. *Journal of Mathematical Psychology*, 47, 122–131.

Schwenk, C.R. (1984). Cognitive simplification processes in strategic decision – making. *Strategic Management Journal*, 5, 111–128.

Solnik, B. & Zuo, L. (2012). A global equilibrium asset pricing model with home preference. *Management Science*, 58(2), 273–292.

Stein, S., Gerding, E.H., Rogers, A.C., Larson, K. & Jennings, N.R. (2011). Algorithms and mechanisms for procuring services with uncertain durations using redundancy. *Artificial Intelligence*, 175(14–15), 2021–2060.

Sun, B. (June 2011). *Limited Market Participation and Asset Prices in the Presence of Earnings Management*. Board of Governors of the Federal Reserve System – International Finance Discussion Papers. https://pdfs.semanticscholar.org/5e4e/2e2cdafb92b0c872e7 7f654d87832bddaa0c.pdf.

Swiecki, T. (2017). Determinants of structural change. *Review of Economic Dynamics*, 24, 95–131.

Teoh, S., Welch, I. & Wong, T. (1998). Earnings management and the long-run underperformance of seasoned equity offerings. *Journal of Financial Economics*, 50, 63–100.

Terán, J., Aguilar, J. & Cerrada, M. (2017). Integration in industrial automation based on multi-agent systems using cultural algorithms for optimizing the coordination mechanisms. *Computers in Industry*, 91, 11–23.

Vu, K. (2017). Structural change and economic growth: Empirical evidence and policy insights from Asian economies. *Structural Change and Economic Dynamics*, 41, 64–77.

Wakker, P. (2001). *Prospect Theory: For Risk and Ambiguity* (Cambridge University Press, Cambridge, UK).

Wang, T., Winton, A. & Yu, X. (2010). Corporate fraud and business conditions: Evidence from IPOs. *Journal of Finance*, 65(6), 2255–2292.

Wang, Z. (2012). *US-listed Chinese Firms in Credibility Crisis: Who Are They? Where Are They?*. Working Paper.

Wang, Z. (2014). *The Role of the Director Social Networks in Spreading Misconduct: The Case of Reverse Mergers*. Working Paper, Columbia University, USA. www.columbia. edu/~zw2160/Zigan%20Wang_Job%20Market%20Paper_Columbia.pdf

Wei, W., Wang, J., Chen, X., Yang, J. & Min, X. (2018). Psychological contract model for knowledge collaboration in virtual community of practice: An analysis based on the game theory. *Applied Mathematics & Computation*, 329, 175–187.

Wu, Z., Zhao, R. & Tang, W. (2014). Optimal contracts for the agency problem with multiple uncertain information. *Knowledge-Based Systems*, 59, 161–172.

Xianwu, Z. & Lihui, B. (February 9, 2012). Variable interest entity structure in China. *China Legal Insight*. www.chinalawinsight.com/2012/02/articles/corporate/foreign-investment/variable-interest-entity-structure-in-chinal.

Yang, G. & Liu, X. (2018). A commuter departure-time model based on cumulative prospect theory. *Mathematical Methods of Operations Research*, 87(2), 285–307.

Yang, L. (2010). *Essays on Prospect Theory and Asset Pricing*. PhD Dissertation, Cornell University, USA.

Yogo, M. (2008). Asset prices under habit formation and reference-dependent preferences. *Journal of Business and Economic Statistics*, 26(2), 131–143.

Young, R. (February 21, 2013). Federal communications commission regulations impose $142 Billion in compliance costs: More on the way. *Regulatory Report Card, #1*. Competitive Enterprise Institute. https://cei.org/sites/default/files/Ryan%20Young%20-%20 FCC%20Regulatory%20Report%20Card.pdf.

Zhang, L. (2017). *The Investment CAPM: Forthcoming in European Financial Management*. http://theinvestmentcapm.com/InvCAPM2017March.pdf.

Zhu, T., Lu, M., Shan, Y. & Zhang, Y. (2015). Accrual-based and real activity earnings management at the back door: Evidence from Chinese reverse mergers. *Pacific-Basin Finance Journal*, 35A, 317–339.

Ziegler, S. (2016). China's variable interest entity problem: How Americans have illegally invested billions in China and how to fix it. *The George Washington Law Review*, 84, 539–549. www.gwlr.org/wp-content/uploads/2016/03/84-Geo.-Was.-L.-Rev.-539.pdf.

Zohar, A. & Rosenschein, J. (2008). Mechanisms for information elicitation. *Artificial Intelligence*, 172(16–17), 1917–1939.

Zou, B. & Zagst, R. (2017). Optimal investment with transaction costs under cumulative prospect theory in discrete time. *Mathematics and Financial Economics*, 11(4), 393–421.